D1474472

A Guide
to Professional Architectural
and Industrial
Scale Model Building

A Guide
to Professional Architectural
and Industrial
Scale Model Building

GRAHAM DAY PATTINSON

PRENTICE-HALL, INC., Englewood Cliffs, New Jersey 07632

Library of Congress Cataloging in Publication Data

Pattinson, Graham D.
  A guide to professional architectural and industrial scale model building.

  Includes bibliographical references.
    1. Architectural models.   2. Engineering models.   I. Title.
NA2790 P3   720' 228   81-13892
ISBN 0-13-370601-X   AACR2

Editorial production supervisor
and interior design by   James M. Chege

Cover Design by   Diane Saxe

Manufacturing buyer   Joyce Levatino

Printed in the United States of America

10 9 8 7 6 5 4 3

ISBN 0-13-370601-X

PRENTICE-HALL INTERNATIONAL, INC., *London*
PRENTICE-HALL OF AUSTRALIA PTY. LIMITED, *Sydney*
PRENTICE-HALL OF CANADA, LTD., *Toronto*
PRENTICE-HALL OF INDIA PRIVATE LIMITED, *New Delhi*
PRENTICE-HALL OF JAPAN, INC., *Tokyo*
PRENTICE-HALL OF SOUTHEAST ASIA PTE. LTD., *Singapore*
WHITEHALL BOOKS LIMITED, *Wellington, New Zealand*

To my wife, Izzy, whose continued tolerance, understanding, and whole-hearted assistance have kept fired the inspiration to complete this work.

Contents

Preface

This book was written to provide a comprehensive guide to professional architectural and industrial scale model building. It is addressed to builders and users, both actual and potential, some of the principal ones of whom are listed below in alphabetical order.

Architects and engineers (with or without their own model building facilities)

Advertising and display firms

Building designers and contractors

Career model builders as independent contractors

Government architectural, engineering and urban planning offices

Hobbyists

Instructors and students in the fine arts and crafts, architectural, and civil and structural engineering departments of schools and colleges

Interior designers

Landscape architects

Libraries

Motion picture and television study property departments

Museums (reproductions and miniature dioramas)

Real estate developers

To dispel any esoteric atmosphere surrounding this specialized craft, it is appropriate to create some background through an historical précis and to list some of the reasons why these models are valuable to the user.

Recorded history tells us of the use of scale models thousands of years BC. Most of these ancient forms were of articles used during the life of the deceased and buried with him. As time approached the birth of Christ, evidence indicates the burying of a model of the deceased's house with the owner to shelter his spirit in case no residence could be found in the land of hereafter. In ancient Britain, before the arrival of the Romans, there apparently was a society of model builders whose works have been recovered. Scale models of some of the great cathedrals built during the Middle Ages were used by their architects as practical supplements to the then inadequate drawings. Sir Christopher Wren, 1632–1723, the famous British architect, is said to have used scale models of his projects.

In modern times models are used more and more as their benefits become more widely understood. The generic benefit is the immediate, understanding response to an object in three dimensions. This expedites a meeting of minds between two or more observers who might have different interpretations of the subject from two-dimensional media alone. It is safe to say that drawings and renderings are often misunderstood, making a model mandatory. I recall a model I once built for a board of directors specifically for the reason that they could not obtain the correct concept from the voluminous drawings of the project. The model performed its mission.

Because of the generic benefit, it is economically sound to build scale models for the purposes indicated below. These not only help to justify the existence of the craft, but, more importantly, should help to add inspiration for any interested reader, whether he or she wants to teach model building, render a professional model building service, work as a model builder in a professional office, or practice the craft as a hobby.

Scale models can be indispensable aids in saving time and money by helping to:

Analyze architectural, structural, and functional design, space, and topography

Sell projects, products, processes, and systems

Finance through fund raising campaigns

Win court cases

Train employees and students

Educate the public

Satisfy zoning, planning, and other commissions

Where time and money saving are not of the essence, scale models can be constructed to:

Decorate an entrance, lobby, or display booth

Entertain the hobbyist and the public

Satisfy scholastic requirements (as for an architectural thesis)

I have constructed models to order for all but the last of the above purposes, thus proving them in practice.

The continued building and use of scale models throughout the world are convincing testimony to their important contribution to human progress.

Glendale, California   GRAHAM DAY PATTINSON

1

Introduction

STRUCTURE

This book is structured as a comprehensive guide for those contemplating or practicing a career as independent contractors in architectural and industrial scale model building. It is presented primarily from a professional standpoint. Here the term "professional" makes use of the dictionary definition "vocational" as opposed to "avocational" where the hobbyists, for example, may practice without time limitations, quality requirements, or anticipation of monetary compensation for their efforts. This distinction is made because of the disciplines necessary to produce to the specifications of a second party a product of a quality high enough to justify paying for a professional service. These disciplines are expressed or implied throughout this book as prerequisites to authentic results.

Format: As noted in the Contents, this book is divided into chapters including construction tips and supporting information pertaining directly to model building, as well as some thoughts at the end for the independent career-minded reader on organizational subjects. Chapter 49 includes some photographs of representative models. These models are referred to throughout the text. The photos are all placed in one chapter since one photograph may be referred to several times for different reasons in separate chapters and because each model is a one-time event with its own peculiar problems probably never to be duplicated. I feel very definitely that confining your attention to how a particular model was made is conducive to tunnel vision. You should develop panoramic sight and keep an open mind to enable you to tackle sucessfully any individual one of the endless construction problems that are possible in this craft. It is more instructive, for example, to give construction tips for making various shapes and sizes of columns than it is to explain how "the columns in the photograph" were made when you will never be called upon to make them. The photograph simply shows another example installed in a finished product. An Appendix (Ch. 50) is included to list miscellaneous information such as outside production sources.

CROSSTALK

Since all model building procedures are closely related if not interdependent, it would be impossible to establish clear cut construction subjects sufficient unto themselves. Therefore, some interchapter reference is necessary for complete understanding of the procedures under discussion. You can hold page-flipping to a minimum by noting that many references are merely convenience leads to subordinate information, such as references to the materials and tool chapters. It is hoped that this crosstalk will not be as confusing as that sometimes encountered in electronic communication. Cross-reference was chosen as the lesser of two evils, the other being cumbersome repetition.

LIMIT OF SCOPE

One hundred models could be built, and each one would have its peculiar requirements and problems; it would be impossible to cover every combination of architectural or industrial specifications in one book. Also, it would be superfluous to attempt to describe completion of specific models since we would be duplicating construction tips for the sake of one or two new or different applications of materials or methods peculiar to a given model. On the other hand, it is helpful in any work of this nature to have examples to the extent necessary to illustrate the construction methods generally applicable. Model A, B, etc. will be used, where appropriate, for this purpose, the first one appearing in Ch. 8. These hypothetical subjects will be presented with more or less formal delineation and with information extraneous to the immediate construction tips but necessary to your having a "concept of the whole" as discussed in Ch. 6. Untitled models or sections of models will also be used to help explain a procedure.

SIMPLICITY

Simplicity is stressed in suggesting solutions. Sometimes alternate solutions are given. Where more complicated methods are included they are there to show how computed dimensions and angles, for example, can be used to satisfy the requirements of "split-hair" accuracy (Ch. 3).

Because the model builder must be able to work in any one of numerous scales, the description of each scale would be superfluous. Illustrations are drawn purposely without scale unless otherwise noted. Most of the sketches are in isometric and schematic form, perspective being used only where necessary to intelligible viewing. The principle or procedure being depicted is more important than the scale of the illustration or its artistic quality. On the other hand, references are made to specific scales to help you visualize the sample project and to supply clarifying discipline toward understanding the procedure being discussed. Illustrations are numbered consecutively within each chapter and are referred to by a chapter number followed by illustration number, as "Fig. 23-1."

PREREQUISITE ABILITIES

It is assumed that you who are anticipating an independent career in model building or expect to construct scale models for any reason, have the ability to read drawings, mentally visualizing the subject in three dimensions, manual dexterity, a modicum, at least, of artistic ability, and a fluid imagination, all flavored with patience; so no detailed instructions are given for "drawing interpretation," "using a mat knife," "mixing paint," etc. Since tips cannot be given to cover every application of every material, or every method for solving every construction problem, reliance must be placed upon your imagination and ingenuity, as the need for other solutions arises. Though the professionals must follow prescriptions of a client, their creativity can have wide latitude in execution.

EXPERTISE

Though most of my 25 years' experience has been that of constructing projects emanating from architects' offices, these and other sources have produced projects of widely varying nature, all of which should be included in an architectural model builder's expertise. Though formal scientific training is not necessary, don't doubt for a moment that you will be presented with sophisticated projects to tax your knowledge of physics, chemistry, electronics, and mathematics. Expertise in these fields will accumulate as you progress. Refer, for example, to Ch. 49, Photo 1, and you will see that architecture was secondary to industrial facilities, animated hydraulics, and electric lighting. In this case I even had to make my own drawings (for client approval) from which to build the model. So the field is not quite as narrow as it might seem at first blush. You will have to put on your engineer's hat many times to execute complicated shapes and systems in scale. These creative challenges are what make the craft so fascinating.

GUIDES

Construction tips are intended as guides that have been proven in practice. They are not intended to constitute the only answer. One of the intriguing characteristics of this craft is the freedom the model builders can give to their imagination in discovering, through experimentation, a better way or a better material. It is hoped that the tips herein will inspire such imagination. If tips or advice are repeated, it is done to stress their importance. Whenever specific products, services, or sources are mentioned, there is no intent to exclude substitutes. They are simply examples of those that have been beneficial to me. Materials and methods are continually changing and improving as new sources arise and expertise becomes more sophisticated. I have tried to confine myself to basic principles which should hold up as long as scale models are built by human hands.

2

Types of Models

Along with the specialization that is becoming widespread in other professions, due to the varied approaches required to solve increasingly complex and sophisticated problems, model building also finds itself specialized. The subject of this book is one branch, the words "Architectural" and "Industrial" being applied through usage to cover numerous subtypes to be discussed later in this chapter.

Though all branches are interrelated in varying degree, those not covered as such in this book are "Engineering" models and "Prototype-Product" models. Each of those deserves their own study and manual. Engineering (a general term confined here by usage) model building concerns itself principally with the physical operational layout of complex chemical and electronic processing facilities such as petroleum refineries, marine exploration and drilling towers, and atomic, solar, and wind energy plants. You might say that because a luxury has become a necessity engineering model building has come of age. This branch has proven its worth to the point that study models are now made and finalized prior to making working drawings as the most expeditious approach to solving the complicated layout problems peculiar to its subjects. These models are often placed on site to guide the contractors. For those interested in this branch, references are given in Ch. 50. Note here an example of the interrelation between branches. Upon completion of the engineering study or construction model, you may be called upon to don your "Industrial" hat and build a display model of the whole installation including headquarters and outbuildings, civil work, landscaping, cars, and human figures. I have supplied architectural components for such a model. See Ch. 49, Photo 5.

To save space, the phrase Prototype-Product branch is used here to include models of vehicles for air, sea, and land, wind-tunnel models, patent models, miniature furniture, trains, toys, industrial designer's furniture and appliance models, etc. Note that this category includes full scale mock-ups such as the clay models made of automobiles before production. The prototype is really a model, a three-dimensional pattern to establish a standard even though it is not a scale model in the usual architectural sense. Where esthetics are of primary import in devising attractive conformations to house or allow a function, as in the case of an automobile or telephone handset, the suggested reference for those interested would be one of the many excellent art schools where models are the order of business in conveying concept. Another highly specialized category in this branch is that including spacecraft and satellite models, requiring the engineering expertise to serve the space laboratories.

Returning to the subject of this book, it is well right at the start to establish some sort of conceptual discipline to help prevent misunderstandings in your relationships with clients. Webster's dictionary closes its definition of "architect" with "...hence, the deviser, constructor, maker, or creator of anything." This opens the door to confusion even before we have had a chance to consider the architect's products. Forgetting literality, however, we can rely upon common usage to tell us that our principal client is an architectural school graduate certified to practice the professional service of designing and supervising the construction of buildings and other land improvements. Unfortunately there are no literal, definitive words to establish clear lines of separation between model types, so we have to rely upon accepted terminology, the knowledge of which will help you to communicate satisfactorily.

Listed below are some of the principal terms I have found in use over the years, followed by some necessarily loose definitions to help you establish a conceptual guide. They also help to indicate the breadth of the architectural-industrial branch of model building.

Models may be:

1. Study	11. Lighted
2. Display	12. Structural
3. Presentation	13. Schematic
4. Industrial	14. Section
5. Topographical	15. Breakaway
6. Site	16. Reverse scale
7. Miniature	17. Interior
8. Sales	18. Exterior
9. Contour	19. Product
10. Animated	20. Equipment

Items 1 and 2 are probably the most literally definitive of the lot, implying the use to which the model will be put and thereby usually indicating the extent of the architectural or other detail shown.

1. A *study model*, as the name implies, is usually made for the architect, designer, or engineer for in-shop analysis of mass relationships, traffic flow, land conformation, material and process routing, office and production line arrangement, utilities location, security provision, etc. Where buildings are involved, they are probably in block configuration only, covering their floor plan area in scale, and might be supplied loose to permit studying different arrangements. Where a product or a piece of equipment is the subject, the model would show overall shape in scale size as a preliminary concept without detail. A site in a valley would probably be preliminarily graded, with open contours to give your client an opportunity to read elevations quickly and allow cutting and filling to arrive at a topographical solution. An interior study model of a structure might have movable partitions, block form equipment and furniture, etc., to help your client arrive at the most satisfactory arrangement for efficiency and security. Window openings might be in detachable frame form, making their location adaptable to interior arrangement. In multilevel structures, the floors might be of clear acrylic plastic to allow study of interlevel facilities such as stairways and utility ducts. Any display of study models would normally be confined to the owner's representative responsible for the subject development. See Ch. 49, Photo 29 for example of a display quality study model.

2. A *display model* is normally a finished product with architectural and other detail shown to the extent allowed by the scale and budget. Some block buildings could appear as existing facilities to differentiate between construction phases. The grading is usually smooth-surfaced; all the colors of the life-size project are there; accessories such as cars and human figures are installed, where the scale permits, and the model is landscaped. It is usually supplied with an acrylic cover for display protection. Before continuing, it is well to point out that you should always keep in mind that a study model may be returned later for completion as a display model. If your client indicates this possibility at the start, methods of construction can be adjusted accordingly

to allow the most expeditious finishing later.

3. *Presentation* is a term never encountered in my experience with clients, but one which is apparently used in other localities. In my opinion, it is one of the least descriptive of terms since *any* model can serve as a presentation medium. The members of a church parish, for example, would probably be presented with a display model with architectural detail and landscaping as an aid to fund-raising. On the other hand, the building committee of that same church might have first been presented with a study model of the same project completed or detailed only to the extent necessary to show the architect's concept of requirements. Local use in other parts of the country may have established this term as a concept more definitive than that in my experience.

4. *Industrial models* are those of manufacturing plants, processing facilities, quarries, sanitation fills, etc., where the architectural detail, if any, becomes subordinate to the purpose of the project and plays a relatively small part in the overall picture. See Ch. 49, Photo 7.

5. I confine the term *Topographical* generally to models in small scale of large areas of land, containing any grading and improvements. A model of a large real estate development, an extensive area of natural terrain, or of a town or city could be called topographical.

6. A *site model* is any one including an area of terra firma, but the term is usually confined to a small scale model of an entire site of ownership, as opposed to a larger scale model of a portion of that site holding a single element of improvement such as an administration building of a large complex.

7. *Miniatures* are scale models in which every practicable detail is shown, as in an historic townsite, an amusement park, or interior of a living room in a private residence showing period furniture and complete furnishings. Practicable detail here means all detail reasonably possible with available equipment, considering the scale. Technically any model could be called a "minia-

ture" because it is a small scale reproduction (visually) of the real thing, but the term here is confined to those which might be said to be the result of a conscientious effort to attain *complete realism* (Ch. 49, Photos 8 and 28). They will be few and far between in your career because of the extremely high prices necessary to cover the effort. Fortunately extreme detail is not required for fulfilling by far the greater number of purposes for which models are built.

8. *Sales models* are, as the term implies, for attracting customers (Ch. 49, Photo 12). They can be anything from a display model of a church to raise funds for the project to a scale model of a swimming pool, perhaps with circulating water, to convince homeowners that they should have one in their back yard. Display site models of real estate developments and larger scale models of individual dwelling units, with lift-off roofs have both been used countless times to promote sales, both before and after the project has been started.

9. *Contour models* are those showing open contours for study of terrain, and are ordered usually where considerable changes in natural grade will have to be bulldozed into finished grade before structural improvements can be built. They can be constructed using either the horizontal or vertical control methods (Ch. 9) or the contour cutting method (Ch. 10).

10. *Animated models* are those containing automatic movement of parts or accessories, usually electrically actuated. An operating HO railway, an activated sales model (Ch. 49, Photo 2), or a model with flowing water are examples.

11. *Lighted models* obviously contain provision for lighting of interiors(Ch. 49, Photo 53), street lamps, etc. They may employ black light for special effects, or fluorescent, incandescent, or neon sources. They may have hidden spot lights trained on features of the project. An airport tower might have a flashing light on the roof, thus making it animated also.

12. *Structural models* are those in which the structure of improvements is left open to

view for the observer's analysis or appreciation of structural system (Ch. 49, Photo 3). The framing system of a private residence is a good example.

13. *Schematic models* depict processes, systems, methods, or layouts using nonauthentic elements without regard for final location except to the extent necessary to explain or demonstrate principles. A good example would be a model of a piece of property split by a freeway on which your client can move symbolically shaped blocks in an effort to determine the best manner and location of freeway crossing (Ch. 49, Photo 13).

14. *Section models* are used to aid in esthetic or structural analysis of a portion of a building, a single facade, an entrance architectural screen, a portion of a colonnade, etc. These are sometimes called stage set models when they are concerned with a single vertical plane or facade as on a moving picture lot (Ch. 49, Photos 14 and 15).

15. *Breakaway models*, as their name implies, come apart for viewing of interior planning or structure (Ch. 49, Photos 17, 18, and 19). A common breakaway model is one of a private residence with lift-off roof.

16. *Reverse scale models* are blowups of items which in life size are too small to be self-explanatory. A good example is the blowup of a star element of a transducer (Ch. 49, Photo 2).

17. *Interior models* are built to depict interior arrangements, facilities, furnishings, etc., as an aid toward obtaining the best space use or interior decoration. They are built with or without regard for the exterior treatment (Ch. 49, Photo 20).

18. *Exterior models* are by far the most common kind, with interiors shielded from view.

19. *Product models*, used mostly for sales demonstration, are important where the life-size item is too small or too large (Ch. 49, Photo 27) to show satisfactorily on a conference table. I have built models of a lighted electronic score board, a lighted corporate sign, and an advertising sign with movable surface to indicate changeability of copy.

20. *Equipment models* can be made for sales purposes (product models) or as accessory items for display or demonstration models. These would include a set of various pieces of service equipment that could be disassembled for air transport (Ch. 49, Photo 27).

Note that in these descriptions and definitions, no attempt has been made to interrelate the various types. Any expression of the many possible combinations would take up more space than the effort was worth, and only create confusion. The fact that a contour model, for example, could also be considered a topographical model or a site model is obvious. The main point is to become familiar with descriptive model terms commonly used, even though they cannot be applied in a literally exclusive manner. When all is said and done, study the drawings and specifications to the point of complete understanding and construct what they prescribe, considering ultimate use, whatever your client's descriptive term might be.

3

Accuracy and Authenticity

Accuracy controls *authenticity* which is the goal of at least every scale *display* model building assignment. Though the algebraic sum of minor inaccuracies may not destroy authenticity of the finished product, it is appropriate to devote a short chapter to the importance of accuracy before discussing procedure or construction tips with respect to component parts.

"Accuracy discipline" would be a better expression, since *split-hair accuracy* is not required in most cases, as long as it is not needed for visual authenticity. Always think accuracy, keeping aware of the specific and cumulative effects of inaccuracies as you proceed. If you are faced with a site plan for a model to be used as evidence in court, you should consider using trigonometric functions to "close your survey," so to speak, in layout. This is true particularly where drawings of existing property are incomplete. I have on occasion gone out to the subject property armed with a tape measure and camera. The use of trigonometric functions in layout provides an acceptable and understandable means for recording how you located the various elements so that, as an expert witness, you can readily convince the court of your accuracy. I remember a case during

which I was asked to indicate on a blackboard to a jury, how I established my bearings and distances. My notes saved the day. The slightest error in elemental relationships, for example, can allow the opposition to shoot down your model as inadmissable evidence, thus damaging your client's case. Let your good judgment be your guide in any particular project. Remember, the *notes* alone help to prove you used precision methods and add credence to the created impression that you built an accurate model.

Here is an excellent example of the importance of knowing, before starting, your *client's purpose* in obtaining the model. Again, if your client is going to use a study model, for example, to aid him in appraising clearance allowances in a traffic flow situation, special attention should be given to accuracy of dimension so that the client can place a scale against an element and read exactly what the drawings prescribed. The client's study is often the means for determining changes, and any inaccuracies on your part are likely to confuse the issue.

On the other hand, no one is likely to criticize your natural lake shoreline configuration because the cutting tool slipped slightly off-pattern in a place or two. Because of naturally changing water levels, the pattern itself could probably be questioned at any given time. If you inadvertently cut a building wall 1/4″ too short, you would have to do it over again if you couldn't patch on with the joint hidden, but if your parking lot turns out to be 1/16″ out in one dimension, consider taking up the difference in the width of an adjacent planter as long as the changed relationships do not destroy visual authenticity. Always consider how such minor discrepancies will affect later installation of other components. Generally speaking, *minor discrepancies* will be harder to camouflage in structures than in civil work. A 1′ scale difference in the located end of a road gradient up the side of a mountain would not spoil the scene in otherwise unimproved terrain, but one of two separated entrances higher than the other on the same side of a building would be obvious sloppy workmanship. Remember that the importance of the discrepancy will be affected by the scale of the model.

A common trap is the *cumulative effect* of small differences. Assume, for example, that you have a 40-story building to construct. You have cut the walls and installed the spandrels at floor edge locations. For the floor stock you have selected Masonite which is slightly thicker than the scale thickness of the floors, but since this is an exterior model, you are not concerned because the extra thickness will be hidden by the width of a spandrel. If you should take the floor-to-ceiling measurements from the drawings when you construct the core sections (for sandwich construction), you will find during assembly that the floor edges will gradually approach the top of the spandrels and become visible. If the floor thickness is only 0.005″ greater than the scale thickness, the 21st floor will be 0.10″ higher than it should be, and the roof will wind up being close to 1/5″ too high. The correction, of course, lies in the lowering of the core sections or changing the floor material. If you have sanded off 0.005″ from each core section but one, save the last to absorb any minor errors accumulated from your sanding.

Sometimes during the relatively simple carpentry of base assembly, the frame will seem to grow when you join the corners. When in doubt, check through dry assembly before you join the corners. Particularly in the case of small scale (1/32″ and

smaller) assembled components, the result will be minutely larger than scale because of glue, paint, and/or lack of microsanding or cutting.

A basic assurance against error, of course, is the use of a *sharp pencil* or scribe with the point at the exact line of a carefully placed *measuring instrument*. If you have twenty 9′ parking spaces to line between two planters on a parking lot, check first to be sure that the distance between planters is 180′. If not, see Ch. 26. If the total distance is correct, place your scale accurately and leave it in position until you have made the 19 pencil dots. If you have a line of specified length to plot at a given bearing, crosscheck your bench marks by meeting yourself coming the other way. That is, check the terminus of the line by taking measurements from that point to other points on the layout. Remember, the plotting of a bearing with your *protractor* a fraction of a degree off will mean an error in the location of the terminus in proportion to the length of the line.

For measuring thickness of material and dimensions of small components, the precision jaws of *calipers and micrometers* (Ch. 36) are more consistently definitive than is the visual matching of edges with markings on a *scale*, whether the measuring system be English or metric. See Fig. 15-7 and accompanying text that point out the practical impossibility of attaining accuracy in the literal sense. The extent to which you apply accuracy discipline is the key first to structural matching and authenticity and second to acceptance or discard of results.

Follow the practice of continually viewing the model as a whole. This can reveal errors through obviously *incorrect relationships*. You have not only the accuracy of a component structure assembled off the base to worry about, but also the accuracy of its placement on the base in relation to other elements.

In closing this chapter it is well to point out that although you should always keep in mind the fact that accuracy controls authenticity, there are times when only *suggested* authenticity is in order. Where, for example, it is impractical because of scale or budget to reproduce architectural decoration with strict authenticity, *model builder's license* is justified by your ability to suggest the real thing.

4

Scale

Since *scale* is inseparable from the subject of this book, it is important to point out some accepted concepts and discuss applications.

EXPRESSION

I do not mean to ignore the metric system by confining my examples to the inch-foot (or English) system. However, restricting use to the system with which I am more familiar will expedite explanation and avoid unnecessary confusion. All scale expressions indicate ratios, and there are conversion tables readily available for those of you interested in translating to metric equivalents. An excellent handbook covering the use and application of the metric system in the architectural field is listed in Ch. 50.

Scale will usually be expressed as a fraction of an inch equaling one foot. Thus, 1/4″ scale means that 1/4″ measured on the model equals 1′ on the life-size project, or a 40′ dimension called out on the drawing (Ch. 5) would be 10″ (40/4) on the model; 1/100″ scale means that 1/100″ measured on the model is equal to 1′ on the project, or a 25′

dimension called out on the drawing would be 1/4″ (25/100) on the model, and so on. Decimal expression is handy when establishing a model "inch" or a vernier setting on a machine tool. Decimals for the above scales would be 0.25″ equals 1′ and 0.01″ equals 1′, respectively. A scale inch at 1/4″ scale is equal to 1/48″ (1/4 × 1/12) or approximately 0.021″. There being 12″ in 1′, you multiply the model foot (in this case 1/4″) by 1/12 to obtain the model inch.

A variation in the fractional expression is sometimes encountered, usually in other than the architectural and related professions. A 1/4″ scale model could be expressed as a 1/48 scale model or a 1:48 scale model, meaning that the dimensions of the model are 1/48 the size of those on the project. At 1/8″ scale, 160′ on the ground would be equal to 20″ or 1′8″ on the model. At the equivalent 1/96 scale, 160′ would also be equal to 1′8″ (160/96) or 1.67′. In the first case you arrive initially at inches by dividing 160 by 8 and then convert to feet by dividing by 12. In the second case, note that the immediate answer is in the same units as those of the project. Note also that you can obtain the "rational" expression by multiplying the denominator of the fractional inch expression by 12. Since all expressions of scale indicate ratio, there is no definitive word to differentiate the two, but relying on school day expression of ratio formulas, I call the alternative rational scale. Rational scales are found on U.S. Coast and Geodetic Survey and other maps and are expressed as 1:2500, 1:2400, and so on with no mention of units since they are the same on each side of the semicolon regardless of the unit chosen in considering distances. For example, 1″ on a 1:2500 (1/2500) scale map would equal 2500″ on the ground. Under the metric system, a commonly used rational expression such as 1:500 means that 1 mm equals 500 mm, or converted to the standard meter unit, 2 mm equal 1 m.

IMPRESSION

Other than being permitted the errors discussed or implied in Ch. 3, you must be allowed flexibility in using model builder's license to obtain the proper scale *effect*. Some examples are given here as a guide to your judgment in future situations.

Back-up Items: Items such as light bulbs, fluorescent tubes, transformers, fans, switches, wiring, and the "works" of an animated model should all be buried out of sight behind structure or in a deepened base. If necessary, include such things as transformers in a box separate from the model, a clumsy situation at best. If there must be street lamps, inform your client that the scale will have to be large enough to accept grain of wheat bulbs or provision for fiber optics. Life-size objects such as switch handles protruding through model grade are great scale destroyers! A good example of a violation of these principles can be seen in Ch. 49, photo 1. The model has life-size rotometers rising from the edge of the base to show fluid movement. This treatment was important to the purposes of the model, but a deeper base could have removed the visual obstruction below grade. Another example would be perimeter black light fixtures to light up features of the model surface treated for this purpose. In any case, paint the fixtures black.

Illusion: Scale can sometimes be an illusive thing. Generally, scale should be adhered to for accuracy and authenticity (Ch. 3), but, depending upon your experience and judgment, an out-of-scale item might *look* to be in scale and therefore be acceptable. Landscaping can give scale to a model. Trees

in nature come in all sizes and shapes; so a given pine tree may serve as a sapling at 1/8″ scale and a mature tree at 1/32″ scale. (Ch. 25). If you become entranced with a perfectly formed "oak tree" twig, for example, consider its completed size before you place it in the patio of your private residence model. Technically it may be in scale, but look gross on the model and therefore better saved for a larger scale model or larger planting area later on. If you have a 6″ curb to show at roadside, remember that 6″ at 1/32″ scale is only 0.015625″, calling for material of that thickness. Sheet vinyl of 0.015″ thickness would be acceptable since the 0.0006+″ difference would not be noticed. Sometimes items a bit larger than scale are necessary to make the item discernable to the viewer. An obvious example is the installation of a full grown tree in place of the landscape architect's prescription for a seedling (Ch. 25).

Accessories: These items can add scale to a model. An automobile helps the viewer relate a known life-size image to the building against which the automobile is parked. Strategically placed human figures accomplish the same thing as well as give life to the model.

Simplification: In the interests of time and dollars simplification can often be employed without destroying good impression. In a large 1/32″ scale model of a multiunit housing development, for example, consider leaving out the windows and casting the units with architectural configuration, in plaster (Ch. 24). Be sure to include features such as chimneys, and add authentic roof treatment since most viewing will be done from above. The roofs and chimneys will give authentic character and landscaping will tend to hide the fact that the windows are not there. I have successfully followed this procedure with great saving of time and no serious loss in overall effect. Of course if a miniature (Ch. 2) is required, or the scale is 1/16″ or larger, such simplification would not be permissible in a display model.

Mixed Scales: Requests for executing parts of models in larger scale than that of the basic model should be discouraged because of the wrong impression such procedure can give. An example is exaggerated contour intervals to make the mountains more dramatic. If your clients insist on different scales, make sure that they understand the possibility of *their* client's confusion.

DETERMINATION OF SCALE

Architects and other clients used to working with models will probably prescribe the scale at which the work is to be done. But part of the model builder's service should be suggestions as to the best scale under a particular set of circumstances. Obtain answers to such questions as: "For what is the model going to be used?"; "What is the size and character of the ultimate display area?"; "How much detail do you want to show?"; "How do you plan to transport the model?". In one case the desired scale will dictate the size, and in another the desired size will dictate the scale. Remind your client that doubling the scale will quadruple the size. The more impressive larger one may require a sectioned base for handling (Ch. 7). Too large a single base model will make working in the center difficult, particularly if you have things like columns to install. If a single oversize base is required, consider making center components off-base and installing the finished product in arms' length situations.

RECORDS

It is useful to record on a blackboard converted key measurements as a ready reference to aid you in establishing scale thicknesses of materials for such things as decorative fins on the facades of a high-rise building, window mullions, etc. If the model is to be at 1/16″ scale, for example, record the fact that 1′ = 0.0625″ and that 1″ = 0.005″+. Such notice can save confusion particularly when you have two models going at once or in a crash program situation.

MEASURING INSTRUMENTS

Use rulers divided in the scale at which you are working (Ch. 36). It is obvious that 1/8″ on a standard ruler is 1′ at 1/8″ scale, but at 1/50″ scale, an engineer's scale is mandatory. Remember consistency when working with rational scales. Though no units are specified, they are the same on each side of the semicolon or in both numerator and denominator of a fractional expression.

LIMITATIONS

It will be obvious that the required scale of a particular model will affect the amount of detail practically possible and often dictate the methods of construction. Prior knowledge of the physical and practical limitations inherent in materials, processes, and procedures can forestall futile and excessively time consuming efforts toward miniaturization. Unfortunately there is no magic formula. Guided by manufacturers' specifications and instructions covering a particular material, by far the greater part of this knowledge will come from experience through trial and error. This is so because of the applications peculiar to this profession. As an example, the manufacturers of contact glue do not put out their product to serve as guy wires or ropes to support a circus pole at 1/32″ scale. After testing for reasonable display durability, this was my solution in an amusement park model (Ch. 49, photo 9). The glue was pulled with a sharp instrument from one anchor point to the other.

Until you learn what a particular client expects from you in extent of detail, explain any limitations that might be controlling at a given scale. Unless the client wants a miniature (Ch. 2), don't fall into the economically unsound trap of overdoing detail. You will find it at times very easy to become carried away in your struggle for realism, not only delaying delivery but also giving your clients more than that for which they are paying.

To spark your line of thought on the subject, a sampling of applications is given below to indicate the extent to which scale can predetermine or limit the use of materials, processes, and procedures. Each subject is covered further in the indicated section.

Steps: (Ch. 15) At 1/2″ scale, 1″ is equal to about 0.042″. A riser would be, at 6″, 1/4″ high, to be topped by a tread made from 0.020″ vinyl. The nose of the tread could just break the top edge of the riser to give a realistic effect. Each tread would be supported by two strips of 1/16″ illustration board (Ch. 35); the strip nearer the front of the tread serving visually as the riser. This piece construction obviates the use of a sandwich system of 1/4″ thick riser material, the riser surface of which might have to be lined for a finished appearance. At 1/8″ scale, 1″ is equal to about 0.010″. A 6″ riser would be 1/16″ high, the approximate thickness of lightweight illustration board, and calling for a sandwich construction. Be sure that the riser edge of the illustration board has been sanded smooth and has sharp edges. For a refinement you could line the top surface of the illustration board with 0.005″ vinyl to serve as a separate tread for appearance. At 1/400″ scale, the steps would become, at best, lines in the walk.

Railings: (Ch. 16) There can be no fast rules here because of the multitude of variations possible in support and decorative configurations. At the larger scales, say 1/4″ and larger, railings can be assembled on site where straight, upright poles can be inserted into the pavement or ground. Decorative iron work may complicate this simple picture, in which case layers of acid-etched material (Ch. 17) should be considered. At the smaller scales, acid etching is the only satisfactory answer, unless you can symbolize (Ch. 28) with strips of lined clear 0.005″ vinyl. Below 1/32″ scale, leave the railings out unless the budget will allow your getting out your microscope!

Walls: (Ch. 18) Considered here are only those walls of which the thickness is open to view, such as garden walls, walls around the perimeter of property, or those in a breakaway model (Ch. 2). At 1/4″ scale and larger, consider using hollow construction with illustration board to save weight and provide easy piercing for openings. Thick materials such as plywood may have surfaces that will require treatment. A 6″ thick wall at 1/4″ scale could be made from a lamination of two layers of lightweight illustration board. Heavy weight illustration board will provide a 9″ thick wall at 1/8″ scale. Curved garden and perimeter walls can be formed with strips of 0.015″ vinyl for a 6″ thickness at 1/32″ scale.

Trees: (Ch. 25) Because of the almost endless variations provided by nature, trees do not pose the same limitation because of scale problems as do the manmade structures. The model builder has considerable freedom of choice of materials, scale limiting the armature material only since the foliage will usually be the same material. Exceptions might be palm and pine trees. At 1/4″ scale, a perfect oak tree trunk can be found among the dried twigs of various plants around the garden. The available metal armatures are very versatile. At scales such as 1/100″, an orchard can be made from pins dipped in ground cover material, any lack of trunk texture and shape being camouflaged by the overall scene.

As a parting admonition for this section, continue viewing your model as a whole as you progress through assembly of components. As you view keep "scale" in mind. If a prescribed tree looks too dwarfed by an adjacent building wall, pull it out and plant a more mature one, etc.

5

Drawings and Specifications

In the final analysis, no matter what your expertise in building to scale, a model will be only as accurate as the drawings and specifications from which you build it. Insist on complete information. Don't guess. Obtain a site plan that includes all of the area you are required to model, floor plans, elevation drawings and sections of all structures, details of critical structural elements which will be visible on the model, door and window schedules, color and texture specifications, civil work details, and a landscaping plan with a plant schedule. "Complete information" does not necessarily include foundation, electrical, or mechanical drawings, since as a "miniature" contractor, you won't be pouring concrete, or installing plumbing or wiring (except for model purposes only as in a lighted model, Ch. 29). There are, however, cases where such information is helpful if for no other reason than to let you know what you are leaving out. Drawings not directly applicable sometimes help to create an intelligent feel for the project as a whole.

EXISTING STRUCTURES

Existing structures required on the model may include those both inside and outside the subject property line. Be sure to obtain the necessary information for their construction even if you will indicate them only in block configuration. In the absence of available drawings, site plan foundation outlines and photographs can help you and your client agree on dimensioned sketches for the purposes of the model. Beware of proceeding unilaterally in such circumstances. You might have to do something over at your own expense. If portions of a freeway are to be shown, particularly if an overpass is involved, some research at state highway department offices might be necessary. Be sure to include in your time estimate a provision for time spent there (Ch. 44).

CONTOUR MAPS

Contour maps (drawings) may be part of the complete information necessary. They will be considered further in Chs. 9 and 10 on grading.

RENDERINGS

Artist's color renderings can aid in establishing an intelligent feel for the project as a whole. They can help to create atmosphere. Mention any obvious structural differences from the drawings to your client, to be sure the latter are correct. Don't be led astray by rendered details. Follow the drawings. The rendering may have been made during a conceptual period before the drawings were finalized. In any case, the perspective necessary to an artistic result can mislead the eye dimensionally.

DIMENSIONS

As a general rule, follow the printed dimensions on drawings rather than your scaled measurements. Your experienced eye will tell you when to cross-check. I usually make quick additions of elemental dimensions to see that they add up to the over-all dimension. Bring any errors to the attention of the architect. This not only obtains the correct figures for you, but also may save contractor confusion later on.

SCALE OF DRAWINGS

Square and indicated radius corners and returns do not require drawings in the scale of the model since a simple computation can convert the drawing dimensions into usable units, but where a site plan, for example, shows compound curves in the civil work, request drawings in your scale so that they can be traced, saving valuable redrafting time. A contour map supplied for the purpose of building a model showing abrupt and complicated changes in grade must be in the model scale to allow expeditious completion. If you know that the property is flat with an even slope from one end of the project to the other then this requirement is not necessary, but when you start building mountains and valleys it becomes very important as will be evident in Chs. 9 and 10. The natural water line of a lake is another good example of the need for drawings in the scale of the model. I have run into the problem of reproducing a compound curved roof where the working, structural drawings were necessary in the model scale even though all structural members were not necessary to the completion of the project. For an example see Fig. 20-4.

PATTERNS

If drawings must be cut up for ease in obtaining patterns, request such drawings in duplicate so that you will have a complete, undisturbed reference throughout the project. Sometimes floor patterns are glued down to show space arrangements in lieu of three-dimensional wall and partition construction. Be sure you have a clean set of drawings for this purpose. Of course it is sometimes handier to trace drawings in the working scale than to cut out patterns which are hard to handle. I have traced many road and walk configurations directly onto the material to be used in large, small scale site models. (See Ch. 13.)

PRELIMINARY DRAWINGS

Quite often you will receive drawings marked "preliminary" or "not for construction" meaning that they are not complete enough or approved for the contractor or that certain elements have not yet been drafted in final form. Proceed as though the drawings are final for model purposes, reminding your client that you can incorporate changes if informed in time, and keeping in mind that any changes to work already done can bring additional time charges under your contract (Ch. 45). This "preliminary" period is often the most economical time for starting a model, and cooperation with your client can forestall reconstruction by delaying work on elements where changes are likely to occur.

DIVIDED DRAWINGS

Because of paper size limitations, you will occasionally receive a site plan, for example, in two or more sections where the scale is too large for single sheet presentation. These sections will have division lines so that you can accurately join them into one sheet. After assembly, I usually draw model area limit lines, trimming off excess paper except where I anticipate the need for selvage in plotting layout bench marks (Ch 8). I think the best method in joining drawing sections is to trim along match lines (division lines), and butt-join the sections with transparent tape. This avoids double thicknesses and underside "flaps" that catch on table edges, etc. Use a duplicate set of sections for patterns, saving the composite drawing for record and reference during the job.

FOREIGN LANGUAGES

Drawings in other than your native tongue can be disconcerting to say the least. Many elements will be obvious from the "picture," but where your language skills are inadequate for certain interpretation, rush out to your local bookstand and purchase a pertinent dictionary to help you translate. The dictionary may also ease in clarifying communication with your client. Retain this dictionary in your reference library (Ch. 43).

CARE OF DRAWINGS

During a long job with a large number of drawings, let your assistants pull separate sheets for their use at working locations, but maintain a policy of returning the drawings, in order, to the stack. This policy not only helps to maintain efficient organization, but also helps to preserve the drawings for continual reference. I maintain a table for drawings only, and I remove all staples to permit easy access to separate sheets. For a number of years I followed the practice of labeling and filing rolls of used drawings in case a severely damaged model was returned for repairs, etc., but this practice is really unnecessary and causes increasing use of valuable storage space. Probably 99 percent of repairs will be made to models where reconstructed configurations will be obvious from memory and the undamaged portions. Before you destroy drawings, be sure to retain those the client wants returned.

SPECIFICATIONS

The term "specifications" could be used to describe all prescriptions used by the model builder to accomplish his or her mission, but it is used here to include detailed information not generally found in the architectural or structural drawings. These are such items as materials, texture, and colors. The natural materials such as granite, marble, slate, etc. will have their own texture or configured surfaces; so try to obtain samples of specified materials to aid you in duplicating their appearance. Pictures of manufactured surface

textures, such as salted or pebbled concrete, "cobble stone," etc. will serve as guides. Mental concepts of colors are almost impossible to communicate verbally; so have your client submit color chips for you to duplicate. Sometimes you can obtain ready mixes to save time, but clear any slight differences with the clients. From experience you will be able to establish your standard colors for such things as asphaltic concrete, concrete for sidewalks, grass, etc., but for architectural colors and textures, submit samples of your interpretations before applying them. It is much easier to install numerous window mullions after painting than it is to repaint after installation! Tips on textures are given in Ch. 33 and on paints in Ch. 32. Landscaping specifications are covered in Ch. 25.

NOTE

To prevent confusion because of ambiguity of terms, the following definitions are established for this book.

Elevation: Drawing or picture of what the observer sees standing on grade looking at a building; for example, a picture of the vertical aspect of a building or other structure or feature.

Elevation: The height of a point or horizontal plane above (+) or below (−) a designated zero or base elevation on an architectural or civil drawing (Ch. 9).

Height: The difference in elevation between the top of a structure and the grade upon which it stands, as in a building "40′ high."

Altitude: The number of feet (or other units) a point is above sea level as shown on contour maps of natural terrain.
   Should the two meanings of "elevation" not be obvious, I will specify.

6

Planning

Planning must be continuous throughout the project, from the time you negotiate the contract to the day the model goes out the door. As a very important aid in planning, find out from your clients at the start the purpose of the model. Discussing this purpose will help your clients decide on type and scale, if they don't already know. At least your questioning will bring up alternatives which might prove better for their purpose. Also it is a good idea to learn something of the purpose of the life-size project. The fact that it is a medical facility would explain the wheel-chair ramped entrances. If it is a manufacturing facility, knowing what they manufacture will enable you to have a more intelligent approach to construction of characteristic components.

CONCEPT OF THE WHOLE

This concept of the whole is very important. A thorough grasp of the whole picture at the start will save time and headaches as you get into the job through enabling you to establish a logical sequence of events. Cool your enthusiasm for diving in and study *all* the drawings carefully so that you won't construct yourself into a corner later on. Inject your thinking into the project as though you were the owner. Answers to such questions as "Why did my architect put the loading dock there?" or "What is the purpose of the enclosure at the far left corner of the property?", etc. help you have an intelligent approach in the interests of producing the best model possible considering time and budget. It may not happen very often, but model builders have been known to bring critical errors or conflicts to light through their conscientious studying of drawings. Obviously this is the most economical time to discover errors — before the contractor has started to pour concrete. By all means ask questions to clear up items you do not understand from the drawings. Don't guess. On the other hand, remember your client is busy, and it is not only time-consuming but embarrassing to ask dumb questions, bringing the response remembered from school days: "Read the problem!" Study the drawings completely and be sure you grasp the whole picture.

PATTINSON'S LAW

Planning helps you to establish an efficient sequence of events. However, keep in mind Pattinson's Law: "Every time you set out to do something, you have to do something else first." This seemingly facetious admonition suddenly becomes important when you realize you have painted yourself into a corner and that freeing yourself is going to take valuable extra time. I learned the hard way to keep questioning the sequence of events. Continually ask yourself such questions as: "What should I do to the base before installing those buildings, the installation of which would prevent or make harder to do?"

Apparent violations of Pattinson's Law in construction tips do not invalidate it. It is clearer to the reader to complete a subassembly, for example, without confusing the explanation with descriptions of ancillary items which in practice might normally be included concurrently. Where important, I will point out the violation.

FLAW LAW

Another law which, because of its pessimistic if realistic connotation will be mentioned here only. The Flaw Law states that: "Whenever you accept a piece of material based upon inspection of one surface only, there is likely to be a flaw on the other side making it unusable or requiring a time-consuming repair." A piece of plywood may have an open cavity running in from one edge that will cause it to collapse under pressure at an interior point. A panel of scrap illustration board may have part of the surface lamination torn away on the other side. The vinyl stock from which you are cutting a garden wall may have a hard to remove or cover stain on the other side, etc. One of the most frustrating situations is where you have shaped a piece of acrylic leaving the masking tape on for protection only to find a chip or structural flaw upon removing the tape. Fortunately this does not happen often. Look for flaws in model base framing so that your mitering of corner joints will place a flaw on the inside. As a general rule be as sure as you can of your material's flawless condition before spending a lot of time on it.

PREDRAWING PERIOD

From time to time, you will be faced with a situation where the architectural and structural drawings are not ready for your purposes, but a model is required as soon as reasonably possible. In such cases establish with your client the area to be included and make the base (Ch. 7). Do all possible filling and sanding, and give it the first coat of paint. As soon as you can obtain finished grading, select, cut and mount the adequate thickness and shape of urethane foam for contour cutting (Ch. 10), or otherwise start building up the base up to grade using the horizontal or vertical control method (Ch. 9). In the absence of knowledge of location of improvements, you can at least make the perimeter walls for one of the Ch. 9 methods. If you can determine from available information the expected highest point on the model, whether top of mountain or building penthouse, consider adequate height clearance and order the acrylic cover (Ch. 39) and shipping crate (Ch. 40) if required. In other words, put to immediate use all available information to expedite later completion. If existing buildings are to be included, get started on these whether they are to be in block configuration or display form. Use this time to locate drawings of the section of freeway to be included — a sometimes frustrating search in state engineering offices! If you are still waiting for drawings after the above tasks have been completed, consider making trees, or ordering human figures and cars and painting them. When the project drawings finally arrive, you will have a head start toward avoiding a crash finish.

DELIVERY

Be sure that you and your client understand the method of delivery to be used to prevent last minute confusion and possible ill will. During my early station wagon days, I delivered a lot of models, but experience has shown that the client pickup is the better way for several reasons. Your vehicle may not be adequate. You lose construction time on other projects. You have to consider in-transit insurance. If your client does not have adequate transportation, even though your contract (Ch. 45) is FOB your shop, offer him the service of arranging for delivery by a public carrier.

My cratemaker will pick up a model, pack it, and ship it where crating is necessary.

CONTINUOUS PLANNING

Keep planning in mind at all times to stay out of trouble. As you gain experience, priorities will tend to become automatic, but beware of unusual situations where even the most experienced can fall into traps where surgery is the only way out, thus losing valuable time. Planning with respect to materials, methods of assembly, etc. is continuous no matter what the expertise because every model is likely to have its peculiar snake in the barrel ready to nip you if you are not alert. For example, note any subsurface items, such as swimming pools, for which you will have to raise the finished grade off the base to accommodate. Plan your time to the extent possible within the available working time. Try to get a reasonable cushion of time beyond that expressed by the contract dollar time so that the delivery date will allow for a bit of the unexpected. Even if you have all the drawings take care of as many as practicable of what might be considered closing operations at the start of the job to prevent tag ends from hitting you in the face at the last minute. For examples, see "Predrawing Period" in this chapter. During a job where more than one person is working on assembly components, have them crosscheck to be sure all the parts will fit together when completed. One person's methods or materials, though normally acceptable, may not jibe with those of a coworker in a particular assignment. Dimensions also may be off just enough to require time consuming redo even though individually they are within acceptable tolerances. Thus continuous planning results in effective teamwork.

7

Bases

SYSTEM

Model bases should be flat, solid, and durable. After all, they are the supports for considerable investments, and for that reason alone, they should be given serious consideration. It would be foolish to anchor a $5000 high-rise office building model to a single slab of 1/2″ plywood which has probably at least a slight warp, or will eventually acquire one. After various trials, I have standardized on a hollow-door-type system which has proven very satisfactory over the years. There is no worry about solidarity, and bracing can be added where required to give added assurance. Holding down weight is important, but the system described below has proven to be a successful compromise.

CONSTRUCTION

Cut a piece of 3/8″ good-one-side, standard interior plywood in the shape of a rectangle, for example, with dimensions to agree with the size of the area to be included in the model. Allow for a 1/4 to 1/2″ border around the property line, and, if the property has to be raised above the plywood

surface to accommodate basements, transformers, fans, etc., provide for an additional 1/2″ border of plywood to help prevent damage on placing or replacing the acrylic cover (Ch. 39). When you purchase 4′ × 8′ plywood panels, get them as flat as possible, so you don't have to pull warp out in construction. Attach this model base to a frame of standard 1″ × 2″ white pine (or redwood if white pine is not available) (Ch. 35), constructed with 45° miters at the corners which are glued and secured with corrugated fasteners (Fig. 7-1). Use white glue (Ch. 34) and finishing nails (brads). The frame should have a lip of about 5/16″ around the perimeter of the plywood for esthetics and to provide a bearing for an acrylic cover if required (Ch. 39). Turn the assembly over and crossbrace, corner to corner, with the same stock from which you made the frame. The crossbracing can be glued to the underside of the plywood to hold it until you can nail it from the top surface. Over this assembly, glue and brad a piece of 1/8″ untempered Masonite (tempered Masonite for contour cutting, Ch. 10), so that its edges are about 1/8″ inside the frame perimeter. Turn the base over again and nail through the plywood into the crossbraces. As a nailing guide, draw a pencil mark

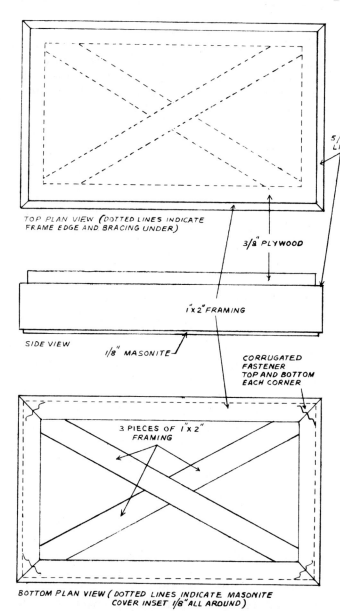

TOP PLAN VIEW *(DOTTED LINES INDICATE FRAME EDGE AND BRACING UNDER)*

3/8" PLYWOOD

5/16" LIP

1"x2" FRAMING

SIDE VIEW

1/8" MASONITE

CORRUGATED FASTENER TOP AND BOTTOM EACH CORNER

3 PIECES OF 1"x2" FRAMING

BOTTOM PLAN VIEW *(DOTTED LINES INDICATE MASONITE COVER INSET 1/8" ALL AROUND)*

FIGURE 7-1 *Standard base construction.*

HANDLING PLYWOOD

For those of you not used to handling common Douglas Fir plywood, beware of splinters for the sake of esthetics if not fingers! Because of the grain configuration or direction in the top lamination, splintering may occur along its edges. Immediately glue down, with white glue, any splinters that cannot be sanded off without disturbing the edge profile. This will obviate later time consuming cutting and filling to restore the edge.

BASEMENTS

Where there are one or more subfloors to indicate, such as the entrance to a basement parking garage, cuts can sometimes be made in the plywood to accommodate the lower plane, but consider that the bracing may have to be relocated from its standard X form to clear. Where basement requirements are extensive, or just as deep as or deeper than the base frame, raise the model surface an accommodating distance up off the plywood. Don't wind up with the basement floor lying on the base Masonite. The flex in the Masonite between braces may disturb your installation.

ODD-SHAPED MODEL AREAS

If the odd shape of a contour model, for example, reveals unused plywood, cover the exposed surface with illustration board (Ch. 35) or fill and sand the plywood to camouflage the grain and provide a smooth painting surface. If there is a problem cutting the illustration board to the shape of the model perimeter, consider lining the entire plywood surface before mounting the model. The open model base surface often can be used for the client's descriptive signs.

BASE SHAPE

Except in very rare cases, the best shape for a model base is a rectangle (or square) regardless of the shape of the property being modelled. This has been at least tacitly agreed to by every client I can remember. In spite of its structural importance, a base is only a support element. It is not part of the display and should visually play as small a part as

against a straightedge, corner to corner so that it follows the approximate center of the bracing edge underneath. If you do not hit the exact vertex of a corner with the end of a bracing piece, put a guide mark on the outside of the frame before you cover with masonite. Fill and sand the plywood edges and slightly chamfer the frame corners. In cases where the model is small, say 2′ × 2′ in size, consider making the frame with the 2″ dimension horizontal instead of vertical for better esthetic balance in the final result. The corners of the frame can be reinforced with luggage-type bumpers where you anticipate continual transport, but this is usually not necessary.

possible. A rectangle is the most practical shape with which to subordinate the base's presence. A base shaped to an odd configuration of a piece of property distracts from the subject it supports. A rectangle is also easy to handle and crate for shipment. The rare cases justifying violation of these principles would be where a specific shape was required to fit a display location, or where the open area of base plywood was so extensive as visually to overpower the subject and be considerably larger than the space needed for descriptive information. An example of the latter type of exception is the case of a modelled triangular area where the open corner of the base should be truncated to reduce excessive unused plywood.

BASE FINISH

Most clients concur that a model base should be "painted out" as much as possible, and for that reason all extra-model surfaces should be painted matte black. If the client has a panelled room display area, they may desire a frame to be in one of the popular hard woods, which can be accomplished through the use of strip veneer. When carefully applied, this veneer can look for all intents and purposes like the solid product (Ch. 35). In my opinion, it is unnecessary to make the frame out of walnut, for example, which is much harder to work than white pine, more expensive and adds nothing to the finished appearance. Cabinet work is present only to support the model and should be considered only as a necessity to a more important end.

DIVIDING A MODEL

If the model must be divided for ease of handling and shipping (because it is larger than about 4' × 6') provision must be made when constructing the base for establishing the division or divisions compatible with configurations of the finished model. Make divisions so that they will fall along the edges of straight roads, for example, so that they can be camouflaged as easily as possible. Try to stay away from improvements where you would have to cut through a structure or be so close that the continual assembly and disassembly would cause damage. Where a jagged division becomes necessary, try to take advantage

of straight sections of roadway or side walk (Fig. 7-2). Warning: When you divide the plywood base consider the amount of material the saw blade is consuming so that you don't reduce the overall dimension when the sections are pressed together. Remember that you will have to shape the 1″ × 2″ pegged frame members at the joints to agree, at least approximately, with the edge configuration of the plywood. Glue together strips of 1″ × 2″ stock so that one bandsaw cut will provide mating halves at peg locations. Assuming three pegs will be sufficient, temporarily hold together each set of mating supports as you drill a hole through each to accept a 3/8″ wooden dowel peg. Before continuing, remember that all pegs will have to be mounted so that they are not only horizontal (parallel to the plywood) but are all parallel to each other. Otherwise you will not be able to join the model sections. Force a peg with white glue on it into one side of each of the mating pairs of supports and slip each mating half back onto its peg, reaming the open hole sufficiently to provide a snug slip joint. Turn the base over and mount, with white glue, each mating pair of supports in its location across the closed joint of the plywood so that all pegs are on the same side of the joint and so that each mating support half is slightly back from its edge of the joint. When mounted, you should just be able to see the peg in the crack between the supports when the plywood sections are held tightly together. Remember to mount the pegs so that they are parallel! Along the joint edges of the plywood between the pegged supports glue on each side a sufficient number of frame sections (slightly back from the edges) to provide sufficient solidarity to the assembled sections. Turn the sections back over and nail the plywood to each edge support piece as well as the X bracing for added security.

Where you do not have convenient breaks in plane or texture across the model as you do in Fig. 7-2, make straight cuts across unstructured property in such a way as to minimize visual disturbance by the closed joint. If you should have to cut through a structure, that being the only thing in the way of an otherwise well-camouflaged joint, try to divide the structure at a line of change of plane where a joint could normally be. As a last resort consider plugging in the affected facility after the base has been assembled. This is awkward because it requires transporting separately a possibly easily damaged unit when the base sections are separated.

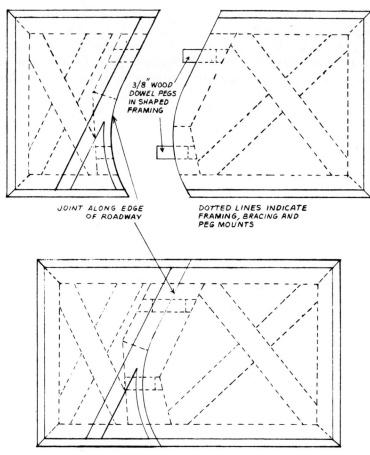

FIGURE 7-2 *Dividing a model.*

TRUENESS OF BASE

Obviously the best assurance of a flat model base is to assemble it from flat and straight components. I stress these qualities each time I order lumber, explaining the reason for the apparent fussiness, and I have had good cooperation from suppliers. Flatness is particularly important for contour models which shouldn't rock when pushed under the cutter to give varying results at a given setting. Often the brads and glue of assembly will pull out minor gradual bows in the plywood panels or leave only an imperceptible rise at one corner not seriously affecting an architectural model.

If you should be stuck with an obviously bowed plywood panel, before waiting for the next delivery, consider trussing out the bow. I have done this with success with the following technique. After assembling the base with the outside radius of the bow toward the framing and before adding the bottom Masonite liner (Fig. 7-3), pick out two opposite extreme ends of the bow at the frame perimeter and mark them. Leaving an un-

obstructed line of sight between these points pile weights on the base X frame until the bow is flattened against the work table (which of course should be flat). If you don't have sufficient weights, hold the bow flat while you temporarily brad the plywood to the table surface using opposing angle insertions at key locations. At each marked end of the bow screw in part way two 1/2″

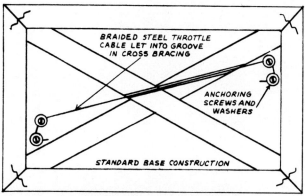

FIGURE 7-3 *Trussing a base.*

#10 wood screws through steel washers about 1″ apart. Wind the end of a length of braided steel cable such as automotive or motorcycle throttle cable one and a half times around a screw and drive it home. Wrap the cable around the other screw and cinch it. Pull the cable across the base toward the other pair of screws and cut a groove in the X frame where it passes to bury it flush with the surface. Wrap the cable around the second set of screws and tighten them enough to allow the cable to slip. Catch the free end in the claw of a carpenter's hammer, and using leverage, pull the cable as tight as you can with one hand as you tighten the screws wth the other. Remove the weights (or clinching brads). The plywood should remain acceptably flat against the table. Clip off the excess cable and add the bottom liner.

8

Layout

The subject of layout is placed here, following the subject of bases, since layout is logically the first operation in the sequence of model building events, and the base supplies the terrain to be developed.

You could say that layout is to the model builder as site location is to the surveyor. In a simpler way you are doing just that. You locate a bench or reference mark and establish locations of natural and constructed objects in correct relationship.

BENCH MARKS

At least one bench mark should always be established as a permanent reference point on the site plan and it should also be plotted on the model base. An example is the intersection of two perimeter street curbs at right angles to one another. If the curb is curved to change direction, extend the curb lines beyond the corner until they intersect. This is a point you know will not be covered during construction. Assuming the model edges are the center lines of these two streets, plot the bench mark on the model using right angle site plan

measurements from the model limit lines. You will then be able to plot or check the plot of improvements on the model from the two curb lines each parallel to a model edge. For reference, I have often used two lines at right angles to each other (parallel to model edges) drawn through the center of the model area on the site plan and on the model, being sure to maintain some evidence of these lines as they are being covered by improvements.

If the site plan is in the same scale as the model, the features of the site can be punched through onto the base and the punch marks connected by pencil lines. If you are doing this on an illustration board covered base, the pin punch marks are better than carbon tracing which is sometimes difficult to remove. In any case, establish at least one reference point common to both site plan and model. It is your anchor to prevent drifting away from specified relationships. There are no hard and fast rules with respect to this initial or flat terrain layout, nor are there such rules with respect to the uneven terrain layout to be discussed later. Every model will be different. As you gain experience you will find that your bench mark need be only mental as in the case where your installation of a flat plane of street curb-sidewalk-planter material at the correct distance from the edge of the model will automatically provide reference for location of subsequent installations. The curbs will supply any number of bench marks as needed, and even under split-hair accuracy requirements you could still truthfully say that your bench mark was the curb intersection at a street corner. Just keep the bench mark principle in mind at all times even though you do not have to plot the point.

MODEL A

As an example of this initial layout on flat terrain, model A is introduced as our first hypothetical assignment. Information extraneous to the immediate subject will be given to create a whole picture

atmosphere and indicate the items that must be included in the model builder's planning.

Let us assume you have a contract to construct a 1/16" scale exterior display model of a manufacturing plant and administration building (Fig. 8-1). It is an expansion plant of a company that makes irrigation equipment for agriculture. They own adjacent property which is being held for future facilities. Initially unused space in the 14-story administration building will be leased to others. Note here that I make no attempt to relate the manufactured product to the illustrated facilities or apparent space use. The assumption of product is given only to bring out the importance of gaining knowledge not only of the purposes of the model but also the reason for the project. The company could be making furniture, toys, etc. the knowledge of which helps establish an intelligent atmosphere in the mind of the model builder.

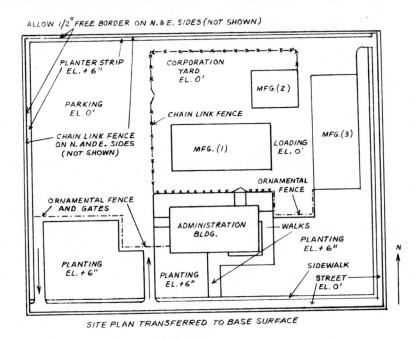

SITE PLAN TRANSFERRED TO BASE SURFACE

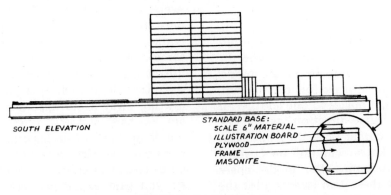

FIGURE 8-1 *Model A.*

Knowing something of the manufacturing process became mandatory in the case of the model shown in photo 1 of Ch. 49 of a liquid fertilizer plant for which I had to make the drawings. This is an unusual case, but it points out the importance of the concept of the whole discussed in Ch. 6.

The base frame for model A is to be the standard black matte finished white pine (or redwood) (Ch. 35). An acrylic cover (Ch. 39) is required, and since the model is to be shipped across country, a crate (Ch. 40) will be required. You are to arrange and pay for the shipping, billing your client for these extras over and above the contract price. There is an extra allowance for acid etching for the ornamental fencing.

The subject of model A is to be on a level (flat) piece of land, measuring $3' \times 4'$ at $1/16''$ scale. To these dimensions add one half the width of the frontage street or $25'$ and of the one along the east side of the property or $15'$. This is usual practice to help orient the setting and allow for some vehicular traffic activity. Along the north and west sides include a $1/2''$ border to prevent damaging the perimeter planting and fencing when placing the acrylic cover. A $5/16''$ lip formed by the perimeter frame under the plywood base will result in overall dimensions of $38\ 11/16'' \times 50\ 1/16''$. Your drawings of course would have complete dimensions for construction of the model. I purposely am holding their expression to a minimum to prevent confusing with numbers your understanding of procedure. Such numbers as the assumed scale, size of base, and other key dimensions are presented only for the purpose of helping you, along with the illustration, to form a mental picture of the subject. Another orienting dimension might be the height of the administration building with 14 floors. Assuming a minimum of $10'$ from floor to floor and a 3.5' parapet, the building would be 143.5' high, or about $9''$ high at $1/16''$ scale.

You have made the base (Ch. 7) and desire to line the plywood with illustration board to provide a smooth, grainless surface with which to work as well as to provide slight texture (Ch. 33) for the roadways and parking areas. Cut the size needed to cover the plywood from a standard $40'' \times 60''$ sheet of heavyweight illustration board to avoid joints and attach it to the plywood surface with contact glue (Ch. 34). White glue could be used but its water base tends to buckle the illustration board unless the board is completely covered with glue and weighted down overnight, consuming valuable time. If you have to use smaller

pieces of illustration board, place the joints so that they occur, if possible, under planted areas, along fence lines, etc. A slight sanded bevel away from the joining top surfaces will sometimes help obtain a tight joint.

Remembering Pattinson's Law, delay laying out the site until the base receives its initial finishing treatment. As we saw in Ch. 7, sand the illustration board flush with the plywood edges of the base, filling the plywood with spackling paste (Ch. 35) where there are gaps in the laminations. Check the frame joints, slightly chamferring all sharp edges and corners. When filling with spackling paste, close with a slightly convex surface so that the fills can be later sanded down flush when dry. After sanding, spray the perimeter of the base with a flat black paint such as Krylon (Ch. 32), being sure to include the edges of the illustration board and the edges of the bottom masonite cover which are inset from the frame edges. Spraying the base at this point will obviate having to mask later to prevent spattering the model. Since so much of the area is driveway or parking, paint the illustration board a macadam gray (Ch. 32), assuming that all vehicular surfaces are AC (asphaltic concrete). The AC paint will cover any spatter on the illustration board resulting from spraying the frame. If necessary, the frame can be touched up at the last minute with a brushed on coat of black matte latex (Ch. 32).

LAYOUT OF MODEL A

Assuming that you have a site plan in the same scale as that of the model, cut the site plan along the centers of the two streets and allow the $1/2''$ border on the north and west. Place the result on the illustration board so the edges match and with a pointed instrument punch through key line intersections. Make punches just strong enough so that you can read them. Otherwise you may have to fill holes. Join these points so that you duplicate the shapes on the drawing, using a hard pencil lightly applied. As mentioned previously, you won't have to plot a formal bench mark in this case, but you can still consider the intersection of the two curb lines as your controlling reference point at elevation zero. In fact, you wouldn't have to trace or punchmark anything, relying on your placement of the sidewalk layer of material at the specified distance from and parallel to the model edges to establish reference points. This will be done in

Ch. 9. This layout problem is about as simple as you will find and has been kept so in order to present some of the basic principles involved. Model A will be left for the time being so that I can present some tips on layout on uneven terrain.

UNEVEN TERRAIN

As the model area becomes more complicated, with considerable changes in finished grade, extensive areas of uneven natural grade, or really mountainous country, you will often find it necessary to don your civil engineer's hat to complete layout with acceptable accuracy. Any layout of hillside facilities during your flat terrain layout such as that for model A would be a waste of time because the hill will cover your plots. The only useful indication on the flat or level area of the site would be perhaps the lowest contour line where the hill hits even grade. Further, you cannot, for example, lay a drawing in the scale of the model down over a range of hills and expect to extend accurate locations of facilities. The unevenness of the terrain will distort the extension. If the hills have been contour cut (Ch. 10) or made using the horizontal control method (Ch. 9), you can very likely "eyeball" critical locations on the open contours, checking distances from points easily identifiable on map and model. Normally contours will be left open until they have served their purpose as an aid in layout. If you forgot Pattinson's Law and filled the contours prior to layout, or the surface is one resulting from the vertical control method of grading (Ch. 9), then you will have to take a different approach.

Before continuing, so I won't be accused of putting the cart before the horse, it should be pointed out that though hill construction is discussed in Ch. 9, an exemplary completed hill is included here as a medium to allow presentation of all layout tips in one section.

LOCATOR TOOL

Assume you have a series of column supports for an aerial tramway to install on a finished (smooth) mountainside (Fig. 8-2). The gradient is fairly steep and the ground surface quite uneven; so some sort of surveying aid is necessary for accurate placement. I have made a simple but effective tool for this purpose. See Fig. 36-8 for a complete descrip-

tion and assembly and see Fig. 8-2 for part numbers for use on this assignment. Figure 8-2 illustrates the use of this tool along with a homemade adjustable angle (Ch. 36). In an attempt to offset the tendency of prose to make procedure seem more complicated than it really is, the use of the locator is described in separate, numbered steps.

1. Pick a flat area convenient to the tramway location along one side of the model base frame and attach with screws the mounting bracket (Part 1) so that the pivot rod (Part 5) hole is at right angles (vertical) to the model base.

2. Assemble the tool at any convenient height so that you can locate the vertical stop (Part 4) to accommodate the notch in the end of the deadarm (Part 3). Screw the stop vertically to the frame. All screw holes can be filled later when you are putting on finishing touches.

3. Measure the distance from the edge of the base plywood to the center of the pivot hole in the mounting bracket (Part 1) and from one end of the base plywood to the same point. Plot this location on the site plan as a bench mark and draw a line from this bench mark through each column location (Fig. 8-2a). Note that this bench mark will be outside the model area since the locator is mounted on the base frame. Note also that though it is normal to have a site plan in the same scale as that of the model wherever contour reproduction is involved, any difference in scale will require conversion for plotting the bench mark on the site plan. Any difference in scale will not affect the angles in which we are interested.

4. Place the adjustable angle on the drawing with the vertex at the bench mark and the lower right leg parallel to the edge of the model area. Place a piece of $1'' \times 2''$ stock under the upper left leg (Fig. 8-2a) as a spacer to fill the vertical offset of the two legs. Hold the tool down as you adjust the edge of the upper left leg and flush spacer to agree with the line you have drawn through the location of the first column support and tighten the pivot screw.

5. Nest both arms of the locator tool in the fixed angle of the adjustable angle tool (Fig. 8-2b) and tighten the wing nut (Part 10) to

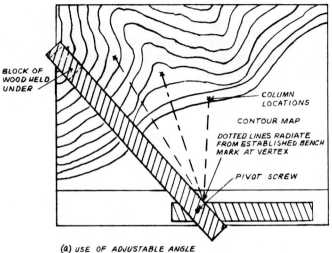

BLOCK OF
WOOD HELD
UNDER

COLUMN
LOCATIONS

CONTOUR MAP

DOTTED LINES RADIATE
FROM ESTABLISHED BENCH
MARK AT VERTEX

PIVOT SCREW

(a) USE OF ADJUSTABLE ANGLE

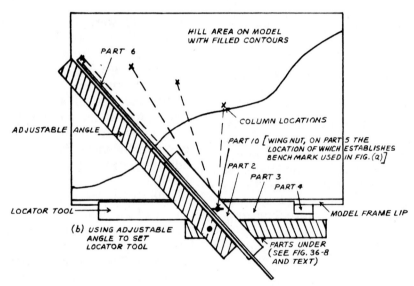

HILL AREA ON MODEL
WITH FILLED CONTOURS

PART 6

ADJUSTABLE ANGLE

COLUMN LOCATIONS

PART 10 [WING NUT, ON PART 5 THE
LOCATION OF WHICH ESTABLISHES
BENCH MARK USED IN FIG. (a)]

PART 2

PART 3

PART 4

LOCATOR TOOL

MODEL FRAME LIP

(b) USING ADJUSTABLE
ANGLE TO SET
LOCATOR TOOL

PARTS UNDER
(SEE FIG. 36-8
AND TEXT)

FIGURE 8-2   *Use of plotting tools.*

hold the locator arm holder (Part 2) and the deadarm (Part 3) down against the collar (Part 7).

6. Extend the locator arm (Part 6) to the distance measured on the site plan from the bench mark (center of pivot rod) to the desired location of the first column support, adjusting the height of the pivot rod (Part 5) in its bracket (Part 1) so that the end of the locator arm just touches the hill surface on the model. Be sure the deadarm (Part 3) is against the stop (Part 4).

7. Cinch the pivot rod (Part 5) in the bracket and mark the point where the tip of the locator arm touches the hill. If all the column supports are in a straight line, you may be able to locate intermediate columns

along a straightedge held against the two terminal columns located with the tool. If not, you may have to locate them all with the tool.

ELEVATION LOCATOR

Note that the locator tool can be used also for establishing heights. I remember the configured line of roller coaster supports in uneven terrain which of course had changing top elevations. After checking the level reading on the base along the perimeter frame of the model to establish parallel control, I taped a small level to the top of the locator arm holder (Part 2), and, after plotting horizontal locations, I inserted each column to the height at which the locator arm was set. This was quickly accomplished by setting the tool to the difference between the elevation of the bench mark and the prescribed elevation of the support column top. In such application be sure that there is no considerable sag at the end of the locator arm below the pivoted end of the locator arm holder. Refinements included a vertically drilled guiding hole in the end of the locator arm through which I could push the piano wire columns into the base. Do not confuse this use of the locator tool with that of the height gauge described in Ch. 36 (Fig. 36-7). Use of this gauge will be discussed later in this section.

Don't let the number of parts in the locator tool discourage you. That and the adjustable angle have saved me a great deal of time, justifying the initial effort of construction. You can quickly make locator arms (Part 6) of different lengths to accommodate different model distances, and you could make an adjustable angle tool without serious loss of time each time the need arose for different arm lengths. The principal advantage of the locator tool is the automatic control provided by its horizontally fixed and vertically adjustable fulcrum for any installation within its reach. An aerial tramway could be on the left, a roller coaster on the right, and some other column-supported structure in the center. The only change you might have to make would be slipping in a longer or shorter locating arm as you moved to the next location.

ALTERNATE METHODS

The infinite number of terrain configurations and facility relationships likely to confront the model builder makes impossible a complete discourse on the subject of layout, but these exemplary tips should help you in the planning process. Obviously if a point to be plotted on a mountainous site lies on a flat mesa, you can place a properly oriented site plan of the same scale, or a cut-out section thereof, on the mesa and punch through the point. Even in rough terrain with filled contours you can sometimes eyeball a location with reasonably accurate results by comparing contour configurations on the site plan or contour map with the shape of the finished surface on the model, letting tight convolutions lead your eye right to the spot. Consider here the use of the model. If split-hair

accuracy (Ch. 3) is required, your plotting by visual comparison might toss out the model as unacceptable evidence in court even though you "hit the nail on the head."

A curved trestle across a lake can be plotted through a template made from a site plan of the same scale. Cutting the shape of the lake out of the drawing should give you a guide for location and orientation. If you have established the location of the top and bottom supports for a ski lift in a straight line on the surface of a steep slope where the support intervals are not the same, consider the use of a Profile Plotter (Fig. 36-9) for locating the intermediate supports. Cut out the profile drafted and hold it between the top and bottom supports on the model and mark the indicated locations.

Vertical Plotter: This is another useful tool for locating facilities on a model and is so-named to differentiate it from the locator tool discussed previously. See Fig. 36-14 for construction. Unlike the locator tool this tool is handheld (or clamped) against the side of a model to locate points on steep slopes at the model edge. It usually will have to be moved for each plot. On the site plan draw a line at right angles from the desired point to the indicated edge of the model. Measure the length of this line and the distance from the intersection of this line with the model edge line to the nearest corner of the model area. Mark this distance on the model as the point at which you place the center line on the tool shaft against the model side (Fig. 8-3). Place the horizontal arm in the free hole nearest to the hilltop and the vertical marker in its hole in the arm. Slide the arm out the distance from the shaft to marker as measured on the site plan and push the marker down to plot the desired location. Be sure the marker is parallel to the vertical center line on the shaft. Note that you can check elevations also with this tool.

Height Gauge: This tool is handy for checking relative heights of facilities already installed on the model. See Fig 36-7 for construction. The tool is made to straddle the model, and after the spanning straightedge is levelled, the sliding gauge is moved over the questioned facilities. Comparing readings on the gauge taken from the roofs of each of two buildings, for example, will tell you whether they are relatively correct in height. Sometimes illusion will make relationships look wrong and this gauge will help you check.

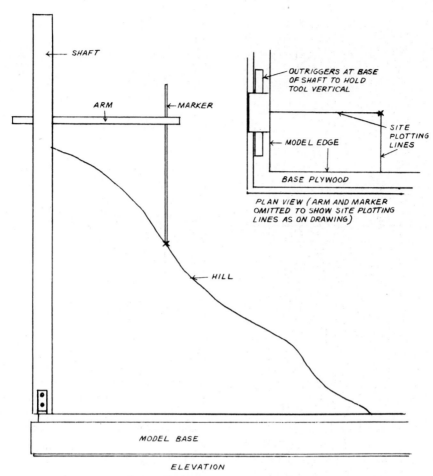

FIGURE 8-3 *Use of vertical plotter.*

PLOT CHECK

Your first and easiest verification of a plot is visual. Does the relation of the plotted point to nearby facilities, terrain features, civil work, etc. appear to be in agreement with the site plan? If something looks wrong, replot using either surveyor's aid described previously in this section, or counter-check from another side of the model. A third rough verification can be obtained through the use of a mentally constructed right triangle (Fig. 8-4). Plot a bench mark on a convenient place on the model edge that you can readily transfer to the site plan. On the plan measure the distance from this point to the location of the facility the plot of which you are checking. This is the base of your hypothetical triangle. Subtract the elevation of the bench mark from that of the facility. This will give you the vertical side of the triangle. Since the hypotenuse of a right triangle is equal to the square root of the sum of the squares of the other two sides, you can arrive at length of the gradient

from the bench mark up to the facility. Check this against the reading on a ruler or measured strip of vinyl, etc. held on the model between the two points. The two should agree.

As a closing admonition with respect to layout on uneven terrain, if you took advantage of open contours to help plot facilities, be sure that your site markers (such as straight pins) are inserted far enough into the surface to prevent losing your plots when the contours are filled or sanded off.

OTHER LAYOUT TIPS

Lakes, streams, and waterfalls are relatively easy to locate because the contour configuration on the site plan (or contour map) reproduced on the model will be an obvious guide. Street car tracks running parallel to the edge of the paving and concentric with the curves can be located by drawing a drafting compass point along the edge of the street material. The resulting lines will be a

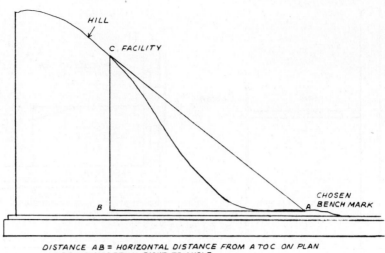

DISTANCE AB = HORIZONTAL DISTANCE FROM A TO C ON PLAN
ABC = CONCEPTUAL RIGHT TRIANGLE
DISTANCE BC = ALTITUDE OF C LESS ALTITUDE OF A
DISTANCE AC = $\sqrt{AB^2 + BC^2}$

FIGURE 8-4 *Triangular check of location.*

guide for scoring at the smaller scales, such as 1/32″ and for construction at the larger scales. Railroad bed material cut from a pattern can be placed and oriented in one piece by locating each end. Where you have a number of houses to locate as on a tract development model, cut out the road material to include driveway stubs. When this configuration is mounted, the driveways will serve as automatic house locators. Private facilities such as backyard swimming pools and separate garages can then be placed in proper relationship with the houses after a couple of simple measurements. Layout of items which, at the scale of the model, can be accomplished two-dimensionally such as grout lines for brick, tile, or concrete block, parking

space designations, surface designs, street traffic lane divisions, etc. are covered in Ch. 26.

In closing this section it is appropriate to remind you that no subject in model building is ever closed. There is always hope for the better way mentioned in the introduction, so let your imagination flow. As an example of how trial and error can produce improvements, the first pivot arm in my locator tool was a system of nesting brass tubing to allow vertical adjustment. This was not as satisfactory as the threaded rod because the friction between the pieces of tubing was not strong enough to hold a set height. Those of you who are machinists might want to make the whole tool out of aluminum.

9

Grading

Before going any further it is well to forestall any confusion arising from my sequence of construction tips. It is normal to start with the simple and progress to the more complicated when illustrating application of procedures. This was done in Ch. 8, where model A was introduced as the simplest of subjects. Where different construction methods are available to attain basically the same result, however, it seems less confusing and cumbersome to cover all methods, using appropriate illustrations, and then to backtrack to exemplary projects starting with the simplest of applications as is done in this chapter returning to model A as the subject.

There are two general conditions of grading: natural and finished. The terms appear to be self-explanatory, but in order to prevent possible confusion, it is well to establish concepts in this respect. The contractor's "finished" grade is that which is established during the construction process, the contractor's movement of earth through cutting, excavating, and filling. Though it may end up practically the same as the natural grade as in the case of a piece of naturally flat ground graded and paved for a parking lot, the end product would still be considered "finished." Any grade left un-touched, such as a portion of foothills, would remain natural grade at the completion of the job. All of model builder's grading could be considered "finished" since he or she has constructed the foothills as well and any inprovements, but the terms used here refer to the contractor's concept.

ALTITUDES VERSUS ELEVATION

Visualize an uninhabited hilly area which is to be modelled and is to include proposed improvements. You have received a site plan showing finished grade contour lines connecting those of natural grade disturbed in the cut and fill process to obtain access roads, parking areas, building pads, corporation yards, and areas to be landscaped. The highest point in the area is the top of a hill at altitude 740' (see the note at end of Ch. 5). The lowest point is at altitude 420'. See Fig. 9-1 for a schematic illustration of relationships. You won't be concerned with the altitude of the hill, but you will be concerned with the difference between the lowest visible point to be modelled (420') and the highest point at 740' or 320' pro-

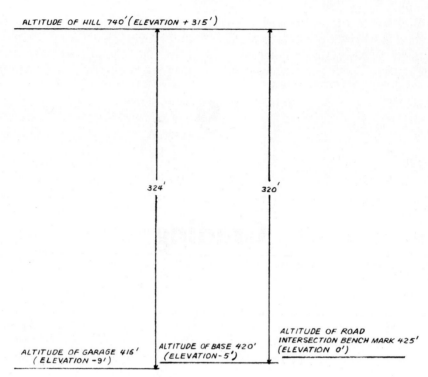

ALTITUDE OF HILL 740' (ELEVATION + 315')

324'

320'

ALTITUDE OF ROAD
INTERSECTION BENCH MARK 425'
(ELEVATION 0')

ALTITUDE OF GARAGE 416'
(ELEVATION -9')

ALTITUDE OF BASE 420'
(ELEVATION -5')

FIGURE 9-1 *Vertical relationships.*

ducing, at first inspection, a model 20" high at 1/16" scale. Upon further analysis you find that the lowest finished surface grade is at a road intersection at an altitude 425' and that the floor of an underground parking facility is at altitude 416', meaning that the model will have to be raised off the base 4' (scale) to reflect the difference between the garage floor level and the lowest visible grade to be shown (420'). As is common practice to simplify expression of relationships, your client has designated the road intersection bench mark at altitude 425' as elevation zero and all other altitudes as plus or minus elevations in relation thereto. This results in the top of the highest hill becoming elevation +315' (740' – 425'), the garage floor –9' (425' – 416'), and the lowest visible point –5' (425' – 420'). The total height of the model will then be 324' (315' + 9') or 20-1/4" at 1/16" scale. These numerical gymnastics are presented to stress the necessity for planning (Ch. 6) from the start. A thorough analysis of the site plan will often reveal structural requirements not obvious upon cursory inspection when your mind is anticipating methods of constructing that building facade. Pattinson's Law contains a useful admonition. If you cornered yourself through not noticing the garage excavation, using a saber saw (Ch. 36) you could cut a hole in the plywood base assuming you still had

the unobstructed area to permit it. The relative expediency of cutting the basement (Ch. 7) versus raising the model is secondary in this discussion to stressing the continuing need for elevation analysis.

CONTOUR MAPS

Contour maps are generally not needed where the entire property includes improvements the elevations of which will be indicated on the architectural drawings showing mostly flat planes at different elevations connected by steps or ramps. A contour map of a large, warped-for-drainage parking lot might be useful, but spot elevations on the architectural site plan would usually suffice for modelling any readable changes in grade. On the other hand, contour maps in the scale of the model are mandatory where hilly or mountainous terrain is included. They should be in the scale of the model to obviate the time consuming replotting of many contour lines in the varying configurations established by nature. Such drawings are a must for contour cutting (Ch. 10). It is always a good idea to ask for them in duplicate to allow cutting up one for patterns. Be sure all superinscribed finished grade contours are ultimately connected to their relative natural grade contour lines. The cutting or tracing tool has to be told where to cut or trace. This continuity is often obvious as along the sides of a canyon fill, but can become very confusing and time consuming because of crowded inscription in the area. If there is any doubt at all, have your client's civil engineer complete the connections for you.

ELEVATION CHANGES

There are two general methods used in effecting elevation changes in model construction. The first is *structural*, and the second involves *contour cutting*, the latter being described in Chapter 10 because of the special equipment required.

STRUCTURAL CONTROL

The structural method includes two systems of elevation control: *horizontal* and *vertical*.

Horizontal Control: Horizontal control is obtained by stacking, or laminating, layers of material of contour interval thickness, at the scale of the model, cut to the configurations of the contours on the map, using a suitable adhesive for the bond (Fig. 9-2). I have found that contact glue (Ch. 34) is best for this purpose. It gives a fast, secure bond and avoids buckling. Weight can be reduced by cutting out the centers of each layer except the top one, being sure to allow enough underlap with the one above and enough material to provide a solid stack around the outside perimeter. To fill the contours, apply plaster (Ch. 35) of a thick cream consistency using a spatula. Build up the covering with several coats, and when the last coat is dry, sand the surface smooth. While the last coat is wet, you may want to insert pebbles, etc., for rock formations, or sculpt such formations (Ch. 25). If the material used in building the contours is nonabsorbent, consider inserting pins at intervals of about 2″ over the surface to give the plaster an anchor. Plaster will stick to itself, but it will tend to chip off a hard, slick surface. Be sure that the stack at the outside perimeter of the model has a smooth, vertical surface. Fill and sand where necessary so the finish paint will camouflage the laminations. If you want to line the exterior sides of the stack with illustration board or vinyl, remember you will have to cut notches in the top edges to agree with the steps in an open contour situation.

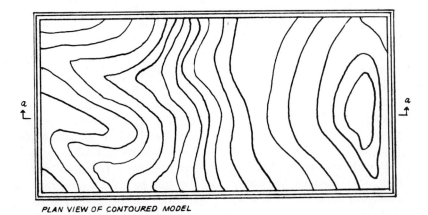

PLAN VIEW OF CONTOURED MODEL

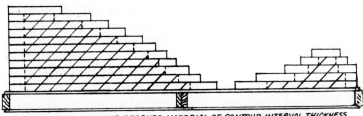

SECTION *a-a* SHOWING STACKED MATERIAL OF CONTOUR INTERVAL THICKNESS. HATCHED AREA INDICATES MATERIAL REMOVED TO REDUCE WEIGHT AS WELL AS SAVE MATERIAL.

FIGURE 9-2 *Horizontal control grading.*

It is obvious that the thickness of the material used at a given scale is controlled by the contour interval, so try to establish an interval which will allow a standard, readily available thickness. If you want to use a contour interval different from that specified on the drawing, such as double the interval on the drawing to allow the use of a thicker material, clear this with your client, particularly where the contours are to be left open. Filling, for the usual display model, will usually hide any evidence of a reasonable change in interval. At 1/100″ scale, for example, a 1′ contour interval would require material thickness of 0.010″. At this thin gauge vinyl would be better than Strathmore paper (Ch. 35) because of the stiffness of the former and its nonabsorbent qualities. Even with contact glue, the paper would tend to produce a lumpy result, which would be accentuated by paint when the contours are to be left open. At 1/16″ scale you could show 1′ contour intervals with lightweight illustration board (Ch. 35). The first of these examples covers a very unusual situation but it points out the hazards when using very thin materials. In locating a material of scale thickness, remember the cumulative effect of stacking out of scale thicknesses. Fifty layers, each 0.005″ out of scale thickness, will result in a mountain 1/4″ too high or too low.

The difficulty of material cutting with any reasonable dispatch is an important consideration. The prospect of cutting 25 layers of 1/8″ Masonite, for example, to create a hill covering a few square feet of area would immediately drive me to consideration of other methods. Let your judgment be your guide. In my opinion, the only advantage of this method for mountain building is the automatic production of accurate open contours for study purposes where no surgery will be required. Its disadvantages far outweigh its advantages. The weight, even when hollow, increased by the covering of plaster when filled, the problem of finding a relatively easy-to-cut material at scale thickness, the large amount of material required, the difficulty in reworking open contours in a study analysis, and the laborious tracing and cutting of contours constitute the principal objections. It is described here in an attempt to be comprehensive, and to pay respects to probably the first method considered at the dawn of model building. The horizontal method of mountain building should be quietly laid to rest and exhumed only for the simplest of assignments such as the building of occasional berms in landscaping, the layering necessary to obtain correct elevation of walks,

curbs, loading platforms, etc., and the construction of steps at scales no larger than 1/8″. Without the necessary equipment (Ch. 10), it may be the only convenient method open to you for showing unfilled contours.

Vertical Control: This method in its pure form produces only a smooth surface. It is obtained by using vertical structural risers to support a covering surface the elevation of which is controlled by the plotted and cut configuration of the top edges of the risers. In its simplest form, this system can be found in the raising of the ground floor of a model up off the base to accommodate underground parking or the electric components of a lighted model, for example. An egg-crate support or blocks of 4-lb urethane foam under a loading platform would constitute vertical control. Stair risers could be a literal example. Contouring of natural, hilly terrain becomes a bit more complicated than elevation of improvements, but still quite simple when following the steps described.

Assume that you have to build a 1/16″ scale exterior display model of an apartment house complex. All buildings and other improvements are on land that has been graded flat (except for drainage warping not considered here). Across the rear of the property there is some hilly terrain that you decide to construct using the vertical control method since there is no need for the study of open contours. The natural hills are going to be left alone. (See Fig. 9-3.) You have at the scale of the model, and in duplicate, a site plan on which the contours are shown. The lowest altitude (L) forms the edge of the flat, improved area, and is at the same elevation. When cutting the heavyweight illustration board (Ch. 35) liner for the improved area, cut the edge at the toe of the hill so that it follows the same configuration as that of the lowest altitude contour line on the site plan. This will permit a tuck-in space for the hill surface material edge in making a tight joint as shown in Fig. 9-3b. On the site plan, which will appear as Fig. 9-3a inside the property line, draw riser lines in the manner shown across the contour lines so that they will include all critical configuration changes and close enough to provide adequate support of the surface by the risers mounted at the line locations. Use 2″ as a general separation guide, realizing that some lines will fan out from a common location. Number these lines, 1, 2, 3, 4, etc., for riser identification purposes. You will need the three backing plates shown as A, B, and C on

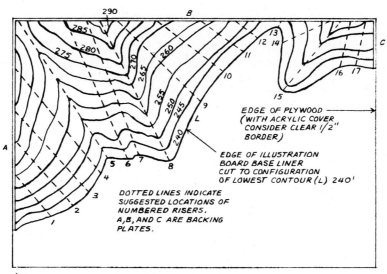

(a) CONTOURED SITE PLAN PLACED ON BASE PLYWOOD TO ILLUSTRATE LOCATION OF CONSTRUCTION ELEMENTS.

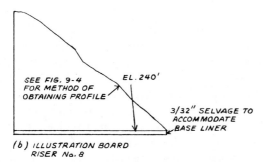

(b) ILLUSTRATION BOARD RISER No. 8

FIGURE 9-3   *Vertical control grading.*

Fig. 9-3*a*. Starting with backing plate A, lay one edge of a piece of heavyweight illustration board along the property line on the site plan at side A so so that one corner is at the intersection of side A with side B (See Fig. 9-4). At each intersection of a contour line with the property line along side A make a pencil mark at the edge of the illustration board, and from each of these marks draw a line on the illustration board perpendicular to its edge and long enough surely to include the vertical distance from the lowest to the highest altitude. If the lowest were 240′ and the highest 290′, then the backing plate material needed would a maximum of 50′ high or 3-1/8″ at 1/16″ scale. Be sure to add 3/32″ (the thickness of the heavyweight illustration board forming the liner) to provide the tuck-in space mentioned previously. At say 3-1/2″ from the top edge of the backing plate draw a line parallel to the edge of the illustration board resting on the property line on the plan. This will indicate the bottom of the backing plate. Draw a guide line 3/32″ above this bottom

line and parallel to it. This will provide for the thickness of the liner on the improved area. Starting at one end of the indicated backing plate area on the illustration board measure up from the base line along each of the vertical lines a distance to represent the height of each contour and mark the location. Connect these points to give the top edge profile of backing plate A and cut it out along this profile line, edge of liner line, and base line. Follow the same procedure for the other two backing plates, B and C. On your belt sander sand 45 degree miters at the two joining edges and with white glue (Ch. 34) mount them on the model with the outside surfaces at the property line. This will result in a three-sided, open topped box mounted on the plywood base. The same system of dimensioning and profile marking is used for each riser with the riser material laid along its riser line on the plan except that they will be trimmed at their property line ends by 3/32″ to accommodate the thickness of the backing plates. Cut out the hilly area from the site plan 3/32″

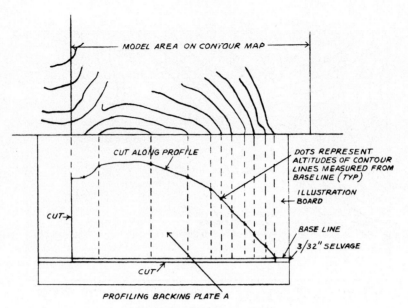

FIGURE 9-4 *Riser profiling.*

inside the property line and along the lowest contour line. Place this pattern on the model surface inside the backing plates and mark the intersections of the riser lines with the lowest contour line on the edge of the model base liner and at their termini on the inside surfaces of the backing plates. If you don't install each riser as you make it, number them to correspond with the numbers indicated on the edge of the base liner and at backing plate termini to speed assembly. The risers are glued down vertically between these numbered points. Note in this case (Fig. 9-3) you may not need all the risers shown for support, but you may need them all to establish authentic surface conformation. Also in other cases where the risers are actually a foot high or higher, you may want to put in braces, generally at right angles to and between the risers for rigidity. Be sure these braces are not so high that they disturb the surface configuration when covered because of their opposing position.

When the plates and risers are firmly in place, the next step is to cover the area. Those of you who have worked with model railroad scenery may be familiar with hard shell methods where the strangth of your ad lib mountain surface lies entirely in a thin shell of plaster. That may be fine in your home basement, but remember here that you are not building a mountain out of your imagination but one which is a replica of existing terrain to the specifications of a client who is paying for your efforts. To assure client satisfaction, not to speak of your own peace of mind, always build with *accuracy* and *strength*. In this case the plotted

edge configuration of the riser tops provides the former, and the method of construction provides the latter. Don't be afraid to add a little weight in the interests of rigidity. It could be embarrassing as well as image destroying to have a finger hole poked through a flimsy surface. I learned my lesson the hard way. In the early years I made an acrylic carrying case for a study model, relying on a simple weld for the handle. The handle snapped off, and the case collapsed on impact. Needless to say, it took a while before I did anymore work for that client.

Forgetting such things as papier mâché and the like, the most practical material for the surface liner is window screening, either plastic or metal. The latter provides the benefit of more readily staying where you form it. Aluminum will avoid rust, but this is really not a serious hazard since the plaster and paint will cover any such spots. Start at one side, and, with common pins with their tops bent to right angles to hold the screen, fasten a piece of screen big enough to cover the area. Push the pins into the center of the top edges of the illustration board backing plates and risers, being sure that the points do not penetrate the outside surfaces. Here is one reason that heavyweight illustration board was used. To gain more anchoring width, you can glue strips along the inside surfaces of the backing plates, trimming the top edges to agree with backing plate configuration. Inside the perimeter backing plates, I have found that small carpet tacks are good for anchoring the screen to the risers. As you proceed across the model pull the screen taut as you pin or tack, adding any additional risers to aid in obtaining configurations missed in your original plot. With scissors trim the screen closely to the outside top edges of the backing plates, and trim and fit the wire edge into the joints where the risers meet the edge of the illustration board improved area liner. Check for tag ends. With a spatula apply a thin coat of thick cream plaster (Ch. 35) gently pushing the plaster into the screen holes to provide a good anchor. Let this coat dry and add coats as necessary to obtain a complete coverage. Sand off any objectionable tool marks or lumps. Note here you may have incorporated some rock outcropping as mentioned previously under description of the horizontal control method. (See Ch. 25, Landscaping.)

Before continuing, it is well to cover any question with respect to accuracy (Ch. 3). You probably have already realized that as soon as the surfacing was added to the risers, the hills were made "fatter" by the thickness of the screen and plaster. The thickness of the base liner was matched by extending the bottom of each riser and backing plate 3/32"; so the starting points are in agreement. From my experience, the out-of-dimension thickness of the screen plaster will not destroy visual authenticity, but it is always wise to be aware of such discrepancies. If you anticipate a legal evidence situation you can run a test combination of the screen and plaster before installation and accommodate the thickness. In any case, keep notes to back up your procedure or reasoning. From a practical standpoint even as much as 1' of added material at 1/16" scale will not destroy visual authenticity of a display model under normal circumstances as long as the surface conformation is correct.

Alternate Methods: If you have a lot of pieces of wooden dowel stock of 1/2" diameter and larger to get rid of, they can be substituted in place of the illustration board risers. Install backing plates as before. Draw a 2" square grid over the site plan and punch line intersections through into the plywood as guide points for gluing in the dowel pieces cut to the length equal to the differences in elevation between the plywood and the altitudes shown on the drawing nearest to where the grid lines intersect. This is not as accurate as the riser method because grid line intersections may not be located at significant changes in contour line configuration. Keep your eye on the drawing as you install the dowels, and don't forget to include the extra 3/32" in length to agree with the edges

of the base liner. Hammer the tacks through the screen into the centers of the dowel tops to avoid splitting.

A second alternate method eliminates the dowels and the illustration board risers indicated in Fig. 9-3. Trace the contoured section of the site plan in the model scale onto the plywood at the hill location and use these transferred contour lines as guides to gluing down the edges of strips of heavy weight illustration board cut to widths equal to the scale differences between the altitude of the plywood and that of the contour lines. These are glued down perpendicularly on edge along the contour lines they represent. You could say that the result is a three-dimensional contour map, ignoring the open spaces between contours. Bend each strip to the general configuration of the contour line before gluing with white glue to prevent its fighting installation. Where there are sharp changes in direction such as in the canyon areas, it is better to cut the strips at the change location for ease of mounting. Scoring with a matte knife at right angles to the length across the surface at the outside of a curve will make the forming of the strips easier and help prevent opening up the laminations in the illustration board. Cover with wire screen as you did previously. This method, when done carefully, theoretically should provide the most accuracy because the supports are the actual contours, but you may have already thought of the limitations. Where the area is large or the height of the mountain is more than a few inches, it becomes clumsy to form the wide strips and mount them vertically, not to speak of the gross waste of material. Confine this method to relatively gradual slopes in small areas.

Combination Method: This method could be called a combination method because it results in open contours (horizontal control method) and is vertically built up (vertical control method). The system involves the vertical offset lamination of strips of material obtained by cutting along the contours on a contour map glued to the material surface (Fig. 9-5). The width of the strip will of course depend upon the distance between two adjacent contours, and the height (thickness of material) should be just large enough to allow a vertically overlapping glue joint with the next strip below and a freestanding vertical surface equal to the contour interval. Probably the easiest to handle material is rigid 4-lb urethane foam. Since this will be cut with a knife to avoid loss of

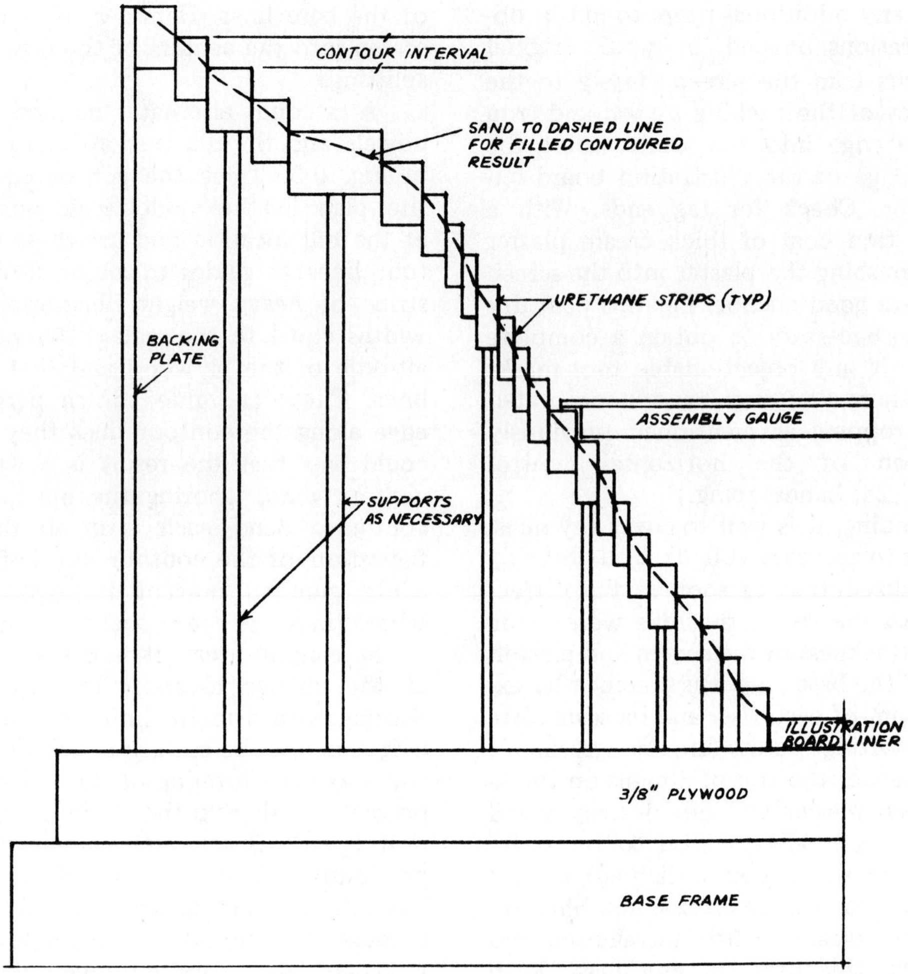

FIGURE 9-5 *Combination method.*

material, I would limit thickness to about 1/2″ which is approaching the limit of knife throw in my Cut-Awl (Ch. 36). In the absence of a power tool, use a thin, serrated edge paring type knife (a hacksaw blade will remove material and what you want is a slice). The joints will mate; so you do not have to be too particular about keeping the knife exactly vertical. Referring to Fig. 9-3 build the backing plates as you did for the methods previously described and install them on the model. Assume for this example that the contour interval is 1/8″ at the scale of the model (2′ at 1/16″ scale) and that no contour line is closer than 1/8″ from the adjacent ones. Using a temporary glue (Ch. 34), affix the contour map (site plan at the scale of the model) to the surface of the 1/2″ rigid urethane and trim the edge along the lowest contour (Fig. 9-3). Then cut the first urethane strip by cutting along the next higher contour line. Remove the paper and glue this strip to the plywood base against the edge of the heavyweight illustration board liner establishing the improved

area. Slide a 1/8″ sanding guide on the liner along this strip as you sand it down to one contour interval (1/8″) above the liner surface. The next two strips will have to be sanded off in the same manner to get a 1/8″ clear contour interval. Beyond the third, the 1/2″ depth of the strips will clear the plywood base when obtaining this interval. Glue the strips together with contact glue (Ch. 34), using a 1/8″ thick mounting (spacing) guide as shown in Fig. 9-5. If a strip breaks in handling simply glue the pieces in place separately. In fact, because of flimsiness due to length and thickness, you may want purposely to cut them into sections before mounting. As you assemble, use light finger pressure to test the composite rigidity. When you are about 2″ off the base, start putting in supports in various places. These can be dowels or strips of heavyweight illustration board. As you approach the top you may have to use tweezers to install supports in the narrow remaining open space between the last installed strip and a backing plate surface unless you have provided **for removable** backing plates. Glue the ends of the strips to the backing plates as you proceed to give added anchorage. If you come out with a small gap at the top because of material lost in cutting, simply make the last two strips a little wider than the map shows to fill the gap. To "fill" urethane contours the neatest way is to sand off the "steps" down to the joints of "tread" and "riser" as shown by the dotted line in Fig. 9-5. That is why the lowest contour strip was mounted one contour interval *above* the liner instead of even with it. Ch. 10 will explain this principle further. The top edges of the backing plates are already smooth surfaced since they were made as they were in the discussion of the vertical control method. They probably could be supplied that way during your client's study period as they will match the edge of the urethane when the latter is sanded off for display purposes.

You have probably already sensed the limita-

tions of this method. If the contour lines are too close together as in a steep gradient you will not be able to cut strips, unless you can skip enough lines to accommodate. Also, if the contour interval becomes too small, it will be difficult to make them evenly readable on assembly. It is a slightly clumsy method for great expanses of contouring even though you can cut the strips into sections. The more pieces you have the more susceptible the system is to errors demanding corrections resulting in a messy open contour result.

MODEL A

Returning to model A, introduced in Ch. 8, and duplicated as Fig. 9-6, the only grading exercise confronting us is the establishment of certain areas

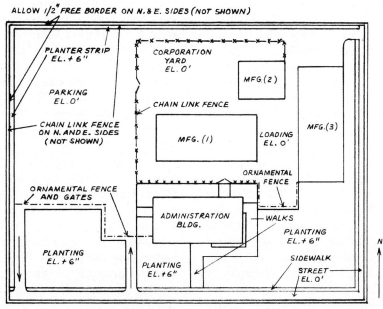

SITE PLAN TRANSFERRED TO BASE SURFACE

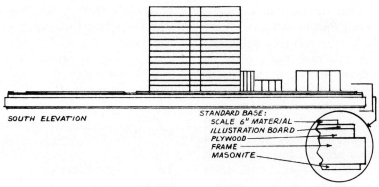

FIGURE 9-6 *Model A.*

at a level 6″ above the overall base liner level at 0′. Drainage warping is ignored for purposes of this illustration. The crosshatched areas on Fig. 9-6 indicate the raised areas. In this simplest of grading problems, the obvious solution is the horizontal control method or the gluing down in each area a single layer of material 0.03125″ thick (6″ at 1/16″ scale). You could use sheet vinyl of 0.030″ thickness, but because you would prefer a warmer and minutely textured surface for lawn areas, you decide on 0.030″ Strathmore paper (Ch. 35). Note that this thickness is 0.00125″ short of 6″ at 1/16″ scale, but that small amount of difference will not destroy visual authenticity and might be made up in glue and paint. Cut out the crosshatched shapes as shown, hold them in position on the model base, and trace their outlines with sharp, hard pencil lines to serve as glue limits and positioning guides. For mounting these shapes, apply contact glue (Ch. 34) to both surfaces and let dry. When applying the glue to the macadam gray base liner, push the brush carefully up to the guide lines so that glue won't be visible beyond the edges of the Strathmore. Small amounts of excess glue not yet hard can be rolled off much in the same way you roll off rubber cement. Be careful not to disturb the top surface of the illustration board liner. When the glue is dry, carefully line up one edge of each piece of 6″ material along its guide line so that as you progressively lower it onto the model, it will exactly fill the previously traced area. Use the longest side of each piece in the initial lineup. In the case of the two planter strips along the north and west at the perimeter of the property, hold down one end with a finger as you grasp the other end to control straight placement. This indicates that it is better to apply two meeting strips than one including a right angle change of direction. When all pieces are down, seat them with blows of your fist to assure overall adhesion. Incomplete application of glue may show up in the form of bubbles when you paint the absorbent surface. In case of bubbles, later see Ch. 42. Considering Pattinson's Law, there are times when it is better to paint components before installing, but in this case prior painting would curl the Strathmore making it harder to glue down. Note that sometimes when it is difficult to apply glue within a designated narrow area such as the planter strips, you can get by with application to the part only. If these strips were 4′ wide, then the outlined area on the illustration board liner would be 1/4″ wide at 1/16″ scale making glue application not too difficult, but if you had to lay down strips 1/16″ wide, then the

one-sided application of glue makes sense. Weight them down before the glue has dried to assure adhesion. For laying out curbs and walks, see Ch. 13. Note that the added layer of material automatically gives us 6″ curbs at the streets, a normal situation. The driveways enter the property at street level (El. 0′) so no ramped grading is necessary at the sidewalk. The sidewalk pedestrian steps off a curb to cross a driveway.

Before leaving model A, consider the effects on construction approach of different scales. Ignore the effects on overall size of the model for this purpose. At 1/32″ scale, you could use 0.015″ Strathmore or sheet vinyl for the 6″ layer. At 1/8″ scale you could use lightweight illustration board since it is approximately 1/16″ thick. At 1/4″ and larger scales you start to run into difficulty in locating scale 6″ thick materials. At 1/4″ scale, you could use 1/8″ Masonite, but that has a poor surface for painting and landscaping. The thicker materials add weight which you should avoid as much as possible. You could laminate two layers of lightweight illustration board to obtain a 6″ high curb at 1/4″ scale, but here and larger go the vertical control route. At 1/4″ scale, raise a single layer of lightweight illustration board with an egg crate of 1/6″ stripwood (Ch. 35) with the outside strips even with the edges of the illustration board. The subject of curbs is so closely related to this form of grading that it is briefly considered here to complete the picture. The curbs at 1/16″ scale can be shown most satisfactorily by drawing a "concrete" paint-filled drafting pen along the edges of the 0.030″ material used to show the +6″ grade (Ch. 26). If you wish to use this method at 1/4″ scale, be sure that the outside edges of the stripwood egg-crating are exactly flush with the edges of the grading material or you will show a horizontally laminated curb. You can forestall this by gluing the outside riser strips to the grading material before mounting to ensure a flush joint, but the better way at the larger scales is to cut the grading material a curb-width short and add separate curb material either in formed stripwood or in a vertical lamination of strips of sheet vinyl (Ch. 13) to make up the curb thickness. Your judgment should tell you which method to use under a particular set of circumstances.

MODEL B

To illustrate some of the more complicated problems in grading, model B is shown (Fig. 9-7). The subject is a proposed community hospital facility

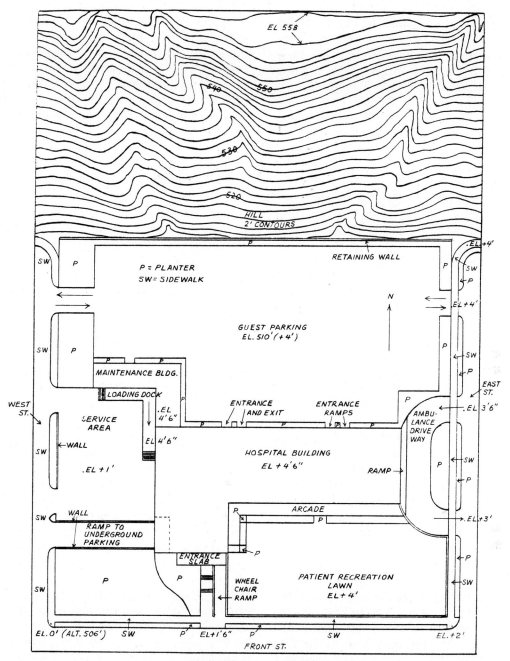

FIGURE 9-7   *Model B.*

to provide both medical and convalescent services. A group of local business men and doctors have purchased approximately 3-1/2 acres against the foothills, and have engaged a firm of architects to develop the property in phases. The approved Phase 1 of the project is reflected in the site plan shown in Fig. 9-7 which represents a scale drawing reduced to convenient size so that all the elements are in correct relationship. The guest parking and foothill areas to the rear are available for later development. The directors desire a 1/8" scale exterior model with an acrylic cover for study and display,

to create interest among the community, and to help in raising capital improvement financing.

Since grading construction procedure is the important consideration here, numbers are given only to the extent necessary to help you define your mental picture of overall size and level relationships. The property is in the shape of a rectangle measuring 320' × 480', or 40" × 60" at 1/8" scale. There is a 6' sidewalk along three sides, a 4' planted parking strip along Front and East Streets, 14' of street on each side, and 20' of Front Street. This, with a 5/16" lip all around, will bring the overall dimensions of the model to 46-1/8″ × 64-3/8″, well within a standard plywood panel size without the necessity for base division. With a 2′ contour interval, the highest natural grade altitude is 558′. Establishing a bench mark as elevation 0′ at altitude 506′ at the southwest street corner, the highest graded point will be +52′ on the hill area at the rear limit of the model (558′ - 506′). There are to be two buildings in Phase 1, the hospital building and a one-story maintenance and supply building. The hospital building will have 10 floors with a heliport on the roof. With 12′ floor to floor, the elevation of the roof will be +124′6″, and the building will be 15″ high standing on its +4′6″ pad. Mentioning the buildings will help you to acquire the necessary overall concept discussed in Ch. 6. Note that the hospital roof is considerably higher than the highest elevation of the hill to the rear; consider this the highest point when ordering the acrylic cover (Ch. 39).

Grading: Before firing up the bulldozers, take a visual walk around the property to help determine the best approach to grading. This is in effect what you would do in following the precepts of Ch. 6. Moving east along Front Street, the city planting strip and sidewalk are at +6″. This 6″ curb appears wherever a street surface exists. The planting area at the southwest corner of the property starts at sidewalk level, rises to +1′6″ at the building entrance walk, and warps up as a bank to the top of the steps at the level of the entrance slab at elevation +4′6″. The entrance wheelchair ramp rises between its own curb and the retaining wall holding up the patient recreation area from +1′6″ at the sidewalk to the same entrance level of +4′6″. The recreation area wall with top of wall (TW) at +8′ extends south from the building to the sidewalk, east to the East Street sidewalk, and north to the ambulance exit which it borders in a curve back to the building. The Front Street sidewalk and city planting strip slope up to elevation +2′ at the southeast corner of the property and then north to +3′ at the ambulance exit, and +4′ at the ambulance parking area entrances. Continuing north the contoured hill rises from +4′ (altitude 510′) to +52′ (altitude 558′) at the rear of the property. Flanked by planted banks, the exit from the parking area slopes down to +2′ at the sidewalk of West Street. The northerly planter is limited by the end of a retaining wall extending the width of the property along the north edge of the parking area (elevation +4′).

Continuing south along West Street the sidewalk passes the exit from the service yard at +1′6″, the entrances to the service yard and underground parking at +1′ and then down to +6″ on top of the curb at the southwest corner of the property, the starting point of the tour. The hospital and maintenance buildings each have a finished floor (FF) elevation of +4′6″ and loading docks at the same elevation. With a service yard elevation of +1′, the 3′6″ to the dock surfaces will facilitate loading and unloading to and from standard delivery truck beds. The peristyle on the south side of the hospital building with an FF (finished floor) at the same elevation as that of the building has an apron sloping down 6″ to +4′, the elevation of the recreation area.

The lowest point in the model, -7′ at the underground parking entrance, was not considered in determining the depth of the acrylic cover since it is not necessary to raise the model off the base to accommodate it. This single underground depression can be effected by cutting a hole into the base plywood. Seven feet at 1/8″ scale is only 7/8″, requiring a floor level well within the depth of the 1″ × 2″ framing. The only conflict will be one leg of the X bracing in the base (Ch. 7). You have received a site plan in the scale of the model in two sections (Ch. 5). Keeping Pattinson's Law in mind, before you assemble the base, trace on the base plywood the line where the underground parking entrance ramp meets the sidewalk, the side limits of the ramp outside its retaining walls, and the building wall line. Expand the hole indication inside the building so that the cut edges of the plywood back under the building will not be visible at the entrance. In showing a 9′6″ traffic clearance, the bottom of the header at the building entrance will be 2′6″ above the elevation of the plywood surface. See Fig. 9-8 for a schematic section, and a plan of the hole shape. Guide your saber saw along the sides of the ramp just inside the lines so that you can later sand the edges down flush with the covering material or liner. This extra thickness provided by the plywood will add to the support of the retaining walls of the ramp. Paint the cut edges of the plywood under the building a matte black for camouflage. When installing X bracing, cut a notch out of the top edge of the conflicting leg to clear the area and provide a support for the ramp (Fig. 9-9), and install a piece of 1″ × 2″ with an added wood strip to form a shelf to support the end of the ramp at -7′. Note that all of this exercise is best done after you have installed the X bracing and before

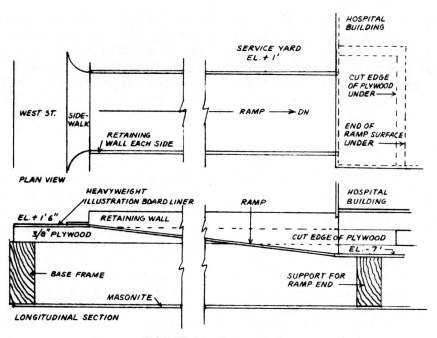

FIGURE 9-8 *Ramp scheme.*

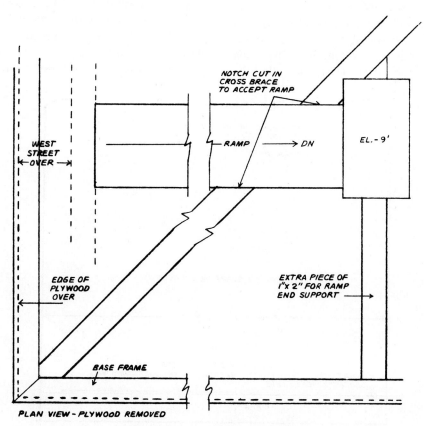

FIGURE 9-9 *Clearance for ramp.*

you add the bottom Masonite cover. Since the conflicting leg crosses the ramp toward the street end, you can cut out the relieving notch from the top or plywood surface. When you have completed the base assembly and performed the necessary filling and sanding, you are ready to consider layout and overall grading.

Liner or Covering Surface: The important first step in this process is to determine the material and its thickness with which you will establish the most prevalent finished elevation. Figure 9-7 shows this to be El. +4' over most of the guest parking and patient recreation areas. Since the vertical control, or riser method will be the most efficient way to establish this level, a material thick enough to hold span between risers and pliable enough to stand slight warping as at vehicular traffic accesses is required. Heavyweight illustration board (Ch. 35) seems to fill this bill. Its laminated composition won't stand small radius bends, but it is anticipated here that the straight slopes required will not separate the layers. The goal is to cover as much area as possible without joints in the material. The largest standard available sheet of heavyweight illustration board in my experience measures 40" × 60"; so it is obvious that one sheet will not include all the finished graded area from the lowest contour of the hill area south to the edge of the model. This area measures 330' (N-S) × 364' (E-W) or, at 1/8"

scale, 41-1/4" × 45-1/2", (overall dimension of 46-1/8" – 5/8" lips) requiring the use of two sheets of 40" × 60" material. From the 60" dimension of the first sheet cut a piece 45-1/2" long, resulting in a rectangular piece 40" × 45-1/2". Place the site plan over this piece so that the *property line* on the south and the model limit lines on the east and west match the edges of the illustration board. Using carbon paper, trace the bottom contour line (Alt. 510') of the hilly area on the north on the illustration board. Cut the board along this line, and along the bottom (property line) edge, notch out the width of the retaining wall limiting the south border of the patient recreation area, resulting in a covering surface shape as shown in Fig. 9-10. From the second sheet of illustration board, cut a strip 45-1/2" × 3-3/4", the width being equal to the width of the south sidewalk, planting strip, and street, 30' divided by 8 or 3-3/4". On assembly, the only obvious joints will be across the city rights of way on the east and west sides of the model at the south property line. Most of the remaining property line joint will be camouflaged by changes in surface treatment and change of plane.

Layout: Layout (Ch. 8) poses no serious problems in this case because the drawings at the scale of the model (1/8") can be traced directly on the plywood base and liner. Use carbon paper because punch marks alone on raw wood are difficult to

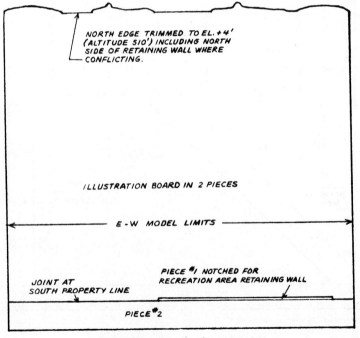

NORTH EDGE TRIMMED TO EL. +4' (ALTITUDE 510') INCLUDING NORTH SIDE OF RETAINING WALL WHERE CONFLICTING.

ILLUSTRATION BOARD IN 2 PIECES

E-W MODEL LIMITS

JOINT AT SOUTH PROPERTY LINE

PIECE #1 NOTCHED FOR RECREATION AREA RETAINING WALL

PIECE #2

FIGURE 9-10 *Surface cover.*

read, and you are not concerned with indelibility as you were on the painted surface model A. Also, there are no mountainside installations to plot. Trace all the finished grade configurations as shown in Fig. 9-7 on the plywood base, including the lowest contour line (El. 510′) at the toe of the hill and make elevation notations as shown on the site plan. All these lines will ultimately be covered up, but they are necessary as guides for placement of the elevating material or risers. Make this same tracing on the illustration board liner, noting that the north edge has already been cut along the 510′ (+4′) contour line and that the south edge, notched out for the retaining wall on the east, is the south property line (Fig. 9-10). Again, we are not concerned about indelibility of carbon paper tracing, since the surface is still unpainted.

Surface Cover Breakup: As a material and time saver, the logical method to use for establishing finished grade levels is the vertical control method throughout most of the improved area, but before

you start cutting risers consider breaking up the surface cover to facilitate effecting abrupt changes in grade. This will help you install risers of the correct length and most efficient direction, guided by the pencil layout previously accomplished. See Fig. 9-11 for an indication of where you will cut or crease the cover. Front Street and its sidewalk and planting strip are already on a separate strip of illustration board since we had to use two sheets of the material to cover the area. Cut East Street off as indicated by the solid line at the inside edge of the curb. With a 6″ wide curb, note that this will make the actual planter strip width 3′6″. Cut slots out as shown to accept retaining walls on the east and west sides of the patient recreation area to meet the slot across the front already cut when you cut the outline of the base cover (Fig. 9-10). Also cut a slot for the screen wall between the service yard accesses. Cut out and save (as filler patterns) the areas marked "P" (planter) except where peeling off the top lamination is more convenient. The holes will be filled with urethane foam so no risers should

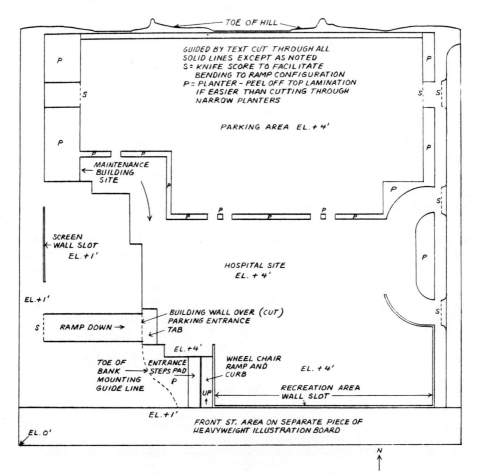

FIGURE 9-11 *Surface cover breakup.*

appear across the openings. Cut out and discard the rectangle indicating the wheelchair ramp. On the west side score, with a mat knife, the dotted lines shown at one end of each of the two vehicular ramps. This is where the slopes start down, and the scoring will allow even change of direction. On the north ramp, cut all the way through at the street. The sides were cut when you removed the planter areas. Cutting this ramp tab at the street is to accommodate the fact that the hypotenuse of a right triangle is longer than either of its two sides. In other words, when you bend down the tab to meet the street, it will tend to pull away from the joint because of foreshortening. The open joint can be filled later with spackle (Ch. 35). Rather than confuse the issue with a complicated table of stretchability of various materials spanning areas at various gradients, it is more practical simply to alert you to the problem. In the case of the ramp at the north end on the west side, the approximately 1′ in 15′ slope is not very steep, but to avoid the tendency to pull the street edge in from the plywood base edge, cutting is advised. The ambulance exit ramp on the east side of the model probably can be left attached to the sidewalk since the slope is only about 1′ in 60′. In cases like this, you can always make relieving slices later if you can't stretch the assembly. As standard operating procedure in scale model building so often dictates: Try a method and if it doesn't work, change it! At the underground parking ramp, cut through on the solid lines shown which are outside the retaining wall to be installed on each side. Note that the tab extends under the building an arbitrary few inches to rest on the shelf made previously when installing the bracing and has a T end to give visual continuation. When you have determined the thickness of the building wall material, trim the bar of the T so that it will have a snug fit. Cut the solid line at the north and east sides of the service area as shown and across the north end of the entrance walk at the entrance slab facing Front Street. This tab will go under and support the

steps. As a check, because you have previously cut an underground parking entrance hole in the plywood base, be sure that the tab cut at the same location in the illustration board cover matches this hole. Score the dotted lines and cut through on a curve the north and south sides, from sidewalk to street, of the three driveways off East Street. This is to form entrance apron tabs which will be sloped down to meet the street.

Maintaining Relationships: Before proceeding, consider the effects of adding liner or surfacing materials to the plywood base and to levels above or below that base. Remember that when you add the *same* thickness material to the base as that which you add to structure built to the specified elevation above that base, you have maintained correct relationship because you have increased all surface elevations equally. This is illustrated in Fig. 9-12. Don't fall into the trap of building structure to specified elevations above your established base *liner* and then adding liner material. The resulting elevation will be too high by the thickness of the material, and relationships with surrounding correctly installed facilities will be distorted. Particularly where the liner (cover) will reflect grade changes, establish the flat, even surface of the raw plywood base as your 0′ bench mark for all vertical control. The slots were cut for walls in Fig. 9-11 because it is easier to establish level top of wall elevations from the established 0′ level than it is from sloping ground. The retaining walls at the underground parking ramp cannot be bottomed because they extend below the base plywood, but the even gradient will make it easy to cut the bottom edges of the walls to fit the slope of the ramp on which they will rest.

Risers: Risers now have to be added to the plywood base (vertical control method), and profiled to reflect the elevations shown in the areas defined by the guideline tracing. It is a good general practice to start around the edge of the model, particularly where you have separate strips of cover (liner)

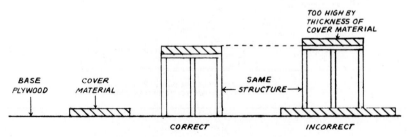

FIGURE 9-12 *Level relationships.*

to mount, since this will confine your interior work within an established area to help you maintain correct relationships. A good place to start in the case of model B is the street along the east side of the property. Along a 60″ edge of the second sheet of 40″ × 60″ illustration board used in making the liner (Fig. 9-10) mark off the distance from the intersection of the 510′ contour line with the model edge to the southeast corner of the plywood base. About 5/8″ from the edge and parallel to it, draw a line on the illustration board which will indicate the bottom of the riser glued flush with the edge of the plywood. The 5/8″ width of riser strip will be just enough to include the highest elevation along its length (3′6″ or 7/16″ at 1/8″ scale). Plotting so that the top or finished surface of the illustration board will face the outside of the model when the riser is installed, mark the distances from the pencil line toward the edge to represent the elevations as indicated on the site plan. Connect these marks with a pencil line and cut along this line. Then cut out the strip along the straight line first drawn. Note that this is the same procedure followed previously in the discussion of vertical control. See Fig. 9-13. At the south end of this riser bevel a 45 degree angle which will meet vertically the same bevel on the east end of the riser installed along the south edge of the model. Note that the grading configuration was cut before the riser was separated from the sheet of illustration board. This is done because it is hard to hold a narrow strip while cutting a wavy line. Also note when plotting elevations along a riser, the places where the change in elevation is obviously abrupt to a higher or lower plane which may obviously be level before a slope appears again. In the riser just discussed, for example, the +3′6″ elevation at the north end at the curb base would continue to the

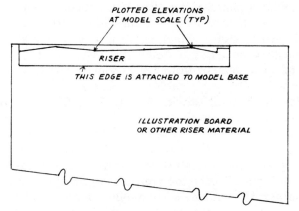

PLOTTED ELEVATIONS
AT MODEL SCALE (TYP)

RISER

THIS EDGE IS ATTACHED TO MODEL BASE

ILLUSTRATION BOARD
OR OTHER RISER MATERIAL

FIGURE 9-13 *Cutting risers.*

back side of the curb (which curves eastward) and then notch at right angles up to +4′ to continue at that elevation across the city planter strip and sidewalk. Make a duplicate of this first riser, adjusting for the slight difference in the north end where it passes under the sidewalk area. These two risers will take care of the East Street which is 14′ wide or 1-3/4″ at 1/8″ scale. Glue the interior one along the curb line parallel to the first one which is flush with the edge of the plywood.

The third riser will be glued down parallel to the first two along a line just inside the curb to catch the east edge of the liner from which the street has been cut (Fig. 9-11). This will have the same configuration as the first two except at the driveways the top edge will be notched down to receive the aprons sloped down to street level from the sidewalk. Otherwise this riser will be 6″ (1/16″) wider (higher) than the first two to help form the curb. A duplicate of the third riser, without the driveway apron notches, will be glued down generally under the location of the sidewalk.

Follow the same procedure along the south and west perimeters of the finished graded area except that there are no traffic aprons to street level. This means that the sidewalk and sidewalk-planting strips can be added to the street surfaces using lightweight illustration board (Ch. 35) to form the 6″ curbs (horizontal control method). The driveways off West Street pass *through* the sidewalk 6″ below the surface of the latter. It is probably safe to say that the normal entrance involves ramping up to the sidewalk level, but this alternate is shown here to show a different, street intersection type condition where the pedestrian steps off a curb to cross the right of way as was done in model A (Fig. 9-6). Each of Front and West Streets will have its set of risers in triplicate. Be sure that the outside risers are configured so that the good (white) surface of the illustration board faces out and that mitered joints are made at the southwest and southeast corners.

When the street risers are glued down, you can mount East and Front Streets which are separate pieces. For a quick, sure bond, apply contact glue (Ch. 34) to the entire undersides of both street strips and to the top edges of the risers involved. When joining, be sure the outside edges are flush with the top outside surfaces of the outside risers as you bring the glued surfaces into contact because the bond will be immediate. If you should get caught glued out of correct location see Ch. 42. Light sanding of the street edges will often correct slight differences in plane. Cut a

9'6"-wide strip of lightweight illustration board (1/16" or 6" thick at 1/8" scale) and glue it flush with the inside edge of the Front Street surface (for sidewalk and parking planter), being sure that the ends will be flush with the curbs of East and West Streets. Along a straightedge score a line 6' from the property line edge as an aid in later designating sidewalk and planter strip areas with paint. Now that the two streets are down, you should begin to have a feeling for relationships both horizontal and vertical. You can't install West Street yet because it is attached to areas for which the risers have not been put down.

Before setting your sails for a run through the remaining risers, dig up Pattinson's Law to prevent goofs. Upon analysis, you will find that most of the remaining risers will be strips of illustration board (heavyweight) 4' (1/2") wide from end to end, and that side-exposed risers will occur along the north and east sides of the service area, serving as walls of the loading dock and building below ground floor. Where such exposure occurs, be sure you mount the riser walls so that you will view the white or good side of the illustration board in the finished model, that the exposed corners are tight, mitered joints, and that they are flush with the cover (liner) edges. Note that the wall riser will have a 2'6" (3/16") notch cut out of the bottom edge to span the underground parking entrance and provide the 9'6" clearance from the ramp. Also any doors, such as for a freight elevator, should be indicated in exposed riser walls before mounting. See Ch. 21 for methods of indicating. There is likely to be a bit of trial and error fitting of the exposed riser walls. Glue the segments down with contact glue on one surface only (so that they can be moved if necessary) carefully following your previously plotted guide lines. Place a temporary wall against Front Street at the patient recreation area as an assembly stop and place some 1/2" thick strips of 1" × 2" wood frame material temporarily across the guest parking and building areas to support the cover while fitting. Remove and replace the cover until you are satisfied that you have the riser walls located correctly. If you have not done much shifting, the one surface glue application will hold by pressing the risers down. Remove the cover and install the remaining risers including the necessary sloped risers at the guest parking and ambulance exit driveways. With the service area at generally El. +1', use the horizontal control method and laminate a riser with two pieces of lightweight illustration board which is 6" (1/6") thick. Cut one thickness

to the shape of the area allowing a loose fit. Glue this to a second sheet and trim to the configuration of the first. Since you have a large area at one elevation, and since the small change can be effected with readily available material of exact thickness, this method is faster than the vertical control method using numerous pieces of 1/8" thick strip wood. Add an additional piece of lightweight illustration board at the yard exit so the liner will ramp up to +1'6". At the joint between the planted area and Front Street at the southwest corner of the model use a shaped stripwood riser to be sure that the two planes meet exactly. Otherwise in the planted area you can use the same method used in the service yard except that you would use several pads of single thickness or laminated lightweight illustration board at key spots. The cover would be warped down over these pads, leaving the hole at the corner of the building open for insertion of urethane foam. When you have the entire improved model area risered, it should appear similar to Fig. 9-14 without the cover. Except where exposure demands precision in installation of risers as on the east side of the service area, there are no hard and fast rules covering egg-crating. The goal is *support*. To be safe, I have always followed the practice of supporting all edges first, with the risers just back from the edge of the cover in unexposed areas and then egg-crated to avoid possible parallel ripples from settling. Heavyweight illustration board that is 3/32" thick should span at least 4" without sag. You very likely could span a much larger area under normal conditions of humidity, but it is better to be safe than sorry. In my early years I once spanned about 6" with *light*weight illustration board, and after the model was finished I noticed in certain light that there were parallel waves between the parallel risers — a disheartening sight to say the least.

With a paper cutter (Ch. 36), cutting 4' (1/2") strips of illustration board and gluing them down with white glue is much more a tedious job than a lengthy one, but if doing this over about 8 sq ft of area gets to you, try one of the following methods. On your table saw, cut strips 13/32" thick from your stock of scrap 1" × 2" framing pine. Chop the result into lengths of about 3" and glue them to the centers of approximately 4" square pieces of heavyweight illustration board, giving you the 4' high risers that you want. Scatter these "tables" over the area to support the cover. Another alternative is to mount squares of 1/2" plywood, if you are not concerned with the

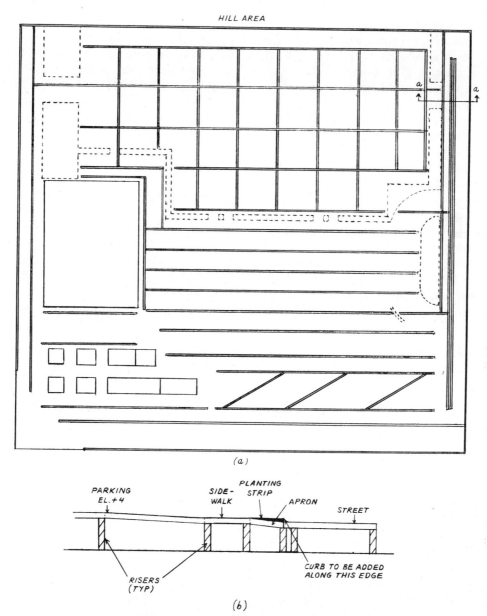

FIGURE 9-14 *Risers installed (and Sec. a-a).*

extra weight. Better still, if you have a supply of 4-lb urethane foam, cut out blocks of convenient dimension and slice 1/2″ thick pieces on your bandsaw. With any of the above methods I find it a good practice to use the illustration board strips around cover perimeters to ensure a solid mount at the edge of the raised area and provide a finished appearance.

Mounting the Cover: East and Front Streets have already been mounted as discussed previously. Turn the remaining cover over, and with a mat knife score across the ramp at the building line so that the T end can be bent up horizontal to rest

on the shelf provided (Fig. 9-8). Place the cover on the model dry so that West Street fits the west edge and joins correctly with Front Street. Weight the service area down so that the cover will not shift as you check the joints at exposed riser wall areas and those at East and Front Streets. Through the hole above, press the underground parking ramp onto its shelf and trim or add material to the bottom of the T crossbar to obtain a snug fit inside the riser wall at the entrance. When you are satisfied that all is well, apply contact glue to the entire underside of the cover and on the top surfaces of all the risers, including the shelf at the T end of the underground parking ramp. You don't have to wait until the glue is dry before mounting the cover, but it probably will be by the time you apply it to all the risers. Here is one of the advantages of contact glue. Some of the white glue, if used in this case, would be dried to a state of uselessness by the time you got around to putting the cover down. Over dry contact glue, place pieces of newspaper (brown wrapping paper is better) except over the West Street area. This will give you a chance to force slight adjustment if necessary on first contact. Clamp a backing to the lip along West Street snuggly against the plywood edge, lower the southwest corner against Front Street (at the inside edge of the sidewalk). Hold this down as you push West Street against the backing as you lower the entire edge. Push in the service area to a tight fit with the loading dock and building riser walls. When you are satisfied that the western area is lined up, pull the

shield and smooth the rest of the cover down onto its risers, hitting the cover surface with the palm of a hand to cinch it. Press down the underground parking ramp into place, as well as all driveway ramps. Cut 5'6" (11/16") strips from lightweight illustration board to serve as the sidewalk segments along West Street and glue them in place along the property line. Remember to round the ends at the driveways. The curbs (Ch. 13) will bring the total width to 6'.

Building Slab: The 6" building slab to bring the first floor level to +4'6" is cut out of lightweight illustration board as shown in Fig. 9-15. Provision is made for 6' of planter and entry approach along the north and east sides of the maintenance building and along the north side of the hospital building. On the east, the slab extends in the form of a ramp at the ambulance entrance. There is a 10'

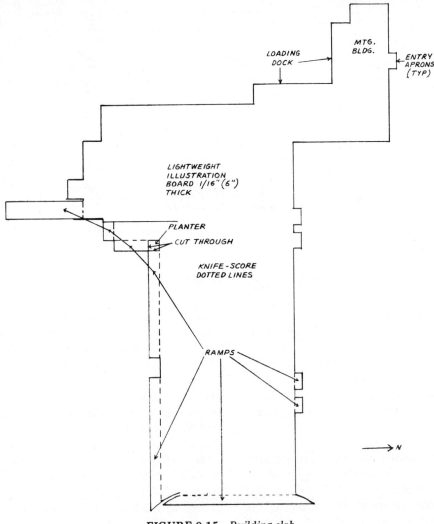

FIGURE 9-15 *Building slab.*

wide peristyle against the inside of the L on the south side of the hospital building with a 6′ ramp down to the patient recreation area. The slab covers the configuration of the entry porch with a tab to form the wheelchair ramp to Front Street against the patient recreation retaining wall. The slab also extends to cover the configuration of the loading dock at the service area. When the slab has been cut, turn it over and taper sand the ramp ends except the Front Street wheelchair ramp as suggested in Ch. 13. These are at the ambulance entrance, across the east end of the hospital at an indicated entry on the north side and at the peristyle. On the top surface score, with a mat knife, a break across the start of each ramp area. Carefully bend these ramps down slightly below the bottom surface of the slab so that when glued down they will form tight adhesion at their tapered edges. Where the planters occur in the slab, notch them out. Their outside edges will be defined by the curb (Ch. 13). Fit the slab dry on the model checking to see that the front wheel chair ramp tab will make a tight joint with the rear side of the Front Street sidewalk. Trace the rear and east sides with a pencil to provide a glue guide and apply contact glue to both surfaces, let dry and put the slab in place, pushing all ramped surfaces down to curbs (Ch. 13) at grade. Fill the planter cutouts with urethane foam trimmed to provide tight fits with cover edges and sand the surfaces down to match the grade. This concludes the subject of grading as it applies to the improved area of model B. Note that our grading included not only the use of bulldozers, skiploaders, and scrapers, but also involved surfacing of guest parking area and driveways, construction of underground parking facilities and loading dock, and installation of sidewalks and ramps. You have, in effect, constructed the foundation of the hospital building and mainteance building as well as 95 percent of the civil work.

Ancillary Civil Items: Model B project presents an excellent example of what I mean when I say in the Introduction (Ch. 1) that it is impossible to separate construction tip subjects into sections sufficient unto themselves. The contractor very likely would include curbs and gutters (Ch. 13) along with surfacing, expansion joints and textures; so they should be recognized under "Grading" with reference to pertinent chapters to prevent unnecessary repetition. Retaining and screen walls (Ch. 18) and exterior steps (Ch. 15) fall into the same category. Provision therefore must be made

during grading, but their special construction tips are better placed in separate chapters. Landscaping (Ch. 25), which certainly is based upon grading, is better left, as in real life, until all construction has been completed and is probably the most easily isolated of all the subjects. A certain amount of repetition is unavoidable in the interests of continuity and clarity. Tips on ramps included in model B were given in this section though their general coverage is in Ch. 15. This is to help cut down page flipping while you are in the midst of building the model.

Pattinson's Law: Following the extremely important principles of efficient sequence of events, I have tried to obey Pattinson's Law in presenting tips in this section. You may have noted an apparent violation in not painting the guest parking surface before installing the building slab or in not providing for camouflage of the visible joint between the cover and the riser walls at loading dock and underground parking entrance. The general rule is to paint opposing planes of different colors before joining, but here it seemed wiser to cover up any splatter of black paint applied to the model edge surfaces after the latter had been accomplished following installation of all grading including the hill area to the rear of the property. Any AC gray paint smears on the edge of the building slab will be covered by the separately applied curb. Camouflaging of the joints is best done after assembly, and this is covered in Textures (Ch. 33).

Natural Grade: Though you may want to construct the buildings off the model, this is a good time to grade the hill area at the rear of the property without structure in your way and to allow finish painting of the entire model perimeter before proceeding with the finished grade areas. Assume that a 4′ retaining wall has been installed across the north edge of the guest parking area at the 510′ altitude contour line (El. +4′) (Ch. 18).

Considering the model size of the area (44-1/2″ X about 22″) and the height of the countouring (6″), the vertical control method seems to be the one to use here. Follow the tips as presented under Vertical Control in this section, being sure to catch all critical changes in direction of contour lines. Suggested locations of key risers are indicated by the contour configuration in Fig. 9-7. Add others to give support and authentic configuration to the finished product. When all grading is done, spray the outside edges of the model with matte black Krylon (Ch. 32). Include the edges of the underliner of Masonite, the frame, lip and edges of the plywood as well as the perimeter risers and street edges and the backing plates at the hill area. Doing this now will obviate having to mask later when improvements are finished.

Drainage: You may have wondered why no indication of drainage facilities was made during the grading of model B. Usually drainage warping of such surfaces as the guest parking area is incidental to the goal of authenticity because its lack is not noticed. If such warping is considerable, considering the scale of the model, then the risers or other elevating media should be adjusted to show it. Along East and West Streets in model B, there probably would be drainage outlets in the gutters on the upstream sides of driveways. If these are important, they can be shown by removing the top white layer of illustration board (for example) in the configuration of the opening and treating the area as indicated in Ch. 13.

You will at times be presented with grading problems much trickier than those covered in this section, but I believe the understanding of some of the basic principles will aid you in finding solutions to more complicated challenges all of which could not possibly be covered in one book. The next chapter will show you how a contour cutting machine can make a breeze out of grading in general.

10

Contour Cutting

Contour cutting naturally falls into Ch. 9, Grading, but because of the peculiarities of method, material, and equipment, it has its own separate chapter. The procedure involves the transformation of a model land surface into a three-dimensional configuration in a soft material by following with a vertically and horizontally controlled cutting tool the contour lines on a civil engineer's drawing. The material must be soft enough to allow easy milling and firm enough to hold the cut shape. See Ch. 49 photo 10 for example of unfilled contour model.

MATERIAL

In my experience rigid polyurethane foam of 4-lb density has proven to be the most satisfactory. Lighter grades of the same material are too susceptible to damage and do not have the density to permit as good a definition of edges and corners. The foam is of cellular composition and comes in various colors depending upon the source. It can be easily cut, sawed, and sanded to sharp edges. Within limits it can be compressed as required to make minute changes in elevation or to accept components

tapped into selfconfigured cavities. It can be glued with the standard glues such as contact, white, or 3M spray without dissolving. It spray paints well with the latex paints (Ch. 32), leaving the desired landscaping texture. It requires only reasonable care to prevent gouging or chipping by carelessly swung tools, grabbing finger nails, etc. Its dust tends to cling to everything requiring a collecting and disposal system working along with the cutter. In this respect check with the manufacturer as to its toxicity and flammability, and to be on the safe side wear a mask or respirator when cutting. With an efficient vacuum system I have never found it necessary to wear a mask, but "different times in different climes" may change the situation. Hereinafter this material will be referred to as "urethane."

METHODS

To give you a choice, three mechanical methods are briefly described as to principal characteristics with advantages and disadvantages. The possibilities of sophisticated electronically or photographically controlled methods are not considered here as being unreasonable means to produce the same result considering the expected available space and volume of business in basically a handicraft profession.

Pantograph: This method involves tracing with a stylus a map at any convenient scale, the tracing being transferred through a system of proportional arms to a frame-supported cutting tool adjustable to cut to the scale of the contour interval. The main advantage lies in the remote control of accurate results from a handy size drawing smaller than the model area, but the complications of structure combined with the necessity for precision mechanics eliminate this system from contention. Unless you have expertise in mechanical engineering and construction and can spend the time perfecting your own pantograph, the components or the entire assembly would have to be purchased outside at a cost probably not justified for a small shop. In other words, the expected volume of work would not be sufficient to return the investment within a reasonable time.

Reversed Drawing: This popular procedure includes tracing with a stylus the contour lines on a model-scale reversed or mirror image drawing mounted on a table directly below the urethane suspended overhead. Moving the stylus moves a mobile frame with the cutting tool mounted at its upper end. The system's main advantage is the remote control cutting of unobstructed urethane in blocks of any thickness starting with the highest elevation, thus usually obviating the necessity for considering the cutting depth capabilities of the bit. (See objection 4 following.) In planning my approach, I anticipated the following objections to this method:

1. The requirement for an overhead frame to support the urethane with the problem of accurate replacement should the material have to be removed for some reason during a job.

2. The mechanical problems of making a rigid but light mobile tool holding frame with vernier height control and tracing stylus in accurate vertical relation to the bit.

3. The indefinite control of cleanoff between widely spaced contour lines and of waste. "Waste" in this chapter means unneeded material outside the contoured area.

4. The hazard in certain cases of steep gradients where the depth of the bit would cause con-

flict between the tool chuck and contours already cut.

5. The gross waste of urethane arising from cutting blocks of material thick enough to include the lowest and highest elevations. See "Layer Method" later in this section.

6. The difficulty of dust disposal.

7. The lack of ready visual appraisal of tool bit location and the mental "twist" of having to think in reverse while tracing the mirror image drawing.

Rather than fight the foregoing anticipated faults I switched to a permanently located tool system which, with its minor faults, has proven to be very satisfactory.

Pattinson Mill: This tool is basically a stationary, overhead vertical mill with vertical vernier control within the limits of the length of a geared piece of steel screw stock adjustably clamped to a hollow tubular shaft. See Urethane Mill and Fig. 36-12 in Ch. 36 for a more complete description. The urethane model stock is pushed under the mill bit usually after mounting the material on the model base. The contour map at the scale of the model is temporarily glued to the urethane surface, and the cuts are made using the contour lines as guides.

DUST DISPOSAL

Continuous urethane dust disposal during cutting is a must so that you can see what you are doing, not to speak of keeping it off everything in the shop as well as out of nose and throat. The Pattinson Mill has a Sears shop vacuum hose attached to the top end of the hollow tube shaft and routed along the support frame down to the tank at the end of the table. Inserted into the base of the shaft I have a plastic pickup shoe which extends at right angles to curve around the chuck to pick up dust as it is cut. Provision is made so that this shoe can be raised and lowered to follow the depth of cut with a thumbscrew to hold it in place. This keeps close to 95 percent of the dust out of the air. The dust that falls in place I pick up periodically with a household tank vacuum cleaner under the table with its hose suspended on a hook. I moved its switch to the nozzle for accessibility. When cleaning the model be careful not to chip contour edges with the metal nozzle. Using the plastic attachment nozzle and drawing it toward you will help prevent this. It is a good idea to keep the table reasonably clean, also so that built-up piles won't be pulled by the sliding model base to conflict with the runners and cause friction.

Note the validity of objection 6 to the reversed drawing method. To keep the dust from continuously falling on the drawing you are tracing you would need a flexible vacuum hose attached right at the bit location; an exercise more difficult by far on a mobile tool than on a stationary one. The only alternative is to blow the dust out of the area creating a further collection problem.

CUTTERS

Since the size of the chosen tool bit will control the amount of urethane that can be cut at the maximum depth setting, it is well to establish some principles in this respect. As you increase the length of the bit to increase the number of contours cut during one run, and reduce the diameter to allow cutting into narrow V's of sharp changes in direction of contour lines, the danger of whip arises. In other words, as the shaft becomes more flexible at high speeds the end of the bit will tend to turn in a circle with a diameter larger than the diameter of the bit, causing a cut farther than indicated by the contour guide line, not to speak of the danger of ultimate breakage. The material is relatively soft, and with the proper tool, cuts like cheese, but it is reasonable to establish a compromise on the safe side and avoid worries about the hazards just mentioned. With this approach, I have settled on standard four flute, 1/4", 5/16" and 3/8" end mill bits with a 2" cutting length. Actually you can cut to a depth of approximately 2.2" taking advantage of the disappearing flutes cutting a soft material. By setting the tool to a depth just beyond that required for a given number of contours which, according to the scale, can be cut in 2", you can automatically provide for cleanoff at the top if desired or required.

Note that the sacrifice of close cuts into narrow V's of contour lines in the interests of the mass of a 5/16" bit, for example, is made up for to some extent through being able to clean off large areas of tread between contours faster than with a smaller diameter tool. I have on occasion changed to a 1" diameter bit for fast cleanoff purposes, being sure that the bottom edge of the larger bit was at the same level as that of the smaller one. This can be done with assurance when the two bits have the same length and are set into the chuck at the same

setting of the vernier scale. Cutting bits will give long life, but it is well to have a spare to use when sharpening becomes necessary. Keep the flutes clean at all times for cutting efficiency, noting that they will pick up slight amounts of the adhesive used to secure the drawing to the urethane.

CUTTER SPEED

With the Powerstat speed controlling transformer set at a low speed, increase the speed of rotation until you can just comfortably and steadily cut the urethane with the bit buried in the material and with steady pressure against the base of the model. This speed will depend upon the cutter, its sharpness, and the density of the urethane. No specific rpm can be given, but you will be able to determine the minimum effective speed from experience and feel of your own situation. If the bit tends to slow down under moderate pressure, turn the speed up a notch.

SELVAGE

As a general practice I usually allow for an arbitrary 1/2" to 1" of uncut urethane as a solid base to the urethane against the plywood of a contour model. Thin and wide contour risers and treads around property sloping gradually are susceptible to damage particularly if the glue application was not complete and the urethane has slightly curled up off the plywood upon being relieved by the cutter. Selvage will help keep everything in place. The amount advisable depends upon how steeply the material rises from the edge. A precipitous cliff could rest on no more than say 1/4" of uncut material and provide adequate support. I believe that most distributors will have saws; so after studying the contour map you are about to use, decide on the desired selvage and add it to the thickness when ordering.

MODEL C

To explain the use of the Pattinson Mill, assume that your client has a piece of property to develop. It is in the shape of a rectangle with one corner truncated in a curve (Fig. 10-1). The unshortened sides measure 3600' and 4800'; the lowest altitude is 350' and the highest is 950', resulting in a dif-

(a)

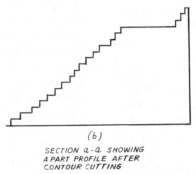

(b)

SECTION *a-a* SHOWING
A PART PROFILE AFTER
CONTOUR CUTTING

FIGURE 10-1 *Model C (and Sec. a-a).*

ference of 600′. The client has decided that a contour model at 1/100″ scale would be a useful medium for study and later display purposes. This results in the requirement for a 7″ thickness of urethane (6″ in scale plus 1″ selvage). You have received two 1/100″ scale drawings of the area. One will be used in cutting, and the other will be held as a reference since the first will be destroyed in the modelling process. The contour interval is 10′ which, at 1/100″ scale is equal to 0.10″. No roads, buildings or other improvements are to be shown at this time, and the contours will be shown open (unfilled) to aid your client in establishing elevations for later development.

Base: Construct the base as in Ch. 7 making the plywood component 37″ × 49″ to provide a 1/2″ protective border around the urethane and using *tempered* Masonite for the bottom liner to provide a hard, slippery surface. When assembling the base, make certain that the result is as flat as possible to forestall rocking as you push the base under the cutter. A minute rise at one corner can be ignored since the base will stay in one horizontal plane resulting in consistent contour relationship, any minor overall bow being unnoticeable in the finished product, but any unevenness which permits movement under slight vertical pressure must be avoided. During construction if you notice a definite bow in the plywood consider using a truss as discussed in Ch. 7 before discarding it.

Two Procedures: A contour model can be cut out of a single block of urethane or layers of a thickness that can be handled by the length of mill bit without leapfrogging. The term "procedures" is used here to avoid confusion with overall term "method" as the reversed drawing method or Pattinson Mill method. "Procedure" is thus a subtitle under "Method." Model C will be built under each procedure, revealing the advantages of the layer procedure as cutting progresses.

Single Block: Order a standard 4' × 8' panel of urethane 7" thick. Check dimensions, and using a saber saw with sufficient blade travel (Ch. 36) cut off 36" of the 8' length and then cut at the curved property line at the southwest corner (Fig. 10-1). Cut just outside the lines, being sure to hold the blade as vertical as possible to avoid cutting into the property area. Carefully sand down to the lines with grater and sanding sticks (Ch. 36), using a carpenter's square to aid you in making the sides vertical. Urethane sands easily; so take care as you approach the desired result. Apply contact glue or a 3M spray glue (Ch. 34) completely to the bottom of the urethane and the plywood base within the property lines, and glue this shaped block of "property" to the base, being careful to center it within the 1/2" free border. Once the dried contact glue on each surface comes together, the block will adhere immediately; so have a helper guide the block into place. If no helper is available, temporarily nail a strip of 1" × 2" white pine framing material, or other suitable material, along a 1/2" border line on the plywood as a guide stop for the matching edge of the urethane. Holding the block between outstretched arms lower it as horizontally as possible, centering it against the stop immediately in front of you. If the glue is completely dry, you can cover the plywood except for a starting strip of glue with brown paper (Ch. 35). Holding the block at a low angle, center one edge against the stop over the uncovered strip of glue, and pull the strips of paper consecutively as you lower the urethane into place. Using a hammer against the protection of a piece of scrap plywood, go over the entire surface of the urethane, pounding it into good adhesion. Check the joint all around to be sure. Taking into consideration the porosity of the material, complete glue coverage should assure complete adhesion. Apply more glue with a spatula under a raised corner, for example, and weight the

area overnight. Turn the assembly over on a flat table, taking care not to chip urethane edges, and wax the Masonite liner with a good grade of wax (Ch. 35). Note that all brads are countersunk or flush to permit a sliding surface, not to speak of preventing scratches on your client's display table. Polish the wax, and apply the same wax to the table runners.

Turn the assembly over onto the milling table and cut one of the drawings along the property line. The result should exactly cover the urethane surface since the model limits are to be these lines. Recalling that the cutting bit will handle a maximum of 2.2" cutting depth, this will include 220' at 1/100' scale. Taking 200' as the cutting range, 950', the highest point in the property (southeast corner of Fig. 10-1) less 200' equals 750', the first contour to cut. This will require 2.1" of tool length representing the elevation difference of 200' plus 10' to account for the first contour cut. The extra available 0.1" will allow for trim at 960' on the top surface to clear off any previously unmeasurable differences in the urethane block. Lower the bit to the maximum depth against the side of the urethane 2.2" down from the top surface. Turn the adjustable vernier scale to 0 and clamp the tool shaft. Attach the auxiliary scale (discussed later in this chapter) so that altitude 750' is exactly under the wire marker. This scale will be your anchor in case the vernier spins free and you loose your setting at some time during a course and when you leapfrog the bit down to the start of a subsequent course. Using an X-acto type knife (Ch. 36) cut the drawing along the 750' contour, resulting in two relatively small pieces to be glued to the urethane for the first run. These are a rough triangle at the southeast corner of Fig. 10-1 and an oval shaped piece at the northwest corner. As a guide in positioning, hold the entire drawing on the top of the urethane as you glue these pieces down. Use rubber cement or some other temporary adhesive applied to the paper only. I have found 3M's #77 spray adhesive satisfactory for this purpose.

Make the cuts along the 750' contour edges of the two pieces of drawing and clean off all waste at this tool setting. Unclamp the shaft, and without disturbing the vernier disc turn the handle to raise the bit one contour interval of 10' or 0.10" (to 760' on the auxiliary scale). The vernier scale accounts for 0.050" per revolution; so two revolutions are necessary for each contour interval. Cut the drawing pieces along the 760' contour lines and peel off the strips of paper. Make the next mill cut following the 760' lines and proceed as before until all contours on these two pieces of drawing have been cut, resulting in a plan view as shown in Fig. 10-2. Note that the top of the mountain to the northwest is at 820' (considering the bottom of the bit as the elevation cut, to be explained later); it was completed before the other mountain with a maximum elevation of 960'.

Next, cut the remaining drawing on the 550' contour line (Fig. 10-1) and glue the V-shaped piece down on the flat, cleared 750' level so that the 750' contour edge fits against the first riser in the urethane cut on the first course. Don't worry about minor differences between the edge of the drawing and the urethane. Nature is never put on paper exactly. Release the shaft of the mill and turn the tool bit down to the 750' level so that the bottom of the cutter just touches. The vernier scale should read 0, and the pointer (wire marker) should be at 750' on the auxiliary scale. Push the model out of the way and turn the handle so that the cutter bottom goes down 40 turns of the vernier (40 × 0.050" or 200'). This is the start of the second series of cuts or contour line 550' (with the auxiliary scale pointer at that altitude). Note that the bit was lowered exactly 200' this time since you want to arrive at the top cut at 740' with exactly one con-

tour interval between the last cut and the 750' level at which the first series was started. Completing this series will result in a plan view as in Fig. 10-3. Completing the third series after gluing down the remaining 200' of contoured drawing on the 550' level will result in a completed contour of the property as shown in Fig. 10-1.

OBJECTIONS TO BLOCK PROCEDURE

Now that Model C has been cut from a single block of urethane the immediate opportunity arises to appraise the faults of the block procedure with a view toward their elimination if possible. Without a deep-throated industrial type bandsaw with the capacity to handle thick blocks of material, handling, cutting, and accurately trimming a 7" thick block of urethane can be a time consuming and arduous process. The one curved edge configuration as in Model C presents no serious problem, but imagine a free-form or multisided piece of property where you are required to cut to the property lines. Next, referring to Fig. 10-2, note the extent of the white area representing a 2" thick piece of urethane

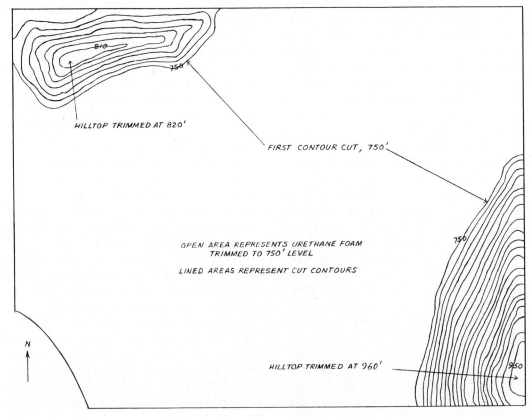

FIGURE 10-2 *First cut, block procedure.*

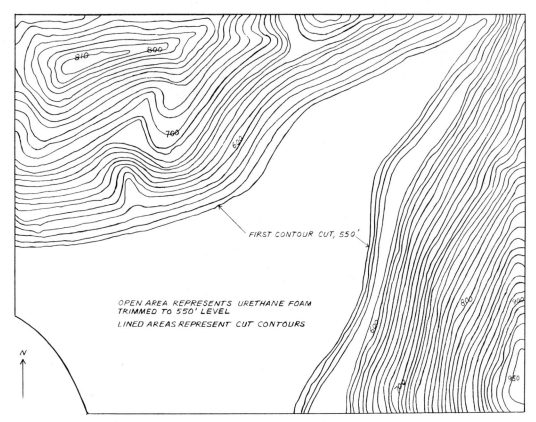

FIGURE 10-3 *Second cut, block procedure.*

ground to useless dust. This must be close to 20 board feet, which in slab form would be more than enough to make the two mountain tops shown. This represents a wasted cost not to speak of the time consumed in the clearing. Lastly, the leapfrog cutting in series presents the hazards of error in tool setting. The mill will accurately do what you tell it, but if you give it incorrect information you could wind up with the necessity for a bit of sticky and time consuming surgery. Note that the reversed drawing method eliminates this leapfrog cutting, but still the same amount of material clearing is required, and the adapting of this method to allow use of the layer procedure next described to save material, would, in my opinion present a clumsy problem of resetup. An unusual case where a filled contour model cannot be covered with ground cover to hide urethane layers next discussed, may require the single block procedure in spite of its drawbacks.

Layer Procedure: This involves stacking pieces of urethane of a thickness which can be easily handled by the length of the available mill bit, (in my experience 2″) starting with a bottom layer thick enough to include selvage. In the case of Model C,

cut and trim a 3″ slab of urethane to the same perimeter configuration as that of the 7″ block used in the block procedure just described, and glue it to the base. Temporarily glue the drawing to the surface of the urethane and cut off the paper along the 350′ contour, the lowest and first to be milled. Set the bit down the side of the material 2.2″ from the surface representing the level of the 350′ contour. 2.2″ will give you 21 contours to include elevation 550′ plus one contour interval to allow cleaning off the top surface (after removing the drawing) usually necessary since exact thickness of the material cannot be counted upon. If this first layer thickness were correct throughout, you would be able to include a total of 22 contours with the last one at 560′ instead of 550′. This in turn would allow a trim in either of the next two layers required to finish the model. If the two top layers both required trimming then you would have to add a small button of urethane to the stack to reach contour 950′. Don't fall into the trap of creating a layer joint between contours just to save material. Always end a layer at a contour line level. As in the block procedure, cut the contours in sequence from 350′ to and including contour 550′, assuming for the sake of this illustration that you performed

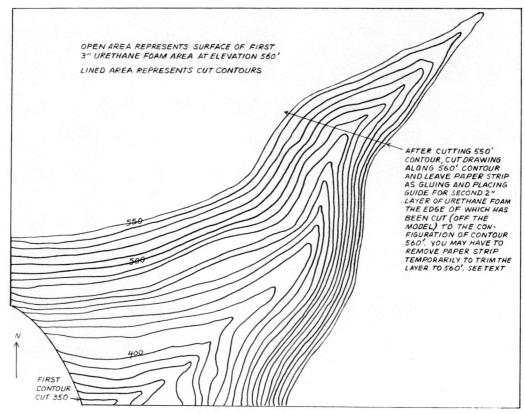

OPEN AREA REPRESENTS SURFACE OF FIRST
3" URETHANE FOAM AREA AT ELEVATION 560'

LINED AREA REPRESENTS CUT CONTOURS

AFTER CUTTING 550'
CONTOUR, CUT DRAWING
ALONG 560' CONTOUR
AND LEAVE PAPER STRIP
AS GLUING AND PLACING
GUIDE FOR SECOND 2"
LAYER OF URETHANE FOAM
THE EDGE OF WHICH HAS
BEEN CUT (OFF THE
MODEL) TO THE CON-
FIGURATION OF CONTOUR
560'. YOU MAY HAVE TO
REMOVE PAPER STRIP
TEMPORARILY TO TRIM THE
LAYER TO 560'. SEE TEXT

550

500

N

400

FIRST
CONTOUR
CUT 350

FIGURE 10-4   *First cut, layer procedure.*

an exemplary trim at altitude 560' but do not have to consider trim in the two top 2" thick layers. The result from cutting the first layer will appear as in Fig. 10-4. The drawing was removed to allow trim discussed previously. Cut the drawing at contour 560' and reglue the strip of paper (between contour 550' and 560') along the 550' contour on the model. This strip will serve as a positioning guide for the second layer as well as a glue stop. Glue the remaining drawing to a 2" thick layer of urethane, and with a saber saw cut it along the edge of the drawing which is the 560' contour. Apply glue over the entire uncut surface of the first layer, stopping about 1/8" from the paper strip guide, and do the same on the bottom surface of the second layer, stopping about the same distance from the contour shaped edge. This is so that if the model contours are filled by sanding the surface smooth (to be discussed later in this chapter) you will not reveal beads of glue which are difficult to remove without damaging the joint. When the second layer is adhered to the first guided by the paper strip, pull off the strip and cut the drawing along contour line 570', the starting level for the next series of cuts. Move the tool bit up two contour intervals or 4 turns to 570' remembering that you have already cut contour 560' in cutting out the second layer with a saber saw. Cut the remain-

ing drawing (glued to the second layer) at 570' and cut the second course in sequence ending up at 750' to result in the model appearing as in Fig. 10-5. Follow the same procedure with the third layer consisting of two small pieces as shown in the white areas of Fig. 10-5, and end up with the completed model appearing as in Fig. 10-1.

Note that through the layer procedure the three objections to the block procedure have been eliminated. These were the difficulty of handling thick blocks of urethane, excessive waste, and leapfrog cutting. In comparing the efficiency of the reverse drawing method with that of the Pattinson Mill method, it is fair to point out that the latter has the peculiar requirement for adhering the drawing to the urethane and for sequential trimming of paper between contours. From experience this does not appreciably add to the time, and in my opinion still leaves the vertical mill method far ahead of the alternate.

PREPARING FOR DELIVERY

Now that model C has been cut to specifications, thoroughly vacuum all surfaces, do any patching necessary to restore damaged contours, sand off

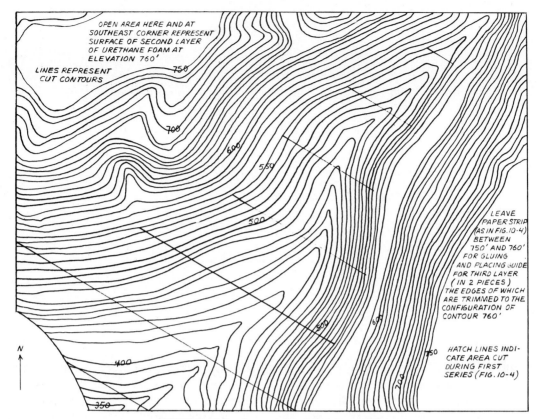

FIGURE 10-5 *Second cut, layer procedure.*

any small excess urethane "spikes" missed by the mill, fill any cavities in the edges of the plywood base with spackle (Ch. 35), and sand smooth, check the outside edge flushness of layers of urethane if the model was constructed using that procedure, sand off any roughness on the open plywood area at the arc of the property line, and slightly chamfer frame edges, etc., in preparation for painting. Before painting, it is well to bring up here the possibility that you may want to line the sides of the urethane with lightweight illustration board to protect against gouging or to cover flaws in the urethane, etc. This is usually not necessary with the 1/2″ free border all around, and paint will usually satisfactorily camouflage areas which have been cut out and plugged with urethane pieces sanded flush. Lining can be an arduous task, particularly where you have to cut contour configuration into the top edges to match the urethane edges. Paint all except the contoured surface with matte black Krylon (Ch. 32), which is the quickest way to accomplish coverage. With a handheld mask of cardboard, moved as you proceed around the model, and by spraying *up* at the edges, you will have little trouble keeping the Krylon off the contoured surface. When this is dry, using a similar masking shield, spray the contoured surface with a neutral green latex paint, being careful not to puddle the paint. PPG's "Grass"

latex is generally acceptable. Any splatter onto the black can be covered with brushed on black matte latex over the Krylon. Install the acrylic model cover (Ch. 39) if one has been specified.

Now that model C is ready for delivery, attention can be turned to various additional tips, conditions which will come up in your contour cutting career, and some variations in model requirements.

AUXILIARY CUTTING BOARD

With the memory of the cutting of model C fresh in your mind, this is a good place to discuss the auxiliary cutting board and the conditions under which it becomes useful. I use a 4′ × 4′ × 3/4″ piece of flat plywood lined on the underside with tempered Masonite waxed as was the bottom of model C. Attach the Masonite with contact glue. You may want several such boards of different sizes, but I have found that 4′ × 4′ is a good compromise considering handling and useful area.

Where the required one piece base is too large to handle on the cutting table, divide the urethane and cut each piece separately on the auxiliary board, being sure to use the same vernier settings for joining sections so that contours will meet ac-

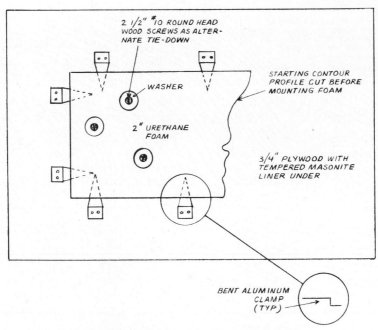

FIGURE 10-6 *Auxiliary cutting board.*

curately. Taking advantage of the selvage at the bottom in the block procedure or in the bottom layer of the layer procedure, you can fasten the urethane to the board with aluminum clamps as indicated in Fig. 10-6. These are made out of about 0.0625″ aluminum sheet obtainable at your hardware store. Obtain the material hard enough to hold shape while doing its job. Cut out clamp shapes with your metal shears (Ch. 36) and bend them into the configuration shown in Fig. 10-6. Drill two holes in each for wood screws to hold them firmly against the board. You can also use this system in the upper layers of the layer procedure as long as you can insert the clamps under the contours to be cut, holding the lower contour areas down with your hand while cutting to ensure against the material's raising. Unless you are going to line the perimeter of the model, fill the slits made by the clamps with slivers of urethane and sand them flush.

Where the stack of the layer procedure becomes too high to clear the throat of the Pattinson Mill, or it is just handier to cut separate layers on the auxiliary board, each layer in turn can be mounted on the board with screws inserted vertically through the urethane into the plywood at convenient locations sufficient to hold the layer flat. I use 2-1/2″ #10 round head wood screws through 1-1/4″ steel washers to hold down 2″ urethane. Longer screws may be necessary in the first layer considering selvage thickness. Place the screws just beyond the highest contour to be cut to avoid conflict with

the mill bit. If, because of contour configuration, you can't use more than one screw, for example, through the highest area and there is too much lower area to hold down with your fingers as you cut, pick a few other spots in as high an area as possible for additional screws. In this case you will have to cut around the washers, later trimming the "columns" of urethane and adjacent contours by hand. You will also have to fill the screw holes not covered by the next layer. If you arrive at the top of a layer with less than a contour height left, remove the pertinent screws to allow peeling off the remaining drawing without tearing. Then replace the screws and trim the top around the washers. Remove the screws and sand off the buttons of urethane.

If you want to try cutting small pieces of urethane without benefit of clamps or screws, friction obtained with slight hand pressure will usually cause the board to move with the material to prevent "sanding" off the bottom of the piece being cut. Another holddown for relatively small pieces is a frame of wood strips temporarily nailed to the board so that the urethane is held snugly in a socket.

If your saber saw is sick or nonexistent, you can trim the edge of a 2″ layer to the starting contour configuration on the mill. Place the layer level on some scraps of urethane on the auxiliary board, and adjust the height of the bit so that its length spans the thickness of the layer. No vernier settings are involved. Hold down the material with your hand as you guide it past the bit along the edge of the glued on drawing cut along the starting contour line.

PROPERTY LINES

Model C was cut at the property lines which conveniently outlined a rectangle except for one corner truncated on an even curve. When you have to contend with property lines which change direction often resulting in a multisided shape, point out to your client that the time of cutting the model can be reduced by shaping the urethane perimeter to a square or rectangle large enough to include the property. This will require that contours on the drawings be extended to include the entourage and that some means of indicating property lines be used. White nylon thread wrapped around common pins has proved to be a simple, effective solution. Tie the thread to a pin and insert it to the head at any convenient intersection of property lines. Plot by inspection and measurement the locations of every change of direction and push pins in part way at each of these locations. Play out the thread, pulling it just taut, as you wrap one turn around each pin in sequence. When you return to the first pin tie the thread to it being sure to keep the thread taut. Inspect the circuit and where the thread spans free of the urethane, as across valleys, with the point of a pin against the thread twist it into a single wraparound and push the pin in all the way. Be sure to insert the pin so that the lowered thread is in the proper line of that leg of the property line without cutting into contour edges. With a small brush paint each pin head with the same paint used to spray the model. This will eliminate the shine and camouflage the anchors. Use the same system to outline lots in a proposed housing development, or tap in, edge first, strips of white vinyl until flush with the urethane surface.

SHARP DIRECTION CHANGES

Note that as indicated in Fig. 10-1 there will be many contour lines changing direction with radii much smaller than that of the milling bit. I follow the practice of approaching these narrow vertices until the bit touches on each side of the V, ignoring the sharpness of change. If it should become a critical point, you could run over the completed

model with a fine cutter to reduce the radii or cut out the excess material with a sharp pointed knife. In my experience, no case has arisen where the client thought this necessary. The subject is mentioned here to prepare you for the contingency.

PROXIMITY OF CONTOUR LINES

Though the drawing of Fig. 10-1 is a no-scale, much reduced representation for illustrative purposes, it brings to our attention that situations will arise where contour lines are so close together in a steep mountain slope, for example, that it becomes difficult to cut every one with accurate definition. Where the slightest wander of the cutting bit would ruin the next contour above, consider with your client the advisability of cutting every other, or even every fifth, contour, depending upon the requirements. Fifty contours can be cut in half the time it takes to cut one hundred; so it makes sense to consider the problem from a cost point of view also. Where the model is to be finished by filling the steps or by sanding them off, as long as the integrity of profile is maintained, intervening equally spaced contours can be eliminated with no ill effects. The principles here are illustrated in Fig. 10-7.

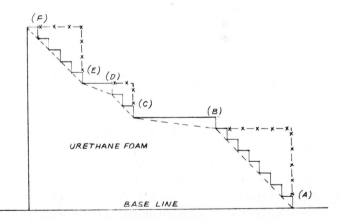

STARTING WITH BOTTOM OF MILL BIT ON BASE LINE, CUT CONTOURS (A) THROUGH (E) AND CLEAN OFF THE TOP AT (F) RESULTING IN URETHANE INDICATED BY STARRED LINE. TO CLEAN OFF WHEN YOU FINISH SAND TO DASHED LINE. NOTE THAT 11 CONTOUR CUTS HAVE BEEN ELIMINATED WITHOUT DESTROYING INTEGRITY OF SLOPE. NOTE ALSO THAT THIS CONFIGURATION PROBABLY WOULD NOT HOLD TRUE AT ALL LOCATIONS AROUND THE HILL NECESSITATING THE CUTTING OF MORE CONTOURS THAN THOSE ABOVE, BUT THE EXAMPLE SHOWS HOW EXAMINATION OF THE CONTOUR MAP CAN OFTEN SAVE CUTTING TIME. BE SURE YOUR CLIENT DOESN'T WANT EVERY CONTOUR SHOWN FOR STUDY PURPOSES BEFORE FINISH SANDING.

FIGURE 10-7 *Eliminating contours.*

CONTOUR INTERVAL

A closely related subject is contour interval, which, if too small at the scale of the model, will require cutting fewer than every one. My mill can cut at any setting of the vernier gauge, but because of the relative softness of the material, and the freehand method used under the system, as you approach a small contour interval of, say 0.020″, you start to lose continuous definition because of uncontrollable minute movement. I have never run into a situation where my client insisted on such minute definition. Contour intervals much less than 0.050″ are impractical not only because of the limitations of the machine system, but, particularly when close together, they are also hard to read for study purposes. Where minute detail is required for study of relatively small areas where improvements in the property are anticipated, intervening contours can be cut in these areas only and feathered out within the larger intervals of the general terrain. Again, overall integrity of profile in the finished product is the practical requirement.

FINISHED GRADES

When clients ask you for open contour models of property to be developed, be sure that they understand the fact that any finished grading is much more economically cut into the original construction than is cutting and filling afterwards. They very likely want natural grade only to help them decide the location of improvements, but you do no harm to your reputation by showing interest in the most economical approach.

Building pads, for example, can be cut along with the general grading with any between normal contour lines feathered off on each side of the finished graded areas. Location and elevation control will automatically be present when buildings are added. Be sure your client has completed the drawings given you to reflect the meeting of finished with natural contour lines. The civil engineer probably knows how he or she is going to provide for access, drainage, etc. even though this is not reflected on the drawings, but the model builder's tool bit has to be told which line to follow. Guessing is frowned upon for obvious reasons. If you receive back an open-contoured study model (such as model C) for finished grading, consider the extent of the property affected before insisting that the model would better be done over in place of

surgery. This is a matter of judgment under the peculiar circumstances. If it is decided that surgery is practical, cut out the affected areas shaped to squares or rectangles to include the planned junctures of finished and natural grades. Make carefully executed cuts with a sharp serrated knife or hacksaw blade held vertically into the affected terrain to a depth of about an inch below the lowest level involved. Since this natural grade will be discarded, you can hog it out with a curved blade such as a grapefruit knife, being careful not to disturb the top edges of the cavity. With a sanding stick with sandpaper glued to an end, smooth off the bottom of the cavity to provide an even bearing for the urethane plug you will make to fill the excavation. You can also cut the cavity using the mill. Place the model on the cutting table, raise the bit above the approach to the area to be excavated, lower it into the center of the area to the desired depth, and mill out the material without violating your perimeter knife marks. You can leave the radius in each corner and shape the plug to conform. Cut and sand a plug of urethane to fit snugly with a flat top slightly higher than the highest contour included. Contact glue this plug into the cavity with glue at the bottom only, to be sure no glue appears after the cut. Temporarily glue the piece of drawing at the same scale as that of the model to the top of the plug oriented so that the contour lines are directly above their continuation on the urethane around the perimeter of the cavity. After setting the tool bit to the lowest contour to be cut, mill the plug in the normal manner, matching contour ends with those previously cut. The joints can be camouflaged with ground cover if the model is to be finished for display. If the plug has to be cut off the model, mount it on your auxiliary board in a socket of wood strips as discussed previously.

DIVIDED MODELS

I have contour cut urethane blocks measuring 4′ × 5′ in size. Depending upon the number and complications of contours this is about the comfortable maximum. You could enlarge your table with extensions to maintain constant bearing during cutting gyrations of larger bases, but in spite of the ease of sliding on the runners, the greater inertia of the added weight might get to your shoulders after a few hours of this exercise. The bigger bases are also clumsy to handle in more situations than the cutting. A 4′ × 8′ model might be acceptable in one piece since your client has the transportation and space to handle it, but this size would require dividing the urethane. If the base is also split you can of course contour cut each section mounted on its section of the base. If not, then cut each section on an auxiliary board as previously discussed. With two such boards you can cut each section at even vernier setting to assure match at the joint and obviate having to reset the tool at the starting point a second time. If you can anticipate improvements, make the division in the urethane so that it passes as much as possible through open territory, following the principles mentioned in Ch. 7.

TRIMOFF

The trimming of the top surface of a block or layer of urethane less than a contour interval above the last contour cut has been touched upon during cutting tips for model C. After experience with your supplier whose cutting equipment does not ensure exactly 2″ thicknesses, for example, it is best to follow the practice of lowering the bit at least one contour into the selvage for the first course to guarantee the number of contours planned on. In the upper layers, simply count on one less contour than a 2″ thickness should allow. This may mean an additional layer at the top of the mountain, but its usually relatively small circumference will not require any considerable additional material.

LAYER JOINTS

Here are a few more tips on joining layers covered previously under the layer procedure. Instead of the strip of paper left on the layer below, you can, through inspection of your reference copy of the drawing and measurement, orient the milled edge of the next layer and then spray the starting tread with the same paint you expect to use over the entire model surface. The contrast will give a gluing guide. It is admittedly hard to confine a spray to a line about 1/8″ in from the edge of the guide, but with the help of a paper shield in one hand you can use 3M's #77 spray adhesive without serious concern about its appearing later at a sanded off joint (discussed later in this chapter). A bit of revealed spray glue will not cause the mess that contact glue will. The underside of the layer to be added should also be sprayed in a like manner. Wait until the

spray is just tacky on both surfaces and joining will give you a contact glue like adhesion.

BEFORE AND AFTER MODELS

Sooner or later you will probably be asked to build a single model of a site in hilly terrain, including removable plugs to show natural grade as well as after development configurations. If the model is small, the finished grade situation covers most of the area, and/or the contours are simple, consider with your client the economy of doing two complete models to show the two situations. Remind the clients that they will have to remove the acrylic cover every time they want to change a plug on a single model.

Assume here that the size of the model, the complicated contours, and the fact that the improved area is a small part of the whole, dictate the advisability of a single model with removable plugs. If the improved property happens to fall near the edge of the model, then the free side of each plug will make them easy to slip in and out. If the plug area is surrounded with permanently mounted urethane, then a bit of gymnastics will be necessary. In any case, remember to cut out the removable pieces before mounting the whole block or first layer if using the layer procedure on the plywood base. Contact glue where it is not wanted can be a mess to clean up. If the plugs are thick (deep), sand-relieve all sides of interior plugs from about 1/2″ down from the surface. This will prevent galling on removal and still allow a visually tight joint at the surface. Don't of course taper the visible edges of a plug slipped in from the side, since this would leave gaps in the side of the urethane block. Contour cut these plugs in place as you did in the case of the fixed change plug described previously under "Finished Grades."

Plug Removal System: It is normally difficult to provide secure, camouflaged means for pulling out interior plugs—those that are surrounded by permanently mounted urethane; so some provision for lifting must be made. A simple cam shaft with cams has worked well for me. See Fig. 10-8. The system consists of a piece of 1/4″ or 5/16″ wooden dowel inserted through the urethane block, across the center at the bottom of the plug cavity into a bearing socket at the other side. Drill a hole through the handle end of this dowel (which should be inside the free border edge) and insert a finishing nail, to act as a turning level. Holding it level and

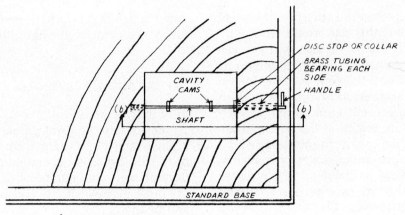

(a) PLAN VIEW OF PLUG CAVITY

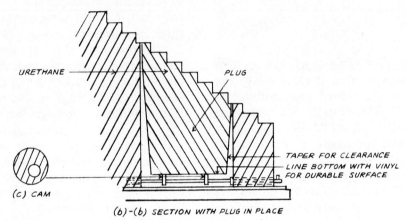

(b)-(b) SECTION WITH PLUG IN PLACE

FIGURE 10-8 *Plug removal system.*

straight, carefully push the other end (sharpened on your sander) through the urethane, across the cavity and into the other side a few inches, twisting as you push. A plastic or wooden mallet will help drive the dowel through. Remove the dowel; cut it to length and flatten the end with chamfered edge. Cut two pieces of brass tubing just long enough to make bearings. They don't have to be as long as the shaft hole and socket. The tubing size should be just large enough to allow free but not sloppy turning of the shaft. Place one bearing on the shaft and work it into the outboard hole, using the shaft as a guide, until the outside end is flush with the surface of the urethane. Push the shaft through to the cavity and slip the other bearing on, to be driven into the socket in the same manner. Friction should hold the bearings, but to be sure, add a swipe of contact glue on the leading edge of each bearing before inserting it. Remove the shaft and make two cams as indicated in Fig. 10-8c out of wood or acrylic so that they have a snug slip fit on the shaft. Also make a stop disc, or use a large washer, which will be held by a brad through the shaft to prevent the latter from slipping out beyond

the base free border edge. Drill a hole in the shaft at the right place for the disc or washer holding pin.

Final Assembly: Insert the shaft into the cavity. First, slide on the stop disc or washer, then the two cams. Shove the end of the shaft into its socket, slide the stop against the inside surface of the cavity nearer the handle, and insert the holding pin in the shaft. Then position the cams on the shaft so that the eccentricities are in the same longitudinal plane and a balanced distance apart. Mark these positions and slide the cams enough to allow gluing at the marked positions. Replace the cams, lined up, over the glue.

Plug Level: You will need just enough cam action when you twist the shaft with the lever handle to raise the plug enough to permit grabbing its sides. Line the bottom of the plugs with vinyl over the cam-contact areas to provide smooth friction surfaces. The cams in time will wear away the urethane if the latter is left bare. If the bottoms of the plugs are too high when resting on the low sides of the cams, progressively sand off the bottoms until the surfaces meet exactly the surrounding terrain. If too low, add the required amount of material. Paint the visible end of the shaft matte black, and you are off to the races.

FILLING CONTOURS

Most display models will have smooth ground surfaces; so the contours will have to be filled in. This could be done with plaster, but it is a messy and unnecessarily time consuming job adding weight and producing a surface into which it is difficult to install trees, for example, in a neat and efficient way. The practical solution to contour filling is to sand off the steps to the vertices formed at right angles by the treads meeting risers. See Fig. 10-9 and Ch. 49 photo 7 for example. You might be concerned about removing all that "dirt," thus making the hill smaller. It is true that the hill *will* be smaller, but consider *how* it is smaller. Since distance a–a (Fig. 10-9) between risers on opposite sides of the hill is equal to distance b–b between any other two opposite points on the same risers, then the contour lines will be in the same location horizontally whether they are at the tops or bottoms of risers. In other words, by sanding, the hill simply has been pushed vertically into the ground by the amount of the length of one riser or by one contour interval. Always thinking of the *bottom* of the tool bit being at the elevation of the contour line being cut will forestall confusion. To maintain the correct relationship between the elevation of the top of a hill and the elevation of contiguous finished grade at the base of the hill, for example, where urethane foam is to be installed against an established illustration board surface liner, cut the urethane block to a depth that will reveal one contour interval of height above the finished grade at the joint. Figure 9-5 illustrates this principle which holds true whether the urethane contours are assembled as in the combination method of Ch. 9 or cut on the Pattinson Mill. Where you cut the entire model base from urethane foam, don't forget to cut the first natural grade riser higher by the thickness of the liner material you expect to use on the finished grade. See Fig. 9-12 to help you recall this principle.

When you are finishing a model for display, don't be too hasty in sanding down all the contours. Remember Pattinson's Law, and the fact that once the surface has been smoothed off, you have lost ready elevation control. When you are satisfied that all finished grades have been established, trace the edges of roads you have cut out (Ch. 13) and sand down their cavities. Then glue down the roads permanently. Leave installed roads alone. Any catching of edges, etc. may tear them loose since the grainy urethane does not provide a gluing surface as firm as that provided by other materials. These will serve as orientation guides in placing buildings on their pads in proper relationship. Points on the roads can be used as bench marks for locating all improvements, including landscaping, thus saving a lot of time in head scratching as to where a row of trees starts and its bearing, for example. Establish floor levels for all buildings before sanding off contours around their pads. This is particularly important where a "finished" contour crosses a pad where adjustment has to be made to provide a level surface. Maybe the floor cantilevers from the higher elevation, necessitating filling under the free end, etc. Leave the natural grade of the surrounding terrain open until the last. Being able to spot an elevation otherwise hidden may save headaches during your improvement process. Remember you can always sand off a contour, but you cannot readily add it back on. For sanding use sanding sticks and small pieces of fine sandpaper pressed with a finger into concave places in the contour configuration.

MODEL B

Consider the time-saving advantages of cutting urethane foam to provide not only the naturally

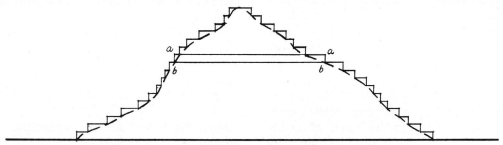

FIGURE 10-9 *Filling contours.*

graded hill of model B (Fig. 9-7) but also the finished grades of the improved areas. A sufficient depth of urethane would eliminate the necessity for cutting a hole in the plywood to take care of the underground parking or building accommodation up off the plywood. All the separate risers would be eliminated since all grades could be cut or sanded to their relative levels in a solid slab above or below a 0 bench mark as established in the vertical control method of Ch. 9. The 0 elevation would simply be a tool setting high enough to include the –7′ at the underground parking entrance.

Assume you have in stock a 4′ × 8′ × 2″ slab of 4-lb foam. At 1/8″ scale 2″ equals 16′ or more than enough to accommodate the highest improved dirt elevation of +4′ and the lowest of –7′ (1-3/8″). Selvage as such is not important here since there won't be any low-lying open contours to protect, but in the interests of expediency the extra 5/8″ is not a serious waste. Revealed urethane around the model perimeter can be lined with vinyl more for appearance than protection since it all will be horizontally covered with liner material. Cut the urethane to the size of the complete model area including perimeter streets and glue it to a base whose plywood surface is 1″ larger in both dimensions to provide a 1/2″ free border all around. This will help to protect the urethane perimeter of the hill, particularly when replacing the acrylic model cover. Note that this free border could have been provided for model B in Ch. 9, but it was not as important since the hill was protected by illustration board backing plates.

Contour Map: Use the site plan submitted in duplicate at the scale of the model as a pattern medium. Tack glue it to the urethane and cut out areas to be milled just as you cut along contour lines in model C. These will show the natural contours of the hill at the rear of the property as shown in Fig. 10-10 which is a duplicate of Fig. 9-7. These are the required guides for the cutting tool. In the improved areas contour lines if shown at all will not be as obvious because they become stacked around level areas enclosed by geometric construction. The elevations at contour intervals on the face of a retaining wall location, for example, appear in plan as a single line because they are all in the same vertical plane. This is the same condition that appears in the case of a natural vertical cliff or escarpment. Using spot elevation indications as along the streets, you can in effect establish your own guiding contour lines interpolating within the length of an obviously even gradient and establish your own contour intervals to the extent required to facilitate

later sanding to a smooth slope. From the nature of the indicated construction you know that there is a vertical drop from the dirt level of the parking area (+4′) down to the dirt level of the service yard (+1′); so the edge of the pad becomes your contour line against which to cut the cavity with the bottom of the bit 3/8″ below. Any contour interval less than 3′ at this location would be pointless.

In some cases it is easier to cut only top and bottom elevations of an even slope and sand down the intervening urethane to connect. In others it is easier to cut the whole distance at the bottom elevation and later fill with a shaped piece of material. Define the Front Street grade of model B, for example, by cutting at 0′, +1′, +1-1/2′, and +2′ along the property line from west to east and then fill the contours by sanding Front Street smooth using the filling procedure previously described in this chapter. Obtain the sloped support for the wheelchair ramp on Front Street by cutting in from the sidewalk at elevation +1′6″ to the edge of the entrance slab at +4′6″. Later fill this cavity with a triangular block of urethane to meet the top and bottom of slope. The same approach would apply to the adjacent entry steps which are made off the model and installed as a unit. At the service yard extend the +1′ level to the West Street sidewalk from the inside surface location of the building wall, and to the outside of the south retaining wall of the parking entrance ramp. Inside the building line cut a convenient rectangular cavity at –7′ to support a disappearing garage level. Make this cavity so that it extends say 1/2″ on each side of the entrance against the inside surface of the building wall. Fill the ramp space between its retaining walls with a block of urethane and sand the slope from the sidewalk level down to the –7′ level. Follow a similar procedure at the vehicular street entrances, cutting back at street level to the parking area edge to provide for ramps being formed by tabs of the liner material (next discussed) with or without support depending upon the flexibility due to length. At the service yard accesses, form ramps of the liner material. The loading dock can be later added as a separate unit to the service yard level.

Each of an apparent olio of procedures is available to fit a peculiar situation, all variations of which would be impossible to describe here. As you become familiar with working with urethane the most expeditious solutions will become obvious.

Liner: Except at the open planting areas the urethane in the improved section of the model is supportive only since all tread surfaces must be of a

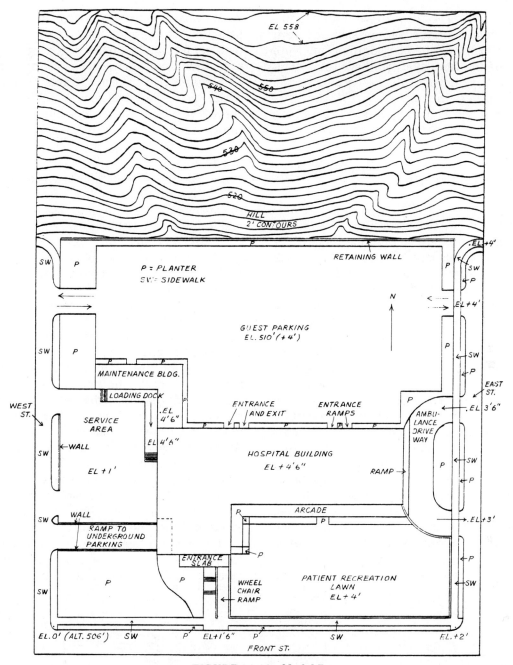

FIGURE 10-10 *Model B.*

smoother, harder, and denser material than the foam. As in the vertical control edition of model B (Ch. 9) 3/32″ thick heavyweight illustration board is a good candidate for a liner the surface of which will be considered at the same elevation as that of the urethane to which it is applied. Be consistent in adding this same material wherever a liner is called for to maintain correct vertical control. See Fig. 9-12 for an illustration of this principle. For the least amount of urethane cutting, consider the top of the foam to be at +4′, the largest area at one elevation in the improved section of the model.

The levels above this liner will be established by adding 1/16″ illustration board to form sidewalks, building pads, and the planters in the guest parking area. This is the horizontal control method used on model A.

Hill: Trim the edge of a 2″ thick piece of urethane to the configuration of contour 510′ so that it matches the first layer around the perimeter of the model and glue it against the north edge of the liner at the guest parking area, also at 510′ (+4′). Make your first mill cut at the 512′ contour line after raising the bit 1/4″ (2′) above the liner surface and continue using the layer procedure to top off at 560′, 558′ being the last contour cut. Note that the top of the first layer will have to be trimmed at less than a contour interval because of the 3/32″ selvage against the liner of that thickness at the bottom. Fill the contours by sanding off the steps as previously described in this chapter.

REAL ESTATE DEVELOPMENT

As a final example of the versatility of urethane foam, it seems appropriate to describe its use in a display model at a scale larger than that of contour model C and smaller than that of model B.

An excellent example of the time-saving use of urethane foam is its application in a small scale model of a real estate development where there are to be 60 houses with recreation facilities. For mental definition, assume the scale is to be 1/20″, resulting in house pads in the 2″ to 3″ square size. The houses are along entry roads on a slope; so terracing is required. You can readily imagine the extent of grading necessary to obtain 60 accurately located house pads, not to speak of road gradients and planting areas. With the structural methods described in Ch. 9, it is estimated that the grading process would take about three times as long as the urethane cutting method. Consider all the risers to make and place accurately, for example, and the forming of a surface liner to arrive at the specified ground conformations between houses. Using a finish grade site plan in scale, the entire property can be cut into urethane foam, resulting

in automatic elevation control and workable surface for cutting and filling as well as an excellent texture for landscaping. Referring to Fig. 10-11, note that a cut riser remains at the uphill limit of each house pad in order to maintain a level foundation area. This will require filling on the model and/or retaining walls depending upon specifications. At small scales such as the one under discussion, with 1′ contour intervals, a great deal of satisfactory filling can be accomplished with landscaping materials to camouflage the transition. This project is a prime example of the need for retaining the open contours until all critical levels of improvements have been established. I follow the practice of sanding or milling house pads in rows where sequential changes can be easily kept track of and of holding off open terrain sanding until all improvement levels (e.g., for structures and roads) have been established. As an aid in not becoming lost among the contours, stick a pin with an elevation tag in at every fifth contour, for example, in the area being worked on. If you use 0.020″ sheet of vinyl, for example, for roads, the urethane should technically be milled down 0.020″ to absorb the additional height because you cannot conveniently raise the uncovered areas as you did in model B to keep elevation relationships accurate. Where you can't camouflage the 0.020″ open edge with landscaping, take a block of wood and a hammer and tap the vinyl into the foam flush with the surface. At the smaller scales such hair-splitting is not worth the effort because the extent of the violation does not visually destroy authenticity. Here is a case where you can justifiably chalk it up to model builder's license unless, of course, you are facing a nitpicking opposing attorney in court.

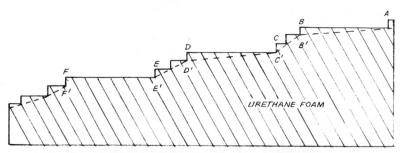

A, C, AND E REPRESENT THE MAP CONTOUR LINES AT THE DESIGNATED ELEVATIONS OF THE HOUSE LOTS A-B, C-D, AND E-F (BOTTOM OF MILL BIT).

THE DASHED LINE INDICATES THE NORMAL SANDED CONFIGURATION TO REFLECT CLOSED CONTOURS ON NATURAL TERRAIN, BUT TO MAINTAIN LEVEL LOTS IN THIS CASE, SAND OFF ONLY THE STEPS BETWEEN LOTS AS FROM B' TO C' AND D' TO E', AND TREAT THE DOWNHILL LIMIT OF EACH LOT (B, D, AND F) AS INDICATED IN THE TEXT.

FIGURE 10-11 *Housing development pads.*

MISCELLANEOUS TIPS

Routine: To help prevent errors, establish a routine procedure to follow during a contour cutting exercise. Immediately following a contour cut, raise the bit one contour interval in preparation for the next cut. Do this consistently, fortified by an eyeball check each time you approach the start of a cut to be sure that you actually did raise the tool. This may sound a bit like asking you to put on galoshes over your rubbers, but the routine pays off in saving the costs of surgery.

Auxiliary Scales: Particularly where you have to move the vernier scale of the Pattinson Mill out of sequence during a cutting job, an auxiliary scale is a handy convenience for maintaining control. Using your shop mill (Ch. 36) for accuracy scribe scale contour intervals on a strip of .020″ vinyl and pencil in the range of elevations (altitudes) you will be cutting. See Ch. 36 under "Homemade tools" for scribing set up. Tape this strip to a strip of aluminum mounted vertically to the movable shaft of the Pattinson Mill. Use a piece of piano wire as a marker attached at one end with a machine screw to the fixed body of the Pattinson Mill so that the wire crosses the scale parallel to the scribed altitude indications. Set the Pattinson Mill bit to the first contour elevation you will cut, the vernier scale at zero and attach the auxiliary scale so that the first contour elevation visually falls behind the marker. At the end of the job note the scale of the model on this auxiliary scale and file it for possible future use. The auxiliary scale is especially valuable for the single block procedure because of the leapfrogging of the cutter between runs. The temporarily attached scale with all altitudes noted will obviate your having to count revolutions of the vernier scale when lowering the bit to start a new course.

Test Runs: Whenever starting a run in a new layer of urethane on an auxiliary board make a test run through a piece of scrap to be sure that the interval is correct. If the new layer is the first one cut off the model base, you will have to establish a new 0 on the vernier. On subsequent runs using the same surface the test run will verify this reading. As you gain confidence in yourself and your mill, testing becomes less mandatory, but don't forget that a wrong interval during a course will throw your whole mountain off.

Approach: Always cut in against solid urethane as long as possible. Don't leave isolated thin strips of foam on the edge of the contour below. The mill bit may snap these off at first contact tearing a pit at the base. For the same reason don't isolate sub-hilltops until you have to. Leave the peninsula in as long as possible, and before milling off a spike taller than it is wide cut most of it off with a knife by hand.

Sharp Points: Where the mill did not make a smooth transition as prescribed by the contour line on the drawing, sand off sharp points with a manicurist's emery board which has an adjusting flexibility.

Flush Contours: Where the bit inadvertently slipped in to the next contour line above, redefine the upper one with right angle cuts with a knife.

Islands: Islands left in a large cleanoff area should be cut off with a knife close to the base and then sanded flush.

Unwanted Glue: Too much spray glue used to hold the drawing down on the urethane will sometimes leave residue when the paper is pulled off. This can usually be pulled off with tweezers. If you have a small lump that seems to want to pull the urethane with it, wait until you have spray painted the model and then try sanding it off. The dried paint will help prevent pulling as you sand. Just enough glue to hold the drawing in place will prevent this situation. The same glue appearing at sanded off contour joints is usually in not enough quantity to cause problems if you were not too lead-fingered on the spray button near the layer edges. Small bubbles can be pulled off with tweezers. Unwanted contact glue is a more serious problem, particularly at layer joints where you should have stopped your glue brush back from the edges as previously mentioned. Small beads can be pulled off without serious damage, but if you are confronted with a glue line at the joint, accept it and cover it hopefully with ground cover. Continuous soaking with a swab dipped in solvent (MEK, Ch. 35) is a long process, the unpristine result being hardly worth the effort. Accidental drops of contact glue can be removed immediately by twisting it off wrapped around the end of a pointed stick or scribe. Spread out a remaining amount carefully so as not to fill the pores of the urethane, and peel off a film as it dries. Don't try to rub it off. Filling the pores will create a permanent spot, and be accentuated by paint.

Vertical Joints: The best way to camouflage permanent vertical urethane joints without benefit of ground cover is to rub the two pieces together before gluing. The mutual abrasive action will create the best mating. This of course can be done only along straight joints. In anticipation of such a joint, provide selvage along the edges opposite the joint to absorb any lost material in the "sanding" process so you won't wind up with short dimensions.

Filling Plugs: If you are faced with an accidental deep dent or gouge, use a knife to cut out the area in the form of an including square or rectangle, and fill the cavity with a plug of the same urethane with contact glue around the bottom end only. Carefully shape the plug with a sanding stick and slightly taper the sides so that when tapped in place the material will join as tightly as possible. Sand the excess plug material flush. Paint will help to camouflage the accident, and ground cover (Ch. 25) will hide it. A plug in the black painted vertical surface of the perimeter will hardly be noticed.

Filling Paste: I have never been able to duplicate the natural surface of urethane exactly, but based upon the tenet that a filled crack is better than an open one try a little putty made by mixing urethane dust with the paint you are going to use in the area. Press the putty into the crack without compressing the surface, let it dry and sand off. Generally speaking this approach is not as satisfactory as the filler plug next above because the different texture of the dried putty will create a patch more obvious than the plug.

Cracks: This type of unwanted opening occurs when, for example, a tongue of urethane is snapped off accidentally when gluing a cut model layer to the base. Without disturbing the naturally mating surfaces, carefully press them together as you mount the two pieces. If you add contact glue to each, keep the glue well below the model surface so you won't have to contend with squeezed out beads of adhesive. If you are not allowed the luxury of ground cover (Ch. 25) to hide the crack on a sanded (filled contour) display model, try the following procedure. While your spray of overall background green paint is still wet along the crack, sift urethane dust from your vacuum cleaner tank lightly along the crack just enough to cover. As the paint dries, lightly and evenly with a finger push the dust over and into the crack to hide it. Let the model dry and mist the crack area with the same paint to color any urethane dust still obvious. Repeat this process if necessary to obtain the condition where

only you notice the crack because you know it's there. Without landscaping or other improvements to hide a crack accept the impossibility of complete obliteration.

THINK "URETHANE"

Whenever you have a grading problem think "urethane." There would obviously be no point in using the foam where the overall area is flat with a few level planes which can readily be built up using the horizontal control method as in the case of model A, discussed previously, but where risers are necessary to obtain sloping gradients or multilevel planes, urethane foam is the logical answer. Even in the absence of a contour cutting mill, you can make risers out of it in time-saving large pieces, berms for landscaped areas, islands in a lake, even sculpture for the park, etc. Its porosity gives good "earth" texture over a wide range of scales. It can be used to fill planters, and trees with sufficient free trunk can be mounted without glue. Where surgery is required to effect changes in a lined surface, you can cut through illustration board and excavate urethane foam with relative ease. After you have fought the stubborn edges of installed illustration board risers which have to be lowered, you will appreciate the blessing of this material.

EASIER DONE THAN SAID

If all the verbiage in this section overcomes you, remember that when you start performing these operations, you will find that they are easier to do than explain. I have tried to keep the presentation of these tips as simple as possible. I know they work with a practical minimum of complications. If they lead you to better methods that will prove again that there are more ways than one to skin the proverbial cat.

BENEFITS FOR THE CLIENT

Last, but not least, your client can cut and fill an open contour urethane foam model to his or her heart's content to reflect solutions to access and drainage problems and to establish desired relationships of finished building sites. When models are delivered, supply the clients with scraps of foam for their filling exercises and remind them that a serrated knife blade or hacksaw blade and sanding sticks are satisfactory surgical tools.

11

Aerial Photo Backgrounds

USE

The use of aerial photographs of large areas of generally flat terrain as model base covers can be an effective and economical way to obtain setting and entourage for study purposes. Models of structures in block configuration at the scale of the photograph are mounted on the photograph in the area to be developed for studying relations of a site to surrounding facilities such as freeways, related industrial sources, commercial outlets, etc. By the use of removable plugs, different concepts of improvements can be shown. Photographs of the model tend to make the topography in the aerial photo pop up with an overall three-dimensional effect. An ideal use for such a quickie model might be where the architect wanted a three-dimensional medium to help a client decide on one of two widely separated sites for improvement. Such a model could help city planners decide upon arrangement of proposed additional facilities in a civic or cultural center. All existing facilities would be shown in three-dimensions. See Ch. 49, photo 22 for an example of an aerial photo model.

Because of the small scales necessary (say, 1/100″

LIMITATIONS

or smaller) to permit coverage of large areas in a manageable size, this type of model can be not much more than conceptual. Though the architect might derive some help from a space use and arrangement point of view, the more helpful study medium is one where the setting and entourage are structured to provide a complete three-dimensional picture. This is true even though the study of architectural design is momentarily subordinated by the limitations of small scale to mass and arrangement studies. Though your expertise should enable you to "put a hat on a gnat" if required, the small scales required in aerial photo models prevent convenient study of architectural design.

Aerial photo models are generally not good public display media because even though the improvements shown have accurate block configuration, the two-dimensional photo setting is relatively dead to the viewer.

A structural limitation lies in the fact that an aerial photo cannot be stretched more than minor amounts to cover changes in grade. Here we are up against the basic principle that the hypotenuse of a right triangle is longer than either of its two sides as discussed in Ch. 9 with respect to the driveway ramps in model B. Since the amount of stretch possible in a given photographic paper is a finite amount, the scale of the model must be held to one where the changes in elevation do not require more than that amount for continuous coverage without cutting and patching — another reason for 1/100″ scale or smaller. Generally speaking confine this medium to relatively low, rolling countryside as a maximum change in elevation condition. Hills too high or gradients too steep can result in a patched up mess.

Modern photographic processing can hold distortion to a minimum, but you probably will not be able to match exactly the edges of two photos in a mosaic situation. Better matches can be had by making joints away from the edges of a frame if overlap is sufficient.

CONSTRUCTION

You have a contract to construct a 1/100″ scale aerial photo background model for presentation to a city planning commission for their study of locations of a proposed high-rise office building in their civic center. The area is generally flat with a slight rise to a series of knolls at one end of an established rectangular perimeter; so all conditions fall within the aforementioned limits. A clear, composite photograph has been supplied on thin paper, large enough to more than cover a 3′ × 4′ model base. No acrylic cover is required.

Construct the base as indicated in Ch. 7. Since the terrain is mostly low-rolling, there is no point to attempt grading as described in Ch. 9 and 10 except that through the use of a bit of horizontal control, a few of the knolls will be formed out of urethane foam and glued in place. Line the base with heavyweight illustration board and trim the edges flush with the plywood. Spray all the perimeter with matte black Krylon (Ch. 32) being sure that the illustration board edges are covered. Orient the photo on the base and trim off the excess, leaving about 1/8″ selvage for final trim after the photograph has been mounted. Weight the photograph to hold it while you apply two pieces of masking tape at right angles to mark each of two corners of the illustration board at the end farthest away from the knoll area. Apply contact glue across the underside of the photo at this marked end and across the illustration board.

Make the band of glue about 1″ wide. Holding the marked corners taut between two hands, and guided by your thumbs on the intersections of the pieces of tape and your fingers underneath at the plywood edges, mount the photo in place and rub or tap it to firm adhesion. Roll the photo out all the way, weight it down and pin prick through the apparent crests of the knolls the elevations of which have been determined by your client from a civil map, assuming toes of slope for this purpose. The highest one will be 1/2″ above the illustration board. Taking advantage of the reverse roll set in the photograph to keep it out of your way, unroll it down on contact glue applied with a brush as you proceed. When about 6″ from the knoll area, stop applying glue and form the knolls. Cut pieces of urethane foam of appropriate thickness to the configurations of the toes of slope established previously and glue them in place using the pin pricked crest centers as guides. Then sand each one down to height with even slopes to their bases. Place a waterproof cover over the model under the dry photo and with a sponge, water soak the photo in the knoll areas. With slight pressure on a damp sponge and a tug at the free edges of the photo, form it over the knolls. Don't get too muscular or you will tear the photo. Note any excess photo paper resulting from this forming, raise the photo and apply white glue over all the free area and push press it down over the rest of the model base. White glue is used here to be compatible with the water-soaked photograph. Weight down any white glued places over flat ground and continue to form the photo over the knolls with fingers and sponge. At this time slice any excess paper bubbles with a razor blade, carefully remove any excess paper, and press the edges down to butt joints. Apply weights wherever possible and continue to press the photo down until it dries sufficiently to hold. Rubbing the soaked areas with toweling will speed up the process. Keep checking the photo edges which tend to curl up. When dry, trim the selvage from the model edges.

Improvements: Install the existing buildings of the civic complex at their proper locations on the photograph. These will be in block form, painted a neutral gray. The proposed additional high-rise building could be made with a distinguishing color or composition (Ch. 18) and should remain loose so that it can be moved to different locations during the planning study. Note that since every spot in an aerial photograph can't be recorded as on a plan because of angular distortion, you will have to ignore "tilting" buildings, for example, when you attach improvements and concentrate only on where the foundations are.

Patching: If you run into situations where you do not have enough photo paper to cover a hill or depression, slice the photo and let it separate to conform. Make cuts along edges of improvements to keep the patch from being more noticeable than necessary. Don't cut down the middle of a street, for example. When the edges of the hole are glued down, cut and fit pieces of scrap photo with at least the same shading if not compatible subject matter. At cliffs, slice the photo at the top edge and press the down side of the cut onto the base past the riser installed to form the cliff. The face of the cliff should then be shade painted to camouflage the surgery.

Embellishments: Sometimes your client will want to stress certain topographical features in the entourage of the developed area such as a freeway overpass. Cut along each side of the freeway to include the overpass and across one terminus. Fold the overpass back and cut along each side of the underpassing street. Fold the two ends back and excavate a cavity to reaccept these ends glued

down with a patch to fill the gap underneath the freeway location. Glue back the freeway tab at its free end and you have an effective three-dimensional site.

Automobiles at the scale of the photo placed around and in the improved area will give a feeling of activity.

Minute pieces of landscaping material can sometimes improve the setting.

From these examples, you can see how there is a wide range of embellishment possible, limited only by your imagination. Always keep in mind, however, that your embellishment program may be "gilding a lily" which by itself is sufficient unto the purpose of the model.

FEASIBILITY

Based upon local research, it seems that the cost of an individual print of an area is about 1/4 the cost of a first run photographic mission, and well within the budget of projects justifying model work. This is of course assuming that most metropolitan areas of any considerable size have already been photographed, allowing subsequent prints without the initial higher flight cost.

12

Water and Its Containment

Water, whether in natural or man made containment, could be included in Ch. 25, Landscaping, but it is included early in the text to place it in logical structural sequence. It is often necessary to excavate for the installation of water, and this can be awkward after finished grades have been established in the neighborhood and more so after structures have been installed. A discussion of real water is intentionally omitted here since it is very seldom used. It will be touched upon in Ch. 30.

Water in real life adds visual appeal to the landscape, whether it be in the form of a swimming pool, bird bath, reflecting pool, pond, lake, reservoir, mountain stream, river, waterfall, fountain, or ocean. So water in a display model, whether as a feature or a landscaping detail, must be given serious attention in the interests of gaining the same appeal in the miniature scene.

MOVEMENT

The bodies of water usually presented as modelling challenges are, in real life, seldom static. If the water isn't flowing, there is probably at least some surface disturbance. Even a bird bath may have some breeze-activated ripples. As this movement increases to river rapids, waterfalls, and ocean waves, water becomes increasingly difficult to reproduce authentically because the model builder must *stop* this movement (as camera shutter stops action) without losing the appearance thereof. The builder must some times even *create* a feeling of movement on the surface of an apparently quiet reflecting pool or mountain tarn to avoid an unnatural piece-of-glass look. By taking such license, the model builder does not violate nature. The tarn is simply "photographed" during a windstorm!

With the exception of fountains, vertical waterfalls, and breaking waves to be discussed later, the key to creating a feeling of water movement lies in surface disturbance. At whatever the scale of the model including water I have found that the best, generally applicable way to create this disturbance is through stippling the surface with clear vinyl glue (Ch. 34). Other than occasional pourings of casting resin (Ch. 24) or pieces of clear vinyl or acetate at the very small scale installations, the surface involved will best be clear acrylic. Remove the cap from the clear vinyl glue tube, and holding the tube vertically tap on drops of glue continuously over the entire surface, blending the edges of the drops and let dry. Practice will tell you how much finger pressure to apply to the tube. If you get too much glue, back off the pressure and break up the puddle with the same woodpecker action. Watch for captured air turning spots of glue cloudy. Break these up with taps of the tube tip, adding just enough glue to blend out the cloudiness. At the base of a waterfall, for example, be a woodpecker in disappearing concentric circles. Waterglass (sodium silicate) can make things look wet, but is not as durable as the vinyl glue which can do the same thing. At very small scale, an overspray of clear Krylon (Ch. 32), allowing the spray to fall on the surface, can create the desired minute disturbance, but the critical control required here makes glue stippling with the head of a pin more attractive.

AUTHENTICITY

Particularly in a display model, try to avoid stylized or amateurish appearance. Some of you may be model railroad hobbyists where the primary consideration is rolling stock and not professionally executed scenery. Where you might satisfy yourselves and your friends with a lake of painted material with a gloss finish coat or of blue mirror, remember here that you have to satisfy someone who is making a considerable investment in a professional product demanding as much realism as practicable. Try to obtain the degree of authenticity which automatically blends the result realistically into the landscape. An important key to authenticity is a suggestion of *depth* which requires a clear medium of some thickness. You can get reflection from a painted, opaque surface, but the necessary suggestion of refraction is absent. As a goal, consider your model as a three-dimensional photograph of the actual scene.

JOINTS

If you must have a divided base (Ch. 7) for shipping and handling purposes, be sure to avoid breaks in water whenever possible. There are fewer distractions worse than a lake or other body of water with a joint across it! Even consider a separate plug for the model after assembly to include the entire lake. If you can't avoid a joint because of available size of material, for example, try to place the joint

at the narrowest part of the body of water and under a bridge. Consider casting the lake (Ch. 24).

COLOR

Nature's specifications give the model builder a fair amount of leeway in the chosen color of water, but consideration should be given to the actual conditions being modelled before picking the range. Pure water, itself, has its own light blue color, but this is overshadowed by the results of mineral content, algae, plant life, color of the container, depth, and light reflection. Deep ocean on a clear day is dark blue, and with varying amounts of overcast can be green to slate gray. As the water becomes shallower, the greens predominate. The ocean over tropical white beach sand can be turquoise. Much the same variations appear in a small, still lake. Dark rock bottoms will tend to offset the green around the shallow edges. Swimming pools can safely be tinted turquoise, varying the density from deep to shallow water. Rivers are usually cloudy because of silt carried, and the color of the bed will also affect the water color. Rapids, waterfalls, and fountains will appear predominantly white because of aeration. The container of a reflecting pool may be painted black under architectural specifications, making the water appear black.

If water exists and will remain on the property to be modelled after improvements are made, the best advice to give here is, if possible, to visit the property on a sunny day and allow your artistic talents to carry the colors to your model. A display model is more attractive when constructed showing sunny, springtime conditions than those of somber winter. In the absence of a visit, study color photographs, and don't forget your clients' specifications. They may require samples for approval.

MARINE LANDSCAPES

Unless your assignment includes a diorama as seen through the hull of a glassbottomed boat, don't waste your time on marine landscapes. How many lake or ocean bottoms have you seen while standing on a shoreline or even from the top of a shoreline cliff? A Bermuda beach scene may reveal white sand at an underwater shoreline, but you are not going to see that sunken galleon unless you fly over it on a sunny day; so avoid being unrealistic, and save time to boot. A clear mountain stream can be another kettle of fish which, incidentally, you may see hiding under a rock. A clear pool of sufficient size to warrant the effort may require bits of animal, vegetable, or mineral matter on the bottom before the water is installed, but don't overdo it. There is plenty of charm for the public in realistic miniaturization above the waterline without letting your imagination get out of bounds.

SCALE

Because of the liquidity of water, and therefore its uncontrollability outside of confinement, a peculiar problem of scale arises. We not only cannot scale down a water molecule; we also cannot scale down practically a spray of *drops* of water. What is the size of a 1/16″ scale drop of water? The drops being miniaturized are so uncontrollably varied in size that we might say that water has no scale. At the larger scales, we might indicate a "splatter" with authenticity, but, generally speaking this would not be worth the effort. We can, however, scale down the size of container, height and width of waterfall, obtain a fair representation of fountain or ocean spray, and make things look wet.

EXTENT OF AUTHENTICITY

This phrase is used to describe the amount of time and effort applied to the modelling of any body of water. The extent of the effort toward authenticity will depend upon the scale and the planned use of the finished model. From our general concept of a *study* model, you might assume that a small lake on such a model at 1/8″ scale, for example, would require nothing more than a painted indication of the scale size in the correct location. On further questioning, you find that your client wants to study esthetic effects of the relation between the lake and the buildings proposed at its edge; so, though the buildings may be in block configuration only, you will have to make the lake of display quality to reflect those buildings. Otherwise the scene would be "dead." On the other hand, a 1/100″ scale *display* model of a large development might show simple, underpainted rectangles of acetate or clear vinyl at swimming pool locations because the scale is too small to justify more authentic miniaturization. Based upon our conclusion that water has no scale, you might

show ocean white caps, for example, very close to the same size at both 1/16″ and 1/8″ scale. The former were shown under stronger wind conditions! A 40′ wide river would probably take no more effort at 1/8″ scale than one at 1/16″ scale. The former just has a bigger container, holding more water molecules all of the same size no matter what the scale.

CONSTRUCTION TIPS

This is the first section in which display quality improvements are installed in grading other than flat terrain as in model A of Ch. 8. For this reason it is appropriate to state that though the general intent of this book is to discuss one proven method of construction under a given set of circumstances, alternate methods are mentioned, where appropriate, to give you subjects for investigation in your search for the better solution.

Because contour cutting facilities (Ch. 10) will not always be available, some improvements, as the 1/16″ scale swimming pool in this chapter will be installed using the vertical control method (Ch. 9) to lead you to solutions of other installation problems using this method. It will be obvious to you that this pool could have been supported in a cavity cut into urethane foam.

I have found clear acrylic, clear vinyl, and casting resin satisfactory materials to use in simulating water. There are of course other materials such as the various potting compounds; so if you want to play the field and experiment in this respect, check with your local hobby shops and chemical friends for likely subjects.

SWIMMING POOLS

Being probably the most frequently required model water facility, swimming pools will head the list in presenting construction tips. You will notice that most of the stress is placed upon display quality which involves the greater effort, reliance being placed upon your ingenuity and judgment in simplifying for study model purposes. This approach will hold true throughout the discussion of water modelling.

Small Scale: A 20′ × 30′ swimming pool at 1/100″ scale would measure, on an engineer's scale, 0.2″ × 0.3″. Paint on one side a piece of clear acetate or

0.010″ vinyl a suitable blue (aqua, turquoise, etc.), and from this piece cut a pool shape slightly larger than the above pool dimensions. Next, cut the shape of the deck area out of single ply Strathmore (Ch. 35) or other good bond paper, and cut out a rectangular hole 0.2″ × 0.3″ at the pool location. Single-ply Strathmore is 0.007″ thick, meaning that about 9″ of concrete will show above the water line. Visually this should not appear too gross. After the decking is painted the specified color and scored for joint pattern, (Ch. 26), glue the blue piece of plastic, unpainted side up, to the underside of the decking, using the overlap to accept contact glue around the edge, being careful not to allow glue to appear beyond the coping. This assembly is then glued on the model. Embellishments could include shade-painting the underside of the "water" to indicate deep to shallow ends of the pool and disturbance of the surface to indicate ripples lightly with a scribe or by applying vinyl glue. In the latter case, be careful not to overdo it. A very thin, finely stippled coat should suffice.

Large Scale: Here we will jump to an arbitrary 1/16″ scale to exemplify a more extensive construction process. Figure 12-1 shows a schematic longitudinal section of a pool measuring 20′ × 40′, indicating the shape desired. The chosen scale will result in a model pool measuring 1-1/4″ × 2-1/2″. Cut a piece of 1/2″ thick clear acrylic to the pool dimensions, and, from about 10′ (5/8″) out from one end, sand one of the polished surfaces to slope up to the other end to a depth of 3′ (3/16″). This will establish the deep and shallow ends. At the shallow end, undercut steps on your mill either across a corner or all the way across, depending upon specifications. Polish the sides, ends, and bottom, to a degree that does not leave any obvious scratches. These surfaces can be left with a frosted appearance since aberration would normally confuse the eye looking below the surface. An unobstructed, fine sanded, matte finish tapered up from the deep end will help give the feeling of depth. Spray the

bottom, sides, and ends with color in the turquoise range (Ch. 32), making the deep end darker graduating intensity toward the shallow end. No formula is possible here, trial and error being the best teacher.

Assuming your grading has been done using the vertical control method (Ch. 9), cut a hole in the surface liner for a moderately snug fit of the pool. Too snug a finish will rub the paint off the pool when you install it. On the plywood beneath the hole, build up a flat platform to receive the deep end of the pool so that the pool surface is either flush with the liner surface for an added deck and coping, or the top-of-coping-to-water distance below the liner surface. If this distance is to be 6″ then the pool surface would be 1/32″ below grade, and the edge of the illustration board (for example) liner will have to be painted around the pool cavity. At the shallow end, under the first (top) step tread vertically glue a support strip to the plywood to hold up this end of the pool. When installing the pool, tack-glue it with pinpoint drops of contact glue on each of the deep end corners and underneath the first step tread at the shallow end to adhere to the support mentioned previously. Press in place and leave alone. Too much glue or disturbance after positioning will tend to remove the paint. If you have to add coping and decking, cut the hole so that its edges *just* break the pool edge to cover up any possible cracks that may occur between the acrylic and the surface liner. Disturb the pool surface by stippling with clear vinyl glue to form ripples. Embellishments could include a diving board made out of 0.010″ sheet vinyl by gluing a strip of the material to a standard support or to the one in the specifications. A ladder at the deep end could be formed using fine wire showing one visible rung at the water surface. Curve each of two pieces so that they rise from the coping edge about 3′ and then bend down to the water against the coping edge. Two holes drilled with a pin vise (Ch. 36) should hold the coping ends of the wire, and the rung should hold the other ends. The fact that you cannot insert the ladder below water surface will be

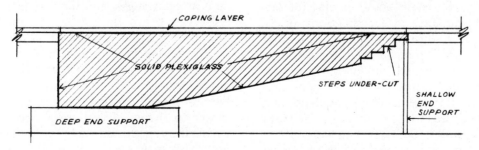

FIGURE 12-1 *Section of swimming pool.*

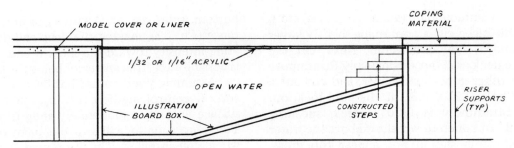

FIGURE 12-2 *Section of swimming pool.*

camouflaged by the ripples formed previously. Add some activity with a rectangle of vinyl, brightly painted and scored as a rubber raft glued to the pool surface. You can even add a sunbathing beauty (Ch. 27).

As the scale becomes larger, you can see how clumsy the block of acrylic could become. At 1/2″ scale, the block for this pool would measure 10″ × 20″ × 4″ thick (for an 8′ depth), making it a special purchase and impractically heavy. In such a case, we should abandon the preferable solid block approach in favor of a surface sheet of 1/32″ (or 1/16″) stock *just* large enough to be suspended over a cavity in the base liner. Note how the depth of this pool requires at least 4″ clearance between liner and base plywood. This seems like a lot of grading exercise, particularly if the pool is the only reason for raising the finished grade off the plywood, but there is no other way to obtain authenticity. The clarity of swimming pools makes scale depth mandatory. The acrylic should be as thin as possible to hide visible edge effect. Polish the edges and don't let them run under the coping any farther than necessary. The stippled surface will help to camouflage. See Fig. 12-2 for a schematic drawing of the assembly. Make an open-topped box out of heavyweight illustration board with the interior dimensions those of the pool. To provide all around support, make all sides the full 4″ in depth and insert the bottom within this frame, sloping it up from the deep end to result in a configuration like that of the acrylic in Fig. 12-1, except that the shallow end would extend to the shallow end wall under where the steps show in that illustration. Construct the steps to specifications at the shallow end out of illustration board. Note that underwater risers can be higher than the standard 7″ because of water-created buoyancy. Don your artist's hat and paint the interior of the box in varying shades of turquoise depending upon depth and location. Tint the steps too, since you will be viewing them under water. Cut a rectangular hole in the finished grade liner on the model to accept

snugly the outside measurements of the pool box. Clear away any obstructing grading risers, being sure that the edges of the liner have sufficient support. Mount the pool in this cavity so that the acrylic pool surface will be flush with the liner surface. Lightly tack-glue (with contact glue) a piece of clear acrylic cut to dimensions to allow a minimum of support by the top edges of the pool all around. Add about 1/4″ thickness of coping and deck material so that the edges of the coping lap the edges of the acrylic and are vertically in line with the inside surfaces of the pool beneath. You can build up this decking with vertical risers of illustration board to obtain the approximately 6″ from water to top of coping distance. This procedure assumes that the area will accept the added 1/4″ of material, according to your initial planning. If your plan called for installing the pool as part of the grading exercise, then you could have raised the liner enough to accept a filler strip around the acrylic edge under the liner, making further additions unnecessary. This reminds us again of Pattinson's Law and *planning*. Disturb the pool surface with vinyl glue as you did with the 1/16″ edition, except that in this case you do not have to be quite as dainty with your stippling because of the larger scale. Embellishments could be the same as in the case of the smaller pool, except that you can install the ladder before adding the acrylic, running the straight top ends of the wire through holes drilled in the Plexiglass as you install it. Then bend the wires up over the coping, inserting the ends into drilled holes. The bottom ends would be bent at right angles and inserted into the pool wall a few feet below the surface. You will have to add the above surface rung or rungs *after* installation.

Swimming pools come in all shapes and sizes, but the same methods of construction generally apply regardless of perimeter configuration. A kidney shaped or free-form pool will just take longer to shape. If you are presented a pool with an island, you should show its foundation as specified. This may mean cutting a hole in the acrylic through its full depth. Waterfall and cascaded supply will have solutions suggested later in this chapter. Sometimes wading pools or saunas are installed in the immediate vicinity of the main pool, presenting no unusual problems. If they are water-connected to the main pool, try to cut the acrylic to include such connections to avoid joints unless you can hide them under a bridge over the connection.

BIRD BATHS

Because of the small size of the standard decorative garden bird bath, you probably will never have to model one at a scale below 1/32″. That could be executed with a spot of glossy light blue paint on the top of a stand. When, in your judgment, the scale becomes large enough, you can confine your method of the solid acrylic system used in the case of the 1/16″ scale swimming pool. At 1/2″ scale, for example, sand a 1″ diameter disc of 1/8″ acrylic so that one large surface has a rounded or bowl shape, leaving a slight vertical edge to prevent chipping. Press this disc into 4-lb urethane foam, carefully sanding out with a hemispherical ended stick, the cavity until the surface of the disc is sufficiently below the surface to allow shaping the rim. Paint the sanded face of the disc with your chosen blue tint and tack-glue with contact glue into the cavity. Cut the urethane following the outside edge of the disc far enough away from the disc to allow sanding the shape of the container. When you have obtained the required shape, fill the urethane with thin plaster (Ch. 35). When the plaster is dry, finish sand to a smooth surface, paint to specifications, and mount the bowl on its pedestal. For activity disturb the surface with vinyl glue. Note: Your Jay's Nest (Ch. 35) may contain a wood button just right for the bowl.

REFLECTING POOLS

These are usually design-motivated structures installed as part of the architectural setting. They are often shallow pools, not more than a few inches deep, contained in concrete basins. They may be flush with grade, permitting your insetting a piece of underpainted acrylic of scale thickness into the deck and adding a frame of strips of acrylic or close-grained wood such as bass wood (Ch. 35). If they are raised, simply build up a supporting platform for the scale depth acrylic "water" and

deepen the frame to specifications. From their definition these pools are supposed to reflect; so unless otherwise directed do not disturb the surface.

PONDS

Natural country ponds are discussed with lakes. The ponds here are the concrete-contained fish ponds installed as part of the landscaping plan. They may be as much as 2′ deep, have free-form shapes, and contain flora and fauna. The solid acrylic method can be used as in the case of the 1/16″ scale swimming pool, or the thin sheet-over-cavity method, particularly where you want to include some bottom configuration and flora simulation. These ponds are usually dark because of bottom gravel, plants, fish, and other little creatures; so stay away from the light blues we've been talking about and think about browns and dark greens. Even on a solid acrylic pond you can float lily pads cut out of green paper and glue protruding reeds to the surface. Because of circulating water, indication of movement should be applied to the surface, even if just in the vicinity of water inlets. As the scale increases, and the budget calls for it, you can pour casting resin with embedded fish, plants, etc. (Ch. 24). Raised sides of free-form ponds can be laminated vertically using sheet vinyl, with the first layer welded with acrylic cement to the shaped edge of the acrylic "water," or horizontally by cutting a traced shape out of layers of illustration board or solid acrylic. Use the easier method depending mostly on scale. Cutting a ring out of acrylic would be more satisfactory than trying to laminate vinyl to get a 1/8″-wide curb or pool side, and would not require filling to hide the layer edges.

LAKES

The subject for discussion is a spring-fed lake in the foothills of a wilderness park area with mountains on the north and west. A mountain stream approaching from the northwest runs over a waterfall into the lake. See Figs. 12-3 and 12-4 for schematic illustrations. The lake covers between 6 and 7 acres and is to be installed on 1/32″ scale model. This results in a roughly rectangular area measuring 18″ × 16″. Streams and waterfalls will be discussed later, but a beach area on the east side is considered

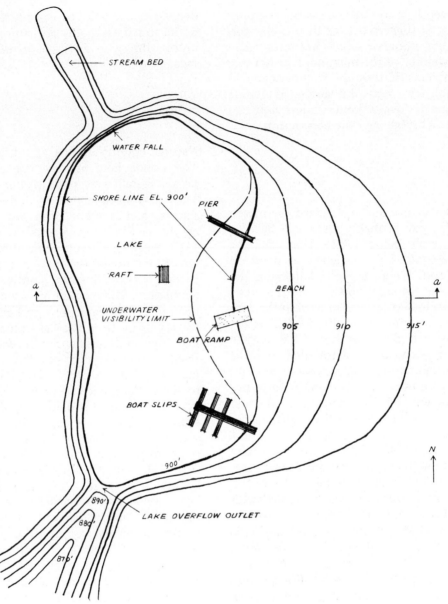

FIGURE 12-3 *Lake installation.*

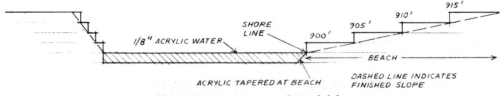

FIGURE 12-4 *Sec. a–a through lake.*

where a small boat ramp is to be installed as well as a small pier, a few boat slips for summer residents, and a swimmer's raft. See Ch. 49 photo 57 for an artificial lake.

Contour Map: The entire model terrain has been cut from urethane foam using a 1/32" scale con-

tour map or drawing (Ch. 10). You are interested here only in the lake area where a mean waterline of the lake shows as contour line 900'. This is represented by the lake outline shown in Fig. 12-3. It has been decided to use 1/8" clear acrylic for the water since you are not concerned with the configuration of the actual lake bottom which is naturally invisible except at shallow edges. Depth gradient will be taken care of by shading the painted underside of the acrylic.

During the cutting process, assume you have cut up from the southwest to and including the 900′ contour shown in Fig. 12-3 at the lake overflow outlet at the southwest corner. Note that the mean water level of the lake is also at 900′, a contour which closes on itself. Using your papercutting knife, cut out the drawing along this waterline and set this lake-shaped piece of paper aside to be used later as a lake pattern. Record the 900′ setting on the mill, raise the bit to clear the uncut urethane, and sink it back to the recorded 900′ level into any convenient spot in the lake hole indicated by the contour map. Cut out this entire lake cavity carefully following the cut edge of the drawing, and then continue cutting the remaining higher contours as normally, starting with 905′.

Acrylic Lake: With a few pieces of double-faced tape, attach the lake pattern cut out of the drawing to a sheet of clear 1/8″ thick acrylic and trace the outline with a scribe. Cut out this lake shape on your bandsaw and file trim any burrs. Don't worry about minor errors since the shore line will actually change through the seasons.

Beach and Lake Cavity: Remembering from Ch. 10 that the bottom of the cutting bit is considered to be the level of the contour line being cut, you will have to cut the lake cavity deeper by the thickness of the acrylic to result in a water level at 900′. Before doing this, mark a visible underwater beach extension on the urethane as indicated by the dotted line in Fig. 12-3. If you are not guided by underwater contours which would show on the lake pattern indicate a reasonable area of shallow water. Place the acrylic lake in the cavity, and with a wax pencil trace this shallow water limit line on the surface. This will be a guide to sand-tapering the underside of the acrylic at the beach area to accommodate the beach gradient as it extends from the shore line.

Remove the lake, and, after setting the model under the cutter again, lower the bit the thickness of the acrylic (1/8″) below the previously recorded reference setting (900′) and carefully cut out the material which will be replaced by the lake. Carefully follow the already cut shore line (900′) except at the beach area where you will follow the arbitrary underwater beach slope limit line drawn previously. This will produce a tongue of urethane projecting into the lake socket. Sanding this tongue down at

a slope to match a taper in the acrylic will indicate the visible underwater terminus of the beach.

Forming the Beach: Sand the beach area carefully down from the water line to the arbitrary beach slope limit using fine round-edged sanding sticks to help prevent chewing up the urethane foam. Try to get an even slope all along the beach area, noting that as you approach the lateral limits the slope will become steeper until the limit line blends into the water line. Next sand the underside of the acrylic lake, starting at its edge and sloping up to the guide line you previously traced on the other side (surface). I have found the top of the belt sander good for taking off the greater part of the material before handsanding to limits. As you approach a knife edge at the beach shore line, test fit by placing the lake in position. Sand the acrylic until you get a snug fit in the cavity. Be careful not to chip the shore line edge too sharply to destroy authenticity of water lapping the shore. A few chips can be sanded or filed into a more natural configuration. The next step is to polish the sanded acrylic (Ch. 24). Turn the lake over on a flat, firm surface, with the water surface down (to guard against further chipping of the knife edge), and polish with wet-or-dry sandpaper (Ch. 35), starting with a 400 grit, for example, and ending up with a 600 grit. The finer the last grit, the easier the finish polish on the wheel where you have to be doubly careful not to chip the shore line. Round off any obvious sharp transition between sanded slope and the acrylic surface at the limit line. No harm is done by sanding beyond the line since any objectionable marking can be polished out. The idea behind the polishing is to obtain transparency at the water's edge where you can see the sandy bottom.

Painting the Lake: Since this lake is only 4′ deep at most (1/8″ at 1/32″ scale), it is necessary to obtain a visual feeling of depth by shade-painting the under surface, using the same principle used in the case of the 1/16″ scale swimming pool previously discussed. Assuming the lake is quite deep throughout most of its area, start at the center with a deep blue carried almost to the west and northerly shores where very steep slopes enter the water. Shade this into greens, gray-greens, with a little brown blended in from the northeasterly shore down around the south edge where it is all relatively shallow. Leave the beach area relatively clear with a mist transition to deeper water. As noted previously, there is no fixed formula here.

Your knowledge of nature's specifications in the area and practice are the key guides. I have completely removed all the paint on occasion and started over again.

Beach Urethane: Paint the beach the specified sand color, here including browns since we underpainted the lake using that color at the shallow areas. Spray painting (Ch. 32) will help ensure against filling the pores of the urethane. You may find that the 4-lb urethane will give adequate course sand appearance without further treatment. If not, spray the area with clear Krylon (Ch. 32) and immediately sprinkle on some sand of the specified color. Spread it finely and evenly, using a sieve, in two or three coats if necessary, to prevent congealed lumps.

Installation and Finish: Glue the lake in its cavity using contact glue sparingly, tacking it in place around the edge so that no glue will be seen, and no paint disturbed. When you dab the painted surface with glue, leave it alone thereafter! If pressing the lake into position disturbs a spot of paint, you may be able to exercise modelbuilder's license with a shoreline tree hanging over the water. Disturb the lake surface with clear vinyl glue as described previously in this chapter. Do small areas at a time, blending in with preceding applications before the glue sets hard. Wavelets at the beach shore line can be suggested with a linear application of glue and light brush strokes of thin white paint. Carefully sand down the perimeter contour steps to water level and you are ready for landscaping that area, and installation of facilities. Note that under concept of the whole planning (Ch. 6) you would normally consider the stream and waterfall concurrently with the lake because they are closely related, but as mentioned earlier, these are discussed separately for clarity of construction tips. For example, when you disturbed the lake surface to show ripples, those around the base of the waterfall would be in radiating circles.

Boat Slips: Improvements and facilities installed in and around bodies of water are, because of their peculiarities, best included in this section. As a diving board was included under "Swimming Pools," tips on certain lake facilities are included here. For indications see Fig. 12-3.

Boat slips to accommodate a dozen small sail boats can be made from a single piece of 1/8″ acrylic by cutting to the shape shown in Fig. 12-3.

If less than 4′ to water is specified, sand down the finished shape to the required thickness. Paint this form to indicate painted wood, score on planking indication, and glue it down in place on the lake surface as though it were supported by floats underneath. A floating system will adjust to changes in the lake level, and a ramp approach should be installed so that its outboard end will slide on the slip assembly surface as the lake level rises or falls. See Ch. 27 for suggestions with respect to boats.

Boat Ramp: A boat ramp for trailer-launching small boats would be a concrete slab laid far enough into the water so that buoyancy will float the boat off the trailer. This can be made from 0.010″ sheet vinyl, painted a concrete color, and slipped under the shore line edge of the lake. Lift the lake edge just enough to clear so that you won't chew up the urethane beach. Carefully press the assembly down to be sure the waterline touches the beach.

Raft: A swimmer's raft is supported on floats anchored off shore. It probably would be made of heavy planking mounted on a frame and have a couple of short, one or two-rung ladders hung over the side to help swimmers climb aboard. Simulate the planking by scoring painted vinyl.

Pier: A low, 10′ wide wooden pier is supported by concrete pylons embedded in the lake bottom. With your pin vise (Ch. 36) and wire drill, drill holes through the acrylic of the lake in support configuration. Clip the heads off common pins, sand the clipped ends flat, and tap them into the lake bottom through the acrylic to the prescribed height. This height should be high enough so that the pier surface would surely be above water at its highest level (the height of the natural outlet spillway at the southwest corner of the lake). The deck could be made from scored bass wood (Ch. 35), painted according to specifications, and an indication of railing could be added (Ch. 16). With a height gauge made from a strip of sheet vinyl, check the even height of the pylons and glue down the deck centered on the pylons. Embellishments could include a float at the end of the pier with steps, and row boats tied up in anticipation of fishing expeditions.

Alternate Methods: If the above lake were to be made using the *vertical control* method (Ch. 9), it is advisable to install the acrylic simulation in the correct location supported by risers to give the correct water level *before* the surrounding terrain is built up. Hold the unpainted lake in position on its risers with a weight while you install the risers for the surrounding country configuration around its perimeter. Tuck the ends of these risers under the lake edge to help support it and provide a snug transition from dry land to water. The beach location would be sanded out of the underside of the acrylic as you did previously, and the beach could be formed using lightweight illustration board (Ch. 35) supported by risers cut to fit the configuration of the cavity in the acrylic and lined with sand. Be sure you extend the beach far enough under water so that the opaque depth effect painting will hide the edge. This beach shape could also be hand-formed from a piece of urethane foam which is a useful material even though no contour mill is available.

The lake could be made by *pouring resin* into the urethane cavity (Ch. 24) but in my opinion nothing is really gained by using this method. You would have to shade paint the lake bottom to obtain the feeling of varying depth, because there is no way to shade-dye the resin in solution. You could form the clear resin lake in a separate mold and shade-paint the under side as you did with the acrylic but why go through the mess and extra time? The casting method makes sense where you have to show an intricately shaped water's edge at rip-rap, or where ocean breakers are required. These will be discussed later.

RESERVOIRS

These naturally fall into the "Lake" category, but because of the various man-made provisions for containment, they are discussed separately. In case of a central urban reservoir where the water level is controlled by inlet pipe valves, the model builder would be faced with simply an oversize swimming pool with retaining walls instead of coping and deck. This discussion will be confined to dammed up lakes out in the country. These dams can be built of reinforced concrete, or rock or earth filled.

CONCRETE DAM

Our example of a concrete dam will be one at 1/16" scale spanning a deep, symmetrical, truncated V shaped gorge cut over the centuries by a river. To establish a bit of atmosphere, assume that

the dam will be the feature of a model to be constructed for the U.S. Corps of Engineers in a wilderness setting. The scale of 1/16" is used to give you reason to show authentic configuration and to give you some construction activity more extensive than that required in a topographical model at a much smaller scale. Refer to Figs. 12-5, 12-6, and 12-7 for schematic illustrations of the system. Even though these drawings and others used in this discussion are not in scale, where space permits an attempt has been made to show correct proportions as an aid to visualization. With the length of the dam being 16 times the width of the superimposed roadway, Fig. 12-5, for example, obviously had to be foreshortened across the page to allow easily readable relationships up and down the page.

Considering the scale, the size of the dam will be assumed to be of a size permitting a rectangular base measuring 3' × 4', a size easy to visualize. Most dimensions will be multiples of 16 to simplify explanation. A dam 128' high, 224' across the stream bed, and with a straight line distance between banks of 512' at the top, would produce, at 1/16" scale, a model dam 8" high, 14" across the stream bed, and 32" across the top. The dam will run parallel to the 4' base dimension, and the lake formed behind will run off the model across the 3' dimension. This will provide about 16" of mountain space divided between each end of the dam. About 12" downstream will be allowed for an approach view. Since most concrete dams are arched against the stream flow for the purpose of obtaining maximum resistance to water pressure, this example will be arched. The 20' wide top will have a 32' paved, two-lane roadway built up and cantilevered evenly over each top edge. The roadway will be edged with sidewalks, concrete parapets, and railings. This will be a link in a mountain road. Provision for overflow will consist of an opening between the roadway and the top of the dam. Controlled spillways will be provided below the expected water line. The foundation at stream bed level will measure 148' thick (parallel to the stream bed) with an overflow diversion skirt at the downstream base to prevent erosion.

Contouring the Base: Using a 1/16" scale contour map, cut the contours in urethane foam (Ch. 10), using the layer procedure to save material and to allow cutting a complete thickness of 2" stock. Upstream below the water line cut across the gorge to form a cavity to accept the toe of the dam face. After the dam face has been installed, this cavity can be filled with urethane to provide continuous

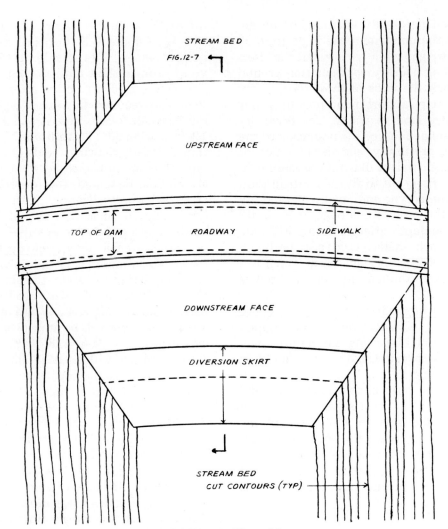

FIGURE 12-5 *Plan of dam.*

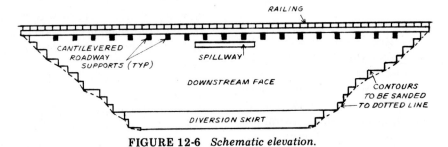

FIGURE 12-6 *Schematic elevation.*

support for the lake. Anticipating a lake made from 1/8″ acrylic, terminate your cutting vertically in the lake area at the level 1/8″ below the water line to form a lake-shaped cavity as in the case of the mountain lake discussed previously in this section.

Dam Construction: After the base has been contoured, consider the dam itself which is assumed to meet all geographical, geological, and engineering requirements in a hypothetical situation. Here is

an excellent example of the need for planning (Ch. 6), keeping in mind Pattinson's Law, in order to arrive at the most expeditious sequence of events. Analyse the assembly to find five main components (Figs. 12-5 and 12-6): the top surface of the dam, two dam faces convexly battered upstream and concavely battered downstream with a specified 2-to-1 slope, a diversion skirt at the base of the downstream face, and a roadway superimposed across the top surface. The top is defined

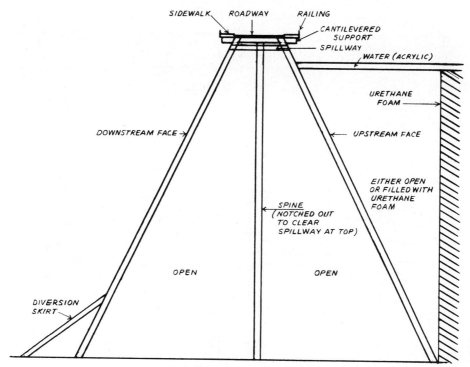

FIGURE 12-7 *Section of dam.*

by two level plane curves concentrically spanning the gorge at an elevation 128′ above the stream bed. The two faces are curved planes installed at a slope. The cross section of the dam (Fig. 12-7) is an isosceles trapezoid (ignoring the diversion skirt).

Normally you would receive complete information including the results of all computations critical to construction, but it is assumed here that for some reason computations on your part are necessary. A professional model builder has to be ready for all sorts of structural situations; so I feel that it is beneficial to demonstrate how, with a little analysis of known values, you can compute yourself out of a corner. Obvious methods available to you in construction of this dam without calling on Pythagoras and his ilk are initially ignored for this purpose. Here is another good example of a case where computations and notes could support the accuracy of your model as evidence in court even though use of such computations was for your verification only.

Dam Top: We decide to start with the top surface, not only because it is the simplest component, but also because with it you can construct a rigid spine against which to install the faces without disturbing the exact site. The roadway is another curved, level plane that can be added after the dam

has been constructed. The engineering drawings show that the radii of the upstream and downstream edges of the dam top are 416′ and 396′ respectively. These are shown schematically as R-1 and R-2 in Fig. 12-8. Draw two parallel "bank" lines on a sheet of heavyweight illustration board 512′ (32″) apart. This is the straight line distance between banks at the top of the dam. On the outside of each bank line draw a parallel line to provide 1/4″ of selvage to bury in each bank. With the center on a line drawn parallel to and half way between the bank lines, scribe arcs with the radii of R-1 and R-2 and R-3, extending them to the selvage lines. These radii are 26″, 24.75″, and 25.375″, respectively. Cut out this arced dam top and lay it aside after locating the ends of the center line at the banks. Insert common pins into the urethane to mark these anchorage points.

Spine: To help support the dam top and to provide a rigid spine at a fixed location, an unseen model component will be made in the form of a vertical plane glued to the center of the under side of the top between banks of the gorge. Here enters some basic geometry and trigonometry. Note from Fig. 12-8 that you have the radius of the top of dam center line arc R-3 (406′ or 25.375″) but do not have its length. That is needed to cut the correct amount of material for the spine element to be

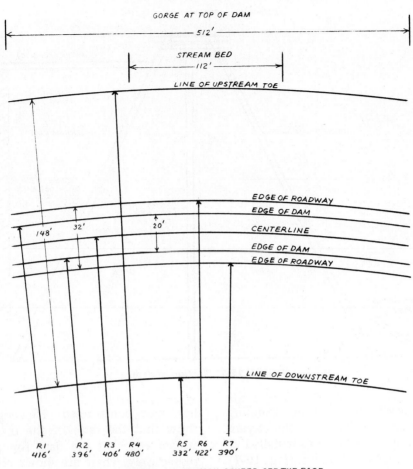

GORGE AT TOP OF DAM

512'

STREAM BED

112'

LINE OF UPSTREAM TOE

EDGE OF ROADWAY
EDGE OF DAM
CENTERLINE
EDGE OF DAM
EDGE OF ROADWAY

148'   32'   20'

LINE OF DOWNSTREAM TOE

R1   R2   R3   R4   R5   R6   R7
416'   396'   406' 480'   332' 422' 390'

ALL RADII TO COMMON CENTER OFF THE PAGE

FIGURE 12-8 *Critical measurements.*

installed on a curve. Refer to Fig. 12-9 for this purpose and for later computations of the same nature. The standard letter designations will be assigned different values depending upon the dam element being computed. The extraction of certain elements of Fig. 12-8 and setting them out separately as Fig. 12-9 is to simplify explanation and avoid the confusion of many lines and figures. The arc shown in Fig. 12-9 can represent any one of the arcs in Fig. 12-8 depending upon the one of which you are determining the length. A key to the letters in Fig. 12-9 follows:

A = Length of arc

C = Chord of arc

a = Angle subtended by an arc and its chord

b = Angle subtended by 1/2 an arc and 1/2 its chord

R = Radius = Hypotenuse of a right triangle

B = Base of a right triangle or 1/2 chord (C)

D = Leg of right triangle perpendicular to its base (B) = Center line of stream bed

Sin b = B/R

  a = 2b

A = a/360 × 2 × π × R

Returning to the spine element, arc A in Fig. 12-9 represents the center line of the top of the dam. Its radius is R-3 in Fig. 12-8 or 406' (25.375"). The length of the chord (C) of this arc is 520' (32.5") which is the top of dam span between banks plus 0.5" of selvage. You need angle a, the angle subtended by the chord and arc. Sin b = B/R. B = 1/2 chord C or 16.25". Then sin b = 16.25/25.375 = 0.64039. My slide rule calculator shows this to be the sine of 39.8212 degrees. Trigonometric tables will give you degrees, minutes, and seconds, but the calculator uses decimals to simplify expression. Answers will be rounded off to two decimal places as the maximum eyeball plotting limit. From Fig. 12-9, a = 2b or 79.6424 degrees. With this

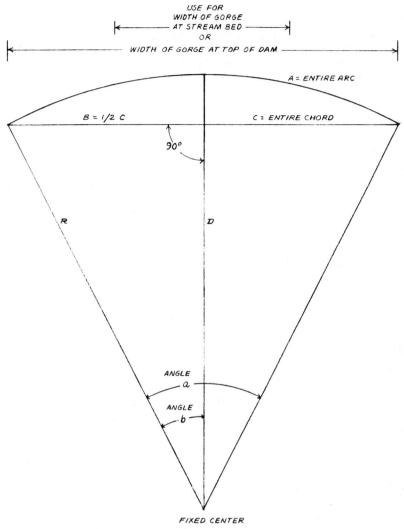

FIGURE 12-9 *Multi-purpose diagram.*

information, you can determine the length of the arc (top of spine element) by using the formula: Length of arc = a/360 × 2 × π × **R** where a is the number of degrees in the angle subtended by the arc and its chord, π the ratio of the circumference of a circle to its diameter (a constant of 3.1416), and R the radius of the arc. The number of degrees in a circle is 360. Substituting the known values, you have:

Length of arc = 79.6424/360 × 2 × 3.1416 ×
25.375 = 35.271889″

or 35.27″. This is the length of the top of the spine element.

Considering Fig. 12-9 a schematic plan at the bottom of the dam, chord **C** becomes 224′ (14″), plus 0.5″ selvage or 14.5″, one half (or 7.25″)

of which is the length of the new triangle side B. Side R (R-3 of Fig. 12-8) remains the same at 25.375″. Following the same procedure you used for determining the length of arc at the top of the dam, you find that angle b = 16.6015 degrees making a = 33.203 degrees. Substituting the known values, you have:

Length of arc = 33.203/360 × 2 × 3.1416 ×
25.375 = 14.704889″

or 14.7″. This is the length of the bottom of the spine element. Note that this arc is almost a straight line since the straight line distance between banks at this location is 14.5″.

On a sheet of chip board (Ch. 35) draw an isosceles trapezoid (Fig. 12-10) with a top side 35.27″ long parallel to a bottom side 14.7″ long

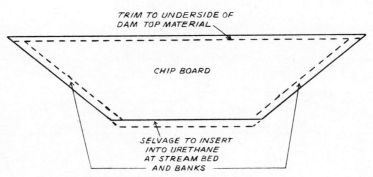

FIGURE 12-10 *Spine element.*

and a height of 8″ (128′ at 1/16″ scale). Add an arbitrary 1/4″ of height to the bottom for selvage to insert in the stream bed and reduce the height at the top by 3/32″ to accommodate the thickness of the heavyweight illustration board dam top made previously. Mark the selvage guide lines and cut out the resulting figure. Contact glue its top to a centerline drawn on the underside of the dam top. Place this assembly at the dam site with the chip board vertical and the termini of the top centerline matched with the pin markers in the urethane banks. When satisfied that the position is correct, pull the spine and glue it back permanently. This will provide a firm backing against which to install the dam faces which are next on the agenda.

DAM FACES

The dam faces present the peculiar problems arising from curved planes meeting other curved planes at a slope. This requires arcs in the ends of the faces with radii different from those of the top of the dam and toe anchorage, and the lengths of the chords of these arcs to arrive at material widths. The height (length of slope) is also required, being longer than the prescribed height of the dam that could be used for the spine element in a vertical plane. The computations needed then for drawing the shape and size of the dam faces are:

1. Radii of arcs of the top and bottom edges of the trapezoidal faces to give the arced shape of these edges which meet the curved edges of top and curved toe anchorages.

2. The lengths of the chords of these arcs to provide the widths of material at top and bottom.

3. The height of the faces (length of slope) to provide the length of material.

Upstream face: To avoid confusion, concentrate first on the upstream face. Before attempting computations, in order to get a handle on the various elements, place a cross section of the dam cleared of superstructure in an imaginary cone (Fig. 12-11). This is the main part of the section shown in Fig. 12-7. Figure 12-12 shows a portion of the cone split down the side and spread into a flat plane. This will help visualization.

The base of the cone will have the same radius as that of the arc of the upstream toe, 480′ or 30″ R-4 in Fig. 12-8), because its circumference follows the shape of the dam. This makes the center of the cone the same as that of the radii indicated in Fig. 12-8.

The radius of the bottom edge of the upstream face material is equal to F-1 as indicated in both Fig. 12-11 and 12-12. Since the radius of the base of the cone is 30″, the prescribed 2 to 1 slope of the face makes the height of the cone 60″. Therefore:

$$F\text{-}1 = \sqrt{30^2 + 60^2} = 67.082039'' \text{ or } 67.08''$$

The radius of the top edge of the face material is equal to F-2 which is equal to F-1 (67.08″) less F-3. To obtain F-3, the height of the face material, find the hypotenuse of the right triangle formed by the vertical, dotted line in the dam section of the cone. The base of the triangle is equal to R-4 less R-1 (Fig. 12.8) or 30″ − 26″ = 4″. The height of the triangle is the height of the dam or 8″. Therefore:

$$F\text{-}3 = \sqrt{4^2 + 8^2} = 8.9442719'' \text{ or } 8.94''.$$

F-2 then equals 67.08″ (F-1) − 8.94″ (F-3) or 58.14″. The arcs at the top and bottom of the face material (lying flat in Fig. 12-12) have the same lengths as those of the upstream top and toe of the dam, but they have larger radii (F-1 and F-2) with resulting flatter curves and longer chords (top

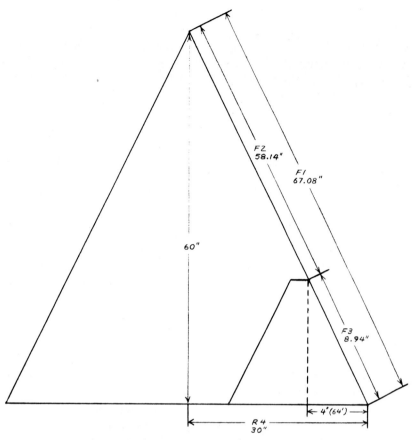

FIGURE 12-11 *Imaginary cone.*

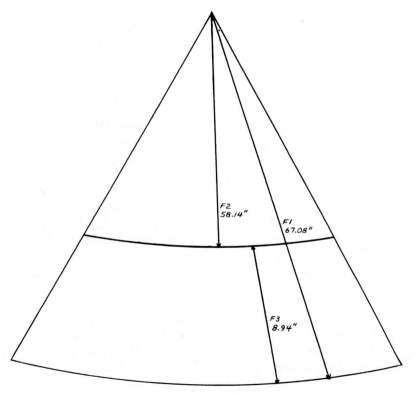

FIGURE 12-12 *Cone split and rolled flat.*

and bottom widths of face material). To find the lengths of these chords first determine the length of arcs at the top and toe of the dam by using Fig. 12-8 and 12-9 as you did in computing the lengths of arc for the spine element. Assign these values to the arcs of the face material and use the length of arc formula, working back with the new radii F-1 and F-2 (Figs. 12-11 and 12-12).

For the upstream arc of the top of the dam R (Fig. 12-9) = R-1 or 26″ (Fig. 12-8). C (the distance between banks at the top of the dam) = 32″ + 0.5″ of selvage or 32.5″. B = 1/2 C or 16.25″. Sin b = 16.25/26 = 0.625, the sine of 38.6822 degrees; so angle a = 2b or 77.3644 degrees. Then:

$$\text{Length of arc } A = a/360 \times 2 \times \pi \times 26$$
$$= 77.3644/360 \times 2 \times 3.1416 \times 26 = 35.106931$$
$$= 35.11″$$

For the upstream toe, R (Fig. 12-9) = R-4 (Fig. 12-8) = 30″. C = 14″ + 0.5″ of selvage or 14.5″. B = 1/2 C or 7.25″. Sin b = 7.25/30 = 0.24166, the sine of 13.9849 degrees; so angle a = 2b or 27.9698 degrees. Then:

$$\text{Length of arc } A = 27.9698/360 \times 2 \times 3.1416$$
$$\times 30 = 14.644986$$
$$= 14.64″$$

Using these lengths of arc for the top and bottom edges of the face material, substitute them in the length of arc formula including the radii F-1 and F-2 (Figs. 12-11 and 12-12) to find angle a (Figs. 12-9 and 12-12).

Top of Material:

Length of arc	=	$a/360 \times 2 \times 3.1416 \times$ F-2
35.11	=	$a/360 \times 2 \times 3.1416 \times 58.14$
35.11	=	$365.31 \times a/360$
a	=	$360 \times 35.11/365.31 = 34.6$ degrees
b	=	1/2 a = 17.3 degrees
Sin b	=	B/R (F-2)
0.297375	=	B/ 58.14
B	=	$0.297375 \times 58.14 = 17.289382$
C = 2B	=	$2 \times 17.289382 = 34.578764$ or 34.58″

This is the width of the top of the upstream face material.

Bottom of Material:

Length of arc	=	$a/360 \times 2 \times 3.1416 \times$ F-1
14.64	=	$a/360 \times 2 \times 3.1416 \times 67.08$
14.64	=	$421.48 \times a/360$
a	=	$360 \times 14.64/421.48 = 12.5$ degrees
b	=	1/2 a = 6.25 degrees
Sin b	=	B/R (F-1)
0.108867	=	B/67.08
B	=	$0.108867 \times 67.08 = 7.3027983$
C = 2B	=	$2 \times 7.3027983 = 14.605596$ or 14.61″

This is the width of the bottom of the upstream face material.

On a sheet of heavyweight illustration board draw a center line across approximately the center of the 30″ dimension of a standard 30″ × 40″ sheet. On this line lay out 8.94″, the height of the face. (See Fig. 12-13). At right angles to and through the termini of the indicated 8.94″ draw the chords just computed so that the centerline passes through their centers. The length of the top chord is 34.58″ and of the bottom chord 14.61″. Anchor the illustration board so it won't shift, and with a straightedge extend on the table top the centerline above the top of the upstream face configuration being drawn so that your compass (Sec. 36) can accommodate F-1 or 67.08″. Draw an arc of this radius so that it passes through the ends of the bottom chord, and from the same center draw an arc with a radius of 58.14″ (F-2, Fig. 12-11) so that it passes through the ends of the top chord. You will then have the shape and size of the upstream face as in Fig. 12-13. Mark the selvage guide lines 1/4″ in from each side and cut out the figure. Before gluing in place, sand-taper the top edge to make a mating joint with the top of dam edge.

The downstream face can be computed using the same procedure except that for visualization, place the cone upside down with the dam on the outside so that the shape of the cone will conform to the opposite slope of the face (See Fig. 12-14). The height of the face will be the same (8.94″) as that of the upstream face since a cross section of the dam, ignoring the diversion skirt, is an isosceles trapezoid (Fig. 12-7). The base of the cone now has a radius equal to R-2 (24.75″), the radius of the downstream top edge. This makes the height of cone 49.50″ (2 to 1 slope). F-1 = $\sqrt{24.75^2 + 49.50^2}$ = 55.34″. F-2 = 55.34″ − 8.94″ = 46.4″. These are the radii of the arced top and bottom of the

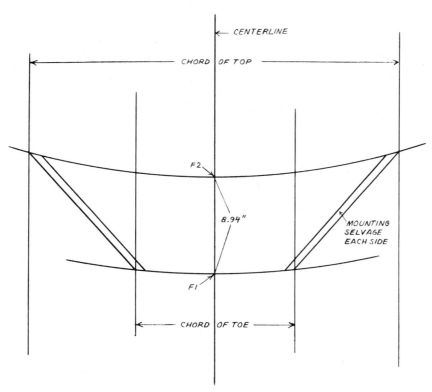

FIGURE 12-13 *Upstream face.*

downstream face material. The lengths of these arcs are equal to the length of arcs of the top and toe of the downstream side of the dam as was the case upstream.

Referring again to Figs. 12-8 and -9, R of Fig. 12-9 = R-2 of Fig. 12-8 or 24.75″. C of Fig. 12-9 = 32.5″; so B = 1/2 C or 16.25″ as before. Sin b = 16.25/24.75 = 0.65656, the sine of 41.038 degrees; so angle a = 2b or 82.077 degrees. Then:

$$\text{Length of arc A} = 82.077/360 \times 2 \times 3.1416 \times 24.75$$
$$= 35.45''$$

For the downstream toe, **R** (Fig. 12-9) = R-5 (Fig. 12-8) = 20.75″ B = 7.25 as before. Sin b = 7.25/20.75 = 0.34939, the sine of 20.45 degrees. Angle a = 2 × 20.45 or 40.9 degrees. Then:

$$\text{Length of arc A} = 40.9/360 \times 2 \times 3.1416 \times 20.75$$
$$= 14.81''$$

Find angle a by using the length of arc formula (as you did for the upstream face) with the cone radii F-1 and F-2.

Top of Material:

Length of arc	= a/360 × 2 × 3.1416 × F-1
Therefore 35.45	= a/360 × 2 × 3.1416 × 55.34
a	= 360 × 35.45/347.71
	= 36.702999 degrees
b	= 1/2 a = 18.35 degrees
Sin b	= B/F-1
0.314821	= B/55.34
B	= 17.42″
C	= 2B = 34.84″,

the width of the top of the downstream face material.

Bottom of Material:

Length of arc	= a/360 × 2 × 3.1416 × F-2
Therefore 14.81	= a/360 × 2 × 3.1416 × 46.4
a	= 360 × 14.81/291.54
	= 18.29 degrees
b	= 1/2a = 9.15 degrees
Sin b	= B/F-2
0.159	= B/46.4
B	= 7.3784816
C	= 2B = 14.76″,

the width of the bottom of the downstream face material.

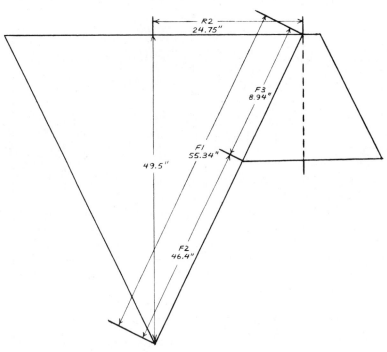

FIGURE 12-14 *Imaginary cone.*

With the developed information draw the downstream face as you did for the upstream face, cut out and install to complete the main part of the dam. Note that the top and bottom arcs are both bowed in the opposite direction from that of the upstream face since one face is convex and the other concave.

Diversion Skirt: With information similar to that given for the dam faces, the diversion skirt also could be computed, but having exemplified with the faces the occasionally required computation procedures it seems superfluous to continue the mathematical gymnastics. You would draw the arc of the skirt on the downstream face material before mounting the latter as a guide to mounting the former. Cut out a strip of the top lamination of the illustration board of the face to form a socket to provide a tight joint with the top edge of the skirt.

Water: The 1/8″ thick acrylic lake should be cut and trimmed to a pattern with the underside shade-painted in the same manner as was the lake discussed earlier in this chapter. Except perhaps for a shelf here and there the lake will be deep, calling for an overall dark blue reflecting a sunny sky. Occasionally along the banks blend in some greens to relieve the monotony. The special consideration here is the joint where the water line meets the face of the dam.

First fill the cavity that was cut to accept the upstream toe. This replaced foam will provide a continuous and consistent support for the lake. The top layer of the fill should conform generally to the configuration of the cavity. You can hand-sand the arc of the dam face in sections.

The best approach to establishing a tight fitting, even arc in the acrylic where it meets the dam is a slow and methodical one. One chip or misfit in over 32″ will ruin the appearance; so take your time. As a guide, figure the radius of the dam face at the water line and draw it on a piece of light-weight illustration board cut out to make a pattern which can be adjusted to a tight joint before tracing it on the acrylic. With the elevation of the upstream toe and that of the water line given, the difference will be the height of the water line (depth of lake). The established 2 to 1 slope of the face means that the horizontal distance from the water line to the toe is equal to one-half this height. Deduct the result from the radius of the upstream toe (Fig. 12-8), and you have the radius of the water line arc. Trace the final corrected pattern on the lake pattern, accurately oriented and located, and when you cut the acrylic cut just outside the arc line to allow sanded adjustment. Taper the arced edge to conform to the dam slope, avoiding a razor edge which is easily chipped. Again, take your time. Round off the taper on the bottom to camouflage the change of plane. Finish with wet-or-dry sandpaper and paint this edge along with the underside of the lake. Before gluing the lake in with contact glue, choose spots around the edge (except at the dam surface) where the lake rests solidly with no spring. At these points apply contact glue to both surfaces and let dry. Mount the lake finally with finger pressure at the glue locations and don't disturb thereafter. There will be no glue at the dam edge, but should a spot of pulled paint be objectionable, consider an overhanging tree on the bank. When you disturb the water surface with vinyl glue this will camouflage minor disasters.

Roadway: Cut the roadway as indicated in Figs. 12-5, 12-6, and 12-7 out of heavyweight illustration board, assuming that the 3/32″ thickness provides scale thickness of road edge. Adjust the radii to accommodate later adjustments of parapet or railing structure so that the total width will be to specifications. Add arcs of 0.030″ vinyl at each edge to form the sidewalks and approximately 6″ curbs. Mount this assembly concentrically on a solid block extension of the dam top to the specified height, checking the elevations of the mountain roadway at each end. Leave the prescribed opening under the roadway at the center of the dam for overflow spillway. Add the required concrete parapet and railing (Ch. 16), and the cantilever supports under the road edges. Fill open joints with spackle (Ch. 35). Probably all but the railings can be painted a concrete gray. The latter can best be treated before installation.

Spillways: Gate controlled spillways appearing in the form of cavities in the downstream face of the dam were purposely omitted in the sequence of events to avoid confusion in the computations of the dam faces. These would normally be installed prior to assembling the dam.

ALTERNATE METHODS

This dam construction project has been a good medium with which to show how mathematical methods can help obtain structural answers and be a check and guide for your mechanical efforts. With each model project usually presenting at least one peculiar challenge, the time consumed in empirical effort can often be shortened by drawing on your knowledge of basic geometry and trigonometry. There is nothing as conclusive as carrying out a procedure to determine whether or not it will provide the answer, but with time being

of the essence, make use of every tool at your disposal to cut down the amount of trial and error. Consider your knowledge of the mathematical approach as another tool.

Assuming normal and complete information from your client, the subject dam could have been constructed in one of several ways. Following the same assembly procedure used after computing shapes, the length of spine element could be found mechanically by bowing a flexible strip of wood or cardboard along the arced centerline of the dam top. With the spine installed, the faces could be shaped by holding them against the top edges and tracing the arced profiles. A little trial and error adjustment to an approximately radiused diversion skirt could accomplish that element against a firmly installed face.

You could use the vertical control method with illustration board risers parallel to the stream bed and cut to a trapezoidal profile with notches in the top edge to hold the top of the dam. The intervals between risers could then be filled with urethane foam and the surface covered with vinyl or plaster.

After interpolating contours on the dam faces in the drawing, you could cut the whole model out of urethane foam with the Pattinson Mill or similar cutting tool and then cover the sanded smooth surfaces with vinyl.

To obviate the lengthy process of shaping an accurate arc at the lake edge, you could construct the upstream face so that the visible upper part just overlapped the edge of the acrylic. The objection to this method is that it is hard to camouflage the fact that the water extends into the surface. This is often acceptable in the case of swimming pools where a gutter or overhanging trim can cover the fact, but against an open, obviously single plane surface, lapping tends to destroy authenticity of appearance in my opinion. A third method is to pour the lake in casting resin. The lake bottom should be unobstructed by joints and must be painted to hide the material surface since it is difficult if not impossible to shade-paint the resin. Resin can be poured in layers with different tints, but the total thickness must be at least 1/2″ to help prevent cracking of a lake measuring about 32″ × 24″, thus adding to weight.

Earth-Filled Dams: Most of these can either be cut into the urethane base along with the surrounding contour cutting or formed out of urethane foam and added to the model. Depending upon the local geography, geology, and hydraulic problems, filled dams are made from a great variety of soil and rock combinations, but as model builders we are interested only in the surface configuration and treatment. In an analytical display, a cross section might show the composing core and outer layers designated by colors and texture, but particularly in our branch of model building, a complete dam would usually be shown as a part of the landscape. The stored water can be shown as in the case of a concrete dam, with special consideration given to the water-dam face transition. If the upstream face includes heavy boulder rip-rap, and the scale is large enough to make a natural appearing acrylic joint awkward, the lake can be poured using resin (Ch. 24). Remember that with this method you will have to shade-paint the lake bottom prior to pouring and include the supplying stream, if included, in your pour. Sometimes this is the only satisfactory solution. The dividend is the natural way the resin will flow into rip-rap cavities. Concrete spillways for controlled overflow and anti-erosion diversion skirts can be cut into the urethane foam and lined with illustration board or sheet vinyl.

MOUNTAIN STREAMS

If a mountain stream is included in the drawings submitted for the purpose of building a model at 1/200″ scale of a large housing developement, for example, consideration must be given as to whether or not the stream should be shown. A 10′ wide stream at this scale would be 0.050″ wide, or at best, a little wider than a pencil line. If the stream is to be a part of the developed landscape then the effort would be worth the time involved, even though the stream might have to be made large enough out of scale to make its presence obvious. If the stream is left in natural, undeveloped surroundings, then why show it at all? Chances are that you can hide the bed with overhanging trees. This seems like a minor question, but it will come up some time resulting either in your spending a couple of hours cutting, painting, and blending into the landscape a minute strip of vinyl or ignoring the stream and saving the time.

   If a minute stream such as the one in the last paragraph must be shown, cut a strip of 0.020″ sheet vinyl to the configuration of the stream bed and a little wider than the water course. Paint the strip an earth color, and, down the center, overpaint a light blue or blue-green line. This can be done with a fine brush or a drafting pen (Ch. 26). Use subdued, matte colors so that a blue line on the model doesn't pull your eye away from model features. Where the stream is not open to a blue sky, it will be naturally darker toward the grays with plant-growth green along the edges. Glue this strip to the urethane or to the plaster if the canyon has been constructed using the vertical control method (Ch. 9). Camouflage the edges with ground cover (Ch. 25). Before installing, spray the strip with clear Krylon (Ch. 32) if you desire to simulate a wet surface.

   As the scale becomes larger, or the stream is a feature as one emptying into a park lake, more attention will have to be given to its execution. A 10′ wide stream at 1/20″ scale would measure 1/2″ wide, calling for a treated strip of 1/16″ clear acrylic cut to the width of the stream in the drawing configuration. Note here that no selvage is left on each side of the water course because you do not want the water to appear to be running below ground at the banks. This installation is similar to that of a lake discussed previously where the "water" is held in a socket so that you can obtain a feeling of depth by shade-painting the underside of a transparent material. Where you can't press this acrylic strip into a Pattinson Mill contoured urethane foam base to create the socket, because you have used the vertical control method of grading, trace the strip on a piece of lightweight illustration board (Ch. 35) wide enough so that you can conveniently blend the banks into the entourage. Following the traced lines, cut the two bank strips and mount them on the model so that they will butt against the edges of the acrylic thus forming a socket for the stream. In your planning you will have provided for this installation in the stream bed depression during your grading. Lightweight illustration board will be flush with the surface of 1/16″ acrylic, so if you want to create banks sloping to the water's edge, use heavyweight illustration board or laminate material to the bank height and taper the water edges as required. Do your tapering *before* you glue in the stream or you stand the chance of scratching the acrylic. Shade-painting the underside of the stream using a spray nozzle will be difficult because the stream's average width is only 1/2″. In this case you may be satisfied with an overall neutral blue-green, shading longitudinally into darker blues at deep pools. If not, use a brush, and, after donning your artist's hat, blend wet paint as you alternately apply several different shades.

Surface Disturbance: In creating surface disturbance in a stream, keep in mind the difference in the type of movement compared with that in a lake, discussed previously, or at sea, to be discussed later. Wind-swept disturbance results in ripples up to swells where the water molecules move up and down in place, but in a stream, the molecules are all moving in the direction of flow, the only real surface disturbance being caused by obstructions such as rocks, dead tree trunks caught along the edge, etc. where the molecules are forced to change direction. You can use the same vinyl glue you used on the lake (Ch. 34) but the overall stippling should be replaced by more elongated applications around obstructions. If over an unobstructed stream bed the surface seems too glasslike before installing, apply a thin overspray of clear Krylon, letting the droplets fall on the surface. Go easy so you won't wind up with simply a complete layer of paint to defeat your purpose! The relatively deep pools found along the route may very well look like glass in nature. These may be lightly stippled with vinyl glue as though a breeze were blowing across them.

Rapids: Rapids or white water occur where the stream runs swiftly and appears to tumble down a distinct change in gradient of the bed or through a rockbound gorge not easily eroded. Rock and boulders in the water's path churn up foam and kick up spray, both white because of aeration. In the case of the $1/20''$ scale stream, sudden changes in gradient can be indicated by heating and bending the acrylic strip prior to any other treatment. Be sure that the stream's socket in the model surface is formed to fit this configuration. At this scale, a rocky stream bed can be simulated by pushing or pulling up the acrylic surface with firm applications of a hot soldering iron (the small, pencil type, (Ch. 36) with a chisel point). Heat and flame will consume acrylic; so don't hold the iron against the surface longer than necessary to raise the "rock." Make the cavity, from which you dug the rock, on the downstream side. Where large boulders are called for, melt holes through the acrylic with the iron pressed against pebbles chosen for indigenous colors. This is better than drilling concentric holes because the tighter fitting setting hides the visible thickness of acrylic at the rock, and the molten material hardened around the rock can be incorporated with the simulated disturbance. Paint the minute rocks you pushed up with the iron to match the inserted pebbles and add touches of white paint where the water would be broken up. Streaks of vinyl glue can create the water "folding" between boulders.

RIVERS

You probably will never be called upon to model the complete width of a river like the Mississippi, at least in any scale large enough to show detail, but you may have to model a stretch of a bank. From erosion over the centuries, rivers tend to have wider and flatter beds and run more slowly than mountain streams. They are not as clear as mountain streams because of thier silt content, so consider this when you paint the underside of an acrylic river. In their mountainous reaches, rivers can have rapids just like their small sisters, and you can follow the same principles in their execution as you did just previously. When cutting a river bank, be on the lookout for connected backwaters the configuration of which should be included in your pattern.

Alternate Methods: Streams and rivers can be poured using casting resin (Ch. 24), but unless the expanse or length warrant it, I do not believe that this method is worth the trouble. If a marine landscape is in order, then it makes more sense because you can show actual objects *in* the water as they would naturally be. Rocks, plant growth, and even fish can be mounted in place for a single pour or on top of the first of two pours to create varying depths of location. Remember that if you pour a stream, the gradient of the bed may be steep enough to allow the resin to run away from you! In such cases make provision for tilting the model base until the resin has had a chance to set in a level position.

WATERFALLS

The rapids discussed under "Mountain Streams" and "Rivers" could technically be termed waterfalls, but the subject here includes only those with generally free-falling water as seen in the photograph of one at $1/32''$ scale in Ch. 49, photo 31. Assume you have a $1/16''$ scale waterfall to construct as a break in a 20' wide mountain stream. You have cut the stream out of clear $1/16''$ acrylic and have painted the under side to give color and depth. The pool at the base of the falls could be deepened below the acrylic socket depth for marine landscaping, but because of the surface disturbance caused by the falling water, any interesting effect would be mostly lost. Break the acrylic straight across the point where the upstream edge of the pool is to be the end of the stream above. When the two strips of stream have been positioned so that they line up vertically at the falls, remove the upper piece and round off the waterfall end on the top side. This is as much for camouflaging the end of the acrylic as it is to create an effect of water starting to fall over the edge of the precipice. Polish this rounded end and mount both stream strips in place. The falling water is executed with contact glue. Insert the tip of a piece of pointed dowel into contact glue thinned to about the consistency of molasses; touch the pool at a point along the line where the water would fall, and draw up a "hair" of glue vertically until you can rub the point of the dowel at the curved end of the upstream acrylic and thus attach the top end of the hair. Keep doing this until you have enough water falling in the right configuration. Let the glue dry completely and paint the whole falls white, taking care not to break the glue hairs. With clear vinyl glue, make concentric ripples moving away from the point of impact in the pool and coat surrounding rocks to make them look wet. A judicious application of wisps of white cotton will give the effect of spray. Even though colored, I have used the contact glue for waterfall simulation because it seems to have more stability for the purpose than the clear vinyl type. Given enough starting supply, it will pull out to about any extent required in model building. No mention has been made of the rock formation at the falls. This is because such geological formations are discussed in Ch. 25.

FOUNTAINS

Fountains are left to the last of fresh water facilities because they are the hydraulic orphans of model building. I have never seen a model fountain that really looked like a fountain. They can be simulated, but stylization is about all you will accomplish. I have had them spun out of glass, used shredded plastic, etc. with no satisfactory results. The infrequent requirement for fountains in my experience has probably limited my research, but unless one of you has the magic formula, my advice is to tell your client the water has been turned off prior to maintenance of the pools! The nonauthentic results aren't worth the time and effort in my experience, but this is not an automatic damnation of all model fountain research and development. Also, some clients will be satisfied with a skillful simulation because they feel the fountains should be shown even though they have to be in stylized form.

OCEANS

Large lakes, such as the Great Lakes, and ocean fronts present distinctive problems to the model builder principally through swell and wave activity. In their absence, a sheltered marina, where the only obvious disturbance would be tidal surge, could be executed in the same manner as was the lake discussed previously. You might find more varied facilities along an ocean front than you would see around a mountain lake, but the same principles of pier anchorage, boat ramp and slip construction, etc., would apply. As mentioned previously, you should consider pouring resin where extensive rip-rap appears, (see Ch. 49 photo 23) or there is an extent of rocky shore line where authenticity requires an appearance of flow around multishaped surfaces. Tidal pools of clear resin can be poured independently of the ocean into cavities in the rocks, and where the acrylic method is used, small pieces of the material will serve the same purpose. Don't forget surface disturbance with either method — vinyl glue stippling in the case of acrylic, and disturbing the surface of the resin with a tool before it hardens. Since any modelled ocean will appear along an edge of the model base, make provision for covering the joint between acrylic ocean and such base, or for confining the liquid resin. A 1/2″ high heavyweight illustration board dam around the model base location of the ocean will also serve as a finishing surface when the resin of that depth has set.

Waves and Breakers. As a variation from the installation of relatively quiet, sheltered, lake-like portions of ocean, assume you have a 1/8″ scale model to construct of an open bay with sandy beach, curving around to a headland with rocks and tide pools at its base. (see Fig. 12-15) Construction methods will have to be adjusted to include swells approaching shore where they break up into waves. The 1/8″ scale will provide sizes large enough to require detailed execution. In other words, you can't fool anybody with simple artistic suggestion. You have to *build a wave.*

Before tackling the job, I advise study of the real thing. If you are lucky enough to be near a coast, take some time out and contemplate nature from the top of a cliff overlooking the ocean. Note the continuous approach of swells, with a depression of equal amplitude between each two, and how they finally curl over into breakers, creating foam and spray, spending themselves in a rushing sheet of water up onto the beach before sliding

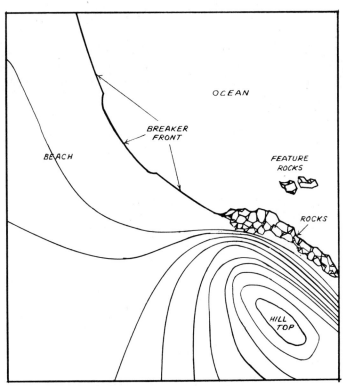

FIGURE 12-15 *Ocean shoreline.*

back to meet the next onslaught. Note the activity around the rocks and tide pools, the latter being transparent to allow a bit of marine landscaping. Along with watching nature at work or studying marine photographs in the absence of the live scene, it is helpful to know some of the basic facts about marine hydraulics. Friction between wind and water is the principal cause of ocean waves (swells); their wave length, amplitude, and frequency depending upon the intensity and duration of the wind. Until broken into a white cap or breaker at the shore, the water molecules do not move in a linear (horizontal) direction. They move up and down within the amplitude of the wave. This explains why a cork will tend to stay in one location as the swells raise and lower it in passing. When the waves reach a point offshore where the depth is less than the wave length, the system slows down and the wave length and amplitude decrease. When the depth becomes less than the amplitude, the troughs slow down more than the crests, causing the latter to break in varying positions along the shore. This is indicative of the effect the overall conformation of the ocean bed can have on wave activity. Note how waves break some times far out to sea when they hit a reef, and how little breaker activity there is along a shore where the drop to depth is steep. Here is a good example of how knowledge of the subject

being modelled can increase interest in the project and contribute toward attaining maximum authenticity.

Beach Model: Returning to our beach scene to be done in 1/8″ scale, it is evident that the best way to construct the ocean is with liquid resin poured into a mold containing surface disturbance including, ripples, waves, and breakers. The model has been graded in urethane foam (Ch. 10) as schematically illustrated in Fig. 12-15. The lowest contour cut in the ocean area is the water level (mean high tide). Remember in the case of the lake, a contour cut was made 1/8″ below the water level to create a socket for 1/8″ acrylic. Here it is decided that 1/2″ of resin will provide stability and depth, as well as ease of handling; so the model will be placed under the cutter and a cavity 1/2″ deep cut into the water level, following the outline traced along the edge of the hardened resin ocean made as indicated below, showing for simplicity a single, broken line of breakers.

Make a lightweight illustration board pattern to just exclude the tide pool area and just include the leading edges of the breakers. Place this pattern on the model to make sure your limits are reasonable considering your inland grading. Square off the pattern at the model edges to allow a trim liner for the edge of the hardened resin. This liner can

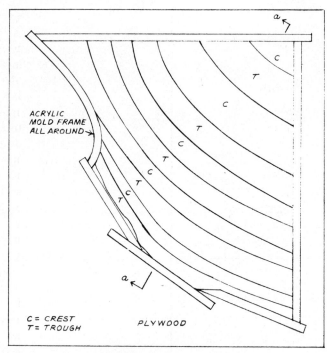

FIGURE 12-16 *Ocean mold.*

and be sure the plaster has settled solidly on the plywood. The 1/2″ thickness of plaster has no relation to the 1/2″ of resin about to be poured for the ocean. It is just coincidentally a practical thickness for both mold and product. When the plaster has firmed up, remove all but the wave front plastic strips, and, with a steel ball-shaped burr, cut grooves parallel to the wave front across the plaster about 1/8″ deep representing a positive amplitude at 1/8″ scale. The winds will produce varying results; so use your best judgement as to amplitude and wave length. You are not concerned with frequency since the setting is static. Make these grooves (which will be the swells in the resin) as smooth and even as possible. You can make a depth measuring jig from acrylic, continually checking your grinding with a hand power tool, or you can run the mold under the same burr held by the Pattinson Mill (Ch. 36) which will automatically control depth. Check the spindle speed on a trial run and don't try to take too much plaster at one pass. Remember the Pattinson Mill is built for cutting *soft* material. When you get to the grooves that will form the breaker tops, note that the acrylic strips left in this area will help to prevent chipping away the plaster at the location of the thin wave edge. After you are satisfied that all your grooves are finished properly, with a concave-edged trowel made from 1/8″ acrylic having a radius equal to that of the grooves, apply 1/8″ of plaster to the spaces between the grooves. These "humps" will form the negative 1′ amplitude of 2′ amplitude waves in the resin. When all is dry and sanded smooth, a section profile should appear as in Fig. 12-17.

be a continuation of the one used around the rest of the model or can be camouflaging strips of vinyl with ends flush with the urethane surface if no general edge liner is used.

Mold: Flip the pattern and trace it upside down on a flat piece of 3/8″ or thicker plywood which will serve as a plaster mold base (Fig. 12-16). The pattern is reversed since the underside of the resin when poured will be the surface of the ocean. Cut some strips of 1/4″ acrylic 1″ wide and score a centerline lengthwise on each to act as a plaster pouring guide. With contact glue, cement the strips vertically around the pattern trace, placing them just outside the lines at the model edges to allow for possible resin shrinkage by providing a slightly oversize mold. Make tight butt joints, overlapping the strips confining the broken wave front, using contact glue so that you will be able easily to disassemble the mold frame. Pour the plaster up to the centerlines on the perimeter strips, shaking the whole assembly slightly to remove any bubbles

Casting: Replace any 1″ wide acrylic strips you removed to allow the grooving for swells and breakers. With contact glue attach them tightly to the plaster mold so that there will be no resin leaks. Note that except where the plaster humps occur, you will have 1/2″ free acrylic above the previously scored centerlines. Assuming you have provided for three planes of breaker front in the single line of breakers, make, out of acrylic, three plugs which you will suspend in the resin to create

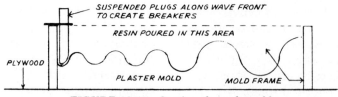

FIGURE 12-17 *Section through mold.*

a hollow arch behind the breaker fronts as indicated in Fig. 12-17. The rounded edges of the plugs should have radii a little less than that of the breaker grooves in the plaster mold so that the breaker arches will have enough thickness to prevent chipping. Make these plugs high enough so that you can insert wires into the ends to reach across the mold sides to suspend the plugs say 1/32″ above the bottoms of the breaker grooves to allow resin flow underneath. Note that the leading lips of the breakers will be against the acrylic sides of the mold along the breaker line.

Seal the plaster thoroughly and apply mold release to all interior mold surfaces (Ch. 24) including the breaker plugs. A rough calculation of volume will guide you to the adequate amount of resin and catalyst. As you stir in the catalyst, add tinting pigment blue or blue and green, by the *drop*. These pigments are strong, and you should retain clarity, realizing that the ocean bed will be shade-painted to give opaque depth. Start the pour by partially filling the breaker cavities and suspending the breaker plugs therein. Continue to pour, jarring the mold slightly to remove any bubbles, until the resin has just reached the tops of the acrylic strip sides. Holding the mold level, lift slightly, and drop it on the table a few times to be sure you have removed bubbles and that resin has filled the gaps underneath the breaker plugs, and between the plugs and the mold sides. Let the pour cure overnight or until the resin is hard. Then carefully work out the breaker plugs and break away the sides of the mold so that you can remove the resin ocean from the plaster.

Place the ocean on the model and trace the bottom edge. Place the model under the contour-cutting bit and cut out the 1/2″ deep cavity to hold the ocean. Using the lightweight illustration board pattern cut previously, peel off the top (white) lamination of paper and glue it to the bottom of the cavity to hide any possible visible granular ocean bottom of urethane. This surface will be easier to shade-paint than the urethane surface. Unless you are creating a Bermuda-type white sand bottom, make your shading transition from deep water dark blue to the lighter blues and greens of shallower water intense enough so that you will not "see" the bottom. Before tack-gluing the ocean in place, inspect the breaker edge to see if you have to add any resin particularly at the transitions between breaker front planes to cancel abrupt, unnatural changes. Carefully sand down the slope of the beach as it approaches the ocean side of the breaker arches (edge of ocean cavity) so that there is clearance between the beach and the falling edges of the breakers. Assuming that the natural graininess of the urethane will serve as sand, paint the beach with indigenous colors and glue down the ocean, being careful not to leave visible spots of glue. Using a separate mix of untinted resin, paint the beach with it, starting at the back walls of the breaker arches and continuing up to the water's edge of the just previous collapsed breaker. For variation fill with resin the space between breaker tip and beach part of the way to indicate progressive collapse. In these areas, build up a bit of resin to indicate the bounce of the breaker edge from the beach. Tint all water edges with white, adding minute whisps of cotton wool where appropriate to create natural activity. A mere suggestion is better than a wad!

Consider the rock area to be at the edge of deep water, the rocky face dropping abruptly into the sea. This will add variation in eliminating beach-type breakers. Starting at the transition from beach to rocks, cover the joint between ocean and rocks with pebbles of suitable color and size, noting any feature rocks shown in the drawings. Though scale finally controls, you have considerable leeway as to sizes of pebbles. Let your sense of proportion guide you. Using a soldering iron, you can "melt" rocks into the ocean surface and can make rock formations with plaster along cliff faces and between pebbles to form tide pool depressions. In these depressions pour clear resin after painting them to agree with surrounding colors. If your casting included vertical throws of water, back these up with suitable rock formations as though they caused the throw. Paint the tips white and add small amounts of cotton wool for flying spray. If the casting did not include this surface disturbance, pile up additional resin at rock barriers staying with it until the resin gels enough to hold it in place. Let resin run between the rocks and stipple a smooth-surfaced ocean with vinyl glue to break up a mirror surface. Embellishments could include such things as marine life placed in the tide pools before pouring the resin. Wet the rocks with resin or vinyl glue.

With the vagaries of the weather and infinite differences in coast line conformations, there can be no formulae to apply strictly to a given area to be modelled. No one is likely to call you on lack of split-hair authenticity as long as you keep in mind the basic physical laws mentioned previously. It is safe to advise to keep amplitudes and wave lengths in a proportion which results in a rolling rather than corrugated appearance of the system.

Alternate Method: In the smaller scales, you can carve and sand a separate piece of urethane foam into a wave and breaker system. After mounting, seal the foam with thin plaster to obtain a non-porous surface, shade-paint to ocean colors, and cover with several coats of resin and catalyst, staying with it to keep it from all running into the troughs. Paint it down over the carved out breaker arches and tint with white as was done in the case of the 1/2″ thick pour. The reason the urethane is sealed is to avoid seeing a porous bottom through the thin resin. Even though we can actually see the bottom, optical illusion should hide it.

You can make a series of breakers as over a reef area with consecutively mounted strips of breaker cast in resin. Joints are hidden by the arch of the next seaward breaker. It is well to mention here that cracks in resin cannot be invisibly filled, but they can be quite well camouflaged with additional resin and surface disturbance as in a broken up series of breaker fronts with different lengths. Put on your genius hat!

CONTROL CHANNELS

These will vary from small, concrete hillside development ducts to prevent erosion and mud slides, through large county flood control channels to open metropolitan supply aqueducts. Sometimes rivers will have stretches of concrete lined banks to hold their course. Most of these structures will be at grade and made out of concrete with vertical or sloping sides depending upon their location and purpose and easily made from illustration board or vinyl, depending upon scale and size of visual edges. If you are presented with the job of constructing an ancient Roman-type of aqueduct, see Ch. 14 where discussion of bridges will give you some hints. An unlined drainage ditch at the smaller scales from say 1/16″ down can be pressed into a urethane surfaced model using a piece of wood shaped to the cavity configuration. Outline with pattern and knife point and then use consecutive punches overlapping to give a smooth bottom. I make small water channels by laying out the course with common pin markers, connecting the pin locations with shallow slices of a serrated knife and then inserting strips of rigid sheet vinyl about 1/4″ wide (depending upon depth of channel). The bottom is then formed in the same manner as the drainage ditch just described and then lined with spackle or plaster smoothed with form-

ing tools. You can ensure parallel sides by inserting common pins through a site plan in scale, clipping off the pin heads and then pulling the plan straight up off the pins. Don't make the vinyl sides wider than necessary surely to provide scale depth of channel. Even with the guiding knife grooves, excess width will tend to make the vinyl wander from vertical as you pound the strips in with a miniature hammer.

Where water is to be shown, follow the tips mentioned earlier under the various containers. If a flood control channel is to have wall to wall water, make the bottom out of acrylic. If there is to be a trickle down the middle, let a bead of vinyl glue do the job or pour resin being sure to hold the model level until it sets! Water running out of a free end of a drainage pipe will tend to twist or fold as it falls; so adjust your water material accordingly for realism. A terraced supply aquaduct whether for aeration purposes or simply to get water from A to B, will probably have some white water conditions. Logging and mining sluices with rounded bottoms are probably most easily poured to fill the cavity and allowed to set in a level position before being placed in location. An amusement park flume ride at the small scales of around 1/32″ can be made by painting a strip of 0.010″ to 0.020″ vinyl a turquoise blue and vertically edging it with the same material welded on with acrylic solvent to form the trough. See Ch. 23.

ICE

An ice-covered lake or pond (with skating surface) can be made with translucent white acrylic of 1/8″ thickness. The translucency will give a more authentic appearance than the opaque stark white, but treat the bottom of the lake if necessary to avoid conflicting shadow. Form icicles with "drips" of vinyl glue touched where esthetically necessary with white paint.

SNOW

There are numerous materials you can use for snow. Two successful ones are white flock and a heat treated and expanded mineral called Perlite. Check with your local building materials sources for plaster extenders and lighteners probably under different trade names. You can get white flock at hobby and craft shops. Be sure that it is not the shiny variety. The clear spray glues are best for application (Ch. 34) as well as clear Krylon which is shiny and must be matte sprayed where obvious through the snow. As with all granular applications, the key to success lies in thin, even coats of adhesive to avoid soaking the material which is sifted through a strainer. Too much adhesive will create unnatural lumps, and brush applied glues tend to result in ridges. Successive light sprays are best, assuming that you can safely mask the surrounding areas (Ch. 32).

13

Surface Traffic Ways

STREETS AND ROADS

Probably 95 percent of the streets and roads you will have to model will be of the asphaltic concrete (AC) type, and most of these will be perimeter streets along the sides of the sites including the feature subjects of the projects. It is common practice to show half the width of an average city street at the edge of a model. This helps to provide a frame for the site, allow vehicular activity, and with the street name shown, orients the viewer.

Materials: For the larger common scales from 1/16″ to 1/4″, I have found that cold pressed heavyweight illustration board (Ch. 35) can be used successfully for both AC and concrete. Both materials have a fine texture normally used to support vehicular traffic, and illustration board seems to have a similar texture visually acceptable at any one of several scales. Hot pressed illustration board is too slick for this purpose. Heavyweight board is generally prescribed because its 3/32″ thickness provides more stability then the lightweight material which is approximately 1/16″ thick. At the scales smaller than 1/16″, you can use

sheet vinyl because the texture has for all practical purposes disappeared. You very likely can find other satisfactory materials for street and road surfacing, but you won't go wrong using the two mentioned here. I have seen models which included streets made from Masonite which is not only harder to work but lacks the texture needed in the larger scales giving it a hard and cold appearance. It is also harder to paint.

Support: Particularly where the vertical control method of grading is used, care has to be exercised to prevent wavy street construction. Around the edge of a model, a street would be supported by the perimeter risers on one side. The other side should be supported by a riser or risers mounted parallel to the perimeter, the number depending upon the span of street to be supported. When in doubt, add another riser! I have followed the standard of a maximum of about 3″ to 4″ between risers, a bit on the conservative side with heavyweight illustration board, but having lived through a wavy surface too late to fix it, I'd rather be safe than sorry. Longitudinally placed risers can be shaped easily to follow the street grading without gaps. The surest support is solid urethane foam which will be present when the grading has been cut with a mill (Ch. 10). Here, lightweight illustration board can be used where texture is required because support is continuous. If you wish to mount the road surface flush with the surface of the foam, make a trace cut along the edges of the street before pressing it down to form a cavity. This will prevent tearing the foam and make forming impression easier. Sheet vinyl road surfacing, because of its thinness, can usually be left glued to the surface. Landscaping will camouflage the minute change in plane. The same principles of support apply in the cases of ground level parking areas and their transitions to street level. Though a parking area may have an AC surface, the ramped areas across the sidewalk and planting strip will usually be of concrete. Knife score the ramp at the outside edge of the sidewalk and bend the tab cut to rounded curb configuration down to the street. A neat joint can be made with the street by undersanding the tab to accommodate the slope and insert the end into a socket cut into the street material. If illustration board is used, sand the street end of the ramp just to the underside of the top paper lamination. This will assure an unragged edge at the joint. Any minor foreshortening because of slope can be camouflaged with spackle (Ch. 35). If the slope is a steep one, you may have to install a separate piece for the ramp in order to have it long enough to cover the length of gradient. Support for overhead traffic ways is discussed in the next chapter. Brick and cobblestone streets can be made with paint and scoring. Considering the scale, check out the availability of textured papers the embossing on which, aided by scoring and paint, may just fit the bill. Rural gravel roads can be reproduced with sandpaper or sprinkled on fine sand, depending upon scale. Both can be brought to authentic appearance with oversprays of the right colors of paint. Dirt roads can be made by applying thin coats of plaster, running a "vehicle" over the wet surface and dry-brushing the dried result with earth colors. Wet the wheels of your vehicle so that the plaster won't adhere to them as they form the ruts.

Curbs: Curbs can be painted on the edge of a planted area (Ch. 26) or made as separate elements. Curbs of concrete against concrete can be designated by scoring, but this is hardly worth the effort at scales of 1/16" or below. This is true in the case of model A (Fig. 9-6) where there is no planted area at the street curb. Along the entrance and exit driveways, however, note that curbs should be indicated at the edges of the planted areas. Where curbs are indicated by paint, be sure that the material being curbed has sharp, smooth edges. At scales above 1/16" it is a good idea to define the curb with a knife score the width of curb distance in from the edge. This will help stop the two colors of paint at a sharp meeting line. Sometimes a peeled off top layer of illustration board over a planted area will be a satisfactory way to establish this definition.

Where scale and situation justify the effort, street curbs can be formed by adding strips of material to the edge of the material installed to create a curb height elevation above the street. Generally it is better to confine your application to solid strips of wood or vinyl since long stretches of lamination present the problem of camouflage of layer joints. At 1/8" scale, apply 1/16" × 1/16" stripwood (bass or white pine) to the edge of the +6" sidewalk level, being sure that you have cut back the liner material creating that level to accommodate the added width of curb material. For methods of making corner bends in the wood see Ch. 24. In the absence of a concrete gutter as discussed later in this chapter, paint the two exposed sides of the curb material before installing it with contact glue. If there is to be a concrete gutter, you can easily paint both elements after installation. At 1/16" scale, you can get by with 1/32" high 0.030" vinyl for a 6" curb. The 0.00125" will never be missed!

Gutters: Gutters can be designated by scoring the street the scale distance from the curb and extending the concrete paint to this score. If storm drains must be shown, you can cut a cavity back into the edge of the curb surface and paint the cavity black. Where the drain is in the gutter surface, peel off the top layer of illustration board, paint the cavity black, and insert a piece of acid-etched material (Ch. 17) authentically symbolic of the actual configuration. Particularly at the small scales (1/16" and smaller) trying to show these drains is usually impractical and incidental to the whole model picture.

Drainage Crown: Generally speaking unless you are showing a complete street at a large scale, showing grading to reflect the rise toward the center is not necessary. Consider partial perimeter streets flat for model purposes since the slight rise to the edge of a half street (at most) would be insignificant.

Suburban Streets and Roads: One of the most common improvements requested for a contour model is the road system usually including a portion of the public road serving the area and the branches there from serving the property to be improved. Probably in nine cases out of ten, the material for this purpose is sheet vinyl of 0.015″ or 0.020″ thickness for stability and flexibility. Most models of real estate development are at small scale because of the amount of terrain to be covered. Most of them at least initially are open-contoured for study purposes, and at this stage curbs and gutters are usually not required. Using carbon paper (Ch. 35) trace the road system on sheet vinyl through an in-scale site plan, getting as much of the system on one sheet of plastic as possible to avoid joints. Where joints are necessary, try to confine them to natural divisions such as the points of transition between the main public road and service to the property being modelled. The most expeditious method for obtaining an accurate road system is as follows. Trace one side of each road segment *carefully* to establish an accurate configuration. The other side can be traced in short sections for later orientation only. With a mat knife or scissors cut along the guiding trace and using a drafting compass set to road width, draw the steel point along the cut edge allowing the pencil point to draw the other edge which is cut in the same manner. This will assure even road widths. Small radii intersections can be eyeballed to connect segments. Be sure the compass points are held in a line at right angles to the edge guiding the steel point. Otherwise you will wind up with too narrow road widths. When you are tracing, note that the accurate trace will vary from one side of the road to the other. When you arrive at closed rectangles of roadway, for example, establish the most convenient guiding road edge as you proceed. This method is important in the case of narrow roads where inconsistent widths are obvious. Orient the system on the model, which has been painted the chosen overall countryside green, and tack-glue it with contact glue at a sufficient number of contour steps to hold a smooth configuration. (See Ch. 34 for sensitivity of vinyl to contact glue.) Don't try to force the vinyl into the joints between contour treads and risers. Your judgment and trial and error will tell you how much excess length to leave when cutting the roads out to accommodate the three-dimensional road bed. Glue the whole system down and then trim excess off with the scissors at the correct termini. If you haven't already sprayed the system

with your standard macadam gray, you will have to use a brush after installation. It is easier to get a smooth paint job with the spray since the vinyl is not absorbent. The tack-gluing will hold adequately for study purposes and will allow easy removal should the model be returned for display treatment. After the model has been spray painted, I usually put down the road system before anything else required since it helps in layout as mentioned in Ch. 8. Obvious house locations on graded pads, for example, are verified by stub driveways cut out as part of the system.

Parking Areas: These are included under "Streets and Roads" since they will almost always be made from the same materials as extensions thereof. Curbs and islands are usually raised structures defining parking areas and amount only to attaching material of the correct height and width to the parking area surface. Paint concrete items of this nature before attaching them to an AC surface, being sure that the glue is confined under pressure to the underside of the curb or island. The layout of parking stalls is covered in Ch. 26.

Shoulders: This typical road feature is usually a little wider than a car width and the standard means for providing emergency parking at roadside. They may have the same surface treatment as the roadway or be made of gravel or just graded soil. A concrete freeway may have AC shoulders or turnouts where the motorist with a disabled vehicle can escape from traffic. Where hard-surfaced, the space can be made as a continuation of the roadway material, and painted for any contrast of surface. Where gravel or soil appear, cut the roadway to designate the change and fill the shoulder space with sand of a grade to satisfy the scale, or fill the area with spackle and paint the appropriate earth colors.

WALKS

Sidewalks: These are seldom put down as separate items since they can be defined by scoring, curbs, or change in texture in the same material that establishes the elevation of adjoining facilities such as stores along a city street, the front lawns of private residences, etc.

Entry walks, entry slabs, loading docks, malls, courts, patios, decks, waterside wharfs, etc. are also usually extensions at the grade of surrounding or adjacent material. Otherwise, if not connected by ramps, the only real structural concern might be steps which are covered in Ch. 15. The real life materials can generally be reproduced by the surface treatment of illustration board or vinyl with paint (Ch. 32) and surface disturbance with lining or scoring (Ch. 26) or texturing (Ch. 33). A *peristyle* around a building, a *colonnade*, or an *entrance portico* as at the ambulance entrance of model B (Ch. 9) would probably be extensions of the ground floor of the building.

Flagstone Patio: Approaching the ultimate in authenticity is a flagstone patio at 1/2″ scale with an attached garden walk. The stone I have used is a rosy-hued shale whose strata can be separated to produce smooth surfaced flagstone. It has become rare in Southern California, but check with your local building material suppliers for a similar product. Make a shallow cavity the size of the walk and patio configuration and deep enough to accept the thickest stone chip. Line the cavity with redwood strips. In your planning you should include provision for this by using solid urethane foam as support so the cavity will be a cinch. With a hammer make enough chips to supply your project. The sizes should range from about 6″ to 2′ (1/4″ to 1″ across). From your assorted supply of chips lay compatible shapes out to fill the cavity so that there is a fairly consistent mortar space between them. When you have completed your arrangement, remove the flagstones in order as you place them in the same arrangement on a piece of plywood or illustration board. Mix enough plaster with water base black paint to get a mortar color. Fill a few square inches of the cavity and pour the plaster mix until it is just below the tops of the confining redwood. Immediately start laying the flagstones in order, pressing them in level with the headers. Use some sort of straightedge wide enough to span the walk or patio area so that you can maintain an even level surface. Wipe off any excess plaster from the stone as you proceed. Wet the "trowel" to keep the plaster from adhering to it. The reason for small plaster mixes is to keep the unused portion from drying hard during the laying process.

If you are determined to lay flagstones in the absence of suitable rock compressed by nature, texture-paint (Ch. 33) a panel of lightweight illustration board to the desired stone effect and cut up the stones as in a jig-saw puzzle. These can be glued down, and the spaces can be filled with the same mortar used with the real stone.

Decking: Open decking such as that found in private residences and made of separated 2″ × 4″ or 2″ × 6″ wood stringers poses a time of construction problem because of scale. At 1/8″ scale, 1″ is about 0.01″; so you can see how impractical literal authenticity becomes at smaller scales. If time and money permitted, you could, at 1/8″ scale, assemble such a deck with strips of 0.020″ thick vinyl with spacers of the same material, but at the smaller scales confine your efforts to scoring illustration board or Strathmore paper depending upon the depth of the structural members. The scores would represent the openings between stringers and could be accentuated with rubbed in black ink after the wood finish had been applied. Wiping off the excess ink while still wet can give the deck a weathered appearance.

Separate Walks: These include those between buildings and other facilities, garden walks, those through a city park, etc., and present no special structural problems aside from cutting the chosen material to size and shape and gluing down according to specifications. Narrow walks across open areas should be cut as suggested for narrow roads mentioned previously to control even width. A free-form walk across a level, small scale park area, for example, might be scored with a double scoring tool (Ch. 36) in an illustration board surface, possibly presenting a lengthy painting assignment unless you wanted to mask the whole area. A better solution could be a separate walk cut from thin Strathmore paper (Ch. 35) where the slight change in grade would not be objectionable.

RAILWAYS

Some of the model railroad scales are at least close enough to the standard architectural and industrial model scales to permit use of hobby shop track. This can usually be purchased in sections already mounted on ties, thus saving considerable time in installing a railroad freight spur, for example. Few models will have complete rail systems. S gauge is 3/16″ scale; O gauge is 1/4″ scale; HO gauge is near enough to 1/8″ scale to get by; as TT gauge is to 1/16″ scale, and as Z gauge is to 1/32″ scale; so check with your favorite hobby shop before setting out on a lengthy track laying exercise.

At 1/32″ scale, I have indicated urban trolley car track by double scoring a paved (illustration board) surface with a double-bladed knife (Ch. 36). The actual rails were buried in the pavement, so there was no point in attempting to lay it in three-dimensional form. A complete narrow gauge system of railroad at the same scale was made by laying out the configuration on a sheet of heavy-weight illustration board and scoring the track position with a double-bladed knife used for the trolley tracks, adjusted to the larger gauge. This scoring was gone over with a mat knife to deepen and ream the scores to accept strips of black 0.010″ vinyl used for the rails. Using the center of the span between rails as the center of the road-bed, the latter was cut out with a mat knife so that the edges were tapered down to ground. The road-bed was painted a granite gray and lightly over-sprayed with matte black Krylon to give the effect of gravel. Groups of ties were shown at random by ruled lines in brown ink. The time for showing all the ties was not justified under the circumstances; so it was assumed that the hidden ones were covered with gravel. Approximately 1/16″ wide vinyl strips were then inserted in the scored cracks with the aid of a small wooden mallet and a depth controlling gauge made by laminating two pieces of stripwood separated by a piece of 0.010″ vinyl recessed to the desired height of rail. Slightly chamfer the inside edges of the wooden pieces to allow easy positioning over the rail, and tap the other end of this tool

until the wood hits the roadbed. Where you have difficulty in sinking the rail into the roadbed, go over the score with a mat knife, carefully wiggling it from side to side to ream the slot. In the absence of prior knowledge or a model railroad library, go to a railroad freight yard and study a switching system, the reproduction of which can be done with the same mat knife grooves and insertion of vinyl rail. Also note the configuration of spur track bumpers to stop stored cars. At road intersections, fill the space between the rails with the road material brought up to the outside of the rails to bury them.

When laying 1/8″ (HO gauge) track, which will be preassembed with ties, lay it down by section over contact glue of a syrup consistency brushed over the entire width of roadbed and immediately sift on ballast sand purchased with the track. Tamp the ballast down with a piece of wooden dowel or other suitable tool and let dry before vacuuming off the excess. Don't try to lay too much track at once. The one surface application of glue may dry before you get to it. After this operation you can drive in hobby shop spikes through the ties for secure mounting. You will probably find prepared roadbed also at your hobby shop, if you do not wish to make your own.

Authentic storebought items are often cheaper than your time!

14

Raised Traffic Ways

Raised traffic ways include all structures, both vehicular and pedestrian, which are supported in some fashion above grade or span a depression in grade. These include *freeway overpasses* and *ramps, bridges, trestles, causeways, elevated railways, baconies, decks, piers,* and *catwalks.* Adding marine *breakwaters* and *moles* may still not make the list complete as far as specific terminology is concerned, but it is complete enough to include the principal structures with which a model builder can expect to be faced. Note the probable prevalence of simple post and beam construction. The only intricacies of construction will arise where multielement support systems must be shown as in the case of trestles and some bridges. As model builders we are not concerned with stresses or how far down we have to go to find bedrock, but we *are* concerned with authenticity of appearance (Ch. 3) and anchorage and durability (Ch. 19).

FREEWAY OVERPASSES

Many models in an urban setting will include a portion of freeway and even some suburban de-velopment settings will have a freeway running along one side some of which will be shown if for no other reason than the orientation of the viewer. Perimeter roads and streets will likely require overpass construction. Since these structures are usually incidental to the feature of the model, you may be faced with the problem of locating the drawings necessary to authenticity of your result. I have found local state engineering offices very helpful, but be sure to include a time allowance for such research in your contract. To augment available information, I have on occasion gone out armed with camera to record structural and ornamental configurations. Don't forget that line of sight and perspective can fool you, and unless you want to end it all before the model is finished, I advise staying out of the fast lane!

A simple overpass is exemplified in Fig. 14-1. Think of a rectangular box the bottom of which carries the surface street and the sides of which support the top which is the freeway span over the opening. Under the vertical control method of grading (Ch. 9) you will have used vertical risers to support the freeway on each side of the surface street beneath, keeping in mind the thickness of the freeway material as it affects finished eleva-

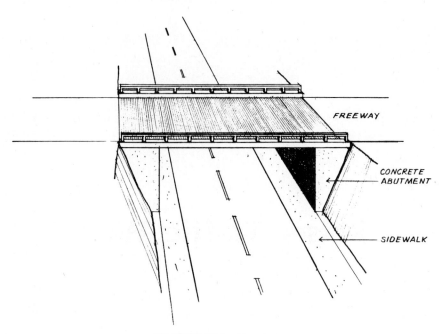

FIGURE 14-1 *Overpass.*

tion. Place the risers out far enough to support any paved shoulder included, but in from the edge to allow tuck-in filler by the dirt banks along the sides. See Fig. 14-2 for the system. Where possible, to avoid joints, prepare the surface street complete with sidewalks and gutters in one continuous stretch of material and install it. Then install the concrete abutment faces on each side of the street and brace them with sharp cornered returns of the same material at the freeway edges. The ends of these returns will be buried in the dirt banks along a plane in specified relationship to the freeway edges overhead. Lay the freeway down in a continuous trip across the opening. It is much neater to score a joint to define a change in surface treatment, for example, than it is to make the actual joint which introduces flush support problems. If you have to make a joint, make it over solid ground farther down the road. If the edges of the freeway illustration board or vinyl at the overpass are too thin, provide for the addition of thin strips of the right width to attain authenticity. Chances are good that you won't have to thicken the freeway over its entire width at the overpass since no one will be able to see underneath. After the overpass has been installed, add the prescribed curb and railing or parapet (Ch. 16) along the side edges. To make the banks under the vertical control method install triangular risers at supportive intervals to establish the final configuration and gradient. If the scale is small and you do not have more than, say a few inches to a

foot of each of the four banks to construct, you can fit in slabs of illustration board, chip board, vinyl, etc. Your own judgment should tell you when to use the wire and plaster method. Plaster will of course result more easily in a rough, dirt finish for planting than will the cardboard surface to which you may have to add plaster anyway. The most satisfactory banks can be made with scrap pieces of urethane foam glued to close the bank areas and then sanded to the finished bank configuration. Here is a good example of the versatility of urethane foam of which you should always carry a supply even though you do not have a contour cutter. Through its granularity, you have a ready-made dirt surface at any scale.

If you have graded the base with a Pattinson Mill, using urethane foam, the cut for the overpass, the banks, and the freeway support will already have been formed, obviating some construction details. The abutments can be glued to the face of the urethane at the cut, and the banks can be finished by sanding off the steps.

These tips should lead your imagination into handling the many detail variations you are apt to find in overpass construction. For example, the cut might be a wide, shallow slope of uncovered earth with support columns running on each side of and parallel to the surface street. The overpass may be one of a stack of overpassing ramps suported by an apparent maze of columns. An important consideration here is your method of anchoring the columns securely and vertically.

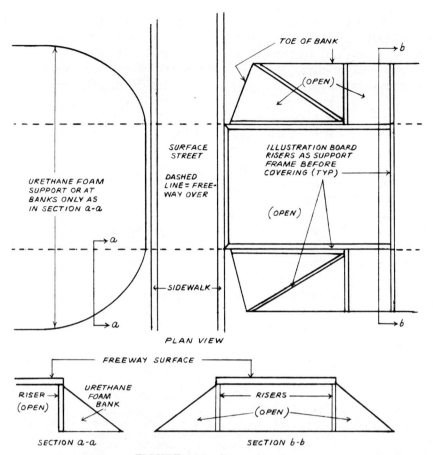

FIGURE 14-2 *Support system.*

Even with a thickness of urethane foam to give rigidity, it is better to mount a row of columns in holes drilled through the plywood base. Once you have disturbed a hole through the urethane to correct an error in location, the relative softness of the material makes rigidity harder to establish. Before installing the columns (Ch. 22) be sure you have shaped their tops to accommodate the direction of the ramp. With holes all the way through the plywood, you have a certain amount of leeway in height adjustment, a very important time saver in a lengthy multicolumn exercise. If the columns have splayed tops, you should have secure gluing surfaces to hold the driveway. If in doubt, consider drilling a hole of a size to provide a tight friction fit of a small box nail in each column top. Countersink the nails to the thickness of the top lamination of illustration board and fill the cavities with spackle (Ch. 35) or make the driveway in two layers, covering the nail heads with the second layer after installing the first. Another method is to push the driveway down over the tops of the columns down to the correct height, sanding off the column top flush, and then covering the as-

sembly with a second layer of driveway made out of vinyl or Strathmore paper cut to the first layer configuration. The trick in this case is to be sure that the holes accepting the column tops are exactly in the correct location. Consider the slope of a ramp or overpass when installing railings along the sides. The posts should be vertical, necessitating acid-etching (Ch. 17) to conform. If you run into trouble with column location in your layout, refer to the tips in Ch. 8. Ramps will be discussed more generally in Ch. 15.

BRIDGES

As with so many model subjects, the history of bridges and their development, since some Roman engineer built a timber arch over the Tiber around the second century BC, would be a fascinating subject to pursue, but we must stick to the main course of this book and leave such research to more leisurely times.

Almost like buildings, bridges come in all

shapes and sizes, some of them supporting buildings as did a London bridge in 1600 which had shops and dwellings from one end to the other. Compared with the number of buildings, the number of bridges in existence is minuscule; so you probably will not be receiving a great many contracts to build models with bridges as the main event. On the other hand, bridges at small scale can very well be included in the landscape; so some consideration should be given to their construction. From the model builder's point of view, bridges can be divided into two categories which, for want of better adjectives, can be labelled "closed" and "open" to describe their main support structures. The former include solid masonry bridges made with brick, stone, or reinforced concrete, covered bridges, and pontoon bridges where the supports float on water. Open bridges include the uncovered steel frame bridges constructed in geometric configurations to provide a balance between tension and compression. These are found in the steel arch, steel truss, cantilever, and suspension bridges. Figure 14-3 illustrates some examples. To provide height clearance for marine traffic, bridges will have mechanically or electrically activated adjustable sections such as those in draw bridges, lift bridges, and swivel bridges.

Single Arch Masonry: Refer to Fig. 14-3a for the subject of an assignment to construct a single arch stone bridge over a 30′ wide stream, which runs across a corner of the property for which you have a contract to build a model. For the purpose of construction tips, the scale is not specified so that variations in approach can be presented over a range of different scales. It is assumed that the grading has been done with a contour cutting machine, with the contours still open (Ch. 10) and that the stream has been installed (Ch. 12). First of all, break the structure into elements. There is an arched shape which could be considered the core of the bridge. There

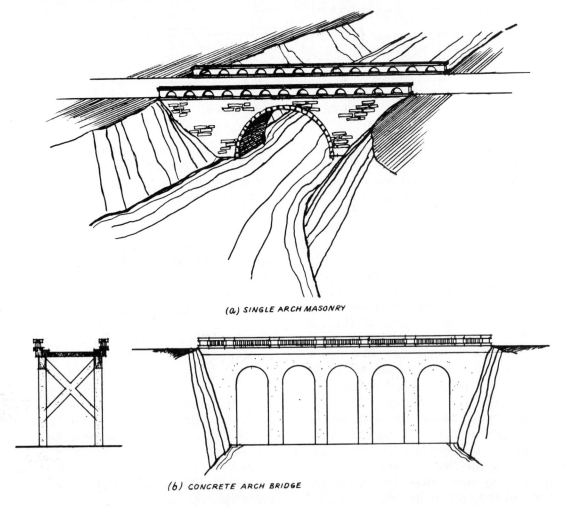

(a) SINGLE ARCH MASONRY

(b) CONCRETE ARCH BRIDGE

FIGURE 14-3 *Bridge types.*

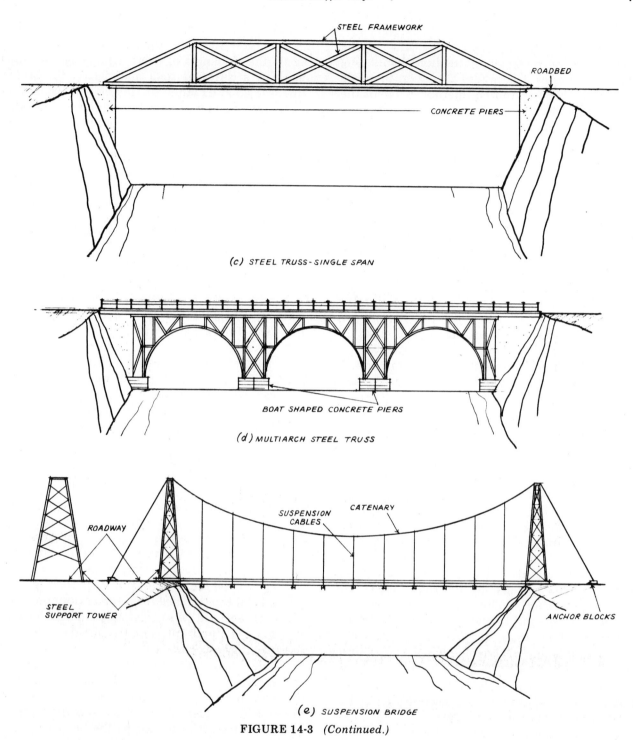

(c) STEEL TRUSS-SINGLE SPAN

(d) MULTIARCH STEEL TRUSS

(e) SUSPENSION BRIDGE

FIGURE 14-3 (Continued.)

are two side and one arch liner or surface on which to reproduce the appearance of stone. There is a road over the top and an open arched parapet on each side of the road. As far as the stone is concerned, we do not care whether the actual construction methods are ancient or modern. A stone veneer over a reinforced concrete core will give the same visual effect as a shaped pile of field-

stone. Consider what you have on hand to provide a readymade arch. At 1/16″ scale, a 2″ diameter mailing tube would be fine. At 1/100″ scale, search through your "Jay's Nest" (Ch. 35) for an arch of the right diameter or close enough to allow camouflaging the difference. How about a piece of brass tubing cut in half? At the smaller scales, a piece of pine with an arch filed in with a rat tail file would do the trick. At the larger scales, drill a hole through a piece of pine and cut the wood across the diameter of the hole, laminating several thicknesses if necessary to obtain the scale width of the bridge. Another method is to cut the two bridge sides out of 0.030″ sheet vinyl and connect them with an arched piece of the same material. *Lightly* heat treat a piece of vinyl of the scale width to aid in setting the right curve of the arch and then trim off the excess length. Attach the vinyl pieces with acrylic cement (Ch. 34). With whatever you make the bridge sides, leave the ends square so that you can bury the excess in the urethane banks, rather than trying to cut the ends to the bank profile. This will give sure closure and mounting. Still another method, favoring the reproduction of the stone faces, is to make a one time mold and cast the core (Ch. 24).

Realizing that the rock faces will measure probably anywhere from 6″ in diameter to horizontally laid slab faces 2′ long, the method of treatment will depend upon the scale and the surface of the bridge core. At the very small scales, say 1/32″ and smaller, you probably can get away with treating the core surface whether it be wood or plastic, but a wooden core at 1/16″ scale or larger should be covered to hide the grain with a veneer of Strathmore paper on which you have indicated the rock texture to hide the grain. In any case, paint the veneer or core with the desired rock colors (Ch. 32). Place the veneer stock on a sheet of illustration board to obtain some resiliency, and with a round-pointed scribe or stylus press in the rock face shapes, thus forming the mortared joints and making the rock faces stand out in slight relief. Follow the indentations just made with a pen and thinned out gray latex paint to indicate the mortar. At the very small scales pencil lining alone will suffice. When you cut the veneer to shape, try to line the arch so that the grout lines meet reasonably at the corners or joints of arch and side planes. This becomes more important as the scale becomes larger.

Now that the main bridge structure has been completed, install it on the model, excavating the urethane banks to obtain a snug fit. Any discrepancies between the arch surface and the stream can be camouflaged with bits of ground cover such as "water grass" and "moss". When installing the bridge leave it slightly higher than the top edges of the banks so that you can seat it flush with a wooden mallet after placing the road over the top. Glue the roadway down with contact glue, checking the desired slight overhang at the

rock faces. In your planning you will have taken into consideration the thickness of road material versus the thickness of overhanging edge, possibly requiring a different road material on the bridge. This is a good example of violation of Pattinson's Law: my not mentioning this earlier shows what can happen without whole concept planning.

The open-arched parapet can be made by cutting circles accurately along a centerline in acrylic of the right thickness and then cutting the material through the hole centers as you did in one of the methods for making the bridge arch. Establish the roadway over the bridge by scoring the edge of the AC if the entire surface is not concrete, and paint the edges a concrete color from the inside of the parapet line out.

Multiarch Masonry: Figure 14-3*b* shows a multi-arch reinforced concrete bridge which can be modelled following procedures similar to those just discussed except that columns are added. Assume the columns are in a double row with X bracing between each pair at right angles to the roadway. If 100′ columns at 1/16″ scale have a peculiar shape in cross section and/or taper then the quantity of eight would justify casting (Ch. 24).

Note here that in anticipation of installation of this bridge you should plot the column locations during your original layout and drill holes through the plywood to take a slip fit of 0.030″ piano wire or small box nails which will be inserted in the column bases during the casting process. This will help to insure accurate location later and establish the correct elevations of column tops. If you use the vertical control method of grading (Ch. 9) and the distance from top of column to the base plywood will be so great as to make the length of plaster column precariously fragile, build up their mounting points with blocks of wood with the holes drilled therein. This will cut down on the length of column needed. If your grading is to be cut in urethane, press the first layer down over the blocks to identify location and then turn it over to cut cavities to accept the blocks. Be sure in either case that the tops of the blocks are below the lowest finished grade of the model in the column area. In the case of vertical control grading, you can punch clearance holes in the wire and plaster surface over the mounting points. When you reach the column locations on the map during urethane contour cutting, punch in holes with a piece of dowel to mark clearance holes to be drilled later. Filling the openings around the installed columns at the ground surface should not pose any serious problems. With either method of grading you can close the openings with bits of urethane foam.

When installing the columns, press them in carefully *straight* down to prevent breakage. Apply excess contact glue on the ends to transfer some of the glue to the mounting points and then remove the columns to let both surfaces dry. When dry, press the columns back in place with a careful tap on each column top to insure a firm glued joint. Immediately fill the clearance gaps at the ground surface to help hold the columns vertical. Make the X braces out of illustration board, laminating to obtain scale thickness. Cutting an X without joints will make the bracing easier to install, and illustration board is not only easy to cut, but when undisturbed will provide secure support. Attach these braces with contact glue, gently squeezing each column pair together to establish tight joints.

The importance of installing the columns first lies in the relative ease with which the bridge can be located accurately. Though you will often find it more expeditious to construct an entire building away from its location and then install it on its pad or foundation, where the foundation of a structure consists of many separated elements as the eight columns of this bridge, better control is maintained by building the foundation on the model and then adding the superstructure. Added to the problems of installing a finished bridge with at least slightly flexible legs is the difficulty of accurate location in raised grading which does not allow even surface mounting.

The next operation is to construct the roadway supporting arcade along each side. Each row should be made out of one piece to result in monolithic continuity, eliminating the problem of joints between arches. These can be made by cutting *straight* rows of holes in wood or acrylic and then cutting the material lengthwise through their centers. The material should be of a scale thickness that covers the column tops according to specifications. If the material is too thick, sand the arches down to scale. If it is too thin, you will have to laminate. If the arches are made from wood, you may want to sand them down slightly to accept a lamination, on the visible side, of vinyl to hide the grain. Mount the arcades with contact glue, first checking trueness of location on each column and the height considering where the roadway is to meet the banks of the gorge being spanned. If the joints between the arch bearings and the column tops have decorative relief, add this using vinyl, thread, etc. to obtain the specified

configuration. Often this can be accomplished most easily by adding caps to the columns before installing the arches, keeping in mind the resulting overall height which might require sanding down the column tops if they were not made short enough in the first place. If no decoration exists, fill any joint openings with spackle and sand down to a visibly flush condition.

Assuming that the roadway element has a stepped edge as in the section of Fig. 14-3b, you can make the roadway by laminating material of different widths. If combinations of available illustration board, vinyl, or Strathmore paper do not result in the correct thickness according to the scale of the model, in the case of a straight bridge you can run a strip of acrylic the width of the topmost layer through your table saw at adjusted settings to obtain the stepped edge configuration. Be sure to run each side of the acrylic through the table saw at each setting to obtain a consistent result. If the thickness of the acrylic is slightly oversize, cut the steps starting with the top, leaving the bottom riser to be sanded or milled off to obtain overall correct thickness. After checking it for fit on top of the archways, you can finish the roadway element off the model where it will be easier to install the railing. If you want a warmer, more paint-absorbing surface, cover the acrylic or vinyl with a thin gauge of Strathmore paper which should not be enough to disturb dimension to any considerable degree. This is a matter of judgment. At 1/32" scale a visible 20' of roadway would be only 5/8" wide allowing you to ignore lack of texture on the harder materials, but at 1/16" scale and larger, a warmer material may read better. Further, you must consider the specifications for the road surface beyond each end of the bridge. It may match that on the bridge, even if just in appearance.

Before continuing I feel it important to point out what a good example this bridge discussion is in defining the the purpose of this book as stated in Ch. 1. I could attempt to recall and record every tip resulting from experience and still not obviate the necessity for your using the tips presented as a guide to your finding the "better" method to fit your particular situation with your particular model. Model components are often so immediately interdependent and so varied that it would be impossible to cover every combination at every scale. Let your imagination flow!

The railing for this concrete arch bridge (Fig. 14-3b is more of a parapet than a railing because of its massiveness (in the interests of safety). As the section shows, it is made up of a raised, flat bridge edge and a double row of posts between reinforced concrete stanchions and capped with a rectangular steel box railing. The sticky element here is the double row of posts which, depending upon scale, will have to be acid etched (Ch. 17) or assembled. At 1/8″ scale where an inch is about 0.010″, a 2″ post would mean acid etching 0.020″ thick material resulting in square posts. Have your supplier etch posts terminated top and bottom by bands of the same material. This extra material can be buried in the base and top material of the parapet in two parallel rows. A completely assembled parapet would involve first punching in the base material post centers with a scribe mounted in the chuck of your mill and then drilling holes to accept piano wire or wooden dowel depending upon scale. Sand the posts to equal height by using the sizing jig described in Ch. 37. Note the possible conflict between specifications and available shape of posts. There is no such thing as round acid etching, and piano wire is round only. At the smaller scales visible authenticity is not in serious jeopardy because of conflicting shape as long as your client is made aware of the situation. At the larger scales, consider broaching the mounting holes to accept square posts. The panoramic view demands the consideration of all possible solutions to arrive at a balance between the most accurate and the most economical. There is nothing more accurate than acid etching, but does the cost justify the expenditure for the railing for one bridge, for example? An automatic "No" answer may be changed when you consider not only the time saved on the job at hand but the possible use of excess material being used "free" on a future assignment. See Ch. 17 for further discussion about the process.

Covered Bridges: These bridges found in rural New England should not pose any particular construction problems when you consider them house shells on bridges. Those constructed for a modern theme park can have configurations and decorative embellishments to try patience and imagination (Ch. 49, photo 9). I have made them with cupolas on the roof, cantilevered outside walkways, etc., but since there are no standard themes on which to anchor construction tips, rely on your bridge building expertise plus imagination when following the drawings presented.

Pontoon Bridges: These are usually temporary facilities to get construction crews or military commanders and their equipment across a stream. These bridges are principally a system of flat boats or inflated rafts anchored across a waterway over which is laid some sort of treadway.

Open or Steel Framework Bridges: Such bridges, unless they are model features, can become economic snakes in the barrel to the unwary submitter of a proposal. Specific time should be allowed for their construction unless your client agrees that they can be simplified. If construction can be simplified through acid etching, then their cost should be included in your price or accepted as an "extra". There is no magic formula.

Figure 14-3 shows some samples of steel bridge configurations, each one of which includes at least some intricate steel framing. The *steel truss* or box girder bridge of Fig. 14-3*c* could fairly easily be made from strips of vinyl formed into an open work box over the bottom of which runs the roadway whether for railroad (Ch. 13) or automotive purposes. Make the sides and top separately and then assemble with the sides attached to the sides of the roadway. Use acrylic cement for constructing the lattice work and you won't have to worry about oozing glue to clean up around each joint. The concrete supports at the bridge ends can be incorporated in the vertical control method of grading or inserted in the banks when the grading was done by contour cutting. Make them out of vinyl at the small scales (say 1/32″ and smaller) and out of illustration board at the larger scales. Note that the arch supports at Fig. 14-3*d* are boat-shaped concrete footings in the stream bed. These are probably best made from solid acrylic which can be shaped on your belt sander. They can be cut in the stream or glued to the water surface depending upon the realism demands of scale. One of the problems with a *suspension bridge* as at Figure 14-3*e* is the effecting of the catenary with the appearance of being under tension. This is true under the conditions of the most usual scales since most threadlike cables will not have enough weight suspended to make them taut. The solution is to preform wire to a fixed catenary curve with straight runs beyond the towers. The vertical cables holding up the roadway should be lengths of finer wire glued in place, an operation which can drive you at least into extra trips to the water fountain, the number of trips depending upon how many catenary sections it takes to span the area being bridged. To obtain wire smaller than 0.015″ piano wire and still get pieces that will remain straight, anchor one end of softer wire in your vise, wrap the other end around a piece of dowel and exert a steady pull until you can feel the wire stretching. From this exercise you can obtain straight pieces. Another source is a brush with bristles near enough in scale to get by.

If you want to put on your engineer's hat and try for some additional structural authenticity, try the following method for a suspension bridge. On a piece of illustration board make a drawing of an elevation of the bridge in scale. See Fig. 14-4. Cut a piece of lightweight illustration board with the width equal to the distance between the tops of the towers. Cut one end the shape of the catenary and glue the piece to the drawing so the edge follows the curve on the drawing. At the tower tops on the drawing insert pins just far enough away from the edges of the added illustration board so that fine nylon thread will pass through the opening. Wrap an overlength piece of the thread around the catenary shape on the drawing surface and up around the pins. Pull the thread taut and weight the ends to hold the tension. Along the line of the road edge on the drawing tack-glue a strip of 0.020″ vinyl as wide as the thickness of the roadway. At each point where a vertical cable meets the catenary, glue the end of a vinyl hair of 0.010″ vinyl cut on your paper cutter. Use one of the cyanoacrylate or "magic" glues (Ch. 34) with pinpoint application and let dry. Then carefully pull these vertical cables along their guide lines on the drawing across the width of the vinyl strip, one by one. The vinyl hairs will tend to curl; weight the ends so that when they are taut the catenary will not be pulled away from the illustration board form. Glue each cable across the vinyl strip with acrylic glue which will weld vinyl to vinyl. Almost dry-brush apply the

glue to get just enough for a quick weld. When all has set, release the plastic strip by running a knife blade under the edge and remove the assembly. Trim off the excess vertical cables at the bottom edge of the roadway side strip and glue the latter with contact glue (two surfaces) firmly to the roadway edge. Repeat the operation for the other side of the bridge. At the catenary cable anchoring points insert common pins so that the heads are just free enough to allow wrapping the cables around them. Gently guide the cable ends over the tower tops, one by one, and wrap them around the pins, immediately applying "magic" glue to hold them. When dry, the pins can be forced in further to create more tension. Be sure that the tension on each side is the same to keep the vertical cables vertical. Snip off the excess cable and cover the pin locations with the specified concrete anchor blocks. Though nothing has been mentioned about color of the cables, it is assumed that you would use black thread as the nearest steel finish unless the specifications show another color of weatherproofing coating.

Remember that if you are obtaining acid-etched material for steel open work, be exact in your submitted drawings because you will not be able to flex the resulting shapes in the plane of the material to correct an error. You can chop off acid-etched railing stock to length, but there is no way you can change the shape of a fixed arch!

Among the bridge types not illustrated are the steel arch where the arch rises above the roadway apparently suspended between its legs, and the can-

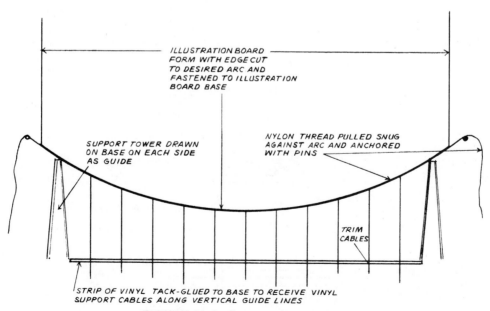

FIGURE 14-4 *Catenary construction.*

tilever which consists of elongated steel frame triangles with the bottom apexes resting on concrete foundations and the side apexes connected with horizontal trusses. Combinations will also be found where the towers of a suspension bridge will be of reinforced concrete to support the catenary. The movable section bridges over marine waterways will, 99 times out of 100, be shown in static condition by the model builder; so they will not appreciably add to the already discussed problems of open steel work. In closing the subject of bridges, though you are obviously to build to specifications presented by your client, some of the railroad hobby publications may give you some ideas about execution.

Trestles: These are usually constructed to carry rail traffic and can be extremely intricate in bracing—an organized pile of sticks. Figure 14-5 shows a fairly simple version I once made at 1/32″ scale. The wooden 8″ poles were made out of pieces of 0.020″ piano wire, and the bracing was made out of 0.010″ vinyl strips. The concrete foundations were made from blocks of wood painted concrete color. The rails, laid over open ties, were strips of 0.010″ vinyl as were the components of the side railings. The entire trestle, except for the founda-

tions, abutments, and the rails, was painted a dark brown to simulate wood. The grading was done with the Pattinson Mill; the foundations and abutments were inserted in the urethane foam and anchored with contact glue. As the bracing becomes more complicated, consider breaking down the assembly into planes which can be acid-etched and then assembled with considerable saving of time. At scales larger than 1/16″ you will run into the maximum thickness limits for acid-etching, requiring lamination of the acid-etched material to obtain the scale depth of structural elements. Crossbracing applied to the surface of braced members rather than being let in will require separate runs. You might find a standard crossbrace configuration on the trestle which would allow a sheet or sheets of etched material from which you could cut the braces as needed. At 1/8″ and 1/4″ scales, don't discount the possibility of trestle kits from your local railroad hobby shop. Even just a few parts from a kit might be adapted to your specifications to save time and money.

Causeways: These could be considered continuous, elongated low bridges across marshy ground too unstable or too wet for surface mounting of roadways. Generally, the drawings submitted will

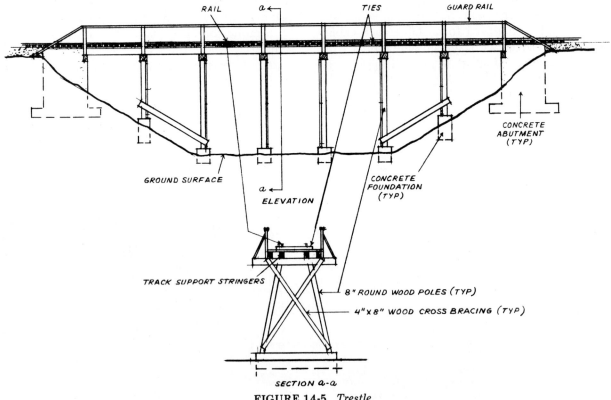

FIGURE 14-5 *Trestle.*

show a standard, bridge-type roadway with parapet/ rail side barriers raised on concrete blocks to clear the shallow waterway, swamp, etc. They should not pose any problems not covered previously in discussing raised traffic ways.

Elevated Railways: Often found in urban areas these can be considered continuous steel frame bridges with a series of short spans of post and beam construction strengthened by necessary reinforcement of open brace work. Their multilegged construction will require finishing of the surface over which they run before mounting supports. In an urban model, lay out the route and column locations before the model has any building or other three-dimensional installations in the vicinity which could make construction difficult. The support structures will have to be made on the model; install them early even though you add the railbed later.

Balconies: These are covered more extensively in Ch. 18, but are mentioned here since they are actually raised, pedestrian traffic ways. They are more appropriately covered in connection with floors of which they are, in effect, an extension.

Decks: Decks are in the same category as those discussed under Surface Traffic Ways in Ch. 13, except that they are here raised above the ground as enlarged balconies on stilts. Residential decks are usually made of wood with solid, waterproofed flooring warped for drainage or open, slatted flooring, both supported on columns to concrete foundations. The columns are often steel pipe which can be modelled in brass tubing or piano wire, depending upon the scale. Square, wooden columns can be cut from stripwood and glued to "concrete" blocks of wood or acrylic. Where the ground below slopes away from the building, the easy way to establish a flat, even plane across the column tops is to insert excess column length into a urethane foam base or into holes drilled in the plywood base as in the case of the bridge supports discussed previously in this section. Visible foundations can be built up around the column bases at ground level with pieces of illustration board, boxing in the columns. An egg-crate of supporting beams can be made from stripwood or vinyl and then installed as an assembly so the beam intersections rest on column top centers. The flooring is then laid over this and the railings attached around the perimeter on three sides.

A *pier* was discussed in connection with the recreational lake in Ch. 12. At scales larger than

1/32", supports can be made from wooden dowels and bracing from vinyl, stripwood, or acrylic. Where you do not have a broach large enough to allow inserting square supports into your lake or ocean, drill round holes with a diameter equal to a pole side dimension and file them square. Apply the walkway made out of scored basswood (Ch. 35) to simulate planking or paint illustration board and score in the plank joints. A pipe railing can be made from acid-etched material or piano wire. If the model has a seaside feature, consider pouring a resin ocean after you have the pier installed. Disturb any annoying meniscus contact around the poles with a scribe. This occurs where capillary action draws a liquid up the sides of a container.

Catwalks: Catwalks are steel treadways raised to working levels around and through manufacturing facilities in industrial plants. They can be on supporting columns or cantilevered out from the equipment to be serviced. Their construction, in general, will be similar to that of steel bridge work already discussed, with due consideration given to acid-etching to speed up accurate assembly at the smaller scales. For the treads themselves, you may find punched metal stock at a specialty hardware store that will serve your purpose. This comes in different designs with different size openings. Acid-etching is a natural solution.

Breakwaters and Moles: These items usually found at ocean side are generally disciplined, elongated piles of rocks from a visual and model building point of view. A breakwater per se will not necessarily have a road or railway on top as a mole does, but since harbor-forming breakwaters often have access roads to lighthouses at the end, they are included in this section. The main consideration here is the construction of the battered, rock sides. At all the scales large enough to make configuration obvious to the viewer, construct a truncated triangular base from wood or illustration board, continuing the sides to the base below the water line. Shade and dry-brush paint the surfaces in the colors of the rocks to be used. Choose the gravel or pebble size and color to be used, depending upon scale and specifications. Brush on a fairly thick coating of soupy contact glue so that it just laps the top edges of the slopes, and sprinkle on the chosen gravel to cover all visible glue, pressing it on to make good contact as you proceed. Don't try more than about one foot at an application or the glue will dry while you are adjusting the gravel to get maximum coverage. You can fill persistent gaps later with separate pebbles over additional glue. The rocks should come up to the edge of the traffic way on top as though the latter were superimposed. The best shore line here is accomplished through pouring of resin (Ch. 12) which will fill the gaps around the uneven rip-rap.

At very small scale, you can get by with laying the mole or breakwater on an acrylic ocean where the rip-rap would be nothing larger than very fine gravel or sand.

15

Elevating Traffic Ways

Elevating traffic ways are the means by which pedestrians, animals, vehicles, and goods move or are moved between planes at different elevations. They include *ramps*, *steps*, *stairways*, *ladders*, *elevators*, *escalators*, and *tramways*. A highway climbing through a mountain pass could technically be called an elevating traffic way or ramp, but to establish an arbitrary distinction, this would be considered under Surface Traffic Ways in Ch. 13 as part of a continuing road network. My distinction confines ramps to specific local transitions of relatively short extension.

RAMPS

These have been touched upon as components of illustrative model B, Fig. 9-7, which included pedestrian ramps at the entrances and patient recreation area as well as automobile ramps at the underground parking entrance, down from the guest parking area at the rear of the property, and at the ambulance entrance. The most common ramp is the transition from street to sidewalk level. Pedestrian ramps are usually on grade

and of low gradient to make negotiation as easy as possible. Vehicle ramps are on grade, over closed sides with the space underneath being used for other purposes, or elevated as at freeway transitions mentioned in Ch. 14. These can be steeper than pedestrian ramps as is the garage entrance on model B.

An important consideration in constructing any ramp is the method of handling the joints at each end. Because of the small size of joint indication in the life size subject, anything larger than a knife score will look gross at any of the popular scales. At the smaller scales, it is better to fill any separation with spackle (Ch. 35) and sand it flush. There is no way to escape some sort of joint since a change in direction is involved. Whenever possible maintain continuity of material at the top of the slope by breaking the material at a knife score since this not only gives you control but also obviates having to place a support exactly under the joint. If the ramp termini are both in the same sheet of material, you may, with a very shallow gradient, be able to knife score the underside of the material across the lower end of the ramp and break it *up* as you broke the top end *down*, without any visible foreshortening because of the greater length of the hypotenuse of a right triangle compared with its base. As the gradient becomes steeper, you will have to cut the material all the way through at the lower end and fill the gap. When you can, cut the ramp tongue longer than necessary and later trim to fit as you did with the overlaying building slab piece of lightweight illustration board to make the entrance wheelchair ramp for model B (Fig. 9-7). There the only reason the first covering layer ramp material was removed was because the ramp gap was to be covered independently. My standard lower end joint between driveway ramp and street consists of sand-tapering the underside of the end of the ramp down to the first or finish lamination in the illustration board and then countersinking this end into an exact slot formed in the street surface by removing a strip of surface lamination. This makes an easily camouflaged connection. Where you have to install a separate piece of ramp material to span the gap, slightly sand-taper the ends according to the gradient to help close the two joints.

Another consideration, particularly in the case of pedestrian ramps, is surface texture (Ch. 33). Most are provided with some sort of nonskid surface to provide grip regardless of weather conditions. This is accomplished through the use of separate disturbed-surface runners or mats or through treating the concrete, for example, while still wet. Salt will create small pits as though the surface had been shot-blasted. Pebbles can be scattered to create surface disturbance, or the wet concrete can be combed to create a minute corrugated effect. For salted concrete, try smacking a rasp held against the surface of a separate ramp piece removed from the model with a rubber or plastic mallet. Do this at random locations, being careful not to break your rasp. Another method is to be a woodpecker with a scribe point (the same action used in applying vinyl glue to disturb a water surface). Try dry-brush stippling with a slightly darker paint over a concrete painted ramp. If the sides of the ramp will hide out-of-scale thickness, make the ramp out of a shallow tray filled with plaster tinted to concrete color and sprinkle on gravel or pebbles while the plaster is still wet, pressing the application in with a flat trowel to get an even, pebbly surface. Note the specifications, considering the scale, and let your imagination have free rein. At 1/16″ scale, sand sprinkled over wet paint may do the trick. At the smaller scales, even paint stippling may look too gross. A plain surface tread is better than a splotchy one!

Before closing the surface or underfilled ramp discussion, it is well to remind you of the obvious need for support in some cases where the ramp spans an open cavity as in vertical control grading. Finger-pressure test the ramp before you glue it down. When in doubt, add a triangular riser or risers to prevent any sag. The garage entrance ramp in model B would be supported by the enclosing wall on each side.

Freeway Ramps: Freeway ramps have the distinction of being more extensive than the usual ramps found within the confines of an individual enterprise (Ch. 49 photos 32 and 33). They may be curved, banked, or dipped to follow the ground configuration to save the cost of elevated even gradient support. They may be elevated on reinforced concrete columns as touched upon in Ch. 14, and they may be vertically interlaced to handle complicated direction changes where two or more freeways intersect.

The schematic plan shown in Fig. 15-1 represents the simple on and off ramp situation where the ramps on grade follow the toes of the freeway banks from the local or city street up to the freeway surface. These ramps are likely to be AC surfaced with elongated approaches at the top to permit easy infiltration into freeway traffic. Note that all four ramps can be cut out of the same piece of material thus avoiding joints at the freeway. This is important particularly where the elongated approach results in long points in the ramp material fostering lamination separation to mess up an otherwise clean, tight joint. Vertically tapering the ends meeting the local street will help the joint situation. Here again contour cutting will have provided solid support to make vertical risers unnecessary.

A knotty construction problem can arise where a freeway on ramp dips down the side of a hill to curve and then run up in normal ramp fashion to join the freeway. The plan can be misleading because it distorts the length of the steep slope and the shape of the curve to cut in the material used. The engineering drawings are a must so that you can study elevations and gradient profiles as well as determine beginning and ending of curves at stated radii in order to enable you to determine the plane shape and size of the ramp. Hopefully you will have the engineering drawings in the scale of the model so that you can trace profiles for risers for vertical control grading. Solid, graded urethane foam should be of great assistance in helping you to form the installation. Since illustra-

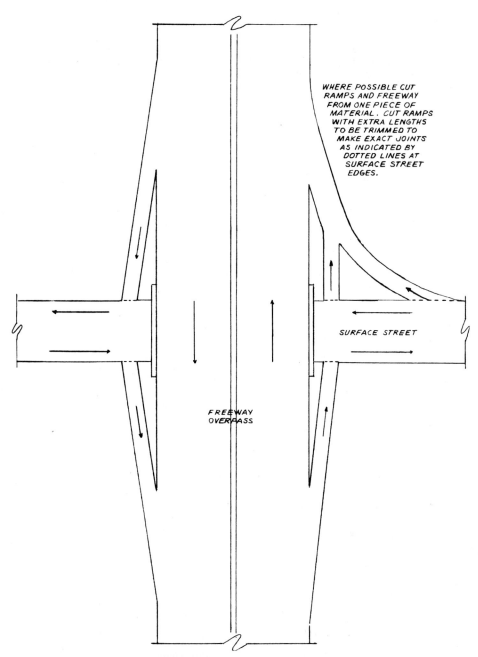

WHERE POSSIBLE CUT
RAMPS AND FREEWAY
FROM ONE PIECE OF
MATERIAL. CUT RAMPS
WITH EXTRA LENGTHS
TO BE TRIMMED TO
MAKE EXACT JOINTS
AS INDICATED BY
DOTTED LINES AT
SURFACE STREET
EDGES.

SURFACE STREET

FREEWAY
OVERPASS

FIGURE 15-1 *On and off ramps.*

tion board is not suitable for bending into tight curves, lay out the plane shape of the ramp on chip board (Ch. 35) and cut it out. Soak this in water until it is saturated and weight it down over the shaped risers or contoured urethane until it dries. A spray of clear Krylon (Ch. 32) will help seal the ramp configuration. To improve the surface, trace the ramp shape (before you soak it) on Strathmore paper. This will serve as a covering surface for painting an assumed AC color. Chip board does not have the finest of surfaces for finish treatment. Glue the ramp shape into

place being sure that you will have flush joints at the top and at the freeway, considering the addition of the Strathmore. This may require cardboard shims under the chip board at the connection with the thicker illustration board. Place the surface liner over the ramp being sure that it fits exactly. Then, starting at the top, progressively glue it to the chip board with complete surface covering applications of contact glue, smoothing the top down with the palm of your hand as you go to avoid wrinkles and bubbles.

To enlarge on the discussion of elevated ramps

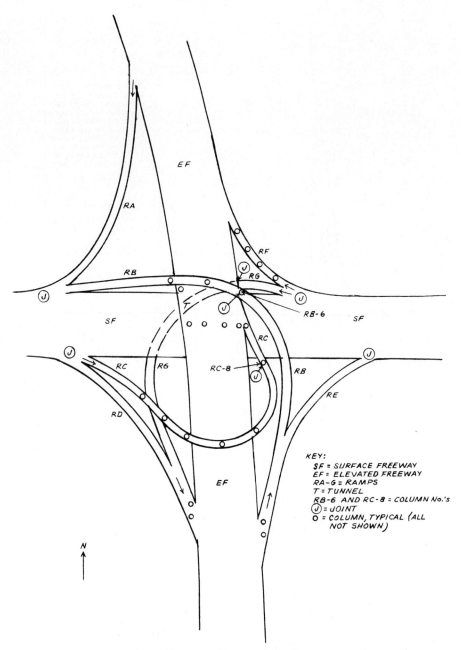

FIGURE 15-2 *Freeway interchange.*

as mentioned in Ch. 14, consider a system where these ramps are incorporated in a large metropolitan interchange (Fig. 15-2). Methods of mounting the supporting columns were mentioned in Ch. 14, and the same principles apply here with the added challenge of several rows of columns running in different directions. Assuming here that the terrain is generally flat, except for raised freeway beds graded by the highway engineers, you won't be hindered in column placement by the deep overburden present in the case of the multiarch bridge in Ch. 14, but because of the

complexity of the system, their location should be plotted during your initial layout. Don't wait until you have other structures in the way! Number the column locations on the drawing and place the same numbers on the plotted points on the model. This will be a time-saver during possible confusion later. Use a series of numbers for each ramp and label each ramp with a letter. Plot "R-B2" will mean the second column up from the starting point of ramp B, etc. Even though the subject of the model is on flat ground and there is too little planted area to justify contour cutting, you can still use urethane foam to build the surface freeway bed on the heavyweight illustration board base liner.

Figure 15-2 shows a simplified hypothetical interchange without overpasses, bridges, or surface streets. The omitted elements have been covered in Chs. 13 and 14. Also, the ramps have purposely not been stacked, as in the Los Angeles four level "mix-master," so that elements under discussion will not be hidden in plan view. Surface freeway side banking is omitted for simplicity.

Cut and shape the roadbed for the surface freeway (SF), and cut in the tunnel (T) (Ch. 22), which may or may not have to be finished all the way through depending upon visibility allowed by the scale. At least the concrete entrance and exit frames will have to be shown, and these can be made from vinyl. Glue this roadbed in place.

In all model surface liner construction, the ideal is to obtain continuity of surface by using a single sheet of material. This controls location of transitions and avoids joints. In the case of this freeway exchange this is possible only to a limited extent for several reasons. If the visible edges of the freeways are thicker than those of the ramps, then you would have either to use a separate material for the latter or choose a ramp material of scale thickness and laminate the freeways up to scale. The second consideration is the presence of conflicting courses. You obviously cannot, for example, cut ramp R-C out of the surface of the elevated freeway (EF) without creating an awkward gap to fill in the latter. The third consideration is the effect of forcing the base of a right triangle into its longer hypotenuse. As mentioned previously, you can sometimes force a low gradient out of a level dimension without objectionable distortion, but as the scale increases so does the foreshortening over the same span. The solutions are to cut one end of the ramp, preferably at the bottom or ground end, and install a filler piece, to install a separate ramp of the correct length, or better still to extend ramp cuts wherever possible beyond plan length to provide trimming selvage at joints. Mark the plan lengths on the free ends of the ramps as later guides.

Assuming a 1/16″ scale model with vertical separations of traffic ways as much as 18′ (1-1/8″) or more, the following is one solution that has a minimum of separate pieces. Ask for a plan drawing at 1/16″ scale since varying radius curves are difficult to plot with specified relationships (Fig. 15-2). Assume the basic ramp thickness is 1′ and the freeway thickness 2′, meaning that lightweight

illustration board can be used with a lamination of the same material for the freeways. Trace the drawing twice completely and twice for the freeway underliners. From one complete tracing, cut the surface freeway (SF) as though no ramps existed except include part of ramp RB to column RB-6 at the east edge of freeway EF and ramp RC between the surface freeway (SF) and the south edge of the same freeway to the east or right side of the elevated freeway at column RC-8. This violates the principle that joints are better made on the ground rather than at free-standing locations as at columns RB-6 and RC-8, but it seems the best solution here. From the second complete tracing cut the elevated freeway including all ramps except the parts of ramps B and C just cut with the surface freeway (SF). Include the stub of ramp RG to the east side of freeway EF. Later add a piece to connect this stub with the north end of the tunnel to meet the piece approaching from the south. The south tunnel approach can be cut to the west edge of the elevated freeway (EF) at "T". It will be inserted under the surface freeway after trimming to installed visible length. Where column-supported ramp pieces meet at columns, trim them so each joining end rests on half a column top. Note that you will not have much selvage if any to trim at column RB-6. Laminate the freeways with the material cut from their tracings to bring thickness up to specifications. Even though the edges of the surface freeway in the locale of Fig. 15-2 will not be revealed except perhaps at the tunnel entrances, laminating lightweight illustration board is a simple operation to ensure rigidity.

The number of columns involved will make you think of casting, but this will not be worthwhile unless most of them are configured to a shape not affected by changes in height. Even though stock materials will satisfy most requirements, there may be a few identical configurations calling for casting (Ch. 24) if only to ensure consistent result. If the columns are round, you probably can find wooden dowel, brass tubing, or, at the very small scales, piano wire to serve the purpose. If the columns are square, consider cutting them out of bass wood. Square columns should be broached through the surface illustration board for security of installation. If the column tops are splayed, consider casting the largest splayed form and then sanding to the smaller sizes. These could then be glued to the tops of shortened columns to fill out their heights.

To simplify discussion, let us assume that all

the columns are round and that you have wooden dowel stock to include the several diameters needed. Mount the surface freeway (SF) on its bed with contact glue. Drill all column holes through the plywood base so that they provide a snug slip fit, except for the columns at the center of the elevated freeway (EF) supporting ramps B and C. These two columns should be inserted through the illustration board so that the bottom ends are flush. Where holes are drilled in illustration board, with razor blade and sanding stick remove the raised hole edges caused by the drill bit.

Cut all columns about 1/2" oversize from the dowel stock of the diameter to fit their locations and place their designated number on the bottom of each. On your sander, shape the tops, or the added splayed forms to agree with banking and gradient angles according to the drawings. Glue the splayed forms on the pertinent column tops and insert the columns in their holes just enough to hold them. Paint them all a concrete color, and when dry press them in to the right heights and circular position. Where a snug fit is absent, pull the column out slightly and brush on a coating of glue (either white or contact) before repositioning the column. Where footings or pedestals appear at column bases, as at the center columns in the freeways, these can be formed by tack-gluing vinyl forms around the columns and pouring plaster. Carefully smooth out their surfaces between columns. When the plaster has set, remove the vinyl forms and paint the footings concrete.

Lay the elevated freeway-ramp system on its column system dry. Weight the freeway to hold it temporarily and test the positions of the ramps, threading ramp G on the south under ramp C and into the tunnel. When all seems to fit, remove the elevated system and brush contact glue to catch column tops on the underside. Apply contact glue to all the column tops and mount the system. Mount the extension of ramp G on the north side of the surface freeway so that it disappears into the tunnel, and the section of ramp B where it crosses the elevated freeway (EF).

To make this interchange complete you would, of course, have had to consider section profiles of the roadways to determine structural shape. You would have installed the parapets, railings, curbs, gutters, directional signs, etc., covered in other chapters. The important lesson to learn here is the total time saving made possible by spending time at the outset to plan the most economical sequence of events in any construction complex. When you add to your natural skill as a hobbyist the discipline

of time and dollars, your choice of the most expeditious procedures becomes very important.

Parking Ramps: These inside structures are provided to accommodate customers of shopping centers, department stores, etc. They usually have the requirement of transition between levels within a restricted area. Complete floors are often tilted to lower ramp gradients, and even though you are making an exterior model, the ventilating openness of parking structures will often make the showing of interior configurations necessary. An underground parking facility might require showing only the entrance with the roadway disappearing inside, but if coiled level changes are visible, these can be made by splitting "doughnuts" of the scale material used and warping them so that the ends are joined and tangents provided for access to each floor. The coil may be open in the center for ventilation or enclosed as an oversize column perhaps housing utilities. In an open, above grade parking structure the sequence of structural events will for the most part depend upon the column support system to be discussed in Ch. 22.

STEPS

Steps do not usually pose any serious structural problems since they are basically series of flat planes terraced to allow easy movement from one level to another. They can be made using the grading methods of horizontal control, vertical control, and contour cutting. They also can be made by cutting a material like acrylic on a mill or by pouring plaster into a form. The method chosen in any particular case will depend upon the scale, length of gradient, location, configuration, and whether or not the steps are open or closed. The material used in the life-size system will also have a bearing on the procedure. Open steps are those where the risers are not continuous across the treads, and/or the sides are not confined by closing structure.

One of the principal criteria in judging finished steps is trueness of alignment. Though a particular set of steps may be simple to make extra effort should be applied to obtaining accuracy of tread depth and riser height as well as evenness of the sides, particularly where they are open. Consider the configuration a set of parallel lines where the slightest deviation will stick out like a sore thumb.

Before discussing some examples, I present one of the common comfort formulas in step and stairway construction. The figures that stick with me are 7 to 7.5″ vertical distance from tread to tread and 17 to 17.5″ as the sum of riser and tread dimensions. We have all seen variations from this relationship, but it has been helpful to me as a guide in appraising an installation. Knowing, for example, that a riser over 8″ high becomes uncomfortable will help you decide whether or not your model builder's license in filling a slightly off vertical space violates authentic appearance. If, after following the specifications of the drawings, you find that you are off 1″ at 1/16″ scale, no one will notice a 0.005″ shim under the bottom tread, but 0.020″ extra thickness of tread at 1/4″ scale would require adjustment of the rise. I have, on occasion, unnoticeably warped the top level down to fill the gap. Be sure you have the correct number of risers!

The *horizontal control* or layer method is a handy solution to most closed step installations at scales no larger than 1/8″. At 1/32″ scale, you could get away with 0.015″ vinyl lamination, keeping in mind that there will be cumulative error of about 0.003″ per riser if each is actually 7″ high. Six risers would result in a noticeable gap of 0.018″ or the equivalent of one riser. If you can't shim up the bottom level conveniently so that the ramp is not noticeable, laminate each tread with bond paper. If splitting authenticity hairs is in order in the case of closed wooden steps, barely reveal the edge of the paper beyond the front edge of the vinyl to form the nosing often found in such steps. Common concrete steps will have risers in the same plane from tread to tread. At 1/16″ scale, the same principles apply. A 7″ riser would be approximately 0.035″, calling for 0.030″ vinyl plus paper or 0.005″ acetate. The concrete steps at the entrance to the hospital in Fig. 9-7 would span a rise of 3′ (4′6″ at the building pad less 1′6″ at the sidewalk) allowing five 7″ risers. The extra inch is absorbed by ramping the entrance walk up from the sidewalk. The utility steps at the ends of the loading dock rise 42″, allowing five 8″ risers from a 2″ upward warp at approaches. Maximum riser height is often used in such situations where the run must be kept to a minimum. This increases the ratio of riser to tread. The 7″ (0.073″) risers at the entrance could be formed with lightweight illustration board plus 0.010″ vinyl, being sure that the lamination at the front of each tread is filled. The 8″ risers would require 0.020″ vinyl lamination. At 1/4″ scale the con-

venient limits of the layer method become apparent because the laminating approaches the awkward stage. A 7″ riser at 1/4″ scale would be approximately 0.147″ which could be made up of heavyweight illustration board (0.094″), 0.030″ vinyl, and 0.020″ vinyl, with 0.003″ paper added, or with two layers of lightweight illustration board (0.125″) with 0.020″ vinyl, leaving 0.002″ to be camouflaged through assembly. At 1/2″ scale and greater, other methods become more practical. One of the main points to consider with the layer method is the riser surface. Illustration board has a tendency to be fuzzy at the edge, particularly when disturbed. A sharp knife cut will give you a good surface with sharp corners, but pay attention to this requirement as you assemble.

The *vertical control* method at 1/2″ scale and larger involves constructing the steps much in the same manner as that used by the building contractor. The treads and risers are separate pieces supported by carriages and stringers which are boards on edge notched out in a stair configuration so that one leg of each right angle notch is horizontal when the board is sloped to the gradient of the system. Carriages are the rough lumber supports underneath the steps. Stringers, supportive or not, usually form the side closures. Here, consider stringers to be performing both services. At 1/2″ scale, a 3/4″ plywood tread could be made from 0.030″ vinyl or 1/32″ acrylic with the minute differences being made up for in cutting the six 1/4″ strips to form the remaining riser height. These riser strips can be made from material of offscale thickness (illustration board, vinyl, or acrylic) when not open to view. Be sure you consider the thickness used when you cut the stringer or other supports so that the riser-tread relationship will be to specifications. Where nosing is present, round the front edges of the treads and assemble so that the risers are inset the scale amount from these edges. If you were building the entrance steps on model B (Fig. 9-7) at 1/2″ scale, install the retaining wall against the bank on the west side and the wall enclosing the left side of the wheelchair ramp on the east side. Glue a notched stringer against each wall and place a triangular support with notched hypotenuse in the center of the space. Then assemble treads and risers with the former flush with the top edges of the latter since there is no nosing in these concrete steps. Actually there probably would be steel angles at the front edges of the treads for protection of the concrete, but these won't show on the model. Finish sand the top joints of tread and riser, filling where necessary to give a monolithic effect after painting.

Contour cut steps are not practical at less than 1/16″ scale. Below that scale the time consumed in cutting the finely defined levels could easily be shortened by inserting a layered step system into a cavity in the urethane. If the scale and surrounding configuration warrant such cutting along with the rest of the grading, keep in mind that the step treads will not be a contour interval apart. Separate settings of the mill will be necessary; record where you take off from the limiting contour at the bottom of the steps. You can feather out the step contours on each side into the grading since the presence of steps indicates a finished display model on which all contour steps will be sanded off. Strips of thin material are then glued against the risers and on the treads of the urethane configuration to form the steps. Remember that the urethane treads and risers must be undersize to accommodate the added material.

I have found the machine shop mill (not the Pattinson Mill) an excellent tool for cutting closed step stock. Always cut more than you need so that you can have some available for the next model with the same scale and step gradient. Choose a suitable block of acrylic and sand off one edge at an angle equal to the step gradient. Mount the block on the mill table with doublefaced tape, tapping it down with a mallet to obtain a secure hold. Use your judgment as to when you should provide selvage outside the bit operating area so that you can use clamps. I have found the tape method secure enough for most jobs. After cutting the steps in the sloping side of the block, cut off the specified width slightly oversize on your bandsaw. Sand the system to width and length on your belt sander. Insert this triangle into the prepared cavity on the model, considering the side walls, curbs, railing support, etc., discussed in other sections.

Poured Plaster Steps: See Ch. 24

Curved Steps: Curved steps (either concave or convex) present no particular problems since the only change involves increasing or decreasing radii curves in the tread faces from bottom to top, and, in the case of built-up systems, the bowing of the risers, which are usually made from vinyl. With an indexing table on your shop mill, you can even cut these out of acrylic within limits.

Open Steps: Open steps such as found in garden transitions to decks, and in steel industrial systems, have open riser spaces. The usual redwood garden steps will probably be open-ended also. An important consideration here is the visual authenticity of the visible stringers. Where the scale becomes so small that reading openness is difficult, forget the stringers and use the layer method discussed previously. The utility steps at the ends of the loading dock in model B (Fig. 9-7) might very well be of the open, steel type instead of the previously considered closed concrete system. The treads in these are usually enclosed in solid (unnotched) stringers on each side or run into the wall on one side with a stringer on the other. As a concept consider them thick ladders with wide rungs tilted to be level at the gradient of the system with a handrail added.

Urethane foam steps cut out of a solid block are generally not satisfactory because of the softness of the material and the fact that you have to fill the visible pores with plaster. I have used them at 1/4″ scale as a quickie way to get steps down to a basement entrance where the steps are closed on both sides. The closure allowed filling any chipped out places in the urethane with spackle.

STAIRWAYS

For the purposes of this book, stairways are those systems which generally have length of runs equal to the distance between floors in a building and longer. Most of them are found indoors, such as those in private residences, theaters, concert halls, civic buildings, etc. Stairways provide access and serve as fire exits in office buildings. Those outdoors include upper floor accesses against the wall of a building, fire escapes, and industrial systems between levels and catwalks around machinery, utility equipment, storage tanks, etc.

Interior Stairways: Interior stairways will probably not very often be required from the model builder in the architectural field because by far the greater number of assignments will be for site and exterior construction with interior detail hidden from view. There will, however, be cases where an exterior model will reveal the interior of stair wells in office buildings, or open parking garages with just parapets at each level. Interior arrangement models will reveal the stairway systems, and I remember once building a design study model of a spiral stairway or "winder" in contractor's terms.

Though your imagination could carry you through the construction of a building stair well aided by tips previously given with respect to steps, one very important consideration is the expected visibility of your effort. There is a natural tendency in constructing a primarily exterior model to try to save time by installing only those portions which will be visible. Except for obviously hidden elements, you very likely will not know for sure the minimum requirements until the model is finished. My warning from experience is not to try to outguess the viewer's eye. Particularly where a standard concrete scissors stair system is behind a substantially transparent glass wall, build the entire system. It will be easier than trying to install only visible pieces. A scissors system is one where individual flights reverse direction between landings. Install the landings at their designated locations first. Then connect these landings with the flights against the interior wall of the well. They will all be parallel in a vertical plane. Add the railings to this half system and, after mounting the railings (Ch. 16) on the outside system of stairs, install it with the flights running in the direction opposite from that of the first system. Consider cutting the stairs out of acrylic on your shop mill as discussed in the case of the previous steps. Cut the solid block of acrylic behind the stairs and parallel to the gradient and sand the back to specified thickness.

If you are fortunate enough to receive a contract to construct an interior model of a historic Southern mansion with a curving stairway, carefully note all visible dimensions of structural extensions. Sturdy simplicity of construction is the goal, but if the treads are nosed over the stringer be sure to select a tread material of the scale thickness. This may seem elementary, but without thorough planning and analysis initial concepts are often full of flaws. This is particularly true where ornamentation confuses the issue. Where the scale is very small you can usually beef up hidden construction and line it with scale surfacing.

SPIRAL STAIRWAY

In the case of the dam in Ch. 12, it was assumed that all the information was not available for some

reason so that you were driven to computations not usually necessary. This was done to show how your knowledge of basic mathematics can produce solutions to structural problems and can be employed as an auxiliary tool to check your work. In this case a hypothetical *spiral stairway* will be used as a medium to give you at least a superficial indication of how the engineer might have developed such a facility. Even though you have all the structural drawings enabling you to count the number of treads and even trace the tread shape from an inscale detail, dimensions and computations will be given as though you were doing the engineering. As a model builder you will not usually have the time during construction to question why an element was designed in a certain way. Your mission is much the same as that of the contractor—to construct according to prescribed specifications. On the other hand, an accumulated knowledge of basic engineering principles can make your approach more intelligent and the job more interesting. As in the case of the dam (Ch. 12) you are not concerned here with strains, stresses, loads, etc. but the visible result must be authentic. This demands that engineering principles be considered even though the materials used are for the most part only representative of the real thing. Intermittent use of the common fractions and their decimal equivalents will be used to stress the necessary familiarity required with both expressions.

Assume you have a 1/4″ scale spiral stairway to construct for installation in your model of a proposed bank lobby interior (Fig. 15-3). This stairway is to run from the ground floor counterclockwise to a mezzanine floor 12′ above. The mezzanine edge skirts three sides of the lobby, in a U shape. When making the mezzanine floor out of 1/4″ acrylic, make the leg of the U containing the stairway access separately so that you won't have to contend with the mass of the entire mezzanine when assembling the stair system. Visualize this model as a box with one side open. The top of the box would be the second floor with the mezzanine inserted between that and the bottom of the box or ground floor. Recalling Pattinson's Law, you would have established an efficient sequence of events; the following tips will ignore the area other than that occupied by the spiral stairway. You probably will decide to leave the top or second floor off until last in order to have unobstructed access to the interior. The ground floor carpet would be laid before final installation of the stairway.

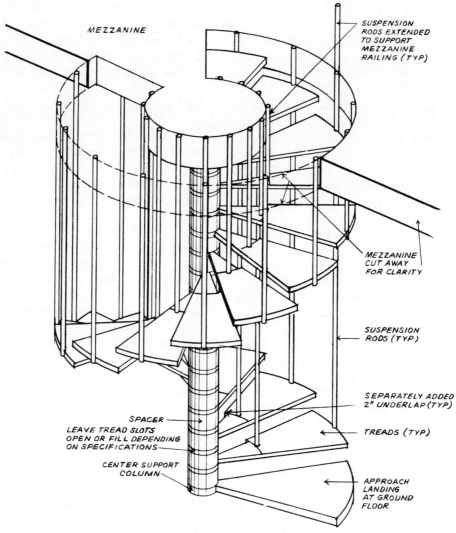

MEZZANINE

SUSPENSION
RODS EXTENDED
TO SUPPORT
MEZZANINE
RAILING (TYP)

MEZZANINE
CUT AWAY
FOR CLARITY

SUSPENSION
RODS (TYP)

SEPARATELY ADDED
2" UNDERLAP (TYP)

TREADS (TYP)

SPACER
LEAVE TREAD SLOTS
OPEN OR FILL DEPENDING
ON SPECIFICATIONS

CENTER SUPPORT
COLUMN

APPROACH
LANDING
AT GROUND
FLOOR

FIGURE 15-3 *Spiral stairway.*

Note that the scale of 1/4″ is probably the smallest to be used for a design study only. Depending upon the subject, the larger the scale, within limits, the easier it is to read in the conference room. Here it can be assumed that the bank lobby is only one of several subjects to be displayed in a group, demanding a limit to the size of each unit. More important, the scale is large enough to require the assembly of many components suggestive of the dexterity required in doing so. The system is 10′ in diameter. The risers (except the top one) are open, and the treads, 1″ thick, are cantilevered from a center supporting round column 12″ in diameter except for the top tread which is attached to the mezzanine floor edge at the access opening. The column runs from ground floor to the mezzanine. The leading edge of each tread overlaps 2″ (in

a vertical plane) the rear edge of the next tread added to the rear edge of each tread (except the top one) between the inner and outer limit of useful traffic way. Note that this additional tread would be included in the manufacture, but since its rear edge forms a line not on a radius of the common center of the system, it is initially ignored here in geometric analysis and pattern making. Each tread is supported by two 3/4″ steel rods suspended from the ceiling and held rigid by the hand rail system which includes sling braces to hold the treads transversely level. This sling structure can be ignored in the model. One suspending rod is passed through the center of the tread 24″ from the center of the column at the inner limit of the traffic way, and the other is clipped to the center of the outer perimeter. Access to the mezzanine is through an arced opening enclosed by railings except at the stair access. The tread material is tile laid in a steel frame which can be accomplished with paint and scoring.

Note the small difference which can be visually tolerated and absorbed in construction. With 7.5″ risers, there will be 19.2 (144″/7.5) in 12′ and 18 treads. The 0.2 riser or 1-1/2″ (1/32″ at 1/4″ scale) will be the height of an approach landing on the ground floor. The 3/4″ steel rod would be 0.0156″ at scale; so you can safely use 0.015″ piano wire. The tread thickness of 1″ is 0.0208″ calling for 0.020″ vinyl. The 12″ diameter of the center column is equal to 0.25″ or 1/4″ allowing the use of brass tubing or wood dowel of that diameter. These include good examples of the use of model builder's license where standard, not easily resized materials can be used in structure without seriously affecting authenticity of appearance. The difference in thickness of the tread material, for example, will be made up for in paint.

One of the important considerations in spiral stairways is the diminishing tread width as the treads approach their common center. Smaller than normal treads can cause accidents, so the area of travel should not extend toward the center any farther than where the usable tread depth is no less than the minimum allowable considering riser height. The comfort formulas are of course violated as the treads become deeper toward the perimeter of the circle. Comfort is sacrificed to design with some relief provided by the hand rails. Following the comfort formula mentioned previously in this section, the 7.5″ risers will require a minimum usable tread width of 10″ or as close thereto as the geometry of the system allows. Since the minimum tread is located at the inner limit of usable traffic way it will be at a point 24″ from the center of the supporting column.

Treads: The key elements of this system are the 18 treads which must be placed accurately so that their sequential progress follows a rising counterclockwise coil around a central column in an imaginary cylinder 12′ high with an interior diameter of 10′. The 19 spaces each measure 7.5″ from tread to tread (6.5″ between 1″ thick treads), with a 1-1/2″ high approach landing at the lobby floor to complete the total height of 144″ or 12′. To establish the size and shape of the treads calculate the number of treads with a chord width of 10″ at 24″ radius that can be included in a circle without overlap which is ignored for this purpose. Refer to Fig. 15-4 which is included for geometric representation only. The outer and

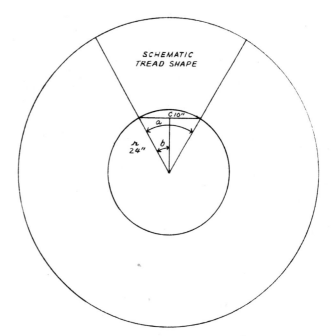

FIGURE 15-4 *Geometric aid.*

inner circles represent the perimeter of the system and the inner limit of usable traffic way respectively. Anywhere on the inner circle draw a chord to represent the 10″ minimum tread width. Draw a radial line through each end of the chord from the center to the outer circle to form a tread shape. Also draw a line perpendicular to the chord through the center of the circles. This will form two equal right triangles. As you determined using Figs. 12-8 and 12-9 for the dam in Ch. 12, compute angle a which equals 2 times angle b.

$$\text{Sin } b = \tfrac{1}{2} \text{ chord } C(B) \text{ divided by } r,$$
the radius of the arc subtended by the chord
$$r = 24'' \quad \text{and} \quad C = 10'' \text{ Then}$$
$$\sin b = 5/24 = 0.20833$$
the sine of 12.0247 degrees
$$a = 2 \times b = 24.0494 \text{ degrees Then}$$
$$360/24.0494 = 14.969188$$

or the number of treads you can get into a circle without overlap, each tread having a chord width of 10″ at 24″ radius. The nearest whole number is 15, so from a practical stand point, use 15 as the number of treads necessary to fill the circle. The difference of approximately 0.03 will cause a negligible prorated reduction in the desired 10″ minimum comfort tread width. 360/15 = 24 degrees, the angle to draw to make your tread pattern.

The drafting you do now will have to be in scale and accurate since it will produce the desired treads to install on the model (Fig. 15-5). On a sheet of 0.020″ vinyl draw two concentric circles with radii of 1/2″ (2′) and 1-1/4″ (5′). With the largest protractor you can find in your tool crib (for maximum plotting accuracy) plot 24 degrees anywhere around the larger circle. Connect these two points with the center of the circles and with dividers (Ch. 36) set to the chord distance between the points where these radial lines cross the circumference of the larger circle, repeat this distance around the circumference. You should fill the circumference with 15 equidistant light punches which when connected to the center result in 15 pie-shaped sections that are the treads. If the dividers do not exactly span the last space, start over. Follow this same procedure with a second pair of circles to provide the additional 3 treads required to make 18, the quantity required for the stair system.

Before cutting out the treads paint the circles the tile color. With a knife compass (Ch. 36) score the tile grout lines starting with the 24″ radius circle. Between there and the center paint the column supported ends of the treads black or other specified metal finish color. Redefine the circumference and radial lines as cutting guides. With a mat knife lightly score the radial grout lines to match the intensity of the curved lines made with the knife compass. Cut out the 18 treads and add, with acrylic cement, the 2″ (0.040″)

underlap strip of the same vinyl across the traffic area on the rear edge of each. Paint the additions the tile color, and with a mat knife, eyeball the continuation of the grout lines. The treads can be framed with a drafting pen (Ch. 36) using the same paint you used to finish the tread center ends. If the purely supportive inner ends of the treads are perforated for esthetics or weight-reduction, consider several holes drilled with a wire drill and pin vise to simulate this. Be consistent with hole placement.

In the center of the 24″ arc on each tread drill a hole to accept the 0.015″ piano wire suspension rod and in the center of the outer end file a small notch for the same purpose.

Support Column: Tips will be given on two ways to make the center column which holds the inner ends of the treads. The simplest involves the grooving of a length of wood dowel with accurately spaced grooves deep enough to provide a good bite on the tread ends, still leaving enough solid core to prevent easy breaking. Set up your mill or lathe with a 0.021″ or 0.022″ jeweler's saw blade with saw height or a stop to allow a cut 1/16″ deep as you roll the 1/4″ dowel under or against the blade. This will leave a solid core of 1/8″ diameter which should be ample for strength. Move the index or vernier 7.5″ (0.156″) between each groove cut completely around the dowel. Cut 17 grooves since

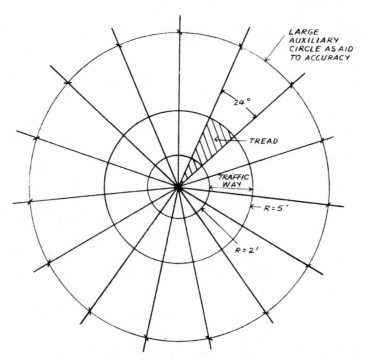

FIGURE 15-5 *Tread pattern.*

the top tread will be supported by the edge of the 1' (1/4") thick mezzanine floor. In the absence of machine tools to handle the dowel column you can assemble it with spacers of telescoped brass tubing (Ch. 36) slid down over an uncut piece of 1/8" tubing mounted as you would the dowel. Coat a length of 7/32" tubing with contact glue and twist it into a length of 1/4" tubing to obtain as much binding glue coverage as possible. Inside this assembly slip a length of 3/16" and inside that 5/32" tubing, providing a built-up tube with a 1/16" wall held together with contact glue. This tube will be cut up on your bandsaw (or hacksaw) (Ch. 36) to form the spacers.

Spacers: Before you cut any spacers refer to Fig. 15-6 which represents a sketch you might make to help you determine the number and height of spacers required. Also, knowing that the total of the increments must equal 12' (3") such a sketch helps you to prove the accuracy of your developed individual dimensions much in the same manner that you add up the dimensions of components to prove a total shown on your client's drawings (Ch. 5). Starting at the ground floor note that the first spacer must be 8" high since it includes the height of the approach landing which is 1-1/2" high. Above this there are 16 spacers at 6-1/2" or the 7-1/2" riser less the standard thick-

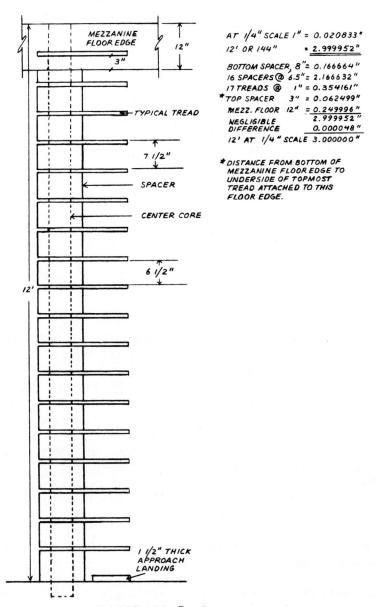

FIGURE 15-6 *Proving measurements.*

Item	Height or Thickness	Computed at ¼″ Scale	Used	Quantity	Totals Life Size	At Scale
Mezzanine	12″	0.249996″	0.25″ (1)	1	12″	0.25″
Top spacer	3″	0.062499″	0.0625″ (2)	1	3″	0.0625
Tread	1″	0.020833″	0.020″ (1)	17	17″	0.34″
Spacer	6.5″	0.135415″	0.135″ (2)	16	104″	2.16″
Bottom spacer	8″	0.166664″	0.167″ (2)	1	8″	0.167″
				Totals	144″	2.9795″
				Should be	144″	3.0000″
				Difference	0	0.0205″

Add shortage of 0.0205″ to bottom spacer and approach landing.

(1) Use material of standard thickness.
(2) Must be cut to size.

FIGURE 15-7 *Analysis table.*

ness of tread, 1″. The top spacer is 3″ high to fill the interval between the 17th tread and the underside of the mezzanine floor. The 18th tread is within the thickness of the mezzanine floor increment. The sketch is simple and the reasoning elementary, but all is not beer and skittles. Where many small dimensions must be effected in shop so that their total fills a fixed space, lack of precision can play havoc with your assembly because of accumulated differences. These are supplied by various gremlins such as a misread measuring instrument or too heavy a hand with tools. A belt sander can in a flash remove a few thousandths which can usually be camouflaged upon installation of a single component, but multiplied by many components can result in adding to the contents of your waste basket.

Figure 15-7 shows how even conscientious analysis of procedure can result in a difference to be absorbed. For example, establishing a practical limit to reading measuring instruments automatically causes differences by reducing decimals to three places. This added to the other gremlins results in a formidable force against your accuracy discipline. All this is not to belabor the accuracy and authenticity discussed in Ch. 3, but to make you aware of the obstacles against attaining acceptable compromises.

In the case of the spiral stairway add the calculated difference of 0.0205″ to the bottom spacer and the same amount to the approach landing to maintain the prescribed 7.5″ riser. Feel fortunate if adjusting for this difference results in spanning the 3″ flight with an acceptably snug fit. Stack all components dry before assembly to determine any final adjustments needed.

From the previously prepared tubular spacer stock cut the 18 spacers a bit oversize on your bandsaw by carefully rolling the stock against the blade as you hold it against a wood stop. Provide some sort of catcher to prevent the cut-off spacer from flying across the shop. Between each cut sand the end of the stock flat. To hold each spacer for sanding to dimension you will need three adaptations of the sizing jig listed in Ch. 37, one for the bottom spacer, one for the top spacer which is only 1/16″ thick, and one for the 16 intervening spacers. The general procedure is to drill 1/4″ holes (for a snug fit of the tubing) through material of the same thickness as the spacer depth and then glue this material to a wood block backing to form spacer sockets. For the bottom spacer drill a hole in a piece of say 3/16″ acrylic, cut out a button including the hole and sand it down to 0.167″ thick checking with your calipers as you proceed. With the polished side out glue this to a block of scrap white pine framing material with contact glue around the perimeter of the hole. Do the same out of clear 1/16″ acrylic for the top spacer. The intervening 16 spacers can be gang-sanded pressed into 16 holes drilled in a single piece of acrylic as long as you can size the complete piece evenly. Try adding 0.010″ vinyl to 1/8″ acrylic before drilling the holes. This will give you the required 0.135″ thickness. The reason for having a polished acrylic surface toward the sander is to let you know when the first scratch appears indicating spacers of the desired height. As mentioned previously, dry stack the treads, spacers, and mezzanine floor to determine any adjustments needed to make up the total 3″ distance from lobby floor to mezzanine.

Site: The next exercise on the program is to prepare the location of the stairway. On the prepared section including the stairway at the mezzanine

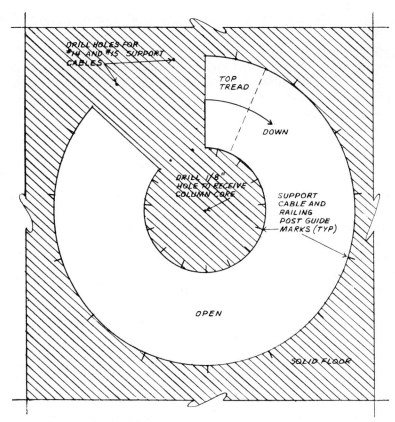

FIGURE 15-8 *Mezzanine configuration.*

locate the specified center and draw or scribe two concentric circles around this center, one with a radius of 2′ (0.5″) and an outer one with a radius of 5′ (1.25″). This reproduces the tread pattern circles (Fig. 15-5). Establish the top terminus of the stairway with a radius line drawn from the center to the outer circle. This is the line of the topmost riser. Plot the center line of each tread (15 in number) around the outer circumference and indicate by radius lines extended beyond the circle to be used later for locating the tread support rods. See Fig. 15-8 for illustration. Clockwise from the terminus line establish the mezzanine floor opening to provide at least 7′ head clearance for people using the stairway. Since the mezzanine floor (Fig. 15-6) is 1′ thick, 7′ clearance requires that the opening start at a line directly above the nose of the tread nearest to 8′ below the mezzanine floor, or the 13th tread down from the top (8 × 12″ = 96″; 96″/7.5″ riser height = 12.8″) This means that the arc cut through the mezzanine floor will leave two tread widths of solid flooring since there are 15 treads in the circle (Fig. 15-5). Drill and file out this opening. Drill holes at the centers of the arcs of the two treads represented by the remaining solid portion of the mezzanine to accept the piano

wire rods supporting the 14th and 15th treads from the top. Tread 16 is supported by rods suspended from the mezzanine floor at the centers of the ends of tread 1 mounted against the floor edge directly above. Treads 17 and 18 can be supported by the same rods supporting treads 2 and 3 since the pairs are vertically in line.

Drill a 1/8″ hole through the center of the mezzanine section including the stairway, and after locating it on the ground floor, use the hole as a guide to drilling the same size hole through the latter. These holes will support the ends of the uncut center of stair support column over which you will slip the spacers to hold the treads.

Assembly: Small or intricate model components are generally best assembled off the model whenever possible. This stairway is only 3″ high, and, with 17 cantilevered treads to install in spiral configuration it would be handy to be able to turn the assembly to a comfortable line of vision and access as it progresses. Tack the 18 spacers down on double-faced tape (Ch. 35) and paint the exterior surfaces with matte black Krylon (Ch. 32) or other prescribed finish. Cut 30 pieces of 0.015″ piano wire a little over 3″ long and sand one end of each flat. Stick 26 of them into urethane foam to hold them while you spray them black also. The remaining 4 will be painted after installation since friction through the mezzanine floor would scrape off the paint. Cut a piece of 1/8″ brass tubing 3-3/8″ long to serve as the column core. Flatten and trim both ends and insert it into the lobby floor to the latter's 3/8″ thickness. Slip on the bottom spacer and the mezzanine floor section so that the top of the core is flush with that floor and adjust to fit the space in the lobby. Any excess can be pushed farther into the lobby floor. Remove the mezzanine section, raise the bottom spacer enough to allow application of contact glue at floor level and then let it slide back in place. Note that with brass tubing you could solder this spacer to the column, covering the core thoroughly with flux so that the solder will flow into the joint without external evidence. When the spacer has set, pull the assembly out and insert it in a jig base of 3/8″ plywood as an assembly support. Establish a radial starting line on the plywood to mark the location of the bottom tread. Clip off 1/16″ of the pointed tip of each tread to accommodate the diameter of the core. Place contact glue around the core the height of the second spacer, on the edge of both spacers at the estimated tread location and on the tread tip top and bottom. When dry, place the tread against the core on the bottom spacer and clamp it down with the second spacer, being sure that the front edge of the tread is on a radial line from the center of the core. This can be checked with a square placed on the radial line on the plywood jig base and compared with the location of the center support rod notch at the outer end of the tread. If you decide to solder the spacers in place, remember that you won't have any twisting adjustments later to help you line up treads radially. Proceed in the same manner until you have 17 treads and all spacers mounted. Be sure that the only material which underlaps the tread above is that of the added 2″ discussed previously. Trim the 18th tread to fit the mezzanine access opening and glue it to the edge of the floor 7.5″ (0.156″) from the top surface. At right angles to the mezzanine section glue vertical risers of heavyweight illustration board to the jig base to support the section's cantilevered end when glued in place on the support column. Visually check the assembly as a whole. If the first tread is correctly positioned radially, check the others in sequence with a small square of vinyl pushed along the leading edge of each to be sure that it lines up the full length with the rear edge of the one below (ignoring the underlap strip).

Install the inner support rods first. Note that since there are 18 treads and only 15 can be included in a circle without overlap, three pairs of treads will be supported by rods in common, hence 30 rods instead of 36. Push the unpainted ones through the solid part of the mezzanine floor and paint with a brush after installation. Be careful when inserting a rod into the hole in a tread. If you run into resistance, file a point on the wire, push it through, clip off the point, carefully sanding the end flat with a miniature file (Ch. 36), and pull it back until flush with the under surface of the tread. Since you have only 0.020″ thickness of tread, put a pin point of cyanoacrylate glue (Ch. 34) at the joint to hold it. Contact glue will make a mess in such a small application. Use the guide lines drawn on the mezzanine floor section to glue the top ends of the rods to the mezzanine floor edge, trim the excess and file jagged ends flush. When all inner rods are in place, install the railing as close to specifications as possible. This may be a couple of strands of fine wire or involve a configuration requiring acid-etching (Ch. 17). Railings will be discussed in Ch. 16. Add the outer rods and railing, paint the unpainted rods and install the assembly on the model. It has been assumed that you would have treated the lobby floor and ceiling at the mezzanine beforehand. Add the approach landing and any required floor finish and railing on the mezzanine after filling the four rod holes and the top of the core of the support column.

A third way to construct the support column involves the making of spacers out of solid 1/4″ acrylic rod with holes drilled through the centers of each to allow mounting on a core. I find that these should be drilled on a lathe to assure accuracy of centers. The telescoping brass tubing is a natural, storebought material with which to solve the problem without the aid of such a machine tool.

EXTERIOR STAIRWAYS

These include those that are used as a means of access to upper stories against the sides of buildings or to a balcony along the front of a motor court, etc. They are found as fire escapes, winding around a storage tank, against a shoreline cliff at a beach, or between levels of an industrial catwalk system. I find no hard and fast distinction between exterior stairways and steps. They both present the same basic problems to a model builder, those of establishing flights of level, equispaced treads along the hypotenuse of a right triangle between levels. I think of steps being built into grade and stairways as mostly freestanding, often with open risers.

Particularly where there are landings at intervening accesses to the structure, consider extending the structure floor at these points to form the landings and provide established termini for the individual flights of stairs. This is far easier than constructing the complete stairway independently so that the landings are at the correct levels. The finite termini of sections also reduce the effects of cumulative differences to single flights forestalling their accumulation over the complete system. This was brought out in the discussion about the spiral stairway. Even if the landing is only a spot to rest your legs, fastening the landing to the wall first will supply the same control over the gremlins.

A closed riser system such as that of the flights mentioned earlier with respect to the visible interior stairway is usually easier than one where the treads have to be mounted individually. At the smaller scales such as 1/32″ and 1/16″ and in the absence of a mill, consider gluing stepped carriages cut out of vinyl to vinyl stringers and mounting the treads and risers of the same material between two such assemblies, or at very small scales, gluing folded paper to a stringer on each side, following a pencil indication on each stringer of the stepped configuration. If the risers are open in the case of the carriage-stringer assemblies simply leave the risers out.

At 1/4″ scale you can make an excellent open-risered flight by stacking triangles of 0.030″ vinyl holding the stack in a vise (Ch. 36) under a horizontal mill armed with a jeweler's saw blade the thickness of the vinyl treads plus a thousandth or two for slip fit. Each triangle is a right triangle and the stack is placed in the vise so that the bottom leg is parallel to the mill table. Cuts are then made vertically into the hypotenuse edge which has been cut to the stairway gradient. The depth of each cut is equal to the tread width and spacing is controlled by the vernier adjustment to provide consistently accurate riser heights. Cut with a mat knife, each triangle parallel to the hypotenuse just beyond the bottom of the saw slots to hold the riser tongues together. Attach each carriage strip to a 0.010″ vinyl stringer with acrylic cement (Ch. 34) and assemble the flight by inserting the treads, all cut to the same length, into the slots formed at each side by the carriage-stringer assemblies. Hold the ends of the treads in their slots with acrylic cement. Trim off excess material at the back of the stairway and cover the

visible edges of the carriage-stringer laminations with strips of 0.010″ vinyl cut on your paper cutter (Ch. 36). Continue the same process with pairs of carriage-stringer laminations until you have all flights necessary for the system.

To build a stairway from bottom to top around a cylindrical storage tank in your industrial model first establish its path by making a pattern out of heavy paper, vinyl, or even lightweight illustration board if the tank is large enough to allow its easy bowing. Mark the points of start and finish of the system on the material held against the tank surface with the bottom of the material even with the bottom edge of the tank. Flatten out the pattern material and draw a perpendicular line from the bottom through the indication of the top terminus. Connect the top terminus mark with the starting point and you have a right triangle with the hypotenuse representing the path of the stairway. From the drawings determine the horizontal distance between tread centers which is actually the length of horizontal arc between them. Plot these centers along the base of the triangle starting half a tread width from the bottom terminus of the system. For consistent accuracy use dividers, repeating the fixed distance between the points of the instrument. You should wind up with a number of tick marks equal to the number of treads in the stairway, the last one being half a tread width from the top terminus line or upright leg of the triangle. At each tick mark draw a line perpendicular to the base of the triangle up through the hypotenuse to transfer these tread centers to the stairway's path. Cut the pattern material along the hypotenuse, hold the pattern against the curve of the tank and punch the tread centers into the tank surface.

If you for some reason have to do some figuring to obtain tread centers and shape of treads, on a piece of lightweight illustration board draw a circle with a radius equal to the outside diameter of the tank in scale. From the same center draw a larger circle with additional radius equal to the length of the treads (width of stairway). On the inner circumference mark the starting and ending termini of the stairway and draw a line from the center through each point to enclose the arc it spans. Draw these two lines through the outer circumference. Draw the chords of the arcs and with a scale measure the length of one of them. Divide this length by twice the number of treads required (to get tread center spacing). If the quotient is too far from a rational number at which to set your dividers accurately, try doing the same with the other chord. If the quotient is still too fractional to plot with ease, make your own scale by dividing the chord length into the required divisions by using the method described in Ch. 26. In any case you should divide either chord exactly.

Draw lines from the center through these points on either chord, and you have established both the tread centers and tread patterns if not the treads themselves. At 1/2″ scale lightweight illustration board should be about right for tread thickness which would have the indicated choice of pattern material to use at the scale of the subject. Note that the procedure followed here is similar to that used in the case of the spiral stairway treads except that in this case you are not concerned with angle measurements because you have an established distance around part of a circle.

Cut out the arc of illustration board containing the treads, and before cutting out the treads place it against the base of the tank between start and finish of the stairway system and draw vertical lines from the marks representing tread centers up the tank side through the pathway traced using the pattern triangle. The intersections are the points to punch into the tank surface.

At each of these punches, with a wire drill in a pin vise (Ch. 36), drill holes to accept piano wire tread supports with a snug fit. Consecutively insert these supports with sand-flattened outer ends and with the inner ends dipped in contact glue. Push them in flush with a block of wood the width of the stairway held against the tank surface. In the absence of acid-etched railing stock mount an L shaped piece of wire at railing post location, the bottom of the L forming the tread support and the upright forming the hand rail support with a sand-flattened end. The hand rail could be constructed with strips of vinyl or wood. See Ch. 16 for a discussion about railings. The shape of the treads should help you mount them radially (without overlap) with their centers on the supports. Apply contact glue to both support and tread and let dry before mounting. To help prevent tilting place a pinpoint of glue on the inner end of each tread just before mounting. The landing at the top can be cut out of the remaining double arced area formed during the drafting exercise on the lightweight illustration board.

LADDERS

Ladders are fortunately an infrequent occurrence in model construction. My experience has been with occasional maintenance access ladders placed vertically against the exterior wall of a manufacturing plant, to the roof of a penthouse structure, or against industrial storage or processing equipment, etc. I have often been fortunate enough to find a casting or stamping to fill the bill. When working at the railroad scales, check out the hobby shops. Even if you have to buy an entire kit to get ladder stock, the price will likely be less than the cost of your time to make it. The next time you order acid-etching (Ch. 17), consider including drawings of ladder stock at various scales to provide a small inventory. Acid-etched material can be stacked to obtain desired thickness, and the stringers can be added to to reflect inset rungs. The swimming pool ladders in Ch. 12 are relatively simple because of the one or two visible rungs, but where you have to make one with numerous rungs you will see why it becomes a sort of nuisance accessory.

At the smaller scales (that is 1/32″ and smaller) hold down two strips of vinyl parallel on double-faced tape (Ch. 35) and add vinyl rungs guided by rung interval parallel lines drawn at right angles to the stringers. Attach the rungs with acrylic cement. Remove the assembly carefully from the tape with a knife blade, turn it over and trim the excess rung lengths with a razor blade as you press down on the joints to prevent breaking. As the scales become larger, drill rung holes in strips of vinyl, acrylic, or strip wood and insert pins or piano wire rungs first finished to flat ended rung lengths using a sizing jig (Ch. 37). You can make metal ladders with rungs soldered between stringers, accepting the hazard of solder lumps to be filed off without breaking joints. Use a hot, pencil iron (Ch. 36) and the best electronic solder preferably with brass stock which heats faster than piano wire. The best joint areas are clean ones requiring little if any flux which tends to spread unwanted solder beyond the joint.

ELEVATORS

Even in interior model work (Ch. 31) elevators are usually hidden from view behind closed doors within enclosing shafts; so they are not a common challenge. If the scene includes the activity creating atmosphere of open elevator doors with people entering and leaving, the model builder is faced with nothing more than a boxed in area behind an opening, with due consideration given to sliding door configuration and overall surface finish and decoration. One modelled type of elevator is the one carrying passengers up the exterior of a building to a penthouse restaurant, for example, where the drama of open space transport is the reason for the exercise. See Ch. 49, photo 35. A solid block of acrylic, polished and "metal" trimmed to specifications makes an excellent cab. This is placed in a slot the sides of which hold the hidden cable system. Scoring can indicate the doors at each floor. If the scale is large enough to justify the effort, make the cab in the form of an acrylic box and include human figures inside. Another visible elevator is one travelling in a square or cylindrical cage up the side of a building under construction to haul workers and materials. Working elevators are touched upon in Ch. 30.

ESCALATORS

Escalators are the moving stairways found in department stores, air terminals, etc. where large numbers of people have to be moved continuously. In the usually static model form, they present no particular structural problems since they can be shown as closed-riser stairs sandwiched between two solid slabs topped with a rounded strip to simulate the moving hand rail. Some systems have opposing escalators side by side. Mill the steps along the hypotenuse of a solid right triangle of acrylic shaped to specifications. Line your wooden effort with vinyl to hide grain. In the absence of a shop mill, you can notch out the steps with a bandsaw and file and sand to finish, or follow one of the procedures mentioned earlier with respect to steps and stairways.

TRAMWAYS

Tramways can be either surface located or aerial. Examples of the first are the San Francisco cable cars and the cable drawn means for travelling up the side of a mountain as to a ski lodge. These are both of the railroad family allowing you to indicate or lay track as suggested in Ch. 13 with a slot between the rails to house the cable. Note that the mountain tramway will likely have cars including seats that are in step configuration to make them level against the steep gradient. Examples of the second type are ski lifts and amusement park aerial rides, both discussed in Ch. 23.

16

Fences, Railings, Screens, and Trellises

FENCES AND RAILINGS

Since there is no convenient clear cut distinction between fences and railings, the terms will be used interchangeably for the purposes of this chapter. They each involve post-and-beam construction and can be protective, decorative, or both.

The criteria necessary to successful model fence and railing construction are straightness of course, uniformity of interval, and verticality of posts. In relation to the whole of a scale model their aspect is almost two–dimensional, and a crooked course or post can spoil the picture just as an obviously crooked line in a rendering can detract the eye from an otherwise attractive scene.

Posts: The primary key to successful installation is creating accurate post holes or mounting centers. If you are mounting fence posts in urethane foam grade, as along a property line, make guides from strips of vinyl with one edge shaped to the course of curves and straight runs and plot centers along this edge. If the posts are piano wire these may be inserted vertically into a urethane base with extra length, obviating the use of glue. Be sure the top ends are flat. To obtain verticality, aid eyeballing

with a jig made from a piece of stripwood with a hole drilled vertically through the end and thickness equal to the height of the posts above grade. Press each post in through the hole until it is flush with the jig. At the larger scales where you might use round or square wooden posts, point the bottom ends evenly to help direct insertion. Disturbing the urethane holes may make gluing mandatory to hold the posts straight. Where the urethane is lined with illustration board, vinyl, or other hard surface paving, with a scribe punch drill-starting indentations along lines drawn on the surface with centers indicated. Small drill bits tend to wander; be sure to punch accurately and hold the hand drill (Ch. 36) *vertical* until the bit just clears the paving. Where you are drilling through paving only in the absence of urethane foam you can take advantage of the under cavity, and push through extra post length to the correct above grade height. Fix with contact glue (or white glue in the case of wood and cardboard) and clean off the excess appearing at the post base. If the liner (paving) is mounted on the plywood base, special care will have to be exercised to drill all holes exactly vertical because of the unadjustable rigidity of the material. Where you cannot use a square broach (Ch. 36) to ream holes for square posts, drill holes just large enough to take the diagonal dimension of the square and fill the gaps at the surface with spackle (Ch. 35).

As a general rule always drill post holes for secure and accurate mounting. If you find an occasional hole out of line as you complete the fence or railing, consider eliminating those holes and clip and sand flat the ground ends of the posts affected, allowing them to rest on the surface. The rigidity of the remaining posts in the ground will likely hold the system securely. This will obviate the mess resulting from trying to redrill or ream the out of line holes.

Some prefab fencing or railing at 1/32" scale can be surface mounted with contact glue on even surfaces. Under some circumstances you may have to surface mount posts. These should have at least 1/8" diameter to provide sufficient contact. Both ends will have to be flat and the lengths sized, requiring a sizing jig (Ch. 37) similar to the one used for the tread spacers of the spiral stairway in Ch. 15. It is sometimes difficult to get these to stand up straight because of minute obstructions of glue or unevenness in sanding. If the posts are mounted on illustration board, don't disturb them with a careless swipe of hand or tool. You may break the top lamination of the surface.

Follow the same principles with railing posts as at the side of steps cut into grade, around a balcony or stair landing, along pedestrian guide lines, etc. Where holes must be drilled close to structures, keep Pattinson's Law in mind to prevent an overhanging eave, for example, locking you out of drilling holes around a balcony edge. Note that where the underside of the railed surface is visible, the posts should be sized and flattened at both ends with the bottom ends pushed in flush with the underside. This will assure maximum purchase provided by the thickness of the railed structure and prevent ragged post ends becoming visible. This same post treatment is necessary where posts are attached to a structure edge as in the case of the outside stairway in Ch. 15. Before gluing these posts in place, file shallow notches on centers to guide correct mounting. When drilling post holes around the top of a building for a parapet railing, consider the material used for the parapet. Make drill bit guide punches in acrylic and when drilling the edge parallel to the surface of illustration board, clamp the board at each hole location before drilling so the bit will remove material and not spread the laminations. Don't try to punch in standard pins for posts or you may cause a bulge at each post location.

Fence and Railing Design: Structural and decorative configurations of fences and railings are so varied that it would be impossible to do any more than scratch the surface in trying to compile a comprehensive list. There are, however, a number of tips to help you solve most problems of execution.

Probably the most frequent fence type presented will be the chain link, consisting principally of wire mesh attached to a pipe frame. These fences are found around industrial property for security and enclosing small industrial areas such as transformer yards. They are found around tennis courts and other sports areas and are used as protective barriers around private residences. They keep Fido in and intruders out as well as prevent the neighbor's kids from falling into your swimming pool. They can hardly be called decorative, but buried in shrubbery they provide an unobtrusive protection. I have found the most reliable supply of mesh to be in brass filter cloth which comes in different size meshes from the hardware store. The smallest holes available may be out of scale and the material will be too thick, but the finished effect is authentic enough to forestall criticism. To reduce any chance of bulkiness, use the bound edge at the top of the fence and omit any pipe framing other than the supporting posts. Cut it to size with scissors following the link rows for a straight line. Spray it with matte aluminum Krylon, being careful not to fill the holes, and attach it to the posts with contact glue or one of the cyanoacrylate glues (Ch. 34). Doors and gateways can be indicated with fine strips of vinyl applied to the surface in the shape of the opening frame. Another source of suitable material can be found sometimes at your favorite department store. For a 1/20" scale model including many tennis courts, I found some rayon elastic braid which served the purpose well. Before cutting it to height, spray it with clear Krylon to prevent unravelling and install it relaxed. Any tension will reduce the width and hence the height of your fence. I have also found hobby shop material prepared for this purpose, but the supply has not been reliable. Check with your local hobby shops, because the material has not been as bulky as the filter cloth.

A serious problem with post and rail fences is the insertion of rails between posts. A top rail of piano wire, for example, can be installed on preinstalled posts with contact glue, but except for very short runs, the entire fence should be assembled off the model, using, in the case of piano wire, soldered joints. Figure 37-4 should help with this. Use a sizing jig for dimensioning the let-in rails after soldering the top rail to the posts. Accuracy here will provide fixed spacing. In a common X frame decorative fence, insert vinyl X's between rails and posts. In any case where you are limited to acceptably out of scale materials, be sure the size relationships between components are correct to prevent visually compounding the problem.

Continuous picket fencing can be assembled off the model by applying strips of vinyl to a top and bottom rail and the whole assembly glued to the installed posts. The pickets will hide the fact that you have not let in the railings as specified. You can further camouflage by leaving out a picket at post locations and applying slightly thicker strips to accentuate the posts.

The so-called Armco road barriers can be simulated with strips of vinyl attached with suitable spacers to stub posts.

Again, do not ignore your hobby shop when you are working in the model railroad scales. Even if you have to buy a whole kit or kits to obtain adequate quantity, you may find just what you are looking for ready to paint and mount. The cost will be far less than the value of your time saved.

Short runs of simply configured railing or fence can be cut from 0.010″ vinyl at the small scales. Use a mat knife and cut with a scoring motion. Particularly if the vinyl is cold, trying to "chop" through the material will sometimes cause the vinyl to chip and ruin your design. In vinyl wider than the fence or railing is high (including post extensions) lay out and cut the interior configurations first and then cut the outside profile. This will avoid fighting the flexibility of rails as you cut them to even size. Mounting the entire vinyl strip on double-faced tape will help hold the fine bridges of the design as you cut out the openings. Starting at one end of the finished product, gradually work it off the tape with a knife edge. At the post locations add vertical strips of vinyl to provide the three-dimensional effect of let-in railings. I confine this method to short runs because it is relatively so time consuming to get consistent widths with straight, even edges.

Another method for longer runs is to mount parallel strips of vinyl cut on your paper cutter (Ch. 36) on double-faced tape and insert vertical spacers slightly narrower than post widths at post locations. Over these spacers attach strips of vinyl of post length with acrylic cement (Ch. 34) to provide mounting depth at the bottom. If both top and bottom rails are let in, extend the tops of these strips the specified distance above the top

rail. When set, carefully peel the assembly off the tape, turn it over and mount matching post strips forming three layer posts. If the posts extend above the top rail, fill with vinyl of rail thickness so that these extensions will appear solid. Do the same to fill the bottom ends. Add cut out vinyl designs between posts, using the slots provided by the narrower than fence post width spacers (the centers of the post sandwiches) as mounting sockets.

Considerably long runs of grapestake fencing present the excessive time consuming task of mounting individual strips of wood or vinyl to a frame. Unless the scale and prominence demand it, I have gotten by successfully with scored vinyl painted with varying intensity of paint to simulate wood. If the frame side is not obvious to the viewer, you may get by with scoring only the front side and just painting the back surface. If the scale is at least 1/4″ or larger, consider the use of hobby shop scored bass wood which comes in various scoring centers and, to my knowledge, a minumum of 1/32″ thick. This will be scored on one side only, and the uniform scoring precludes a natural, split stake appearance. At 1/2″ scale, if time, temper, and dollars are all in tune, assemble splinters from a life-size grapestake on a 2″ × 4″ or pipe frame, and no questions will be asked.

Sloping railings such as those along the sides of steps and stairways present the problem of angle between vertical posts and railings parallel to the rise. When flattening the top ends of the posts, guide them against the adjustable miter slide on your belt sander so that you will have the properly angled surfaces on which to glue or solder the top railing. This means that when you insert the posts they will have to be turned to accepting position.

Most decorative fencing across sloped ground will be stepped so that horizontal assemblies can be mounted with the top railing of one assembly or section lower than that of the section above on higher ground.

When installing railing on posts mounted on a curve, try to establish the approximate radius in piano wire before attaching it to prevent its fighting adhesion at post tops. Obtain sufficient length by dry bending it around the post line before trimming and finishing the ends. Attach one end first with contact glue applied to both surfaces. After fixing the other end held just above the post tops, apply contact glue to post tops and eyeballed locations on the underside of the railing. Let dry and press into place. With the approximate radius bent into the rail this method should result in a stable assembly. Follow a similar procedure with vertical curves as along the sides of an arched bridge.

Wrought iron type fencing and railings with intricate designs are best accomplished through acid-etching (Ch. 17). At 1/32″ scale, I have found fine lace acceptable as balcony railings after checking with my client as to the different designs. Size such material with a light spray of clear Krylon (Ch. 32) to stiffen it.

At a small scale such as 1/32″ you can simulate occasional railings with strips of clear vinyl or acetate. Carefully scribe in the design with a metal scribe and rub on black paint to fill the indentations. Do this on the outside surface only as on the railing for the outside building stairway in Ch. 15. Such faking is generally frowned upon in professional circles, but is acceptable where one or two such structures are incidental to the overall scene. Where such railings are extensive or prominent, acid-etching (Ch. 17) is the only answer, considering relative economics along with the desire for authenticity.

The railing for the spiral stairway in Ch. 15 would probably be attached to the inside surface of the suspending rods with the hand rail separated from the plane of the rods for finger space. Parallel rails could be made from vinyl strips attached to the rods, but because of the curvature, any designed segments should come from your acid-etching source.

Property line fencing can often be eliminated from the model particularly if it is of the chain link type. Other than the fact that it is usually near the edge of the model and susceptible to damage, this functional bit of authenticity can detract from the bird's eye view of the scene. The model is obviously of a specific piece of property the limits of which are evident in the form of streets, planting, etc. Ornamental fencing is justifiably included in deference to design, but security fencing alone can be superfluous along a naturally defining edge of trees and shrubbery. Chain link fencing around athletic areas is a necessary element of the facility, but check with your client before spending the time to place the same fencing along the property line of a small scale model of a large area as that of an amusement park.

SCREENS

Architectural screens are used as sun shades, indoor and outdoor area dividers, visual barriers around mechanical facilities, or simply applied to a bare wall to decorate an otherwise stark area enclosure. They, as well as the trellises discussed later in this chapter, are included here since they involve principles similar to those of railings and fences. You may not be concerned with a line of posts, but you are still faced with modular sections including sometimes intricate designs. The scale, depth, character and intricacy of design, and quantity will determine whether you should build up, cast (Ch. 24), or rely on ready-made materials or acid-etching (Ch. 17).

The larger hardware stores will carry perforated metal sheeting in various designs used as household heating outlet covers, etc. Sometimes one of these can be used as is, or as a basis for further treatment to satisfy model requirements. The basic limitation of lack of depth might be overcome by stacking or making a sandwich. Acceptably representative substitutes, cleared by your client, can often save many hours and outside costs. If it were not for model builder's license, reasonably applied, some models would have to cost far more than they do.

Built-Up Screens: These items will be exemplified by two samples as indicated in Figs. 16-1 and 16-2. Figure 16-1 shows a relatively simple screen made out of wood as an area divider in the entrance landscaping of a commercial building. The scale of the model was 1″ = 1′, making the components easy to handle and assemble. As an assembly guide, a pattern of the screen at model scale was drawn on illustration board flat on a flat table. Eight wooden stops were glued, two at each corner of the drawing, to the illustration board to hold the screen frame. Since all components had the same dimensions except for length, stock strips were cut from clear white pine with a sharp cabinet table saw blade. All pieces were then cut slightly oversize after squaring the end of the stock on the belt sander before each cut. This provided finished ends to place against the stop of a sanding or sizing jig (Ch. 37) to obtain equal group lengths. Note that all right angle corners are mitered to avoid visible end grain which is unsightly and difficult to seal. The frame was made first after all pieces were examined for nicks and splinters, and after finish sanding with fine sand paper with a flat approach to avoid rounding edges. All pieces were assembled dry to be sure of fit before applying white glue sparingly to prevent its oozing out the bottom and sticking to the illustration board. Note that in assemblies of repeated configurations the best control is found in assembling like patterns consecutively to be sure they are the same even though in different locations. In this case each of the four corners has a matching rectangular shape diagonally across the screen. When all pieces have been assembled and have started to set, carefully run a thin spatula under the screen to release any spots where the glue has adhered to the illustration board. Let the screen dry and finish sand both faces with fine sand paper attached to a flat piece of illustration board bigger

than the screen. Before spraying the screen to the specified color, fill the wood with a light spray of clear Krylon (Ch. 32) being careful not to let excess run into the interior corners to spoil the sharp right angle joints.

The second example of a built-up screen is illustrated in Fig. 16-2. This represents a section of a decorative sun shade on the hospital building facade shown in Ch. 49, photo 24. The illustra-

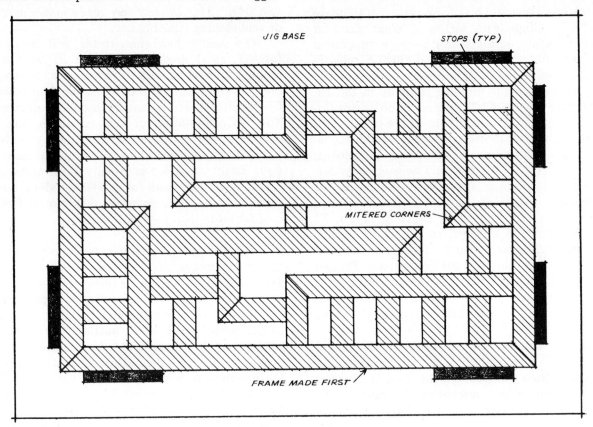

FIGURE 16-1　*Wood screen.*

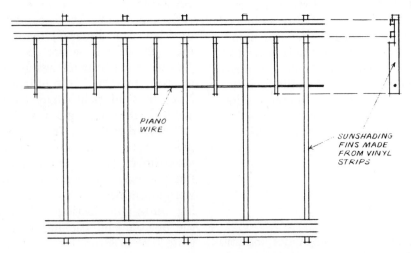

FIGURE 16-2　*Building facade screen.*

tion is larger than the 1/16″ scale of the model to provide easy visualization. The screen was made up of interlocking strips of vinyl of specified thicknesses gang-cut on a shop mill with a piano wire rod holding the ends of the short fins. There is no point in going into more structural details than those shown by the illustration since this is an original design probably never to be repeated. The value of its presentation lies, along with the wooden screen just discussed, in illustrating the varied challenges with which you will be faced. Sometimes even acid-etching (Ch. 17) won't come to the rescue because of many varied planes.

Cast Screens: Architectural screens, whether they are free-standing area dividers or decorative sun shade treatments of building facades are sometimes better cast than built up or acid-etched. The principal reason for this is the relatively large bulk or depth involved in the configuration. Chapter 17 will reveal that intricacy of design is duck soup for the acid-etchers, but this process is practical only where the design is shallow and the surface is generally in one plane. Where thickness varies, where the surface is in varying planes and shapes, or where the bridges are sculptured, and more than one unit is required, the most expeditious route to multiple authenticity and consistency is through casting. This is true even if the casting is confined to certain parts only, thus requiring later assembly. The time consumed in making the master can be considerable; so keep this in mind when making time estimates.

Two very different screens involving plaster casting are illustrated in Figs. 16-3 and 16-4. Figure 16-3 shows a precast concrete unit as one of many

placed as sun shades along the facade of a research center building (Ch. 49, photo 25). They are, in effect, individual window "eyebrows." The scale of the model was 1/16″. As in the case of the second screen (Fig. 16-4), only the casting master will be considered here as it will be used later in Ch. 24 as a mold making subject. The master of the first screen was carved out of white pine, and then sanded and sealed to prevent adherence of mold material. If it is easier for you, carve such forms in two sections, taking advantage of grain direction in each and then glue the sections together, blending and filling the joint with spackle (Ch. 35) to make the assembly monolithic. The resulting plaster castings could, with a bit of dress-up sanding, be left in their natural state to represent white architectural cement.

The one of six modules of an area divider screen (Fig. 16-4) obviously presents some problems of casting the entire assembly because of all the cavities and undercuts. You might make two half-masters as though you sliced the entire module from top to bottom parallel to the faces so that these masters matched perfectly when put together, and then make two molds. This seems extra time consuming and presents precariously thin halves, the delicacy depending somewhat upon the scale. The alternative is to build up the screen of six modules, taking advantage of casting as many components as possible. Other than rectangular framing, there are 60 ellipsoids with three-layer caps top and bottom, and 72 flat, splayed spacers.

Make the screen frame from acrylic to include all six modules. This framing will include the module ends inserted between the two parallel top and bottom strips six modules in length. The

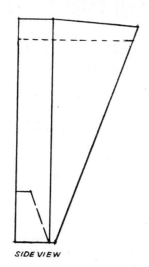 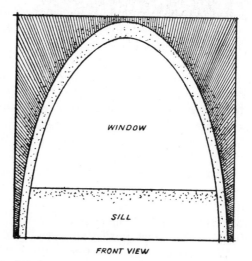

SIDE VIEW   FRONT VIEW

FIGURE 16-3 *Window eyebrow.*

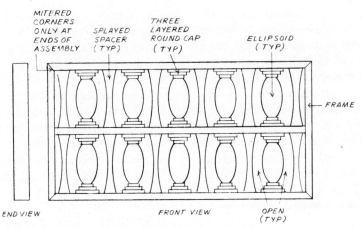

FIGURE 16-4 *Area divider.*

horizontal module dividers are also included, all components being joined with acrylic glue (Ch. 34). Note that mitered joints are not necessary since you are not concerned with grain. Be sure that all components are of the specified length. A sanding (dimension) jig (Ch. 37) will help ensure that all module ends are the same.

In the absence of 60 ellipsoidal beads of acceptable shape and size in your Jay's nest (Ch. 35) or in a local costume jewelry store, these can be cast from a master. Two master caps could each be made from 3 sizes of washer obtained at a hardware store, discs cut from 3 sizes of acrylic rod, punch-outs from a variable die punch, or they could be shaped on a lathe. A splayed spacer master could also be made for casting. For making the master spheroid see Ch. 24. Spray the finished master with clear Krylon to seal it against sticking to the mold material. Attach a contact glue assembled or lathe-formed cap to each end of the ellipsoid being sure that you have secure joints. Contact glue applied to both joining surfaces should be sufficient. Try this assembly for size in several places in the screen frame. If it slips in with a slight pressure it is just right.

An acrylic master of the flat, splayed spacers can be laid out directly on the material since its configuration is formed by two opposing arcs of a circle the radius of which should be in the drawings. You won't need any release treatment for the mold.

As a screen assembly guide, draw parallel lines on a sheet of illustration board to represent alternately spacer and ellipsoid centers, making the lines of any convenient length longer than the screen is high. Repeat these lines until you have enough to cover all six modules of the screen. Temporarily anchor the screen frame over these lines at right angles to them and centered so that ends of each module falls on its centerline. This set up will make it easy for you to eyeball even positioning of the cast parts.

As in the case of the two built-up screens, these two examples of screen assignments where plaster casting comes to the rescue should help inspire your imagination into solutions to the many varied configurations presented in your model building career.

TRELLISES

Though the first image thought of upon hearing the word "trellis" be one of the redwood open frame work attached to a blank wall to encourage a vine or an espaliered pear tree to soften the scene, the term here includes all lattice work. This is found not only for the purposes just mentioned but also as roofing for colonnades and pergolas, building entry canopies, and as the perimeter walls of gazebos or summer houses. It is often found in outdoor screening dividing garden areas or around a service yard. The material used is generally wood in strips of various sizes assembled in simple geometric patterns.

At most of the common scales, the garden vine trellis can usually be made from strips of vinyl painted the specified color. Depending upon scale and prominence, I have found that a suggestion only is necessary since it will be covered with landscaping material.

The roofing for a pergola or colonnade is often constructed with $2'' \times 4''$'s or larger laid with overhang on top of and at right angles to beams connecting the column tops. As an aid in obtaining equal spacing, first place a cross member at each pair of column top centers and then fill in the intervals. Any misplacement will be confined to sections. Place a vertical stop along one side to maintain even overhang. Obtain equal length of cross members with the old workhorse dimension jig (Ch. 37).

A 1/20″ scale lattice residence entrance canopy is an assembly challenge to try the patience of Job, particularly when you have a large number to make. An example is shown along with a description of the assembly jig in Ch. 37.

17

Acid-etching

In spite of the fact that acid etching is but one of many processes and methods found in this profession, it can be, on occasion, such a boon to the model builder that it deserves its own chapter. It logically follows Ch. 16, since by far the greatest application will be found in the items discussed in Ch. 16. See Fig. 17-1 for a few examples.

Unscientifically expressed, the process involves acid eating through metal such as sheet brass, bronze, or stainless steel as allowed by a treated photographic stencil, or photochemical machining. The etching can be done all the way through the material or to a controlled depth. See Appendix for a source.

The uses for this process are limited only by your imagination. Different configurations can be stacked for varying depths of architectural screens, for example, or the same configuration can be stacked simply to obtain greater thickness. If the thickness is greater than a few layers of the acid-etched material, such as a 1/4″ scale area divider, sandwich a core of urethane foam between two pieces of the material exactly opposed and file out the openings. Put contact glue on the etched material only so it won't obstruct and tear the urethane during filing. To accentuate fence posts,

add strips of vinyl on each side of those included in the etching. This will give the effect of railings and decorations of thinner stock than that of the posts. Chapter 16 points out the difficulties in establishing straight and true runs of fencing, and after looking at Fig. 17-1 it becomes obvious how beneficial this outside process can be not only in the saving of time but also in accuracy of result.

To obtain a quote or order an acid-etched supply of a particular railing, etc., submit a drawing clearly showing your requirements and the relationship of the scale of the drawing to the size of the finished product desired. In most cases the drawing should be at a scale larger than the model scale to make it easy for the supplier to interpret. See Fig. 17-2 for an example of such a drawing as submitted with pertinent information. Note that the etchers are not interested in life-size dimensions. The extra post lengths are to allow about 1/8″ below grade for mounting, leaving about 6 scale inches between grade and the bottom rail. This selvage will depend upon the surface in which you are mounting the fence. If it is to be inserted into urethane foam, for example, you should have more for adequate anchorage. You can always trim an excess. You will probably receive the fencing in a 6″ × 12″ sheet

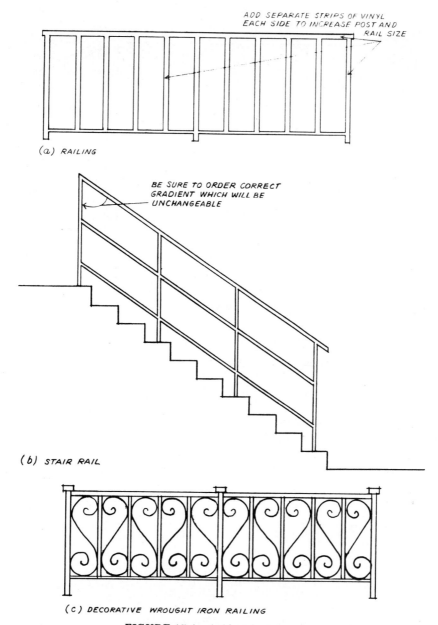

FIGURE 17-1 *Acid etched samples.*

out of which you can cut the length of strips desired; based upon your order of 2 linear feet, you will have a considerable supply left over. This will probably be the minimum order your supplier will accept. Always consider ordering an excess of a common design so that you will have a "free" supply for the next job requiring the same thing since the initial set-up cost is by far the greater part of the price. Figure 17-2 shows a simple design for explanatory purposes. If you have a run of New Orleans wrought iron railing to reproduce, the drawing will take a little extra time, but there is no other way to obtain an authentic result. Remember that

if you have an arched bridge or stair railing, be sure to submit the correct radius or gradient, because you cannot vertically bend the finished product to fit.

Relative to the cost of standard model materials and outside services, this is an expensive process; you won't be calling your acid-etchers every time you need a couple of inches of railing. If your accumulated supply of overruns does not have exactly what you need, a substitute may be acceptable. Keep track of each order with a filed sample so that you can reorder a particular design at a cost far less than the first run which contained the set-

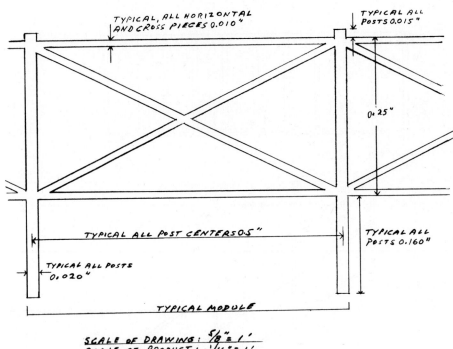

FIGURE 17-2 *Sample drawing.*

up charges. Find out from your suppliers how long they keep the stencils. When the drawings show a large amount of intricate railing or screen, point out to your client that you are including provision for acid-etching in your proposal as not only the best means for obtaining consistent authenticity but also the most economical considering the quantity that would otherwise have to be handmade.

18

Floors and Walls

Model floors and walls are structurally so closely interdependent that they are included together in one chapter. In a modern high-rise building, the walls may be simply hung on or set back from floor edges of a structure which depends upon internal steel and concrete geometry for its strength, rigidity, and durability. The building would stand without the walls. In the box method of model building, the continuous walls constitute the building itself with perhaps only occasional hidden floors serving to support the walls vertically and maintain building shape. In the sandwich method the wall segments between floors could be the only support for the latter. As in all model construction, establishing concepts in relation to the life-size subject will help you to organize efficiently your approach to an assignment. The more efficiency, the more time saved, and the larger will be the black bottom line of your profit and loss statement at the end of the year.

Multistory structures are the introductory examples here since having mastered their assembly, subjects with one or a few floors and accompanying lesser expanses of walls will, in general, present no new problems of the floor to wall relationships.

FLOORS

Floors are obviously "traffic ways" and as such could have been covered in Ch. 13 or Ch. 14. They are set out here as a separate subject because of their generally repetitive installation within the confines of buildings and because they are so often used by the model builder merely as hidden elements to help hold a model together. Based upon the premise that most of your model work will be of an exterior nature, by far the majority of floors will be installed for structural purposes only. As long as they are not seen, they neither have to be of scale thickness nor have finished surface treatment. The only prerequisites are that they be made of rigid material strong enough to do their supporting job and that they be placed at correct floor intervals so that the edges will not be seen. Though it is probably safe to say that because of cores, partitions, and solar or reflective fenestration no building is transparent, be alert for see-through areas such as that between exactly opposite ground floor entrances and exits. If the scale is large enough to permit an obvious view of the lobby, its floor may require some authentic treatment. At 1/16″ scale where a viewer has to "stand on his or her head" to see through the building, some neutral color will probably suffice. When in doubt, set up a quick dummy assembly for eyeballing to help you determine the extent of interior detail required. A building constructed using the sandwich method where the floors extend beyond the glass line for balconies or sun control and the fenestration is clear glass some interior treatment obviously will have to be considered. This is especially true if the building is to be lighted (Ch. 29).

Floor Materials: These should be rigid, not subject to warping, and provide clean, sharp, edges. I have found Masonite, illustration board, and acrylic to be satisfactory materials, their use depending upon the type of model. In a sandwich building at 1/16″ scale, 1/8″ Masonite will give a sharp 2′ thick edge. Be sure that the material is smooth on both sides. The untempered product may have a "waffle" surface on one side. I like illustration board because it is stiff enough to hold even over moderate expanses, is easy to cut with a mat knife, holds a fine edge with careful handling, and has a good painting surface. Lightweight illustration board can be laminated to obtain scale thicknesses in 1/16″ increments. Acrylic is good for lighted ceilings (Ch. 29). For more on materials see Ch. 35. At scales of 1/32″ or less, that old work horse high impact sheet vinyl comes to the rescue.

Floor Sizing: A very important consideration is the duplication of floors of exactly the same size and shape. Purely structural floors must hold the building box true from top to bottom, and visual floor edges must line up perfectly. One out of line will cause an obvious blot on the landscape. As a general practice make the first floor as a pattern to be traced for all the rest. When laminating illustration board, glue a pattern floor to an oversize piece of the next layer with contact glue applied to both surfaces and carefully trim with a mat knife to the pattern edges. Finish the assembly with hand sanding if necessary. Always be careful not to disturb the laminations of the illustration board itself. To hide obvious joints not covered by painting, line the edges with vinyl, adjusting size to allow the added thickness if considerable. One way to get final trueness is to bolt the stack of floors together with pieces of 1/4″ steel screw stock (Ch. 35) (as long as the two holes in each floor will not disturb an interior view) and run all four sides against your

belt sander. An even few thousandths undersize is better than jagged floor edge profiles.

Decorative Edges: It would of course be futile to try to discuss all possible configurations, and hopefully you will not be faced with "Corinthian" profiles, but a few tips may lead your imagination toward at least simulation of complicated shapes. A right-angled stepped edge can be accomplished by running the floor vertically through your table saw with a different setting for each run. Be sure to run each floor through at each setting to maintain consistency. Avoid illustration board which has a tendency to be fuzzed up by the blade. Another method is to laminate the floor with different sizes of material to create the steps. A concave edge can be accomplished by filling a slotted edge with spackle or plaster and "troweling" it with a piece of acrylic formed to the specified radius. Attach a stop on each side of the trowel to control depth. Be sure plaster will adhere to the floor surface. Coat the groove with a light coat of white glue (Ch. 34) as you apply plaster if there is any doubt. Rounded, convex edges can be made with halfround bass wood from your hobby shop supplier (Ch. 35). Some more complicated edges can be simulated with a scribe or dental tools (Ch. 36) in wet plaster, an arduous and time consuming process. When you are confronted with an ogee or more complicated molding type edge, and the scale justifies the effort, consider carving a few inch master out of white pine or bass wood and casting it (Ch. 24). The master should include one complete module of decoration to simplify the operation. Cut the floor edges back far enough to allow plaster strips deep enough to avoid breaking during installation. To hide the joint between applied castings and the floor material, consider lining at least the visible floor surface with a bond paper so that its edge becomes a part of the decoration. A beaded edge can be made with uniform beads strung on nylon thread wrapped around the floor edge formed in a convex shape mentioned previously. A right-angle notched edge can be made by gang-cutting strips of acrylic indexed on a shop mill. See Ch. 49, photo 37 for an example of a configured floor edge.

The foregoing tips apply literally only where the scale is large enough to justify the time expended. As the scales become smaller, rely upon your model builder's license to apply your skills of suggestion (Ch. 3) down to the point where no decoration at all need be shown. As always in such situations draw upon your good judgment as to what extent you should go in obtaining authenticity. Unless you know your clients, point out any limitations to execution so that they will not be disappointed. You are likely to find designers whose architectural decoration is their star of the show!

As an exemplary exercise, assume you have a 1/16″ scale exterior display model to build of a high-rise office building (Fig. 18-1). The building is to be constructed on a raised pad to form an entry court and pedestrian traffic way at first floor level all around and to help accommodate underground parking and form a setting. Detail dimensions will not be given since numbers would unnecessarily confuse the issue, but for the sake of establishing concept, the building will have 40 floors and a utility penthouse on the roof. The rectangular shape of the model will measure

9-1/4″ × 13-1/4″ and will be approximately 30″ high. To aid your concept refer to Ch. 49, photo 34, realizing that this example is not specifically pictured. For future reference this model will be labeled HR 1.

The exterior walls are in effect to be of bronze solar glass in one vertical plane from ground floor to top of parapet with anodized aluminum spandrels at floor levels and an opaque cap applied to the glass plane at the top to terminate columns similar to those in the photo referred to. All floor edges are contained; the box method of construction is called for. To get the most use out of this subject (HR 1), a variation of conditions will be cited to show how prior planning (Ch. 6) is necessary to establishing the most efficient use of materials and methods. Of immediate interest here, such planning will help decide whether structural floors are needed or not, and if so, how many. If

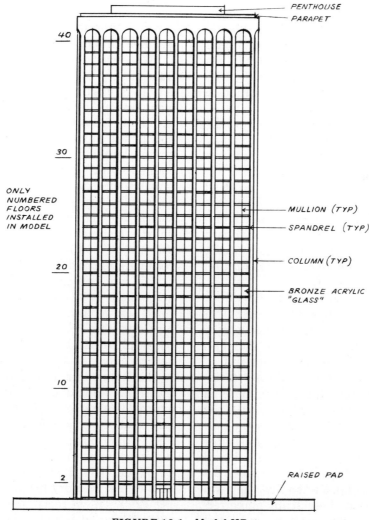

FIGURE 18-1 *Model HR 1.*

the building is to be electrically lighted, that will require construction peculiar to such a facility. Lighting will be discussed in Ch. 29; this edition of HR 1 will not be lit. Considering the height of the model, what provision must be made to prevent disaster when the model is jolted or tipped? The answer is the tie-down rods discussed in Ch. 19. Should 1/16″ or 1/8″ bronze acrylic be used? Both boxes with good welded corner joints would stand rigidly by themselves, the 1/8″ walled one more securely with its almost 0.090″ additional welding surfaces at the 45 degree mitered corners. Since the corners of HR 1 are not column-wrapped to help the welds (as they are in the photo previously referred to), relying solely on corner welds with 1/16″ acrylic would be a bit precarious to say the least. One accidental whack with a janitor's broom handle in the display area could snap the joints open. But since there are no fins or projecting mullions for which to cut mounting grooves and weaken the thinner 1/16″ acrylic and some wrap-around security in the building cap, it is decided to use the lighter material and fasten the walls to structural floor edges to back up the corner welds. If less extensively, this should be done also with 1/8″ acrylic as added insurance in a 30″ high structure with little or no corner reinforcement.

Returning to Model HR 1 in addition to the ground floor and the roof it is decided to install the second, tenth, twentieth, thirtieth, and fortieth floors as structural members for security. Note that this choice is arbitrary. There are no fixed formulae. It is simply a matter of taking advantage of all reasonable bracing allowed under the circumstances. On the heavy weight illustration board ground floor pad already installed on the model, locate the building position with corner orientation marks and complete the surface treatment (Ch. 33). Extend the treatment over the building first floor area if for no other reason than to kill any light reflection off the white surface. The bronze acrylic walls will thwart any casual peeping Toms trying to see into the lobby. Make a pattern floor out of heavyweight illustration board and cut the remaining four floors to match out of the same material so that they will all just slip horizontally into the bronze acrylic box building. Assuming for the purposes of this example a central rectangular elevator and utility core, cut strips of illustration board (heavyweight) wide enough to fill the spaces between structural floors and placed so that they will be behind spandrels. From these strips make rectangular frames to form core sections and paint them as well as the floors with a mat brown paint

to forestall any possible reflection. Locate a core outline on one of the floors and gang-drill two holes along the longer center axis as far apart as possible within the core area but still within the interior perimeter of the penthouse which will cover the nuts on the tops of the tie-down rods (Ch. 19). Center one of the floors within the building location on the ground floor pad and trace the holes. The roof will be taken care of separately since it will be of a size different from that of the floors. Center the appropriate core frames on the top and bottom surfaces of the second floor and glue in place with white glue. On the top surfaces of the tenth, twentieth, thirtieth, and fortieth floors do the same with their sections of core. The one on the fortieth floor should reach the level of the underside of the roof. To assemble these subassemblies into one floor–core assembly, glue them together on a table top with the floor edges backed up against a stop as in Fig. 18-2. Note that a slightly out of line core section will not be seen, but that it is very important to get all floor edges lined up for true insertion into the building.

Whenever there is a chance of objectionable transparency of a building particularly where clear acrylic is used, the assembly just discussed can be made opaque by inserting black matte finished fins extending from the corners of the core to the corners of the building. With little or no corner cover on the building facades, be sure the fins are thin enough to fit snugly into these corners and not reveal their edges. This floor–core assembly will be installed in the building under "Walls" to be discussed later in this chapter. Note that the anticipated attachment of floor edges to walls is through the use of contact glue. Where you have facade configuration to hide the heads such as the columns in this case you can drill holes through the acrylic at locations to be covered and insert small, countersunk screws, brass escutcheon pins, or common pins into the floor edges. Illustration board floor edges will satisfactorily take the common pins only, and be sure that the holes are opposite the center of the floor edges. For screws and escutcheon pins, illustration board floors should be made with an added framing of white pine or bass wood, being sure that the spandrels will hide the greater thickness. Notch out, punch, or drill relief in the backs of the columns to accept the pin heads.

Model HR 2 will designate a 1/16″ scale example of a 15-story headquarters building measuring 12″ × 18″ in rectangular plan. The floor edges extend beyond the glass wall line for sun control, calling for the sandwich method of construction.

This building type is illustrated in Ch. 49, photo 38. The building is to be erected on grade with a perimeter walkway all around and is to be modelled with display quality showing exterior only. Since the glass is clear, provision will have to be made to prevent transparency by painting the entire floor surfaces between core and glass line a matte black and by fins to the corners as mentioned previously. This building could well be built on the model site since there are not two separate assemblies involved as with model HR 1. The 2′ thick floors should be made from 1/8″ acrylic or Masonite for rigidity and scale of the visual floor edges. The core sections in this case can be of any convenient size since they will not be seen, but consider distribution of floor support along with the glass. If the building is to be tied down with rods (Ch. 19) there should be some support near these rods so that cinching down the building will not create a swayback situation. If you are relying on glue only, place solid blocks within the core sections to provide gluing surfaces in addition to the top edges of core frames and window walls. These blocks can be made from scraps of model base framing.

Make the floors to agree with a pattern floor as made for model HR 1. Here fit is not important, but the vertical line up of edges is just as important as the fit in the model assembled using the box method. There is a single line of columns through the floor extensions in this building; gang-drill holes there for on your drill press. If the columns are square, the holes should be broached to accept them unless you feel you can satisfactorily fill the curved edge cavities. When broaching be sure that you control the insertion of the bit so that one side of each square hole is parallel to the floor edge otherwise the column will be cocked at an angle. The reason for installing continuous columns is to ensure line up which is frustratingly difficult to do with separate column pieces between floors, not to speak of the mess that can be encountered when trying to slide in column sections with wet glue on each end. The walls will be box frames made from acrylic as described later in this chapter under "Walls". The violation of Pattinson's Law here is committed to expedite tips on floor laying. Using the floor pattern punch mark and drill holes in the ground floor pad to take the bottom column ends which will help to anchor the building thus obviating the use of tie-down rods unless you want the added assurance of stability during anticipated shipment. From your column stock (either square brass or hardwood round dowel (Ch. 35)) cut four columns long enough to give you selvage to press into

the ground floor pad when tapping the tops down flush with the roof surface upon completing assembly. Against the bottom of each floor and the roof, glue an acrylic wall frame. Use contact glue at the top corners only of each frame, pressing it in correct position against its ceiling. Let each wall frame and floor set long enough so that they will stay together and then line up the wall edges visually by dry-stacking the floors horizontally against a stop as you did for the floor–core assembly in Fig. 18-2. Do this with the floors in the same sequence as on the building site. Tap one of the four cut columns into each of the four corner holes in the ground floor through the corresponding holes in the second floor after mounting the core frame (and blocks, if necessary). Mount the core frame (and blocks) on the second floor and press and tap down the third floor and wall over the guiding four columns. Do this to and including the roof. Slightly chamfer the leading edges of each column and add a little soap for lubrication. Tap each one through its holes starting with the roof. Take your time. A snug slip fit will tend to cause galling. If galling builds frustration to the boiling point, forget the sledge. A solution will be found under "Galling" in Ch. 22. The columns will have to be painted after installation since assembly would scrape the paint off and make them harder to push through the holes. Depending upon the specified roof texture (Ch. 33), the column tops may be punched just below the surface and the holes filled with spackle and sanded flush, or you could cover the entire roof with bond paper or a sheet of vinyl inset slightly from the roof edges. A gravel roof will cover a multitude of sins (Ch. 20).

Warped Floors: Warped floors such as those sometimes found in parking structures are best formed with thin materials which will easily conform to supportive blocking or framing configurations. I speak only of considerable, obvious warping short of the definite ramping as covered in Ch. 15 but more evident than the usual slight drainage warping found in parking lots which is camouflaged by model scales and therefore not worth effecting. To obtain a 1/8″ thickness, for example, it is better to mount a single layer of lightweight illustration board first and then laminate with a second layer of the same material than it is to try to make heavy-weight illustration board conform with 0.030″ vinyl added to bring to thickness. If you should run into what I call a roller coaster situation, soak chip board (Ch. 35) in water and tack it down over the structural form (Ch. 24). When dry, brush on

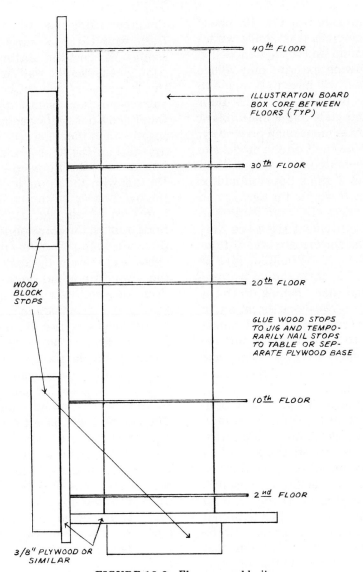

FIGURE 18-2 *Floor assembly jig.*

plaster to cover and fill unwanted depressions, sanding the plaster smooth. If floors of similar shape are supported on columns above the ground floor, make the supporting shape as a separate element off the model until you have all floors formed. Spray the dried chip board forms with clear Krylon to seal them where only occasional support is anticipated. Papier mache and fiberglass methods are not considered here since you won't be confronted with anything more precipitous than a rolling situation.

Small Scale Floors: These can be indicated by the use of Chart-Pak or similar tape or vinyl applied as spandrels. In a 1/100″ scale model of an industrial park, for example, the floors in a high-rise building can be indicated by warping 1/32″ tape around a polished block of acrylic. The extra width could represent spandrels. For more realistic effect, laminate polished acrylic building shapes with 0.020″ vinyl to show cantilevered floors or those ending at the wall plane depending upon the design. When assembling buildings for a 1/32″ scale model make hidden floors thicker than scale to provide maximum gluing or welding edge surfaces. At open entry ways, notch back the floor to give the impression of continuation of grade into the building.

Balconies: Balconies could also be considered raised traffic ways (Ch. 14) but are included here because they are usually extensions of the floors which they serve. Interior balconies such as that in the bank lobby containing the spiral stairway discussed in Ch. 15 can be floors unto themselves, but by far the greater number presented as model subjects will be those on the exteriors of buildings. Whether they are separately applied to the building exterior or formed by floor extensions similar to the overhangs in model HR 2 discussed in this chapter will depend upon scale, size, and quantity. Balconies are sometimes formed by cavities in the exterior wall enclosed on three sides creating ceilinged areas with the open parapet or railing side extending very little if any beyond the facade of the building. Balconies around the corner of a building or extending along one side could call for a combination of box and sandwich construction. The walls of the box would terminate at the ends of the balconies which would be projecting tongues of the floors sandwiched between their own separate wall sections. Depending upon the feasibility of hidden internal support in an exterior model, the balconies could be separate strips extending inside just far enough to be held by a vertical strip of material holding their inside edges. This would obviate installing every floor. Single balconies (one for each apartment) in a high-rise apartment complex are best applied to the exterior walls. With a few floors, the cutting and notching out of extending balcony floors in sandwich construction is generally not too grossly time consuming and the balconies are automatically lined up, but in the case of many floors, forget it! To help install the balconies temporarily affix strip guides vertically with the floor levels marked. Horizontal trueness can often by eye-balled, but with multibalconied facades use horizontal guides also. If the balconies are enclosed by solid parapets and the scale is small (1/32″), consider making T shape vinyl forms and bending the top bar of the T to form the enclosure.

WALLS

Walls are generally vertical structural elements erected for the purposes of enclosing, protecting, and defining areas, as well as acting as structural supports for elements within the areas. They are usually described as to constituent material used rather than as to shape. An exception would be a "battered" wall with a truncated triangular shape in cross section. This shape is often used in the case of earth filled dams, for example, to provide strength and stability. Walls can be described as to their use, such as retaining wall to contain a slide-prone earth bank along a freeway cut. There are crenellated, turreted, and buttressed walls which indicate types of configuration, but unless you are confronted with an historical model of some medieval cathedral or of a fort for the French Foreign Legion, you are not likely to be as concerned with structural profile as you are with surface treatment (Ch. 33). As to constituent materials, there are walls of stone, brick, concrete block, wood frame and plaster, glass, etc., each one described by the material used. But here again the model builder is mostly concerned only with size and authentic appearance. Requirements for building a model wall by laying scale bricks, for example, are so remote that construction tips on the subject are omitted.

Wall executions in scale are as varied as the possible number of different architectural and structural treatments would indicate. Some of the basic structural methods will be described here with no attempt to cover all the possible results of designer madness.

Wall Materials: Wall materials in model building fortunately do not have to be as varied as they are in life-size construction. Acrylic, illustration board, wood, and vinyl are the model builder's mainstays. The key to variation is surface treatment. Acrylic is useful where large glass areas are called for as in the case of high-rise office buildings. It can be used in many situations where the walls are made opaque by surface treatment, with the windows masked off during the treatment to show fenestration that can be surface framed and mullioned. It can be used wherever a smooth surface is called for as in the case of reinforced concrete retaining walls, garden walls, etc. It is indispensable for transparent study situations where opaqueness would hide the main subject. Examples of this use are transparent partitions in an interior arrangement study model and in transparent buildings included for mass relationship studies where the feature of the model must not be hidden from view. Solid blocks of acrylic are excellent for small scale study models where polished surfaces can be left unpainted or otherwise covered to indicate fenestration. *Illustration board* makes a fine plain plaster surface as is, or a concrete block garden wall with paint and scoring. You can laminate illustration board with acid-etched material (Ch. 17) to form special surface treatments, or add plaster to "rough it up" at the larger scales. It is easy to cut for window openings, and holds rigidity over most model expanses. *Wood* is useful at small scales where solid sheets of bass wood can be used for walls requiring wood surfacing. The fine grain obviates worry about out of scale markings. I have used scored 1/32″ bass wood for the walls of 1/20″ scale private dwellings in a real estate development. This was obtained already scored from a model supply house to simulate the actual scored plywood used in the project. Bass wood or white pine are good for filler material in building up wall thickness at the larger scales and of course for showing uncovered framing in a residential structural model. *Vinyl* can be used for walls at the smaller scales such as 1/32″ where its rigidity, almost automatic sharp edges, easy window cutability, and easy joining are of great advantage. The mirrored walls found as the exterior skin of commercial buildings can be satisfactorily simulated with mirrored acrylic which is discussed in Ch. 33.

Returning to model HR 1, the floor–core assembly having been made, the next step is to construct the walls of the box out of 1/16″ bronze acrylic. Leave the masking paper on to prevent scratching until you have to remove it to effect the facade treatment. With a sharp plastics blade on your table saw set to 45 degrees, cut the four building sides to specified width (in this example two at 9-1/4″ and two at 13-1/4″). Take it *slowly* and steadily to prevent chipping. When you have cut one edge of each of the four oversize pieces, run each pair through with the same setting against the bridge so that they will match exactly. With flat, square bottom edges, cut the tops flat and square at a height equal to the overall height of the building less the sum of the height of the parapet plus the thickness of the roof (say 1/4″). See Fig. 18-1. The top of the acrylic will then form a ledge against which to cinch down the roof (Ch. 19).

Aided by temporary masking tape to hold the assembly together, make a dry run assembly test to be sure that the walls will fit snugly around the prepared floor–core assembly. If the box dimensions are correct, sand or shim the floor edges to fit if necessary. Peel off the masking paper from the outside surfaces of the acrylic walls and lay them out on a flat, clean surface with the three adjoining edges in building sequence. At 1/16″ scale 9-1/4″ represents 148′ and 13-1/4″ represents 212′; so with 16′ column centers, there will be ten and fourteen 4′ square columns on the narrow and wide sides of the building respectively. The outside edges of the first and last column along each side of the building will fall at the edges of the acrylic, forming in effect a notch at each corner of the building. With a steel scribe score the acrylic building sides 2′ (1/8″) in from the edges from top to

bottom and then lay out and score the 16′ (1″) centers in between. Between these column center indications make *light* scores from top to bottom as mounting guides for the mullion strips (Ch. 21). Lightly scribe horizontally across all walls, which are lined up together as previously mentioned, the bottom edge indication of all the spandrels. One by one, tack weld with acrylic cement one end of each vinyl mullion at the top of the wall and hold down selvage at the bottom with a weight or masking tape so that the strip follows its score line. Holding down the mullion with a scribe point as you proceed, carefully wick in acrylic cement the entire length. Be careful not to get cement on the acrylic outside of the mullion. Only practice will tell you how much to have on your brush with each application. See Ch. 34. When all mullions have been installed, lay out the spandrels made from matte black vinyl one by one. These could be 4′ (1/4″) wide and 4″ (0.020″) thick. Tack down one end, and with a razor blade cut out the section of mullion and remove it where the spandrel crosses. Retack snapped loose ends of mullions as you go. The reason for lining up the walls in sequence is to be sure the spandrels will meet at the corners ensuring consistent location all around the building. When all the spandrels have been welded down, trim all ends at the wall edges back 4′ (1/4″), and cut out 1/4″ sections centered on the column scores. This is so the columns will rest flat against the acrylic from top to bottom. In other words, you have cut the spandrels into the mullions and the columns into the spandrels. Check the ground floor end of the walls to be sure you have indicated with vinyl strips any door headers or other entrance configurations.

Continuing with exemplary assumptions of dimensions, make the building cap from 3/16″ acrylic and laminate on the outside surface 1/16″ acrylic to form the parapet. The cap and parapet assembly will appear to wrap around the building with 45 degree joints at the corners, thus giving strength to the corner wall joints. It, along with the columns, will be faced with "granite" treated 0.010″ vinyl (Ch. 33). Don't final trim the cap and parapet pieces until you can fit them around the assembled building.

From the sequential arrangement of the four walls at the mullion and spandrel location, pick two adjacent walls and stand them up at right angles against a right angle jig made from 1″ × 2″ framing stock tacked to the table. The point of the jig's joint should be flattened so that it does not project into the corner being welded. Hold the two walls against this jig with weights so that the 45 degree edges meet tightly and squarely. During any acrylic welding exercise, keep everything away from the immediate location of the joints so that the cement will not wick out over the material being joined. Remedial procedures are given in Ch. 34. Holding the tops of the walls together with your fingers, wick in with a brush enough acrylic cement so that it will run as far as possible down the joint. Keep doing this against the corner and along the vertex inside until you have filled as much of the joint as possible. The perfect joint is hard to attain because once the wicking has stopped you cannot get any more cement beyond it. I would accept an 80 percent weld as a good one, and it should be possible to get more with such thin acrylic. Let this assembly set before moving it and do the same thing to the other two walls. Carefully brush on contact glue back of the spandrel locations where the structural floors will be joined and do the same around the edges of all the floors. When dry, stand up one of the wall pairs and press in the floor–core assembly into the right angle. Then press the other pair of walls into place and cement the acrylic joints. Except at the top and bottom you won't be able to apply cement inside because the floors are now in the way, but the holding power of the contact glue will make up for any lost weld. Clamp the cap and parapet strips level at the right location and draw a razor blade against the bottom edges to cut the mullion ends being lapped. Remove the cap pieces and snap off the excess mullion ends. If you got a good weld you may have to do a bit of scraping to get them off. When all the cap area on the walls has been cleared, finally fit the cap so that the 45 degree joints meet exactly. Clamp the cap pieces in place and attach them to the walls by wicking in acrylic cement. Pattinson's Law has been violated again by not applying the granite facing before installation. This treatment (of 0.010″ vinyl in this case) is discussed in Ch. 33.

The next exercise on the agenda is to make the roof out of 1/4″ acrylic (or Masonite) to hold rigid against the pressure of the tie-down nuts (Ch. 19). Cut the material so that it just slips into place inside the parapet. Using the marked hole locations on the ground floor as a guide, drill two holes in this roof to accept the tops of the tie-down rods (Ch. 19). Make the penthouse out of illustration board, pencil trace (or scribe trace in the case of acrylic) the exterior profile in place on the roof, and paint it the specified color along with the inside of the parapet. Except for the

columns (Ch. 22), the granite and roof treatments (Ch. 33) and the tie-down system (Ch. 19) model HR 1 has been assembled.

The window walls for model HR 2 assembled using the sandwich method are made from strips of clear 1/16″ acrylic welded together with 45 degree corners in the same manner used for model HR 1. Before welding the strips to form the window walls between floors, lay out the strips in groups vertically for each side of the building so that mullion installation will be lined up floor to floor. Any horizontal members should also be installed so that they meet at the corners.

There are two variations in procedure worth mentioning with respect to facade treatment of high rise buildings such as that represented by model HR 1. Without confusing the prose with dimensional figures, assume that instead of the columns there were vertical fins projecting from the glass plane from top to bottom. These fins could be made in the form of vinyl strips of a thickness nearest to scale welded to the acrylic wall. To provide a secure mounting in a straight line, cut grooves at the specified centers in the acrylic wall and make the vinyl strips wider than scale by the depth of the groove. Use a jeweler's saw blade a couple of thousandths oversize so that the strips will easily slip into the grooves. If you had planned to use 1/16″ acrylic for the walls, consider the possibility that the grooving will seriously weaken the strength of the walls. A guiding groove need provide no more than a certain mounting location, but you would be ensuring sufficient rigidity by using 1/8″ acrylic instead. For an adjustable sliding square as an aid in cutting the grooves see Ch. 36 under that title. If there are also horizontal sun shades, you might have to make grooves at right angles to the fin grooves necessitating cutting in either the fins or sun shades to form the egg-crate configuration. The other basic variation involves painting the spandrels on the back of the acrylic to provide the often used continuous glass surface of the facade. This means that you have to lay the walls on their faces and mask the window openings before painting. Sometimes the spandrels will be defined by raised frames on the exterior surface requiring grooving as mentioned previously. Use 1/16″ acrylic if possible to hold any visible distortion (because of distance between painted spandrel and "glass" surface) to a minimum. Also consider using the pin or screw attachment of wall to structural floor edges (if the heads can be hidden) because the glue on the spandrel will tend to remove the paint. If you are stuck with the glue (no pun intended), apply contact glue with as few swipes of the brush as possible to the painted surface and let it completely dry on both surfaces before attaching the walls to the floors. Press the joints together once and leave alone. If the Gods are with you, your spandrels will not be destroyed. The use of 1/8″ acrylic for the walls might obviate the use of structural floors, relieving you of the nervous strain caused by the paint-glue combination. This situation is expressive of the frequent need for compromise determined only by your best judgment based upon experience.

Admittedly not being able to "cover the waterfront" in one book, I will skip to the other end of the spectrum and submit some tips on constructing the many different buildings for a 1/32″ scale model of a theme amusement park. "Theme" indicates different eras of history or different locations on the earth, calling for different architecture indigenous to time or place. No part of any building can be duplicated. I will concentrate on walls, a subject of this chapter, which are after all the main backdrop for architectural configuration and decoration. Floors as a subject have been discussed, and roofs will be discussed in Ch. 20.

What is the most expeditious way to accomplish say two dozen different buildings? They could be made in block form using wood or acrylic, but the time consumed in carving the many shapes, finishing the surfaces, and providing for a feeling of depth at openings and behind windows are some of the objections to that method. Furthermore this is to be a display model requiring all detail reasonable at the scale; so the only solution is to build them wall by wall. Because of minuteness of parts and because of difficulty in reaching sites on the model base, these buildings are best constructed on a work table and then mounted complete. As a compromise between the largest welding edge surface and ease of cutting, cut the floors out of 0.020″ vinyl, notching out behind openings at grade to indicate level access. Cut the floors at their interior profile, and separately affix each floor with a spot of contact glue to a small holding base of heavyweight illustration board on which the building will be built. A good material for all walls is 0.015″ vinyl. With thin clear vinyl or acetate attached behind window openings, this would reveal approximately a 5″ deep frame and sill, but model builder's license in this case will not grossly violate visual authenticity. From experience this possibly out of scale element would not even be noticed except by a critical engineering analyst. On a

scrap slab of urethane foam mill out or cut on your table saw a series of parallel grooves to serve as a quickie wall stock rack. As you need a certain height of wall, cut matte vinyl strips and store the unused portions in grooves labeled with the life-size widths so you can use them on later buildings as particular widths repeat themselves. Hold a wall section snugly against its floor mounted on its holding pad as you wick in acrylic cement with a small brush (as you did when assembling the walls of model HR 1). Use butt joints, generally making the front walls lap the ends of the side walls. Save painting by brush until all walls have been assembled. The colors will vary so much that there is no point in trying to paint stock, and any paint falling on a joint surface will prevent welding. Where there are columns (Ch. 22), hopefully you can add a 0.015″ slab to the bottom of the floor extended to the limits of an entry pad, etc. to accept the column bases. On grade this would create about a 5″ step riser. When all walls have been installed with required added configurations, and all windows are in, remove the building from its holding pad with a knife blade and fit it on its site to check for correct mountability when the building has been completed with roof. You can add the roof at this point or wait until all buildings have been walled. The important consideration is the establishment of some sort of routine which will speed up accomplishment.

Retaining Walls: Retaining walls against a possibly unstable embankment are usually of reinforced concrete and serve an important functional purpose without decoration or esthetic shape. They can be modelled with acrylic, illustration board or vinyl, depending upon the scale of the model. If the finished grade is the top surface of urethane foam, they can be inserted into the foam to the correct depth with no concern for fitting to ground configuration. In the case of vertical control of grading (Ch. 9), they should be anticipated and base mounted to assure level tops. Curves of large radii can be brace-mounted into shape using illustration board or acrylic can be heat formed (Ch. 24). The retaining wall at the toe of the slope on the edge of the parking lot in model B (Fig. 9-7) represents a type that could be made out of reinforced concrete block with an architectural cap and just high enough to define an improved area with the secondary purpose of preventing debris from encroaching. A sea wall is another example of a retaining wall to keep wave action from eroding land's end.

Space Walls: Space walls include all those whose purpose is neither to retain or support. They include privacy and security walls around property and decorative space dividers as in a garden. They are often capped with contrasting materials and can be perforated in decorative fashion. As mentioned previously, the constituent material is reflected in surface treatment by the model builder (Ch. 33). Construction using one of the materials noted previously is the subject here. Perforations can be accomplished by drilling and filing to square openings. Walls down a slope may be stepped, maintaining level tops of each section. These may be made by cutting the steps out of continuous material or by installing separate sections where the joints can be accepted. Gradual curves can be executed by bending vinyl as it is inserted into urethane foam, by laminating chip board as indicated under "Warped Floors" or by heat forming acrylic (Ch. 24). Relatively small radius planting alcoves can be formed with pieces of tubular items such as brass or cardboard tubing, or at small scales simply by bending pieces of vinyl with round jawed pliers. Columns appearing in the system are usually best effected by adding material on each side of the wall at their locations and filling any overlap at the top. This avoidance of breaks in the wall course will obviate joints and make your installation more stable.

Wall Thicknesses: Thicknesses in scale are important only where the top of the wall is seen and may have to be effected by laminating or hollow door construction at the larger scales. In exterior models of structures, the thickness generally need be only that sufficient for strength and rigidity, but in models of interiors scale wall thickness becomes important, as it is with space walls just discussed. For this reason it is a good idea to memorize thicknesses of standard materials. Heavyweight illustration board, for example is 3/32″ thick; lightweight illustration board is approximately 1/16″ thick; Masonite is readily available in 1/8″ and 1/4″ thicknesses, etc. You can get acrylic as thin as 1/32″. At 1/2″ scale, a 9″ thick wall would be 0.375″ which could be made up with a sandwich of two layers of lightweight illustration board with pieces of 1/4″ stripwood in between. When preparing such a wall, be sure that the stripwood framing is made continuous around window and door openings and along the visible wall top. For appearance sake, you may want to line the top with vinyl to cover joints. Partitions in a manufacturing plant layout, even though they be transparent for viewing purposes, should be of scale thickness for proper space analysis purposes.

MISCELLANEOUS TIPS

Floors: If the underside of any floor at a visible edge will not be seen, use material no thicker than that which will ensure structural rigidity and build up to specified thickness with a fascia of vinyl or other suitable material. This can be a time-saving solution where, for example, you have a 1′ thick elevated, multidirectional walkway system to construct between facilities at 1/4″ scale. Heavyweight illustration board is much easier to cut than any usable 1/4″ thick material, and the prescribed thickness can be obtained with a fascia along all visible edges. This fascia can also serve the dual purpose of hiding railing mountings.

Where visible floor edges must be thinner than the necessary structural support material, laminate the entire floor and extend a layer or layers to create the specified visible thickness.

Walls: At the larger scales where you have to obtain wall thickness by laminating or framing consider using 4-lb urethane foam sandwiched between vinyl or illustration board for a lightweight result. If the wall area is too large for cutting single slabs of foam on available equipment, cut it in sections against a suitable width-establishing bridge on your table or bandsaw. Glue sections together with spray glue (Ch. 34) so that the area is slightly larger than that of the finished wall. Cut the liner material to specified wall size and cut out matching door and window openings. Glue one liner to the foam with contact or spray glue and trim excess foam to liner edge along two adjacent sides being careful to keep the edges square. This is so you can mount the second liner to the other side with edges and openings exactly opposite. Trim the remaining selvage to liner edges and cut out the foam to the opening configurations. Close visible edges with vinyl, or, at the openings, with authentic wood framing.

19

Anchorage and Durability

ANCHORAGE

I once air-freighted a model of a high-rise apartment complex to Honolulu, and during the trip
one of the towers snapped loose and rolled over
the landscape causing general havoc. I was also air-
freighted to Honolulu to repair the damage and
was graciously permitted by Mrs. Joann Morse, a
local model builder, to use her model shop facilities, thus plugging the holes in my traveling tool
bag. In addition to the structural damage, some
flax seed used for an unremembered reason in the
landscaping had sprouted in that humid climate
producing a bumper crop. So the lawn had to be
mowed.

This example is given to stress the importance
of adequate anchorage. A high-rise building may
seem perfectly secure in its glued down location
on a model sitting on a table top, but keep in
mind that the model will be tipped if not jarred
at some time during its useful existence. The top-
heaviness of a tall building much taller than it is
wide will tend to follow the laws of gravity with
sometimes grave results. A building constructed
in layers (the sandwich method), without the bind-

ing effect of a continuous outer skin, will be
particularly susceptible to lateral forces.

Aside from conscientious gluing, burying an
extension of perimeter walls in the basement, etc.,
one of the surest methods for anchoring tall building is with rods of 1/4" or 5/16" screw stock extending from roof through the plywood base.
(See Fig. 19-1) The size of stock will depend
upon the weight of the building and the number of
rods that can be used. Returning to model HR 1
(Ch. 18) which has been constructed in anticipation of this system, at the previously traced hole
locations on the ground floor pad drill two 3/8"
holes to pass through the base plywood and insert anchor nuts (Ch. 35) which have both external
and 1/4" internal threads. With a deep basement,
glue the slot in the top of the nut to the screwdriver blade as an assist in finding the hole in the
plywood, and screw the nut in *vertically*. These
will provide permanent anchorage which cannot
be knocked out by the end of the rod as you
search for the hole from the top of the building.
The beveled entrance in the nut will help you find
it. Other anchor nuts have a T shape with burrs
on a flange hammered into the *under* side of the
plywood into a friction grip hole. When using these,

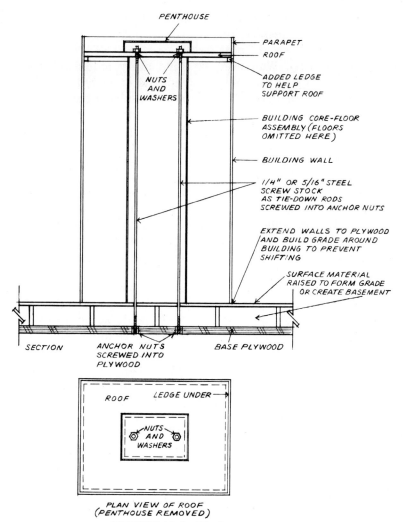

FIGURE 19-1 *Tie-down system.*

go easy when you are locating the hole with the blind end of the rod or you may knock them out. The best way to secure this kind is to insert them into separate blocks of wood securely fixed to the plywood base surface in exact location to capture the T heads. Remember to install them before you put your ceiling on the basement to prevent locking yourself out.

Place the building on its pad using the corner marks as a guide. Insert the roof and drop the rods down through the roof and holes in the floors. When you feel and hear contact with a nut, mark on the rod above the roof the approximate depth of the nut plus a little more. Screw the rod down to this mark. When both rods are screwed in, mark on each a point just above the thickness of a tie-down nut. Remove the rods; cut them at the marks and trim the threads so that they will accept nuts. Replace the rods, place thin steel washers over the ends, add the nuts and cinch down the building

until it is snug. Only feel and judgment can tell you how tight to make the nuts, too tight and you may spring a joint, too loose and the building will shift when moving the model. In this case to help prevent shifting, glue down a small square block of acrylic inside each corner if it can be hidden by the exterior columns. Another way to accomplish the same thing is to peel off the top layer of the illustration board pad in a strip of wall thickness width so that the building will rest in a very shallow groove. Every model will have its own configurations. A revealed top of foundation might serve as a wall locator, etc. Other than the security provided, one important advantage of the anchor rod system is that it permits easy removal of the building for adjustment or repair. The roof can be removed to replace a light tube if the model is so equipped (Ch. 29).

Lower buildings such as the approximately 10″ high model HR 2 with its relatively large floor area do not have such precarious center of gravity problems, but in the case of sandwich construction it is wise at least to tie the window walls and floors together to keep them from shifting. Whenever there is no penthouse to hide the tops of the rods, consider cinching against the first floor below the roof leaving the latter removable.

Stress has been placed on anchoring high-rise buildings because they are the most obvious and most prevalent candidates for extra protection. Thought should be given to anchorage beyond that which is visible for any structure with a small bearing considering its height, weight, and mass. A 1/4″ scale water tower sitting on spindly legs should have the legs inserted into the supporting surface, etc. Firmly glue down accessories such as cars, buses, and trucks so that they won't become missiles during shipment of the model, not to speak of preventing your client's child from walking off with a pocket full. Fix that top-heavy spreading oak tree so it won't acquire a lean the first time the model is tipped to pass through a door way. Attach everything so that you could turn the model upside down, bang the bottom with your fist, and have nothing fall off except a bit of ground cover. In fact I follow the practice of lifting each corner of a finished model and dropping it to find any weak spots before the client does.

DURABILITY

Build every model so that it will stand up far beyond its expected useful life. It is often easier to build a substantial structure than a flimsy shell, taking advantage of hidden space for extra bracing. All the materials mentioned in this book should provide durability when properly used. Obtain complete glue coverage at joints. Protect the ends of streets at the model's edge with strips of vinyl where the material is illustration board. This will help to prevent tearing open the laminations by a clumsily removed acrylic cover, for example. Frame and acrylic cover corners can be protected with right angle steel braces. Sink addenda such as chimneys, flag poles, fountains, etc. into the surface so that they won't snap off at the first whack of the base against a door frame.

In landscaping (Ch. 25) stay away from organic materials as much as possible. A strong dried twig of just the right size and shape may be fine for that big Eucalyptus tree but lichen will dry out to crumble to the touch no matter how much of a glycerine soaking it has had.

When your model has been built to high durability standards all you have to expect from your client is reasonable care.

20

Roofs, Chimneys, and Gutters

ROOFS

Roofs are described either by structural shape or by the material used on the surface. The purpose of this chapter is to submit tips on construction of roof shapes, the surfacing being left to Ch. 33 in conformity with the policy of holding repetition to a minimum. Construction will be confined to that necessary to exterior appearance, excluding decoration and extension of interior components such as beams and rafters which can obviously be add-ons to the subject being discussed. Seldom will you be called upon to model rafters, purlins, beams, struts, etc., in a gable roof or the necessary steel work necessary to support a clear span roof over an arena. Some interior considerations are given in Ch. 31.

Figures 20-1*a* through *q* show some of the popular shapes a few of which will be discussed as structurally representative examples along with some special shapes to exemplify the types of individual design challenges with which you may be faced.

Flat and Shed Roofs: These are shown in Figs. 20-1*a*, *b*, and *c*. The flat roof is generally level ap-

pearing with a slope of no more than 1 in 20 or warped for drainage. The roof of model HR 1 (Ch. 18) is an example where drainage warping is ignored because of scale. Note that flat roofs may be enclosed by parapets or have an eave, calling for materials to provide scale thickness at the visible edges. The surfacing is usually of built-up composition (such as tar paper and gravel). Shed roofs have an obvious slope, the degree depending upon the application such as on a tool shed or carport or covering a one-story extension of a private residence where a gable would conflict with upper windows or simply as part of the architect's design including a sloped ceiling underneath. The surfacing can be composition, shingles, slate, or tile depending upon the degree of slope, location, and the use of the building.

Folded Plane Roofs: This term is a generic description for all roofs formed by pairs of planes meeting at an angle (called a dihedral angle). Figures 20-1*d* through *n* show examples of obviously folded plane construction. To exemplify procedure refer to Fig. 20-2 showing a private residence of which you have to construct the roof for a 1/8″ scale exterior model (model R).

Note that a basic key to the concept when tak-

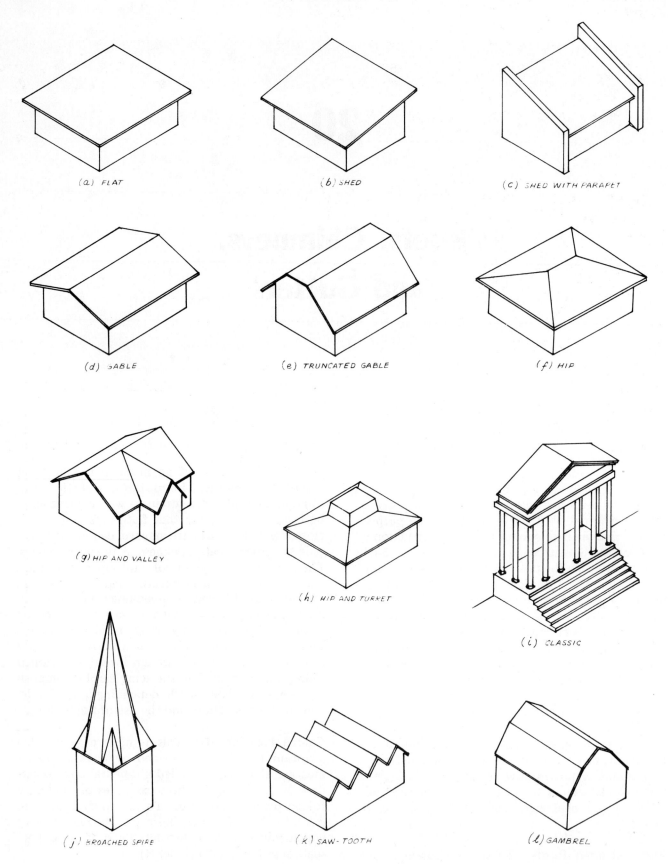

FIGURE 20-1 *Roof types (a) through (q).*

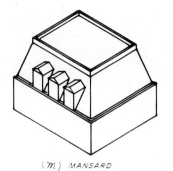

(m) MANSARD

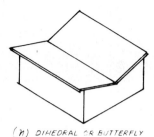

(n) DIHEDRAL OR BUTTERFLY

(o) CLERESTORY

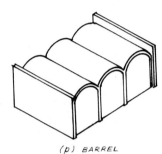
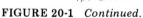

(p) BARREL

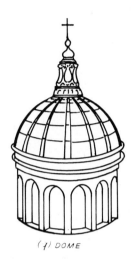

(q) DOME

FIGURE 20-1 *Continued.*

ing dimensions of a sloped surface from a plan, is that the third dimension, height, must be included. This means that you are dealing with right triangle hypotenuses longer than the horizontal measurements would indicate. You normally will not have to call on your friend Pythagoras since you can scale sloping distances from elevations and sections included in the drawings when you are computing overall flat shapes to cut and fold into roof configurations. For model R cut a ceiling to fit flat over the tops of the walls so that it extends beyond the wall lines all around the depth of the eaves. This will form a soffit closing the eave space between the roof edge and the wall. Such soffits usually include screened vent openings for attic ventilation. The ceiling material could be lightweight illustration board with the edges sanded to accept the slope of the roof. Since no extension of the roof structure appears beyond the level of the soffit, you can assemble this roof on your work table away from the model. Following the precepts of Ch. 19, use your model builder's license to strike a balance between rigidity and scale when choosing the roof material. Even 0.010″ vinyl is about 1″ thick at 1/8″ scale, but since no edges will be visible, use 0.020″ vinyl and sand the soffit edges back enough to hold scale depth of soffit. Cut out the main roof shape and two separate hip shapes. Lightly sand taper the underside edges of the hips and the edges of the main roof so that the

hips will not fall through when installing and so you will get snug joints. Glue down on the ceiling triangular braces as shown by the dotted lines in Fig. 20-2. These are made out of lightweight illustration board. Though the triangular shapes will tend to be selfsupporting, these braces will help to provide a rigid mounting. Braces under the main and subordinate level ridges are not shown to prevent confusion. Paint the brace under the main ridge a matte black to stop reflection through the dormer windows. Score along the top surface with a mat knife at the ridge line so that you can break the roof into its triangular form. Carefully fold the two roof slopes together so that you don't snap them apart at the ridge and cut through rectangular holes to take the walls of the dormers. Remember that you are cutting through a slope so the holes will be slightly deeper from top to bottom than the vertical wall height as viewed in the elevation. This cutting of both holes through the double thickness of roof material will assure that front and rear dormers are exactly opposite. Mount the main roof using contact glue on all surfaces. From each end through the hip opening hold the ceiling down tightly so that the roof edges will be flush with the edges of the soffit. Make the four dormer side walls out of 0.020″ vinyl. They should be just a little wider than the openings are tall and extend from the center brace under the ridge to the bottom of the roof openings. Notch the bot-

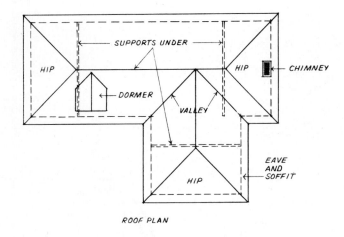

ROOF PLAN

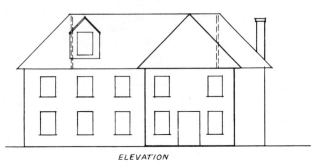

ELEVATION

FIGURE 20-2 *Model R.*

tom excess height (width) so their vertical front edges are flush with the roof material at the bottom. Glue the rear (inside) ends to the ridge brace (running parallel to the ridge) with contact glue and weld the outside surfaces to the sloping roof edges with acrylic cement. Paint the insides of the walls black. Cut the dormer roofs, scoring and breaking them at their ridge lines and fit them dry over the walls with prescribed eave and slope. Note that the rake is parallel to that of the hips. Set these dormer roofs aside for later installation of the windows (Ch. 21). In one of the hip shapes cut the chimney hole so that the chimney can be inserted to the top surface of the ceiling for secure mounting, and mount the hips with acrylic cement obtaining joints as flush as possible. Any minor discrepancies will be covered by the shingles (Ch. 33). Make the house extension roof and hip in the same manner used for the main roof and hip and mount them. Note that here you are not concerned with visual effect of depth as you are with the dormer windows; the extension roof can be attached to the main roof without cutting a hole. The roof should now appear in plan as it does in

Fig. 20-2 without the chimney. You might question the use of 0.020″ vinyl for the dormer roofs because you can see the edges in elevation, but assume here that the addition of molding trim would increase the overall thickness to the approximately 2″ revealed by that size stock.

The broached spire in Fig. 20-1*j* is an octagonal cone with a pyramidal section at each corner of the cone to fill the square area supporting the base. As in all model work, scale plays a part in determination of the most expeditious route to result. This spire can be made by casting with the master inserted in the mold point down, but unless you have more than one to make, the master can serve as the finished product. In any case you can shape the spire by sanding solid material or assemble it from illustration board or plastic triangles, adding the broaches as separate configurations. When sanding a spire scaled to less than 1″ long do it on the end of a length of square wood or acrylic stock to facilitate handling and then cut off the product. Mark a base line around the stock, mark a center in the end, and sand two opposite sides parallel until you reach the center at the specified slope. Do the other two opposite sides until you wind up with a four-sided pyramid. Then sand pairs of opposite corners in the same manner until you have an even sided octagonal cone. This procedure will help you keep control of the shape. If assembling a cone, slightly sand-taper the edges to provide tight joints where the triangles meet. If you use illustration board be careful not to separate the laminations at the points causing a fuzzy tip of the spire. The broaches are best assembled since you can make eight identical triangles to fit the sloping faces. This is easier than trying to sand four identical shapes out of solid stock unless you want to cast them using a single sanded effort as the master (Ch. 24).

The saw-toothed roof (Fig. 20-1*k*) results from a multiple folding of identical planes supported on saw-toothed walls. At the smaller scales, compute the total length of material required and score the ridges in vinyl with a mat knife. Carefully fold at each ridge line so that you don't separate the plastic. Span the walls using intervening support or not depending upon the length of span and the rigidity of roof material used.

The Mansard roof in Fig. 20-1*m* was developed by the French architect Francois Mansard to obtain upper story occupancy in the face of wall height limitations. The feature is a truncated pyramidal shape outlined at the top with a vertically sided parapet (or railing). Assemble the dormers or shape them out of acrylic leaving the front surfaces polished (Ch. 24) for fenestration to be mullioned (Ch. 21), and add the roofs.

Prompted perhaps by aeronautical thinking, I violate a generic term by applying "dihedral" to the V shape in Fig. 20-1n. The roof reminds me of a pair of airplane wings with positive dihedral. This shape is found mostly in walkway canopies between facilities or along railroad passenger loading platforms where the support is a row of single posts under the vertex with gussets, plain or ornamental, at the column tops at right angles to the roof course to help support it. As in any railing situation (Ch. 16) or column mounting (Ch. 22), a key to successful assembly is flat-topped posts of exactly even height. At the smaller scales you can simply glue the vertex to piano wire posts. At larger scales you can file V's in the tops to accept the roof angle. When the scale allows, use the score-and-break method for forming the roof to obviate having to handle two planes with a glued joint.

The clerestory roof in Fig. 20-1o is representative of all roofs where planes are separated (usually by fenestration) for light and ventilation. Sometimes the upper plane is sloped and the lower one level as in the case of multiple clerestories found on some factory buildings. In an exterior model consider making the fenestration material as a supporting element extending to the floor below.

Solar Roofs: As the world approaches exhaustion of fossil fuels, more and more attention will be paid to the collection of solar energy to provide heat and electricity. This means that at least until central generating plants can be made efficient enough and large enough to supply segments of the population as large as a city, reliance will be placed on selfsufficient residences and commercial and industrial buildings. The logical place for collecting equipment is on the roof for both electricity and heat, which, for the model builder, means in effect a form of folded plane roof construction. Photo 41 of Ch. 49 indicates the sawtooth configuration of both the voltaic and the collector arrays. The angles shown are 45 degrees from the horizontal for the cell and collector panels facing the sun. The surfaces of the reflector panels are at 35 degrees. These angles are chosen in relation to the latitude location of the installation. The arrays can be made from strips of high impact vinyl, scored lengthwise and folded to form selfsupporting inverted V's. The voltaic panels are left

in natural polished black (with suitable vertical panel dividers), and the collector panels are sprayed with bright aluminum Krylon over which are laid black piano wire lengths horizontally to simulate water pipes. The rear slopes of the arrays are painted with bright aluminum Krylon to simulate the surface's reflecting light and heat onto the panels of the next following array. I have tried aluminized mylar for the reflective surfaces, as used in the real installation, but it was found to be too susceptible to scratches and the slightest disturbance of the surface on which it was mounted. The bright aluminum spray enamel was much more satisfactory and did the job in the model. The arrays are mounted on what, for model building purposes, amounts to a standard flat built-up roof, the only portions of which will show are walking space borders around the arrays. At 1/16" scale, the use of sand in these areas is superfluous, even though you would use it if the arrays were not there. Residential solar water heating facilities will probably change fairly rapidly as the state of the art becomes more sophisticated; no attempt will be made to outguess the progress. But it is pertinent to mention a simple installation with which I have had experience. In effect, it is a large, flat skylight-type glass or plastic cover over a box set into the sunny slope of a gable roof. The box is lined with reflective material, which, with the greenhouse effect, concentrates the sun's heat onto a grid of black, continuous water piping. Spray the inside of the openfaced box with bright silver Krylon and install black piano wire or metal rod, bent to the specified configuration, to simulate the water pipes. Then attach an acrylic cover.

Curved Roofs: These include curved plane or barrel roofs as illustrated in Fig. 20-1p, domes as illustrated in Fig. 20-1q, and variations where the curvature is compounded by varying radii. Note that Fig. 20-1q could represent an entire building or a cupola on top of a larger roof. The dome itself could also be an entire building as in the case of a geodesic dome.

Barrel roofs can be like the curved panel roof in Fig. 20-1p or inverted with the concave side to weather as in Ch. 49, photo 42. With the convex side to weather consider laminating a row of wooden dowel stock of the scale diameter sanded to produce two flat sides and bottom. If you cover the surface to provide an eave, place a shim double the thickness of the covering vinyl between adjoining dowels to give clearance at the joints. If the end walls are transparent or partially so, cut the dowels shorter than the building depth, paint the ends black, and make the walls out of acrylic. I have often found sections of mailing tubes suitable for such configurations. You have to consider filling joints in the cardboard, but the desired shape is preformed for you. Where just shells are required for either convex or concave surface to weather, with the roof resting on columns, for example, consider forming them (Ch. 24) in the absence of available ready-made shapes. A good example of the occasional challenge you will receive is shown in photo 42 of Ch. 49. The inverted barrel roof shown was cantilevered from each side of ridge beam structures deep enough to close the inboard ends of the individual inverted half barrels or troughs. See Fig. 20-3. The top edges of these structures were horizontal. The radius of each individual section at the outboard end was greater than that at the main ridge resulting in a sloped bottom of trough for drainage. The form to cut was a trapezoid with inboard and outboard widths equal to the length of the arcs at those locations formed by the installed shape. This short description of a part of a finished model which you will never be called upon to duplicate is in violation of my tenet expressed in Ch. 1, but since any hypothesis would also require a nonstandard shape and assembly, the roof in the photo referred to provides a word and illustration saving subject.

Domes: Domes can be hemispherical or more or less of a sphere. They can be spheroidal in shape, or the profile displaying curves of varying radii. From the model builder's point of view they can be hollow or solid depending upon visibility of the interior, the scale, and whether or not the surface or parts thereof are transparent or translucent. In the interests of saving time, first consider your Jay's Nest (Ch. 35) and the local stores before worrying about how you are going to form a dome. A rubber beach ball may have the exact diameter. Check the wood door and drawer pulls at your hardware store. I once found a child's hollow transparent plastic ball with water and a duck inside that gave me the specified hemisphere. The duck flew off to deeper ponds. Your plastics supplier will probably have a range of small solid acrylic spheres. A ping pong ball may be just right. Armed with calipers (Ch. 36) cruise your home dressing table or local cosmetic counter. To save buying 25 gallons of "Trailing Arbutis," buy one bottle and use the cap as a master for casting (Ch. 24) to get duplicates. If you are dexterous with belt sander or lathe, form a master on the end of

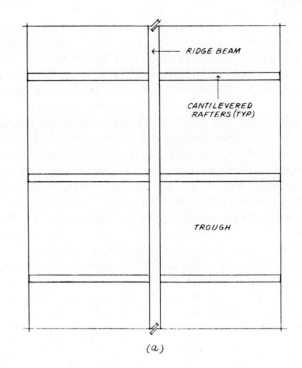

(a)

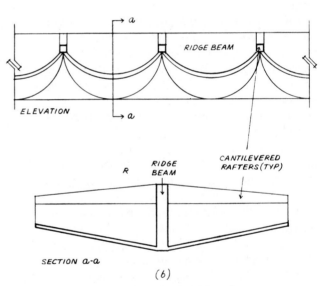

FIGURE 20-3   *Barrel roof.*

wooden dowel of the specified diameter. Transparent domes up to about 6″ in diameter can be heat pressed on your drill press (Ch. 24). They can be painted for opaque canopies (Ch. 49, photo 42). Small skylight domes can be formed on a small vacuum machine (Ch. 24). Solid and hollow domes of almost any configuration and size can be constructed using profile parts (Ch. 24).

The foregoing olio of items is indicative of how prodding the memory, aided by imagination, can save hours of construction time. Get everybody within shouting distance in on the act and your neighbor may come up with an old toilet bowl float for that dome.

Geodesic Domes: Geodesic domes are so named because of employment of the principles of geometry of great circles around a sphere. Great circles have the same diameter as that of the sphere. The shortest distance between two points on a sphere is the length of the shorter of the two arcs of the great circle passing through the two points. Intersections of three or more great circles not passing through the same opposite poles of the sphere form spherical triangles. The triangle being the only truly rigid shape is the ideal structural unit for a selfsupporting dome to be used as a building shell, but before any structural drawings can be made, some sort of guiding discipline must be established to enable the engineers to determine the dimensions, shape, and number of flat panels needed for the dome. To do this a polyhedron is visualized inside the sphere so that the required number of great circles can follow the edges of the faces of an icosahedron, for example, which has 20 equilateral triangular shaped faces. The resulting spherical triangles are then broken down into as many smaller equilateral triangles as possible to represent the structural polyhedron which comes closest to a spherical shape. The edges of the flat triangular faces are then chords of the arcs formed by the great circles, and are computed to obtain the sizes of panels to be used in building the dome. For those interested in the subject see Ch. 50 for suggested publications.

There is no fast way to make a geodesic dome model. At the smaller scales, such as 1/32″ and below, try etching with a scribe aided by templates on the surface of a hemispherical shape of acrylic. If the dome is to be opaque, paint the dome first and scribe through the paint. At the larger scales where the size results in say a 6″ diameter or greater, have a dome-shaped plug spun (Ch. 24) and construct the dome out of individual sections of acrylic using the plug as an armature and cover the joints with framing made from strips of acrylic cutting in the intersections. This is an arduous task but the only route I know of to authenticity. Use acrylic at least 1/16″ thick to get good joints and still not be obtrusive to the eye beneath the surface. Make a sanding jig to obtain edge taper to permit maximum edge contact at the joints.

Compound Curve Roofs: Curved roofs such as that shown in Fig. 20-4 will require the engineering drawings in scale to give you profile patterns

at critical stations. To help establish a structural base, make the initial ribs as long as possible. Make them out of illustration board or chip board, filling intervals with ribs of opposing direction to make the assembly as rigid as possible. Further discussion of this type of model will be found in Ch. 24.

As roof shapes become more complicated than those exemplified in this chapter, first analyze the whole assembly, picking out the principal or main elements to be done first as a base on which to construct the satellite assemblies. Often what at first glance appears to be an impossible maze of planes or curves can be broken down into relatively simple repetitive modules.

CHIMNEYS

Chimneys being for the most part obvious, partly free-standing, vertical appendages, will have to be indicated by the model builder down through the smallest of workable scales. Even a study model of an industrial project at 1/100″ scale could include a bank of chimneys made out of 0.020″ vinyl. Because of environmental considerations the banks of huge industrial stacks are becoming a thing of the past as the requirements for recycling and scrubbing become more stringent, but until it is decided that Homo sapiens cannot tolerate a bit of wood smoke from the friendly hearth, we will fortunately have residential chimneys to include in our work.

Materials: Materials include acrylic, wood, vinyl, and, if cast, plaster (Ch. 24). Chimneys need not be hollow except to the extent the scale reveals their interior. At 1/20″ scale, for example, I have painted black openings on chimney tops. As the scale increases, consider drilling or carving out a shallow cavity and painting it black to indicate the flue. Some chimneys will have round flues extending above the masonry. These can be made by inserting short pieces of brass tubing of scale size into holes drilled into the tops, inserting them into the wet plaster chimney just poured into its mold (Ch. 24), or by simply gluing tubing rings to the tops.

Shapes: Shapes of residential chimneys usually present no structural problems in their standard rectangular form. Where chimneys are attached to the outside of a residence, variations may include

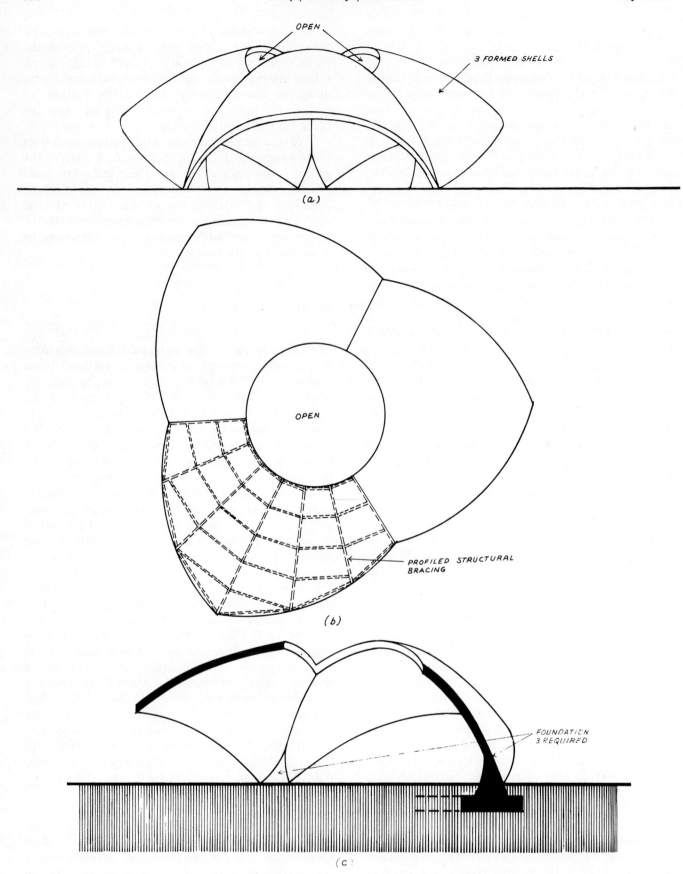

FIGURE 20-4 *Compound roof: (a) elevation, (b) plan, (c) section.*

widened bases (to include interior hearth dimensions), and caps slightly larger than the chimney. If the scale or material make it awkward to cut out the base expansion, consider adding a separate piece or pieces, hiding the joints in the texture (Ch. 33) or by covering the whole assembly with vinyl.

Textures: Textures are discussed in Ch. 33, but it is appropriate to point out here that you will run up against all sorts of finishes. I have made chimneys with wood paneling, shingles, stone, plaster, or brick, depending upon the cosmetic prescriptions of the client.

Installation: Installation of through-the-roof chimneys requires solid mounting so that they cannot be flicked off by a careless hand or snapped off by a crash of the model against a door jamb on the way to the display area. In the case of model R earlier in this chapter, literally insert the chimney through the roof to be anchored on the attic floor or even farther down if necessary. Where a chimney is attached to an exterior wall, you may have to notch out an eave to accept it. Wherever possible, insert tall industrial chimneys into the base material or into the building served. Where the visible limit of the base is at grade, indicating a subterranean source of smoke, simply gluing the base to illustration board is inviting a repair job. An accident may tear up the top lamination of the illustration board, complicating restoration.

GUTTERS

Unless you have been engaged to construct a miniature as described in Ch. 2, experience has told me that roof gutters and down spouts can safely be omitted in most architectural work as incidental to the display. In any case, such facilities are not worth the time and effort in any scale below 1/4″. You can usually find tubing (brass, plastic, or soda straws, etc.) suitable for round down spouts, but if the configuration is square or rectangular, they are best made from strip wood with cavities cut at down spout joints to simulate openings. With the broadening availability of supplies for industrial model work, check with sources such as exemplified in Ch. 50 for plastic tubing shapes if your requirements are voluminous. The gutters at eaves present greater problems in the absence of the outside manufacture of hemispherical channel stock. For the standard rounded gutter at 1/4″ scale, drill a hole that will just accept 1/8″ brass tubing through wood as thick as your drill bit will handle (Ch. 36) and cut the wood lengthwise through the hole resulting in a hemispherical groove. Cut on the outside of an established diameter line so that the thickness of the blade will not destroy the hemispherical shape of the groove. Increase the length of groove by laminating several pieces of drilled wood. Securely glue the 1/8″ tubing into the groove so that it will not rotate and sand off the exposed half on your belt sander. If the tubing wall appears grossly thick, try filing the exposed edge to a thinner aspect. If important at the larger scales, shaped gutters can be formed as noted in Ch. 24. If you use sheet copper for example you can solder the joints at the corners and between sections. Drains in flat roofs can usually be satisfactorily indicated by surface treatment — a scored black spot at the smaller scales and an inset of acid-etched material at the larger scales. This latter method is similar to the procedure for street gutter drains in Ch. 13.

21

Windows, Skylights, and Doors

Though different in construction and materials used, windows, skylights and doors conveniently fall into the same chapter as standard building openings.

WINDOWS

To place you in what might be called a window frame of mind, consider the types of windows by form (not necessarily by use) with which you could be faced during your career. There are *fixed panes*, with or without mullions, used in all types of buildings. The so-called "picture" window in a private residence is a good example. There are *curved* windows for which the glass has been formed into an arc. It is common practice, however, to attain curvilinear shapes by the use of contiguous flat planes each of which forms a chord of the arc being spanned. *Double-hung* windows consist of two adjacent, offset panes whose sash slides vertically in grooves in the frame. When closed, the bottom of the sash of the upper half toward the outside of the building just overlaps the top of the sash of the bottom half. Sliding is often as-

sisted by weights hung on cords within the window frame on each side. *Casement* windows with either wood or metal sashes are hinged vertically to swing out or in. The popular metal sashed *sliding* panes move in top and bottom grooves in various combinations. There may be two overlapping panes; one sliding pane on each side, movable to overlap a central fixed pane; etc. *Louvred* or jalousie windows consist of horizontal slats of unsashed glass activated in unison by levers in the frame. Each slat is held at the ends by clamps which swivel to open or close so that the bottom edge of each slat overlaps the top of the next slat below. *Transom* windows are usually rectangles of glass the sash of which is hinged on the top or bottom. This type might be found at grade for light and ventilation in a residential basement playroom. *Tubular* windows such as that on a light house or on the top of an airport tower are usually made up of separate flat panes in a manner similar to that of a bay window mentioned previously. *Stained glass* windows are found most predominantly in churches and mausoleums where religious themes may be depicted in multipaned glass of varying colors. *Obscured* windows are those which are treated in various ways to obtain transluscency without transparency.

Though the different types of windows will require different construction approaches by the model builder, note that except perhaps in large scale miniature (Ch. 2) work, they will not have to open or close. You might, for example, show a double hung window open, but it will be in a fixed position. This is simply another case where knowledge of the real life object helps you to model with visual authenticity.

I believe it is safe to dispense with *window screens* right at the start by saying that they will never be required. Even at scales of 1/2″ and larger, the available metal and cloth meshes are technically out of scale, and, in any case, will tend to blot out the windows, making a screened private residence model, for example, look as though it had its eyes closed. Model builder's license permits the use of the meshes for chain link fencing with acceptable authenticity, but in that use there is no concern about hiding an important element behind the mesh.

Scale "Glass". In professional model building there are few insurmountable obstacles, given time and budget, to attaining at least reasonably accurate scale results. One true obstacle is the thickness of window glass. At the commonly used scale of 1/8″, for example, 1/4″ plate glass would be 0.003″ thick at most, making it difficult to find transparent material stiff enough to be useful. Fortunately the edges are hidden; at least in exterior work you can get away with materials much thicker than they should be. The front surface of the glazing can be installed at scale depth of sill, and what is behind cannot be seen. Even in interior work (Ch. 31), usually done at the larger scales, the frames can be imperceptibly deepened on the inside to offset the out-of-scale thickness of the "glass" if doing so is important to visual effect.

Study Models: Study models are the common media for land use and mass analyses generally do not require through-the-wall openings in the buildings. The same is true in line-of-sight studies for proposed real estate developments where houses are necessary in block configuration only, to prove such things as whether or not a house across the street will block a resident's view. Where a small scale conceptual study model of a proposed industrial park, for example, is dressed

up with landscaping for display purposes also, building walls can be made from clear solid acrylic as indicated in Ch. 18. Windows are then indicated by opaquing the surrounding areas with paint, tape, or strips of vinyl. When the focus shifts to individual buildings the scale will likely be 1/4″ or larger to make facade studies easier to read. Where interior space use allows flexibility in fenestration, you may be called upon to furnish several concepts in panel form with windows finished to display quality. Initially you can supply a block type building (or a single pertinent wall) with detachable window indications in the form of vinyl or acrylic shapes backed with double-faced tape, using just enough tape to ensure adhesion. Where fenestration has been settled upon to the extent that drawings are made, a complete facade can be cut out of the drawing at the scale of the model and glued to the model wall. This is good for in-shop study only since in contrast to a three-dimensional building mass, the affected wall will look flat. Also, a window perforated wall with no glazing will make a building look empty.

Display Model: Windows will be discussed here with tips given for accomplishing some of the common types to fortify your imagination in solving the occasional special problems. Mullions are discussed separately later in this chapter. Additional tips applicable to interior work will be covered in Ch. 31. Glazing materials which I have used successfully are clear vinyl, acetate, polystyrene, and acrylic (clear, color-shaded, and mirrored). An important objective is to obtain material that is stiff enough to maintain an even surface over the window opening. At 1/32″ scale and smaller you could probably use cellophane to cover a window opening, but a naturally rigid material is easier to handle.

Three basic methods for assembling windows are shown in Fig. 21-1. I call them basic since they do not necessarily take into account facade treatments. They are useful in establishing glazing-wall relationships most advantageously in systems where several or many windows are mounted within the thickness of the same wall plane. Some individual windows of different types will be discussed later.

In consideration of ease of construction and saving time, wherever possible avoid cutting in multiple windows or masking them for painting to establish opaque areas (Fig. 21-1*a* and *b*). Following the warning in Ch. 6, don't get carried

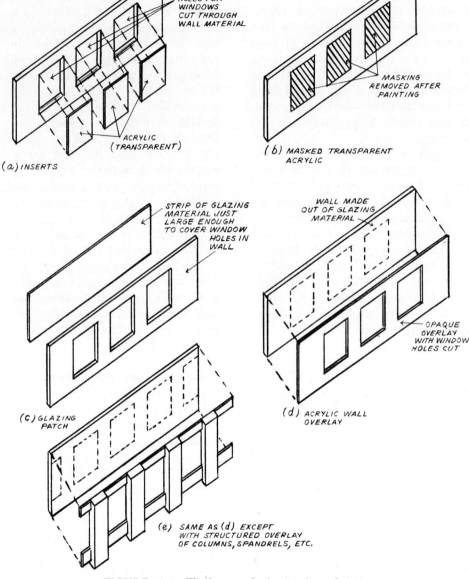

FIGURE 21-1 *Window methods ((a) through (e)).*

away with storebought prepared siding materials which are just the ticket in design and texture but which at the usual minimum thickness of 1/32″ may require cutting in the windows to provide specified visible frame depth or flush glazing. Imagine a 1/20″ scale individual housing development with several hundred windows involved. Consider that your duplicating the texture (Ch. 33) on thinner stock into which window openings can be cut to form an overlay over walls made of glazing material (Fig. 21-1*d*) may take a great deal less time than cutting in individual windows with snug fits. This can be true even where you have to laminate to obtain recessed windows. Masking

with any degree of consistent success is also an excessively time consuming process, particularly where large numbers of windows are involved (Fig. 21-1*b*). This system is good only at scales of 1/32″ or smaller, making it particularly difficult to get consistently sharp edged, even tape masks in the correct locations to stop the paint. Also keep in mind the time consumed in removing all the individual masks after painting. A variation of this method for flush windows at small scale is to make a pattern jig out of vinyl which you place in correct location on the glazing surface and score the outline of the window opening with a sharp scribe. This scoring will stop the paint without the use of masking tape if carefully done and will indicate a window frame.

The method shown in Fig. 21-1c can be used in cases where the wall thickness is equal to or less than the scale depth of frame. In the many varied buildings of a 1/32″ scale amusement park, for example, where the walls are 0.015″ vinyl, the frames will be approximately 5″ deep, but I have found that the technical discrepancy is camouflaged by the overall scene. This is another case where judgment must dictate the extent of model builder's license allowed. If shallower frames are a must, use 0.010″ vinyl (still technically too thick) and brace with 1/32″ acrylic glazing, laminate 1/32″ acrylic with window perforated bond paper (Fig. 21-1d), or mask and paint acrylic as in Fig. 21-1b. Cut the window openings in the vinyl before assembly and cover the inside of them with one of the glazing materials mentioned previously. Here the overlay is the wall and the glazing is added without concern for consistent size or shape since the openings define the window frames. Vinyl to vinyl and acrylic to vinyl joints can be welded with acrylic cement.

Model HR 1 in Ch. 18 is an excellent example of the system indicated in Fig. 21-1e. This method is of course not confined to high-rise office buildings. An extensively fenestrated wall in an exterior private residence model could be made from acrylic as the main structural element, with window areas defined by an overlay of a thickness to provide the scale depth of frame. Here it suffices to say that under this method, the windows are defined by overlays consisting of complete wall area laminations or individual spandrels, sun shades, fins, or columns. Surface treatment is covered further in Ch. 33.

Figure 21-2 shows an alternate method in cases where you want to obtain accurate setback without having to cut the window into a thick wall that was made necessary by scale or structural reasons. Glazing material is attached to the back of the window opening in the overlay material of scale thickness, and this assembly is glued to the main wall through which an opening just large enough to clear the glazing when the sandwich is formed. Note that in all cases where an overlay is used, a controlling mounting edge is provided for added framing and sills if required.

When cutting window openings in bass wood used to simulate plywood siding, carefully cut across the grain first starting at the corners of the desired opening with a progressive slicing action. When you are through the wood, cut the other two sides running parallel to the grain. This will help prevent splitting the entire wall, the danger depending upon the distance between window and wall edge. An additional aid is to drill a hole in the center of each window location before wielding your mat knife. This will provide space into which the wood can move as it is expended by the thickness of the blade, thus removing splitting

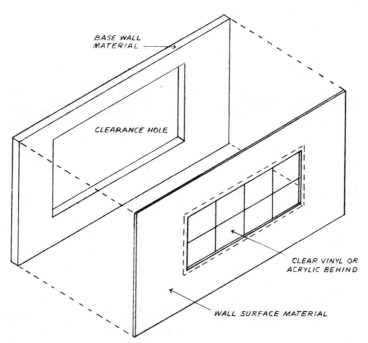

FIGURE 21-2 *Window wall.*

pressure from the material outside the window area.

Where you have windows flush with the surface of added wall treatment such as real wood shingles through which window openings are extremely difficult to cut, add clear acrylic windows to a clear acrylic wall base. (Fig. 21-3). These windows should be of a thickness equal to the thickness of the shingles mounted around them. Mount all the windows in a wall section before adding the shingles. Be sure the window areas and the windows are polished without noticeable crazing, scratches, or masking paper residue. With a scribe (Ch. 36) mark the window openings on the wall base, and for each installation outline two sides of each opening with masking tape as a positioning guide. With an eye dropper flood the window area with acrylic cement and immediately set the window against the masking tape edges and press down steadily to squeeze out the bubbles, being careful to prevent sliding out of position. A few seconds of pressure will weld the acrylic together. You will have to accept a minute bubble here and there. To my knowledge, substantiated by experts, there is no way possible to assure 100 percent clarity in laminating acrylic in this manner. The alternatives are not worth the time to eliminate a few unobtrusive bubbles unless you have no more than a few windows to make under these circumstances. One alternative is to cut window holes in the wall base and trim the edges so that they intrude past the window edges no farther than the width of the frame to be added to the surface. Then place a window evenly over its hole and wick in acrylic cement around the edges. This system will of course reveal the edges

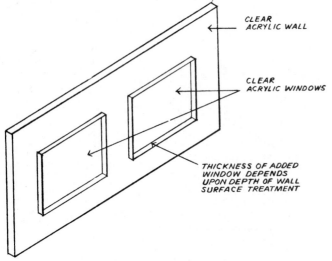

FIGURE 21-3 *Raised windows.*

of the hole in the wall base which should be painted black (to prevent reflection) before adding the window.

Another alternative is to mount 0.010″ vinyl strips no wider than the planned frame at the rear surface edges of the window and weld them to the wall base with a wicking brush. The vinyl strips on the back surface will create a 0.010″ dead air space, possibly to fog up!

A third alternative is to wrap the window edges with vinyl the thickness of the specified window frame and weld the back edges of this frame to the wall base. Use as dry a brush as possible to prevent the cement from wicking out onto the window area, or use contact cement.

Bay windows, of which an example is shown in Fig. 21-4, can be made by scoring and breaking into panels of clear vinyl, or at the larger scales by joining separate panels of 1/32″ acrylic. Bevel the joining edges to conform to the angles and insert strips of vinyl at the joints to simulate framing. These materials can be welded with acrylic cement. Don't let any run onto the windows! Add a layer of vinyl or other suitable material with scale thickness across the base of the window to establish the wainscoting area on the inside. The header can be made in the same manner. For rigidity, form the window around a shaped illustration board floor and ceiling and glue the assembly to the wall which is either painted gray at the window opening or cut through to provide a feeling of depth. Add the folded plane roof drawing on tips from Ch. 20 for guidance. You may be able to obtain the triangular shapes of the panels from the drawings. Otherwise a little trial and error will give you the solution. It will be easier to install the roof after installation of the window assembly when you can use the wall as a backing.

Bowed windows at small scale can be made by welding with acrylic cement clear vinyl around hemispheres of acrylic top and bottom. The stock I have used is 0.010″ vinyl which in my experience is the thinnest it comes in rigid form. Cut the acrylic hemispheres with rectangular selvage at least as wide as the wall thickness as indicated in Fig. 21-5. Glue these hemispheres to the top and bottom of a hole cut through the wall the height of the window and wide enough just to accept both a hemisphere plus the vinyl on each side. Cut the vinyl to a height equal to that of the hole cut through the wall and just long enough to extend to the interior wall surface on each side. Insert the vinyl ends into the wall around the hemispheres and secure it with temporary wedges top

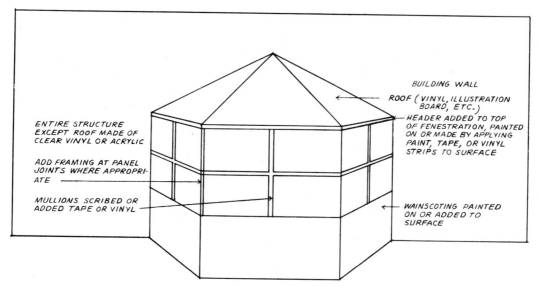

FIGURE 21-4 *Bay windows.*

and bottom. Wick in acrylic cement at the joints with the hemispheres getting as much coverage as possible without letting it run onto the finished window surface. The holding wedges can be made from pieces of 0.010″ vinyl and sand-tapered edges. To offset any concave bows in the sides of the window, apply contact cement with a knife or small spatula from the inside of the building against the sides of the hole and force the vinyl against these sides with a piece of wood tightly spanning the window opening on the inside. Leave the wedges and spanner in until you are satisfied that the assembly is secure.

For a *dormer window* like that in model R of Ch. 20, cut a strip of 1/32″ acrylic wide enough just to cover the wall edges on each side and long enough to touch the attic floor for solid mounting. Slope the top end of each side to fit under the gable roof already made and notch out the sides so that when mounted the sloped top edges will just cover the tops of the walls as in Fig. 21-6. Form the framing out of 0.010″ vinyl (about 1″ at 1/8″ scale) wide enough to cover the wall end at each side and mount the assembly flush with the front ends of the walls and add the roof you set aside in Ch. 20. If the wall edges are in relief according to specifications, set the window back the required distance, make the vinyl overlay to fit inside the walls and fill the space between the bottom of the window and the roof edge at that point.

Tubular windows such as those on the top of light houses can be made from clear plastic tubing or by coiling sheet vinyl (Ch. 24). Check your

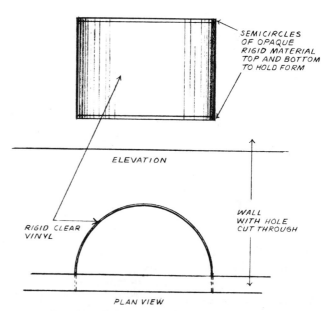

FIGURE 21-5 *Bowed windows.*

Jay's Nest for tubular plastic containers. You may find the answer in a ball point pen refill tube or a tooth brush container. At small scale, consider clear acrylic rod. More likely you will find that the tubular window you have to make for your model of a light house is made up of flat planes forming a polygon in plan shape. In this case follow the suggestions under bay windows just discussed. The top and bottom may be held by male and female patterns cut out of vinyl which provide slots to hold the panel ends.

Stained glass windows such as those you might have to do for a church or mausoleum model present the unique problems of multipane glazing and

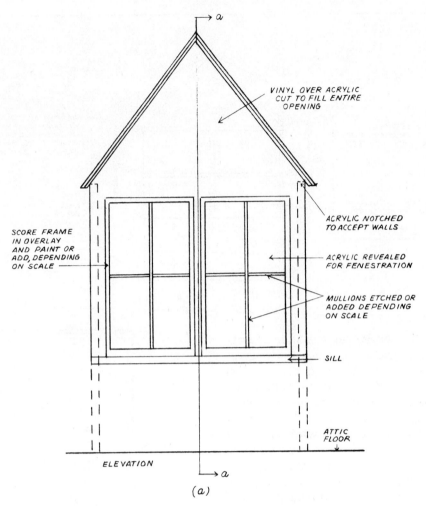

FIGURE 21-6 *Dormer window.*

sometimes intricate mullion configurations. Refer to Ch. 33 for a method of obtaining colored panes. Mullions will be discussed later.

Obscured windows require material treated in various ways to satisfy specifications toward preventing transparency. If you cannot get by satisfactorily with the milky acrylic as supplied by your plastics source, refer to Ch. 33 where surface treatments are covered.

Mullions and frames can be covered by the term "sash", but are separated here since mullions are the principal concern of the model builder. Framing is often visually understood, and camouflaged by the jambs, headers, and sills, but the mullions are obvious. I am probably not far off to say that at least 75 percent of all mullion work will be in the form of scored lines scribed on the surface of the material used for glazing. To get more obvious definition, do the scoring with a knife blade to get even, single grooves and rub india ink or

paint over the surface to fill these grooves. At 1/8″ scale, an inch is about 0.010″; so it is easy to see how impractical the installation of a 1/2″ mullion would be. If it seems important enough to do so, and the budget can stand it, consider acid-etching (Ch. 17) to include the entire sash. In store and building front glazing the mullions are often structural members of sufficient width to permit the use of vinyl strips or architectural tape (Ch. 35). If you use tape, lay it relaxed since any tension will be compensated for by later shrinking and pulling the ends loose. A good practice is to tip the ends with contact glue to ensure adherence. I used a lot of tape at one time but gave it up as a standard solution because of the uncertainty of adhesion over the long pull and the difficulty at times of placing it in straight lines without tension. Where mullions protrude above the surface farther than their thickness, you can either cut grooves to accept vinyl strips or cut the glazing

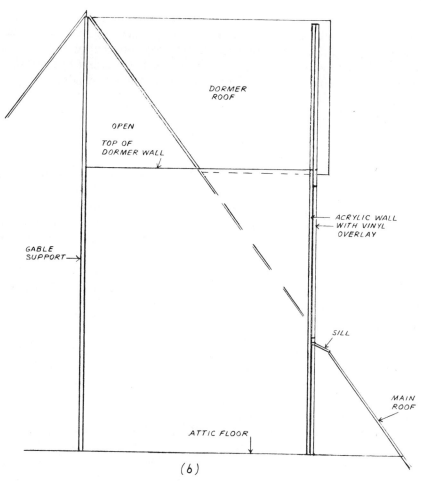

(6)

FIGURE 21-6 *Continued.*

into panes with vinyl strips sandwiched at the joints.

SKYLIGHTS

The term "skylight" defines literally the purpose of the facility: to let in natural light in otherwise dark or shaded areas. They are found in obscure or clear glass or plastic on the roofs of industrial and commercial buildings, over residential atria or interior hallways, in the slope of gable roofs to shed light on artists' studios, over entryways, etc. The clerestory shown in Fig. 20-1o is a form of skylight where one side of a gable roof is raised at the ridge to accept vertical glazing. They are found in saw-tooth shaped roofs of factories where one side of each triangle is glazed.

Structurally speaking, consider skylights as windows mounted at various angles depending upon location and use framing and mullions similar

to those of their relatives. Differences are found in the facts that skylights are usually fixed and their shapes and surfaces can have peculiar configurations. These shapes include single domes (bubbles) and pyramids, multiple repetitions to cover large areas, and gables or tent shapes similar to greenhouse roofs. Their shapes satisfy both architectural design and structural strength requirements.

Assume you have a 1/4″ scale model to build of an entrance canopy consisting substantially of parallel rows of clear plastic bubbles separated by a 3″ (about 1/16″) width of framing members. This flat roof will be supported horizontally on 4″ × 4″ wood posts and framing of no interest for this purpose. The canopy will measure 8′ × 15′6″, and contain 72 acrylic bubbles in hemispheric shape. The outside diameter of each is 1′ making the height 6″. The base of the roof will be 1/16″ clear acrylic. Obtain 72 (plus a few extra to absorb mistakes) 1/4″ acrylic balls (clear) from your supplier and sand each one down to a hemisphere on your belt sander. To do this you will need a jig to hold them so the sanding belt won't spin them in the process and ruin the product. See Ch. 37. Polish the bottom of each hemisphere (Ch. 24) and glue it in place on the roof base using the acrylic glue that comes in a tube. That will give you a better chance of complete, transparent coverage than the liquid cement welding which you wick in with a brush (Ch. 34). Place a drop in the center of the bubble position and press the bubble down on it until you can see complete coverage. Wipe off excess squeezed out glue as you go. You can get an idea as to the quantity of glue to apply by having a dry run with one of the extra hemispheres on a piece of scrap acrylic. As a guide to installation alignment lay out a grid of 1/16″ architectural tape (Ch. 35) or make light score lines with a metal scribe. You will have to paint the opaque frame areas carefully with a small brush after you have mounted the hemispheres.

Because of the free-standing location of the canopy and the small size of the bubbles, clear glue joints of polished acrylic, even though solid, will give sufficient see-through quality to get by. As the bubbles or domes become larger, consideration should be given to installing hollow hemispheres over holes cut through the base upon which they are mounted. This is true even with obscure glass (Ch. 33) if you expect to show light passing through. If you cannot find a suitable bubble or bubbles in your Jay's Nest see Ch. 24 for heat or vacuum forming.

The previously mentioned pyramidal shapes in parallel lines can be cut on a shop mill out of a solid block of acrylic, but you will have the somewhat arduous task of polishing the result to obtain transparency (Ch. 24). Repetitive small, odd shapes are best vacuum formed. Don't forget the possibility that your plastics supplier may have acrylic with a surface disturbed to the configuration you are after, or close enough to be acceptable at the smaller scales. Also don't forget to let your client know before the fact what you intend to do if your solution is obviously not the same as that called for in the specifications. This could prevent a profit absorbing exercise.

The gable or tent-shaped skylights are usually found on the flat roofs of commercial and industrial buildings. They remind one of a miniature gable-roofed house with a glass roof. The glass may be clear or obscure and usually has a small gauge chicken wire insert for added security. For model building purposes ignore this reinforcing element unless the scale is large enough reasonably to permit scoring the screen design on acrylic or clear vinyl and rubbing black paint into the scores to make them stand out. Mount the roof with the scores on the underside.

DOORS

Slab Doors: Slab doors flush with the wall surface are best indicated by score lines and paint. This is where there is no obvious header or jambs. If the door is set back into an entryway, cut the opening in the wall and mount a separate door back the specified distance against the ends of entry walls covering the building wall edges. The entry wall edges will then serve as part of the entry framing with the addition of a vinyl strip at the header location. Whenever headers and jambs are in relief, add strips of vinyl or other material to give scale depth. This slab type of door is probably the one the model builder will run into 95 percent of the time in commercial and industrial buildings and even in private residences as rear and side entrances.

Panelled Doors: At 1/8″ scale and smaller, unless you are building a miniature (Ch. 2) any attempt at adding 1/2″ to 3/4″ deep panels to a door surface is hardly worth the effort. The practical solution is to draw on the design as indicated in Ch. 33. At 1/4″ and larger, it becomes harder to fool the public with a two-dimensional rendition and panel layers should be added. At 1/4″ scale, for example, 1/2″ will be about 0.010″ so vinyl of that thickness can be used. If the scale is large enough, decorative strap hinges can be applied as well as pinhead door knobs. Let your judgment be your guide considering the importance of the door to the total picture. It is sometimes easy to get carried away in a zeal for miniaturization. Such details can look gross if not in exact scale, and are better left off.

Glass Doors: Though *revolving* glass doors have been largely outmoded, you may be confronted with one which can be made by mounting two pieces of clear vinyl or acrylic to the center on each side of a third piece of the same material. Mount it in its container so that the edges of the glazing are not noticeable to camouflage the out-of-scale thickness. Compatible with scale, framing can be accomplished with aluminum paint or applied strips of vinyl. For forming the curved glass container walls, see Ch. 24. *Swinging* glass doors can be framed in the same manner. Polish the edges of acrylic doors (Ch. 24) to help camouflage the thickness and apply glue only at the jambs when mounting. *Sliding* glass doors should get the same consideration with the added attention to the revealed overlapping edges. Below 1/4″ scale, make them out of one piece with a scored division. If you can use 0.010″ clear vinyl at 1/4″ scale, you can get away with a revealed edge since an aluminum painted frame would be about 1/2″ thick.

22

Columnar and Arched
Structures

Since the proven efficiency of the post-and-beam principle, or adaptations thereof, is so extensively applied in construction, the subject of columns deserves a separate chapter. Uniform, plain surfaced, supportive columns are found in structures for all purposes where large unobstructed interior areas are not required, and decorative columns or columnar forms flank entrances and serve as elements of facade treatments (as in model HR 1, Ch. 18); tips on their installation are important to the model builder. As time marches on, we seem more and more to become economic slaves to the dollar sign, necessitating the rationalization of "beauty" into the high-rise maximum-space-use glass box. To a large extent if it is not "economically feasible", it is not built. This means very few Corinthian or Ionic columns, a sad fact that it makes it easier for the model builder who avoids having to sculp capitals of acanthus leaves and scrolls. Fortunately, however, for the practical aesthete (if not for the model builder) there are occasionally still to be found adaptations of Doric and Tuscan column forms, for example, to relieve us from pipe economics. There are also handsome modern, splayed, curved plane capitals to present model building challenges. So even though you

may never be commissioned to build a model of the Acropolis or some ancient edifice in Rome, there are still shapes for which construction tips are in order (Fig. 22-1). Open post-and-beam structures such as pergolas, porticos, peristyles, arches, arcades, and tunnels seem to fall logically into this section since columns in at least suggested form are supportive necessities.

COLUMNS

Column installation for the unwary model builder can turn into one of the largest barrel of snakes known to man. Installing two matched columns in a portico or porte cochere is no problem, but where you have a hundred columns to mount, vertically lined up in rows, it is easy to become a subject for the men in white coats. Planning and layout (Ch. 6 and 8) hold the keys to removing the pain and anguish. Take time to consider the famous "whole picture" and pay attention to Pattinson's Law to prevent painting yourself into a corner or building a boat in a basement.

Before getting into construction tips for multi-

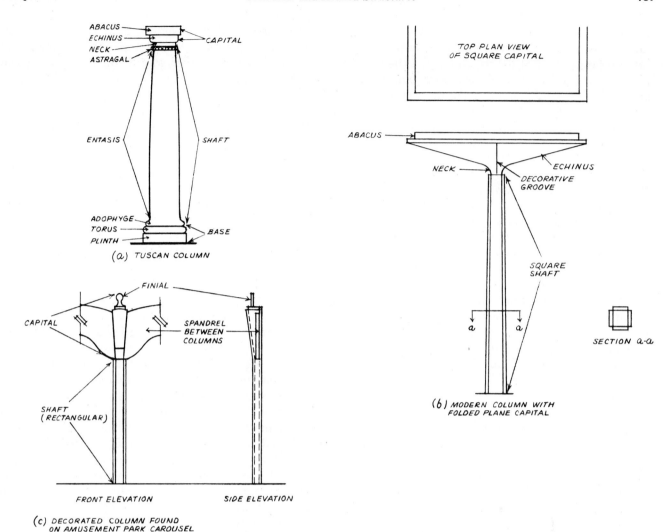

FIGURE 22-1 *Column types (a), (b), (c).*

column projects, there are four subjects that apply generally depending upon the materials and methods employed. They are *sizing, painting, gluing,* and *galling.* The circumstances under which you use these tips will be obvious to you.

Sizing: In the case of floor-to-ceiling butt joint mounting, all columns must be exactly the same length with flat ends at right angles to the length. Violation of either condition will result in a bulged ceiling or floor, a loose column, or a crooked column which will stand out like a red light. Regardless of material, be it piano wire, plastic, wood, plaster, or metal, more than two columns should be sanded in a sizing jig (Ch. 37) as was done for the fence posts (Ch. 16). You may be able to sand two columns individually to get equal length, but as the number increases, gang-sanding is faster and more accurate. Initial sizing is not so important where you can provide selvage to insert into the

base and later raise the columns against a ceiling or trim the tops at roof level.

Painting: Whenever practical paint the columns before installation since it is so often hard to get behind them with a brush and keep the paint from the mounting surfaces. The paint on a wood dowel column may survive insertion through several floor levels, but be prepared for extensive patching after installation in the case of brass pushed through acrylic which will shave the paint off. Patching will be easier, however, than painting the entire column after installation.

Gluing: If you have a row of square wooden columns to install in a peristyle around a building and the butt joint method is used, push common pins into the exact centers of the bottom ends, clip off the pins and file new points for insertion into holes drilled in the base at accurately plotted locations. Put a drop of glue on the bottom end and mount each column, checking to be sure they all line up properly. Just before you install the ceiling, place a drop of contact glue on each column top, and with light pressure against the ceiling level, make final adjustments. The pins will hold the columns in place and provide a stable mount. If the ceiling had to be installed first, put glue on the column bottoms and slide them in starting with a slight angular approach so as to hold smearing on the floor to a minimum. To reduce smearing on the ceiling, force the surface up enough to allow you to apply glue with a spatula. Because of other support to be covered, gluing each column where it passes through a floor in a multicolumn installation is seldom necessary unless the slip fit is too loose to provide the holding friction required periodically in an expanse of floor. In such cases, push the columns through the floor system to a point just before seating and wipe glue with a brush around the columns just above the floor level. Immediately seat the columns and wipe off any excess glue.

Galling: Whenever you try to push any object, in this case a column, through matching holes in a series of separated surfaces, in this case floors, at least a certain amount of galling or binding will occur sometimes to the extent that it becomes impossible to complete the insertion. This is caused by accumulated friction as each layer is reached and by slight unevenness or bow in the column material. Paint will also contribute to the problem. Sometimes a bit of soap or WD40 (Ch. 35) will help, but the best solution is to ream the holes for an easier slip fit. If wood dowel stock is being used, be sure that it is *straight*. If all else fails you will have to break the columns into sections long enough to extend half way through a floor at the ends.

MULTICOLUMN INSTALLATION

As an introduction to this subject, assume you have a display model of a two-story building with second floor balcony to construct at 1/32″ scale. The building whose configuration is shown in Fig. 22-2 is unimportant to this discussion except as it forms a medium for column installation. The balcony wraps around the ends of the building to the extent of one column bay. There is no reason why some other scale couldn't have been chosen except that 1/32″ is an assumed lower limit at which you will normally be required to include architectural detail. Any adjustments to procedures as the scale increases should be selfevident. A plain pipe column has no detail at any scale. The obviously required railings are omitted from this discussion to simplify presentation. The round supportive columns have a diameter of 6″ which, at 1/32″ scale, is equal to 0.0156+″; so 0.015″ piano wire (plus paint) will be authentic. Cut three pieces of 0.015″ vinyl to the rear and side dimensions of the first and second floors and the ceiling (eave), leaving a little selvage at the front to be trimmed later. This is because the columns pass through the balcony so close to its edge that the extra material makes it easier accurately to locate and drill the holes. The model will be assembled off the site because it is

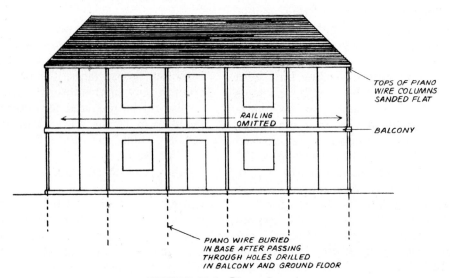

FIGURE 22-2 *Pipe columns.*

easier to work at a table than possibly stretched across the base. Using double-faced tape to hold them together, stack the three pieces of vinyl and locate and drill the column holes to make a friction slip fit of the piano wire columns. Separate the pieces and trim off the excess material according to specifications. Note that the edge of the balcony will be closer to the line of columns than those of the first floor and eave. The first floor will provide a 6″ step at the entrance. Place the first floor in exact location on the model base and punch through the column hole locations. Drill the holes through the graded surface being sure to hold the drill vertical. Complete the building except for the roof installation and mount it with contact glue on the base, checking with a scrap of piano wire to be sure you are lined up with the column holes in the surface grade. Cut enough stock for each column to provide burying excess at the bottom and sand the top ends flat. Note that here a sizing jig is not required since inserting selvage into the base obviates uniform sizing. Install the columns so that their tops are flush with the top surface of the eave and install the roof. Here it is well to reiterate the importance of Pattinson's Law and the continual checking of location and alignment during the assembly of any model or model component. In assembling the building under discussion you would have checked vertical alignment of first and second floor walls and the column holes floor-to-floor. The latter could be done using two pieces of scrap piano wire, one inserted at each front corner. This is a simple case, and the points seem obvious when mentioned, but continued concentration on procedure is necessary to save hours of adjustment.

An alternate situation could be where the columns are simply buried part way into the balcony edge. In this case, drill the holes as before but trim the excess vinyl off through the holes to provide grooves to hold the columns.

A second example of column installation at 1/32″ scale is sketched in Fig. 22-3 showing a section of an amusement park ride raised above grade on the same type of pipe columns used in the first example. This is presented to cover cases where columns must be installed free standing without any ready guide to location or alignment. They must be installed on the model since some of them are in a lake and some on changing terrain involving other structures, making a separate pad on which to install the facility off the model extremely awkward. The columns are to be of 12″ diameter calling for 0.030″ piano wire. The tops of some of these columns will be as high as 60′; we see how important vertical installation as well as alignment is. The approximately 2″ height will make accurate hole drilling mandatory, since the slightest slope to a hole will be accentuated at the top of that column. The model base measures 5′ x 8′, with this ride located near the center of the width and about 3′ from one end. This portion of the ride spans a hill, water, and some paved surface, adding to the difficulty of leaning over the model to drill vertical holes in line. Assuming that you were farsighted enough in your planning, the lake (1/8″ acrylic) was drilled before final mounting in the urethane base, using a plot plan in scale as a pattern. This is much easier than trying to locate holes on an installed lake with edges touching the raised ground of the hill, further complicated by having to assume a spreadeagled position while holding the drill vertical. Drilling the holes in the paving can probably be done easier on the model, hand-drilling *just* through the hard surface (vinyl, etc.) so that the columns can be inserted into the urethane foam beneath, unless, of course, you want to go all the way through into the plywood for security. Be sure you hold the drill *vertical!* The hole locations in the hill of urethane foam will have to be located with the locater described in Ch. 36 since the slopes are too

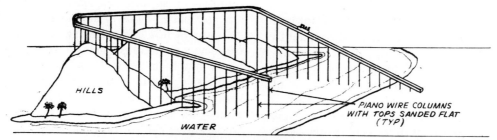

USE OF LOCATING TOOLS (CHAPTER 36)
WILL FACILITATE UNIFORM COLUMN
PLACEMENT

FIGURE 22-3 *Amusement park ride.*

precipitous for a two-dimensional pattern. Cut the columns oversize so that you will have mounting selvage. Sand flat one end of each column as the top bearing surface at the ride track, or trough. Starting at the hill end, insert a column vertically at each pin marker which you set in with the locator mentioned above, and be guided as to height by an overhead elevation gauge (Ch. 36). When you reach the flat areas of the lake and paved surface, you can measure height from such surfaces with a scale, knowing the elevations of these surfaces and column tops from the drawings. Where the columns go into urethane only, as at the hill, place contact glue on the tips before inserting. Where they go into hard surfaces with snug fits, friction should be adequate. When all the columns have been installed, stand back, admire your work, and check alignment. As long as the holes are in line, if a column here and there is off vertical, don't despair. If an offending column is in urethane, pull it and reinsert it with glue since the second installation will ream the hole. If it is mounted in hard material, carefully bend it straight with small pliers gripping the base of the column at the surface. Don't let the column spin or you will be off the other way!

Curved column lines such as those along a double arcade over a walkway can be established with a drafting compass spread to the correct distance from the edge of the walk. Hold the steel point of the compass against the edge of the walk as you move the implement letting the pencil lead side indicate the concentric column line. Then spread the compass to column center distance and leapfrog along the line, making a mark across the line each time you punch the previous mark with the steel point. Note that the column center distance is the length of the chord of the arc between two consecutive centers and not the length of the arc. This chord was determined by spreading the compass to agree with the same points on the drawings in the scale of the model.

Parking Structures: Continuing with multicolumn discussion, assume you have a 1/8″ scale model to build of a four-level above ground parking structure for a shopping center. The roof is one of the parking levels. Ch. 49, photo 44 shows this type of requirement. Except for parapets, the structure is to be open all around, with solid corners enclosing stairways. Access ramps and miscellaneous other facilities, along with stairways, will be ignored to concentrate on column installation. The building will measure approximately 80′ x 140′ requiring 40 columns of 1′ diameter spaced 20′ on center. The two floors and the roof will each be 18″ thick. After considering the problems involved in maintaining straight alignment of columns from floor to floor so that after installation adjustments will not be necessary, you decide to use the continuous column method. Make the floors and roof by laminating, back to back, two pieces of heavy-weight illustration board for each level which, for visualization purposes will measure about 10-1/2″ x 18″ (10″ x 17-1/2″ plus 1/4″ borders all around). This lamination will provide the specified 18″ thickness. On the slab chosen for the roof lay out in pencil the column line grid and stack all three levels using double-faced tape to hold them together temporarily. Place this stack with double-faced tape on the building site, and at each line intersection drill a hole through all layers to take 1/8″ round wooden dowel with a slip fit. Wooden dowel is chosen rather than brass or acrylic because the wood will make it easier to drill the support pin holes discussed later. To forestall galling you should have an easy slip fit in the top three layers, leaving a snug fit in the building pad to anchor the columns. Make a trial lamination and try a 9/64″ bit. Only experience will tell you the size. Sometimes a dull 1/8″ bit will do the job satisfactorily since it will tend to drill oversize. Separate the drilled stack, turn over each layer and sand off any bloom caused by drilling. On the under side of one of the upper floors, note at fairly evenly distributed random about 14 support holes (Fig. 22-4) and cut and peel off approximately 3/8″ diameter discs of the top (white) lamination only of the illustration board at these holes. This will form shallow cavities in the ceiling surfaces to hide support pins inserted through the columns. Do the same at the corresponding holes in the other levels above the building pad. Cut 40 dowel columns long enough to be buried in the base and protrude about 1/4″ above the roof. Bevel the insertion end of each. Pick out the established number of support columns and bevel the other end of each. Note that the number of support columns is not critical since the double thickness of heavyweight illustration board will hold rigid up to as much as 8 or 10 inches without worrying about sag. Facing the building pad, start with the support column farthest away from you and drive it into its hole, being sure that the top will protrude above the roof of the assembled structure. If the friction hold doesn't satisfy you, add glue, either white or contact. Assuming that the floor to ceiling distance is 12′, make a support pin hole

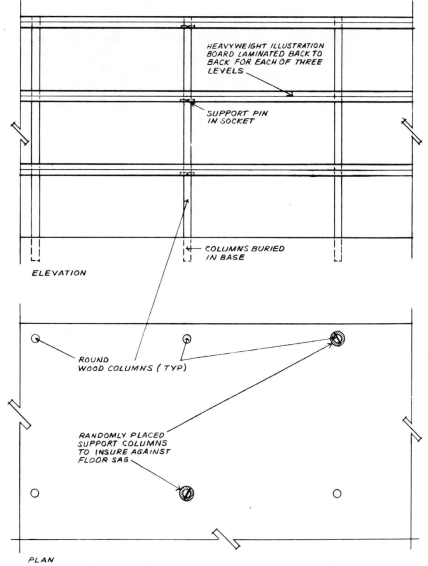

FIGURE 22-4 *Floor support.*

drilling guide by drilling a 9/64″ hole parallel to the greater dimension through a piece of 1″ × 2″ white pine base framing stock and sand down this dimension to 1-1/2″. (Fig. 22-5) Place the guide over the support column just mounted and drill a hole through the diameter of the column to accept a common pin letting the drill bit rest on top of the guide. Push through a pin and clip off each end so that there is a little less than 1/8″ protruding evenly on each side. The pin will rest within the diameter of the cavity in the ceiling and prevent the second floor from slipping down the column. Do the same for the other support columns and work the second floor down over them until it stops at the support pins. Don't forget to remove the drilling guide from the last support column in-

stalled before installing the second floor! Follow the same procedure for the third floor and the roof. For additional security, just before mounting the roof put a coating of white glue around each column just above the support pin.

Now that the building has been assembled on its support columns, tap in the remaining columns, adding white glue to each at the roof level just before driving a column home. If any galling should occur, make spacers out of white pine the same height as the drilling guide Fig. 22-5 and insert them between floors in line next to the offending column. If there is any flex in the cardboard the temporary spacers will help hold the holes in line. With a hacksaw blade saw off the column selvage protruding through the roof and sand

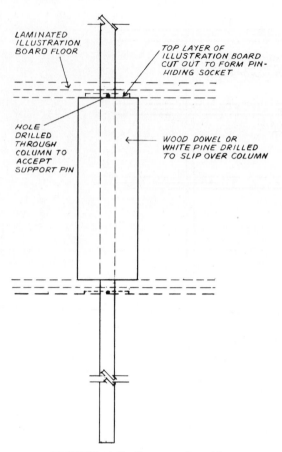

LAMINATED
ILLUSTRATION
BOARD FLOOR

TOP LAYER OF
ILLUSTRATION BOARD
CUT OUT TO FORM PIN-
HIDING SOCKET

HOLE
DRILLED
THROUGH
COLUMN TO
ACCEPT
SUPPORT PIN

WOOD DOWEL OR
WHITE PINE DRILLED
TO SLIP OVER COLUMN

FIGURE 22-5 *Support pin guide.*

them down flush until you can draw a straightedge over the roof without obstruction. To cover the column ends line the roof with 0.010″ vinyl or 2-ply Strathmore paper. Use contact glue on an oversize piece and trim the edges with a razor blade after installation. This added thickness won't destroy visible authenticity particularly since it will probably be hidden by a parapet and fascia.

A variation to the system just discussed could be the requirement for capitals at the ceiling ends of each column. They could be made out of wooden dowel stock larger than that of the columns and slipped over the column tops and secured with glue. This would obviate the need for support pins. In a case where you wanted to avoid anticipated galling, cut the holes through the stack of floors as previously, but this time for a snug column fit. Cut the columns in single floor to floor lengths using a sizing jig (Ch. 37) and drive each one into its hole from the underside of each floor until it is flush with the top surface. Then assemble consecutive floors so that column bottoms are contact glued to the tops of the columns in the floor below. As you assemble the structure double check alignment with a square around the perimeter.

In closing this discussion about a parking garage type structure, remember that some of the columns would be omitted because of supporting structures housing utility equipment, stairways, elevators, etc. Also realize that there will be many parking structures, for example, that will be partially or completely enclosed, thus relieving you of some or all the column gymnastics just described.

Square Columns: Square columns for the structure just discussed would be installed using the same procedure with the addition of the problem of square holes. Cut 1/8″ square columns out of white pine or bass wood, or use square brass rod from your model supply house. The neatest way is to drill 9/64″ holes as before through the levels stacked with double-faced tape and then broach these holes with a 9/64″ broach in your drill press, being sure to hold the chuck from turning so that the hole edges will be consistently parallel to the floor edges. In the absence of a broach, mount the columns in round holes just large enough to take them with a little pressure. Follow the same procedure with the support pins, and when all installed, twist turned columns against a straight-edge to line them up. Fill visible gaps around the columns at floor level with spackle.

Shaped and Decorated Columns: These are exemplified in Fig. 22-1 requiring initial analysis mentally to separate different design elements into constituent parts that can be assembled. This will simplify construction by obviating the necessity for carving the whole column out of one piece. Referring to Fig. 22-1*a*, analyse the Tuscan column as follows. The shaft and neck could be considered one piece over which the astragal (like a string of beads) could be slipped to define the top of the shaft. The plinth, torus, astragal, echinus, and abacus could all be washers of appropriate sizes, or punchouts, flat buttons, etc.

The correct classical terms are used not to make you erudite but as a means for easy identification of the parts for construction purposes. Unless you do nothing but assemble columns every day, if you are like me, the terms will go in one ear and out the other. On the other hand, this is another good example of how your knowledge of terms, processes and products can help you more intelligently to construct any model.

If you are an expert on the lathe, you could turn out the entire master out of one piece of bass wood. The alternative is to carve it out of bass wood or white pine in sections starting with the shaft which could be formed from wood dowel stock on a lathe. If you consider the astragal a disc, include it along with the other five discs and assemble them to form the complete column.

With but one column to support a statue of Lord Nelson in the park, your master will be the final product, but with a row of them to do, the obvious answer is casting (Ch. 24) to get exact duplicates of your effort. With this in view, analyse the column profile again to see what undercuts would make removal from the mold difficult if not impossible. The abacus, echinus, and other discs would tend to lock the casting in, but these could be cast separately. The slight curve in the entasis might be releasable considering the elasticity of Blak Stretchy mold material (Ch. 24) if you decided to cast the shaft and neck together, but why take a chance when you can mold the entire assembled master? The split mold method is described in Ch. 24.

Figure 22-1*b* shows a representative modern curved plane capital and shaft which can't be turned because they are square. This is obviously a three-section column requiring carving a master capital (less abacus) and shaft separately. The capital, less abacus, which is a simple, square element of the capital later added, consists of four curved planes sloping down from the four sides of a square and joining in the curve shown at the base where it attaches to the shaft. The line shown on the capital in the center represents a decorative groove dividing each of the four sloping and curved planes. Note the vertical edge at the top of the echinus. Starting with a square block of white pine or bass wood cut out most of the selvage with your bandsaw, and then, armed with sanding sticks and carving tools (Ch. 36) work out the shape, forming *straight* lines at the plane intersections. The shaft can be sand-formed as a tapered, undersized square in section as shown by the section in Fig. 22-1*b*. The shaft can then be brought to size by adding strips of material to form the open right angles at the corners. The two masters are then molded (Ch. 24). After adding the square abacus to the cast capital, contact glue it to the cast shaft. Most of such columns in my experience were left in natural plaster to represent white architectural concrete, but of course the color will depend upon the specifications. If the joint of the capital and shaft seems too precarious, form a protrusion in the neck of the master capital, file the tip round and drill a shallow hole in the top of the shaft master to accept it. This condition is shown in Fig. 24-3. Contact glue is remarkably strong, and after installation under the surface it supports, the column normally will stay in place

firmly. Your decision concerning such joints will have to depend upon scale and your own judgment from experience. For this type of column see Ch. 49, photo 46.

Figure 22-1*c* shows a form of decorative column used to support a carousel structure. This one was at 1/32″ scale and presented the problem of holding decorative planes in a concentric circle so that the final assembly was rigid and uniform. The circle form consisting of specially shaped columns and spandrels was controlled by cutting a string of columns and spandrels out of one piece of vinyl with a selvage tab on the end of the last spandrel fitting into a notch cut into the first column. This joint was covered by the layers of vinyl added at the columns to obtain column thickness and decoration. The outward splay of the capitals was forced with inserts of vinyl and all construction openings were filled with spackle. Finials were beads placed on points formed in one of the layers of vinyl. Scroll work in such cases can be formed with spackle, being sure to add contact glue to, or punch holes in, a slick surface to give the spackle a binding medium when dry. At larger scales, elements of such columns can be cast and assembled.

These three examples should serve as guides for your ingenuity in accomplishing variations. Corinthian coils at the capital can be formed out of fine wire and then filled with spackle or plaster. You will have to put on your artist's hat for acanthus leaves. The scrolls at the capital of an Ionic column can be formed by twisting strips of bond paper into coils, setting with a spray fixative or clear Krylon and then filling. If the scale is large enough to justify the effort, make vertical fluting by applying strips of material along the column shaft and sand and/or fill the interstices with spackle and use shaped tools to obtain the concave configuration between ridges. If you have a horizontal indexing fixture for your shop mill that will hold a shaft of acrylic rod, run the shaft under a round steel burr of the correct diameter, and turn the shaft one flute width for each run. Doing the same with a shaft of close grained wood will provide guides for hand finishing the flutes where the column is tapered or curved as the entasis of Fig. 22-1*a*.

ARCHES

As valid structural concept, every building arch could be said to be borne on each side by a column even though no column as such is visible. Because of this dependent structural relationship, arches are included in this chapter. Bridge arches were covered in Ch. 14. Curved arches are not prolific occurrences in modern architecture, but even if you expect to model antiquity, whether Byzantine, Moorish, or Gothic, they are all characteristically shaped curved spandrels in one plane between two columns or bearing points. Their basic execution is uncomplicated except perhaps for decoration and shape in some. As in the case of the single arched bridge in Ch. 14, consider first your Jay's Nest for a ready-made hemispherical form. An arched entrance through a wall thicker than the wall material being used can be made by cutting the arch in two separated layers of material and spanning the distance between them at the opening with a vinyl liner of the same width as the wall thickness. In fact this layer method provides the easiest solution in many cases where it is much easier to cut configurations in separate layers of thin material than it is to carve concentric changes in plane out of solid stock. The stepped, tapered depth of a Gothic arch face, for example, is made with layers of material, each one having a larger or smaller opening than the one next to it. Arches, or a series thereof for a colonnade, can be cast in a one-time mold or breakaway form similar to that used by cement contractors when they lay concrete steps (Ch. 24). Construct at least the basic arch shape in the form to give you a solid block into which you can file such configurations as the scallops favored by the Moors. To strengthen a series of arches for that Roman viaduct made in one pour, suspend piano wire, rod or strips of wood lengthwise over the arches in the form.

PERGOLAS, COLONNADES, AND ARCADES

These similar structures are included here because of their columnar composition. Trellis roofing for pergolas was discussed in Ch. 16. Whether the arches be flat (post-and-beam) or curved, the key to success in any of these structures lies in straight, vertically true columns in line at specified centers. Tips on column installation and anchorage were given previously in this chapter; so a few tips on establishing curved arches between them are given here. Solid, curved arches can be made by cutting vinyl fillers and inserting them between columns. If the columns are to appear centered in their capitals, attach a continuous strip of vinyl arches to

the column surfaces on each side and fill the visible cavity with spackle. At the larger scales, a curved colonnade can be poured into a curved form as mentioned previously. Porticos at building entrances, peristyles around an open courtyard, arcades down the side of a church, etc., should be made in close association with the pertinent building construction since they involve a certain amount of fit-as-you-go procedure, but a double colonnade over a walk across an open area, for example, might best be made complete off the model base, walk and all. If you have a curved configuration to accomplish, this is often far easier than working at detail spreadeagled to the center of a large model. Make the walk deep enough to provide secure column anchorage suitable to the scale and size of the columns. This extra "meat" can be buried in the model surface when the assembly is installed. At the smaller scales, laminate vinyl around a curve, cutting the vinyl to the configurations of arch, capitals and friezes (beams) consecutively in each strip. This is easier than trying to form solid material of the specified final thickness (Ch. 24). At say 1/2" scale, you might be able to cut a curved beam out of the correct thickness of acrylic on your bandsaw, thus establishing a firm basic shape to decorate. At almost any scale decorated friezes can be accomplished in vinyl strips punctured for spackle anchorage. Using a scribe, work the design into the spackle and then glue the strip to the beam already installed. The only satisfactory answer to intricate open scroll work, several or many times repeated is acid-etching (Ch. 17). In small or single applications you might be lucky enough to find a lace simulation at your favorite department store, but consider the rigidity of clients' specifications.

TUNNELS

If you consider tunnels as deep arches, they can be accomplished using tubular forms slit to semicircular shape. I have found the various sizes of drawing tubes will often supply the scale answer. If you can't drill a hole through that urethane foam mountain, make a vertical cut on each side of the tunnel area and remove the urethane plug. Lay the roadway or railway and install the tunnel form covered by part of the urethane just removed. Fill the cracks in the mountain as indicated in Ch. 10. Ground cover will complete the camouflage of your excavation.

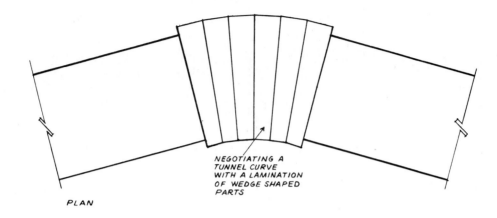

NEGOTIATING A
TUNNEL CURVE
WITH A LAMINATION
OF WEDGE SHAPED
PARTS

PLAN

REINFORCED CONCRETE
PORTAL STRUCTURE

TUNNEL SHAPES: VERTICAL DOTTED LINES REPRESENT SIDES FOR
RAILROAD USE. URBAN TRAFFIC TUNNELS WOULD
PROBABLY UTILIZE COMPLETE ARC TO PROVIDE
SIDEWALK SPACE

FIGURE 22-6 *Tunnel.*

Note that particularly at small scale where no viewer could see through a complete tunnel if he or she tried, make shallow, "disappearing" space holes at each end and paint the interior black. If a through tunnel is required on a curve for a working railway, make the curved portion similar to that in Fig. 22-6. This consists of separate pieces of wood with the tunnel shape cut out and laminated as wedge shapes. Make the tunnel portals shaped as indicated in the drawings. The material could be wood, vinyl, acrylic, or poured plaster, depending largely upon scale.

A railroad tunnel would probably have a shape as indicated by the dotted lines in Fig. 22-6 since a radius of a semicircle large enough to provide vertical clearance will give waste space at each side. A compromise is reached by building the sides as vertical chords of a circle with the desired radius of the arch. An urban automobile tunnel often needs the extra side space for side walks, accessible utility ducts, etc.

23

Industrial, Transportation, and Recreational Facilities

INDUSTRIAL FACILITIES

Complicated petroleum refineries, atomic power plants, etc. may be in the highly specialized realm of the engineering model builder, but don't think for a moment that you won't at some time be confronted with piping systems, motors, pumps, valves, transformers, storage tanks, cranes, scrubbing towers, and railroad facilities, to name a few items of mechanical ilk. Even in the case of industrial plant models where you are concerned mostly with buildings and architecture, you should include in your fund of knowledge at least a basic understanding of mechanical systems and the modelling thereof. You don't have to be an expert in the science fields, but through preliminary discussion with your industrial client a layman's analysis of the particular system or process at hand is a prerequisite to an intelligent construction of the model. This is true even if the mechanical facilities to be shown are only accessory to the main project. Also, if you know why those pipes crossing overhead are there, or why the transformer yard is so located and what it serves, such knowledge paves the way to authenticity in the result. Finally,

the more you know about the model subject the more help you can be to your client which is the name of the game in any professional service.

Assume you have a 1/16″ scale exterior model to build of a manufacturing plant which makes portable electric generators. Without any technical analysis of needed facilities they include for our purposes a transformer yard, an overhead traveling hoist between the assembly and paint buildings, an elevated storage tank, an uncovered piping system on overhead racks, a water cooling tower, and a railroad spur. Since this is to be an exterior model you are interested only in those facilities which are visible outdoors. Interior plant layouts, etc., are covered in Ch. 31.

The first source of pipe system elements which comes to mind is one of the engineering model supply houses (Ch. 50). Even though their smallest scale seems, for most items, to be 1/4″, you may find in this case that their smallest electric motor, for example, will serve for the generators for the group of finished systems you plan to show on the shipping dock. It is a good idea to have an engineering model supply catalog in your reference library (Ch. 43) since you will usually find different sizes of the same item under a given scale.

For the overhead piping use 0.015″ piano wire for 3″ pipe. 0.030″ piano wire will serve acceptably as 6″ pipe; the racks can be made by soldering wide U's of piano wire to posts of the same material. Where the drawings do not show sufficient information about the contents of the transformer yard, refer to a transformer catalog for overall size and configuration. You won't be expected to show every nut and bolt at 1/16″ scale, but you will likely find that adding a few strips of vinyl fins to a shaped block of wood well worth the effort toward authenticity. Tiny beads can serve as insulators, even though they may be actually a bit oversize. In the absence of the right ball, a spherical storage tank can be made using the fin system discussed in Ch. 24, with the supporting legs made out of piano wire. Make the carrying beam for the hoist out of strips of vinyl and glue it to the centers of inverted U support frames made from bent piano wire. An example of a water-cooling tower is shown in Fig. 23-1. This represents the evaporative-type where the hot water is dropped over and past horizontal fins which help to disperse the heat. The cool water is collected in a tank at the base and re-used. The roof plan will reveal cooling fans which draw air up through the system. The fins, creating a type of radiator in appearance, are made by stacking layers of vinyl separated by layers of black acrylic of smaller dimensions than those of the fins. To avoid the problem of camouflaging a flush joint in formed vinyl fan shrouds, search through your Jay's Nest for the right diameter tubing. A plastic pill bottle may be just the right size. Make the fans out of Strathmore paper and set the twist in the blades with a fixative or clear Krylon (Ch. 32). Paint the background black underneath the fans. Be sure to tilt all fan blades in the same direction!

TT gauge is 1/16″ scale; so you can get enough track to make the spur from your local hobby shop where you can find cars and an engine if you want to go that far. Don't forget the bumper at the end of the spur. See Ch. 13 for further tips on railroads.

The items just mentioned of course only scratch the surface of all the possible industrial facilities. It would be impractical if not impossible to cover them all, but these standard few should prime your imagination. Probably the most productive tip I can give is to take a mental inventory of all the odd-ball industrial facilities during your first review of the drawings at the start of the job. Unusual facilities peculiar to a manufacturing process often require attention right at the start to forestall a makeshift substitute at the last minute.

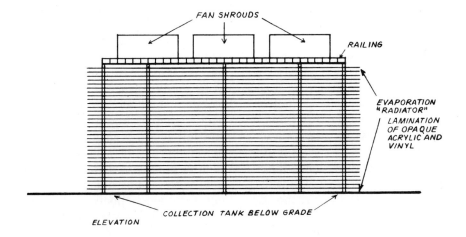

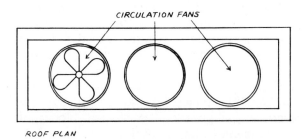

FIGURE 23-1 *Water cooling tower.*

In your planning think of all possible outside sources of items which could save time. A trip to a local toy store and purchase of a 1/4″ scale fork lift, for example, will cost a lot less than the time required to make one in your shop. During your review of the drawings submitted by your architectural client be aware of blank areas carrying the notation "By outside contractor". You no doubt obtained enough information to enable you to include provision for these in your quotation, but don't forget immediately to obtain the detailed information necessary for construction. They may contain a knotty problem requiring some research or experimenting time.

TRANSPORTATION FACILITIES

The common facilities to serve vehicles of land, sea, and air are set out to remind you of some of the identifying characteristics peculiar to their purpose. In design and function study models the vehicles are subordinated to architecture and land use, and need be present only in block form to give scale to the layout. In display models the vehicles peculiar to the facility are necessary to complete the picture and their detail should be developed within reasonable limits allowed by the scale. Only display models are considered here.

Bus Terminal: A 1/8″ scale model of a transcontinental bus terminal should include buses with configuration, color, and markings of the particular line for whom the model is being constructed. Before attempting your own manufacture, check with your client's public relations department. They may be able to lead you to scale decals if not the finished product itself. If they have buses modelled at 1/4″ scale suggest doing your model at that scale to save time. Chances are that the additional cost of the larger model will be more than offset by the saving in ready-made rolling stock. If this approach fails, check hobby shop inventories for HO scale buses (which are acceptable at 1/8″ scale) and toy stores. The wheels should be movable and window glass simulated with transparent material. Mask and repaint where necessary. Sometimes windows and windshields will snap out to save masking them. Hopefully you can find specified colors in Krylon spray cans (Ch. 32) which will shorten repaint time considerably. If your model is for one of the large bus companies, the hobby shop may have identifying decals. In addi-

tion to a couple of buses in the operating lanes, park one or two in their ready slots and one in the service facility area. Build the terminal and outbuildings following the basic principles discussed previously. If the terminal has covered throughway bus access with one side open, show a bus at a loading platform and one just leaving the terminal. Include visible human figures and stacks of luggage, etc. Don't forget representative placement of automobiles in parking areas and on surrounding streets.

Railroad Terminals: Railroad terminals require the same approach as that of the bus terminal with the addition of tractive power units different in configuration from that of the cars. In any case establish with your client a scale which can be satisfied by available hobby shop equipment. Where the subject is a freight yard with train makeup facilities you can imagine the vast difference in time required between laying rail (even if preformed) and laying prepared roadbed as well as that between making cars from scratch and assembling kits. See Ch. 13 for tips on track laying.

Marine Terminals: Ports as a model feature will likely be large enough to require detail in vessels beyond their block configuration as was true in the case of the buses just discussed. Though the sea or lake scape may be token in size, you will still have to pour or otherwise indicate water as discussed in Ch. 12. If you pour resin be prepared to remove any meniscoid effects against pilings or other dock surfaces by disturbing with a scribe or wooden stick along the plane of contact. These occur where a liquid tends to climb a wet surface and fall at a dry surface. Assuming that because of depth any water will be opaque, you can avoid such physical problems by mounting docking facilities and flat-bottomed vessels on the surface. In my experience boats and ships have been much harder to find in scale than automotive equipment. If hobby shop kits don't provide the answer and you can't find a representative freighter or ocean liner at the toy stores, try to find drawings and photographs to get you under way. A trip to the docks armed with camera (and even tape measure!) should at least provide proportion guides not only for seagoing equipment but loading cranes and chutes as well. Hulls need be made only from waterline up. Superstructure can be assembled using shaped blocks of acrylic with windows and port holes masked for painting. Funnels can be shaped out of wood dowel. My dictionary shows an excellent elevation of a capstan. Anchor chain could probably be found at a costume jewelry store. Life boats can be formed out of Strathmore paper or vinyl and davits out of bent piano wire. Just the foregoing items indicate how easy it is to get carried away from time and dollar limits in executing detail. I believe it is safe to assume that items in the entourage of the main subject such as a fish cannery terminating the scene including this marine terminal could be finished in block configuration and paint much in the same manner you show monotone block shapes outside the property in an urban development. Where the ship in this case is as important as the building or loading equipment serving it, there must be a balance between the detail of each. Only judgment based upon experience (and budget) can tell you how far to go toward complete authenticity.

Air Terminals: Airports involve the use of so much open land to provide landing and take-off space that usually a model of a terminal building or buildings will be at a scale too large conveniently to include all the property. The scale of the buildings must be large enough to permit adequate reading of architecture and utility, and the atmosphere can be established by the presence of loading planes and those approaching the take-off runway or taxiing home. Features of the terminal building would include a traffic control tower with 360 degree fenestrated visibility and may include moving walkways at least not completely visible in an exterior model. Other than the movable fixed stairways wheeled to plane side, there may also be telescoping covered passageways for loading and unloading. For airplanes again check with the hobby shops and toy stores for subjects which even though requiring modification will save your construction time. As in the case of the bus line client, check with some of the manufacturers and air lines for model replicas. As in the case of the ships just discussed, the planes should have detail compatible with that on the serving buildings. The toy stores should produce enough small planes to park in a private plane area. Consider the use of the various size round headed pins for runway markers and O gauge accessories for 1/4″ fork lifts and towmotors. For an eyecatching flashing red light on the top of the control tower see Ch. 30.

Space Terminals: Spaceports open up a whole new challenge to the model builder, not necessarily because of the terminal itself but because of the site. For display the diorama is a solution where an open-face box permitting frontal observation only shows the terminal or station suspended by an invisible rear mount against a back drop of an artist's rendition of that part of the universe. An approaching space ship could be mounted the same way. At a necessarily greatly foreshortened distance to the earth, ground facilities are shown with a piggyback pair taking off or a rocket blasting off to rendezvous with the satellite. A key to the effectiveness of such a display is lighting for which Ch. 29 will give you some ideas.

AMUSEMENT FACILITIES

The so-called theme parks (Ch. 49, photos 9 and 30) are probably the epitome of collections of amusement ride structures. About all the variations known to man are usually found at these locations, including all the well-known beach front standards such as ferris wheels, dodgems, and roller coasters. Because of the size of these parks, the site model will usually allow a scale of no larger than 1/32″ for model handling and display purposes. Divided models in such cases can be difficult because of the lack of structure-free area through which to make the division. Though a particular ride may be faster to construct at this scale than one at say 1/8″ scale where more detail is practicable, the smaller scale provides a challenge in arriving at authenticity in the absence of detail. In other words, you have to omit so much structural detail, varying in amount depending upon the nature of the particular ride or structure, the question is presented: "How do I make the facility look like the real thing when I can't possibly include all the cables, braces, etc.?" Generally speaking, the answer lies in visualizing the overall configuration and then breaking that mass concept into its main characteristic components, forgetting the nuts and bolts. Performing this analysis makes possible very realistic results. Construction tips for a few of the out-of-doors facilities are submitted ignoring those such as dodgems for which the building only would be seen.

Flume Ride: This consists basically of boats moving in a trough of water and propelled by the force of gravity down a configured slope after being raised mechanically to an altitude much in the same manner that roller coaster cars are handled. Referring to Fig. 22-3 in the section on columns, you will see a section of such a structure for which you have installed the supports. Though the trough supported by these columns may be round bottomed you can ignore that shape at 1/32″ scale under model builder's license. Trace the bottom of the trough on 0.010″ vinyl using the same plan you used in laying out the support columns. Go as far as you can with available length of material, leaving overlap selvage at the necessary joints and to provide for any extension necessary because you are mounting a plan figure at a slope. Cut out the strips and paint them a water blue color. Carefully sand the edges to obtain flat surfaces and to remove any paint runover that will prevent adhesion. Have a dry run session section by section holding the trough bottom on top of the columns with your fingers to check curves and to decide upon joint location. Joints should be at column tops.

When you have established the location of a section including a curve, for example, glue it in place with contact glue after marking column locations on the under side of the trough to take advantage of the glue's strongest adhesion with dried glue on each surface. Carefully cut the end of a section so that it just bears on a column top where joints will be most secure. Overpaint the water blue with a dry surface color where the boats are to be hauled to the top of the system. When you have installed the complete trough bottom and tied the ends into the terminal buildings check the joints and apply temporary slivers of Scotch-type tape to hold together obstinate joints.

Next cut strips of vinyl to the scale width (height) of trough sides, including the thickness of the bottom. Using your fingers as flush-with-bottom guides feed a strip onto the edge of the bottom of the trough, wicking in just enough acrylic cement (Ch. 34) to give an immediate weld. When your brush supplies too much, blowing on the joint while it is held in place will help dry it. Make the joints at places different from those in the bottom. When the assembly is securely glued, remove the tape patches and with a fine brush paint the sides the prescribed color. The reason for painting at this late stage is to keep paint off the sides for mounting. Paint will prevent adhesion. Make boats by folding paper or vinyl to the specified shape and paint them. They very likely will be rectangular in shape with scow shaped bows. Place these boats at plausible distances, covering joints where possible, and fill them with human figures seated by cutting off their legs.

Roller Coaster: A variation I remember had a vertical, cylindrical "starter" within which the cars were mechanically raised to starting altitude on a coiled track. The track was supported within a circle on racks attached to columns. Make the columns out of piano wire, sand-flatten the tops, and insert them evenly into the base around the circle of specified diameter. Make the racks out of 0.010″ vinyl by pinching strips of the material tightly with pliers around a column size piece of piano wire and cement the ends together with acrylic cement. Slip these racks over their respective columns where friction will hold them while you adjust to establish an evenly coiled path for the rails. When the racks have been positioned a small bead of contact glue on the column will prevent them from slipping when installing the track. With tweezers place a spacer glued to the top of each rack to keep the rails evenly separated. Starting at the level approach at the station, mount a strip of rail made out of 0.010″ vinyl long enough to reach the top of the starting coil and feed it through the column assembly coiling it upward as you glue it with acrylic cement against a spacer at each rack, leaving selvage at the top end. Do the same with a second strip to form the other rail. On flat land lay out the locations for the remaining columns using a pattern. On uneven terrain call on your locator tool (Ch. 36) for assistance both for site and height. Glue the continuation of the rail to the tops of the piano wire columns flush with their tops with as few joints as possible located at the columns. Make the cars in the same manner that you made the boats for the Flume Ride, only this time assemble them in trains. Fill the cars with thrill seeking occupants and throw the switch. Paint the columns white and leave the tracks in white vinyl. Spots of color can be had by painting the cars.

Cork Screw: This is a popular version of the roller coaster where the feature is a vertical "cork screw" loop of track which causes the cars to make one complete lateral rollover. At the beginning of the loop they start to twist until they are upside down at the top of the loop and keep twisting until they reach level track at the end of the loop. The construction is the same generally as that of the roller coaster course, the particular challenge being the forming and anchoring of the loop. One form of support includes three arched girders bridging the course so that they hold the loop of track with suspending cables. The girders are tied together in the center of the arc and are separated in splayed fashion to individual concrete anchors. Form the girder assembly first using piano wire inserted into appropriate blocks of wood or acrylic forming the anchors. Then install the two sections of vinyl track using a spacer under the joined girders at the top to help hold even track gauge. Anchor the approach end of one rail and through trial and error twist it up against the spacer and down to level anchorage where it meets the level track again. When you have established this course evenly, do the same with the other rail maintaining consistent gauge throughout. This takes a bit of gymnastics, but you will find that the stiff vinyl will tend to hold position controlled by the length of the strips anchored at each end of the loop. Fine slivers of vinyl can be used for specified suspension cables. Glue a train of cars just leaving their inverted position to add interest.

Ferris Wheel: Whether this long-standing attraction is mounted in fixed position or on elevating booms, make the identifying feature by cutting out two wheels of 0.010″ vinyl including spokes and hubs. Glue these to the ends of a 1/16″ wood dowel axle slightly longer than the width of the cars or seat containers. Away from the hubs just short of the free-swinging car area glue spacers between opposite spokes to hold the wheel together and allow free entry of the cars. Make the cars out of folded vinyl, paint them in bright colors and mount them between the two rims of the wheel in positions to reflect the effect of movement of the ride. Human figures in the cars will indicate activity in the necessarily static scene.

Spider: A tilting spider ride can be made from acrylic for the three "legs" with cars suspended from rimless wheels of vinyl attached to the ends of the legs. Make the cars from pieces of brass tubing with paper punchout bottoms and parasol punchout canopies pierced by the suspending cables. Single strands of copper electrical wire can be found at about 0.005″ to make plausible cables at 1/32″ scale. The body of the three-legged spider tilts on a central gimbaled mount as it turns.

Carousel: A carousel can be made from vinyl discs with suitably decorated tubular center attached and with cutout horse profiles glued to wires inserted into the base disc and into the rotating ceiling structure hidden by the canopy of the building roof. If the fact that the horses are two-dimensional is not sufficiently camouflaged by the 1/32″ scale, glue profile mates on the backs of the wires and fill the spaces with spackle (Ch. 35). Paint and human figures will contribute to authenticity.

Sky Ride: One form of sky ride consists of a closed loop cable on which cars are hung at fixed distances and which is moved by machinery located in one ground terminal over crosstrees on top of tower structures placed in line across the park property. Square, tapered reinforced concrete towers are formed out of white pine and inserted at their prescribed locations through to the base plywood so that the taper starts at the surface of the finished grade. Make the mounts secure since the nylon thread used for the cable will be pulled taut to exert pressure. Make the crosstrees out of piano wire and glue them into grooves filed in the tower tops. The ends pierce sheaves made out of three layers of vinyl punchouts, the smaller center one of the sandwich forming the groove. At the rear of the interior of the terminal buildings pins are driven into the base plywood and bent over to form hooks. The completed terminal structures are then mounted with holes in the floors to clear the hooks which are not visible from the outside. A loop of nylon thread is inserted through the entry door of one of the terminals and caught on the hook. The two strands are then placed over the supports just outside the entry and continued up over the sheaves at the towers. After weighting one of the strands to keep it in place, loop the other strand through the entrance of the second terminal and catch it on the hook. Pull the two cable ends together snugly and tie them together. The resulting closed loop extending throughout the system is then carefully slipped until the knot is hidden inside the terminal building past a separation maintaining frame just outside the entrance similar to the one at the other end of the run. Make the cars out of vinyl with canopy-holding uprights included in the pattern. Through the centers of the canopies insert wires with hooks bent into their top ends to a configuration which will allow passage over the sheaves. Push the wires just through the car bottoms, and glue the ends of the hooks to the cable at specified distances with a cyanoacrylate glue (Ch. 34).

OUTDOOR THEATERS

Outdoor theaters involve spectator seating as the principal challenge to the model builder, and are discussed next under Sports Facilities which require similar arrangements.

SPORTS FACILITIES

Since most of your career will be filled with exterior model building, stress is placed on tips for open air sports areas. Requirements for indoor arenas for the popular activities will probably be few and far between, so reliance will be placed on your imagination to make any necessary adjustments when you have that "Super Dome" to build with the removable roof! Sports such as football, baseball, track and tennis require accurately accomplished graphics (Ch. 26) for boundary and yardage lines, etc.; so it is a great help to have in your reference library (Ch. 43) an all-inclusive book on area layouts giving the generally accepted standard or official dimensions. I use a booklet put out by one of the sporting goods manufacturers. It has come to the rescue many times.

Grass is important to so many playing fields that it is well to establish if possible standards of execution which can be employed within wide ranges of scale. At scales below 1/32″ where the application covers postage stamp size areas, you can get by satisfactorily with painted surfaces on illustration board or vinyl finished off with stippling (Ch. 33). At 1/32″ scale and larger, there is nothing better in my opinion than 4-lb urethane foam. Even if you have not done the grading in this material, you can always provide pockets to accept a field size portion. It has a texture that seems to adjust itself visually to almost any scale and for that reason becomes a time-saving standard. Grass is discussed more fully in Ch. 25.

Lining can be done with a ruling pen and paint of free-flowing consistency (Ch. 26). Be sure the urethane is well vacuumed to remove all loose dust before painting. If you have a hard time getting sharp lines on urethane, consider inserting strips of vinyl or other material on edge into the urethane. The revealed edges will make perfect lines. Make a knife slice along a straight edge as a guide to insertion, being careful not to make the groove wider than the thickness of lining material.

Baseball base pads can be squares of vinyl or even illustration board if the scale permits. Tennis nets, baseball backstops, and basketball baskets can be made from the materials discussed in Ch. 16. I have made many tennis nets by cutting wire or cloth netting to exact size, spraying it with matte white Krylon, and then gluing with contact glue between two piano wire posts inserted into the court. With cloth netting, spray it with clear Krylon to bind it before cutting, or it may fall apart. Football goal posts can be formed out of wire. For the water sports, skating, hockey, and skiing, see Ch. 12 for swimming pools, ice, and snow. A chair lift in a skiing area can be made following the tips for the Sky Ride discussed

earlier in this chapter. Boundary and slalom flags can be made with wire and triangles of colored paper. Running tracks can be painted illustration board using the color of the actual material used. Tan bark can be fine, dyed sawdust applied over spray glue. The cushions for a pole vault area could be cloth covered squares of sponge rubber or plastic. The scale will dictate the extent of constituent authenticity.

Golf Courses: Golf courses, other than their clubhouse facilities, are 95 percent grading and landscaping (Ch. 25) for both of which urethane foam is ideal. You can delineate the greens by painting them a slightly darker green than the fairways and identify them with hole marking flags. Identify the tee areas with strips of worn looking grass, a ball washer, bench, and occasional drinking fountain. The fairways should be obvious between tree planted areas. Water hazards can be laid as you did lakes in Ch. 12, and sand traps can be designated by white paint in cavities in the urethane or by fine white sand over white paint or spray glue.

Spectator Facilities: Spectator facilities for all the sports consist mostly of rowed tiers of seats, the finish and elaboration of which depends upon the location and use. The bleachers at a local softball park are often open-constructed wooden tiers of benches calling for notched stringers supported by crossbraced studs in a manner similar to that of trestles (Ch. 14). Establish the stringer locations by rows of support posts inserted in the base and add crossbracing as required. At say 1/4″ scale and larger, you can be realistic to the point of using strip wood for construction. At the smaller scales use vinyl strips.

A football bowl can be made by laminating ovals of material of scale thickness, each layer having radii greater than the one below it. Run the assembly over your table saw with varying settings to cut out the access tunnels. Seating for an amphitheater set into a hillside can, at small scale, be cut on your mill in the same manner you cut steps in Ch. 15 out of acrylic. Fasten a curved surface backing jig to the table against which to push the curved block of acrylic to obtain the curved seating configuration. Note that the lines of steps running at right angles to the seating may have to be cut separately and placed in synchronism with the seating blocks obtained by cutting the milled block into sections. You may also indicate the steps by adding additional pieces in line on the one piece seating block. The method used will depend upon the specified configuration. The whole assembly is then set into a cavity formed or cut into the hillside.

Probably the most complicated spectator facilities as far as the model builder is concerned are those constructed for horse racing. The complica-

tions arise because of the combinations of interior and exterior facilities provided. Photo 50, Ch. 49 shows an example of complicated architecture in conjunction with the basic tiered seating just discussed covered with a cantilevered roof. To save repetition refer to other sections for construction tips on the various elements.

24

Casting, Forming, and Polishing

There are two basic reasons for casting. The first arises from a search for the most expeditious way to authenticity in a single model element, and the second from a need for consistent duplication of an element.

Though a valuable aid when the occasion arises, casting is not a day to day occurrence and for that reason care should be exercised to store mold making and casting materials and their instructions in fixed locations to save time when they are needed. Store materials according to shelf-life instructions. Some may require refrigeration. Don't buy more than you need for anticipated current operations, and when you throw away the empty containers, be sure you have a record of content identification and source along with instructions in your reference file (Ch. 43). With up to a year between casting sessions, forgetting the name of the supplier can be as frustrating as forgetting the name of the product. I store casting plaster in an old metal bread box with a half-sliding top and the liquids in their original containers with sealed lids.

There are so many different brands of mold making and casting materials, with their individual characteristics and peculiar instructions that no attempt will be made here to give a complete

course in casting. The supply houses in your area will have instruction sheets to go with the products they handle. *Warning:* until you become an old hand at mold making and casting and can efficiently make your own adjustments and discover "better" ways, *follow instructions explicitly.* You are dealing with chemicals the experts in their fields have developed and compounded; the instructions can be expected to express authority. I have settled on three products: "Blak-Stretchy" for making molds, "Hydrostone" for molds and casting, and casting resin for casting. (See Ch. 50 for suggested sources.) These products have proven satisfactory; no attempt has been made to find others. Check with your supplier to be sure you have at least considered the latest developments. *Blak-Stretchy* (Ch. 50) is a black soupy rubbery liquid which with catalyst in correct volumetric relation hardens into a firmly elastic solid requiring no mold release for the castings. The flexibility permits easy release of the casting and immediate return to mold form for the next pour. Before it sets it stinks to high heaven; so get out the clothes pin for your nose if your olfactory nerves are sensitive. *Hydrostone* (Ch. 50) is a very fine plaster which, when mixed with water, dries quickly into a hard solid which can pass as white architectural cement. It is easily sanded or filed. Drill with light pressure to avoid fracturing and reinforce long thin configurations with wood or wire inserted in the wet plaster to prevent easy breaking. You can cast plaster in a plaster mold with complete coverage of the cavity with a mold release (either purchased or soap). The important thing is to seal the mold cavity surface against adherence by the poured plaster. Clear Krylon (Ch. 32) is effective, or, in the case of a straight sided cavity, make the master oversize and line the cavity with vinyl. Apply mold release between each pouring to be sure. When pouring plaster, be sure that it fills all cavities and that all bubbles are released. Immediately tap the mold against the table and with a small stick of wood poke the plaster into the small cavities such as the chimney of a 1/40″ scale house casting. Pour the plaster to the surface of any mold and screed off any excess with a small straightedge. Shrinkage is minimal. I remember casting a variety of small houses where I allowed 15 minutes drying time before removing from the mold. The time will depend upon size and weather as well as thickness of mix which should be of soupy consistency so that it will fill the cavity without being watery. The best mixing bowl is a flexible rubber one in which you can let the excess plaster dry and then snap the plug into the waste basket by flexing the container. *Don't pour plaster into your plumbing system!* It will harden and require a ream-out exercise. If your mold material supplier does not carry the mixing bowls, try a dental supply house.

Casting resin should be obtainable at your plastics supply source. It is a clear liquid used with a catalyst in *specified* proportion, and there are dyes for tinting. Add dye a drop at a time until you have stirred in the desired intensity. Without caution you can easily wind up with a useless batch of midnight blue ocean water. For a sunny ocean scenario, add a relatively small amount of green to the blue. I have not had reason to cast small objects with resin, confining my use to oceans and lakes. For one pour, restrict thickness to about 1/2″ to avoid cracking in the curing process, or pour the material in layers, letting the heat escape from the prior layer each time. I have not found shrinkage objectionable. The best mixing bowls are paper containers such as drinking cups or ice cream tubs which you can toss out after the mix. Use your mixture immediately since as soon as you have stirred in the catalyst it will start to cure. Do your tinting before you add the catalyst. Curing time will depend upon the quantity and the

amount of catalyst. Follow the suggestions in the instructions for best results.

Numerous references are made to this chapter including some (as in Ch. 12) where on the spot casting tips are given as pertinent only to the subject at hand. This confirms my introductory contention about the difficulty of separating interdependent subjects. So, with resignation to a possible bit of repetition, I will try to present some generic tips here using components from other sections as exemplary subjects.

Waves: The casting of an ocean beach was covered in Ch. 12 as a relatively seldom encountered event including the sculpting of breaking waves. The examples that follow should give you tips that can be more generally applied.

Bridge Arch: (Ch. 14, Fig. 14-3a) Make a one-time mold in the form of an open-topped rectangular box out of acrylic using contact glue so that the inside dimensions are equal to the outside dimensions of the bridge core. You could use wood, but the plaster might pick up the grain configuration, and any absorbent material would require mold release. The core is the bridge less roadway, sidewalk, and railing. Make the mold long enough to provide selvage to bury in the stream banks. Form the arch by bowing a piece of vinyl as wide as the inside dimension of the mold and inserting it against the bottom to be held in bowed shape by pins driven into holes drilled into the base of the mold. You can later fill any cavities made by the pins in the arch surface. Mix the Hydrostone in a rubber bowl, adding water a little at a time until you have a fluid soup. While you are mixing add a little black dye or water-soluble paint until you have a gray mortar color. Pour the mix into the mold, tapping the mold against the table to remove bubbles, screed off the excess against the top of the mold and let dry. When the plaster has set, pry the box apart carefully so that the product can finish drying in the open. Using a little plaster mix in the palm of your hand, fill any cavities formed by bubbles or the pins used to hold the arch form in place. Paint the sides and under the arch the appropriate stone colors (Ch. 32) and with a scribe scratch through the dried paint in stone shapes to reveal the mortar. If the stones seem too uniform in plane chip out small pockets and patch paint. The core is now ready for the road surface and railing.

Steps: (Ch. 15) Poured plaster steps provide authenticity of material about as close to concrete as the model builder will ever get. But this is worth while only where the scale is large enough to justify making a pouring form and where the steps are to have closed risers. At 1/2″ scale, for example, build an open-topped box out of 0.030″ vinyl with the sides notched out to tread and riser configuration as though you were making stringers. Glue bands of vinyl across the riser edges of the box sides and pour a soupy mixture of Hydrostone into the mold thus made. With a spatula, keep the plaster in even tread form until it sets enough to keep it from running out over the bottom riser

frame. When the plaster is firm, break away the mold and fill any bubble holes.

Architectural Screens and Sun Shades: (Ch. 16, Figs. 16-3 and 16-4) The masters for these two mold subjects were constructed in Ch. 16; only their molds will be discussed here. For the master of the sun shade (Fig. 16-3), make a mold form out of plywood, Masonite or even illustration board (Fig. 24-1). Tack-glue with contact glue the four sides vertically to a base of the same material to form an open-topped box with butt joints at the

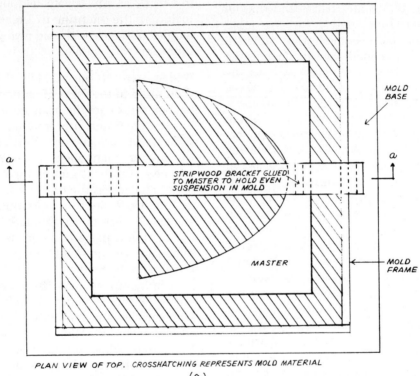

PLAN VIEW OF TOP. CROSSHATCHING REPRESENTS MOLD MATERIAL

(a)

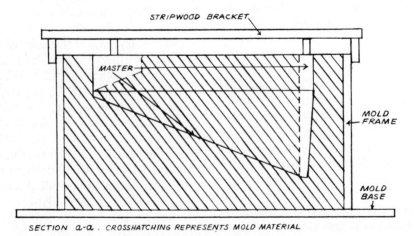

SECTION a-a . CROSSHATCHING REPRESENTS MOLD MATERIAL

(b)

FIGURE 24-1 *Sunshade mold.*

corners and of a size to allow at least 1/2" of mold material around the master on the sides and bottom. This is to provide durability for the mold cavity. Hold the sides with a rubber band.

You may wonder why the one-time mold for the bridge arch just discussed was made out of acrylic and the one here out of practically any rigid material. In the case of the bridge, the formed object was the final product, and it was desired to have smooth sides and sharp corners and to get along without mold release. Here all that is needed is a container for the mold material, the final product coming out of a cavity therein.

Note in Fig. 24-1 that the master was inserted into the mold face down. Positioning is important with any casting master to avoid its being locked in the mold by undercuts, etc. In this case if you put the master in the mold face up the sill would lock it in as would the sloping outside configuration of the "visor". The back of the master should be held just visible in the liquid mold material. To ensure this, glue a small piece of stripwood to the top and bottom of the sun shade and to each end of another piece of wood just long enough to span the sides of the form. Glue this assembly to the master as indicated in Fig. 24-1 so that it will be centered in the mold. You could simply glue a piece of stripwood across the back of the sun shade, but raising the support slightly keeps it out of the way of the mold material.

Suspend the master in the mold so that it is centered and carefully pour the Blak-Stretchy mix until it reaches the top of the form without covering the revealed surface of the master. As soon as the mixture has obviously set beyond the fluid state, remove the sides of the mold to allow air to speed the setting process, and when it is firm carefully extract the master. Let the cavity surfaces set a bit longer to be sure of complete cure and pour your first sun shade. When set, warp-squeeze the mold slightly to break contact, and the casting should come out easily.

Referring to Fig. 16-4, remember that it was decided to cast the spheroids with caps and the flat, splayed spacers, the masters for which were made in Ch. 16. Since the spacers are simply made out of acrylic, you may want to make several masters and set them into a gang mold to provide an equal number of cavities thereby shortening the time to the goal of 72. The 60 spheroids and caps are probably better obtained from a single cavity because of the time required to make duplicates of the one master. Following the procedure discussed for the sun shade, suspend the spheroid in the

mold mix so that only the top of one of the caps shows (Fig. 24-2). Note that the master is locked in because of the top half of the spheroid and the bottom cap. This will require cutting the cured mold in half. Establish a line across the top of the mold through the center of the visible cap surface. With a fine, sharp blade start division of the mold with cuts along the line of equal depth up to and on each side of the cap. With slight thumb and finger pressure force the mold away from the master as you carefully follow its configuration with the blade point. Continue a *single* cut on each side to avoid chewing up the mold. When you have reached the bottom of the bottom cap you should be able to remove the master and allow the mold to snap back into uncut form. This will provide automatic matching of the cut parts for casting. Whether you have this situation or two completely separate mold halves, you should put the mold back in its reassembled mold making form each time you pour to assure proper matching. Any minute ridges in the casting caused by the joint in the mold can be sanded off.

A little more sophisticated approach to keying together two mold halves is to provide for four matching pegs when you pour the mold material. Glue two 1/8" square pieces of acrylic to the bottom of the mold form at right angles to the expected later dividing cut (Fig. 24-2), and do the same at the top of the form where the "pegs" can

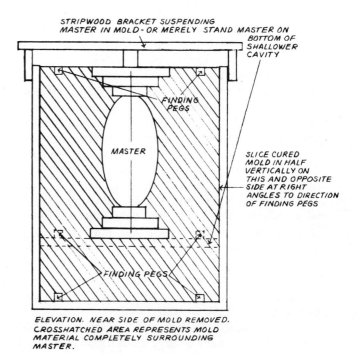

FIGURE 24-2 *Ellipsoid mold.*

be held by friction flush with the tops of the two sides. Separate the pegs laterally so as to escape conflict with the master. When the mold has cured as previously discussed, remove the pegs from the bottom of the mold form and from the top of the mold. After cutting the mold in half glue each peg securely into its slot in either half of the mold so that its extension will find the opposing slot in the other half of the mold when you assemble the latter to cast.

Also in Ch. 16 are other items which might be cast in plaster where masters can be made relatively easily and the components are large enough to provide strength. For example, where you had a considerable length of pergola-type construction over a walkway you might cast a representative duplicated section between columns thus saving the effort of installing a great many evenly spaced crosspieces.

Popular subjects for casting are columns (Ch. 22) because of their shapes and often extensive duplication. Figures 22-1a and b show two columns that are obvious candidates. The Tuscan column in Fig. 22-1a could be cast using the same method as that used for the spheroid element of a screen just discussed, where undercuts are overcome by splitting the mold. The modern column in Fig. 22-1b is shown in its two cast parts in Fig. 24-3. Whenever such a shaft appears too fragile for other than special handling, you can insure against breakage during your rush to assemble the colonnade by inserting a piece of piano wire down through the center lengthwise. Before pouring the mold drill a hole in the bottom of the mold form center to accept a finding pin inserted in the bottom of the master. Insert the master so that its top is even with the top of the mold form. Be sure that there is room for some mold material between the bottom of the shaft and the bottom of the mold form. When you remove the master from the set mold, remove the pin also and use the resulting hole in the bottom of the mold to accept reinforcing piano wire to be held in the center of the cavity each time you pour plaster. Be sure that by measurement and estimation you pull up the reinforcing wire so that its lower end clears any cavity you may have provided in the top of the shaft to accept a male extension in the bottom of the capital. Excess wire through the top of your casting (bottom of the column) can be clipped and sanded or filed flush with the plaster.

Other subjects include small scale residential housing. If you have a large number of houses to do for a residential park at 1/40″ scale, for ex-

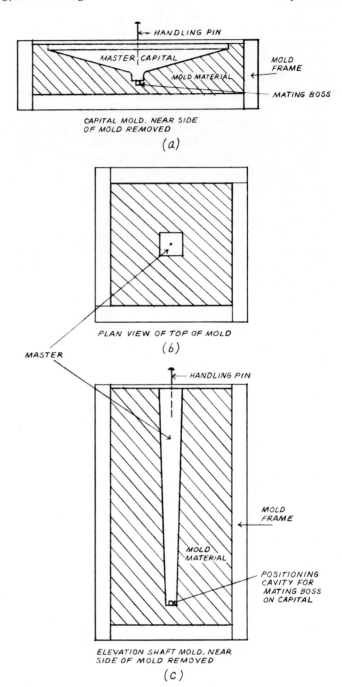

FIGURE 24-3 *Column mold.*

ample, with several different floor plans, make a master for each out of acrylic and make a multiple mold with a cavity for each house. Include the chimneys and roof rakes. Acrylic gives sharp corners and smooth surfaces. As mentioned before, be sure the plaster settles into each cavity. When you add vinyl roofs to the castings and an entourage of landscaping, the windows and doors will not be missed in such a multiple, small scale scene. Accessories such as automobiles in small scale (Ch. 27) can be cast, but the necessary variations in configuration make acceptable masters an arduous task. I gave up this subject gladly when I found an excellent outside source (Ch. 50). Where the scale is large enough to require more than scoring of mortar lines in a natural stone wall, consider sculpting the stone faces on the opposite surfaces of wall-width strips of dried plaster and casting the result for duplication. Here is one case where the master can be part of the final assembly. Be sure to use mold release on the master when you make the mold. For a long wall make two or more masters for surface variations which can also be obtained by reversing the sections when assembling. Glue the sections together with strips of contact glue down the centers of section ends as you mount the wall. Carefully fill the joints with plaster and paint to blend with the natural stone colors chosen.

Mold Release: To reiterate for the novice caster, the hard but flexible "rubber" molds such as those made from Blak-Stretchy do not require mold release. Molds made of porous materials such as Hydrostone plaster must be sealed to prevent the casting material (that is, the plaster or resin) from adhering to the mold. For releasing a plaster cast from a plaster mold I have had success with clear Krylon spray (Ch. 32) or soap applied thoroughly to the mold. For resin casts in plaster molds, polyvinyl alcohol, Teflon-based sprays, or wax can be used. To be sure, when casting resin is purchased obtain the prescribed release for your mold material from the same supplier.

   The foregoing tips do not of course cover all the possible candidates for casting, but knowing the basic methods should open the door to mold making whatever the particular master might be. It is worth reiterating the warning against locking yourself into a mold because of undercuts. Analyze each subject and consider dividing it into releasable parts for later assembly. The flexibility of mold materials such as Blak-Stretchy may let you off the hook with a minor undercut, but even dividing the mold may not be practical with multiple or deep lock-in surfaces.

FORMING

The word "forming" is a bit ambiguous to use as a subsection heading. Casting, just discussed, is literally forming as is contour cutting (Ch. 10) or ramp installation (Ch. 15), but for the want of a better word it is used here to cover the shaping of unusual configurations where the joining, gradual dry bending, or carving of flat planes are not the answer. Forming is accomplished by the use of pressure aided by moisture and/or heat and by the use of the structural method of installing flat planes with their edges cut to desired conformations at critical locations and then filling the intervals. Spinning also can be involved on occasion.

Warping: Very seldom will you have to make a project out of warping a relatively large surface such as a parking lot or garage floor. If any warping has to be shown at all, it can usually be effected by forcing material such as illustration board down against glued joints with wood blocks or risers at key locations. Use weights wherever possible to obviate having to fill tack holes. Where the warp is too much for the wet glue, use carpet tacks instead of brads to prevent puncturing the top layers of the cardboard. If you are careful with a nail punch you can make just a depression at tack locations or punch the heads just through the surface layer to provide a bind for the filling spackle. This is introductory to the case where you are challenged by warping to include ramps in an unbroken surface. Enclose the area with illustration board risers having top edges configured to the changing elevations. This will produce a shallow open-topped box. Within the area fasten blocks of wood with thicknesses corresponding to elevations at critical points or make heavyweight illustration board risers as you did in the vertical control method of grading (Ch. 9). Cut a piece of chip board (Ch. 35) slightly larger than the area to take care of slight increases due to slopes and soak it in water until saturated. Apply white glue (Ch. 34) to the tops of the blocks or risers, place the soaked chip board squarely over the area and tack it down to conform. Use carpet tacks over the wood blocks and weights or pins driven into the riser edges. Let the assembly completely dry, aided by your heat gun (Ch. 36) if you have nothing else to turn to at the moment. When dry cover the area with Strathmore paper (Ch. 35) or 0.010″ vinyl using contact glue (See Ch. 34 for limitations) on both surfaces. This is to cover tack and pin depressions and the less than finished surface characteristic of chip board. A vinyl covering will assure no absorption of any moisture left in the chip board. Trim the edges to be flush with the perimeter risers. If for some reason you cannot perform this exercise on the model, make a duplicate of the shallow forming box on a piece of scrap plywood, omit the white glue and tack down the wet chip board just snugly enough to hold shape. When dry, pull the tacks or pins and spray the chip board with clear Krylon to fix the shape. The result may then be glued to the model without the necessity for fasteners. Trim the edges.

The cantilevered barrel roof discussed in Ch. 20 is another subject for warping. When the flat plane shape of a repeated section has been determined (Ch. 49 photo 42) cut enough sections to make the roof out of chip board and make a forming jig by attaching strip wood to a plywood base as indicated in Fig. 24-4. Note that even though the roof sections are trapezoids, the jig fingers are parallel since the ridges at the roof section joints

are parallel. The simplicity of the jig will allow you to make enough pockets for the entire roof so that all sections can be formed in one operation. Soak the chip board trapezoids in water and carefully bow each one into a jig pocket so the edges are bottomed and let it dry. When removed, spray each one with clear Krylon to fix the shape and glue the edges together with contact glue to form the roof. Note that a section in the jig is upside down compared with its roof position.

Spinning: Spinning by an outside shop can produce opaque hemispherical roofs or the plugs for pressing transparent ones. The process involves a special lathe and skill not justified in-shop where the requirement is not a day to day occurrence. I

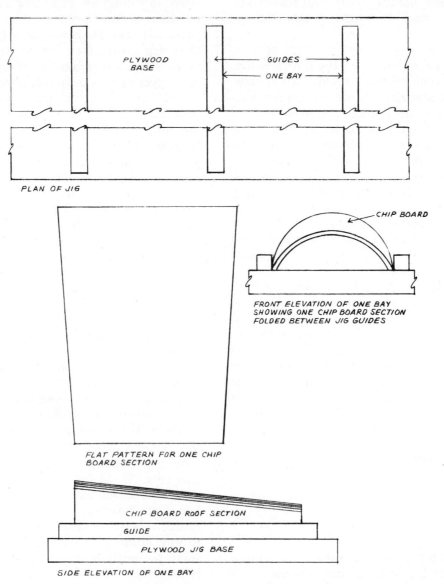

PLAN OF JIG

CHIP BOARD

FRONT ELEVATION OF ONE BAY
SHOWING ONE CHIP BOARD SECTION
FOLDED BETWEEN JIG GUIDES

FLAT PATTERN FOR ONE CHIP
BOARD SECTION

CHIP BOARD ROOF SECTION

GUIDE

PLYWOOD JIG BASE

SIDE ELEVATION OF ONE BAY

FIGURE 24-4 *Barrel roof jig.*

have had opaque domes spun out of aluminum as large as about 10″ in diameter where the only work to be done was the cutting of entrances or windows and skylights.

To make the hemispherical sections of an entrance canopy like the one shown in Ch. 49, photo 42, use the spinner's center in the base of the plug as a guide to inserting a piece of 1/4″ steel screw stock (Ch. 35) to be held by the chuck of your drill press. Cut oversize squares of 1/16″ acrylic. On wood blocks mount a square of plywood with a hole cut out to take the diameter of the plug plus the thickness of acrylic. Heat a square of acrylic in an oven (Ch. 36) until it is soft, immediately place it on the female jig on the drill press, and crank the quill down with steady, firm pressure to push the plug through the hole to stretch the acrylic into hemispherical shape. A trial run or two will indicate the desired depth which you can mark on the depth control adjustment on the drill press housing. Cut away the selvage on the acrylic "hats", trim to specified configuration, and mount the sections in line to form the canopy.

Vacuum Forming: Vacuum forming requires special equipment (Ch. 36). This is another outside service which will come to the rescue if you do not wish to invest in the equipment. I was fortunate in finding a small vacuum machine put out by a toy company. My toy has been great for making 1/16″ scale transparent units for a shaped skylight for example. A thin rectangle of rigid polystyrene is

drawn over a solid master shaped to a hemisphere, pyramid, etc. The individual sections are trimmed and mounted in 1/32″ scale acrylic to form the skylight assembly. If you want more perfection, cut holes in the base acrylic the size of the opening in the vacuum formed section less just enough to provide mounting bearing at the section joints.

Fin Method: The first candidate for this method is the casting master for the spheroid elements of the space divider screen discussed in Ch. 16.

From the drawings make a profile pattern of the ellipsoid, and from this pattern make four acrylic discs (Fig. 24-5). Perforate these elliptical discs with random holes drilled with a small bit. Any one of the miniature wire bit sizes will do. These holes are to hold the plaster filler to be used later. The thickness of the acrylic used will depend on the scale and your judgment based upon the size of the ellipsoid. A thickness of 1/32″ will suffice for several different scales since all you are building is an armature to make obtaining the correct shape easier than trying to sculp the ellipsoid out of solid stock. Cut one of the discs in half, evenly eliminating the thickness of the acrylic used and cement what remains of these halves along the center of a complete disc, one on each side perpendicular to the surface. In plan view this will look like an even cross. Cut the two remaining discs in half as you did with the first one and mount them to bisect the four right angles of the cross. In plan view the result will look like an eight-pointed star or eight spokes of a wheel. Sand-taper

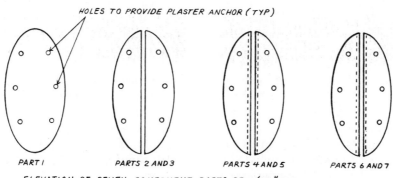

HOLES TO PROVIDE PLASTER ANCHOR (TYP)

PART 1   PARTS 2 AND 3   PARTS 4 AND 5   PARTS 6 AND 7

ELEVATION OF SEVEN COMPONENT PARTS OF 1/32″ ACRYLIC

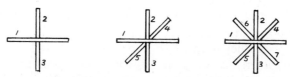

PLAN VIEW OF PROGRESSIVE ASSEMBLY OF PARTS

FIGURE 24-5 *Ellipsoid master.*

the joining edges of the last four pieces so that they will fit snugly in the vertices. Use acrylic solvent throughout. Note that the ends of the ellipsoid are flattened to accept the smallest of the three layers of cap; sand the ends of the armature accordingly. Between moistened thumb and forefinger hold the ends of the armature as you fill it with a mixture of plaster thick enough not to be runny. Use a small moistened spatula to smooth out the configuration provided by the armature. Moistening the spatula will prevent its pulling the plaster. When you are fed up with holding your creation, the plaster has probably set enough to remain in place; set it down to let nature finish the job. When the plaster is hard, fill any small pits, check for consistent configuration, and finish sand any rough spots.

Another good example of subjects for this method is the compound curved roof mentioned in Ch. 20 which has varying radii almost impossible to effect without some sort of station profile control. From the engineering drawings in scale make heavyweight illustration board girders as deep as the roof structure and with edges profiled according to the drawings. Make a girder for each critical location around the roof to catch controlling changes and assemble them into the overall roof shape with wood or cardboard fillers so that each girder is held in correct position. I have found it advantageous to notch out the profile edges and connect them with stripwood beams inserted flush with the profile. This not only makes a secure assembly but also aids in establishing roof surface configuration. Fill in the intervening spaces with urethane foam and sand the whole roof surface smooth being sure not to sand any incorrect depressions. The entire roof may be filled and covered with a light coating of plaster.

Make a spherical storage tank (Ch. 23) in the same manner as the spheroid element of a screen discussed in this section. Another way is to laminate circles of material with varying radii and then fill the steps with plaster or spackle.

Heat is a necessary part of the system in vacuum forming and provision therefore is included in the equipment, but heat also can be applied separately to form acrylic lengths into curves over wood profiles. A propane or acetylene torch can be used, keeping the flame moving over the area of the curve to assure an even distribution of heat. Hold the curve until the acrylic has reset since it has the characteristic of tending to return to original shape. I think the more satisfactory tool is the heat gun which produces concentrated high heat with-

out flame. Flame can consume the material without care. High impact vinyl is usually thin enough so that you can curve it around corners and anchor it to hold shape without heat. If heat is necessary use a heat gun and take your time. Vinyl is extremely sensitive to heat and will suddenly distort to waste basket category with the slightest application. Try hot water first.

POLISHING

Polishing is an operation for which there is little need in the model business except for restoration of acrylic surfaces. Saw-cut edges of acrylic cover parts (Ch. 39) can be polished with a propane torch, keeping the flame moving just until clarity appears. Too concentrated a flame in one spot will round flat edges and consume the material causing a wavy surface. If the saw cut is rough sand first with wet or dry emery cloth (Ch. 35) held over a flat block of wood. Start with a 200 grit and proceed to 400, winding up with 600, keeping the cloth wet at all times to lubricate and prevent burning. The more hand sanding you do the less the flame will have to do. Be careful not to round the edges of desired flat surfaces. With a flat nozzle, try your heat gun in place of the flame thus reducing the risk of burning. Follow a similar procedure to remove deep scratches on the top or side of a cover, realizing that you will probably wind up with a slight depression more obvious to the touch than the eye. Slight scratches can usually be buffed out with a light application of a cloth wheel in your hand drill and polishing compound. For minor scratches try first a little Dr. Lyon's tooth powder on a damp cloth held over a finger tip.

Surfaces of pieces of acrylic small enough to be easily hand held are best polished against a firm cloth wheel mounted on your bench grinder (Ch. 36) and a dry stick of polishing compound obtainable from your plastics supply house. After hand sanding with wet emery cloth to remove roughness, hold the piece to be polished so that the direction of wheel rotation is always away from an edge. This will prevent the wheel from suddenly catching the part to send it flying across the shop. In all precarious situations wear goggles. Only experience will tell you how much pressure to use. Too much pressure will burn the surface, adding to polishing time. Periodically hold the compound stick against the spinning wheel to replenish it and continually examine the surface being polished. Soon you will become an expert, winding up with store-bought surfaces even if with unnoticeably thinner material at the point of grinding.

Your plastics supplier will have a wet paste polishing compound for hand buffing of minor scratches to save your Dr. Lyon's, and a useful tip for hand held pieces with coarse saw cuts is first to hold the subject against your belt sander with gradually reducing pressure. Doing this will produce a smooth matte finish with which you can go right to the wheel, skipping the emery cloth. On the other end of the spindle of my bench grinder I have a soft, dry buffing wheel for which I have found little need. The firm cloth wheel with compound and reducing pressure seem to do the job without further treatment.

25

Landscaping

Remember the statement: Landscaping can make or break a display model. From experience, this is a truism that cannot be denied. Don't wait until the last minute to slap on a few trees as the model goes out the door. Since this is one of the finishing processes at the end of a sometimes long and arduous construction period full of overtime, with your client breathing down your neck, extra effort has to be made to give due consideration to this phase of the work. Include landscaping in your planning from the first time you study the drawings, noting trees, for example, that will require research or special construction methods. During the construction period, while you are waiting for information, supplies, for an area to dry, or a run of columns to set in their molds, set up a separate area not in conflict with the construction area and make trees as the time allows. Place these trees in storage stuck in strips of urethane foam and protected from dust. At the end you will be glad you did. Don't overplant. If you have separate landscaping drawings, follow them, making use of your books on the subject (Ch. 43) to aid you in getting shapes and colors of trees, but don't hide the architecture. I have experienced an architect's pulling out half the trees prescribed by the landscape ar-

chitect who of course would be planting saplings and not full grown trees as required for model purposes. See Ch. 49 for photos containing landscaping.

SEQUENCE OF EVENTS

Though the tips will not necessarily follow the most practical sequence of installation, the best procedure is generally to put down the ground cover first, including the planters, then the shrubbery and flowers and lastly the trees. You can always finish-touch with tweezers under a tree, but with extensive ground cover on a forested hillside, the sequence is obvious. Recalling Pattinson's Law, don't temporarily lock yourself out of installing a critical flower bed by the premature planting of a group of trees.

SCALE

The subject of scale in relation to landscaping is worth discussing because of generally acceptable violations permitted in the literal sense. A case in point would be the impractical requirement that every leaf of even a 1/2″ scale tree be shown in scale size and shape. Fortunately model builder's license is allowed to come to the rescue, camouflaged by illusion as discussed in Ch. 4. The model builder's skill in deceptive application of ground-up materials for foliage makes the scene authentic to the eye. Your ground cover is probably full of "leaves" that are technically too big, but through color, blending, and application, the result without the use of a microscope successfully suggests ivy. Considering the literal scale height and girth of a tree, remember that a sapling at 1/8″ scale could be a full grown tree at 1/32″, the same tree out of your inventory serving a dual application. The pinpoint of paint azalea blossom doesn't look gross when you realize that it is really a group of blossoms, and the actual rock chips used in a hillside outcropping look authentic because there is no visible grain to reveal a violation of scale.

LANDSCAPING BASE

Unless it has been prescribed for some reason, a lot of bare earth showing on a model is not a very attractive part of a display. Showing a bucolic scene including a tilled field prior to planting is one thing, but an expanse of uncovered terrain on a hillside, for example, will look unattractive without some verdure which is likely to be present during at least one of nature's cycles. Just as a model setting is more attractive in spring, summer or early fall, so does the model terrain look better in green than it does in brown. For occasional natural appearing relief, use a dark, matte brown paint in planters around individual bushes, and lighter browns around rock outcroppings in the countryside, blending shades of earth colors to represent those in the actual locale. I have found a muted grass green color to be a successful background for planting in general. Realizing the hazards of trying to impart a mental picture of a color through words alone, it suffices to say that after accomplishing a few model projects you shouldn't have any trouble establishing a standard mix which will be generally acceptable. Your application to illustration board will appear slightly different from that on urethane foam, but if the surface is to be ground-covered, the difference will not be great enough to worry about.

LANDSCAPING MEDIA

The foundation for all landscaping lies in the various materials used (usually in ground-up form) for flower beds, planters, shrubbery, natural underbrush, trees, and ground cover. The subject of materials is covered here instead of Ch. 35 because specific media are so closely related to a peculiar purpose. You might say that the material is the result.

ORGANIC MATERIALS

Organic materials suitable for model landscaping are, in my experience, few and far between. There are many fine shapes in nature that immediately bring to mind their larger editions and so seem ideal for miniature representation, but wilting soon destroys the foliage revealing branching that is not suitable even if dried. There are, however, a few natural products which I have used satisfactorily if not as the perfect answer. In discussing them no intention is meant to discount the possibility of the existence of more or better usable organic materials in your part of the world. Because of the satisfactory use of man-made materials of which there is ready supply, I have given up my disappointing forays into the countryside for answers.

Lichen: Lichen or reindeer moss is harvested in Scandinavia from the trees on which it grows. It has a closely knit texture at the extremities supported by tubular branching which usually has to be eliminated or at least hidden from view when used. The hobby shops put it out treated and colored ready for use, but this is not the economical source for the professional model builder. The best way to get it is in the small bales into which it has been pressed in dried natural form. Carefully pull it apart in hunks and place it in a vat containing a solution of glycerine mixed with a small proportion of water as an extender. As soon as it becomes soft, spread it out on newspaper to allow the water to evaporate. The absorbed glycerine will keep the lichen soft and pliable until it again dries out after an extended display of the model. Pick off a supply of tops for shrubbery and separate them from the rest of the material. Set aside both groups for later dyeing and grinding to be discussed later.

Lichen is mentioned first because it has been a standard model foliage producer for many years. It still is useful as a high volume natural hillside cover, but in my opinion it has outlived its service. Particularly as tree foliage, it has become a cliche. Every time you see a lichen tree, you know it is lichen—it can't be anything else, and this predominance of constituent makes you forget the tree which it represents. It is often difficult to escape the grossness of the heavy, tubular structure under the tips. Other than for occasional shrubbery, the tips are good for some kinds of pines, for example, where bare branches support a bit of foliage at the ends, but by the time you have denuded your supply of prepared lichen tips, what do you do with the bulk of the material left? Grind it up for general wild ground cover previously mentioned. Even with this solution, be prepared to pick off tubes with tweezers because they have been merely squashed by the grinder to return to ugly existence once they have left the machine. Added to the visual objections is the hazard of its eventually drying out and becoming brittle, no matter how much glycerine was absorbed at the birth of the model. Being organic this is to be expected. I have rejuvenated lichen on a model with shielded sprays of glycerine, but it is a losing battle, not worth the effort in the first place. If you can stand the economics, save the tips only in sealed containers for occasional variations in texture in your garden scenes. If you haven't overdone the application, lichen bushes can easily be replaced during a repair and renovating session.

Moss: I have made occasional use of a wild moss sent to me by a friend in the Pacific Northwest. It has branches of minute feathery fronds which have served as planter accents and seem to have a satisfactory model life without treatment. I have never learned the name; so I cannot give further identification, but think "moss," and you may find a gold mine of landscaping materials in your corner of the world.

Nandina Domestica: This material, also called heavenly or sacred bamboo is a member of the barberry family and not a bamboo. Its firm twigs make excellent tree armatures for several scales since they are tapered in profile allowing you to cut the tip for a 1/32″ tree and farther down the stem for one at 1/8″. It is apparently originally an oriental shrub which grows profusely in gardens on the west coast of the United States. Check with your favorite nursery if you are not familiar with it because it is worth having a sack full in your inventory. The stems are straight, and the branching is evenly spaced around them. I pick off the dead

branches as they appear, and no treatment is necessary.

Miscellaneous Twigs: These can be found to serve as feature gnarled oaks, for example, in shrubbery that has been around long enough to become venerable. I have used many dry weeds and grasses pulled from the countryside for eucalyptus tree armatures at 1/16″ and smaller. After making a complete examination of your own and neighbor's gardens, keep your eyes open for subjects on your walks and hiking trips. Look mostly for dead foliage, realizing that the "perfect branching" of a living plant will probably wilt into the waste basket. The hobby shops will have an assortment of dried "trees". The standard, boxed ones that I have seen (and used) are really too coarse for professional use. This is not to say that there are none available which would stack up with the best I could put out, but to indicate the advantages of tailor making trees to fit your particular requirements. Because of this I gave up buying ready-made trees long ago. Air plant has its possibilities for fern-like foliage, but it fits the occasional unspecified shrub accent situation better than it does tree projects.

INORGANIC MATERIALS

Inorganic materials are by far the more satisfactory for model purposes principally because they are everlasting. They are already "dead" so you don't have to worry about disintegration or snapping off a planted tree twig at ground level. You can order cast metal tree armatures (Ch. 50) to satisfy each model requirement as it arises, and there is always a supply of foliage material, as near as your nearest department store, upholsterer, or general merchandiser. Even though this material has to be dyed and ground, you can prepare a sizeable supply in a couple of hours to your own specifications.

Soft Urethane Foam: This is about the most generally satisfactory material for all landscaping purposes. This is the flexible polyurethane foam used in pillow stuffing, not to be confused with the *rigid* foam used in contour cutting (Ch. 10). It is a department store or upholstery shop type of product sold in plastic bags containing chunks up to the size of a ping pong ball. I obtain it in white which does not conflict with any color of dye. Sponge rubber is the nearest similar material in feel and consistency. Coarse grind can provide small shrubbery, or pull the stuff apart in larger hunks for separate bushes. Slicing it or cutting it with scissors will tend to produce flat sides.

Rigid Urethane Foam: Rigid urethane foam dust from your contour cutting process makes great tree foliage with two time consuming disadvantages. Being already ground up at dyeing time, it is a bit of a mess to handle. Probably the most satisfactory way to color it is to spread it out thinly on newspaper and spray it with dye (or paint) using a broad spatula to turn it continuously to get complete coverage. Keep it disturbed so that paint, for example, doesn't hold it in wads. The second disadvantage is the presence of minute shiny particles which the manufacturer tells me are broken up cells. With a layman's skepticism I still would like a better answer because there are certainly more cells broken up in making the dust than indicated by the relatively small volume of reflective particles. In any case if you can't beat it accept it. I beat the situation by spreading the dry, dyed dust out on newspaper and keep disturbing it as I spray with a matte paint spray. In my opinion, it is worth the effort because of the soft, minute foliage it can give numerous trees. Paint will do a better job of covering the shiny particles than dye.

Other Materials: Wood *sawdust* of varying grade can be dyed and used for a change of texture in trees and ground cover. Technically this should be listed under "Organic Materials", but since we never deal with it in other than a dead state it seems to fit here. *Fine sands* can be used for gravelled walks and service areas by being sifted onto a surface covered with clear Krylon, spray adhesive, or plastics glue. Spraying can be done in small confined areas using shields of paper or vinyl and any shine can be killed with a matte spray. Several fine layers are better than trying to cover the area with one heavy application. This will help to prevent lumps. The key is *even* sifting through a fine sieve after an *even* application of adhesive. *Flock* is a material to be used sparingly simply because it says "flock" as lichen tends to speak its name louder than the name of the bush or tree it represents. Use only linen flock or any that does not have a sheen. If the greens seem too "Kelly", try mixing in some gray or black to tone it down. It should be applied with a flock gun over the prescribed adhesive. Your local handicraft shop can guide you. I have given up using it for grass or

ground cover, though it could be used for some of the needle trees to be discussed later.

As in the case of organic materials, you certainly are not limited to the inorganic materials mentioned. I think it would be pretty hard to beat soft urethane foam, for example, but let your imagination flow. Don't discount the hobby shops. Cruise them once in a while looking for new products which are continually appearing. I recently spotted some grass matting which would be great at the larger scales. Though it is not the most economical route for the professional you can always buy packaged ground covers put out in nature's muted colors. When you are in a time pinch, someone else's efforts are often well worth the price.

MATERIAL TREATMENT

For simplicity the tips here will be confined mostly to treatment of soft urethane foam for bushes, flowers, ground cover, and tree foliage. With the prior discussion of dyeing already ground materials, you will see that similar procedures will logically follow with respect to other materials such as lichen.

Dyeing: As you embark on a dyeing session to replenish your supply of foliage, recall your trips through the wilds or just through local neighborhoods on your way to your shop and the gamut of colors with which nature paints her products through the seasons. Other than the almost bright arboreal masses of red, yellow, and brown of fall in some parts of the world, note how the wide range of greens is generally muted and soft (matte to the model builder) from the light greens of new growth through the gray, yellow, and occasional blue greens to the dark and sometimes almost black greens of the forest. The bright colors of wildflowers are repeated and added to by the contents of gardens allowing you to make supplies colored in about any shade you can think of, including the pinks, reds, and whites of blossoming fruit trees.

Since nature has generally ordained matte foliage, we are not out of line in carrying this ordinance to model building. Forgetting nature, spotty, reflective surfaces in a model are distracting because they catch the viewer's eye; unless you have a shiny-leafed holly bush to reproduce as a feature, confine reflections to those expected from your lake or ocean.

Pint cans of concentrated powdered commercial dye will last you through many treatment sessions. Obtain a can of black and one each of the colors red, yellow, green, and blue. With these you can obtain any hue you desire. The black is for darkening and graying. White you will have in the urethane foam. The dyes I use (Ch. 50) are mixed best in methanol, in the absence of which you can use commercial alcohol. A good mixing container is a double depth ice tray made out of aluminum, and useful tools are a pestle made out of a piece of model base framing with a rounded end (if you cannot swipe the hardwood one from your home bar) and a pair of ice tongs. If you do not want to fight the state of dyed hands, wear rubber gloves. Plastic picnic spoons are good for transporting dye from can to mix. As a starter, tilt the pan on a block of wood and pour in a few ounces of methanol. Put in a pinch of green dye and soak a piece of the soft urethane in the mixture after all the dye has dissolved. Squash it with the pestle and then push it up clear of the liquid when fully soaked. Squash out the excess liquid and set it aside on newspaper to dry. Newspaper will aid drying by absorbing moisture. If the result seems like an acceptable new-growth green, increase the amount of solution to accept a fist full of urethane using proportions as close as you can to those of the original mix. For future duplication, keep records by volume on slips of paper together with samples of the results in transparent envelopes. When you have a considerable amount of a mix left over, store it in a jar with a dyed sample attached. As you can imagine, the possible hues, shades, and tones seem endless. If you find you have incorrectly prepared a solution from inspection of a sample dunking, you can usually bring it into line with pinches of the other colors. Trial and error is the only dependable teacher here. After replenishing your ground cover supply, consider runs of pure colors in relatively smaller amounts for planters and flower beds. Leave some urethane in its natural white for blossoms.

Grinding: I started with an old fashioned hand-turned meat grinder, but finally saw the light in an electric salad maker which is nearly perfect for the job (Ch. 36). Try all the disc grids to determine the best grind for your purposes. My standard is a disc with many small round holes. When your last dyeing run has dried feed it through the machine with slight encouragement at the hopper using a pestle, *not your fingers*. For bushes, nibble small pieces off dyed stock and store them separately.

Storage: Buy a carton of clear food-type containers with flexible plastic snap lids. Mine measure 3-5/8″ in diameter and are 3-3/4″ deep. They are stored in a double-depth rack with the front half hinged. Their transparency makes it easy to locate the particular color and grind you want.

When you have a last minute shortage of a given color, try blending some of those you have left before staying up all night for a treatment run. Blending can give very natural effects for such ground cover as variegated ivy, for example. You can also tone down too bright a green with some of darker hue.

INSTALLATION

Ground Cover: From my experience, ground cover is best put down with the old work horse contact glue using a free-flowing consistency, with one exception as noted in the next paragraph. Do small areas at a time, brushing on the glue with enough depth to catch the material immediately sprinkled on by hand or through a sieve. Lightly press the material down as you proceed to get complete coverage and adherence. The glue that I use is brown, but so is the earth under the green base, and it dries matte when put down thick enough to hold the cover. Completely cover such areas as ivy beds to a lush but not lumpy appearance. Where no definite borders are specified, free-form the edges with a slight feathering here and there in lawn areas, around planted trees, etc. On open, natural hillsides, follow much the same procedure, leaving openings of soil, particularly around rock outcroppings. The main goal is to obtain a natural, undisciplined effect with variations in grinds and colors used. After the application has dried you can patch with dexterous use of brush and glue, tapping the material into the patch. Go over the entire area with a vacuum cleaner, holding the nozzle away from the surface. You can save excess material by collecting it in a piece of cheese cloth held over the end of the nozzle.

The adhesive exception mentioned in the preceding paragraph is the use of latex paint on rigid urethane foam to secure the ground cover. Contact glue tends to pull a urethane surface, filling the brush with urethane particles. Use the same color of paint as that used to spray the urethane.

Don't waste your time by trying to get every grain of ground cover stuck down. A finished, landscaped model will always shed a certain amount every time it is moved. See Ch. 39 for model clean-up.

Shrubbery: Shrubbery formally planted consists of separate pieces of treated material put down with tweezers and spots of contact glue applied to the bottoms. If you are installing lichen bushes, be sure you hide or remove any tubular structure. For blossoms, apply minute spots of paint with a fine brush, realizing that each spot will probably represent a cluster of blossoms. Don't overdo it. *Vines* and *espaliered plants* can be made by gluing ground cover material to their supporting vertical surfaces whether they be fences, building walls or lattice work (Ch. 16). If the scale is large enough to warrant the effort, first form branching out of divided picture or electrical wire, burying the bound end below ground after painting the armature brown. As the scale increases, consider tree armatures with the branches trimmed and flattened out to lie against the vertical surface. *Hedges* at 1/32″ scale, for example, can be made from pipe cleaners sprayed and covered with ground cover materials. In the larger scales, try strips of rigid urethane foam treated the same way. For a formal, clipped effect leave even, square corners throughout the length. For unclipped growth, chew out the urethane strip here and there and round the top corners.

Planters: Planters can be ground-surface flower and shrubbery beds, or can be raised structures of wood or concrete. Surface planters in and around a parking lot made of illustration board can be indicated by peeling off the top lamination of the board, leaving the roughed up cardboard underneath as "soil" when it is painted brown. Make curbs out of stripwood (Ch. 35) treated to agree with that in the project. Selfcontained planters can be made off the model out of vinyl, wood, or acrylic. If the depth is too great for planting material alone, fill the cavities first with "dirt" blocks of rigid urethane painted earth brown. Terraced planters as along the edges of steps are best made along with the steps. Paint shaped pieces of wooden dowel to represent terra cotta pots. Drill out the tops to provide soil area.

Trees: Trees, to be made next, will require holes drilled for the trunks in hard materials such as illustration board, but can simply be stuck into a urethane grading, often without glue. In the absence of specifications, plant trees in small groups with varying heights, and, as mentioned previously, don't hide the architecture! When in doubt, ask the architect to visit your shop when you are ready to install the trees to forestall displeasure and save the time of replanting. Trees can make or break the landscaping.

TREE CONSTRUCTION

Tree construction is not particularly difficult or critical when you have free rein in establishing color, size, and shape to fit location, but when you have landscape drawings with tree schedules to follow, the project can become quite time consuming and should be covered in your initial quotation. Here I will give a few basic proven tips on general tree construction followed by my solutions to a few common problem trees and a discussion of considerations when you must follow tree schedules in an attempt to provide literal authenticity. In any case, the governing criteria are height, girth of trunk and foliage, color and shape. Except at an unusually large scale, obviously no client can ever justifiably expect individual leaves or minor branching.

Armatures: Armatures are the backbones of most model trees. They include the trunks and branching untreated and without foliage. They can be organic twigs as previously mentioned, made from multistrand picture or electric wire, or they can be purchased in cast metal form from specialty model supply houses. To reiterate, the disadvantages of the organic twigs, aside from brittleness, are the problems of finding the right twig, and having found it, finding enough of the same thing to build your forest. The stranded wire route in my opinion should be confined to special situations, one of which will be discussed later.

In the long run the most satisfactory armatures are those soft metal castings which can be purchased in varying sizes and shapes from companies such as that listed in Ch. 50. The supplier's catalog will enable you to order, by number, the armatures to fit the job. With tweezers bend and twist the branches into natural configuration and set the armatures out in rows stuck into rigid urethane foam so that they do not touch. The rows will help you count up to the required number. Spray them all with the natural trunk color. If you use Krylon you should again spray with a matte spray to kill the sheen. When these are dry, the final step is foliation.

Foliating: Pick out the suitable ground cover material from your supply and dump the contents of the container into a shoe box or the like. Hold the base of an armature from your treated collection by the selvage mounting peg at the base of the trunk and spray it with a spray adhesive (Ch. 34). Be sure to get complete coverage without overage. Immediately dunk the armature into the ground cover with a spinning motion to get material on each branch. Sometimes you will have to repeat the process to obtain satisfactory coverage, even adding pinches in the center to fill it out. Remember how the tree looked on your way to work, or rely on your reference library (Ch. 38). Most broadleaf trees are open with an airy appearance; so don't make a solid ball on the top of a stick. Collect the finished trees in a slab of rigid urethane foam and keep them out of the way of dust until you are ready to plant. As an armature holder for spray gluing, stick the trunk in a length of brass tubing. Where required, add blossoms by lightly spraying the finished tree with glue and sprinkling on ground cover material of the proper color.

Tree Inventory: As a downtime filler, having your employees make trees for cupboard storage is, in my opinion, a waste of time. No matter how well you isolate them from the hazards of the open shop they seem to become "used" in appearance in a relatively short time. Even with a natural perfectionist attitude, trees made to specific types will likely not be required for some time, and when needed will not be sufficient in number. A few well-protected accent flowering or specially shaped trees might be in order for that future planter, but again, they may not be in the right scale when needed. Much better, spend downtime replenishing ground cover and adding to the various grinds and colors.

Other Methods: These include *piecing together* organic trees by gluing twigs onto larger twigs to serve as trunks. This is satisfactory only at scales large enough to permit branch-accepting cavities or holes in the trunk. The time consumption can be considerable, and there is the hazard of producing a tree that looks mechanical or at least un-

natural. Confine this method to specialty trees few in number such as ancient oak trees where the gnarled, twisted trunks can camouflage your artificial assembly, or a giant sequoia with its massive straight trunk and relatively sparse foliage at the top looking in its natural profile a bit moth-eaten or spastic in any case. The *twisted wire* method is another time consuming stopgap to be used, in my opinion, only where the metal armatures or organic solutions such as *nandina* are not available. It may be the only solution in rare cases where the requirements call for trees such as the weeping willows to be discussed later. If you cannot hide the visible twist in the trunk, dip and redip the trunk in plaster until you get satisfactory coverage, or leave enough insulation on stranded electrical wire to form the trunk. Another solution is to wrap the trunk in florist's tape. Single, shaped trunks can be made from pipe cleaners dipped in plaster. Establish the shape before you cover so that bending won't crack the plaster. If the scale permits use several pipe cleaners bound together at the base. This is good only for stunted trees since each time you bend out a branch you unnaturally reduce the main stem as you increase the height.

PROBLEM TREES

Predominant among those which I label "problem" trees are some of the conifers, the palms, and the weeping willow. I so label them because of the special attention they can require in attaining authentic appearance. You will no doubt find other problem trees indigenous to your area of operations, but I think those included here have sufficient worldwide distribution to make the tips generally useful. If you are building a model of a project in New Hampshire or the north of Scotland you won't be challenged by palm trees, but you could have forests of conifers. Your projects in the temperate and tropical climes may require numerous palms with their accompanying peculiar time charges, and weeping willows will appear in China as well as Southern California.

Conifers: Conifers include the pine and cypress families. The first include the pines, firs, spruces, hemlocks, cedars, and larches. The second includes various cypresses, arborvitae, incense cedars, and junipers. The swamp cypress family includes the giant sequoia and coast redwoods. The arborists among you will think of many species in addition to those given to remind you of the many needle tree challenges possible. Of course, they are not all problems. Some of the closed foliage ones aren't as difficult as a sycamore, for example. Trees like the Mediterranean cypress with their tall, skinny triangular profile, and the tubular incense cedar can be made from pussy willow ends or elongated Q-Tips since no branching is visible. Trim to their uniform shapes and lightly cover with finely ground urethane foam of the characteristic green. *Nandina* makes fine small firs and pines with the Christmas tree shape already made to order.

Except perhaps at very large scales, it is impractical to try to reproduce needle foliage, much less the various forms in which it grows, but you can, through distinctive shape, color, and size, indicate the different conifers with reasonable authenticity. I think a common mental image of a "pine" tree is one with a conical, even-tapered shape, which is not the general rule in nature who has seen fit to produce needle trees in widely differing shapes, from the gnarled, wind-blown Monterey cypress to the sparsely "fuzzed" top of the mammoth-trunked sequoia; from the common image of the hemlock to the tall, skinny pencil juniper; from the tall, ovate shape of the Western white pine to the Stone or Umbrella pine of Italy. So, when you have conifers on your schedule, first look to your reference books (Ch. 43) for the shape, size, and shade of green of the specified variety. Also keep in mind where the tree is grown. The handsome open, spastic shape of a Monterey cypress, for example, grown on a windy coast will change to one of a huge closed foliage bush in a quiet garden.

The open, symmetrical needle trees at the larger scales (say 1/4″ and larger) probably demand the greatest attention of all the evergreens except perhaps for palms. The openness reveals how well you have done in attaining spacing of branches often sprouting from the trunk in groups at the same level. If you cannot obtain characteristic metal armatures, these are candidates for individual construction, unless you can find suitable pine tree kits at the hobby shops. I recently found one for O gauge railway hobbyists (1/4″) scale that has possibilities with in-shop treatment. To get multi-branching from the same level, drill small holes all the way through in a tapered piece of wood dowel and insert as many strands of fine electrical wire as the holes will accommodate. Where the holes can be large enough without splitting the trunk, you can feed opposing strands through to create four branches. Otherwise twist the branch strands together first and insert the ends into the

sockets using contact glue. Where straight through branching occurs, bend one of the branches slightly to avoid a crosstree on a telephone pole look. Pull out single strands to form twigs to accept foliage applied as previously discussed. Hide visible wire twists with heavy paint or plaster and paint, or, before splaying the branches, slide on electrical insulation. Check with your electronics supplier for heat-shrinkable insulation which, over a match flame, will shrink to a tight coating.

An alternative to the twisted wire branching is that made from organic twigs such as those from *nandina* with the unnatural branching clipped off. Note that the trunk used in this case suggests a tree such as the Douglas fir which is tall and straight. If the trunk you choose, whether dowel or a sliver of redwood, does not have enough bark texture, chew up the surface with a knife or rowel (Ch. 36) on an extra thick coat of paint without disturbing the wood.

My previous suggestion that flock could be used in some needle trees is not generally applicable because of the time consumed in effecting a natural appearance. Since the individual filaments defy regimentation about the most that can be expected is the fuzzing of individual twigs to simulate the tubular bottle brush configuration of the needles on a Douglas fir, for example. Having found a suitable armature, either metal or organic, paint it, spray it with spray glue and sift on matte flock all around each branch. To avoid having to scrape off excess flock to reveal wood, brush on thin contact glue only in those spots where the foliage should appear and try several layers to keep the tree from looking like a flocked twig. This method is offered to give you an additional challenge to develop if interested. In my own experience, the result has not justified the effort, but I can see possibilities for some genius to come up with actual needles on a conifer.

I have made many small fir trees (to the Christmas tree image) out of Yellow Bowl pipe cleaners which are shaped like miniature bottle brushes. Paint out the visible wire twist with a fine brush after spraying the tree with the appropriate green. With small scissors snip the branches here and there to obtain a little natural unevenness, and spin the spray-glued armature in finely ground ground-cover material. To obtain required openness apply the scissors again, sparingly since the size of the tree will camouflage authentic spacing of branches.

Palms: Palms for model building purposes may be said to be either fan or feather which are words descriptive of shape of their foliage. Your reference books will show cabbage palms with a variation of the true fan, their fans having a continuous central stem, and a modified fan such as that of the "feathered" date palm. As in the case of conifers, we can confine ourselves at the common scales to obvious generic differences.

Though youngsters may look like runts close to the ground, and the Mediterranean fan palms look like bushes with their multitrunked configuration, most palm subjects will probably have the standard, tall, thin, straight, tubular trunks in various shades of tan undramatically disturbed except toward the tops where dead leaf stubs can add to girth under the green clusters of fans or feathers. The royal palm will show a slightly bulging trunk on its way up, the coconut palm a gracefully curved stem, and the Canary Island date palm a short, thick, rough trunk with a wide headdress of feathers topped by a plume. Otherwise the palm in profile will be a "ball on a stick", the manner of executing the ball being the principal key to authenticity. Model builder's license will protect you from criticism for not being able to effect subtle differences between species in a forest of conifers, but there is no way to hide the difference between a fan and a feather palm except at scales so small that a "ball on a stick" is the only practical solution. For display model purposes the model builder deals in mature trees; even at 1/64" scale a 20' frond will be 5/16" in length, necessitating individual construction of at least the frond outline.

Using a feather palm as an example, cut strips of bond paper or typewriter tissue, painted the correct green, as wide as the length of the fronds plus an extra amount necessary for bonding to a trunk. With scissors snip frond width sections along these strips down to and at right angles to the binding selvage. Shape these sections to the slightly tapered frond shape, and, if scale demands, further snip each section at an angle to "feather" their edges. Cut a strip of this prepared frond stock long enough to make one palm, apply contact glue along the length of the selvage and wrap the selvage (with fronds pointing up) around the top end of a piece of dowel of trunk dimensions painted a bark brown and perhaps rowelled to roughen the bark. Taper the resulting wad of rolled paper at its base with a strip of masking tape, and with a brush paint this wrapped area brown to indicate the stubs of collapsed dead fronds which would be kept trimmed by a maintenance crew. Pull the in-

dividual paper fronds out and down in a curve, creasing as you go to make them hang naturally. This makes a very presentable feather palm. Note that some feather palms have mostly upright feathers imitating a feather duster while others such as the date palm have fronds curving out and down as water does from a circular fountain.

Fan palm foliage requires a different approach since the fans are on the ends of stalks. I recall a considerable number of *Washingtonias* which I made at 1/40" scale by using lengths of braided picture wire containing 12 strands which when pulled out of the braid at one end formed enough stalks to make a fully foliated tree. Stand up prepared trunks and stalks in urethane foam and spray them the bark color. Brush contact glue on the stalk tips. Coat a sheet of bond paper with contact glue and let it dry. Then punch a supply of discs from this paper with a die of reasonably correct scale diameter (Ch. 36). Hold each punchout with tweezers as you snip off two arcs to a common end to form an ovate fan shape. Place it on top of a wire stalk end, glue side down, with the point in line with the wire and squeeze them together to tight adhesion. When each stalk has a fan, slip the assembled palm into a piece of brass tubing as a holder and trunk shield and spray paint the foliage. With tweezers, set the tree in urethane foam to dry. Note that the braided wire trunk was left as painted. At 1/40" scale the resulting texture was hardly noticeable. At larger scales, insert the wire stalks into brass or plastic tubing or leave the insulation on stranded electrical wire to form the trunk. Your imagination will carry you to embellishments as the scale increases. These include the dead skirt under the live foliage and snip-fraying the fan edges for further authenticity.

Again, don't ignore the hobby shops. They may have at least palm armatures as a basis for treatment at the model railroad scales. Also refer to Ch. 50 for a company from whom I have purchased small scale feather palm armatures cast in sections. As mentioned previously, new items are continually coming out, and purchases of ready-made, authentic items can save a great deal of time so important to fulfilling your contracts in an efficient manner.

Weeping Willows: Weeping willows have the challenge of straightforward, updirected branching with pendulous almost cascading foliage; a problem combination to the conscientious model builder. The common hybrid descendants of the original

Chinese species remind me of large groups of daisy chains hanging from some unseen lofty framework with leaves substituting for the daisies. The branching at different levels creates a rounded top effect broken up into sections. The fact that the branching and most of the trunk tend to be hidden from view to the external observer makes it possible to arrive at a fairly authentic image with electrical wire stripped of insulation toward one end to allow bending the strands into pendulous configurations. This armature is then spray-glued and dunked in ground cover of authentic green to make a closed foliage tree. Apply the fine ground cover material in light layers until final closure to avoid chunkiness. To my knowledge there is nothing like a *Salix babylonica* or its descendents in the stores or in nature in miniature form; so put on your genius hat and improve on the above method.

ROCK FORMATIONS

Some countrysides will have rock outcroppings to include in a model, and man-placed rocks may be distributed esthetically as a feature of a landscaped setting. In either case note the type and form of rock so that you can duplicate texture, shape, and color. In a urethane foam hillside you can glue in small chips and pieces of the real rock broken up with a hammer as long as the grain of the rock is compatible with the scale. For a rock face, apply plaster to the graded surface, do a little sculpting, and create rock with paint and brush. If setting real rock in a garden area or as a feature in a park, be leary of great boulders of weather-rounded pebbles which can look gross or out of place because their rounded symmetry prevents their appearing as part of the landscape. The ovate or spherical shape makes it difficult to set them comfortably against adjoining rocks, flower beds, walk edges, etc. If boulders with smooth, rounded surfaces are required, try to find them with flat bottoms so that they will look half buried. An example of a waterfall rock escarpment is illustrated in Ch. 49, photo 31.

WATER

For waterfalls and water in various containers included in landscaping plans, see Ch. 12.

SPECIFIED VERSUS FREELANCE LANDSCAPING

In closing this chapter, I think it important to stress the difference in time and effort required between planting according to the specifications of the landscape architects drawings and according to your own sense of artistry or along with your architect client who has visited your shop for the purpose. It is assumed here that any structural civil work such as walks, ponds, steps, etc., would be installed to specifications in any case, but sometimes confidence in your ability to plant effectively will allow you free rein without being called upon to give the botanical names of the trees and bushes you plant. This allows you to use trees left over from your last job. The architect may suggest a few conifers "here" and a grove of eucalyptus "there" to obtain a certain height, shape, and color without regard for species.

This freelance procedure can be just as effective for display purposes as that requiring the authenticity of the landscape architect's prescriptions, but I have found that particularly in the case of the large models, we are expected more and more to follow schedules. That does have the advantage of providing a guiding discipline to relieve you of wondering what to plant in the various areas. Except for large, easily identifiable bushes, shrubbery is usually no problem as long as you consider size, color, and shape, but trees are a different kettle of fish, and time for research and study should be provided for in your contract. I know that I have literally spent hours tracing botanical names to my reference books and deciding the best way to make a particular tree in large numbers. Don't be overcome by the large numbers of a species prescribed. You can usually cut the number at least in half since you will be planting mature trees.

26

Graphics

It is not necessary for you to be a graphic artist in order to be a successful model builder since your products are of a three-dimensional nature. You should, however, be familiar with a few simple two-dimensional procedures which I have found to be recurring necessities for expeditious progress or simply as cosmetic aids.

DRAFTING

In the architectural sense, all the necessary drafting will have been done for you in the drawings from which you construct a model, but there are times when your drafting arm (Ch. 36) will be put to work.

ACID-ETCHING

Acid-etching (Ch. 17) requires accurate drawings of the subject because the etcher photographs them as a medium necessary to the process.

PATTERNS

Patterns sometimes are a great help particularly where curvilinear shapes with varying radii are involved, and the drawings are at a scale different from that of the model. If this discrepancy in scale includes extensive areas of the model, the best solution of course is to obtain the pertinent drawings blown up or reduced to your scale (Ch. 5).

SIGNS

Signs in scale have very seldom been required in my experience. At 1/8″ scale an inch is about 0.010″ so even 6″ letters are a problem to reproduce neatly and evenly. If you must supply signs for the stores in a shopping center, for example, look for printed matter from which you can make up at least black and white compositions. At the larger scales consider the pressure-sensitive lettering from art supply houses, plastic lettering available

from your plastics supplier, or draft with the aid
of a lettering guide (Ch. 36).

NAME PLATES

Plates describing the model will usually be supplied
by the architect for your installation. These and
street name plates, for example, will usually have
no other than a compatible relationship to the
model scale. The lettering has to be large enough
for easy identification. I have made street name
plates using a lettering guide and with plastic lettering which I have not found smaller than 1/4″ in
size. I don't consider the pressure-sensitive lettering
suitable for this purpose because it is so easily
rubbed off. After all, it is primarily for reproduction. Use contrasting colors or shades on the name
plates so that they will stand out without being
magnetic eye catchers. On an AC surface use off-
white or light gray signs with black lettering; on a
concrete freeway use gray signs, etc.

EDGING

Curbs: Curbs (Ch. 13) can be indicated with a
drafting pen (Ch. 36). Use your standard concrete
paint thinned out and strained (Ch. 32). Dip the
pen in the paint to fill it, wipe off the external excess, and draw the pen along the edge of a scrap of
the same material used on the model so that the
top of the edge is captured by the opening between
pen points. Adjust the opening until you obtain a
line the scale width of curb before "doing it for
pay". If you get an occasional expansion of paint
into the planted area, let it dry and then paint it
out with the grass or dirt color using a fine pointed
brush. With paint of the right consistency and a
good pen, you should shortly become expert in
this procedure. There is no fixed formula. A little
trial and error will get you on the right track.

Window Frames: Window frames (Ch. 21) can be
indicated in the same manner by edging separate
window forms. In fact, wherever edging is required
consider this simple method. If you have a stucco
wall, for example, which requires a wood cap, edge
each side of the top with a drafting pen and brown
paint and then fill in the top with a brush and the
same paint. The thickness of the paint will provide
a slight authentic relief at the edges.

LINING

Mullions (Ch. 21) can be indicated with a drafting
pen drawn against a straightedge. Be sure that the
capability of the drafting pen will permit lines of
scale width.

Traffic ways (Chs. 13, 14, and 15) that are
bricked or tiled can, if the scale is large enough be
mortared with a drafting pen against a straightedge.
Cut and peel off strips of the top lamination of
illustration board and fill the slots with mortar
colored paint. This presents an example of how
important planning is since illustration board is the
only material that will allow this treatment. Painted
mortar lines on a hard surface will tend to look
unnaturally embossed.

Traffic lines in my experience are not a frequent requirement, but where perimeter streets
extend beyond their centers, indicated traffic lanes
if actually present authentically control the traffic
created by the scale vehicles used (Ch. 27). These
lines include those of crosshatched walkways, indicate street parking stalls, direction of traffic flow,
etc. When drawing lines around a curve, make a
drafting pen guide by cutting the arc out of lightweight illustration board. After drawing the radius,
extend the edge of the guide beyond beginning and
ending of curve to assist you in positioning it on
the model. Don't forget to raise the guide off the
surface to be lined so that the paint won't wick
under. All you need is a few buttons of vinyl glued
to the underside of the guide.

Parking stall indication will probably give your
drafting pen the most exercise during its life. Even
where the project's tenant and employee parking
is hidden underground there likely will be visible
guest parking to indicate. For exemplary purposes
assume you have a long, rectangular parking area
to line including four rows of stalls, one along each
edge and a double row down the center (Fig. 26-1).
There is an entrance and exit at each end of the
area; the stalls will be at right angles to the longer
sides of the rectangle. The surface is heavyweight
illustration board painted an asphaltic concrete
(AC) gray, and following Pattinson's Law all raised
surfaces such as curbs and planters have been left
off until the lining has been done. Figure 26-1
shows a portion only of the area. Following the
civil drawings lay out the outside lines of the curbs,
planter locations and moving traffic ways. Confine
your plot to pencil dots as much as possible to
obviate later erasing or repainting. Lay masking

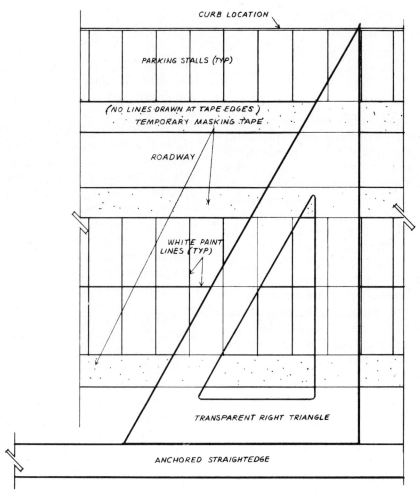

CURB LOCATION

PARKING STALLS (TYP)

(NO LINES DRAWN AT TAPE EDGES)
TEMPORARY MASKING TAPE

ROADWAY

WHITE PAINT
LINES (TYP)

TRANSPARENT RIGHT TRIANGLE

ANCHORED STRAIGHTEDGE

FIGURE 26-1 *Parking stalls.*

tape along the outside of the curb lines and fill the two long driveways between parking stall rows with masking tape. With your thumb nail press down the edges of the tape to make a paint tight joint. Don't press down the entire tape surface or you may pull paint when removing it after the lining has been done. The longer masking tape is allowed to remain, the tighter its adherence will be. Check the straight alignment of the tape edges. If you are not careful in laying it down it will have a tendency to curve. Use multiple dots along a mounting line as guides. With pencil dots lay out on the masking tape along a curb edge the parking stall widths as indicated in Fig. 26-1. Assuming 9′ widths, be sure that the stall area being divided has a length equal to a multiple of 9′. If not, recheck the drawings. The apparent extra width of the last stall may be absorbed by a planter or may be just left that way. If you have to divide an area into so many spaces without regard for

specific dimensions, see the aid discussed later in this chapter.

Temporarily fix a straightedge to the model just outside the parking area so that it is at right angles to the direction of the stall lines to be drawn. With a draftsman's right triangle large enough to span the entire parking area, slide it along the straightedge as you draw a white paint line starting at each pencil point you plotted on the masking tape. Start each line on the tape to avoid starting blobs of paint on the AC surface and continue the motion across the entire width without stopping until you have crossed the edge of the other curb tape. Whether you are right or left handed, slide the triangle away from your lining each time. The thickness of the tape should raise the instrument high enough to prevent wicking underneath. When removing the tape, pull slowly and steadily up and back in a peeling motion to avoid disturbing the surface. Draw a line down the center of the

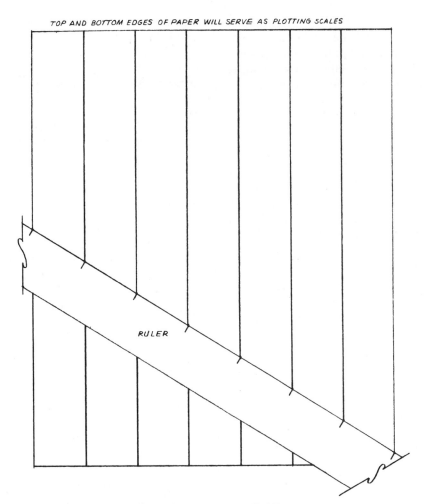

TOP AND BOTTOM EDGES OF PAPER WILL SERVE AS PLOTTING SCALES

RULER

FIGURE 26-2 *Space dividing.*

center double stalls at right angles to the stall lines, leaving gaps at the passthrough driveways. With a fine brush and your AC paint, paint out any paint expansion noted. If you should have to do a line over, completely paint it out with AC paint and let it dry before trying to reline. In one way traffic situations, the stalls will be at an angle. I have often found the sixty degree angle of a right triangle instrument to be the one prescribed. If necessary, make up your own triangle out of a piece of acrylic.

EQUAL SPACING

Say you have a 6″ space to divide into 7 equal spaces. One seventh of 6″ equals 6/7″ or 0.857+″, a difficult dimension accurately to plot using a scale. As shown in Fig. 26-2 draw two parallel lines 6″ apart from top to bottom of a sheet of typewriter paper. Lay a ruler at an angle across these lines so that they fall exactly seven units apart and make six pencil dots to indicate the seven units. Do this at the top and the bottom of the sheet and draw parallel lines through these dots over the edge of the paper. The top and bottom edges will then serve as a scale for use on the model.

SCORING

Scoring of one sort or another is almost an every day occurrence in model building. It involves simply the linear disturbance of a surface with a tool usually against a straightedge. The tools used most of the time are either a knife or a pointed steel scribe (Ch. 36). Knife scribing is done mostly on materials such as illustration board where a shallow cut will facilitate paint color separation with a sharp division. A scribe is used to score mullions, for example, on window material. Knife scoring is used to delineate brick and tile surfaces, for example, cutting just into a prepainted surface. Acrylic sheet can be scored with a special knife (Ch. 36) and then snap-broken along the score.

COSMETICS

Some of the graphic artist's tricks can be used at small scales to create the illusion of relief as in door paneling. Where the scale is too small to justify three-dimensional construction, shade the depressed edges with a pencil to indicate level changes. Draw fine, sharp lines to indicate a delineated surface and then shade the far sides assuming a consistent line of viewing. This same method can be used in ornate decoration which could not be embossed without a microscope.

Shading is done with different paints on a rock or earth face (Ch. 33).

STENCILS

A set of lettering stencils will come in handy at times for painting on identification and directions on model crates.

TRANSFER

Large sheets of carbon paper obtainable at your artists' supplier's are useful for trace-transfer of layout lines on a model base and making patterns. This paper is available also with white "carbon" for dark surfaces.

27

Accessories

By far the most used accessories are vehicles and human figures which give an atmosphere of activity to a model, as well as provide a means visually to establish the scale. My advice to save time and assure consistent authenticity and detail is to purchase accessories outside whenever possible. The specialists have the skill and equipment to produce in large quantities items far better and more economically than you can as a sideline to your model building career. Even if you have the skill to do so, time will not normally allow you to make accurate masters for numerous makes of automobiles, for example, and then cast them in numbers sufficient to fill a parking lot. See Ch. 50 for a suggested source of various items.

VEHICLES

Automobiles: Automobiles cast in soft metal will come, except at the very small scales, with mounting projections on the undersides. Set them out in color groups of random makes in rigid urethane foam to hold them and spray them the different colors with pressure-can enamels. Colors that are not matte from the can should be sprayed with a matte finish to kill any disturbing reflections. Use the standard range of automobile colors avoiding the bright reds and other "atomic" shades which tend to catch the eye. The subduing of reflection is in deference to the difference between the life-size scene and the same scene confined to a few square feet. This is one of the rare educated violations of authenticity. You could spray with your own mixed colors using matte paint, but the pressure cans are much faster, and the matte spray solves the problem.

Punch holes with a scribe in illustration board and vinyl over urethane surfaces to accept the mounting pegs. Be sure you note which end of the vehicle has the peg and add a touch of contact glue to secure it. Display a representative number of cars on the perimeter streets in natural single file in their lanes and a few entering and leaving the property. In front of habitation park a few at the curb. Five o'clock traffic jams will spoil the scene, so stay away from massing. In parking lots substantially fill the stalls without complete occupancy. Show a few cars in the driveways, at the street entrances, and just entering stalls as though employees were just arriving for work or baseball fans were collecting just before the first pitch. A completely filled parking lot has all the unseen employees at their desks creating a dead sea of cars. In a hospital model, show an ambulance just approaching the emergency entrance as though you have just heard the last siren whine or a semi backing into a loading dock in an industrial scene, etc. Even though the scene is not animated, appearances of activity can add interest in a model and thereby better hold attention. Unless you know your client well, and the purpose of the display allows, beware of whimsy such as an automobile wreck with two figures obviously arguing over whose fault it was. This sort of thing may be attention holding in a small scale model of a large urban area on public display, but you may be considered out of order by a board of directors seriously studying land use and architecture.

Industrial and Commercial Vehicles: These will be found at the same source as automobiles. Where appropriate, include trucks of various designs doing their thing. In the absence of required buses and semis at the last minute, you can form the first out of acrylic plastic as described next for trailers, and for the second, chop out the rear top section of an automobile to form a tractor to haul a container shaped out of wood.

Travel and House Trailers: These special vehicles would not be considered accessories in parks as the model feature attraction, (Ch. 49, photo 52) but they are included here as a convenient place to discuss them. They both can be made out of solid acrylic plastic. Obtain plastic of scale height or width if possible and cut it up into pieces of the overall size of vehicle. Polish (Ch. 24) the windowed sides if necessary. Plastic of a thickness equal to the vehicle width has the advantage of providing already polished sides. Shape them on your belt sander and add window size pieces of masking tape in the window and windshield locations. Spray them authentic colors and remove the tape to reveal the transparent areas. Wheels can be made from heavy paper punchouts glued to wire axles or simply to the underside of the body depending upon scale. If there is a wheel skirt, flatten a portion of each wheel and glue it to the underside as though the top of the wheel were hidden. I stress freelancing in this case because I have never found such vehicles ready made at the desired scale. As always check with your hobby shop for solutions before you embark on a lengthy

home-made session. In a permanent-type mobile home park you may have to dispense with the visible wheels, expand a telescoping home, and add awnings, patios, steps, and gardens, all of which take the vehicles out of the accessory classification.

Railway Equipment: See Ch. 13.

Industrial Equipment: Industrial equipment such as bulldozers, forklifts, cranes, and tow-motors such as around airports are usually few in number in any model scene, and will likely have to be made up simply to satisfy scale. I have found a very limited range in toy and hobby shops. I know of an excellent railway crane, for example, at HO scale which could be adapted for an industrial scene at 1/8" scale. This is true of other items which, with a little imagination, can be adapted to your purpose. See Ch. 50 for suggested sources.

Airplanes: I have been fortunate enough to find airplanes in such things as naval aircraft carrier kits in reasonable scale. If you have to show masses of Cessna, Beechcraft, etc. types, not to speak of jumbo jets, discuss availability with your client during initial negotiations, and provide for the time if you have to make even just reasonable facsimiles.

Boats: Boats to fill a marina can be a time consuming problem though not quite as serious as that of aircraft. Occasionally hobby shop kits and the toy stores will have boats which can be adapted without too much difficulty. Thanks to standard hull shapes, a small boat at 1/8" scale can simply be a large one at 1/16" scale, so you have considerable latitude. I have purchased a model ship kit just to get the life boats to adapt for a marine scene. If you have to make them, outline the shape of the hull plan on fine grain wood such as white pine or bass wood, cut out the minimum visible cockpit area and then shape the hull outline, leaving the bottom at waterline level flat for water borne craft since the rest will be hidden. Draw on your imagination for cabins and superstructure. Sails can be made from typewriter copy tissue and masts from fine wire. Indicate bow waves and stern wakes with a fine brush and white paint. Sand the bottoms of sail boats at an angle to provide list with the wind. If you have a lot of the same hull to make for sail boats in a lake scene, consider vacuum forming (Ch. 24).

HUMAN FIGURES

These are available at about any scale from the source listed in Ch. 50. Seated figures have been available at scales of 1/16″ and above. I have cut the legs off 1/32″ scale figures to seat them in leg-hiding locations such as the boats of an amusement park flume ride. The cast, soft metal figures will come with mounting tabs as extensions of one leg so set them up in rigid urethane and spray them all with flesh color whether white, black, or brown. With a fine brush paint on the clothing with the basic colors of blue, green, yellow, white, black, and brown. You can mix colors with the brush as you paint to obtain gray and other shades, the simplest road to variety being different combinations of the same colors on shirts, skirts and trousers. Paint on a few bikinis or shorts for poolside scenarios. If you don't like the existing hat on a 1/8″ scale figure, a few careful twists against your belt sander will remove it. Place the figures at random on sidewalks and patios, leaving or approaching parking lots, in open boats under way, leaving their car at a loading zone, etc. Bend the legs and arms of walking figures and raise the arms of two people gesturing as if they are having a discussion, or pointing at a distant boat from lakeside. These little touches help to create the atmosphere of activity discussed previously. Use a wire drill in a pin vise (Ch. 36) to accept the mounting peg wet with contact glue. The foot will cover the mounting point. If you insist on some subdued whimsy, place a figure looking out of a window before closing up the building.

FLAGS AND FLAG POLES

Effective flags can be made from tissue paper and colored pencils and crimped to reflect wind action before attaching them to their poles made out of piano wire, or finer, depending upon scale. For a terminating gold ball, use a bead or simply a drop of white glue painted gold when dry. *Warning:* If you have flags or pennants flying in a coastal scene with sail boats tacking upwind, don't fall into the trap of showing them flapping in the same direction the boats are traveling.

28

Symbolism

Within the limits of scale, time, and budget, the goal of every professional model builder should be to portray as accurately as possible a real subject. Your expertise in effecting visual authenticity within these unavoidable limits is the corner stone upon which your success will be built. Use your imagination continuously to inspire invention of more efficient methods to obtain a same result.

Because most materials, whether organic or inorganic, don't "come in small packages", for want of a better phrase, we must, as a practical necessity, use *symbols*. We create illusion; we have to be constructively deceptive. If you were building a model of the Taj Mahal, for example, you obviously could not use marble. Even if you could obtain a workable marble veneer, the natural graining itself would be out of scale. Instead, we treat a substitute material so that in appearance there is no doubt as to what it represents. Meeting the challenge of treatment is the model builder's raison d'être. We cannot put needles on a 1/8" scale pine tree or individual leaves on a sycamore, but we can use "symbols" of authentically shaped armatures treated to leave no doubt in the viewer's mind. It would be highly impractical to plaster a model living room wall or lay individual bricks to construct a garden wall, but through substitute materials and texture both projects are visually authenticated through symbols.

The foregoing preamble is introductory to the main point of this section which is the manner of use of symbols. As a long time observer of scale models, I find I have little patience with symbols which are obviously so. Prime examples are trees consisting of paper discs on tooth picks which I have seen as part of the landscaping. Such stylization may be fine in the classroom, but any display (particularly public display) model worth its salt should never lead the viewer into thinking "symbol" rather than the subject the symbol is supposed to represent. Such fake representation on a model reminds me of a copout under the guise of creating an "art form" which should be confined to a dark corner if displayed at all. It is not a scale model.

Another pet gripe of mine is what I call a sanitized model — one *lacking* in symbols. One such model sticks in my mind. It was a sharp-cornered, beautifully executed model of an institutional building on display under an acrylic cover in an architect's entryway. With all due respect to the architecture the model was completely devoid of any three-dimensional landscaping. The building had no setting, no reflective entourage to compliment it. It made me think of something made in a clinical laboratory with white tile walls and glaring lights. To my mind the lack of natural setting made the architecture look sterile. If it weren't for the final, semipublic display atmosphere, I like to think that the model was not yet finished. Perhaps it was purely for architectural analysis, but the excellent workmanship belied any assumption that it was made for study purposes only.

A small model of a building for permanent open display on the desk of the chairman of the board requires sterility as a practical maintenance matter, but as a general rule don't hesitate to add warmth — a natural setting. Don't hide the architecture, but put an espaliered pear tree against that blank wall!

As you progress in your career you will develop your own model philosophy based upon your accumulating experience. I give some of my reaction to experience to help toward that end. A flexible common sense philosophy will help you in giving constructive advice befitting the purposes of the models you are building for your clients.

29

Lighting

Though 95 percent of your models be of exteriors only, many of them will probably include lighting, particularly the high-rise office buildings. Two of the main problems in planning a lighting system are heat and the scale of required visible light sources.

MINIATURE LIGHT SOURCES

A grain of wheat bulb that is approximately 1/8″ in diameter would look extremely gross in the end of a 1/16″ scale street light standard, but it might be hidden behind a lens which had a scale diameter of 1′ in an 1/8″ scale fixture. Since *incandescent* bulbs of all sizes put out a great deal of heat, they have to be well ventilated to prolong their life and keep the surroundings from catching fire. The little 12-volt screw base bulbs are close to 1/4″ in diameter, as are the fluorescent tube shaped bulbs which are 1-5/8″ long. The requirement for miniaturization of lighting sources is fortunately seldom encountered; so you need not worry too much about availability. With the rapid advances in the electronic field, evidenced by such components as light-emitting diodes, by the time you are presented with any spot lighting requirements, it may very well be that cool, scale light sources will be available. Consider low voltage night light bulbs for use with line current as hidden sources of background illumination. I have used them effectively to backlight an altar in a church model, for example. I have found miniature flasher units at the hobby shops for transformed voltage lighting at the top of such structures as airport towers. This is a simple and authentic way to create "animation" (Ch. 30).

POLY- OR FIBER OPTICS

If you have provided for the engineering time in your contract, street lamps, for example, can be the polished ends of acrylic rods through which light is transferred from a hidden, ventilated source, even a household light bulb. To get the maximum light at the lens end of the rod, wrap the rod in aluminized mylar plastic, or coat it with a reflective aluminum paint. The rods can be collected in groups, each group having its own hidden light source. Heat-forming the rods will be necessary to obtain the bends required from source to fixture. It may be necessary to obtain clearance from your client for variations in the design of light fixtures to permit the presence of the acrylic rod, which, if not forming the standard itself, will be run through brass tubing. Scale limitations apply here also, but before you toss out the whole idea as impracticable, discuss your problem with a company familiar with this type of system. Even at 1/32″ scale a 1/32″ diameter light stand would not be too gross, and the resulting spot of light will provide effective simulation.

NEON

Neon lighting is not too satisfactory for models because of the clumsiness of the system and the high voltage necessary to fire the neon gas. I recall neon lighting a 1/4″ scale office building facade with tubing bent to order and connected to a transformer box, necessarily separate from the model, and which weighed more than the model. The smallest tubing available was 3/8″ in diameter and was hidden behind window sun shades. Lighting six floors was accomplished without the hazard of heat which for the most part was confined to the transformer box. With shorter lengths of tubing, resulting in a power source of a mass and weight something less than that of a Boulder Dam unit, this method might have its merits in some situations, but from my experience avoidance is in order. Scale model lighting with neon is in the class of hiring an elephant to pick up a straw.

ELECTROLUMINESCENCE

Since my first contact with a thin 3″ diameter disc which, when plugged into a household outlet, glowed to light your way down the hall in the middle of the night, I haven't had the occasion to pursue the advances in electroluminescence, but I can see great possibilities for it in lighting a model ceiling, for example, without intruding sockets, bulbs, etc., to hide. When you have the requirement for any luminescent surface, check with one of the larger electric lighting equipment manufacturers. You may be able to avoid a battery of bulbs.

BLACK LIGHT

Black light is invisible (close to ultraviolet) light emitted from a special bulb to reflect off luminescent paint applied to the object to be illuminated. The luminous paint reradiates at a wave length long enough to be visible, the paint itself not being visible when applied. The system is good only for special effects in model building, and there is the problem of locating the source fixture without intruding on the model scene. I have acceptably mounted it on a model edge, but the best way is to mount it away from the model in the display area with unobstructed line of sight to the subject. Check with advertising and display companies in your area for sources of equipment.

FLUORESCENT LIGHTING

In the long run standard fluorescent tubes are the best means of satisfying lighting requirements for by far the great majority of models. With air circulating they are a relatively cool source. You will note that when you touch a burning fluorescent tube in an open fixture, it will feel just warm, whereas a lit incandescent bulb may singe your hand. The length and girth of the tube are critical factors, so discuss your requirements with a lighting equipment supplier to find the right tube and compatible accessories such as starters and ballasts. The chances are that you will find a tube length that can be used without too much adaptation of the model structure. Electrical manufacturers such as General Electric and Westinghouse put out catalogues which you should have in your reference library (Ch. 43) so that you can order components by number. Before getting into construction tips, it is well to reiterate the admonition to keep the necessity for lighting facilities in mind from the start—whole picture planning again! Also remember Pattinson's Law so you do not construct yourself out of access to electric component space, or ignore such space altogether.

Assume you have to construct a lighted 1/16″ scale exterior high-rise office building model with walls of bronze acrylic similar to the one discussed in Ch. 18 (Fig. 29-1). You have decided that one tube will do the job and have found one that will extend about 3″ below the ground floor, with the top contacts hidden behind the opaque utility floor wall just under the roof. When con-

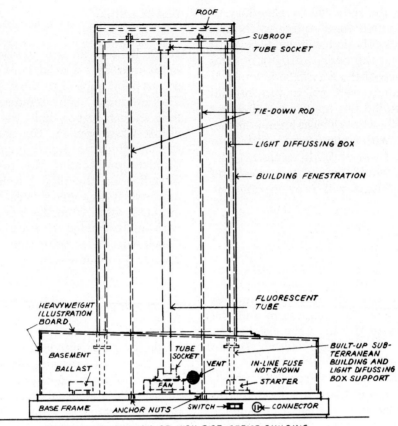

FIGURE 29-1 *Lighting a model.*

structing the base of the model, cut a hole in the 2″ × 1″ frame to hold a male connector with the prongs flush with the outside frame surface. This will allow the power cord to enter the model as low as possible. Use a three-pronged connector to provide a third wire ground from the transformer (ballast) to the power outlet in your client's display area. Be sure to use components compatible with those in the display area and capable of handling the potential at that location. This will probably be a minimum of 110 volts, and in Europe, for example, could be 220 volts. Use a heavy, rubber insulated connector and mount it securely opposite the hole in the frame with shaped blocks of wood so that the mounting will stand continual push-and-pull activity without coming loose. Connect to this plug a length of three-conductor wire and feed it through an oversize hole cut in the plywood base before installing the Masonite bottom on the frame (Ch. 7). The oversize hole is to accept a piece of insulating plastic tubing, separating the wire from the wood. This is similar to running wire-holding conduit through the 2″ × 4″'s in house construc-

tion. Though there aren't to my knowledge any electrical codes for model building, common sense tells us to handle and install all power systems with every reasonable precaution.

Basement: To accommodate the projection of the tube below the first floor, construct a basement of a depth to accept the three extra inches of fluorescent tube and socket with top contacts just below the roof of the building. Note that the 3″ extra length of fluorescent tube is arbitrary for the sake of discussion. The length of the tube will depend upon available size to fit a given height of building. Also note that the basement will have to be deep enough to accept all other components with at least 1/2″ clearance top and bottom for air circulation. If the bottom of the glass of the tube chosen just reached first floor level, you would still have to provide basement space for the other components. The bottom tube socket would then be raised on blocks to the correct height (Ch. 49, photo 54). The sides can be of heavyweight illustration board with top edges cut to the finished grade configuration with sufficient bracing to make the sides rigid and to support the finished grade. Leave the grade-supporting risers out until you have installed electrical components and then fit risers to conform, cutting holes in them where necessary to ensure air flow. Note that vertical control of grading (Ch. 9) is used here rather than a block of urethane foam because it is necessary to have as open a basement as possible for component installation and air circulation. At the center of each side of the model cut a 2″ diameter hole near the base plywood level for ventilation and glue pieces of window screening over them on the inside of the basement walls.

Electrical Components: Electrical components include a fluorescent tube and sockets, starter and socket (unless the tube is self-starting), ballast, fuse and container, heavy-duty toggle switch, cooling fan, and the heavy-insulated three-prong connector previously discussed and mounted in the base frame. I attach the ground wire of the three-conduit power cord to the ballast base being sure of its ground connection in the connector. For inside wiring I use heavy-duty double conduit household wire. The double insulation is scored down the center to make it easy to separate the two sides for single conduit routing. If you are to have any low-voltage circuits for incidental exterior lighting, you will also need a transformer to reduce voltage to 12 volts, for example. This is not an electrical text, so I will not confuse the issue by describing all possible circuits under varying conditions. Tell an electrician just what you plan to do, and he or she will advise you. The previously mentioned catalogues will have various circuits illustrated to fit the components used. In practice I have made each system to stand on its own feet. Even though a repetitive system's circuits are the same for two consecutive models, it is a good idea to start from scratch each time you wire a model to prevent goofs.

Installation: Place the properly rated fuse and holder ahead of the ballast to prevent blowing the fuse of the building in which the model is displayed should any thing go wrong in the display. Mount the ballast on end blocks so that air can circulate all around it as it is the principal source of heat. Wire the switch on the power side of the system and mount it so that the toggle can be conveniently reached through a hole in the basement wall and set in far enough not to conflict with an acrylic model cover. You could have mounted the switch in the base frame alongside

the male plug thus avoiding a second hole in the cover, but this is incidental. Mount the bottom fluorescent tube socket directly in line with the center of the building, and mount the fan so that it will blow up through the building. Since there is only one switch, the fan will run whenever the tube is on which is the way it should be. I have found small, neatly packaged quiet fans at surplus stores, but your local electrical supplier can guide you. Tack down free wire between connections with insulated staples after wrapping the wire in electrical tape at the staple locations.

A self-starting tube may have a single pin contact at each end, requiring single hole sockets one of which will be spring loaded. No starter is required and the ballast will be smaller. The push-in feature will make bulb replacement a little easier than that of the bi-pin tubes which have to be twisted into place, but considering the normal life of a fluorescent tube, this is a minor point. Two objections to the single pin tube are the relative bulkiness of the sockets, considering the usual limited space at the top of the building, and the limitations as to available lengths. A bi-pin tube with starter is used for this discussion.

With the starter mounted near to a basement wall, you can cut an access panel on the illustration board to allow easy replacement should the unit fail. This should be the only reason you would have to have access to the basement, if at all. Hold the panel in place with two small flat head screws screwed into wood tabs glued to the inside surface of the wall.

To avoid running two loose wires up alongside the tube to make top connections, I use the tie-down rods (Ch. 19) as conductors, requiring an insulated mounting. After drilling the holes in the plywood base leave them as locating and clearance holes rather than screwing in the anchor nuts described in Ch. 19 for an unlit model. Cut four 2″ squares of clear 1/4″ thick acrylic plastic. Through the center of each drill holes just large enough to allow a slip fit of the 1/4″ tie-down rod (ignoring threads). Select two square 1/4-20 nuts and two of the four acrylic squares to serve as the bottom layers of the tie-down rod contacts. Enlarge their center holes just deep enough to accept a tapped in fit of the nuts (Fig. 29-2) so that their top surfaces are flush with the acrylic. A tight fit of the nut corners against the perimeter of the hole should prevent the nuts turning, but to be sure, align the nut sides parallel to the acrylic sides and against three sides of each nut drill holes through the plastic to accept small

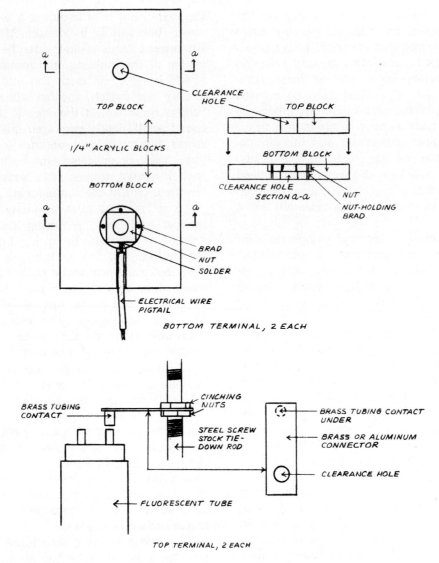

FIGURE 29-2 *Tie-down rod conductors.*

brads with a snug fit. Remove the nuts and from the location of the unbradded side of the nut, file a groove across the surface of the acrylic deep enough to accept a single insulated wire. Do this on both nut-bearing squares of plastic so that the wire will be flush with the surface. Cut two pigtails of wire 2″ to 3″ long and remove about 1/4″ of insulation from each end of each. As illustrated in Fig. 29-2 solder a pigtail to each nut in line with the grooves just filed in the acrylic squares. Replace the nuts in their holes, tap in the brads (three each), and file off excess brad flush with the plastic surfaces. Using a piece of scrap 1/4-20 tie-down rod as an alignment guide, place the other two acrylic squares on their nut-bearing mates being sure that they meet flat with holes aligned. Wick in acrylic cement to weld the two layers together. Trim off any edge mismatch, and

with a conical countersink (Ch. 36) bevel the edges of the holes on the top layers to serve as hole finders when trying to mount the ties rods from the top of the installed building. At the four corners of each sandwich drill holes for wood screws and mount each in location over the holes you previously drilled in the plywood for the anchor nuts not now used. These holes will provide clearance for excess rod length upon final assembly. Solder the free ends of the two pigtails to the proper wires from the ballast, wrap the joints with electrician's tape (or the tubular heat-shrinkable insulation (Ch. 35)), and tack down the wire to the plywood with insulated staples.

When all equipment in the basement has been installed and wired make illustration board risers (Ch. 9) to support the illustration board finished grade cover over the basement. Be sure to leave passageways or cut holes for free airflow drawn by the fan through the vents in the basement walls. Also be sure to support solidly the building by placing risers across the location of the four building corners so that when you cinch the building down, nothing will squash. Rather than have to slope the building wall bottom edges to conform to grade, a much better system consists of a level wooden frame built up in the basement to accept the right angle wall edges through a snug fitting hole cut out of the finished grade surfacing as indicated in Fig. 29-1. The building walls will have of course been made tall enough to provide for the slight amount of subterranean burial. The building support frame will have to be wide enough to hold the bottom of the light-diffusion box discussed later. The burial system will ensure that the building is vertical at all times regardless of what the entourage is doing. The first system is fine for level grading, and when used, don't forget the holes on the basement cover for the tie-down rods and an oversize hole for the fluorescent tube to allow air passage. Glue down the finished grade and put the building in place.

Light Diffusion: This is necessary to obtain equal luminescence over the entire fenestration. (Ch. 49, photo 53) Diffusion is accomplished with an open-ended box of 1/8″ translucent white acrylic made so that it just fits inside the building without touching the walls and high enough to clear the top fluorescent tube contacts. Glue small retainers of strip wood to the support frame to hold the bottom of the box from shifting.

The top electrical contacts (Fig. 29-2) can be made of two strips of brass stiff enough to hold the fluorescent tube vertical. Drill a hole in one end of each strip so that it can be slipped down over the tie-down rod and held in place between two nuts cinched together. On the other end of each strip solder a piece of brass tubing which will fit to make good contact when slipped over a tube pin. Install the tube and adjust the strip connectors by positioning the two clamping nuts on each tie-down rod. Note: The standard top socket shown in Fig. 29-1 requires wire connections to the tie-down rods—a clumsier installation.

SUBROOF

Make a tie-down roof out of 1/4″ acrylic so that it just slips into the building and drill two holes to

accept the tops of the tie-down rods which should now be screwed in place. Install the subroof and turn a nut down on each rod until you have securely clamped the light-diffusing box onto its basement support frame. Follow your sense of snugness required. Too much muscle will crack a seam if not break something. Mark the small amount of clearance you want above the nut on each rod, and disassemble to cut off the rod excess. Dress the new ends so that the nuts will turn on freely. Note that at this point the subroof will not clamp down the building itself, just the light-diffusing box. The building will stay in place of its own weight in its finished grade socket as long as the model is kept level, but as added insurance against sometimes necessary tipping, add retainer strips around the insides of the walls at the same level as that of the top of the light diffusion box. These can be glued on or attached with screws from the outside if you can hide the screw heads behind facade treatment. As an added precaution against the tube's coming up out of its basement socket, at points vertically opposite the contact pins glue on rubber buttons under the subroof to fill the clearance space.

Roof: The roof can be made out of 1/8″ Masonite or even heavyweight illustration board and should slip into the building without forcing. It is held at base of parapet level on a 1/8″ acrylic frame spacer between the top surface of the subroof and the bottom of the roof itself. With contact cement *tack-glue only* these units for easy later removal for repairs or replacing the tube.

Ventilation: Perforate the subroof to allow the free passage of air coming from the basement. A couple of rows of small holes along each side should do the job without weakening seriously the tie-down system. The necessary holes in the roof will be unauthentic but will usually be invisible behind the parapet at normal display height. Consider cutting slots along the roof edges, or if there is a penthouse, cut a hole in the roof the size of the interior dimensions thereof and slots in the top edges of the penthouse walls camouflaged by eaves of the penthouse roof. Don't forget ventilation holes in the model cover.

Other Situations: Other situations involving fluorescent lighting can be as varied as architectural designs and types of projects, but from my experience the foregoing should help to lead you to other solutions to fit other conditions. If there is no opaque top utility floor as in the example presented, or if the opaque building cap is too shallow, etc., then you will have to pierce an acrylic (for electrical insulation) roof with tube and tie-down rods hidden by some superstructure as a penthouse, authentic or not. If lighting is a must, your clients will likely agree to some reasonable field expedients to accomplish that end. Consider the little 6″ fluorescent tubes to fit into small spaces. I have used them to floodlight an open below-grade court, for example.

DISPLAY OPERATION

Always send typewritten instructions along with a lighted model. I usually tape them to the acrylic model cover with a warning not to leave the lights on all night. An electric timer may be in order, to turn them off at a set time. Include in your instructions the type of lighting, how to replace a tube or starter, etc. Stress the fact that the power cord must be disconnected before working on the model.

SAFETY FIRST

Before furling the caution flags, I repeat the admonition to consult with a qualified electrician about your planned components, circuits, and safety precautions. Do this until you are confident that you know what you are doing. Thinking of product insurance, let your broker know about your use of electricity in your models. In the case of any doubt, I feel it wise to wear galoshes over your rubbers, so to speak, by spending an extra hour of insulating and ventilating. Above all, use high quality, matching electrical units with adequate capacities and *always disconnect power sources before working on a system.* As a closing suggestion, whenever it is hard for you to visualize the installation of an approved electrical system as you are building the model, first make a circuit sketch including all the components and their location. Such a sketch would likely be mandatory in obtaining approval from an electrician. Considering the safety of self-preservation, don't fail to include estimated time and material costs of any lighting system in your quotation (Ch. 44)!

30

Animation

Other than lighting (if that can be called animation), 99 out of 100 models in professional architectural model building do not require animation simply because there is nothing germane to their purpose to animate. What is there to animate in a model of a high-rise office building, hospital, library, school, or private residence? You might show some vehicles running, activated by a continuous magnetic belt, for example, but to what purpose? For one thing, the cost would far outweigh the visual benefits, particularly since the static presence of cars in itself creates an atmosphere of activity. Everyone knows what a running automobile looks like; you would be demonstrating nothing.

"Demonstration" is a key word. If there is a system or process that can be best explained through motion, then animation makes sense. If a sales program for a swimming pool manufacturer includes a 1/2″ scale model of an installation, then moving water through it has attention-getting reasons to justify the cost of the embellishment. In any use of scale models as commercial sales tools, movement attracts attention. So, under public relations situations "movement" becomes another key word. A static model of a ferris wheel would not have the appeal that a spinning one would; the amusement park equipment manufacturer feels justified in including the animation. What better way to demonstrate and advertise some railroad company's freight handling system in a confined space than to have running engines making up trains? For public education with respect to their local sewage disposal system, a scale model with water flowing through it will help explain the critical necessity for such a system, the problems involved, and the expenditure of tax dollars, pounds, or whatever the monetary unit might be. An enlightened public is a vital step toward individual cooperation, and movement in a scale model of such a dull subject as sewage disposal will help to hold the viewer's attention.

The above examples are but a few of those that might be given to indicate the advisability of including animation. Because of the many variations in approach and installation in the field of animation, nothing would be gained from construction tips for any one complete installation which probably would never be duplicated. Rather it will be more beneficial to submit some basic information to assist you in getting your imagination and ingenuity into high gear.

WATER

For moving water in a scale model remember you have to recirculate a selfcontained supply, and that you cannot naturally obtain a scale model of a water molecule. Avoid static drops which, in scale, are oversize puddles with no visible containment. For movement consider the fish tank type of pump which you can hide in a raised base, raising it in the same manner as you did for the lighting equipment in Ch. 29. A low voltage pump with transformer is safer than running with line voltage. Use plastic tubing for conduits, with pieces of brass tubing at visible outlets such as those in a swimming pool. A stream source can be hidden in a rock formation as though it were an artesian well. Note here that stream rapids in a model would have to be produced by pressure at the source, creating the hazard of spraying the whole countryside. It is difficult to scale down the movement of water, so confine any flowing water animation to gravity power. Avoid real water lakes. If the bugs don't get you, evaporation will require continual replacement, and even with recirculation, you would need a clumsy fan installation to maintain a rippled surface. Oceans are another case where animation should be forgotten. Swimming pools are the best candidates for moving water, and only where the scale is large enough to make it practical. A good example of the use of water in animation is a 1/4″ scale model of a liquid fertilizer plant (Ch. 49, photo 1) hypothetically designed to be used as a sales demonstration medium. A miniature pump and transformer hidden in the private freight house on a railroad spur pumped "liquid fertilizer" through overhead piping supported on racks throughout the system. The piping was made from transparent plastic tubing so that the flow could be observed. Life-size meters on the edge of the model helped explain the flow. The administration building was lighted and grain of wheat bulbs buried in reflectors atop pieces of brass tubing provided yard lights. Though the static model had sales appeal since the structures, landscaping, etc., were all in scale, the addition of the visibly flowing water brought it to life. The fact that the system was closed avoided any problem of evaporation.

Waterproofing: Waterproofing can be accomplished in various ways. For a swimming pool, solder together an aluminum box, providing for inlet and outlet, and paint it with a waterproof marine paint. If the shape of the pool makes it difficult to form a metal container, construct the shape out of wood or plastic right on the model and line the cavity with resin and waterproof paint. You could even cast one out of plaster. Similar methods apply to stream beds, where you must be sure your waterproofing extends far enough beyond the stream banks to prevent the water from escaping. A stream bed can be lined with flexible plastic sheet such as polyethelene. Paint the surface with colors characteristic of the area, shading according to depth, and glue down rocks for the water to run over and around.

MECHANICAL ANIMATION

Considering that you have a workable scale, about anything can be accomplished in scale animation, given the engineering time and money required. The standard basis for all this animation is the electric motor which is available with about any rating you can think of as to voltage, torque, and rpm. Scour the hobby shops and electronic specialty and surplus stores for the answer to your particular requirement. Sometimes it pays to buy an animated toy just to get the motor. You can make your own gear boxes from watch and clock gears or those from your son's Meccano or Erector set. I have used motors with their own gear boxes incorporated. Miniature drive belts can be made from rubber bands. Special pulleys can be fabricated on your lathe.

A demonstration model of a transducer star element (Ch. 49, photo 2) was made as an open-sided blow-up, with the flexing stainless steel element activated by an electric motor turning a cam from a hidden rear location. Here is an example of work completely devoid of architecture, but indicative of the possibilities in related fields. Another job involving no architecture was a remotely controlled lighted panel to display the flow of gas through a valve system. It was used in court where the attorney wanted to be able to control the lights from a desk away from the location of the easel supporting the panel. The remote control was accomplished by the use of Touch-Plate low voltage components, including a button panel activating solenoid switches in the panel to turn on and off the 12-volt bulbs in a prescribed sequence.

To obtain rotating motion, some sort of motor system is necessary, but as time marches on, control becomes more sophisticated. The Touch-Plate system is a simple and practical way to activate switches from a remote location with safe low voltage. WIith the advent of radio-controlled toys and devices, and remote TV and garage door controls, there is no reason why these wireless principles cannot also be employed in the scale model field.

RAILROADS

Though probably 75 percent of the fun of a model railroad layout lies in the building of it by the owner, you may be called upon to construct a layout at some time during your career. This is an extensive and specialized field with which the professional model builder does not normally have the time or inclination to keep pace, so the best tip I can give is to rely on the hobby shops

for the answers. They will have the knowledge and experience as well as the necessary equipment to help you.

SOLAR ACTIVATION

With progress in harnessing solar energy, models can be expected to show light producing electricity through solar cells mounted on the roofs, etc., and running motors which run animation. Such power could be stored in batteries to light the buildings after dark. Since light alone will fire solar cells, an overhead artificial light source could be used at the model display location. I have seen and used solar cells of various sizes and shapes which might well fit into model arrays as the representative ones shown in Ch. 49, photo 41.

31

Interiors

For the purposes of this book, any time you are called upon to finish entirely or in part the space inside of the perimeter walls of any scale model, you will be performing "interior" work, calling for additional compensation in your contract. Subject of course to the degree of detail required, interior work can easily double the price of an otherwise exterior display model. Interiors open to view such as lower level courts seen through openings in the level above can usually be considered as additional exterior work since they are largely open to the elements, but those revealed by removing walls or roofs (breakaway models, Ch. 2) can pose serious problems in estimating prices. Examine the drawings carefully. Look for raised or lowered ceilings, soffits, and built-in cabinets as well as considering the required furnishings.

AREA STUDIES

Probably the most prevalent purely interior model type is the one used for analysis of space use, equipment, utility, or furniture placement, product

or traffic flow, security problems, etc. The subjects can be as varied as there are kinds of structures. A hospital board may want to study the arrangement of a surgery floor. A manufacturer may want to decide upon the best location of a conveyor belt system in their packaging and delivery department, or Mrs. Jones may want to be able to push furniture around in her proposed living room.

Construction Considerations: These include the presence or not of exterior treatment of perimeter walls, fenestration, split floor levels, fixed or movable partitions, utility ducts and outlets, entrances and exits, security doors, equipment and furnishings, and a scale to strike a balance between ease of handling of the entire model and handling and readability of elements. Generally speaking such studies should be in at least 1/4″ scale to facilitate conference table study.

A basic approach consists of a floor plan glued to a base of Masonite or acrylic plastic with perimeter walls installed without regard for scale thickness or exterior surface treatment. The floor materials suggested provide a smooth surface without filling and sanding. Another solution is to attach the floor plan to sheet vinyl over a *flat* piece of plywood. If the floor plan may be replaced by a changed edition, glue it down with one of the temporary adhesives (Ch. 34). Otherwise use contact glue to avoid as much stain-causing paper absorption as possible. After mounting, spray the drawing with a clear protective coating (Ch. 32). Where windows are to appear, make the perimeter walls out of clear acrylic and line them with 0.020" vinyl with the window configurations cut out. For variable installations, apply two stacked narrow strips of vinyl at each fenestrated wall intersection to provide slots to accept differently perforated liners. For variable door locations, cut the door sizes out of vinyl, paint them a contrasting color and attach them to the walls with tabs of double-faced tape.

Partitions and interior walls should be made to scale thickness and mounted in their indicated locations on the floor plan. If they are to be movable, you will have to provide unauthentic small blocks at their bases to make them stand up.

Power equipment and furniture need usually be no more than blocks of acrylic plastic or wood, identifiably configured, with correct outside dimensions.

Accuracy of Dimension: This is a must no matter what the authenticity of configuration or detail since the size of the space being analyzed is critical. In models of this type you cannot get away with a piece of equipment that is technically out of scale but may appear in scale in a purely display situation. The architect must be able to obtain exact readings with a measuring instrument or the model is not fit for its purpose.

Embellishments: Embellishments include different floor construction, accurately cast equipment and furniture, and surface treatment. One way to provide movable walls, partitions, and equipment that will stay where put is to drill small holes in their bottom edges or bases for the insertion of headless common pins or nails, or wooden dowel pegs with their visible ends sanded to points. Make the floor out of 1/2" to 1" thick 4-lb urethane foam to provide maximum firmness and durability. The smaller the mounting pegs, the longer the urethane will stand repetitive insertion. The objects are then pressed into desired location through the floor plan. Another method is to surface the floor with tin plate covered by the floor plan and then glue small magnets into sockets cut into the movable objects. In my Jay's Nest (Ch. 35) I

keep 1/4" magnetized squares about 1/16" thick. For larger scale installations, consider the hardware store magnetic aids such as the buttons used to hold notes on the family bulletin board. See Ch. 50 for a source of 1/4" scale cast metal shop equipment and furniture, and also for scale piping, valves, ladders, tanks, etc., for your industrial interiors. Surface treatments (that is, textures and colors) are usually of small import in this type of interior model used only as an analysis tool, but embellishments could include the planned colored concrete or tile floor (omitting the floor plan), paneling in the operations manager's office, etc.

Transparent Models: These can be useful for analyzing floor-to-floor relationships. The extent of the transparency will depend upon the subject (for example, department stores, hospitals, or furniture marts), and the arrangement problems to be solved. One wall and all floors (without roof) may be made out of clear acrylic, or the whole exterior may be transparent with opaque interior facilities which can be arranged with access provided by the breakaway system discussed later in this section.

DISPLAY INTERIORS

Any area study type model can of course be made into a display medium either through dressing up the original analysis aid or by building it only for display purposes (Ch. 49, photo 4). A large industrial complex, for example, could include roofless (or transparent roofed) facilities complete with all power equipment and furnishings for employee orientation and training purposes or for lobby and public display. Human figures would help the viewer tune in on the scale. An example of a lighted interior for display purposes is shown in Ch. 49, photo 55. I once made a furnished corporate conference room interior for a joint effort by an architect and an industrial designer (Ch. 49, photo 20) to demonstrate a variable space division system. A translucent ceiling was lit with a battery of fluorescent tubes arranged to give specified light meter readings.

Breakaway Models: Breakaway models are relatively common media for the professional model builder, the extent of detail depending upon available time and budget. The effort is usually confined to space division with a representative minimum of simple furnishings to help explain the concept. The prevalent breakaway system involves a removable roof which is the easiest way to uncover a large area. Examples are shown in Ch. 49, photos 56 and 8, the first showing a round schoolhouse with movable partitions to isolate classes or projects as required, and the second showing the interior arrangement of a small private residence. Note that the schoolhouse can be both a study model and a display model to publicize a designer's concept. The usual private residence model is simply an in-family display exterior with study interior to help the owner understand what the architect has shown in the drawings and facilitate a meeting of minds on any required changes before pouring concrete. The use of such a model can save a great deal of time and money spent on later tearing out foundations and moving walls. Such a model can also help the owner plan the purchase of furnishings.

The foregoing examples of the uses of breakaway models are presented to stress the importance of a few basic construction tips necessary to authenticity and durability. When you attach a roof to an exterior display model of a one-story residence, for example, you are normally not concerned with wall thicknesses or attic authenticity because no one will ever see them. Unless a large glass area permits viewing a raised or beamed ceiling in a lighted model, you simply install enough unauthentic gussets to hold roof shape and attach the assembly to a flat ceiling plane supported perhaps by blocks of wood placed at effective support locations without regard for unnecessary interior walls.

In a breakaway roof model all walls and partitions should be of scale thickness and the top edges finished usually at a consistent scale plate height. Exceptions to a consistent height arise where there is a through-the-attic atrium topped by a skylight, or a raised living room ceiling, for example, where the higher walls help identify the space when the roof is removed. You aren't concerned with authentic wall framing, but make the tops solid and flat with sharp edges. Windows should be installed (Ch. 21) using rigid transparent material as thin as possible with the realization that all sills will be shallower than scale because of the overthick "glass". Cut out the doorways, frame them according to specifications, and glue in separately made doors either in a closed or open position. A movable door can be accomplished with pins inserted top and bottom at the

hinged side. Illustration board wall surfacing will allow you to peel off the top lamination for such things as furnace and air conditioning outlets covered with bits of scrap acid-etched material for grilles.

An important consideration of the roof other than authenticity is durability. It should be able to stand countless removals and replacements and maintain rigidity as a separate unit without warping or easily chewed up corners and edges from handling. Provide locating pegs with location-finding rounded ends so that the roof can be replaced easily and only in its correct position. Depending upon roof configuration, establish solid locations opposite wall tops, and before final assembly hold a structural roof member against the top of a chosen wall and drill matching holes into one of which you can glue a piece of wood dowel. Enlarge the hole in the receiving member just enough to permit a snug slip fit of the dowel peg. Do this in at least three widely separated locations around the house perimeter. If hole drilling is impractical, provide square wooden tongues in the ceiling structure to fit at wall intersections. Sometimes structural house members such as external chimneys will aid in roof positioning.

The ceilings should be finished according to specifications even though they can't be read with the roof in place. Showing the beams in a raised living room ceiling, for example, will help the owner's imagination flow into the enclosed room. Make the atrium skylight out of clear acrylic to reveal its interior when the roof is in place.

A two-story breakaway residence model poses the problem of having to see two levels. Unless the owner wants to push the furniture around on the first floor, suggest a clear acrylic second floor to provide a view of the lower level without a second removable unit.

The breakaway principle is of course not confined to roof removal. Your imagination has probably already carried you to removable walls or portions thereof to reveal manufacturing facilities or interdepartmental relationships. Photos 17, 18, 19 of Ch. 49 show a multilevel civic mall where each level above the underground parking area was removable for demonstration. The proposed buildings were added in clear acrylic to show mass relationships without entirely obstructing the view.

Whatever the requirement, always make removable parts rigid enough to stand on their own feet, so to speak, so that they can be securely keyed into place repetitiously without damage. This follows the good reputation building principle of always constructing to outlast the expected use of the model.

MINIATURES

There are no fixed lines of separation between interiors normally encountered by the professional model builder and the miniatures as defined in Ch. 2, but an arbitrary distinction is made to separate the commercial effort from that of the hobbyist. It is not a matter of expertise but rather of economics. You have all probably seen on display miniatures of period rooms containing authentically configured furniture in the style of Duncan Pfyfe, Queen Anne, Sheraton, etc., and carpets, tapestries, draperies, and upholstery in authentic designs. Considering the time required to make one petit point chair cover, for example, you can realize how prohibitive the price one room alone would be for a single project with a moderate budget. A large interior decorating firm might come to you for a miniature room as part of a permanent adjustable sales display to attract customers to their expertise in coordinating colors and furnishings, but otherwise you can expect to leave this type of work to the hobbyist who can work without considering time or compensation.

You may often be required to supply furnishings in acceptably representative form and in time can become adept at making standard chairs, dressers, tables, beds, sofas, lamps, bathroom and kitchen fixtures and appliances as well as built in cabinets, etc. I have used 1/2″ scale plastic doll house furniture from toy stores to save time by not having to make available ready made items. Don't confuse these with the period miniatures mentioned earlier. These can also be found at toy stores and will probably be confined to 1″ scale. Period furniture is considerably more expensive than what I call symbolic miniatures; so at the time of contract negotiations be sure of your client's requirements. If space analysis is the primary goal, the simplest of block configurations in overall scale may be all that is required. Don't unnecessarily gild the lily to the detriment of the bottom line of your profit and loss statement!

Some tips on making symbolic miniatures are submitted to help you realize how time consuming even these can be (Ch. 49, photo 8). Assuming 1/2″ scale where an inch is about 0.042″, make chairs

by stacking about six seats made out of 1/16″ strip wood, and drilling a hole through the stack at each corner to accept 1/8″ wood dowel legs. Make a chair back by gluing a piece of strip wood to an edge of the seat, and arms out of soft wire. For an upholstered chair or sofa, shape the seat to represent the puffed up effect and cover with a fine material such as velvet. Seats should be 18″ above the floor and sized and shaped to make different types. Beds can be made from blocks of white pine with rounded top edges and covered with cloth or paper as though the bed cover hung to the floor. Before gluing on the bed cover, glue small pieces of shaped wood to the head end to form pillows. To save time, ignore head and foot boards as they are not needed for identification. Tables can be made as you did the chair seats with dowel legs. Chests can be made from wood blocks with lightweight illustration board lids glued on. Add a bead at each corner for legs. Wall cabinets and bookcases can be assembled against the wall by gluing on strips of lightweight illustration board for frame and shelves. Glass fronts can be scored pieces of 1/32″ acrylic. Make books by painting the edges of materials of different thicknesses, cutting out various book sizes and laminating into groups for random placement on the shelves. You don't have to fill each shelf. Drill holes in various size wood dowel "lamp shades" and insert small dowels inserted into bases of illustration board or wood for table lamps. Single thickness lady's compact mirrors will make wall mirrors. Make toilets out of two pieces of shaped white pine with 0.030″ sheet vinyl seat covers and spray with enamel. Make a refrigerator in the same manner, scoring the door division. For concave shapes such as bath tubs, wash basins, and sinks, make molds and cast in plaster (Ch. 24). Save the molds for future production. Spray enamel will provide the porcelain finish. Use 1/32″ clear acrylic for shower stalls with an overspray of clear enamel to frost it. A fire screen can be brass filter cloth sprayed black, and fire dogs can be bent wire. A stainless steel stove top can be tin plate sprayed with a matte spray. Glue on black discs of 0.010″ vinyl for burners. For rugs, carpeting, and draperies use colored or figured papers. Most cloth materials will not hang or lie authentically. Crease the paper draperies and glue them to 1/16″ wood dowel rods supported by wire brackets inserted into the wall.

The foregoing tips are suggestions for relatively fast means for obtaining basic furnishings. In spite of the simplicity each unit should be of impeccable quality and painted consistent with its use. As you gain experience in various scales your methods will automatically settle into standard procedures for which you will have time records to support quotations. At the smaller scales consider making chairs, for example, out of bond paper T's by folding down the arms of the T for legs and the leg of the T up for backs. The result may not have the appearance of "impeccable quality", but may very well suffice for demonstration and space analysis.

STRUCTURAL MODELS

For demonstrating and analyzing structural systems there are no better media than scale models to reduce bridges, office buildings, parking structures, private residences, etc., to easily read conference table size. "Structural" here applies to cases where it is necessary to uncover a normally covered structural skeleton, thus placing the models in an "interior" category.

A good example of such a model is one I once made for a television series during which progress of construction of a private residence was shown, starting with the foundation. The scale was 3/4" which made elements easily identifiable and something larger than tweezer size to assemble (Ch. 49, photos 26 and 28). The framing and finish, both interior and exterior, were progressively shown; so it was necessary to make and install each foundation support, each stud, each plate, each window frame, etc. The foundation and interior support pilings were poured in plaster, and floor joints, studs, and so on were cut to size out of white pine or bass wood. In such projects glue can be the joiner, but nail heads can be indicated with a pencil point for appearance. The extent of this job normally would place it in the realm of the hobbyist because of prohibitive cost, but you may very well be asked to supply at least a framing section sometime during your career for a contractor's display or for a client with a unique structural system to demonstrate. Ch. 49, photo 3 shows a structural demonstration of the support for a solar cell array on the roof of a shopping center.

32

Chromatics

The title "Chromatics" is probably technically too scientific a word for this chapter since you won't be concerned with reflected wave lengths, but it seems a handy cover for the whole subject of color and the media used in scale model building.

In Ch. 28, we stated that the model builder's meeting the challenge of treatment was the raison d'etre that leads to the statement that the most important final aids in attaining visual authenticity are the application of color (discussed here) and the development of texture (Ch. 33). Color is obtained through the media of paint, dyes, inks, pencils, and pastel sticks. These media are used not only for color but often to create texture or the illusion of texture.

I believe every person who is naturally inclined toward this work has the "modicum of artistic ability" mentioned as a prerequisite in Ch. 1. Artistic talent and experience will obviously help, but you don't have to be an accomplished artist to be a success at model building. Experience is a great teacher, and through a willingness to absorb a bit of trial and error time you will likely find a developing hidden talent to lead you to immediate solutions of color and texture problems.

Before getting into materials and methods, it is helpful to review a few accepted facts and definitions to enable you intelligently to follow your clients' specifications. Since you will be directly handling pigments and not light, Newton's seven colors of the spectrum can be reduced to the three primary colors *red*, *yellow*, and *blue*. Yellow *light*, for example, can be combined with blue *light* to form white *light*, but yellow and blue *pigment* will produce green. Red and green *light* will produce yellow light, but red and green *pigment* produces brown. Mention should be made here of the effect that different light sources may have on a color. Assuming that most models will be displayed under fluorescent light (cool white in most cases), you can feel at ease in applying colors in a shop lit by the same source, but be alert to the fact that your matching a client's sample in sunlight may not be as good a match on the model.

Fortunately we do not have to obtain colors in every case by mixing since there are countless prepared mixes available at hardware and paint stores, either already mixed or quickly mixed on order using formula tables. Keep a pigment mixing color chart handy for emergency guidance and a quart can each of the pure (spectral) primary colors.

Hue (color tone) is the quality by which a yellow green, for example, differs from a gray green. *Value* expresses the difference between a light and dark color. *Purity* (intensity) expresses the difference between a spectral or pure color and that color shaded by another as a grayish red. A *saturated* color is one devoid as possible of black and white. *Tints* are obtained by mixing white with a saturated color; *shades* by mixing with black. Black is the nearest we can come to establishing a "color" that absorbs all wave lengths without reflection. It is often spoken of as the absence of color. White is the combination of all the spectral colors as in sunlight.

PAINTS

There are successful model builders who use oil paints, but in my experience there are no advantages to be gained by their use. Their drying, thinning, and clean-up requirements place unnecessary time consuming burdens on the already busy operator. To meet fire-prevention standards, both bureaucratic and practical, accumulated cans of oils have to be stored in metal cabinets, and spraying requires a ventilated booth. A running supply of thinner is also necessary, adding to the storage problems. There is always the hazard of accidental splatter on a model surface. A damp rag to wipe off water-base paints is a much less damaging remover than lacquer thinner which can easily remove the entire finish.

Water-Based Paints: These paints constitute one of the most successful and versatile materials available to the model builder. In usefulness they fall in the class of vinyl, acrylic, and urethane foam, not to speak of the basic wood and illustration board.

Latex paint has been my mainstay for years. It adheres well to all surfaces, and when dry can be washed with a damp rag and a mild soap and is water resistant. It covers well by spray or brush without brush marks. Thinning is accomplished with water as is cleaning of brushes, spray equipment, and hands. It automatically provides the universally desired matte finish. A light spray of pressure-can clear enamel will add the seldom required sheen. It can be patched with the use of a dry brush (see later in this chapter). If it is difficult to cover a spot of a different color (reds,

for example, tend to bleed through) lightly wash the spot with a rag dampened with lacquer thinner first to kill the blatancy or lump and then paint, feathering the edges to camouflage the blending of finish. An accidental chip off a nonabsorbent surface such as acrylic can be repaired by feathering the edges of the gap with wet or dry sand paper and filling with paint. Since most models spend their lives in surroundings protected from the weather you can use either the interior or exterior formulas with good results. I use mostly interior paint because of the greater range of basic colors.

Substitutes in water-based paints include the so-called "poly-vinyl" and "acrylic latex" (exterior) both of which are satisfactory. There is no point here in analyzing formulas since different manufacturers will have their own. I use a poly-vinyl, for example, because I found it ready mixed in an authentic brick or terra cotta color. A little experimentation with water-based paints in your area will put you on the right track. See Ch. 50 for suggested successful trade names. One type is an epoxy paint which I haven't liked for model work because of its resin-like tackiness and the need for soap as well as water in cleaning brushes. Also it does not flow on as well as the others.

Stored in-shop mixes of commonly used colors can be time savers. Most important of these are structural concrete and the macadam or asphaltic concrete (AC) used on streets. Each can be reproduced with black, white, and a chocolate brown, all of which can be bought off the ready mixed shelf. I established mine by laying sample tabs out in the sunlight on sidewalk and parking lot and adjusting to establish a compromise between old and new surfaces. Newly laid AC will appear black, which to me appears too stark, providing too much of a contrast on a display model. A lighter, dirtier gray looks better. This is one place where authenticity has to be tempered with esthetics. Unless your mission is a time and tread worn scenario, cracked sidewalks and chewed up, pot-holed streets are a bit disconcerting to the viewer even though we know they exist. A standard countryside green is another mix to keep on your shelf.

Stored color mixes prepared for specific models already delivered constitute a waste of effort and space unless you want to label the jars with model number and formula. If you anticipate later changes or repairs from a rough life, saving leftover paint makes sense, particularly where considerable time went into attaining an oddball hue, but as a general practice, toss out the excess if you do not want to rent a paint warehouse even though doing so may seem wasteful at the time. You will soon get a fair idea as to quantity needed during a model's construction, and economy will lie in the use of small containers such as baby food jars. The formula on the label of a stored mix can warn you against the use of the contents later as a new mix medium. A particular color in what appears to be a good starting base may forestall your ever getting the new color you are trying to match.

The original quart cans (the smallest supply generally available) will hold paint in usable condition indefinitely as long as they are properly sealed. Keep the lid groove clean, and replace the lid using a wooden mallet to seat it tightly. Screw tops sealed with dried paint can be released from their jars by placing them top down in hot water for a few minutes.

Other Paints: Other paints that you will find useful include the spray can enamels and stains (my concession to the "oils"). See Ch. 50 for proven makes. A set of water-based concentrates is handy for painting human figures, and tubes of ochres and siennas are good for small hue changes during a mixing process.

Spray enamels come in pressurized cans and are indispensable, within limits, for their ease of application. Their limits lie in the facts that the available colors usually will not satisfy specifications on model structures and their finish is glossy. There is a matte white and a dull aluminum. I use a matte black extensively on model bases. Where you can freelance as far as color is concerned such as painting cars to fill a parking lot, an overspray of matte spray (also in pressure cans) will kill the sheen. Where you want to patch a model component sprayed before assembly such as a black facade fin, apply the enamel with a brush after spraying the bristles. Clean the brush with lacquer thinner. The metal primers are matte and can be used as a finish where the color is acceptable. There is a line of metallic finishes including brass, bronze, and copper which come in handy for copper roofing, railings, the spheres on flag pole tops, etc. Follow the instructions on the can to get full use of the contents. If you don't, you will likely run up against a clogged spray nozzle the next time. See Ch. 50 for trade names.

Oil stains are handy for finishing real wood residential siding and shingles, for example, providing authentic components as well as appear-ance. You can use the same stain used on the life-size project. Keep it stirred as you use stain since pigment separation is usually rapid as it sits in the can. Apply it with a rag or brush, the latter usually being the better in model work in order to get the stain into cavities. The brush should have stiff bristles.

DYES

Powdered commercial dyes are needed for landscaping materials. Tips on their use are discussed in Ch. 25. Check with your plastics supplier for acrylic dyes for such items as stained glass windows (Ch. 33), and the same source for resin dyes for water (Ch. 12).

PENCILS AND PASTEL STICKS

Colored pencils (both dry and water-activated) and the colored carbon sticks have a limited use, but a set of each is handy when the need arises. I have lined parking lots with a white pencil though this is not as satisfactory as the paint and drafting pen method described in Ch. 26. The pencil will not give as definite a line as the paint, and you have to keep sharpening it to maintain an even width of line. The pencils are good for patching small spots and for making flags and pennants, signs, and two-dimensional decoration. I have used the pastels to render a mural on a wall and to shade rock formations. If the treated surface is likely to be touched be sure to spray with fixative. The artists among you will probably think of applications beyond my limited use. I have found the child's wax crayons to be unsatisfactory because of the sheen and lack of control of line. The inks and the cartridge pens are a waste of time. The inks give too faint and indefinite results, and the pens, as far as I am concerned, demand more attention than the result is worth. Don't confuse the standard inks with the fixed reservoir, colored ink Magic Markers used by architects and designers in rendering. Their felt tips will provide wood graining and stained glass (Ch. 33).

EQUIPMENT

The best tip I can give here is always to purchase the best equipment. The additional price you pay over that of lesser quality will more than compensate you in usefulness and longevity.

Brushes: Brushes will last for years if they have top grade bristles and are religiously kept clean. One of the big advantages from using water-based paints is the ease with which you can wash brushes under the tap in a few seconds. A set should include the finest point and flat, square ended sizes from 1/8″ up through 1″ to 1-1/4″ in width, all of medium stiffness. Stiff, square ended brushes in the 1/8″ to 3/4″ width range are excellent for stipling discussed later in this section. In one concession to low price, I have found a plastic container of water color brushes handy. The sectioned tube will contain a supply of different sizes for spur of the moment small treatments. When one of these has given up you can toss it in the round file without qualms. Those of you experienced in brushing may have different ideas about shape and stiffness. Some will prefer softer brushes for general painting because they can flow on the paint in larger quantities. I feel I have better control with medium stiffness. In any case, your local artist's supply house can guide you. Good brushes are expensive; don't try to cover all imagined uses in your first purchase. Let your experience demand later additions. In the absence of spray enamel, you may find a house painter's trim brush good for painting model bases, for example.

Spray Equipment: Paint spray equipment is a must for fast, even-coated treatment of numerous model components before assembly, and especially contour models where an overall base coat is required before improvements are added. Brush painting of urethane foam is a tedious process because of the grainy surface. Visible dried brush strokes are not a serious problem with water base paints, but spraying forestalls any doubt. I have found that the standard commercial spray guns (both air and electric) have too large a spray for model work and that the artist's spray equipment (air brushes) does not have sufficient capacity. After much trial and error I have settled on two types of sprayers. One type available at hardware stores is a Crown Spra-tool consisting of a replaceable pressurized can, an 8 oz. paint jar with supply tube, and a molded plastic double cap with button activated spray nozzle. The jar screws into one side of the cap holding the supply tube, and the pressure can snaps into the other. This system provides adequate spray for contour model painting. After each use remove the paint jar and insert the tube into water for spray cleaning the

nozzle. Be sure the air hole through the paint jar half of the cap is open at all times. When you suddenly do not get any action the reason is probably a clogged air hole. The other type of sprayer is an Intermatic compressor-spray nozzle assembly (Ch. 50), a sort of senior air brush. The system comprises a small piston compressor with electric motor and a nozzle cap accepting 1 and 2 oz. paint jars. The nozzle cap is attached to a 6 ft. hose. The motor must be plugged in for spraying since there is no stored air supply. The nozzle gives a fine, confined spray allowing you to spray in tight places (with simple masking) without affecting the surrounding areas. With a little ingenuity you can attach the nozzle component to the cap of a larger jar to obtain more than the 2 oz. maximum provided by the maker. I have found a shop type compressor superfluous for most work (but see Ch. 36 under "Air Compressor") since normal model building assignments do not require large amounts of stored compressed air.

Miscellaneous: Pick a spot on a paint table for location of a heat lamp for quick drying of samples. I have a pile of old business cards for sample tabs. This is important because you cannot accurately compare a wet paint with a dry one. Leave a beer can opener on your paint table for opening paint cans without having to run to your tool cabinet for a screwdriver every time. To help keep paint can lid grooves from filling with paint remove small amounts of paint with the small plastic picnic spoons or wrap wire around a tubular container cap and twist it into a handle to make a ladle. These avoid pouring from the can. Keep a couple of rolls of masking tape on hand for masking next discussed. I find 1/2″ and 3/4″ widths right for general use.

METHODS

Masking: Masking calls for two warnings. The first is to ensure a snug adhesion with a finger nail along the paint approach edge to guard against wicking, and the second is to take care in removal so that you do not pull up the surface or remove the covered paint. Pull one end back slowly in a peeling motion more longitudinal than vertical. If you have an area to mask larger than tape width when you are spraying, attach the tape to newspaper before putting the mask in place. For an alternate definitive break at color changes on soft materials such as illustration board, score the division first with a mat knife and carefully paint up to this score line. Apply the paint so that there is no excess to bridge the score as you approach with the brush. Carefully brush back excess paint from the score so that you don't create a ridge when dry. This method can be used even with the harder materials such as acrylic. Make the score pronounced with a knife and wipe off the plastic dust created thereby before applying paint or you will get a fuzzy edge.

Brush Application: Brush application can generally be made with latex paints of the consistency found in a new can. Brush it on with even, continuous strokes, and let it dry before patching thin spots. If haste makes ridges, let them dry, then sand with wet-or-dry sandpaper, wipe off and repaint . Seldom will this happen with latex. If you are caught with an assembled right angle surface joint as at wall and floor (requiring different colors), carefully paint up to the joint with a small brush before painting the entire surfaces. Always be alert for accidental drips. They will dry as lumps.

Thinning: I have found that thinning with 50 percent water will provide a good spray gun consistency. Strain the mix through a fine screen to remove any clogging lumps. For drafting pen use, thin the paint down until it just flows evenly without spreading. Old paint from your storage shelf where it did not have a perfectly sealed lid can usually be rejuvenated with water and vigorous stirring. Be sure to strain the result.

Dry-Brushing: Dry brushing is accomplished with a stiff, square tipped brush and a minimum of paint. To cover a spot on a completed street for example, put a small amount of paint in the palm of your hand and keep applying it a little at a time until the spot is covered with intermittent short strokes, feathering it into the surroundings. If the original paint is dirty and can't be cleaned with mild soap and water, you will have to paint the entire street over, but the dry brush method is usually a great time saver.

Stippling: Stippling is the vertical, jackhammer motion with a stiff brush, usually dry brush as just discussed. It is a method used to obtain texture (Ch. 33). Use stippling in feathering out a patch, to camouflage definite brush marks.

Splattering: Splattering is done with an even bristled tooth brush. Dip the bristles lightly in paint and draw a small spatula edge toward you over the bristles as you move the brush over the area to be splattered. This spreads varying size droplets onto a base surface to create granite for example (Ch. 33). Experience will tell you how much paint to apply to the brush and how hard to apply the spatula. Keep moving the brush over and above the surface being treated so as to obtain an even spread of droplets. Oversize droplets can be painted out with a fine brush later.

Multiple Component Spraying: When you have a lot of building facade fins, for example, to paint the same color, attach them with tape on a slab of scrap plywood, so that they do not touch. Lean the base against a chair back. When spraying, use even, consistent strokes starting at the top. Use a light coat to prevent runs, let it dry and apply a second coat for complete coverage. If you have a run, smear it with a finger, let it dry and repaint. When painting a group of block houses on a horizontal board, too much paint will adhere the houses to the board, creating skirts of paint that will have to be sanded off their bottom edges.

Spray Patching: Spray patching on an assembled model can be a problem. Where the surrounding area is open enough to allow access, I have used an open tipped cone of paper as a shield. Hold the small end of the cone, with an opening large enough to include the area to be patched, just far enough away from the surface so that some feathering will occur, and be sure the cone will confine all spray at the entry.

Intermittent Painting: Intermittent painting of small parts requires the presence of a jar of water to keep brushes from drying out between applications and a supply of paper napkins, or similar, to remove the water from the bristles each time. Don't leave brushes in water over night. Soft water color brushes will take on a semipermanent bow in the bristles requiring time for straightening the next morning.

Silk Screening: Silk screening involves rolling paint through a silk screen stretched on a frame and has its own techniques out of the scope of this book. It is mentioned here to remind the reader of its availability. In my opinion it has little application in the architectural model field. Only once in over 25 years have I had a screen cut. Among the drawbacks is the fact that you are confined to one color per screen. For a repetitive two-dimensional assignment, a screen might be just the thing, but for a single stained glass window, for example, hand applied dyes are a more economical solution.

33

Texture

This Chapter contains tips on surface treatment to help you toward the goal of attaining authentic texture.

The word "texture" comes from the Latin word to weave and originally described woven material (hence "textiles"), but modern usage includes application to the disposition of constituent particles on or in the surface of any material. Hence, a piece of polished marble might be said to have a smooth, pitted texture. A slab of salted concrete would have a rough, pitted texture, and a concrete aggregate a pebbly texture, and so on. Since you will be dealing with the representation of structural materials in building and architecture, most of the surfaces will have a stable, hard character as contrasted to that of a soft-textured pile carpet, for example.

Texture is here confined to tangible and visual disturbance, or their absence, on and in surfaces of the actual material of the subject being modelled. This is to avoid confusion with constructed surfacing as in the case of an architectural screen covering the facade of a building (Ch. 49, photo 24). A 1/50″ scale model of such a building might appear and feel to have texture because of the minuteness of the added screen, but it is still con-

sidered constructed as on the subject. The material of a concrete block wall with a perforated or cavity design would have a texture, but the overall surface configuration would be considered constructed. Again, for our purposes, the material used for roofing shakes provides the texture; the installation of the shakes or shingles provides structural configuration. As long as you authentically reproduce that which the drawings and specifications prescribe, you might ask "Who cares?", but the discipline of establishing criteria of concept will aid you in communication with your clients. Mental as well as physical organization are conducive to expeditious fulfillment of your assignments. Always initially consider texture as a characteristic of the subject material rather than the model material which is representing it. A tangibly rough texture may be reduced to smoothness at the model scale, but complete knowledge of the subject material will aid you in execution.

Smooth textures such as a plastered wall pose no particular problems since a painted surface will suffice. Even a rough textured plaster wall can be smooth in small scale reproduction since the particles of sand are reduced to invisibility for all practical purposes. There are smooth textured materials, however, that pose a different problem—one of inherent design. Polished or finely sanded wood reveals a generally unidirectional grain, its prominence depending upon the tree from which it came. Polished marble may have veining or mottling depending upon where and of what nature formed it. Polished granite is speckled, etc. In addition to inherent or natural designs there are manufactured smooth surfaced compositions that can have a design or a characteristic visual "feel". These include floor and wall tile, brick, concrete, the various plastics formulations, and anodized aluminum.

The tangibly rough surfaces that may require three-dimensional treatment on a model depending upon scale include concrete aggregates, natural rock formations, gravel walks, stone walls, salted concrete, rough hewn timbers, rough trowelled plaster, rock roofs, gravel roads, railroad beds, and rough formed or adobe blocks.

Tangibly soft textures include soil, landscaping materials, and the fabrics encountered in interior work.

TEXTURING

There are three general methods of obtaining texture. The first is to use the subject material, but this is relatively rare because of the difficulty of working it, weight, and/or the impossibility of finding surface designs in scale even where random sizes are available. The second is to use a substitute material which has a surface closely approximating the real thing. The third method is to line or coat a core or base material of any structurally suitable nature with the material chosen to portray the texture desired. Tips will be given with respect to some of the common textures encountered. These should serve as guides to solutions of other challenges all of which can't be included in one book.

Wood: Wood is probably the most generally usable subject material with its great variety of graining. Sheet bass wood with its almost imperceptible grain makes excellent residential siding and flooring (Ch. 18). The hardwood veneers are excellent for panelling and miniature table tops. You can vary the stains on the lighter veneers to represent various woods. Real wood shingles and shakes are available at 1/4″ scale (Ch. 50). In a structural model you can use cut-to-scale white pine or bass wood for studs, purlins, rafters, and beams without having

graininess to spoil authenticity. Rough hewn lumber can result from knife-chipping white pine or bass wood. Watch the grain so you don't splinter the beam you are fashioning. Redwood can be used for authentic garden structures and railroad tie steps. To weather redwood, rub a little dark brown and black pastel stick into it. Simulated wood surfacing can be accomplished by streak brushing the grain direction with a couple of values of latex paint in the color range of the particular wood you are simulating. Paint the vinyl, acrylic, hot-pressed illustration board, or whatever base material you are using the general color of the wood and then lightly dry-brush on a slightly darker shade to reveal grain. Another method is to dry-brush on alternately two shades of brown, (or another color) before either drys. This will give a blended realistic effect. After painting black vinyl in this manner, score it in the direction of the grain for grape stake fencing. I have had good luck with the draftsman's felt Magic Markers instead of paint. These will give you single strokes of varying intensity on vinyl. With little practice you can obtain wood surfacing about as realistic appearing as the wood itself.

Stone: Stone has a limited use, mostly in landscaping (Ch. 25). It is well to reiterate the warning against grossness. Bury big boulders of rounded shape so that they don't look like eggs sitting on a plate, and avoid large bands of different composition which might be obtrusive eye-catchers. Unless otherwise specified, try to find rocks which at least closely resemble those indigenous to the project locale. If you have free rein, don't, for example, pile granite pebbles in an Hawaiian lava scene. If you have trouble joining rocks in a rock outcropping, consider filling gaps with planting. See Ch. 13 for real rock walks, patios, entryways, etc. Build up a small supply of various kinds of rocks that can be hammered to size if not already in scale. Start with the building material yards and pick up fistfulls on your travels. I remember taking a trip to a beach project to get some indigenous sand and rock for a model. Sand and gravel can be obtained in about any grade desired to fit your scale for sand and gravel roofs (Ch. 20), stream beds and beaches (Ch. 12), and gravel walks and roads (Ch. 13). Except for the aforementioned applications the attempted use of real stone in model building is hardly worth the effort when plaster is faster. A real rock wall laid in a miniature would have its own appeal, but for professional purposes substitute materials can produce the same thing with visual authenticity. With a piece of the real thing before you, paint vinyl the background colors of marble, shading changes with alternate applications of the different colors while the paint is wet. Make deep scratches with a sharp scribe and rub in black paint after the base has dried. Rub so the scratches will pick up the paint and immediately wipe off the excess. Make gray granite liner stock for granite columns by spraying vinyl the base color and then splattering black paint (Ch. 32) to get the varying speckled effect (Ch. 49, photo 11). Follow similar procedures with the other stones. Flagstones and some slate can be accomplished with single colors on vinyl or illustration board. Paint plaster rock outcroppings and escarpments. See Ch. 49, photo 31.

Metal: Metal surfaces are best simulated. I have made copper lined roofs with liver of sulfur rubbed on for weathering (Ch. 49, photo 40), but it is hardly worth the effort when you can obtain authentic simulations with paint on vinyl over-rubbed when dry with streaks of green paint for verdigris. The products of acid-etching (Ch. 17) are brass or bronze giving authentic composition as well as appearance, and aluminum is a good metal for spinning (Ch. 24), but generally you will find your ingenuity will produce metal-appearing surfaces without the difficulty of working and the weight of the subject material. Make bronze anodized building facade aluminum by spraying the back of bronze acrylic with a gold enamel (Ch. 32) and then sanding the front surface with the finest steel wool. You will find that a little trial and error effort will produce about any metal surface you want.

Other Simulations: The old standby illustration board can be the background for a multitude of textures. In its cold-pressed form note that the surface has almost imperceptible grooves or cavities which automatically give a concrete or plaster appearance at any of the popular scales. This is because the casual eye is not cognizant of any scale discrepancies in such a tightly configured surface. At 1/32″ scale, for example, the completely undisturbed surface of vinyl is probably better for a plaster wall, but from 1/16″ scale up to 1/2″ scale, the illustration board will serve the same purpose visually. The 1/2″ scale surface is just smoother plaster. Paint and score illustration board or vinyl for concrete, brick, and tile. At 1/2″ scale and larger consider peeling off the top lamination of illustration board along the joints and filling

the grooves with mortar colored paint using a drafting pen. Become familiar with the various boards and papers sold by your art supplier. He may have a designed paper, for example, which is just what you are looking for. The hobby shops will have stone, brick, tile, and other papers at the railroad scales. Unless they are embossed, I don't consider them as good as in-shop surface treatment which gives a more natural and warmer effect. For slick surfaced tile try hot pressed illustration board instead of the cold pressed. The former has a completely undisturbed texture.

The rough textures that must appear as such on the model because of scale will require a bit more attention than the smooth ones accomplished with paint and scoring. At 1/2″ and larger casting plaster can solve numerous problems of texture. Coat illustration board with it and trowel it while it is wet for rough plaster and concrete. Be sure when applying plaster to a slick surface to provide some sort of binder to keep the plaster from chipping off. As mentioned previously punch holes in the surface of the base material or glue on a layer of fine screen. Don't forget the possibilities of casting (Ch. 24). For salted concrete paint illustration board your standard concrete color (Ch. 32) and tap-punch random holes in the surface as a woodpecker would. For the concrete aggregates, sprinkle sand or fine pebbles (depending on scale) into wet concrete paint. Practice will soon tell you how thick the paint should be. If you have to sculpt decoration on a merry-go-round or a frieze around a building, use an artist's gesso rather than plaster because it will stay soft longer. I have also used spackle and plastic wood filler. Hard casting plaster can be carved with steel burrs in a small power tool (Ch. 36), but this is usually the long way around. The various grades of sandpaper can be used for some graveled surfaces such as garden walks, roadside traffic way shoulders, railroad beds, and roofs with limitations as noted later in this chapter.

ROOF TEXTURES

Roof treatment is important enough to deserve a summary of tips, including some already mentioned under material headings.

Shingles and Shakes: Shingles and shakes at 1/4″ scale are available in real wood (Ch. 50). They are die stamped in pecan wood veneer to indicate varying shingle widths. The self-adhesive sheet is scored for cutting into strips. These strips are applied overlapped so that unit divisions are staggered. Self adhesion is a good time-saving idea, but in practice I have found that because of the spreading caused by the die the strips will squirm into bows against the permanent tackiness of the adhesive resulting in a scalloped installation. Order the sheets of shingles without the glue and apply your own contact glue (Ch. 34) to the back surface of each sheet before you cut the strips. After scoring or drawing to-weather guide lines, apply contact glue to the entire area of roof being worked on. Place the first strip down with its top edge exactly along its guide line and tap into place with a small rubber hammer or mallet. Before installing the next row above, brush on contact glue along the lapped area of the first row for additional insurance against bowing (Ch. 49, photo 21).

Stain the shingles or shakes sparingly with a dry brush (Ch. 32) so that the stain won't dissolve the glue, particularly the self-adhesive type which is very susceptible.

Pecan wood is very tough and relatively difficult to cut across its grain with straight, sharp edges. The spreading caused by the shingle stamping adds to the problem because of its tendency to curve. I have found that cross grain trimming is best done with small scissors along lines drawn freehand while holding a guiding finger against the edge as you wield a pencil in the same hand. Mat knife cutting is best done in a sequential chopping motion with the point. A scoring motion will tend to tear the wood.

The authenticity of real wood cannot be denied, but you can make acceptable substitutes out of vinyl or paper card stock which when painted will look like the real thing, particularly at the small scales. Stack strips of the chosen material in a vise on your mill which should be armed with a fine jeweler's blade. At varying authentic intervals slice the shingle divisions just beyond the anticipated overlap of rows. Even a 0.010″ (1/2″ at 1/4″ scale) separation between shingles will not be obtrusive to the viewer at the larger scales. Slice only within the vise jaw width and then slip the stack to cut the next series until you have strips long enough to span the area to be shingled. If you are applying vinyl shingles to acrylic or vinyl roof stock, you can mount the strips with acrylic cement (Ch. 34). Don't forget the to-weather guide lines. For 1/8″ scale I have found HO railway gauge shingles supplied in the form of a roll of paper pre-slit at shingle widths. At 1/16″ scale and smaller try

scoring a soft material such as illustration board along weather lines and then pushing a tool firmly along a straightedge to squash in a feeling of overlap. Then suggest individual shingles by making random slices with the point of a mat knife between the lap lines. See also "Rowels" in Ch. 36.

Slate and Flat Tile: These items can be made using the same procedure suggested for simulated wood shingles, the color of paint finish identifying the product.

Hemibarrel and S-shaped Ceramic Tile: These items can be made from corrugated cardboard, tubing prepared as for gutters (Ch. 20), or with a crimper (Ch. 36). At the very small scales, shade painting can produce an authentic effect over scored lap lines. Soda straws can be tack-glued along a groove in wood as for brass tubing gutters (Ch. 20) and slit along their lengths with a razor blade producing two half tubes. Cut roof tile lengths and lay them with standard overlap. See also Corrugators in Chapter 36.

Built-up Roofing: Built-up roofing used on flat roofs is made by sifting sand or gravel, depending upon scale, evenly over sprayed wet paint of a tar color (Ch. 49, photo 6). Sand paper can be used where the area is smaller than the size of one sheet. I have found it difficult to camouflage joints. If the natural color is not acceptable, lightly overspray with latex paint.

Metal Roofs: Metal roofs are best simulated using paint on vinyl except for corrugated aluminum obtainable in the railroad scales at the hobby shops. Green paint smudged over bronze paint will produce authentic looking copper roofing affected by age and weather. Apply the verdigris (green paint) sparingly in occasional streaks.

Organic Roofs: These will be few and far between. For *sod* roofs sprinkle ground cover over panels of urethane foam painted the indigenous color. Bundles of straw (broom bristles) down in size to horse hair, brush bristles, or corn silk will help you through a *thatched roof* assignment.

GLASS TREATMENT

Obscure Glass: This material can be simulated with clear acrylic if translucent white does not provide the answer. Spray the clear material with one of the store window "frosters", fog it with clear Krylon (Ch. 32), letting separate light coats dry between applications, or sand it with a grade of wet-or-dry abrasive paper chosen after experimentation on scraps. Try to avoid direction lines. "Pebbled" glass can be simulated with disciplined pin head applications of acrylic or vinyl glue from a tube (Ch. 34) much in the same manner as you stipple a lake surface but with more evenness. Let a row of drops dry before applying an adjacent one to prevent their running together. At 1/2″ scale and larger, check with your plastics supplier for pebble surfaced acrylic. Differences in the product will allow you some leeway in size of surface disturbance.

Stained Glass: The stained glass found in church windows and Tiffany lamp shades involves the use of acrylic dyes on clear acrylic. The detail practicable will of course depend upon scale. If the subject is a scene to be modelled at 1/8″ scale, for example, obtain an 1/8″ scale drawing and trace it with a scribe to etch 1/32″ acrylic placed over the drawing. Use a scribe with which you can etch sharp even lines without burrs. These etched lines will act as stops for separate panel dye applications made with a fine brush. Start with a dry brush to prevent excess liquid from bridging the etched edges of a panel. When dry, fill the lines with a fine drafting pen using a thinned latex paint of a lead color. Instead of dye, try Magic Markers (Ch. 32).

SOFT TEXTURES

Other than the landscaping materials used in landscaping (Ch. 25) soft materials are not a daily occurrence unless you are working on miniatures and furnished interiors. Natural soil in a garden would be considered soft, but for obvious reasons it must be simulated in hard form. The hobby shops have prepared earth materials to sprinkle on an adhesive, but the best solution for garden settings is simply to paint the beds an earth color when they are to be substantially covered with planting. Expanses of country-side earth can be shown at numerous scales with urethane foam suitably painted. Its naturally granular surface lends itself well to the purpose. It can be chewed up for a tilled field or heavily painted for hard-pan. Use a knife blade to fracture the dried up surface around that old water hole in your animal park. Carve it for a landslide down a cliff.

As noted in Ch. 31, most of the cloth materials are too bulky to fold and drape in scale. Some of the fine silks, velvets, and linens will conform satisfactorily for upholstery, but pleats and creases are best made in thin paper for such things as draperies. Finely configured papers may include the answer to your wallpaper requirements.

34

Adhesives

The easily acquired knowledge of the correct adhesive to use for a particular joint is well worth the effort in time and trouble saving. As a general rule to ensure sure and durable joints, use water-based glues only on absorbent surfaces and chemical-based glues on those that are not. Until you become acquainted with properties and hazards, follow instructions on the containers. They mean what they say.

WATER-BASED GLUE

I use Wilhold's white glue exclusively (Ch. 50) simply because it is easy to obtain and there are no functional reasons to change. Among its many uses, its forte in the model business is the joining of wood and cardboard products. The best dispenser is Wilhold's "Glue Bird" which is a plastic bottle with a tapered spout. With continual use, I find the keeping of a nail or pin in the spout to keep it clear a losing battle. Don't fill the bottle full, and after each applying session, hold the bottle vertically and blow out the opening with a few sharp squeezes. You may run into an improved

top with a sliding tip to delay drying out. When making model bases (Ch. 7) run a glue bead along the inside top edge of the frame and on the cross members and immediately position the plywood to obtain an even lip all around. The brads will obviate clamping. Clean up any glue forced on to the lip as you proceed. This glue is very hard to remove once it has dried. In the apparent absence of any satisfactory way to remove dried white glue on plywood, for example, be alert to spills so that you can immediately remove it with a wet paper towel or rag. You can chip dried beads off vinyl and acrylic and other nonporous surfaces, but often the same action on wood and cardboard will dig up the surface, and the heat generated by trying to sand it off will just smear it into more of a mess. Dried white glue on your hands will peel off with the aid of soap and water. When you are gluing two pieces of wood together without nails or screws, clamp the assembly in your vice for a few minutes before using it. When you have a great number of riser tops supporting an illustration board surface (Ch. 9), consider the use of contact glue (discussed next) because by the time you have finished applying white glue to all the risers you may find your first applications dry — a frustrating predicament. When using white glue on cloth materials for such things as upholstery apply thin coats so that the glue won't soak through and spoil your effort. When you are mounting illustration board on edge such as around the perimeter of a model basement, add to security by running a bead of glue along the intersection of the two materials on the inside. You will find incidental uses for white glue such as a drop on the top of a flag pole to form a globular finial. Within limitations you can even do minor embossing and decorating with it. It is not workable the way gesso or spackle is because it is too liquid and dries too fast, but with a little practice you can tap on a string of beads in a building frieze, for example.

CHEMICAL-BASED GLUES

Contact Glue: In my experience contact glue is by far the best all around adhesive for model building. I use Wilhold's which is made with neoprene giving it a beneficial rubber cement characteristic. It can be used to adhere almost anything to anything. Used as indicated by its name, where each surface is coated and allowed to dry, it will make joints as firm as ever required in this profession. Where some aftergluing adjustment is anticipated, coat just one surface and join the parts before the glue has dried. This is particularly useful in tack-gluing for temporary holding purposes, and will allow fairly easy breaking of a joint later for changes or corrections without pulling up material surfaces. Excess contact glue squeezed out of a joint can be peeled off much in the same manner as rubber cement without leaving a stain, but be aware of the problem of contact glue oozing from a urethane foam joint (Ch. 10)! The right time for removal will depend on the temperature and the materials involved. Leave it alone until it is confined to itself without apparent tackiness and then peel it off or erase it with your fingers. If it is too well stuck to a nonabsorbing surface to respond to this treatment, use a little lacquer thinner or contact glue solvent MEK (methyl ethyl ketone). Use this sparingly on acrylic and vinyl which will craze or dissolve with too heavy an application. Be sure all the solvent is removed immediately. Precautions to take when contact gluing vinyl are stated in Ch. 35.

When you are gluing two surfaces together with dried contact glue on each be sure of placement accuracy because you cannot make adjustments after joining. If you have a 4′ X 4′ slab of urethane,

for example, to glue down to a model base, first place it dry and draw a pencil line around the perimeter to record the desired location. Apply glue to both surfaces and let dry to the point where there is no tackiness to the touch. Hold the urethane squarely so that you approach the base with one edge even with the line you drew and then let the material drop into place. Hit a flat piece of plywood with a hammer as you move it over the surface to assure good contact. See Ch. 10 for further discussion of this procedure.

Contact glue is valuable enough performing its manufactured purpose without trying to increase its repertoire, but it will form bridge support cables, for example, by pulling small beads with a pointed instrument from one anchor point to another. The more fluid the glue is the finer will be the cable. Wait until the glue dries before painting it. This is not the most durable installation, but I have had a 2″ test cable stay intact for 2 years.

When you are faced with a long session of small parts to assemble, scoop some contact glue into a small jar with secure lid. This will help save your gallon can supply from drying exposure to the air. See Ch. 36 for a home-made small dispenser jar top. A small, narrow pickle type jar filled with MEK (Ch. 35) is a good contact glue brush holder. Keep about three brush sizes in use. To prevent careless tipping, hold the jar in a section of drawing tube glued to a square of plywood. When gluing large areas such as a model base, pour some glue out of the supply can and spread it using pieces of scrap illustration board as screeds. Big brushes are expensive and must be thoroughly cleaned after each use — a time consuming process. To bring thickening glue back to usable consistency, pour a little MEK into the jar, screw down the lid, and shake until you hear no slop, meaning that the solvent and glue are mixed. For applying glue into small spaces, a glue gun is useful. Mine is like a small hypodermic reservoir and needle made out of aluminum and obtainable at hobby shops. Until you have time to clean it thoroughly after use, store it in a closed jar of MEK. You can reduce the size of the nozzle hole by installing a couple of pieces of telescoping brass tubing (Ch. 35) soldered together and pressed over the needle.

Plastic Glues: Plastic glues are compounded for the purpose of joining specific plastic materials. Your plastics supplier will probably stock all the commonly used ones. The watery, clear acrylic cement comes in small bottles and is wicked into a dry joint with a brush. It comes in various drying time formulations, the choice being up to your experience. Since it dissolves the acrylic surface, the joint actually becomes a weld. Bond puts out a line of complete cements in tubes. I use a clear vinyl glue for water surface disturbance discussed in Ch. 12. Acrylic cement will also adhere vinyl to itself or to acrylic by the wicking method. Where you have large surfaces to join, such as in the special window problem discussed in Ch. 21, Bond's acrylic glue in a tube is another answer where wicking will not flow over the entire surface involved. Polystyrene must have its own particular glue, if you can't use contact glue, but I don't use the material except in vacuum forming (Ch. 24). If you can't immediately blow off an accidental drop of acrylic cement on acrylic plastic, the resulting craze will have to be polished out (Ch. 24). Rubbing will only increase the damage.

Rubber Cement: This material has little use in the model business. In my opinion, its use as a temporary adhesive is offset by the time consuming process of having to clean it off after it has served its purpose.

Spray Can Glues: Sprayable glues such as 3M's #77 are useful for adhering urethane layers and temporarily tacking down a drawing on urethane foam for a contour job (Ch. 10) and are almost indispensable for making trees (Ch. 25). 3M's #76 glue comes in a pressurized can with adjustable spray top. This is handy for controlling application.

Cyanoacrylate Glues: These are the "magic" glues that come in small tubes under various trade names and which can, with just drops (literally) form exceedingly strong bonds. During the occasional use you may find for it follow instructions explicitly. It can immediately glue your fingers together, for example, requiring surgery. Acetone is said to loosen it, but I would just as soon not have to try.

ADHESIVE TAPES AND PAPERS

The common *masking* tape, in various widths, is a useful product, not only for paint masking, but for temporary holddown of drawings, parts, and joints. An important use in parking lot lining is mentioned in Ch. 26. When using, press tight adhesion only along the critical edge, and peel, rather than pull off, to avoid disturbing the surface. This is particularly important where the tape has been allowed to stay in place for a time beyond its immediate use. The longer it is in place, the greater the adhesion. *Double-faced* tape in various widths is handy for temporarily holding together pieces of material for duplicate shaping, etc. Hold the free end down with your finger nail while you peel off the protective paper to the length needed. Always leave about 1/2″ of free-standing paper off the end on the roll, or you may spend some time trying to separate at the next application. Don't rely too much on the *transparent plastic* tapes, such as Scotch tape, which, after all, is for mending a torn book page, sealing a letter or package, etc. It is not supposed to be a masking tape. However bits of it are handy for such things as temporarily joining light materials in the process of assembly. Place it on the invisible side of the joint if possible so you won't have to worry about its coming off in pieces or coming off and falling into an unseen cavity later. The *removable plastic* tapes in a variety of widths and colors used for drawing indications have been used fairly successfully to indicate window mullions, fascia delineation, etc., but beware of the lack of permanency. Don't stretch them when applying, or the ends will tend to lift. Once an end has lifted and acquired a dose of dust, you might as well remove the strip and start over. Put the tape down as slackly as possible with a drop of contact glue under each end of a run. This will help to keep it in place, along with finger pressure applied along its length. Be careful not to disturb its location. The *fiberglass* wrapping tapes have about the same uses as masking tape except for masking. It is very strong. Consider the stability of the surface before applying for later removal which can tear your model apart. The *self-adhesive papers* are not tapes, but fall into this category. If you have found just the design for the kitchen floor "asphalt tile" in your interior model, beware of self-peeling as well as self-adhering as you would in the case of the architectural drawing tapes previously mentioned. Tack the edges down with contact glue in the absence of floor-edge molding to lap the edges of the paper.

GLUE GUNS

The glue guns which supply glue through a nozzle after being melted by a heating coil in a pistol grip tool are not, in my opinion, satisfactory for model work. They are just too clumsy to use for the relatively small area model building requirements.

35

Materials and Supplies

The materials and supplies listed in this chapter are those which I have found useful in applications. No implication is made that those listed are the only ones available for model building purposes. As stated previously, it is hoped that your ingenuity and experience will lead you not only to better methods but also, where necessary, to at least equally satisfactory substitute materials and supplies more readily available in your area. As there is no fixed sequence of use in building a model, the list will be alphabetically (by major category) arranged in groups with comments on use, characteristics, and precautions. In order to gather all items conveniently into one chapter, some repetition is necessary. Exemplary use references will be made to other chapters where identification of materials was necessary to the discussion of procedure. Some items will have housekeeping as well as model building uses. Not all items are starting requirements for a new shop. In fact, you probably will not be buying any model supplies until you get your first model, inventories gradually building up from leftovers of some items and from conscientious buying in quantities to supply continual needs for others.

ABRASIVES

Polishing Compounds: Polishing compounds are necessary for polishing any hard surface. (The most prevalent hard surface in model building is acrylic plastic (Ch. 24).) These polishing compounds are obtainable from your plastics supplier. I use almost exclusively a dry stick which is held against a cloth wheel on a bench grinder (Ch. 36) to transfer some of the compound. A paste compound for minor scratches is useful when you can't take the work to the wheel as in the case of an acrylic model cover. Keep a small can of Dr. Lyon's tooth powder on tap for removing shallow hairline scratches on acrylic.

Sandpaper: Sandpaper in three grades is necessary for smoothing off wood, chamfering the edges of model base frames, and trimming and sizing urethane foam. Keep in stock a couple of sheets each of fine, medium, and coarse for sanding sticks and blocks (Ch. 36). Wet-or-dry sandpaper (or emery cloth) is indispensable for the first operation in polishing saw cut edges of acrylic parts. Obtain a sheet each of 200, 400, and 600 grit for progressive sanding prior to using the bench grinder and polishing compound. You may find from experience that only one of the grades mentioned is necessary to do the job. See Ch. 24. The reason for using water is to provide lubrication and reduce heat. Both kinds of abrasive paper are obtainable at your hardware store. The emery boards (nail files) obtainable at drug stores and cosmetic counters are ready-made sanding sticks for small jobs. A stationery store type hard rubber ink eraser may be all you need to rub out a spot on your roadway, etc. Medium grit seems to be the best all around grade for your belt sander. Keep a new belt in stock.

ADHESIVES

See Ch. 34.

CLOTH

These materials are pretty well confined to interior work (Ch. 31).

Unless you anticipate a long run of miniature interior work, there is no point in trying to stock supplies of velvet and linen, for example. When the requirement presents itself, try the department stores for sample swatches. Buying it by the yard minimum may soon demand your own dry goods department.

DRAFTING MATERIALS

These include a roll of architectural drafting paper, a roll of tracing paper, hard and medium pencils, a ball point pen with black ink, and hard and soft erasers. See Ch. 26.

DYES

The dyes needed are those for acrylics as for stained glass windows (Ch. 21), for resin as in Ch. 12, and for preparing landscaping materials (Ch. 25). The first two are liquids (obtainable at your plastics supplier), and the third comes in powdered form. A suggested source is given in Ch. 50. Magic

Markers, consisting of felt tips on tubes, can often be used in place of the dyes on acrylic and other plastics. See the treatment of vinyl for a wood finish in Chapter 33 as an example. To reiterate, experimentation is the mother of solution.

ELECTRICAL SUPPLIES

The standard components needed for lighting a model are covered in Ch. 29. It is better to purchase such things as ballasts, transformers, switches, etc., as each job requires. An inventory item may not have the correct rating for the next job. When in doubt about an animation project, tell a qualified electrician friend or your electric supplier what you want to accomplish, and let them tell you what you need. Keep a spool of electrical solder and a box of insulated staples on hand, along with some heat-shrinkable insulation.

FILLERS

Either "Syncoloid" or "Dap" spackle is a good filler for cavities in plywood edges, countersunk brad holes, etc. I get small cans at the hardware store and keep the lid on tight between each application to keep the supply from drying out. Fill with a slightly convex surface and sand off even when dry.

HOUSEKEEPING SUPPLIES

Keep a box of fluorescent tubes for replacement purposes. A box of a dozen should last you for several years. Also keep two or three fluorescent starters on hand, unless all your fluorescent lighting is self-starting. I have found that a starter will occasionally have let go when you think it is the tube. Unless your power supply is protected by circuit breakers, keep a small supply of fuses to obviate having to make a trip in the middle of a job when an overload occurs. The best hand soap in my experience is powdered Boraxo. Buy a case of folded paper towels. You will use them continually not only for your hands but often for wiping equipment and cleaning up spills. Buy toilet paper by the case. A jug of toilet cleaner is a must. A box of faucet washers can save a plumber's visit.

JAY'S NEST

After watching a blue jay surreptitiously bury a child's marble, for what purpose I doubt even it knew, I decided that "Jay's Nest" was a good name for the drawer or drawers containing articles of the same ilk. Following the practice of never throwing anything away, collect everything from ball bearings, configured bottle tops, golf tees, punchout discs, various sizes of wooden and rubber balls, various sizes of beads and buttons and an endless assortment of costume jewelry bits and pieces you have garnered from your mother, wife, or sister, or have donated to the cause from your own dresser drawer. Ignore jibes of "Pack Rat". You will be surprised how useful all this junk can be over the years—how many times you can find just the right shaped armature for a model accessory, or a suitable finial for the top of a tower. Among many uses too numerous to list, I remember using a covered wagon off a "dingle" bracelet in a 1/32″ scale child's amusement area.

LANDSCAPING MATERIALS

See Ch. 25.

LIQUIDS

Paints are covered in Ch. 32 with trade names of successful products mentioned in Ch. 50. Glues (adhesives) are discussed in Ch. 34 with trade names in Ch. 50. The following liquids are the ones I have found most useful. I keep them in gallon cans on a paint table which, in my area, seems to be permitted by the local fire department. To be safe, keep flammable items in metal cupboards.

Alcohol (commercial) for minor cleaning and for mixing commercial dye solutions in the absence of methanol.

Contact glue solvent put out by the glue maker or MEK (methyl ethyl ketone). This is for thinning glue that has become too thick in the jar you are using (Ch. 34), and will wipe off unwanted smears. Lumpy mistakes with contact glue are better left to dry slightly and then peeled off. The solvent is likely to spread the error and make a general mess.

Glycerine is used in a 50-50 solution with water to treat lichen received in a dry bale and for rejuvenating lichen landscaping (Ch. 25).

Lacquer thinner is a useful and fast solvent and cleaner. It will clean brushes of dried paint and those used to brush on a sprayed application of pressure can enamel. There is no better way to remove contact glue from your hands at the end of the day with the aid of a paper towel and an afterwash with soap to preserve the complexion. See "Plastics" for removal of stubborn acrylic masking paper.

Methanol seems to be the best medium for commercial dye solutions for landscaping materials. The powder will go into solution faster than with alcohol.

Plastic cleaner will be found at your plastics supplier to clean acrylic (mostly) of finger marks and smudges. There is also an antistatic cleaner for the same purpose, useful where you have a large surface to clean such as that of an acrylic model cover (Ch. 39).

Lubricants: These include machine oil and a silicone spray or its equivalent. Keep a can of 10 weight motor oil with which to fill your oil dispensing can for machine lubrication and the crank case of your compressor. I have found WD40 in a pressure can good for minor lubrication and for cleaning metal parts. Common bar soap or wax will sometimes free sticky drawers.

METAL PRODUCTS

The metal products listed here include items obviously not required on a day to day basis. Those of which the use is not apparent are listed to remind you of their availability for occasional or extra curricular projects. They have all been useful to me at one time or another.

Acid-Etched Material: (Ch. 17) Material left over from past assignments can often be used on current projects. I keep my leftover stock between pages of an unused scrap book to keep it from becoming twisted and bent.

Aluminum: This is a relatively easy to work material useful for all sorts of projects usually not directly connected with model building. It can be found in hardware stores in sheets, tubes, strips, and angles of various sizes and shapes and provides strength and durability where needed. If you have to do much cutting of sheet stock too thick for shears, get an aluminum cutting blade for your table saw. The material is relatively soft and has a tendency to tear rather than slice, so be sure of solid anchorage against the saw bridge and take it slowly. Small stock can be cut on your bandsaw with a metal cutting blade or with a hacksaw (Ch. 36). I have made such items as brackets, electrical contacts, and holddown tongues for urethane foam contouring (Ch. 10) out of aluminum sheet stock. Make an adjustable photographic flood light stand out of telescoping tubing with through peg holes for maintaining a fixed height. Mount the tube in a hole through the seat of a small wooden stool. The easel for the gas flow display (Ch. 30) was made from aluminum tubing with furniture slides to close the floor ends of the frame, and the display box was framed with aluminum angle. Aluminum angle was used for a protective frame for a model base where the client was fed up with having the pine frame repaired after transport. Some stores will have anodized aluminum which obviates painting. For a durable finish, paint aluminum first with a spray primer before adding the color. Corrugated aluminum siding can be found at the model railroad scales in the hobby shops. You may have to buy a building kit to get the metal, but the price will be a lot less than the cost of your time to do your own corrugating.

Anchor Nuts: Anchor nuts are cited in Ch. 19 for holding a model building securely against its base. The ones I use are brass with heavy exterior threads for turning into 3/8″ holes in wood and 1/4″—20 internal threads to accept steel screw stock. I have found them to be a hardware specialty not extensively obtainable; when you locate a source through your store buy a fistful to last you a while. They can be obtained through a Brookstone catalog (Ch. 50).

Brads: Brads are a base building necessity. I use 1-1/2″—16 gauge for nailing down the plywood to the frame and 3/4″—16 gauge for attaching the Masonite bottom. Any lighter than 16 gauge will tend to bend when hammering into Masonite. Keep a small supply of a couple of sizes of heavier brads on hand for odd requirements. The small heads on brads make them easier to countersink for an unobstructed surface than those of regular nails.

Brass Shim Stock: This material comes in various gauges at hardware and machinist's supply houses. It provides a good means for obtaining small scale thicknesses where metal fills the bill and it can be used for filling small openings at joints in model

building. It can be cut and bent to form metal sculpture, or with soldered joints, a watertight liner for a swimming pool (Ch. 12).

Brass Tubing: Your model supply house will have boxes of 12″ lengths of brass tubing in various diameters, each size telescopable into the next. This tubing has uses too numerous to list. It can be column stock, used for light standards, piping, or used for extra curricular purposes such as making a miniature nozzle for your shop vacuum cleaner (Ch. 36).

Corner Braces: These are often chrome plated and used for reinforcing acrylic model covers. They can be obtained at a luggage parts store. Obtain a small sack of braces similar to those described in Ch. 39.

Corrugated Fasteners: These are the easiest means to make secure, corner joints of a model base frame (Ch. 7).

Escutcheon Pins: These are small, round-headed nails of different sizes usually made of brass. Use them to hold down wire screening in vertical control contouring (Ch. 9) to prevent rust from blotching the plaster. Use them where the heads are desired for decorative effect. With the heads clipped off and the top ends sanded flat they can be stanchions or small columns that can be hammered in place.

Furniture Slides: These are the rounded metal buttons used for finishing the floor end of model legs. Some can be snapped into tubular legs and some come with nails incorporated for mounting in solid wooden legs. Use them for domes and storage tank ends in an industrial complex.

Gear Stock: This material comes in short lengths of brass rod with gear teeth cut in lengthwise. You could make your own gears where a specific ratio was required for an animation project, or make a crimper (Ch. 36) for corrugating paper.

Hooks: Hooks in various sizes are good hangers. They come with wood screw ends or with eyelets. I can remember a hook coming to the rescue with block and tackle to raise the removable roof of a heavy model when no assistance was available.

Machine Screws and Nuts: These have numerous uses where wood or sheet metal screws are inadequate or cannot be used for some reason. The ones I use by far the most are size 6 with a 32 thread. Keep several lengths on hand such as 1/4″, 1/2″, and 1″. When too long they can be sanded or cut to length and the ends reflattened. For example, use them to attach chrome corners to acrylic model covers (Ch. 39). Drill and tap the acrylic so you won't have to use protruding nuts.

Nails: Nails are useful for building your own tables, shelves, partitions, etc., but don't have much application in model building. I have used 5/8″ 18 gauge box nails for anchoring recalcitrant model surfaces and in grading work where the heads would be covered. Like escutcheon pins they can sometimes supply the right size shaft for stanchions and columns.

Pins: Pins in various sizes, from the miniature model pins to the large banker's pins, have a wide use. By bending over their tops they can hold wire screen backing for plaster. I have used them to make flag poles and wire mesh fencing supports. I use the standard seamstress pins to anchor nylon thread at changes in bearing of a property line. Use them with glue to cinch down an illustration board finished grade to vertical risers of the same material. This is a case where the heads will be covered. Pins can be used to clear stopped up orifices such as in the nozzle of a paint sprayer. They can be used as small scale tree armatures (Ch. 25). Map pins with their globular heads can be used to make a stylized fruit orchard, or as armatures to be covered with landscaping material for a more realistic effect.

Pipe: Pipe of the plumber's variety can be used for model legs (Ch. 41). A plumber's supply store will usually have facilities for cutting to length and threading to fit into street els attached to the bottom of a model. Have one end of lengths of 1/2″ pipe threaded to accept clamping units from a hardware store. My Pattinson Mill is mounted on a 2″ pipe frame.

Pulleys: Pulleys (or sheaves) can be used to make your own block and tackle for temporarily lifting clumsy or heavy objects.

Screw Stock: Screw stock can be bought in fixed lengths to be cut to size in your shop to tie-down model buildings (Ch. 19). I use either 1/4″ or 5/16″ diameter steel stock with 20 threads per inch,

depending upon the size of the building. You can make your own bolts of any length with a nut replacing the usual head.

Sheet Copper: Sheet copper has little use in my experience except for authentic copper roofing (Ch. 20). You can get it paper thin to cut with scissors.

Springs: Springs can be obtained in packages of different sizes to use for automatic return tools such as the material chopper in Ch. 36.

Steel Angles: Steel angles are sometimes just the thing for bracing joints where glue alone is not adequate. Right angles and flat T's come in various sizes at a hardware store with predrilled holes for wood screws or bolts.

Tacks: Tacks of different sizes have occasional uses where their relatively large heads provide security. They can be used for holding down screen in plaster grading where rust is of no concern. Tack different gauges of screen to wood frames to make sieves to strain gravel and ground cover material.

Tinplate: Tinplate in sheets has uses similar to that of brass shim stock to create metal surfaces. This can be used covered as a floor surface to hold movable furniture and equipment, for example, that contain magnets in their bases.

Washers: Washers are necessary under the nuts in model building tie-down and wherever you want to spread the compression and help hold the assembly together. I keep an assortment of steel and brass washers (both flat and split) on hand. Their extra-curricular uses include column capital parts (Ch. 22) and round structure designation when stacked in a small scale industrial complex.

Wire: Wire should be in every model builder's inventory. Electric and picture wire can be un-braided for tree armatures (Ch. 25). Fine wire bought on spools can be used for cables, railings, and industrial piping. Soft, heavier wire (10 to 12 gauge) can be used for various odds and ends such as temporary hooks to hold up long strips of painted material to dry and repair of a broken hammer handle until you can get around to buying a new one. To take kinks out of wire, clamp one end in your vise, wrap the other end around a piece of dowel, and pull. I have also stretched wire into a smaller diameter by this method.

Wire Screen: I keep a few rolls of window screen for use as a plaster base in grading (Ch. 9) and for making sieves to strain gravel, applying landscaping ground cover such as lichen when I want to forestall having to pick out all the tubular pieces later. A few grades of brass filter cloth from your hardware store will come in handy for chain link fencing, architectural screens, straining paint, etc.

Wood Screws: Wood screws make a more secure mounting or joint than nails. They should be used in such assemblies as a model display table or a shop-made work table. They hold down electrical components in the basement of a lighted model and are good wherever you do not have the space to swing a hammer. They should be used with the angle braces discussed previously. A chart mounted on the door of my fastener cabinet helps pick the right size to purchase when it is not in inventory.

MOLD AND CASTING MATERIALS

See Ch. 24.

OFFICE SUPPLIES

These should be purchased in quantities commensurate with expected use. Purchase such things as file folders, pencils, carbon paper, etc., by the box. Having currently needed supplies on hand is a great time saver and conducive to keeping up with the ever accumulating pile on your desk. Scratch pads are a necessity to be bought in bulk. They should measure at least 4″ × 6″ to hold your endless reminders and computations. Buy stamps by the roll at the post office. Keep a couple of adding machine tapes on hand, and order your next year's calendar refill when the notice appears on your current one. In the absence of a correcting typewriter ribbon I find the dispenser roll of correcting tape better than the liquid. A bottle of stamp pad ink will rejuvenate your pads. Many small items such as paper clips, erasures, staples, etc., will come obviously to mind. The main purpose of this paragraph is to stress the importance of *keeping supplied*. A "nuisance" supply chore is more economically done once every six months than

once a week, to rob you of valuable construction or supervision time.

PAINTS

These are covered in Ch. 32.

PAPER PRODUCTS

Without the many paper products professional scale model building would indeed be a chore if not economically impossible. Both structure and texture rely upon paper in some form. Except as noted all the items listed are obtainable at artist's supply stores.

Bristol Board: Bristol board, a common phrase among model builders, is a generic name of a type of paper and board, most of which has a high rag content and which comes in a wide variety of thicknesses. For years I have used Strathmore's papers from one to five ply. One-ply is 0.007″ thick and four-ply measures 0.021″, so a little searching will usually get you into scale where necessary. These products come with either a slick or matte surface.

Brown Paper: Brown paper is useful for wrapping, pattern making, protective progressive contact between large surfaces covered with contact glue, establishing a clean area for laying out freshly painted components, covering a work space, etc. Obtain a 3′ to 4′ long roll from a paper supplier and suspend it under a shelf on a piece of pipe held at each end by wooden brackets.

Carbon Paper: Large sheets of carbon paper are available at artist's supply stores for covering traced areas in model layout, etc.

Chip Board: Chip board is a common wood pulp type cardboard which, though generally not suitable for finished surfaces, has many uses. I have used it as a backing for a surface of Strathmore paper or vinyl, for patterns, and for support for painting components. It is good for forming curved surfaces (Ch. 24) since it tends to keep the desired shape when soaked in water and left to dry in a jig. I use close to 1/16″ gauge almost entirely, and keep a package on hand for the unplanned need.

Colored Papers: These are used by some for final surfacing; I frown on this because of the danger of accidental spotting either in the shop or by the client. I have never found a satisfactory way to restore a stained surface of this material, whereas a painted surface can be retreated to cover many sins. The use of colored papers is restricted to making such things as pennants.

Illustration Board: Illustration board is one of the basic standbys in model building. I use Crescent board which comes in lightweight form (0.058″ thick) and heavyweight (0.097″ thick). These thicknesses allow practical use for 1/16″ and 3/32″ respectively. It comes in 30″ × 40″ sheets in both grades and also in 40″ × 60″ sheets in heavyweight. You can get cold or hot pressed, the former having a minutely textured surface excellent for streets and plaster walls, and the latter a slick surface. Its construction consists of a medium grade white paper over a lamination of pulp. The laminations are troublesome at times when the edge has been disturbed, but being forewarned about its limitations makes handling no problem. You can peel off the white top layer to outline planters (Ch. 25) and, with care, can peel off layers of pulp for greater depth designation. Illustration board takes paint well and is generally a satisfactory construction material. When covering large areas such as that filled with risers in grading (Ch. 9), use heavyweight whenever possible because of its sturdier thickness.

Napkins: Napkins in folded, restaurant form in a dispenser are excellent wipes to have on your work table to wipe up glue and paint, clean acrylic, etc.

Poster Board: Poster board about 0.040″ thick brings a warning not to use it for finished surfaces. Its white, smooth surface may be attractive, but don't be fooled by appearances. In the early years I tried it as a cover for a model base with disastrous results. The surface disturbs easily, and once it has been distrubed you've had it. Cut it up for patterns and use it for laminating to scale thickness, but be sure it is not the top lamination.

Upson Board: This is 1/4″ thick pressed paper board obtainable at your lumber yard. I was first attracted to it by its even thickness to serve as the core of 1/2″ scale walls. Cutting it with a knife is a chore, and sawing and sanding it will spread paper pulp from here to eternity. So, in other words, be forewarned!

The above list by no means covers all the available useful paper products. It does include the principle ones in my experience and can be augmented by your investigations of artists' supply stores. Each product has its own peculiar requirements, and you may well find textured papers, for example, which I have not had cause to use.

PLASTICS

As indicated throughout this book, some of the plastics materials are of great benefit to the model builder. When you learn their limitations as well as their useful qualities they can be valuable time savers. Through them you can obtain transparency, rigidity, clean, sharp corners and edges, strength of assembly, conductivity, insulation, flexibility, surfacing, and texture.

Acrylic: Acrylic plastic is the most generally used, in my experience. Two popular makes are Plexiglas and Lucite (Ch. 50). The material comes in 4′ × 8′ sheets, tubes, rods, and polished spheres of various diameters. Aside from the clear product, it comes in white and colors, transparent, translucent, and opaque. There are textured and mirrored surfaces. As soon as possible obtain from your dealer or manufacturer boxes of samples of all the acrylic sheet products. These samples are roughly the size of 35 mm photographic slides and are a great help in choosing which one of the several bronze acrylics, for example, is closest to your client's specifications for building fenestration. The clear ("glass") product comes in a wide range of thicknesses starting with the thinnest at 1/32″. You will probably find the most used sizes to be 1/32″, 1/16″, 3/32″, and 1/8″, with an occasional purchase from the selvage bin of thicker material for such things as swimming pools. When you tell your model cover supplier the overall size, he or she will know what thicknesses to make the sides and top for maximum durability. With models measuring as large as 8′ × 8′, I have placed clear, polished acrylic columns as near center as the model will allow to counteract the natural sag of the top of the cover. If you have to buy 4′ × 8′ sheets of 1/8″ thickness or thicker, have your supplier cut them to convenient sizes for your table saw. The thinner materials can be scored and broken using a special knife (Ch. 36) much in the same manner that you break glass using a glass cutter.

You can sand, saw (with a special blade (Ch.

36)), drill, mill, and polish acrylic. It is heat formable for such things as dome roofs (Ch. 20). Its memory will tend to return it to its original shape after being heated. If you are sanding a narrow strip on your belt sander, for example, carefully sand to your score line ignoring the arc the heat is forming. Lay it aside and the arc will straighten out as it cools. Dust acrylic with a soft rag only, with as little rubbing as possible. The material is soft compared with glass, and any abrasive action, even though slight, will scratch it, requiring re-polishing (Ch. 24). Wash with a mild soap and water or plastic cleaner sold for acrylics.

Each side of a welded acrylic display joint should be polished and flat. Structural interior model joints do not require polished edges and surfaces since they won't be seen, but the smoother and flatter they are the stronger the joint will be.

You can safely contact glue wood supports for interior bracing on the back of mirrored acrylic without destroying the mirror treatment as long as you are not too heavyhanded during assembly. Coat each surface with the glue, let dry, and then press on the support firmly without sliding. You can also cement 45 degree corners of mirrored acrylic without obvious joints to spoil facade appearance. This is important where there is no specified framing or column structure enclosing the corner. Polished acrylic will transfer light (Ch. 29).

With all acrylic's versatility in the model building profession, there are two complaints I have involving faults about which you should be forewarned. The first has to do with dimensional tolerance. Be alert to variations in thickness from one end of a $4' \times 8'$ sheet to the other. This will usually be at a gradual taper; so if you try to match a piece cut from one end of the sheet with a piece cut from the other you may find several thousandths difference—enough to be troublesome in precise assemblies. Because of the relatively small areas used in making components, this fault will generally not be a serious obstacle. Just be alert to the hazard. There are closer tolerance versions of acrylic with more consistent dimensions than the "G" version I have used for years, but I haven't found paying the higher price justified.

The other fault which can drive you up the wall in the middle of a rush job is welded on masking paper. Apparently as the paper ages the adhering glue sets into permanency. When I first started in the business the masking paper was heavier, and the adhesive allows easy removal even after 25 years. I have pointed this out to the manufacturer complete with an ancient sample with no response.

Hopefully you will find improvement. I have found a clear plastic masking on mirrored acrylic, and this is easy to remove. The drawback to the plastic covering is that you can't readily mark it with dimension lines as you can the paper. However, it would be obviously grossly uneconomical to throw away all selvage from a current job just because at the anticipated next use the masking paper wouldn't come off without a federal project. There are two solutions. One is to remove the paper from all selvage immediately and store the acrylic carefully where it will not be disturbed causing scratches requiring repolishing at next use. This can be a time consuming process not included in the budget of the job you are performing, but a few pieces with fresh masking paper may make the removal worth the trouble. The other solution is to gird your loins for battle and plan to spend some time letting lacquer thinner dissolve the glue. Don't be misled by those who tell you to use kerosene which is harmless to the acrylic but absolutely useless for removing masking paper with any reasonable dispatch. In addition you have to spend about the same amount of time cleaning off the oily mess left by the kerosene. Cut wall sections, for example, to specified dimensions from the 1/8" acrylic with the stubborn masking paper and place them in a shallow pan. Go over each piece to pull off any easily removable paper and then cover the lot with lacquer thinner. Monitor the soak every 5 to 10 minutes until the paper slides off. Yes, the lacquer thinner will craze the acrylic and roughen the edges a bit, but a 10 to 20 minute soak will not seriously affect dimensions or surfaces. Hold each contemplated joint edge against the belt sander for a few seconds to remove most of the roughness after washing the part with soap and water. If the part is to be painted or otherwise covered, leave any remaining welded paper residue alone. An added thousandth won't seriously affect construction. If the part includes window areas repolish them on your bench grinder (Ch. 24) to take off paper residue as well as the white discoloration caused by the bath. If you have had to resort to a large panel of old acrylic for a model cover, for example, and the paper won't readily pull off, toss in the towel and either wait for a fresh sheet or give the cover dimensions to your cover manufacturer. The latter procedure should be followed in any case in my opinion. Depending upon the tightness of paper adherence, I have found that sometimes hot water will help by softening the adhesive on small parts. During any lengthy boiling of parts on your hot plate you stand the chance of deforming the product with heat. Where time is of the essence, judicious application of lacquer thinner is the best method in my experience. Note that some acrylics will craze faster than others due no doubt to differences in manufacturer's formula. Most of my use has been with Plexiglas and Lucite (Ch. 50), both of which seem to stand the attack quite well.

Industrial Components: Industrial components in plastic can be obtained from such companies as those listed in Ch. 50. Where your products are mostly architectural you won't have much need for piping, pumps, generators, and storage tanks, etc., but obtain a catalog from such a refinery-type supplier. You will find just the right ladder stock some time or the elements to fill the yard of your model of a manufacturing plant.

Fiber Optics: Fiber optics can be useful in certain lighting situations (Ch. 29), where light can be transferred through the plastic fibers to street lamps, for example.

Micarta and Formica: These are two trade names for the hard plastic laminates used for such things as sink tops. I have found little use for these products in model building except for an occasional base for a "permanent" desk top display for a corporate executive's office. In the absence of the real thing, this material would make a good surface plate (Ch. 36) for accurate assembly. Laminate this to a *flat* panel of 3/4″ plywood, for example. Don't try to use it for a cutting surface. It will shorten the life of your blade and soon become scratched beyond repair. Another use would be as a paint table surface since cleaning materials do not easily affect it.

Nylon: Nylon thread and cord are useful articles to have around. They are good for outlining property lines on a contour model and for block and tackle exercises where, for example, you want to suspend a removable roof above the interior to be worked on without chance of damage to a configured joining surface. Nylon has great tensile strength; cables can be drawn very tight. Nylon gears can be used for quiet running animation.

Plastic Screen: Plastic screen for window screening can be used as a plaster base in grading (Ch. 9) to avoid rust from steel wire screen mentioned earlier.

Polyethelene: Polyethelene is found in clear plastic bags for storing landscaping materials, and will

probably be used to protect the model cover you have ordered. Save this sheeting for temporary dust covers for models in process and for covering your equipment when not in use.

Polystyrene: Polystyrene from my experience is low on a model builder's list of supplies. At room temperature it is very brittle, and it requires its own glue for joining (unless you can use the old standby contact glue). Its one claim to stardom is in vacuum forming of small shapes (Ch. 24) because of its fast and even response to heat. Acrylic and vinyl are far better for fenestration.

Polyurethane Foam: This is one of the greatest boons to the model builder ever invented. I use the 4-lb variety exclusively because of its density. The 1-lb grade, for example, squashes too easily. The 4-lb grade can be easily sanded and cut to sharp edges, and its texture makes an ideal base for landscaping at any scale. It can be used for risers in grading (Ch. 9), "dirt" fillers for planters and is a must in contour cutting (Ch. 10). One of its big advantages is the speed with which you can install shaped surfaces to fill large areas where heavy construction does not have to be firmly and accurately supported. It is fairly easily compressed with sufficient pressure to destroy the accuracy of a model office building pad, for example. Within limits, urethane dust makes good tree foliage (Ch. 25). You can carve it with sanding sticks to make freestanding shapes. For additional durability cover the result with plaster. The basic tips for handling are covered in Ch. 10.

Resin and Its Catalyst: These have, in my experience, been used exclusively for water (Ch. 12). For those of you with experience in application, there is no reason why the resins couldn't be used in other casting, as a liner for a real water swimming pool, etc.

Styrofoam: Styrofoam has been used extensively in the past for contouring, using the horizontal control method (Ch. 9), but has fallen to the bottom of the list in favor of the much more versatile urethane foam. If it hasn't it should have because it is absolutely useless in my opinion. For anyone interested I have a stack I'd sell cheap. About any adhesive except white glue dissolves the material, and you have to wait a month of Sundays for that to dry.

Vinyl: Vinyl alphabetically at the end of the list, ranks along with illustration board, wood, urethane, and acrylic as model building mainstays. I use the soft version in the form of clear tubing for liquid movement display in animation. I maintain a roll of stiff 0.010″ clear stock for small scale fenestration. By far most use is of the high impact sheet vinyl which comes in white, black, and colors with a matte or polished surface. Try to get at least one side matte since this is the finish desired 95 percent of the time. The gauges I use are 0.010″, 0.015″, 0.020″, and 0.030″. Vinyl can be stuck to itself and to acrylic with acrylic solvent (Ch. 34), using the wicking method around the edges, but particularly with the thinner stock (0.010″ and 0.015″) trying to flood the contact area with solvent will produce holidays which will show up as bubbles on the display surface of the vinyl. If you have to remove the vinyl because of this after it has been stuck to acrylic, give the assembly the old masking paper bath in lacquer thinner. The lacquer thinner will dissolve the vinyl. It's a mess but sometimes better than making a configured acrylic part over. When you have more than a couple of square inches to laminate use contact glue instead of the solvent. Apply contact glue to both surfaces *evenly*, *completely* and *thinly* and *let dry* before joining. Contact glue will soften and ruin the vinyl if confined while wet. Vinyl is extremely sensitive to heat. If you can't take advantage of its flexibility to hold a curve in mounting an assembly, hold the part in hot water until you can establish the curve. At most heat it over a piece of wooden dowel using a heat gun (Ch. 36). Apply low heat lightly or you may distort the material beyond use even though you have formed the curve. Trim edges slowly on your belt sander. The heat will create an adhering selvage which is best left to cool and then flicked off with a sanding stick. Considerable changes in temperature after installation may produce shrinking at joints or buckling from expansion. In the latter case cut out slivers of material and reglue leaving expansion joints.

When cutting vinyl, draw the knife along the straightedge slowly with slight pressure during the first stroke to establish a cutting line. Too much haste will tend to make the blade take off away from the guide. You can break vinyl by snapping it along a part-way through cut, or you can form a change in plane by one or two knife strokes (depending upon the thickness of the material) and breaking without separation to form the vertical border of an entrance canopy for example. Watch for brittleness when really cold.

No mention has been made of *acetate* because I have found little use for the material. The available thicknesses less than 0.010″ make it attractive for window material, but I have relied upon vinyl and acrylic.

STONE AND PLASTER

This group includes all the sand, gravel, and rocks used in model building. Coffee cans are good for storage of the various grades and colors you will accumulate. The best source other than from your trips to the beach or mountains, is your local building supply company. When making little stones out of big stones, do your hammering on a steel plate inside a stationery size box to confine the shrapnel. The only plaster I use is called "Hydrostone" (Ch. 50). It mixes with water and works well, hardening rapidly into a dense consistency that can be sanded, carved, and drilled. Discuss other similar products with your building material supplier and craft shops for substitutes. You may find another plaster you prefer. Hydrostone accepts latex paints well (Ch. 32) and can be glued with contact or white glue. As mentioned previously, do not pour leftover liquid plaster into the plumbing. It will harden under water creating a stoppage. Let the excess plaster harden in its rubber mixing bowl and snap out the result into your waste basket.

TAPES

Tapes are conveniently grouped here regardless of composition since they all employ the same self-adhesive principle in application.

Architectural: Architectural or draftsman's plastic line indicating tapes come in a wide range of colors and in widths from 1/64″ on up. The most useful have been 1/32″, 1/16″, and 1/8″, principally for window mullions. Lay it relaxed to ensure against curling up of the ends which have been cinched with contact glue.

Binding: Binding tape is a very strong plastic tape occasionally used for holding the larger assemblies together before final gluing. Beware of pulling finish or separating laminations on removal.

Cellophane: Cellophane tape is my generic description of the common clear plastic tapes used in home and office. 3M has one called "Magic Tape" which is excellent for mending torn drawings and other paper products and sealing Christmas wrappings, but avoid it on the model. It is too fragile for holding parts together, and when used as masking tape can be a disaster. It tends to come off in bits and pieces, pulling the surface with it.

Double-faced: Double-faced plastic tape in various widths has adhesive on both sides, one side protected with paper to be peeled off. This is useful for temporarily holding a stack of material sections, such as sheet vinyl parts, together for gang cutting and for holding small components on a board for spray painting. Be sure to leave the end of the protective paper free on the roll for easy separation next time.

Masking: Masking tape is a slightly expandable paper product which is a supply you can't do without. For masking, when you have to protect an area beyond the width of the tape as in spray painting, catch the edge of sheets of newspaper as you apply it and press down the edge of the tape with your thumb nail to prevent wicking underneath. Remove the tape as soon as possible. The longer masking tape is allowed to remain in place the harder it will be to remove. Left long enough it will practically weld itself to the surface.

WAX

This common household item is needed for coating the bottom of the base for contour cutting to aid movement under the mill. Use the slippery kind–not the nonskid variety which helps keep everyone vertical on the kitchen floor. I have found the pure carnauba waxes to be successful. Follow the directions on the can for application. Carnauba is the name of the Brazilian wax palm from which the product comes.

WOOD PRODUCTS

These products have a necessity rating about equal to paper products in model building since they provide the most practical material with which to form the base upon which a model is mounted. They also provide structural members in scale shapes and authentic surfacing such as building siding, roofing, and furniture.

Balsa: This light wood from South America is great for native rafts, but in my opinion it is prac-

tically useless in professional model building. It is too soft to maintain sharp corners. Its fibrous character makes it shred easily, and its surface is easily dented. It squashes easily thus loosing consistent dimension. With other more stable woods available, the use of balsa is a ridulous waste of time.

Bass Wood: In spite of all the stated faults of the beautiful lime or linden trees from which it comes, bass wood is one of, if not the most satisfactory, woods for model building. It is close and even grained and firm enough to permit sharp edges without splintering. At the hobby shops you can find about all the structural shapes, in sheets of different thicknesses, and surfaces configured to all the standard siding systems. The fact that so many wood model building components are made from bass wood is a tribute to and verification of its stable workability. In the hobby shops you are limited to the popular railroad gauges, but sometimes a little imagination will produce scale adaptability. Over the years I have received correspondence from companies who put out some of the basic bass wood shapes in the various professional scales usually prescribed, but I have no need to patronize them. Canvas the model component suppliers (other than railroad) in your area. You may find a time-saving source of beams, siding, etc.

Hardwoods: Generally speaking, the solid hardwoods such as walnut, oak, and mahogany are not of much use in model building because of the difficulty of working them. When a client specifies a solid hardwood base frame, it should not be hard to convince him that a finish of walnut veneer, for example, will accomplish the same cosmetic result without the extra time and cost of the solid material. You can find these veneers in 2″ wide rolls at a hardware store or lumber dealer. The material I have used has a removable paper over a selfsticking back, but I have always fortified adhesion with contact glue to be on the safe side. Apply the strips along each side of the base frame allowing selvage to be trimmed with a razor blade. Then do the same thing on the lip between the edge of the frame and that of the plywood. To be really fancy, line the edge of the plywood also. When trimming selvage cut *with* the grain holding the blade snugly against the edge. Take your time so that you do not cause splintering into the finished surface. The stain used will camouflage the joints. Consider the veneers for interior panelling, flooring, and furniture surfacing where you have a budget for miniature work (Ch. 31).

Masonite: (Ch. 50) This is a hard, pressed wood product which is ideal for model base bottoms (Ch. 7). It comes untempered or tempered, the latter being unnecessarily hard for model building purposes except for contour model bases slid under the Pattinson Mill (Ch. 36). It comes in 4′ × 8′ sheets from a lumber yard. You will find the 1/8″ thickness right for model bases, though you may have occasion to use the 1/4″ stock in other applications. The untempered material may have one surface "waffled". I usually try to keep at least one sheet in stock ahead of current use. Because of its composition it tends to fracture under stress and so is not good for model construction in my opinion. Glued edges, for example, tend to break away on each side of the layer of adhesive pulling the material with it.

Plywood: Plywood in my experience is good only for model bases as far as model building is concerned. It will of course make excellent table tops, shelves, and cabinets. For bases I use 3/8″ good-one-side interior plywood exclusively. The waterproof glue of exterior plywood is not necessary for our uses. Specify "as flat as possible" when ordering the standard 4′ × 8′ sheets, particularly when you are to use it under a contour cutting job. All plywood tends to have at least a small bow or warp which can normally be pulled out by attachment to the frame and Masonite. More serious bows can be trussed out (Ch. 7) if the bow is in your favor. Depending upon the expected use of the model, I either line the exposed plywood with illustration board or sand and paint it. Fill large edge cavities in the lamination with wood to cut down on the quantity of spackle needed. Plywood makes good working table tops because it is firm without being hard enough to cause short life to cutting blades. When the surface becomes chewed up, turn the plywood over or add a new panel.

Stripwood: Stripwood in my experience is simply a name given to include all strips of wood of miniature dimensions. When you can't find bass wood beams, for example, of the scale size required, buy a few pieces oversize and cut them down on your mill or miniature lathe with a table saw set-up, using a jeweler's blade in either case. With thickness dimension correct, you will find it economical to cut widths in this manner from a maintained supply of bass wood of a single width dimension. The prepared structural shapes are well worth the cost of the expert's efforts, but trying to anticipate future needs with an inventory of flat stock of various dimensions is a futile exercise.

White Pine: Because of its light weight and even grain white pine is another boon to the model builder. With white pine unobtainable I once used redwood as a substitute, but it is not as satisfactory for base frames. The standard 1″ × 2″ stock scraps have endless uses for bracing, solid cores for model components, mold making, jig making, etc. Collect the tag ends in a drawer or bin for future use. Strips with holes drilled in them make spare tree storage or holders for prepared tree armatures.

Nominal versus Net Dimensions: Masonite (hardboard) and plywood is sold by the square foot in standard size panels, usually 4′ × 8′. Lengths of white pine framing stock will come as ordered, but the width and thickness will be "net". The nominal 1′ × 2″ will actually measure 3/4″ × 1-1/2″ as finished lumber. This is an easily accepted discrepancy in base framing, but where the drawings specify "rough" beams, for example, in the standard sizes, remember that the nominal dimension is required. In the case of 1″ × 2″ lumber, I have found that the "net" dimension stays consistently at 3/4″, but that the 2″ nominal dimension has varied anywhere from 1-7/16″ to 1-5/8″. Therefore check your stock before cutting pieces for a base frame and bracing to be sure they are all the same size.

Inventories of lumber should be fitted to your expected demand. You probably won't be concerned with the economics of carload lots; so in the interests of available space, maintain just enough to cover the delivery time of the next purchase.

36

Tools

Always buy high grade tools. A midstream failure brings not only loss of time but also the cost of another purchase or repair. Stay away from the often present "bargain" tables in supply houses unless you are satisfied that they contain proven name brands on sale. Bargains are always budget-pleasing goals. They are particularly available in the case of machine tools with a bit of searching. A used mill, for example, can be just as good as new for model building purposes, but be wary. Check out the spindle for run-out, gear lash, condition of slides, etc. Even a second hand machine tool can represent a considerable investment, so if necessary have an expert accompany you for his or her appraisal before commitment.

Tools are listed alphabetically under sub-headings of "Machine Tools", "Power Hand Tools", "Hand Tools, Bits, and Appliances", and "Home-Made Tools" without regard for relative importance which will be mentioned where pertinent.

MACHINE TOOLS

Machine tools include all those that are electrically driven on their own stands or on work tables gen-erally in fixed locations. Steel stands and motors are usually sold separately. Be sure the stands are sturdy enough for the tools they are to hold and that the motors have adequate horsepower and speed ratings. It is better to over power slightly than to be just adequate. Because of the large total investment you probably won't be buying all the tools listed on one mad shopping spree, but except as noted under "Jig Saw", they all will pay for themselves many times over even when used only occasionally. I would purchase the 10″ table saw and 6″ belt sander first, followed soon by the drill press and bandsaw. The bench grinder is a relatively inexpensive item. The others can be purchased as the budget allows and the need arises. I have had rare occasion to do turning; you may want to consider the lathe as a "someday" luxury.

Drill Press: This should have variable speed and a crank-operated table level adjustment. The stand should be of the floor type to allow drilling tall objects. The chuck should have a capacity of 1/2″.

Grinder: Obtain a fairly heavy bench grinder with high speed and high torque. Each spindle end should have wheel mounting facility. Since about 95 percent of my use has been for polishing acrylic plastic, I maintain a firm laminated cloth disc for rouge on one end and a soft finishing disc on the other. Instead of the abrasive discs on the grinder, I use the belt sander for what little tool sharpening I have to do.

Lathe: My small Logan *metal-turning lathe* has not had the use the other tools have, but has justified its presence by occasionally turning round planters, and shaped column masters for casting, etc. I have used it for center drilling, a process difficult to accomplish on the drill press. Though it is always rewarding to have a specialized facililty around when needed, my experience advises not to hock the family jewels to purchase a metal-turning lathe. Because of the relatively soft materials normally used, a good wood-turning lathe might be a more economical acquisition. A Unimat *miniature lathe* has been handy principally for cutting small wood strips to size on its little jeweler's table saw set up. This lathe, only about 18" long, can be stored in a cabinet when not in use.

Mill: An Industro-Lite toolmaker's mill, with vertical and horizontal capabilities, has been well worth the investment. Though not used from day to day, it has been a godsend during specific jobs where small components of complicated configuration could not have been accurately done by hand. Among its many uses have been cutting small scale stair stock, microscoring, and shaping and notching parts for flush assembly as in Fig. 16-2. Different levels on acrylic can be accurately milled as for the undercut steps into a swimming pool, and multigrooving can be accomplished using jeweler's saw blades. This tool more than paid for itself on its first assignment, and though it represents my highest single tool investment, I heartily advise including a mill in your future shopping list. In tune with the guiding purpose of this book it is well to point out that even a toolmaker's mill is not the ultimate in machine tool sophistication. If anticipated business warrants and your budget permits, you might want to consider a machine with greater capability. Though it has done its job well, I have sometimes felt thwarted by the relative shallowness of throat and size of table on the Industro-Lite.

Sanders: Along with the saws, the *6" belt sander* continues to be one of the workhorses of the shop. I use mine in the vertical position exclusively with the adjustable table set at 90 degrees. There is no better tool for sizing, shaping, truing, and finishing

in the majority of operations. Most angular shaping can be done horizontally with the protractor adjustable slide on the table, so you don't ever have to disturb the latter. A medium grit belt seems to be satisfactory for all assignments. A *deburring sander* with a 1" belt is very useful for getting into vertices of angled parts. An *8" disc sander* on a stand with castors can be moved to the work table for lengthy sanding of many small components.

Saws: A *10" Sears-Roebuck table saw* has been humming on demand for a quarter of a century and is still going strong. I keep an all-purpose blade installed as high as it will go and use it for the carpentry part of model building such as cutting plywood, Masonite, and framing. It is also good for slicing urethane foam with precisely even sides not obtainable by hand sanding. Extension frames on each side help support wide stock. An *8" table saw* is maintained for more precise work using a fine-toothed plastic blade for cutting acrylic and for accurately dimensioning components. If you can, get your 8" saw with a micrometer adjustable bridge that can be securely clamped at both ends. Keep two each of general-purpose (wood cutting) and no-set multitoothed plastic blades on hand so you can keep going when one has to be sent out for sharpening. I have never had cause to use some of the specialty blades such as carbide tipped. To you experts maybe this is just a copout to avoid having to change blades for each different kind of material. Next in order of importance is a *bandsaw* with as deep a throat as your budget will allow. Keep blades on hand for metal, wood, and plastic, considering widths versus radii of curves being cut. Last on the list and last in importance is a *jig saw* which is never used except in rare sanding operations where a sanding stick is mounted in the chucks to take advantage of the reciprocating action. It is mentioned since at first blush it appears to be a natural for model building. Other than being able to cut very small radii, it is too slow and too sloppy. Save it for jigsaw puzzle making, but even for that product I would prefer a band saw with a narrow blade.

POWER HAND TOOLS

Belt Sander: A Sears-Roebuck belt sander with a 3" belt has been a workhorse for many years. The majority of my use is in trimming and smoothing edges of model base plywood and Masonite. After cutting these two panels freehand close to pencil lines, lay each in turn on a table top with two edges overhanging and trim them to the dimension lines holding the belt vertically. One or two heavy weights will help prevent the panel from sliding with the pressure of the sander. Because of the usual size of these panels, this is a faster procedure than fighting with a standard table saw. The belt sander will take off wood selvage at a fast rate.

Circular Saw: This tool does the freehand cutting mentioned in the preceding paragraph. Mine is a Sears-Roebuck depth adjustable type with a 6″ blade for general-purpose wood cutting. Establish table top bearing for both sides of the anticipated cut and adjust the blade depth so that it will just cut through the thickness of the panel without grooving the table surface. Cut with a slow steady pressure and a firm grip on the handle and trigger switch. Adjust the cord before starting so that it will follow the saw without getting caught on something in midstream and flip the tool into some unauthorized activity.

Cut-Awl: In effect a cut-awl might be likened to a jig saw where the tool is moved rather than the work. It uses a miniature removable knife rather than a saw blade. The knife is in a swivel mount making it easy to get into tight configurations such as those in contour cutting in the horizontal control method of grading (Ch. 9). The tool is for soft, thin materials such as illustration board, the depth of its reciprocating cut being adjustable by blade position in its mounting bracket. With the general demise of the horizontal method of grading, the tool has fallen into disuse in my shop, but you may think of some cogent reason to cut profiles for which this tool would be the answer. For a source check with craft shops and advertising display people.

Drills: I have two very useful electric hand drills, both from Sears-Roebuck. The 1/2″ drill has speed and direction controllability and is indispensable where you cannot get the work under your drill press. The other drill is a "hobby motor" with interchangeable chucks to hold small bits such as pin drills, grinders, sanders, and polishing wheels. Its uses have included drilling post holes on the model site, carving out cavities in plaster and other materials, and polishing out scratches on an acrylic model cover which you obviously can't carry to the bench grinder. Dremel is a popular make which you can find with accessory kits at hardware and hobby shops. The ideal is one

with an adjustable chuck which will take a range of shaft sizes without having to pick out a chuck every time you change bits.

Router: A Stanley router has been in my shop for as long as I can remember. It was purchased for some extensive grooving job on a model base and hasn't been used since. This is nothing against the tool which might well be used for the same purpose more often in *your* shop. It would be just the tool for cutting shallow clearance cavities in a model base, for example.

Saber Saw: My edition of this useful tool has a replaceable saw blade with a 2″ throw with reciprocating action in a fixed vertical plane. The tool is hand pushed on a flat base steel shoe through a notch in one end of which the blade passes. I use it principally to trim 2″ thick urethane foam to shape for contour model layers (Ch. 10). It can also be used to cut out openings in plywood and other materials. This is another successful Sears-Roebuck tool which has given long service. There are saber saws with a longer throw. I have one that I used to trim 6″ thick blocks of urethane foam until I saw the light. If you decide on a larger tool, be sure it has a shoe large enough to keep the blade vertical or you may cut on a slope into your desired dimensions. With its small stop at the top of the blade, mine would be better off trimming shrubbery and small trees in the garden.

HAND TOOLS, BITS, AND APPLIANCES

At the expense of a lengthy list, I feel it important to direct your attention to the hand tools which I have found to be of value, some if only occasionally. Since you are inclined toward a handcraft career you will no doubt be familiar with most of them. Consider these included to provide a complete checklist as you fill your tool chest. In the interests of brevity, tools are generally described as to character rather than use which will be obvious as the need arises.

Air Compressor: This electrically driven motor, piston pump, and tank assembly has been useful mostly in spray painting as mentioned in Ch. 32. It is not a mandatory appliance but advisable for long runs of contour models where you have 3′ × 4′ and larger urethane bases to paint. Obtain one to provide a reliable 70-lb capability at least, with adjustable outflow. Be sure the tank is approved for commercial use with necessary relief valve, automatic shutoff, etc.

Adjustable Angle: An adjustable angle has a slotted, flat steel arm captured in a slotted steel handle which allows positioning the arm at any angle setting held by a thumb screw. This tool is very useful for duplicating a prescribed angle such as the roof rake to be cut on the top edges of building walls.

Bearing Pullers: These fall into the class of tools which spend most of their time in the drawer but are invaluable when needed to change bearings in machine tools, such as the spindle bearing of a Pattinson Mill. If you plan to do your own machine repair work, obtain pullers to fit the configuration being worked on. I have one which consists of three steel prongs with a handled center screw to bear against a shaft end. The prongs are "hooked" under the bearing.

Bits: Bits form the business ends of your machine and power tools. Without them the tools are useless, and they should be purchased with care to assure efficient operation. Start with as large a graduated set of drill bits as you can afford, starting with 1/16". Twist drill bits should be of high speed steel. Do not waste your money on carbon steel items which are lower in price but far higher in fatality. Good bits should be able to drill mild steel with ease, so with the softer materials used in model building, they will give long service between sharpenings. A starter set of miniature decimal wire drill bits will provide capabilities of drilling fence and railing post holes, etc. Each time you buy a particular size during a job get at least three because they are very brittle and will snap at the slightest off-alignment motion. The flat ended wood boring bits can often be bought in sets cheaper than in individual sizes. These are the ones with the two cutting blades separated by a center guiding screw. For general milling purposes, I have found a 1/4" and a 1/2" end milling bit to constitute an adequate inventory. Only familiarity with the capabilities of your mill will tell you the variations necessary in a given case. Follow the principle of starting out with light cuts in acrylic, for example. Your senses will tell you how much of a bite you can take without overloading the piece being milled or the tool. Obviously, as a general rule, the softer the material, the deeper the cut allowed in one pass. For the

mill bits used in contour cutting, see Ch. 10. Burrs and grinding bits are sometimes useful in your hobby motor for making small cavities and trimming small bits of selvage.These can be obtained from your hardware store in various configurations.

Broaches: Broaches are square (usually), burred steel shafts for making square holes out of round ones as in the case of mounting square columns through a building floor discussed previously. A drill press is a good driver as long as you can lock the spindle to keep it from turning so that the sides of a row of holes will remain parallel. Once the broach has been started, try pressing down with the bare chuck against a cap placed over the top of the broach so any turning of the spindle will be independent of hole alignment.

Brushes: Brushes other than the paint brushes discussed in Ch. 32 are a maintenance necessity as well as dispensing tools for such things as contact glue. I prefer the old fashioned household type broom to the janitor type because of the many obstructions when cleaning up the floor. A long handled dusting brush is indispensable for cleaning work table tops. A dust pan swung on the end of a long wire handle held vertically together with a small edition of the household broom is great for cleaning the floor of the particular cage you are working in. I use small stiff bristled paint brushes for dispensing contact glue and keep them in a jar filled with solvent.

Calipers: Calipers are adjustable measuring instruments of which two kinds are required. One is about 3" long, made out of wood and brass with a brass jaw on the end of a brass shaft which slides into a slot in the wood handle. The jaw meets a mate affixed to the handle, allowing both internal and external measurements. I cannot remember one architectural job where this instrument was not used at one time or another. The other is completely metal with about 12" capacity. A slide jaw is moved on a shaft toward a fixed jaw on the other end of the shaft. This tool is also for external and internal measurements with final micrometer adjustment on the slide for decimal readings. If you must spread your purchases, get the smaller one first in your initial tool shopping spree. The larger machinist's caliper won't be used anywhere near as often. A more sophisticated machinist's caliper has a dial added with the sweep of a hand making measurements easier to read than markings on the slide. Note that "calipers" include the drafting compass appearing instruments which have two duplicate leg points for measuring internal and external dimensions. No scale is included in the instrument. These I have found of little use in the model business.

Calculator: With the ever increasing availability of electronic aids, there is no reason why you cannot include a small calculator in your tool box. Get one with square root and trigonometric functions as well as the standard mathematical capabilities to speed your conversions and solving of geometric figures.

Can Opener: The lever-puncture type of can opener is good to have around for paint can opening and occasional opening of a can of maintenance oil. I have also a thumb screw activated one to accomplish access to a pick-me-up can of soup out of the shop larder.

Carving Tools: Carving tools come in small sets of six different blades. I have found practically no use for them, but those of you adept at carving might well want to execute a sculptured form for a building plaza or carve some architectural decoration out of wood or plaster.

Chisels: Chisels will get much more use in carpenter's tool box than a model builder's, but three sizes from 1/4″ to 1″ have been useful for scraping, hogging, and home-made cabinet work.

Clamps: Clamps of all sizes are indispensable, from the small alligator clips used by electricians to lengths of 1/2″ pipe onto which adjustable jaw units are slid. Get a half dozen each of two sizes of the hinged clothes pin type and the same number of each of different sizes of C-clamps with openings from about 1″ to 6″. Where not much pressure is required, I have used clothes pins themselves as well as the spring loaded metal clips used in the office.

Compasses: Compasses are needed in drafting and layout where circular configurations are required. Get a high quality draftsman's instrument with a removable steel point in one arm and provision for a pencil lead in the other. The fulcrum should be friction tight or the spread of the legs should be adjustable by means of a threaded bar. You can get compass blades which replace the pencil lead for paper circle cutting. Use a compass to indicate

even spacing by recessing the lead slightly and drawing the steel point along a curb face, for example, or along a mat knife score in illustration board. A drafting pen compass is handy where you have curved traffic lines, etc., to draw. The pencil lead leg is replaced by one holding a pen which you can fill with ink or paint. For drawing large circles I have a retractable tape measure with a hole in the end of the tape for inserting a pencil point. At the housing outlet there is a thumb tack under the tape and a thumb screw clamp to hold the tape at the desired radius. The thumb tack is pressed into the center point of the circle to be drawn, and the assembly is spun on this center by pushing a pencil point captured by the hole in the end of the tape. I hesitate mentioning a tool that is apparently a specialty item not readily available, but it has been so useful that it would be worth a little backyard engineering to adapt a regular retractable tape measure to the same purpose. Mine happens to be a gift which was made in Sweden, and I have never seen another one like it.

Countersinks: Countersinks are conical bits for your drill press or electric hand drill for the purpose of recessing screw and bolt heads flush with the penetrated surface. An exemplary use is the recessing of mounting screws in an acrylic model cover. They come in various diameters and conical angle. The ideal of course is to use a countersink with an angle the same as that under the head of a flat head screw, but this is not necessary as long as you can readily bury the screw head without an unsightly cutting ring visible and have enough material thickness left at the screw hole to provide a secure mounting.

Dental Tools: These tools make fine picks, scrapers, and scribes. Pester your dentist for his or her discards. The missing edge or point can be restored on your belt sander for model building purposes.

Dividers: Dividers include those constructed in the manner of a draftsman's compass, only with *two* steel points, as well as those of different sizes and shapes for taking internal and external measurements. The latter will usually have a threaded bar opening control. The compass type is the more useful one in model building, allowing you not only to punch equal spaces but also to etch circles on acrylic plastic or other surfaces where a pencil mark won't show.

Dowel Centers: These are flanged metal plugs with center punches to mark the mating piece. They come in sets of the common wood dowel sizes. A plug is inserted to the flange in a drilled dowel mounting hole, and the positioned mating piece is pressed against the punch to locate the center for drilling the opposite hole. These are handy where you are flying blind. The faster and surer way to mating accuracy is to drill mating dowel holes through both joining pieces at the same time before assembly as described in Ch. 7 covering divided model bases.

Drafting Arm: Because of the small amount of drafting a model builder is called upon to do, this instrument is not indispensable. It consists generally of a double-jointed arm one end of which is clamped to a table edge. The other end holds two rulers or straight edges at right angles to each other in a fixed rotating bracket which has a snap-stop and clamp control for positioning at desired angles as indicated on a circular dial. When locked, this assembly will maintain position regardless of movement of the arm permitting drawing a series of parallel lines, for example. I have found the instrument useful in making drawings for the acid-etchers, space dividing (Ch. 26), etc.

Drills: Hand drills are good to have in your tool box for on-the-model drilling of occasional or very small holes where damage control is easier than with an electric tool. Two of the common types are those where the chuck is turned by spinning a handled wheel on the side of the shaft, and those that have a twist-grooved chuck shaft sliding into a mating tubular element topped by a handle. "Forward", "reverse", and "lock" are controlled by a sliding thumb knob projecting through the female part. Of great use to me on occasion has been a hobbyist's twist drill which has a grooved brass shaft and a swivel top. The drill is activated by sliding a collar up and down the shaft while holding the top. The whole tool is only about 6" long and small enough in diameter to enable you to get into tight hole drilling situations without tearing up the countryside. The chuck is of a size to accept the decimal wire drill bits.

Emery Boards: These are meant for fingernail care and are obtainable at cosmetic counters. They are excellent for fine sanding of small parts or in restricted locations, and seem to have a long life considering they are disposable tools.

Files: Files are a must. Get one each of a good grade of machinist's file with flat, half-round, and round (rat tail) shapes. Also obtain a set of miniature files including all the standard shapes such as square, flat, oval, round, triangular, and flat edge only. Beware of "bargain" sets which I have found to be lacking in "bite" as well as useful life.

Flexible Drive: This consists of a flexible drive shaft in a housing with a chuck at one end and provision for connection to a motor at the other. It allows remote drilling or grinding in small spaces or where you want to avoid the heat and clumsiness of a hand held hobby motor during a protracted session at your work bench. It is an occasionally used luxury item which should be bought only with a hard bearing at the chuck end. I got stuck with a cheap addition whose bronze bushing was worn out during the first job.

Flock Gun: The use of this tool is the only satisfactory way to disperse flock over an area with any degree of evenness. It looks like the standard hand-pump garden insecticide sprayer with a 1/4" tube outlet. You should be able to find one at a crafts shop, assuming you ever want to flock an area in the first place.

Foliage Grinder: After using the old fashioned household hand operated meat grinder for years, I finally bought an electric salad maker with an assortment of grids, and the relief was worth more than the price. See Ch. 25 for use.

French Curves: French curves are useful for developing your own varying curves in a freelance situation or completing prescribed curvilinear shapes graphically. They are draftsman's tools in plastic with edges in curves of varying radii. Several different sizes and shapes will extend your application.

Hammers: Hammers should be included in your first acquisition of tools, particularly a standard carpenter's claw hammer with which you will build your first model base. A small edition of the carpenter's standby will be useful for light work. A hard rubber or plastic hammer is good for pounding on surfaces you do not want to mar. I have gotten a lot of use out of a miniature metal hammer as well as a miniature wooden mallet. Keep a full size wooden mallet in your paint section for sealing paint cans.

Heat Gun: This electric appliance can best be described as an oversize hair drier. It puts out intense heat for paint drying or plastic forming in places where it is not advisable to use a flame.

Heat Lamp: I have an infrared bulb permanently mounted in an old gooseneck table lamp fixture over a small metal stand on my paint table. Its main purpose is to dry paint samples when mixing is necessary to arrive at a client's specifications. If watched carefully, it can also be used for heat forming vinyl.

Hemostats: Hemostats are long-handled surgical pliers with various grasping configurations and finger-hole handles. They will lock as a clamp to hold without finger pressure. Check with a hospital or your favorite surgeon for discards. They are handy for holding material to be painted, holding back that unglued flap so you can work underneath, etc. They are sometimes indispensable in retrieving valuable parts that have fallen into a deep model cavity. If you have no surgical connections, hemostats are available at hardware specialty shops. See Ch. 50 for a source.

High Intensity Lamp: This is a small table stand lamp with a transformer in its base to put out an intense light through a special bulb. They are a great help in working in shadowed model cavities, and should be easily found at lamp, department, or stationery stores.

Hole Cutters: Hole cutters are bits for your drill press that come in two forms. One is in the form of a fixed diameter, shallow metal tube with cutting teeth around the bottom edge. Various diameters are obtainable for cutting soft materials such as plastic and wood. A feature with these is an unobstructed plug out of the hole cut. The other form is similar to a fly cutter with a center guiding drill bit on the end of the shaft which is slotted to accept a small bar that can be set at various radii. An adjustable cutting tool is inserted in the outboard end of the bar. This will give a plug with a tapered edge and a hole in the center.

Hot Plate: The main reason for the presence of this electric appliance is to serve as the heating element for a heat forming oven described later under "Home-Made Tools". You can of course use it to heat up water for your 4 o'clock tea.

Knives: By a wide margin, the star of this category is a mat knife which I think is safe to say has been in use at some time during most of my model building days. My collection from Sears-Roebuck has been very satisfactory. They have hollow handles held together by a machine screw allowing blade replacement. Get a supply of extra blades so that when you have used both points and don't have the time to sharpen them you can make a quick change. There are small editions of this workhorse good for fine, light cutting, some with a sliding blade supply in the handle that keep you in business after you snap off the worn section. Serrated paring and bread knives are good for small cuts in urethane foam. A cobbler's knife with a long narrow blade adjustable for depth in a chucked handle is a useful all-purpose tool. X-acto knives are all right for light work, but will not replace the mat knife. I use an X-acto knife for cutting drawings during contour cutting. Include a Swiss Army type pocket knife for no other reason than that you might need the can opener some time or the leather punch. A surgeon's eye knife will help you with minute incisions. A common kitchen table knife will make a narrow spatula on occasion. Your plastics supplier should have a hooked bladed knife for scoring (scribing) acrylic prior to snap-breaking along a line.

Lettering Guides: These come in sets of various systems. They are handy for sign making in block letters. Mine is a K & E "Doric" with a pantograph arm, one leg of which follows letters pressed in a plastic strip, the other leg tracing with pen or pencil the chosen letter onto the work. I have used mine mostly for street name tags, elevation tags on contour models, etc., where no specified type or size of lettering has been required.

Levels: Levels are convenient instruments with which to check the parallelism of two model segments that are supposed to be parallel either horizontally or vertically. If the instrument is well made you can be reasonably assured that a level reading means what it says, but even if it is not accurate to within a small fraction of a degree, the foregoing check is still acceptable. As long as each surface gives the same reading, you can feel assured that they are parallel, at least for all visual purposes. I use a small carpenter's level with horizontal and vertical bubbles, but the most useful for quick checks has been a little 3″ bricklayer's course line level.

Magnets: Other than being a model supply for

holding furniture in place on a model floor, magnets are good retrievers of iron and steel such as nails and screws that have fallen into an otherwise inaccessible cavity. Two of the most useful are the pencil-like household stud finder and the telescoping auto mechanic's aid with a movable magnetic tip.

Magnifiers: Magnifiers in the form of lenses mounted in a visored head strap will ease the eye strain of lengthy "microscopic" operations. A small lens with handle will help occasionally when you are not sure what you are looking at.

Mallet: See "Hammers".

Micrometers: The term "micrometer" literally could include any measuring instrument which would give fractional readings as in thousandths of an inch. The machinist's sliding caliper mentioned previously could be considered a micrometer. Here we add the very useful C-clamp shaped micrometer or "mike" which can be held in the palm of your hand to measure material thickness up to an inch in thousandths. I use mine continually in search for scale dimensions or letting me know whether I am looking at a piece of 0.015" or 0.020" sheet vinyl. Obtain a top grade instrument for accuracy and durability.

Nail Puller: With a claw hammer on hand, a nail puller is usually not necessary, but sometimes restricted space makes the tool useful. It is simply a small claw on the end of a wooden handle shaft for leverage to remove that bent brad or tack you tried to drive into a partially enclosed corner.

Nail Sets: Nail sets are used for countersinking brads during your carpentry work. Get three sizes to cover the most common brad (or nail) sizes.

Oil Can: A small oil can with squeeze-pump handle will aid you in machine tool maintenance.

Paint Gun: See Ch. 32.

Paper Cutter: This is another indispensable workhorse which saves many hours of cutting strips of vinyl or illustration board accurately with a mat knife against a straightedge. It has a metal-edged hardwood graduated table with a holddown clamp and a hand-activated blade held in compression against a steel edge by a spring at the fulcrum. Get as large a one as your budget and space allow.

Mine will accept the 30" dimension of illustration board and goes to work during every architectural assignment.

Pencil Sharpener: This little gadget would normally be included with office equipment, but since it sharpens many more pencils on the job than it does in clerical work, it is listed here. I have found a hand cranked model completely adequate. If you want to travel first class, electric ones are available at stationery stores.

Pens and Pencils: These include not only the kind used every day in an office, but also a few special items which help the model builder. Acquire a box of hard (4H) pencils for easily erased line indications. Colored pencils were mentioned in Ch. 32. When you do work on drawings and note working instructions, model limits, etc., you will find a four color cartridge pencil useful. This allows you to change color of lead by retracting and extending different lead holders. Probably the most useful pen for actual work on the model is the draftsman's reservoir pen used for lining as in Ch. 26. This is a split point pen with a small screw to adjust the width of opening to allow a larger or smaller amount of paint or ink to reach the surface on which you are drawing. The reservoir is the space between the points filled with the drawing fluid. Get the best you can from an artist's supply store, and *keep it clean.* During a job with intermittent lining chores, keep your pen in a jar of water to prevent paint or ink from drying on the points. There are closed container reservoir pens made for drawing purposes, but in my experience these require more attention than they are worth. If you are a conscientious keeper of pens you may have better luck.

Photo Lamp: If you expect to take your own photographs of your models a used motion picture flood lamp will give you "sunlight and shadow" when mounted on a stand described under "Homemade Tools".

Planes: Planes as used in carpentry have little application in model building. Our lumber sizing is usually done on the table saw. X-acto puts out a miniature plane which you might find useful for minor trimming, but other tools seem better to fit the bill.

Pliers: Pliers of all shapes and sizes are in the workhorse category. The desirable household and mechanics types are the two-position fulcrum, long, tapered point or needle-nose, and curved or right angle nosed. These are for what in the model business might be called heavy work. The curved nose pliers are good for leverage extracting and strong grip installation of common pin fence posts, for example. Other uses will become obvious. Miniature pliers are for occasions where you need more grip than that afforded by tweezers. Get flat nosed, needle point, and round jawed pliers which will help in forming small curves in wire or vinyl strips. The pliers mentioned are basic requirements. Your inspection of hardware store displays will reveal all sorts of specialty pliers one or more of which may strike your fancy as an aid in solving a particular problem.

Protractors: Protractors satisfactory for model building purposes come as clear plastic semicircles with a chord (diameter) connecting the ends of the arc and including a center hole for insertion of a pencil point or fulcrum pin. When using a small edition of this instrument keep in mind that any error in marking a degree reading along the scale etched into the arc will be multiplied as the distance from the center to the point to be plotted increases. To help obviate this problem, obtain two sizes, one of about 6″ in diameter and one of 12″, using the larger one whenever space permits. A field expedient aid is noted under "Homemade Tools".

Punches: Punches of various types and sizes are welcome additions to any toolbox. Mechanics' solid punches or drifts can be obtained in sets of differently shaped tips. When hammer activated they are good for rough hole punching and enlarging, chiseling off dried glue lumps, burying nail tips, etc. Other solid punches include the office types for punching ring binder holes in single, double, and triple hole form. Constructed in a manner similar to that of pliers, the railroad conductor's punch can be found with different punchout shapes. I remember once obtaining parts for an architectural screen with one that had a diamond shaped punch-out. A useful set has been one including a lever-activated punch with top and bottom cavities to accept changeable pairs of mating slugs having different hole sizes, from 1/16″ in small increments up to 1/4″. Aside from punching holes for the hole's sake, the punchouts have made many wheels for built-from-scratch vehicles. For holes and punchouts larger than about 1/4″, you can get hollow, tubular punches to be used with a hammer against a hardwood impact end. Brookstone has a handy hole punch set (Ch. 50).

Razor Blades: Razor blades make fine cutters, choppers, and trimmers in light work. Get a supply of single-edged blades to give you a "handle" edge. You can get different size cutting edges by chipping with small pliers. Sometimes you can find these sold in bulk through mail order tool catalogues. Incidentally, I have never found use for the handles sold to accept a razor blade. Some other kind of knife has always done the job.

Reamers: Reamers come in different sizes, toothed for different purposes for deburring or enlarging holes. Not being much concerned with metal products in the model business, the few I inherited have not had much employment, but they are mentioned to remind you of availability for that unusual case.

Rollers: Rollers are shaped like miniature barrels of solid hardwood held in U frames at the end of a wooden handle. I have used mine for ironing out wrinkles in a thin lining of Strathmore paper immediately after gluing it down, and for any case where nonmarring pressure is required on a surface, as when sealing the edge of masking tape for painting or compressing a smooth cavity in urethane foam.

Rulers: Rulers bring to mind the foot long measuring and ruling devices found in the school room. For similar tools of more use in model building see "Scales" and "Straightedges" following.

Saws: With power saws available for cutting the standard model materials, hand saws will not get much use from day to day. There are, however, several types which should be in your tool box for the occasional special situations. A hacksaw with a few extra blades will make it possible to cut aluminum framing, shorten bolts and machine screws, reduce the size of a corner brace so that it will fit in the model, etc. A hacksaw blade stuck in a handle makes about the best hand cutter available for urethane foam. (See also "Home-Made Tools".) A keyhole saw (long thin blade) will cut a hole in a plywood model base in the absence of an electric saber saw. X-acto puts out a thin bladed fine toothed miniature saw for delicate severing or grooving where the necessary pressure of a knife would be too much for the object being worked on. The thin blade is kept rigid by a stiff spine on its top edge, making straight grooves possible.

Saw Blades: Saw blades were mentioned under "Machine Tools" and "Power Hand Tools" as the business ends of the tools discussed. Here we add jeweler's or slotting saw blades which are approximately 3″ steel discs with toothed edges for use with the horizontal capabilities of your mill with the miniature lathe mentioned previously. Be sure you get them with the hole size to slip-fit onto the arbor of the tool you are using. It is more economical to buy these blades as the current job requires rather than trying to stock up with thicknesses and teeth which you may never use. Over the years I have collected a dozen or more in decimal sizes, the smallest being 0.008″ and the largest 0.125″. On the mill you can gang-groove with two or more blades on the shaft with the proper spacers between. If you are duplicating grooves, be sure the blades are exact mates. A tip for more speed of accomplishment on your mill: disconnect the automatic feed and vernier controls and push the table under the blades, with due respect to the cutting capabilities of the blades and the type of material being worked on. You can make strips out of vinyl sheet with dispatch, for example, but with a block of acrylic, take it easy with small depth changes at each pass as you approach the desired bottom.

Scales: Scales are normally about 1′ (approximately 30 cm) long and made out of wood, plastic, or aluminum. They are flat like the school room ruler or star-shaped in cross section with six different scales provided. Whatever system you are using, English or metric, I think you will find the flat scales the most satisfactory with a maximum of two scales provided on each. I find it annoying to have to keep flipping my star-shaped engineer's scale, for example, to find the 1/50″ scale edge. An instrument which will get continued use is a small steel pocket rule either in English or metric designations. I have a 6″ (about 15 cm) one which I use as a straightedge as well as a measuring device with inch indications in 32nds on one side and in decimal intervals on the other.

Scissors: Scissors will be used now and then for trimming, snipping, cutting out patterns, etc. The most versatile are the pointed, straight-bladed kind in three sizes. Buy a good grade to get durable cutting edges and snug fulcrums.

Screwdrivers: Screwdrivers should include Phillips as well as straight tips, in small, medium, and large sizes. A set of watchmaker's drivers will handle miniature screws. An offset screwdriver combination will help you get into tight places. This tool has fixed stub blades set at different angles in planes at right angles to each end of a short steel shaft so that you can make turning progress by flipping to a differently angled blade. Plastic or hard rubber handles will protect you when working on electrical components. Extra long shanks will help you get into the basement of an assembled model site, and stubbies will avoid obstructions in close quarters.

Scribes: A scribe is any instrument used to etch a material surface usually by drawing the tool along a ruler or straightedge or by light punching at dimensional readings along a scale. The scribe material must be harder than the material being scribed in order to record the effort. Scribes are usually steel in the form of a shaft of small diameter (about 0.125″) tapered at one end to a long sharp point. A scribe is necessary where a carbon pencil won't record as on polished acrylic plastic which is probably the most frequently etched material. Dimensional scribing is usually just heavy enough to read. Heavy scribing, or scoring (Ch. 26), is done, for example, where you want to create a groove to fill with paint to indicate a window mullion or where you want to snap-break a piece of acrylic to size. A common scribe should be available at any tool supply house. Dental tools can be excellent scribes, or make your own to special size and shape as discussed under "Homemade Tools".

Shavers: Shavers remind me of household cheese graters. They both have thin metal working surfaces with many cutting edges created by raised edges of perforations. Stanley puts out a flat bottomed shaver that fits in th palm of your hand and is great for fast removal of urethane foam selvage. They also have a curved one for cavities.

Shears: The shears to include in your tool box are about 12″ long with heavy, relatively short, wide blades and a scissor action. These are for cutting sheet metal principally. I have also shears with extra leverage for metal snipping.

Soldering Irons: Since most of the soldering done in model building is on small parts with little heat transfer surface, you probably can confine your purchase to the small electric pencil type with a pointed tip. This is a good place to remind you that the key to good soldered joints is cleanliness.

When in use, I keep the tip clean by drawing it across a fine sanding stick. Thoroughly clean the surface to receive solder and use a drop of flux. Heat the joint area before applying the solder so that it will flow without creating lumps that have to be filed off. Use a metal iron rack between applications to prevent the iron from contacting flammable materials and burning up the shop.

Spatulas: Spatulas are long, narrow unsharpened metal blades, usually with rounded ends. They are held in wooden or plastic handles. Their stiff flexibility makes them ideal tools for such operations as separating contact glued surfaces and screeding wet plaster. Get one of about 12″ in length and one about one half that size.

Squares: Squares are a must. During every architectural job you will be continually checking squareness of material edges and of assembled components. With all the sophisticated control of settings on machine tools, you can be surprised by a chip of sawdust or an untightened bridge which will affect trueness of result, particularly when you are working against a deadline. The continual checking with a handheld square can prevent many a headache later on when you suddenly realize that that tower, for example, is crooked. Without being able to eliminate prechecked component materials as a cause, you can drive yourself to the loony farm trying to determine *why* the tower is crooked. The short check can be a long time saver. Being able to eliminate squareness of parts confines the cause to assembly. Two parts may have shifted before the glue set, your assembly pad was not flat, etc. A carpenter's square is good for checking model base assemblies and some large area layouts. The carpenter's square consists of two flat aluminum arms fixed at right angles to one another. Each arm is about 24″ long with measurement indications along the edges. This tool can also be used for checking verticality of a building, for example. When used for this purpose be sure the arm against the building is held vertical. Another candidate for the workhorse hall of fame is the adjustable square in two sizes. The larger one has a 12″ steel ruler which slips into a frame assembly which has provision for 90 and 45 degree positions. A thumbscrew holds the ruler in the chosen position. There are fancier editions of this tool — some with more angle positions and some with levels in a circular slide — but I have found the simpler one perfectly adequate. The smaller adjustable square follows the same principle with

a 2″ steel ruler sliding into a columnar handle at right angles and cinched with a thumbscrew. This one will probably be found in the pocket of your work apron every day of architectural model building.

Straightedges: Straightedges are a daily necessity in architectural model building. They give you straight lines, scribes, and scores. They can be clamped to a work table edge to form a solid backing for measuring instruments used to duplicate dimensions, to stop a triangle used to line a parking lot, or simply to form an even backing for assembly. Flat, 12″, 24″, 48″ and 60″ aluminum rulers will get more use as straightedges than as measuring devices, reliance being placed upon scales for measurements for a model. Odd lengths of aluminum from a salvage yard will serve well. I use a hat-shaped beam of aluminum for long lines on a model base and to check trueness of large base frames. Try to find one about 8′ long, drill a hole in one end and store it against a wall hanging on a nail. Flexible strips for transferring curves from drawing to model base can be obtained from Brookstone (Ch. 50).

Surface Plate: A piece of steel plate at least 1/4″ thick, preferably with a ground surface, will serve as an incontestable surface on which to check trueness of assemblies. A piece about 24″ square will serve as its own sturdy, home made table top, or mount it in a permanent location on a level tool table top.

Surgical Tools: Other tools besides the hemostats and dental tools already listed can be useful for special assignments. Ask a local hospital to let you sort through their discards. Your family surgeon should be able to tell you whether or not any are available.

Tapes: Tapes for measuring purposes are those that retract into a coil-containing housing, aided by spring loading. They are often called "Yo-Yo's". Use one to indicate cutting points in model base construction, to locate pieces of scrap lumber and plastic of usable size, etc.

Taps and Dies: These are among those seldom used tools that are a godsend to have around when you need them. They are listed together since the best way to obtain them is in a set which will satisfy most model building requirements. I have gotten the most use out of the taps in threading acrylic and aluminum for machine screws. This is true not only with respect to specific models but also during accessory additions to machine tools and other home made projects. Though you won't often have to make your own machine screws, the dies will clean up threads that have become damaged. Such a set is not a mandatory purchase. You could buy one 6-32 tap with a handle for acrylic model cover corner reinforcements, for example, or even perform the arduous task of cutting threads with the screw itself in soft materials. This is to stress the point of how convenient and time-saving it is to have some of the "luxury" items on hand when needed. In a deadline crisis you could easily spend time equal to the cost of the tap and die set, for example, just trying to find the one tap needed.

Telephone Answering Machine: Particularly when working alone, consider the jobs you might lose because you were out of the shop when the telephone rang. Without a secretary or someone else responsible, a telephone answering service or a recorder makes sense. When you amortize the cost of the recorder it is the more economical of the two if not as personal.

Testing Instruments: Testing instruments are useful at times when you are electrifying a model to determine voltage output of unmarked transformers, amperage drawn, etc. No resistance between two electrical terminals will indicate a break in the line. A combination meter is not too expensive an aid obtainable at any electronics store. Be sure you set it to the correct scale and AC or DC mode when using.

Tongs: Tongs of the ice bucket or vegetable handling type are excellent tools for handling landscaping materials during the dyeing process. They will also help to prevent your going home with hands of a different color.

Torch: A propane torch sold as a combination of a couple of nozzles and gas canister will give you a fairly wide flame for polishing acrylic plastic, for example, as mentioned in Ch. 24. For soldering, an acetylene tank, hose, and adjustable nozzle will give you a more pinpoint flame for single soldering jobs. The electic soldering iron listed previously is the preferable tool for repetitive miniature work. If you desire to braze, get a combination oxygen and acetylene system with dual hose capabilities to provide the required extra heat.

Trammel Points: Trammel points come in pairs as finely machined metal loops attached to pointed shafts. These are slipped over a straight metal or wood bar to form a bar compass which can also be used to check distances between objects or points on a model which has been assembled to the extent that prohibits laying a ruler or scale on the surface. The points are held in position on the bar with thumbscrews. One point should have fine adjustment independent of its position on the bar.

Triangles and Hole Templates: Triangles are clear plastic drafting aids with a 90 degree angle, the other two being either 30 and 60 degrees or two at 45 degrees. Obtain three different sizes of each to enable you to fit the space in which you are drawing. A large one is good for checking settings on table saw and belt sander. Hole templates are also clear plastic drafting aids which contain various assortments of traceable holes of various shapes and sizes. The arcs of round holes are useful for making the change of direction of sidewalk curbs at street intersections, for example, and an ellipse may be just the right size and shape for outlining an architectural screen component, etc.

Tweezers: Tweezers should be included in your initial tool purchase. You will probably collect an inventory of many different sizes and shapes during your career, but the first purchase should include a needle point, both curved and straight, and a flat tip. Long ones will help you reach into cavities, and stubby ones will help in landscaping.

Typewriter: As an economical starter, use the one you had in school, but plan to replace it with a good office electric for expeditious and professional writing of contracts and letters.

Vacuum Cleaners: A vacuum cleaner is a sanitation necessity. Two are a near term goal. One should be a shop vacuum with a large tank on wheels, and the other a small household type for more delicate cleaning tasks such as clearing model streets of dust and ground cover and for removing excess ground cover when applying it. Hold a piece of cheese cloth over the nozzle to save the excess. Both types will come with different nozzles for different jobs. The shop vacuum can be parked by the Pattinson Mill to collect contour cutting dust. See "Home-Made Tools" for facilitating alterations.

Vacuum-Forming Machine: This appliance is required for vacuum molding (Ch. 24) of small parts such as domed skylights. I was lucky enough to find a hand-operated toy vacuum machine made by Mattel who at last check had stopped making them. I replaced the hand operation with a small electric vacuum pump, and with the original heating coil left intact, I have formed many a small part. If you cannot find a similar hobby type machine there are more sophisticated ones on the market.

Vises: Vises include the mechanic's heavy bench type, the small, gimbal action base type which you can clamp to a work table edge, and the type consisting of a miniature thumb screw controlled clamp on the end of a stalk. Check with an X-acto dealer for the last one. In order of importance in my experience, the bench type gets most of the action with the gimbal-based one second. A pin vise is necessary for hand drilling with the small wire bits or as a bit holder to insert in your drill press chuck which won't close tight enough for the miniature bits. A pin vise consists of a miniature adjustable chuck in a metal shaft.

Weights: Weights are indispensable in model building, particularly in gluing operations where clamps cannot be used. Over the years I have collected various sizes and shapes of steel scrap without which it would be extremely hard to operate. I use them not only for gluing weights but also for surface plates, stops and weights for holding components being assembled, and for raising a model off the table to make access easier. You will probably find all you need at a junk yard. Pick up steel blocks of different sizes as well as squares and rectangles of 1/4″ steel plate and a fist-full of small steel strips. See "Home-Made Tools" for making your own weights. Common bricks are not heavy enough in my opinion, and they tent to leave dust, but if you happen to run across a small boulder of convenient size with a flat bottom, grab it.

Whet Stones: These are used to sharpen cutting edges and should be in every tool box. Get a coarse one for primary sharpening and a fine one for finishing. If you want to reshape a blade, do it on your belt sander.

Wire Cutters: Wire cutters are useful in electrical work, beheading and shortening nails and pins, and in any case where a snip will do the job better than a cut. From experience, don't buy cutters smaller than about 5″ overall. The miniatures in this tool category look intriguing but do not have the strength to cut piano wire, for example. You will

be cutting a lot of piano wire; be sure you get a cutter strong enough to handle the hard steel as well as stainless steel. I have gotten considerable use out of large cutters of a size used to cut chain link fencing. The leverage action helps in shortening machine screws and bolts where they are hard to hold in a vise for hacksawing.

Wire Stripper: This tool is an aid in electrical work, making removal of insulation much easier than using a knife. They will have adjustable openings for different size wire and usually a small snipper will be incorporated.

Wrenches: Wrenches at first thought might seem unlikely candidates for a model builder's tool chest, but they are used continually around the shop. You will need end (or box) and Allen wrenches for changing from horizontal to vertical mode on your shop mill and the latter for operation of a Pattinson Mill. A small Allen wrench is needed to change blades in your saber saw, etc. Allen wrenches come individually, in sets, or permanently mounted in handles from which you flip the desired size as you would a pen knife blade. Vise grips and channel lock wrenches are worthwhile purchases along with the original monkey wrench with its screw controlled jaw opening. A pipe wrench will help you assemble a Pattinson Mill frame, install pipe legs on a model, or remove the stopped-up trap under your sink. Get a small end or box wrench for your standard size nuts used on the model tie-down rods. I have found even a small socket wrench set handy at times.

HOMEMADE TOOLS

Since necessity is the mother of invention, there will be many times when your ingenuity will be called upon to develop a special tool or alter an existing one to aid in structural or maintenance solutions. When you can make a tool to have use beyond the initial need, the time spent is more than justified. Included here are some examples in that category.

Adjustable Angle: (Fig. 36-1) This is a quickie field expedient tool where you need arms with a reach longer than that provided by the one in your tool box. Cut two pieces of *straight* scrap white pine base framing stock to equal desired length, stack them evenly, and about 1″ from one end drill

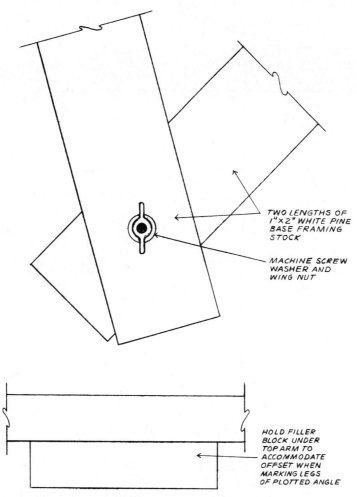

TWO LENGTHS OF
I"x 2" WHITE PINE
BASE FRAMING
STOCK

MACHINE SCREW
WASHER AND
WING NUT

HOLD FILLER
BLOCK UNDER
TOP ARM TO
ACCOMMODATE
OFFSET WHEN
MARKING LEGS
OF PLOTTED ANGLE

FIGURE 36-1   *Adjustable angle.*

a hole through both legs to just accept a machine screw. On the chosen bottom of the assembly, countersink the hole with a flat wood bit just deep enough so that the machine screw head and a washer will not break the surface. Use a washer and thumbscrew to cinch the joined legs at any desired angle. In laying out the chosen angle hold another piece of framing stock evenly under the higher, off-set leg as you make your indication. You probably have already thought of a more sophisticated version of this tool, but until you can get to improvements, fold it up and store it for the next emergency.

Adjustable T Square: (Fig. 36-2) You will note that I omit a T square from the list of hand tools, bits, and appliances. Though it might seem a natural for layout work, I have always used a carpenter's square and other tools instead as apparently better aids. Small, adjustable T squares of various sizes and configurations made up to fit a particular requirement, however, are a different kettle of fish.

Figure 36-2 shows an example of one made to help install shingle strips evenly on a vertical wall. The prescribed to-weather dimension was repeated on the sliding shaft by means of knife scores through punch marks made with dividers fixed at an opening equal to this dimension. In other cases you could simply box in a flat scale or ruler to serve as the movable arm instead of the specially marked strip of vinyl shown. To assure more accuracy in scoring intervals in the vinyl arm than that provided by the freehand use of the dividers, double-face tape the arm to your mill table and use the scoring setup described later in this chapter. After you have used such a tool for its motivating purpose, save it for possible future use, thus saving the time of duplication. The arm in Fig. 36-2, for example could be turned over for making a different interval for another job.

Assembly Box: (Fig. 36-3) As an aid in stacking building floors separated by their core sections

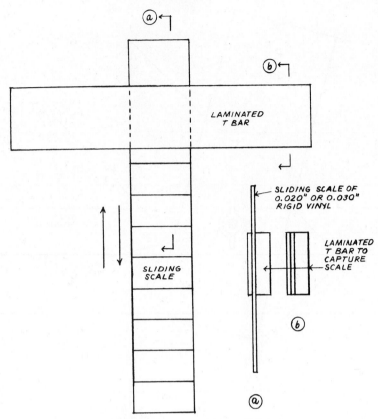

FIGURE 36-2 *Adjustable "T" square.*

make a two-sided open box by inserting panels of 1/4″ clear acrylic into grooves cut at right angles to each other about an inch in from two edges of a square of 3/4″ *flat* plywood. Use contact glue at the grooves and weld the vertical acrylic joint with acrylic solvent. You could use 1/4″ Masonite for the two sides, but the advantage to the plastic is that it allows you to see what is going on from the outside. The size of the assembly box will no doubt be governed by the requirements of the job at hand. Make the first box oversize to accommodate a larger model later on. This aid will help you also in vertical alignment of all sorts of subassemblies.

Auxiliary Scales: Scales can be made to satisfy any specific measuring or space dividing requirement. The auxiliary scale used in contour cutting (Ch. 10) and the adjustable T square are good examples. White high impact sheet vinyl (Ch. 35) is the best material to use. For the method of preparing such scales, see "Scoring Setup" later in this chapter.

Corrugators: (Fig. 36-4*a* and *b*) Corrugators are useful for making small scale simulations of "barrel"

roofing tile or corrugated steel building siding or roofing. The first one involves running paper through two lengths of meshed gear stock of suitable size and number of teeth as shown in Fig. 36-4*a*. I was fortunate in finding two lengths of gear stock at a specialty hardware store with "axles" already installed in the ends of 4″ pieces. If axles are not present, cut them on your lathe or drill center holes and tap them for machine screw axles. I drilled and tapped one axle for a handle as shown. The elongated lower mounting holes are for mesh adjustment and for accepting different diameters of gear stock. The bracket could be made using two standard steel angles instead of the aluminum angle mounted on plywood which was my expedient at the time. Turn strips of brown wrapping paper through the gears being sure to keep it straight. Spray the result with clear Krylon to set it and protect it from later painting.

Figure 36-4*b* shows an alternative where the gear stock is not fine enough for the small scales. With a jeweler's saw blade of scale thickness mounted on the horizontal shaft of your mill cut grooves at scale centers of the tile valleys across a small block of acrylic plastic. Mount this block on a plywood base with contact glue and cut another

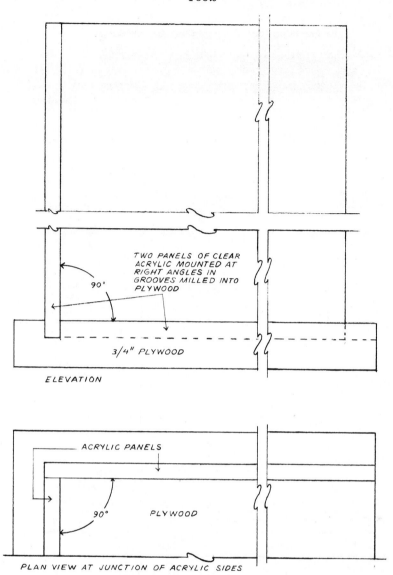

FIGURE 36-3 *Assembly box.*

block of acrylic the same length as the grooves in the first block. Leave this block loose but hold it against the first block as shown with a heavy rubber band. Paint a sufficient stock of bond typewriter paper on one side the tile color and cut it into strips as wide as the groove length. Hold a selvage end of a paper strip between the two blocks as you crease it down over the grooves. Starting at the selvage end draw a scribe firmly along the first groove forcing the paper into the groove. As you progress across the block hold the corrugated result with your fingers allowing the free end of the paper strip to supply the needed expansion into the grooves. Trial and error will tell you what scribe point to use. It should fit easily into a groove without being sharp enough to tear the paper. Your belt sander will give you the right point. Make roof

panels out of 0.010″ vinyl, and glue on pieces of the corrugated stock of the same size. Note that at 1/32″ scale, for example, the valley centers do not have to be *exactly* in scale to appear authentic. This allows a certain leeway in choosing a grooving saw blade from among those on hand. No one will argue about a groove a few thousandths too wide.

Cut-Off Tool: (Fig. 36-5) When you have a lot of strips of vinyl, for example, to cut to the same length, this chopper will obviate having to hold the strips against a ruler or scale for measurement, a process with attendant hazard of unequal lengths. Depending upon the size of the stock, you can cut several at a time to shorten the exercise. Referring to Fig. 36-5, on a base of 3/8″ or 1/2″ plywood measuring about 9″ × 16″, mount two pieces of

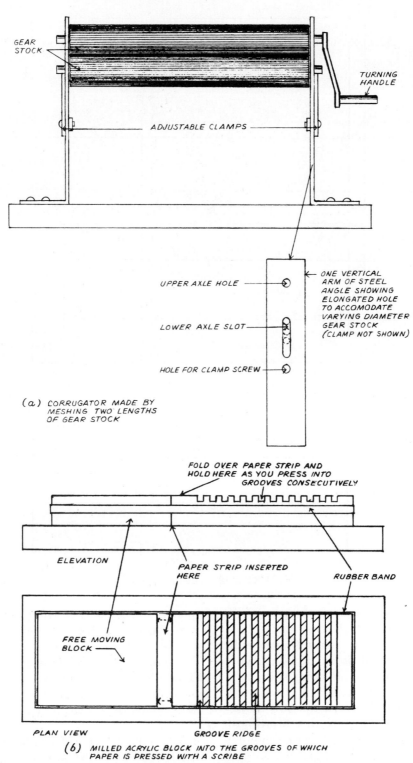

GEAR STOCK

TURNING HANDLE

ADJUSTABLE CLAMPS

UPPER AXLE HOLE

ONE VERTICAL ARM OF STEEL ANGLE SHOWING ELONGATED HOLE TO ACCOMODATE VARYING DIAMETER GEAR STOCK (CLAMP NOT SHOWN)

LOWER AXLE SLOT

HOLE FOR CLAMP SCREW

(a) CORRUGATOR MADE BY MESHING TWO LENGTHS OF GEAR STOCK

FOLD OVER PAPER STRIP AND HOLD HERE AS YOU PRESS INTO GROOVES CONSECUTIVELY

ELEVATION

PAPER STRIP INSERTED HERE

RUBBER BAND

FREE MOVING BLOCK

PLAN VIEW   GROOVE RIDGE

(b) MILLED ACRYLIC BLOCK INTO THE GROOVES OF WHICH PAPER IS PRESSED WITH A SCRIBE

FIGURE 36-4 Corrugators.

aluminum angle about 2″ high and 4″ long with wood screws. These will hold the bearing for the cutting arm and provide stability against side motion. A piece of steel measuring 3/16″ × 1/2″ (or similar) and 8″ long will make a good cutting

arm. Drill through the aluminum angles and the arm to accept a machine screw and nut for a pivot bearing. Drill and tap the other end of the arm for holding a standard mat knife blade with 6-32 machine screws. Flatten a short piece of 3/4″ wood

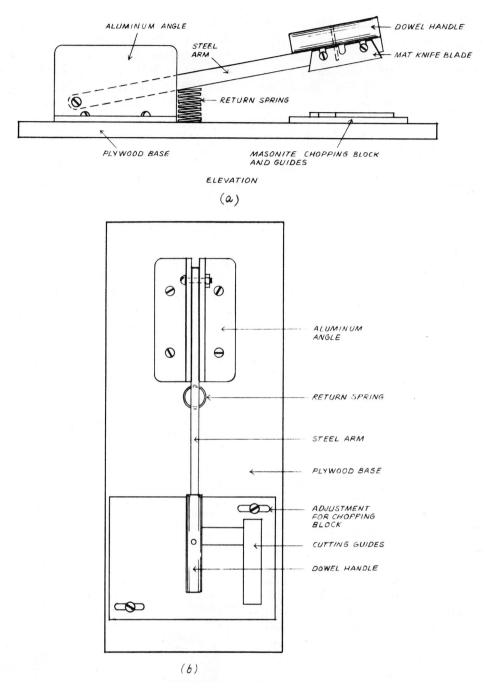

ALUMINUM ANGLE

STEEL ARM

DOWEL HANDLE

MAT KNIFE BLADE

RETURN SPRING

PLYWOOD BASE

MASONITE CHOPPING BLOCK AND GUIDES

ELEVATION

(a)

ALUMINUM ANGLE

RETURN SPRING

STEEL ARM

PLYWOOD BASE

ADJUSTMENT FOR CHOPPING BLOCK

CUTTING GUIDES

DOWEL HANDLE

(b)

FIGURE 36-5 *Cut-off tool.*

dowel so that it will rest on the cutting end of the arm as a handle. Contact glue will hold it, but for more permanence mount it with a machine screw. Underneath the arm at the front edges of the aluminum angles mount a spring with contact glue to act as an automatic arm elevator upon release. For a chopping board use a piece of 1/8″ tempered Masonite screwed to the base through adjusting slots to allow several positions before you have to renew the whole board. Shim the aluminum angles

and/or the cutting board when necessary to cause the blade to meet the board evenly along its length. For a particular job attach pieces of acrylic plastic to the cutting board with doublefaced tape to act as stops. Set the stops to provide products of the specified length. When gang chopping, use a small block of wood, etc., as a holddown to prevent the cut strips from snapping onto the floor. More sophistication could include adjustable stops, hinged holddown, etc.

Compass: For drawing large radius curves on as yet an unobstructed model base, don't forget the age-old expedient of nail, string, and pencil. Drive a nail temporarily at the center, tie a string to it, and tie the other end to a pencil. Wrap the string around the pencil and hold the combination with your fingers as you draw smaller radius curves with the same center. Hold the pencil vertical at all times.

Double Scorer: When you have the requirement for parallel indication as for a railroad track (Ch. 13) make a double scorer with two mat knife blades held in a sandwich of three pieces of acrylic, wood, or Masonite held together with two small machine screws and nuts. Drill the holes so that the machine screws will match the notches in the blades. The center spacer between the blades should be of a thickness to provide scale distance between the score lines.

Edge Scriber: This is an adjustable scribe which allows you to mark material a consistent distance from the edge. An example use is curb indication along street material where a concrete sidewalk meets a concrete curb. The score is made after painting to ensure against filling the score with paint. Cut the head off a $1'' \times 6/32$ machine screw and sand off any burrs created. Place the screw in your vise and carefully bend over one end to a right angle with the shaft. Machine screws are usually fairly soft and easy to bend and break. With pliers hold the hooked end against your belt sander to shape a sharp point. On the other end screw on two nuts, one of which will act as a lock when setting scribing depths. Drill out a small piece of wood dowel of convenient length and screw this onto the undisturbed end of the machine screw to act as a handle. If the length of the point does not permit adequate bearing of the nut against the material edge, shorten the point or place a washer with greater diameter than the nut between the nuts and point, adjusting the nuts to accommodate the thickness of the washer.

Gauges: Gauges are one-time home made tools made out of single or several layers of rigid vinyl or other suitably stiff material to aid in repetitive installations to the same dimension or spacing. A sandwich of rigid vinyl can be made to have a central layer protruding to the open-to-weather distance for installing roof shakes in evenly spaced courses. A strip of rigid vinyl cut to a prescribed interval dimension can serve as a fence post separater. A marked strip of the same material can give you the constant height of a building parapet or distance between traffic lanes. In such repetitive requirements gauges are easier to use than rulers and scales because they eliminate the continual search for the correct reading on the latter, and are conducive to accuracy because of the sequential use of one fixed length or single dimension indication. The adjustable T square (Fig. 36-2) becomes a gauge every time a new setting is made.

Glue Jar Lid: Contact glue will soon film over in a jar when left uncovered, making it useless until stirred or thinned. To help offset this during a continual dipping into the jar during a lengthy assembly of small parts, make a hinged glue jar lid as shown in Fig. 36-6. A shaped Masonite lid is attached with a small hinge to a shaped block of white pine held against the jar lip with a heavy rubber band.

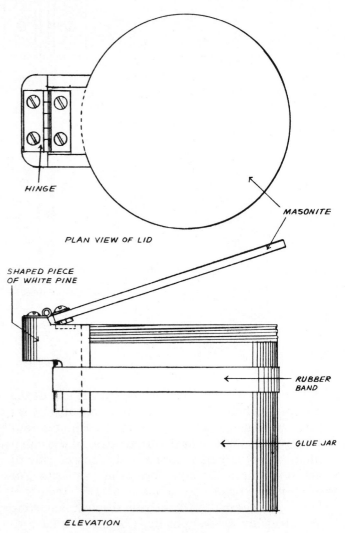

FIGURE 36-6 *Glue jar lid.*

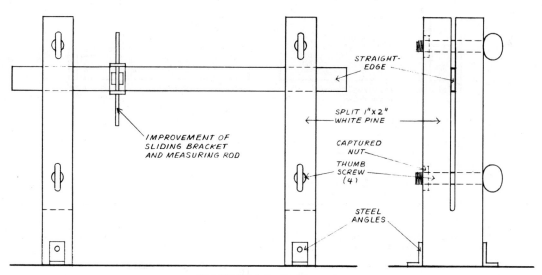

FIGURE 36-7 *Height gauge.*

Height Gauge: (Fig. 36-7) This simple tool can be used to check or establish the elevation of structures installed on uneven terrain. From your supply of 1″ × 2″ white pine, cut two pieces 24″ long from *straight* stock, and on your 10″ table saw, split the 2″ dimension in the center of each piece from one end to about 6″ from the other. The 10″ saw was prescribed because my general-purpose blade produces a slot just wide enough to accept a steel straightedge height bar. On the bottom unsplit end of each piece screw on a steel angle brace against each of the 1″ surfaces so that the legs of the braces are flush with the ends of the wood. These braces are to give one-direction stability while the mounted straightedge gives stability in the other direction. At two places, one near the top and one near the bottom of the slit in each piece drill 17/64″ holes through the 1″ dimension parallel to the 2″ dimension. On one side of each leg countersink the holes to accept a snug fit of 1/4″ nuts driven into the cavities. These nuts will accept the 1/4″ thumbscrews inserted from the opposite sides to cinch the straightedge height bar in place. If your longest straightedge won't span the model base, locate open flat spots on the model where you can place the stands so that the straightedge will be over the location to be checked. The straightedge can be installed at any convenient height parallel to the model base since it is relationships you are going to check.

If one leg rests on elevation 320′, for example, and the bottom of the straight edge is 15″ above the bottom of the leg, then at 1/16″ scale the bottom of the straightedge is at elevation 560′. If the top of the structure being checked is to be at 370′, measure with a ruler 190′ or 11-7/8″ down from

the straightedge over the location of the structure being checked (560′ − 370′ = 190′). If the amount of use seems to justify improvement of the gauge, make an acrylic slide for the straightedge and cement to this slide a grooved piece of acrylic to accept a vertically sliding arm held by friction or a clamp.

Locator Tool: (Fig. 36-8) As discussed in Ch. 8 you will be presented with the problems of locating structures on uneven or mountainous terrain where you cannot plot with normal drafting methods or accurately use patterns. To aid you in this process there are three plotting tools which have been useful to me. To differentiate, I call the first one a "locator tool" which is described here (Fig. 36-8). The second is a "vertical plotter", and the third a "profile plotter", both described later in this chapter in alphabetical order. It is well to reiterate here that since none of these tools is a precision instrument, be prepared with your notes in a court scene or other split-hair accuracy requirement to support your plotting by having used an alternate, back-up method. Both the locator tool and the vertical plotter can be adapted to check altitudes as well as determine horizontal locations. Exemplary use of all three was described in Ch. 8.

Note in Fig. 36-8 that the locator tool parts are first shown as separate, numbered items and than in assembly. The principal material is 1″ × 2″ white pine of which you will pick *straight* scraps left over from your base frame construction. This is the "wood" in the drawing which will indicate whether the visible surface is the 1″ or 2″ dimension by relative size. Heights will vary with the model, but for illustrative purposes 18″ is chosen

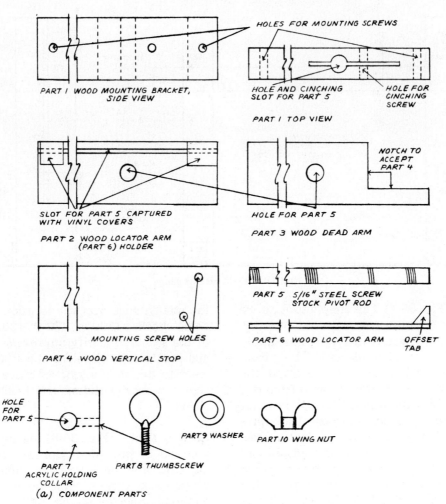

PART 1 WOOD MOUNTING BRACKET,
SIDE VIEW

HOLES FOR MOUNTING SCREWS

PART 1 TOP VIEW

HOLE AND CINCHING
SLOT FOR PART 5

HOLE FOR
CINCHING
SCREW

SLOT FOR PART 5 CAPTURED
WITH VINYL COVERS

PART 2 WOOD LOCATOR ARM
(PART 6) HOLDER

HOLE FOR PART 5

PART 3 WOOD DEAD ARM

NOTCH TO
ACCEPT
PART 4

MOUNTING SCREW HOLES

PART 4 WOOD VERTICAL STOP

PART 5 5/16" STEEL SCREW
STOCK PIVOT ROD

PART 6 WOOD LOCATOR ARM

OFFSET
TAB

HOLE
FOR
PART 5

PART 7
ACRYLIC HOLDING
COLLAR

PART 8 THUMBSCREW

PART 9 WASHER

PART 10 WING NUT

(a) COMPONENT PARTS

FIGURE 36-8 *Locator tool.*

as adequate to provide a reasonable vertical reach. From your supply of building tie-down threaded 5/16″ steel rod cut an 18″ length (Part 5) and trim the ends so that a nut will easily pick up the threads. Cut other parts to lengths approximately as shown. Your immediate model situation will guide you in this, considering cantilevered weight. After initial use you may want to taper parts 2 and 3, for example, to reduce weight and bulk. In part 1 (mounting bracket), drill a 21/64″ hole in the center of the 1″ dimension all the way through parallel to the 2″ side. This hole should be just large enough to allow part 5 (screw stock) to slip through without wobble. Place the part in your vise, and with your saber saw, cut a flexing slot across the center of this hole. This through slot should extend beyond the cinching wood screw (11) so that tightening this screw will squeeze the wood against the screw stock to hold it at the chosen height. Part 1 is screwed to the side of the model base through drilled holes (12) so that part

5 runs vertically through the relative bench mark location chosen on the drawing (Ch. 8). In parts 2 and 3 drill a 21/64″ hole through the 2″ surface. Part 3 (dead arm) will always be set parallel to the model edge and should be just long enough to enable you to set this parallel condition against part 4 (vertical stop) regardless of height above the model base. For part 6 (adjustable locator arm) use a 1/8″ square *straight* stick of white pine or bass wood. This will slide in a slot, cut on the table saw, in the top surface of part 2 so that it will clear the pivot hole. Note that this will require consideration of a fixed, measured offset dimension when plotting because the arm is mounted tangent to the pivot (bench mark location). This can be scribed on a tab glued to project from the end of the locator arm. Cover the slot with a strip or strips of vinyl to hold the arm in place after you have obtained a snug slip fit. On the top of part 2 (locator arm holder) scribe centerlines at right angles through the pivot hole. These will enable you to

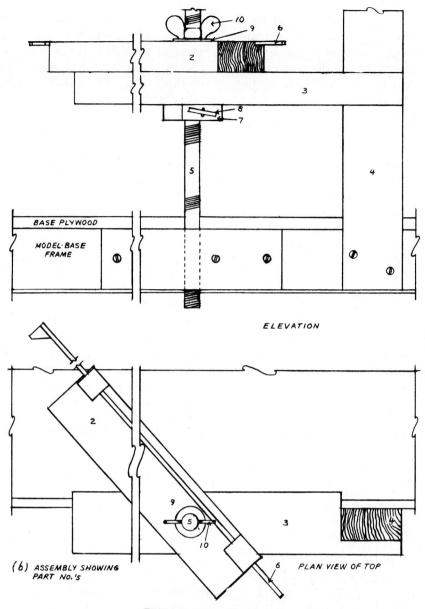

BASE PLYWOOD

MODEL·BASE
FRAME

ELEVATION

(6) ASSEMBLY SHOWING
PART NO.'s

PLAN VIEW OF TOP

FIGURE 36-8 Continued.

establish the offset from the center of the locator arm and also the distance from the bench mark location to the end of the arm or model location of the structure being installed. In the end of part 3 (dead arm) cut a notch just deep enough so that when bottomed against part 4 (vertical stop), which is mounted at right angles to the model base, part 3 will be parallel to the base edge. Thus, no matter the height at which you set the tool to accomodate the terrain, the assembly can be easily set so that one leg of the plotted angle is always parallel to the base edge. For part 7 (holding collar) cut a 21/64" hole in the center of a 1" square piece of 1/2" acrylic and drill and tap a hole

through one side to meet the first hole at right angles and accept a thumbscrew (part 8).

To assemble, screw parts 1 and 4 to the model base frame so that part 4 and the mounting hole in part 1 are vertical at the correct location. Insert part 5 (screw stock) into its hole in part 1 at the height to accomodate the highest point in the terrain including the plot area and tighten the cinching screw (part 11). Next, placing the holding collar (part 7) on the screw stock (part 5), tighten its thumbscrew at a convenient point near the top. Place part 3 (dead arm) so that it rests on the collar with its end notch resting against part 4 (vertical stop), and add part 2 with its locator arm. Lightly hold parts 2 and 3 together with the washer (part 9) and the wing nut (part 10). You are now ready to set the angle and height to enable you to plot the first location. As an aid in doing this, use the adjustable angle previously described in this section. After using this tool refinements will become obvious though not necessary to fulfillment of purpose. A useful addition would be a scale inscribed on the locator arm to obviate having to set it with a ruler each time.

Oven: This seemingly unlikely candidate for a model builder's equipment inventory can be very useful on occasion. In my experience a shop assembled oven has softened acrylic plastic prior to forming (Ch. 24) as its principal claim to fame. I found a home oven or barbecue grille that would rest at the right height above an electric hot plate in a heavy round steel waste basket. Keep an eye on your heating process or you will soon have plastic soup or nothing at all except a gummed up hot plate. To guard against drooping between the grille rods, place the plastic on a thin panel of metal such as a cookie sheet.

Paint Drying Hooks: These are convenient for suspending components which have been painted on all sides. They are made from lengths of soft wire hooked at one end with the other and attached to alligator clips like the ones you use to make a temporary electrical connection. You can hang a row of them along the channel edges of your fluorescent fixture reflectors.

Photo Lamp Stand: See Ch. 41 for construction.

Plotting Square: To accommodate reaches longer than that permitted by your carpenter's square, make a square out of two straight pieces of white pine 1″ × 2″. Glue and brad two ends together flush at right angles, guided by your carpenter's square, and glue a small block of wood in the vertex for strength. This tool can also help you line up the floors of high-rise office buildings, etc.

Profile Plotter: This is an exception to the category of tools of more than one-time use since it will fit only one situation. Where you want to plot or check the plot of an installation on the side of a steep mountain at the model's edge, make a profile out of lightweight illustration board or equally thin, stiff material as indicated in Fig. 36-9. On a contour drawing of the same scale as that of the model draw a line from the installation perpendicu-

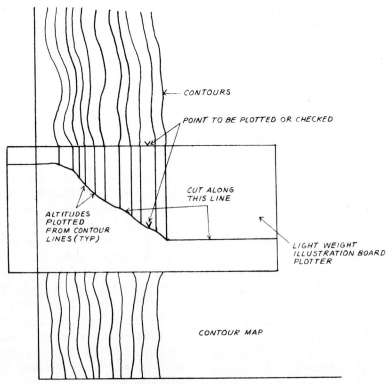

CONTOURS

POINT TO BE PLOTTED OR CHECKED

CUT ALONG
THIS LINE

ALTITUDES
PLOTTED
FROM CONTOUR
LINES (TYP)

LIGHT WEIGHT
ILLUSTRATION BOARD
PLOTTER

CONTOUR MAP

FIGURE 36-9 *Profile plotter.*

lar to the edge of the drawing. Lay the edge of the profile material along this line and reproduce the drawing edge with a pencil line across the face of the material. Hold the material in place while you mark on its edge its intersection with each contour line appearing between the drawing edge and the installation. From these points, using a square, draw lines on the material to represent the altitudes called out on the contour lines and the altitude of the installation. Join with a pencil the tops of these lines. The result will show the profile of the terrain at the location in question. Cut the material along this line and the top half will be the profile plotter used in Ch. 8.

Protractor Extension: This is more of a drafting or plotting aid than a tool since any straightedge on any protractor can be employed as the situation demands. Where you have a long leg of an angle to plot using a relatively small radius protractor, it is safer to place a straightedge exactly across the center and angle indication as a line drawing guide than it is to dot the center and angle indication and then draw a line through the dots. This is simply added insurance against error which is multiplied as the angle leg becomes longer.

Rowels: These consist of small gears of different diameters, thicknesses, and number of teeth mounted in handles for use in texturing (Ch. 33) or for making small equidistant impressions in a regimented manner by pushing them along a straightedge. Obtain gears from clocks and other mechanical devices. For an extra wide gear, chop off a length of gear stock used in the corrugator discussed previously in this chapter. The best handles are made of aluminum or acrylic plastic. Wood is usually too soft to hold the spindles under continued pressure. First cut a slot in the end of the handle to accept the gear width with a slip fit and just deep enough to permit spindle holes. If the gear has a fixed spindle, cut a slot across the end of the handle at right angles to the gear slot to make openings to the drilled spindle holes and insert pins in drilled holes at right angles to the spindle to hold it in place.

The shingle tool referred to in Ch. 33 is a rowel with a special handle to fit the assignment. Figure 36-10 shows a rowel for indicating shingles or shakes at the smaller scales where a reasonable representation is sufficient for visual authenticity. Find in your Jay's Nest a gear with teeth separated an average width of a shingle or shake and with a thickness equal to the open-to-weather dimension

at the scale. Insert one end of the spindle into a hole drilled to slip-fit size near the end of a 4″ × 5/8″ piece of 1/4″ acrylic. Round the end of this handle to trim sharp corners and remove as much meat at the working end as possible without weakening the tool. The spindle should be long enough to go through the acrylic to provide a firm bearing which will take all the pressure. To hold the gear in place, bend a piece of piano wire in a curve the size of the spindle, crimping this loop to clear the thickness of the gear. Hold the ends of this wire with a 6-32 machine screw and washer after drilling and tapping the handle. Note that the wire clip is used instead of another strip of acrylic to eliminate obstruction of line of sight to the point where the gear is scribing the shingles or shakes. Put a drop of oil or WD40 on the acrylic bearing for lubrication.

Sanding Sticks: Sanding sticks are among the most useful of tools and the easiest to make. They can be made in all shapes and sizes with any of the standard grits of sandpaper. They are used for deburring edges, sizing holes, and general finishing. Use strips of wood, acrylic plastic, Masonite, etc., to provide a smooth, hard backing, and cut them to a length equal to the width of the sheet of sandpaper. Place contact glue over one surface of the stick and on an equal width of sandpaper. When dry, place the edge of the stick along the edge of the paper so that the two edges are flush. Tap into good adherence and break the paper by rolling the stick against a hard surface, applying the glue as you proceed. When all four sides are covered, trim off the excess paper with an old knife blade. This will produce a sharp edged sanding stick. Do the same using wood dowel for curve and hole sanding, and glue a piece of the desired grit of wet-or-dry paper to a flat surface for the acrylic polishing process (Ch. 24). A sanding stick of the right grade will do a faster job on acrylic than will a steel file. I have used a piece of 2″ × 4″ wood to make a large sanding stick for the edges of a thick slab of urethane foam, and a right angled sanding stick with one ungritted leg to true up a vertical edge of the same material. Large dowel stock or architectural drawing tubes will make sticks to handle concave curved surfaces. If you want some help in applying sanding pressure to a surface, glue the sandpaper to one of your heavy steel weights. These tools are so easy to make that it won't be long before you have a bushel basket full representing all the many specific requirements of size, shape, and grit.

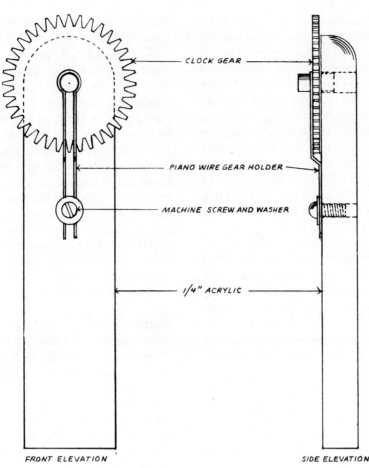

CLOCK GEAR

PIANO WIRE GEAR HOLDER

MACHINE SCREW AND WASHER

1/4" ACRYLIC

FRONT ELEVATION   SIDE ELEVATION

FIGURE 36-10 *Shingle tool.*

Scoring Setup: Whether you want to make auxiliary scales or inscribe decorative lines at specific
intervals on a material, the shop mill can be used to
obtain accuracy and uniformity. Remove the mill
head. Bend a 2″ to 3″ wide strip of 0.0625 aluminum to form a right angle with one leg long enough
to reach from a threaded hole in the vertical mill
stock down to the sliding table set at a convenient
working height. Drill a hole close to the end of this
leg and bolt the aluminum angle to the mill stock
so that the horizontal leg (to be used as a straight
edge) crosses and is parallel to the table. Cut off
the straightedge leg in line with the front edge of
the table. Attach the material to be scored squarely
to the table with double faced tape. Raise the table
so that the material just touches the aluminum
straightedge against which you draw a mat knife
blade to score the material at specified intervals.
These intervals are established by turning the vernier crank to move the table between scores.

Scribes: Scribes purchased as such or acquired
from your friendly dentist have already been dis-

cussed. This is a reminder that you and your belt
sander can make a scribe out of about any suitable
steel shaft with a diameter in the neighborhood of
1/8 to 3/16″, or you can reshape the business ends
of existing scribes. I have made various shapes out
of an old set of nut picks, for example. Sometimes
you will require a rounded tip for an uncut impression or a square one for a groove wider than that
made by a point, etc. Use a scribe made from wood
dowel stock for definition on a urethane foam or
soft surface.

Sliding Square: This is technically not a homemade
tool because I had it made outside to use with the
Pattinson Mill (discussed later in this chapter). The
tool (shown in Fig. 36-11) consists of an 8′ long
shaft of 3/4″ steel screw stock which is clamped
along the edges of a standard plywood panel-
surfaced work table by means of C clamps holding
two aluminum tabs or tongues protruding from
bronze bushed bearing housings holding the shaft
ends from which the threads have been milled off.
At one end there is a handle and vernier scale

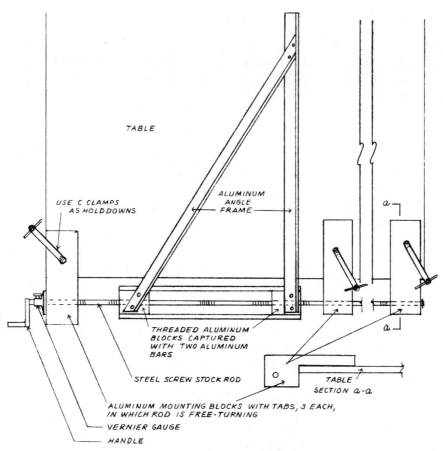

FIGURE 36-11 *Sliding square.*

marked off in thousandths of an inch to 0.050″ or one complete revolution. For rigid support there is a free-sliding aluminum block with tab which can be fastened to the table with a third C clamp at any convenient location. The shaft is turned through two internally threaded blocks to move an aluminum right triangle across the table top. The threaded blocks are captured by two aluminum bars 10″ long, the assembly forming the shortest leg of the right triangle of which the hypotenuse is riveted to form a brace for the 3′ long leg or straight edge side always at right angles to the table edge. The mounting is such that the triangle remains flat on the table top. A panel of acrylic plastic for a building facade, for example, can be doubled-faced taped to the table top and evenly spaced scores can be made against the straightedge leg of the triangle as it is moved by the vernier handle over the panel surface. To make the triangle rest flat on the material being scored, put shims of the material thickness under each C clamped tap.

The initial impetus for my having this tool made was the requirement for slots for mounting vertical vinyl fins on acrylic building facades. I used the Pattinson Mill table and attached a small high speed grinder motor with belt-driven arbor assembly on the shaft of the mill. A jeweler's rotary saw blade was used to cut the slots. The facade panel was pushed under the blade against the sliding square and moved the slot center distance for each cut. The depth of the slots was determined by the vertical control of the mill. Note that if the contour cutting ribs on the table top are fixed, keep a separate panel of 3/4″ plywood handy to lay on the top of the ribs for this use of the sliding square.

Templates: Templates, like gauges, are one-time plotting aids usually made out of rigid vinyl because of its stiffness and obtainable sharp edges. A piece of this material cut to a prescribed radius can serve as a template for inscribing curves in traffic lines, a curve in a fence line, or any curve where a center for a compass is awkward to locate. A template can be cut to reflect correct relationships between small scale buildings in a nonlinear grouping, an oddly shaped planter, etc. The template can be oriented on the model and the cut out floor plans or other shapes traced as a guide for installation on a site difficult to work in with plotting instruments. This is a good example of how seemingly additional effort can save time in the end. A universal template can be made to indicate duplicate window locations on several walls of the same model, cut to reflect a paving design in a building forecourt, etc.

Urethane Grinder: This tool was made by mounting a motor on a plywood base so that the spindle projects into a removable, open-topped plywood box. A hollow, tubular metal shredder is spun on this spindle against blocks of urethane foam fed by hand over a piece of plywood glued at an angle approach. With this tool you can get a supply of ground and tree cover with dispatch.

Urethane Mill: (Fig. 36-12) This tool (the Pattinson Mill) was made outside to my specifications to supply the increasing demand for contour models. Its success is evidenced by the fact that it paid for itself after the first couple of jobs. Figure 36-12 shows the mill mounted on a sturdy plywood-surfaced table on which the model base and attached urethane foam are pushed against a standard "long" end mill bit. The steel ribs on the table top

are to reduce friction against the standard Masonite-bottomed model base (Ch. 7), which for contour cutting is waxed. The 2″ pipe frame holding the mill can be made adjustable for height by mounting the vertical legs beyond the table ends in brackets each including a steel peg for insertion into one of a series of holes drilled in the pipe. A thumbscrew in each bracket would take up any wobble between bracket and leg. The fixed height of the legs mounted on the table surface with street L's and screws was a compromise to speed up getting under way after initial installation and has turned out to be satisfactory for 95 percent of the jobs done since. Extra height can be had by adding sections of 2″ pipe with collars. The hose from the top of the hollow shaft is tied to the horizontal frame member and routed to a Sears shop vacuum cleaner to keep the free dust out of the air. Temporarily cover the ribs with a sheet of plywood to form an unobstructed work table between contour assignments. I believe the drawings are self-explanatory. See Ch. 10 for tips on use of the tool and Ch. 50 for information on available shop drawing for constructing this mill.

Vacuum Cleaner Nozzle and Switch: The nozzle of

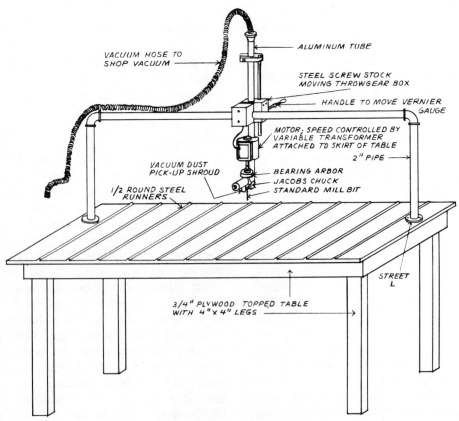

FIGURE 36-12 *Pattinson Mill.*

the household vacuum cleaner mentioned earlier in this section will be too large to allow close cleaning in small areas on a model where you want to clean up bits of loose foliage under a tree for example. Find a common bottle cork which fits the end of the nozzle or make a plug out of wood dowel stock. Drill a hole through the center and press fit a piece of brass tubing (Ch. 35). This smaller orifice can be reduced further by telescoping the next smaller size tubing until you have obtained the desired nozzle size. A little solder will fix the assembly for continual use. Add a short length of plastic tubing for flexibility (Fig. 36-13). To obviate groping for the on and off switch which came mounted on the side of the tank, I cancelled it and taped wires along the hose to include a small plunger switch attached to the base of the nozzle.

Vertical Plotter: (Fig. 36-14) In situations similar to the one described for the Profile Plotter, you can locate and check the altitude of installations near the edge of a mountainous area with a tool made from scrap $1'' \times 2''$ white pine and wood dowel stock. Drill holes at specific distances through the $2''$ surface to accept slip fit $1/2''$ or $5/8''$ dowel. Attach outriggers on the bottom end of the shaft so that it will stand vertical when placed on the base plywood edge or acrylic cover lip against the side of the model. Drill a hole near the end of the horizontal dowel arm of adequate length so that you can insert a length of $1/8''$ dowel with a snug slip fit as a marker. See Ch. 8 for an application.

This is the third of the field expedient plotting tools mentioned under "Locator Tool" in this chapter.

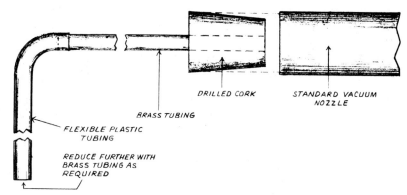

FIGURE 36-13 *Vacuum nozzle reducer.*

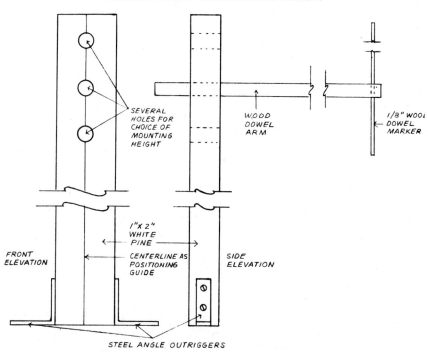

FIGURE 36-14 *Vertical plotter.*

Weights: Weights obtained from the scrap yard and field trips have already been discussed. For self-adjusting weights fill bean bags of canvas or other strong material with lead pellets. Make solid weights by pouring plaster into temporary plywood open-topped boxes. Use a dense, hard plaster such as Hydrostone (Ch. 35). To afford some protection against chipping, cover the dried blocks with 0.030" vinyl. For added weight, include lead fishing sinkers suspended in the casting box.

MAINTENANCE

It goes without saying that proper maintenance of all tools is essential to trouble free operation. It is mentioned here because sometimes long down periods of particular machine tools, for example, tend to bring forgetfulness. Because of sporadic use of such tools as your mill or lathe, it is not practical to "change the oil every thousand miles", much less keep a record thereof, but when you start up an idle tool, try to recall the last time you oiled it; listen to its song, and if in any doubt, give it an injection. A little extra oil won't hurt anything. Before starting up your compressor, check the oil for level and appearance. It will take only a few minutes and may save a frozen crank. Keep aware of the perpetual enemy rust. Use fine steel wool to remove telltale spots and wipe bare steel surfaces with an oily rag. Pieces of flexible vinyl or polyethylene sheeting will protect machine tools from dust and smog while in temporary hibernation.

37

Jigs

Jigs are assembly and process aids which can suddenly become indispensable when their requirement arises. Assembly jigs are usually one-time aids to fit the problems peculiar to a specific model. Process jigs, with adjustment, can often be reused.

You have already been introduced to simple assembly jigs such as the frames for the architectural screen in Ch. 16, the barrel roof in Ch. 20, and the hole spacing jig for column construction in Ch. 22. There is no point in describing numerous jigs in an attempt to cover the field. In the first place it would be impossible because of the unknown problems you will encounter in models to come, and in the second place I believe the more beneficial tips are those which cover the approach to solutions rather than the jigs themselves.

Assembly Jigs: Assembly jigs are means to facilitate putting components together symmetrically and accurately. They are particularly important where you have many identical assemblies to install. A jig can be simply two blocks of wood affixed to a base to hold the main component of an assembly in place while you add the details. It can be a system of weights stacked in such a way

as to permit non-damaging clearance for a partly assembled item while you work on one end, or it can be a temporarily nailed down wooden stop to prevent the assembly from sliding.

An approach resulting in a more sophisticated assembly jig will be exemplified by the hypothetical requirement for 50 lattice-roofed entrance canopies for a residential housing development model at 1/20″ scale. Figure 37-1(a) shows one of these canopies at model size and Figure 37-1(b) shows a canopy blown up for easy interpretation. Analyzing the structure which measures 10′ high overall, 6′ wide between posts, and 7′ 7″ deep overall, you find that there are two rough 6″ × 6″ wood posts, four rough 2″ × 8″ wood beams, and twelve rough 2″ × 4″ wood rafters forming the roof. The rafters are placed 6″ on center standing on their 2″ surfaces and extend 1′ beyond the beams on each side. The beams capture the posts at their outboard ends and extend 18″ beyond the posts. The post tops are 1′ above the beams.

In deciding the best way to make these canopies, there are three possibilities. The first method that comes to mind is acid-etching (Ch. 17) for the rafter beam assembly, but this is ruled out because of the layered configuration. You could

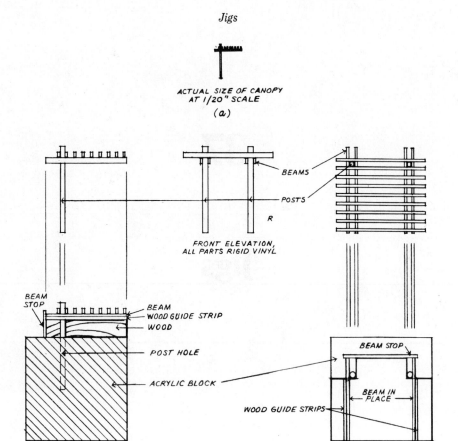

ACTUAL SIZE OF CANOPY
AT 1/20" SCALE
(a)

FRONT ELEVATION,
ALL PARTS RIGID VINYL

BEAMS

POSTS

R

BEAM
STOP

BEAM
WOOD GUIDE STRIP
WOOD

POST HOLE

ACRYLIC BLOCK

SIDE ELEVATION

BEAM STOP

BEAM IN
PLACE

WOOD GUIDE STRIPS

PLAN VIEW

(b)

FIGURE 37-1 *Canopy jig.*

have a single plane etched and add pieces top and bottom for the height of rafters and depth of beams, but you still would have to mount this assembly on two posts 50 times. The second method is casting which is immediately discarded because of the three planes involved not to speak of the small size and delicacy. The third or built up method is chosen as the most practical, using an assembly jig.

The next decision has to do with how much detail, if any, can or should be eliminated at this small scale to obtain the desired effect and to what extent exact scale dimensions can be violated in the interests of using available materials to save time. Since the 6″ centers of all rafters, except the two capturing the 6″ posts, results in a separation of only about 0.017″ it is decided that to keep the desired open feeling of the canopy roofs 8 instead of 12 rafters will suffice, increasing the opening to about 0.025″. With respect to dimensions, the overall measurements should be adhered to as far as possible to maintain the designed relationship between canopy and building, but no visual imbalance will appear if you use standard 0.030″ rigid

vinyl cut for posts measuring about 0.001″ more than 7″ square instead of the specified 6″. Who would question less than 0.005″ oversize in the composite scene? Also, the standard 0.010″ vinyl is only about 0.002″ thicker than the specified 2″ dimension of the rough rafters and beams. This minute difference would help to absorb some of the increased distance between the 8 instead of 12 rafters. Rafter and beam widths (depths) should be cut as near to the 4″ and 6″ as practicable, making them all uniform in length.

Though the foregoing decision making doesn't seem to have much direct bearing on jigs, it is recorded to stress the importance of focusing planning, discussed in Ch. 6, down to the smallest component before proceeding. In this case you can't make the jig until you completely understand the role it is to play. This necessary analytical process will become second nature as you gain experience and find that it is easier to do than explain.

Referring to the jig in Fig. 37-1, drill two holes all the way through a block of 1/2″ acrylic measuring about 7/8″ by 3″ to make a base large enough to handle without disturbing the assembly area. The holes should be just large enough to accept with a slip fit the 0.030″ square vinyl posts with 0.30″ (6′) between them. Cut a piece of pine or bass wood about 1-3/8″ long and 0.30″ wide to serve as a spacer between the columns. Back from one end of this spacer the distance equal to the beam overhang plus the column width glue symmetrically on each side a piece of wood so that the total width of the lamination or assembly block is equal to the rafter length. Across the end of the spacer glue a piece of wood to serve as a beam stop. On each side of the assembly block glue small pieces of wood on the surface to serve as beam aligners, and on at least one side of the block glue a rafter stop to assure evenly lined up rafter ends. To hold the assembly block loose in position, make a socket with pieces of acrylic welded to the base. Put the block in place and plug the bottoms of the holes in the base with pieces of column stock deep enough so that when a canopy post is inserted its top will be 1′ (0.050″) above the beams. A drop of acrylic cement will hold these plugs in place. Be sure the two posts are snug against the intersections of the center lamination of the assembly block and the two side pieces. Place a beam on each side of a post so that their ends are against the stop, and holding them in place with tweezers weld them to the post with a brush applied drop of acrylic cement. Using the guide be sure they are lined up properly. After installing the beams, weld the rafters across them starting with the two capturing the posts, then the last one toward the building entrance end, and then the middle one in the space between the posts and the building entrance. This will help you eyeball the spacing of the remaining four. When the assembly is dry, pull the assembly block carefully out of its socket carrying the canopy with it to be set aside for later tweezer-held spray painting. Note that the assembly block was made out of wood to prevent the cement from adhering the canopy to the jig, and that it was made long enough to provide a finger grip on removal without disturbing the canopy. This type of jig has helped me many times in the face of the requirement for many identical small assemblies.

Process Jigs: Process jigs are usually one-time aids to help maintain uniformity in sizing or shaping numerous identical parts. They can be made adjustable to serve on later assignments making them home-made tools like the cut-off tool described previously in Ch. 36, but for the most part being so easy to make, they are normally tossed in the round file following their service.

One very simple but useful jig (Fig. 37-2) is one where you obtain identical lengths of small dimension strips of vinyl by sliding a few at a time along a wood guide strip to a wood stop and chop them with a mat knife at the end of the guide strip placed at the prescribed distance from the stop. The key to accuracy here is to be sure all the strips to be cut are pushed against the stop each time.

When you have a number of piano wire posts or columns to make all of the same length, the wire cutter will create jagged ends, and it is difficult to obtain consistency by sequential measurement. To help this situation, sand flat the end of the wire stock before cutting a slightly oversize piece each time and place it in a frame as shown in Fig. 37-3 with the flat end toward the stop. When you have accumulated the required number of columns or posts, hold them down close together and glue the second end stop on the base to confine them. With tape, clamp, or fingers, hold the wire pieces in place as you press the jig against the belt sander until all pieces are flush with the edge of the jig. This will produce posts or columns all of the same length and with flat ends.

If you want to make half-round stock en route to roof gutters, for example, drill a hole to take a slip fit of the correct diameter wooden dowel lengthwise through the center of successive pieces of white pine framing stock 1″ × 2″ as long as your drill bit can handle. Thread these onto a piece of the dowel until you have the required length, gluing the successive blocks together as you go being careful not to glue in the guiding dowel. Pull out the dowel and sand flush two sides of the lamination lengthwise so that you can run it through your table saw to cut the hole to leave a hemispherical groove on one side. Adjust the bridge so that the saw blade *edge* is at the hole center

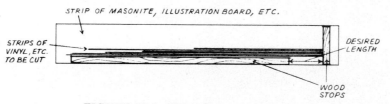

FIGURE 37-2 *Sizing jig—soft materials.*

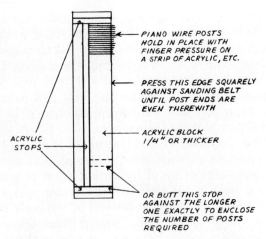

PIANO WIRE POSTS
HOLD IN PLACE WITH
FINGER PRESSURE ON
A STRIP OF ACRYLIC, ETC.

PRESS THIS EDGE SQUARELY
AGAINST SANDING BELT
UNTIL POST ENDS ARE
EVEN THEREWITH

ACRYLIC BLOCK
1/4" OR THICKER

ACRYLIC
STOPS

OR BUTT THIS STOP
AGAINST THE LONGER
ONE EXACTLY TO ENCLOSE
THE NUMBER OF POSTS
REQUIRED

FIGURE 37-3 *Sizing jig — hard materials.*

since its thickness will take that amount of material. Contact glue a length of the dowel into the groove to hold it temporarily from turning and sand it down on your belt sander until the flattened dowel surface is flush with the edges of the groove. If the assembly is not too long, you can sand it in a vertical position as added insurance against turning. To hollow out the half-round so formed, before you unstick it run it under a globe shaped steel burr on your mill. Unglue the product with the aid of a length of piano wire, inserting the wire between it and the holding groove as you carefully exert pressure with your fingers. Erase the glue left on the product with your thumb or use a rag wet with contact glue solvent (MEK).

To assist in soldering piano wire posts to the railing, lay out the latter along the *edge* of a strip of double-faced tape applied at right angles to post center lines drawn on a piece of illustration board (Fig. 37-4). The lines will be guides to perpendicular attachment, and the illustration

board won't absorb wasted heat the way a metal surface will. Acrylic is likely to be melted by the iron and might even grab the joints making the assembly hard to remove. Removing the assembly

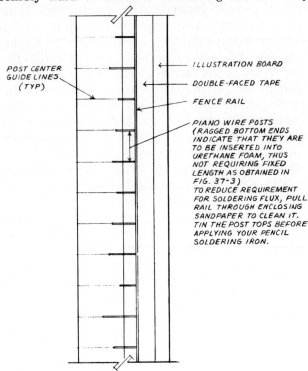

POST CENTER
GUIDE LINES
(TYP)

ILLUSTRATION BOARD

DOUBLE-FACED TAPE

FENCE RAIL

PIANO WIRE POSTS
(RAGGED BOTTOM ENDS
INDICATE THAT THEY ARE
TO BE INSERTED INTO
URETHANE FOAM, THUS
NOT REQUIRING FIXED
LENGTH AS OBTAINED IN
FIG. 37-3)
TO REDUCE REQUIREMENT
FOR SOLDERING FLUX, PULL
RAIL THROUGH ENCLOSING
SANDPAPER TO CLEAN IT.
TIN THE POST TOPS BEFORE
APPLYING YOUR PENCIL
SOLDERING IRON.

FIGURE 37-4 *Soldering jig.*

from the cardboard backing should be easy since the tape is holding the railing only. Another soldering jig consists of an arc of heavy soft wire with an alligator clip affixed to each end. Hold the arc in a small vise; place the parts to be soldered in the clips and bring them into position by flexing the arc ends.

38

Furnishings, Storage, and Sanitation

This chapter is intended as a guide to the necessary furniture, storage facilities, and maintenance items that for the most part do not have any direct bearing on model construction but which serve the day to day needs of an operating shop.

OFFICE

As mentioned previously, set aside adequate space for an office, preferably enclosed not only to keep the sawdust off your paper work but also for at least semiprivacy of telephone conversations and record keeping. A desk and chair are basic prerequisites. Durability is more important than cosmetics. You can probably find a reasonably priced used standard desk with a half dozen drawers (one file drawer) and a swivel chair. Anticipating future accumulation, get at least one four drawer letter size steel filing cabinet with lock, a small bookcase for your source and reference publications, and a typewriter and stand. A briefcase will hold your display photographs in loose leaf binders, and a metal waste basket will handle the never ending flow of trash, received mostly through the mail. Considering the size of your

shop, you may want to consider a telephone extension or at least a large bell that can out-ring the noise of belt sander or Pattinson Mill. Within the confines of your initial budget realize that you may have to record your first year's results from operations sitting on a stool in front of a packing crate, but the above items should constitute a minimum near future goal in the interests of convenience and orderly housekeeping. The convenience of such equipment as an adding machine, photo copier, and telephone answering machine can come later.

SHOP

Work Tables: Assuming that you are starting out alone, you should have at least two 4' × 8' *work tables* on casters, plus one in a fixed location for current drawings and whatever drafting you have to do. See Ch. 36 for a contour cutting table. The 4' × 8' size is good for no other reason than that the working surface can be renewed with a new standard panel of plywood when the original becomes worn out. Metal frames are fine, but my wooden ones have stood up for over 25 years of banging and chopping, so the extra cost is not warranted. At 5′ 11″, I find a table height in the 35 to 38″ range good for working comfort. To help in varying situations, consider making one of your work tables a few inches lower than the other. To hold the assembled sections of a large model of a South American racetrack some years ago, I purchased from a local furniture rental company some 30″ × 8′ × 29″ high picnic tables with folding legs. Stacked in a corner, these have come in very handy on various occasions. I use two of them set up permanently for handling urethane foam panels. A small table on wheels is usefully moved to the immediate work area to hold paint cans, glue bottles, landscaping materials, etc. You will often find yourself in the middle of a clutter of thimblefulls of about everything known to man, and working space is at a premium, particularly where the model covers the table top. A deep shelf along a wall will hold such tools as your 1″ sander, bench grinder, and paper cutter. Make or purchase a sturdy support for your surface plate (Ch. 36). Do your paint mixing, dyeing, and landscape material grinding in a fixed location on a permanently fixed table or counter to confine such messy operations away from the model assembly area.

Tool Stands: Tool stands can usually be purchased to fit the tool if they are not part of the package, but where you have to provide inshop manufacture, be sure that you build them with a good margin of strength and solidarity. I built a mill stand out of wood, using 4″ × 4″ legs and a double thickness of 3/4″ plywood for the base with a cabinet underneath to hold accessories.

Metal Shop Stools: Shop stools with adjustable legs are very satisfactory because of their durability. Because of their continual movement from place to place, high wooden stools tend to acquire loose joints. A few *chairs* and 18″ *wooden stools* will come in handy for working at the edge of a model supported by the picnic tables mentioned previously, supporting paint boards for spraying a number of small components, etc. A home-discarded kitchen seat with fold-in steps has helped to reach a high shelf and provides support for a tired back.

Waste Baskets: Waste baskets should be metal for durability and fire safety and should be located at each working area to lengthen periods of clean floor. A couple of metal containers will serve city waste pickup. Check with your local sanitation department as to size and weight limitations.

Fire Extinguishers: These make common sense and will be required by local ordinance. Check with your fire department as to the types required.

Temperature Control: Temperature control for a comfortable working climate will of course depend upon your location and type of building. As a guide, my Southern California shop in a one-story brick building is adequately heated by a ceiling-hung gas space heater with fan. My "air-conditioning" in the hot summer time consists of open doors with fans.

A large electric wall *clock* will keep you up to the minute. A *radio* or hi-fi will provide background music and keep you up to date with news.

Lighting: Proper *lighting* is extremely important. For working efficiency excess is far better then inadequacy. I use cool white fluorescent tubes in double 4′ fixtures which I obtained secondhand. Be sure to hang one directly over the drawing-drafting table. I have found an old gooseneck table lamp useful for small area lighting at the model site. A high intensity lamp was mentioned in Ch. 36.

Some regulations prescribe posting of certain documents such as Use and Occupancy certificates, Compressor Tank certification, Payroll information, etc. Tack-glue them to a small panel of Masonite and cover with clear plastic for protection, sealing the edges with masking tape.

Hang a *medicine cabinet* with mirrored front over the wash basin to hold basic first aid supplies. Install *paper towel* and *soap* dispensers. An 8′ folding *ladder* is necessary for reaching high shelves, installing light fixtures, and servicing the suspended heater in a high ceiling building. A small *blackboard* mounted on a wall generally visible from all working areas is a good place to record pertinent scale data, etc., during a job as well as a good place for visiting clients to "show you what they mean".

A *refrigerator* keeps resins and catalysts cool. A local appliance store will probably have a small used one still in good working order. An electric *bottled water stand* dispensing hot and cold water is one of the small luxuries welcome to thirsts.

STORAGE

The old maxim "a place for everything and everything in its place" really makes sense in the model building business. You will in a short time gather a collection of almost countless kinds of materials and tools requiring segregation discipline the absence of which can mean chaos. For example, store your landscaping materials within a system consistently maintained in a fixed location; label small drawers and keep only the described contents therein; keep small hand tools in specific drawers, etc. All this consistently maintained fastidiousness has a very practical purpose — *time-saving.* Between jobs put all tools back in their storage location, and all boxes of screws, etc., in the cabinet or on the shelf reserved for them. It is remarkable how a small tool can be "lost" within a small area. With best of intentions you will probably waste some time simply trying to find an indespensable scribe which finally turns up under a piece of scrap illustration board in the litter not yet cleared after the last job. When you are trying to make a delivery deadline, this problem can be a very frustrating and irritating experience, not helped by the fact that you have already accumulated a lot of overtime hours!

Materials Storage: This will generally be obvious as to method or container from the character of the particular items. A few things are kept best under refrigeration; some just stacked conveniently; some in sets of drawers; some on shelves.

Establish a corner of your shop as a permanent location for storing sheet stock such as plywood, Masonite, acrylic, and urethane foam vertically with segregating dividers if possible. Don't fall into the trap of horizontal storage of heavy sheets of different thicknesses. Next time you may want the one on the bottom of the pile! Leave 30″ × 40″ illustration board in its original packaging leaning against a wall. I have a deep closet with deep shelves where I store sheet vinyl, Strathmore and other papers, along with usable remnants of illustration board too large for a drawer. I have partitioned off an area to serve as a general catchall for scrap lumber, plastic, and urethane foam.

It didn't take me many years to collect a veritable olio of cabinets both bought and homemade. The resulting combination is not very chic in appearance but it is practical. If esthetics of furnishings concerns you, try to find an extensive line of cabinets of different shapes and sizes so that as you collect you can match units. I strongly advise the purchase of at least one multidrawered metal cabinet with as many drawers as you can afford and find the room for. The drawers should be about 8″ × 12″ × 2″ deep. Smaller drawered cabinets that can be stacked are also useful for your Jay's Nest contents (Ch. 35), as well as endless other

items. As you progress in your career, the contents of these drawers will become obvious; there is no point in trying to list even a sample collection here. If you maintain the suggested consistent segregation, you'll be able to go blindfolded right to the drawer full of baby food bottles of colored flower bed material. A secondhand wooden dresser is great for storing usable illustration board scraps, pieces of acrylic plastic, metal shim stock, strainer cloth, an album with pages separating leftover acid-etched material, etc. Get dressers with strongly made drawers. Some of the cheaper ones with heavy cardboard drawer bottoms will fall apart. Make cupboards for such things as boxes of screws and bolts one row deep so that you don't have to remove boxes to find the one you want behind. I have a double row of cupboards and cabinets on a discarded work table as a partition to separate paint, paint mixing, grinding, and dyeing of ground cover from the rest of the shop. It is a good practice to keep flammables in metal cupboards in the paint section. This may be required by your fire department, but in any case, an ounce of prevention is worth a pound of cure. Put up shelves just for the quart cans of water-base paints you will accumulate. Make these one can deep. The heavy cardboard file boxes are good for holding various organic twigs and branches for landscaping exercises. You can get these folded flat in cartons from your stationery store. Line these up on a raised shelf providing easy access using the hand holds stamped in the front. Ground cover can be stored as noted in Ch. 25.

Physical Inventories: Physical inventories of materials and supplies should be maintained in quantities compatible with your volume of work. You will probably never be concerned with the economics of "carload lots," so in the interests of your working capital don't overpurchase. It makes sense to buy illustration board by the 12-sheet package, a box of continually used screws rather than the six you need immediately, a stock of several sheets of each thickness of vinyl and Strathmore paper, and a gallon of lacquer thinner, for example simply because the practice reduces the time consuming trips to the store and the periods of waiting for telephone orders, but there is no point in keeping more than a couple of panels of plywood or Masonite ahead because of available storage space if for no other reason. Save obviously usable scraps up to a limit of the containers provided. Otherwise you can reach the situation where either you or the scrap pile has to go. You can somewhat ease the pain of throwing money into the rubbish bin by including, within reasonable limits, the cost of the selvage in the price of the job that caused it.

Hand Tool Storage: This is best solved through the use of a steel multidrawered chest with a lock. I use a Sears-Roebuck mechanic's two-unit chest providing 24 drawers including a deep one at the bottom for electric hand tools. The circular saw, belt sander, and cut-awl I keep in a separate locked homemade cabinet. Except for long straightedges and a carpenter's square hanging on a wall this is an efficient, centralized method for availability and security.

SANITATION

A clean shop is a much more efficient and pleasant place to work than a dusty and cluttered one. The distributed waste baskets should help you and your employees keep the floor free of debris. It is a good idea to have a midstream work table cleaning session during the building of a model. I have found it advantageous to clean up when construction has been completed prior to landscaping which will create its own mess with materials foreign to those used during structural assembly. Place cartons under your table saws to collect at least part of the dust, the accumulation of which increases the fire hazard. During a series of consecutive jobs establish a cleanup time each week so that at least the larger hunks can be removed from the floor. It is much easier to find that small component which fell out of your tweezers when you don't have to sort through a layer of scraps. Periodically have a thorough cleaning session during which you can vacuum all the machine tools as well as the floor, tables, and shelves. During a drive against a deadline, stealing a few minutes of time for cleanup can be a morale builder.

For personal sanitation change to work clothes when you return from a visit to a client's office. Shirts, trousers, and shoes will soon become paint-spotted in spite of all the concentration you can muster against accidents. Along with work clothes, I wear a full-front shop apron as much for the handy tool pockets provided as for protection.

39

Model Covers

Occasions will arise where you want to cover a model in progress which has been temporarily set aside in favor of one with higher priority, or you simply want to keep tool dust off finished surfaces while you are making components away from the base. Lightweight plastic film is good for this purpose. Save the plastic covers you get from the dry cleaners; cut them down one side and tape them together to get coverage. Where an installed high-rise building or other solid structure is not present to support the cover away from more delicate elements, make a quickie saw horse frame out of 1″ × 2″ wood stock to hold up a plastic tent.

POSTCOMPLETION

As indicated in Ch. 42, display covers are extremely important in protecting considerable investments as well as in preserving cosmetic appearance. Clear acrylic plastic covers have proven to be the best means for display protection of scale models. They keep off dust and protect structures, trees, etc., from accidental damage and curious fingers, not to speak of pop bottle and paper cup rings, and other sundry careless treatment.

IN-SHOP CONSTRUCTION

I have my covers made to specifications by an outside firm, but since I at one time made them myself, a few words about working with the material in this application might be of help to those who want to do the same. Considering weight and strength, 3/16″ thick acrylic has proven to be a standard material satisfactory in most cases. Remember that in Ch. 7, a 5/16″ lip is provided in the assembly of the 1″ × 2″ base frame to allow space for 3/16″ plastic plus 1/8″ free space to permit unobstructed placement of the cover. Leaving the masking paper on, cut the top to the size of the model's outside dimensions, using a plastic cutting blade on your table saw (Ch. 36). Peel the masking back an inch or two and polish the edges (Ch. 24). Lay this top aside and cut the sides of the box wide enough to provide about 2″ clearance above the highest element of the model. Cut the two longer sides the same length as the top and let in the ends with butt joints, being sure that they are flush with the ends of the side pieces. This can best be accomplished on a flat table large enough to support the entire cover area and by using weights to hold the sides vertical and in square position. Start at one corner of this box frame and wick in acrylic solvent (Ch. 35) with a pointed brush drawn along both sides of the joint, being careful not to let the solvent run away onto the adjacent surfaces. *Straddle* the joint with your holding fingers so that they don't contribute to a mess! The goal is to flow the solvent at least half way through the joint from each side to obtain complete clarity and avoid bubbles. You are in effect welding; you cannot wick beyond your first application. Refer to Ch. 34 for tips on handling runaway solvent. When the first joint is firm enough to hold, proceed to the next and continue until all four corners have been joined. Leave them alone for about 15 minutes and then place the top on dry to check the fit. Before applying solvent along an edge, be sure that the side is flush with the top the full distance between corners. Long stretches of side material will usually have a slight bow in them. With a spatula-type tool, work the bow out to a flush position, weight the area and apply solvent to hold the side straight. Continue around the top in the same manner and let the assembly rest in place until you are sure that all joints are firm. A good acrylic weld is almost instantaneous, but it is better to be safe than sorry before you flip the cover to allow wicking in solvent along the interior sides of the joints. If you cannot place the cover on the model at this time, peel off the interior masking, turn it over and leave it in place until you can accomplish the finishing treatment.

OUTSIDE CONSTRUCTION

In-shop cover making has proven to be uneconomical for the model builder. It is a field by itself and is best left to plastics houses experienced in assembly of three-dimensional acrylic products. The process is a nuisance side operation, taking valuable time and space from model building. Considering the time saved, obtaining your covers from an outside firm is well worth the expense. Experience with a local firm will enable you to

give them specifications over the phone. The cover will probably be delivered with a protective plastic firm cover, so you can lean it against an unoccupied wall space until you are ready to use it.

COVER COMPLETION

As soon as you reach a break in your model building process, drill two 1/4″ holes at each end of the cover near the top corners. These are for pressure relief during changes in atmospheric conditions or simply to allow continuous equalization. They will help prevent interior fogging. For added security, place chromium luggage angles at each corner at the bottom. These will help to prevent breaking of side seams during handling. I use chromed corner braces 1-1/4″ long on each side and 5/8″ wide, with a 5/32″ hole near each end (Ch. 35). Hold a brace snugly against a corner and scribe the hole locations. Drill and tap the holes to take short 6-32 machine screws so that they do not protrude through the acrylic. Using nuts would mean chewing up the edge of the plywood during placing and removing the cover. Place the cover on the unfinished model and hand punch mark with a scribe hole centers for the mounting screws. These centers should be 3/16″ from the bottom so that the screws will enter the center of the plywood edges. Start with a small pilot bit, drilling through into the plywood, and then ream the holes through the acrylic only with a bit just to allow passage of 1-1/4″ #6 plated flat head wood screws. Your judgment will tell you how many screws to use to prevent the cover from moving when the model must be tipped to go through a doorway, for example. On a 3′ × 4′ model I would use six screws, one in the center of each end and two on each side toward the ends. Countersink the screw holes so that the screw heads will be flush with the acrylic surface. When these operations have been completed, remove the cover and store it, leaving on the exterior masking or replacing the outside firm's plastic film protection until you are ready to button up the model for delivery.

COVER SAG

As the model becomes larger there is a tendency for the cover top to sag increasingly as the expanse becomes greater. When it becomes objectionable, weld a piece of clear acrylic rod to the underside of the top with a length to hold the top level when the cover is installed and as near to the center of the area as you can get without conflicting with model elements. Check with your supplier about relationships. A thicker top for more rigidity will likely do nothing more than add weight, defeating sag correction.

COVER SHAPE

A solution to a sagging top could lie in a curved or dome cover, but these out-of-square configurations, in my opinion, tend to distract the viewer and are therefore not satisfactory.

FABRIC COVERS

These can be for protection of an acrylic cover or for concealing purposes in an "unveiling" situation. I have had a local seamstress make these out of soft cloth, and a local auto upholsterer make a vinyl sheet cover for an animated flow chart mounted on an easel for courtroom display.

It is well to reiterate the importance of performing closing exercises toward the beginning of a model project so that they won't trip you up on the way out the door. It is far more satisfactory to spend last minutes dressing up landscaping or giving the model a last minute vacuuming than it is to have to drill cover mounting holes on the run.

40

Crates

Except for shipments across the local scene, where you can rely on a single, experienced handler, models should be enclosed in professionally made wooden crates for travelling. They are a must for crosscountry transportation.

As in the case of acrylic covers, I went through a period of making my own crates, but soon found that this was not an economical procedure. As do the covers, crates require specialized skills for expeditious execution. Their apparent simplicity can fool you when it comes to proper bracing and padding under specific circumstances. Taking time away from model building to perform an exercise almost alien to the profession is a waste. The experienced crate builder will know immediately how to brace and pad, leaving hand space for model removal, providing for easy access with screwed down top and sides, etc. I have used a firm skilled in packing sensitive instruments, so I have been able to put my models in their hands for crating and shipment without worry.

Be sure that the crate is adequately labelled "This side up at all times", etc. A few "Delicate Instrument" labels are a good idea, because some character will read "Scale Model" and not realize the care required.

When the result of your sweat and possibly a few tears, not to speak of a little blood, is out of your custody, you can't do much to prevent the shipper from dropping it out of an airplane, but with careful crating at least the insurance company will pay for repairs.

41

Display and Photography

DISPLAY

The display of a model is the ultimate responsibility of your client once it has left your shop out of your custody, but to complete your professional service obligations, be prepared to give your client suggestions as to most effective presentation. Be prepared to visit the display area, if necessary, though I have found that most of the time the clients already have the display areas prepared and know just how they want to position the model. Remind them of the points made in Ch. 42, Care of Models.

Line of Sight: One of the most important considerations is the angle at which the standing viewer observes the display. I have found that around 4′ is a good height to suspend a model of a high-rise office building. This permits an oblique view of the ground floor and entourage and a raising of the eye to see the top, a condition similar to standing on the street and looking up. A large, 1/32″ scale model of an amusement park, measuring 6′ × 8′, for example, shouldn't be more than about 30″ high to give the observer an oblique, overall view of the project. Trying to obtain plan views of such models by placing them on the floor is not very satisfactory. There are of course no hard and fast rules, since the size, the scale, and the location can vary to a great extent. Considering these factors, you can place yourself in the position of a spectator and arrive at suggestions to fit a particular case. I have made models for which provision was made to display them on a slope for better viewing by an auditorium audience.

Lighting: The general lighting in the area of the display is usually the most satisfactory illumination of a scale model as long as such light is bright enough to make all parts of the subject readily visible. To augment ambient lighting or to create a feature, floodlighting from directly above is generally the best method. Consider the danger of heat from spot lights (Ch. 42). Though an acrylic cover is accepted as an unobstrusive protective necessity, avoid lighting that creates spot reflections. For special lighting incorporated in the model project see Ch. 29.

Support: The majority of models, from my experience, will be made with a standard base (Ch. 7) and will be displayed on *separate tables* provided by your clients. If you are to supply a table, consider having it made by a cabinet shop enabling you to spend that time on the model. If the table is to be a custom fit support having an odd shape, it is probably better to make it yourself so that you will have certain control over the exact configuration. The most expeditious way to arrive at a neat and serviceable result is to attach threaded leg sockets to a piece of 3/4″ plywood and obtain standard tapered, metal-tipped legs from your hardware store. As the size of the model approaches about 5′ × 7′, the weight will require heavier construction. I have, on occasion, made legs out of 4″ × 4″ lumber set into homemade sockets to provide solid support. Trim the top edges with one of the strip veneers, and, if there is to be open space around the model, line the surface with black Formica or similar material to cover up rough grain. If the table top is to be the same size as the base of the model, you can make a *frame cradle* from aluminum angle, held together with corner angles and machine screws. Square off part of the circular base of a standard leg socket mentioned previously so that it will fit into the frame corner on wooden fillers bolted to the aluminum. The model will then sit on these fillers, one at each corner, and be contained by the remaining free vertical side of the frame. Some situations will require shrouding with a black cloth material around the legs of a table.

Another type of support is the *easel* which is suitable only for relatively shallow demonstration panels or three-dimensional site plans schematic in nature without detailing. The nearly vertical position is an awkward and unattractive way to present a display quality architectural model. Easels can be made from aluminum tubing and angle stock held together in A-frame configuration with machine screws and nuts. Be sure to connect the two A-frames or front frame and rear leg with cord or light chain to prevent the assembly from doing the splits at a critical time! Standard rubber caps on the legs will help prevent sliding.

Since model support involves only carpentry with possibly a bit of mechanics thrown in, your imagination can carry you beyond these tips to arrive at answers to fit your particular cases. For further tips on display area discipline, see Ch. 42.

PHOTOGRAPHY

Include this subject in your continuous planning (Ch. 6), giving yourself adequate time to arrange for professional photography when ordered by your client. I have usually arranged for the photographer to work in my shop, thus avoiding the risk of the extra transportation to his or her studio. The photographer will probably give you a set of prints for your records as mine has done. In any case, I have followed the practice of taking "quickie" shots to be sure that I do have a record before the model leaves the shop. If you are a camera buff with the necessary expertise, you may be able to satisfy your clients with your efforts, but where they do not know of your ability, you can free yourself of the responsibility by turning the job over to a professional. Usually 8″ × 10″ prints of publishable quality will be needed.

As an occasionally used aid in taking my own record pictures, I purchased a used adjustable movie light which I can mount on a length of aluminum tubing supported by an 18″ high wooden stool. I drilled a hole in the center of the seat and through a piece of 1″ × 2″ pine bolted across the two higher leg rungs. The bottom end of the tube rests on a second strip of 1″ × 2″ stock bolted at right angles to the first piece across the lower two leg rungs. With this light adjusted to correct height, I can create morning or afternoon "sun" for shadow effects.

Since the cover will be off during photography, be sure that surfaces are *clean* for the photographer, particularly during close-up exercises. Whisk off remaining bits of ground cover on streets, etc. An almost unnoticeable speck of dust on a 1/32″ scale roof will show up as a boulder in a close-up photograph!

42

Care and Repair of Models

DISPLAY

To protect any model, at least during the life of the purpose for which it was built, it ideally should be displayed with an acrylic cover (Ch. 39) in an air-conditioned atmosphere, out of direct sunlight and any other source of direct heat such as spot lights. Excessive heat will tend to warp structural components, particularly high impact vinyl which cannot be conveniently straightened out after it has been deformed. Heat will also dry out any organic material used for foliage and shrubbery, such as lichen (Ch. 25) so that it will crumble to the touch. High, concentrated heat will also soften acrylic resulting in a sagging cover.

If the model is uncovered, to provide completely unobstructed view, it should be displayed set back behind some sort of barricade out of the reach of curious fingers. I have had models returned with pop bottle rings on the streets, indicating lack of protection. Probably the worst hazard is dust, particularly smog-laden dust, which gradually takes its toll in a dull, smudgy appearance. It takes the life out of a model. If your clients want to display without cover, and they are really interested in keeping the display in top notch condition, tell them that they will have to give it a weekly dusting by some one who can handle a vacuum cleaner nozzle and brush with careful dexterity. See Ch. 36 for a special nozzle. Any ground cover and tree foliage material will tend to shed onto paved areas, and this can be removed with a vacuum cleaner. The frequency of cleaning will of course depend upon the effectiveness of the air-conditioning system and the traffic in the vicinity of the display. Light smudges can be removed from painted surfaces with a damp cloth and a drop of detergent, but a general dull appearance, which sneaks up gradually, calls for return to the model shop for complete refurbishing, including washing, repainting, and any needed damage repairing. In the long run, it is far better to install an acrylic cover. This should be done before delivery of the model (Ch. 39).

Acrylic Cover: Compared with glass, acrylic is a relatively soft material that scratches easily. Covers should be rubbed as little as possible to preserve their uninterrupted clarity. A soft, damp cloth is best for dusting. Finger marks can be removed with a wet cloth and mild detergent.

Scratches require special treatment depending upon their severity, and are discussed later in this chapter. When removing the cover from a model, it is usually a two-person job so that *vertical* movement can be maintained with each person supporting two corners. Beware of warping or twisting pressure that might spring a joint although some protection is afforded by the chrome corner braces (Ch. 39).

TRANSPORTATION

Local: Local transportation includes all moves not calling for a protective crate (Ch. 40). Remind your client that the base frame is susceptible to damage from knocks against door frames, station wagon wheel wells, etc. If there is expected to be a program of continual change of locale, consider making the base frame out of aluminum or place the wooden frame inside a protective metal frame. I have had a model returned for addition of a *steel* frame—a bit heavy but specified. Particularly in the case of a high-rise building model which at 1/16″ scale could be over 2′ high, warn against excessive tipping to get through doorways. You have provided secure anchorage (Ch. 19), but careless tipping can permit gravity to play havoc, depending upon the method of building construction.

Distant: Distant transportation requires the use of crates which are best made by professionals (Ch. 40). This will give assurance that the model is properly braced, padded, and warning labelled. I have air-freighted models across country and to South America safely, with no more than an amusement park Sky Ride car off its cable at the end of the trip.

REPAIRS

Even if it were possible to list every possibly remedy for every possible structural damage to every possible model, such would not be necessary since your own good judgment will tell you how to perform restoration, particularly if you made the model in the first place. Ignoring basket cases where you might as well do the model over, I will note some of the common wounds with remedial tips. These have been known to happen even with cover protection—perhaps *because* of the cover

which was carelessly replaced. The most serious damage can be done when the cover is removed for photography, for example, and not immediately replaced.

Structural damage to feature elements is generally the most time consuming to rectify, and therefore the most expensive. If an awkwardly wielded broom handle has swung against the side of a high-rise building, for example, and cracked the one piece acrylic facade, your client may feel the expense of repair is not justified particularly where the crack is camouflaged somewhat by mullions, spandrels, sun shades, etc. In this case all you have to do is restore the facade treatment. Cut-in mullions can be dug out with a carefully handled scribe or knife blade. Sun shades and balconies made from vinyl sheet and separately applied can very likely simply be removed and reapplied since the spring in the material probably held damage to broken seams. Paint-chipped spandrels can be cut and the damaged section replaced. If mullions were cut through the spandrels, then they are already sectioned for you. I advise resorting to careful patch painting rather than trying to remove a complete building side strip originally applied with acrylic solvent (Ch. 34) which created a weld. If the model is in the early stages of its display career, your client may feel that replacing the cracked facade is worth the effort. In this case, remove the roof and tie-down rods (Ch. 19) and remove the building from the base after first pulling out the fluorescent tube if the model is lighted (Ch. 29). Remove any wraparound corner treatment at the affected corners and carefully work a thin knife blade down from the top at each joint, using a little leverage motion as you proceed to remove the damaged facade. You may luck out! If the weld is too complete, saw the building side out as near to each corner as you can without affecting the good edges of the building. To cut the time of true hand sawing, consider running the whole building against the bridge of your table saw after removing all obstructing surface treatment from the cracked side. In any case you will have the arduous task of sanding off the remaining strips at the corner welds so that the existing surfaces of the good edges will be smooth and even enough to accept the new side. If wraparound corner treatment is to be replaced, you won't have to worry about minor chips and unevenness since such will be hidden.

If someone has dropped a coffee mug on a group of 1/32″ scale miniature (Ch. 2) buildings made from stiff vinyl (Ch. 35), you will probably find that joints only have broken, calling for re-assembly of the original parts and patch painting.

Broken cast plaster columns can often be re-glued unless there is too much crumbling. Fill with wet plaster, sand and repaint before you start hunting for that mold which may have outlived its shelf life.

Crushed railings and fences are best removed and tossed in the round file, depending upon their intricacy and the material from which they were made. If you do not have replacement pieces of a particular acid-etched railing material, try sorting out the tangle in the damaged strip with tweezers, tapping it out flat on a metal plate, and repainting.

Open laminations of illustration board as at the end of a street terminating at the edge of the model can be reglued with white glue (Ch. 34), weighted and then trimmed back about 1/16″ from the edge to prevent further damage.

A bashed in section of perimeter illustration board riser (raising the model off the plywood to accommodate subterranean facilities) should be cut out and replaced unless you can pull out the dent satisfactorily. Try drilling a hole in the center of the dent and pulling the material out. Fill the hole with spackle (Ch. 35). Unfortunately, the cardboard will tend to remember the shape the accident caused, unlike the metal in a dented car fender. If the surface is not too chopped up against filling and repainting, and the damage is near the end of one side, consider carefully peeling back the entire top lamination of illustration board, inserting a new peeled section against wooden stops top and bottom, and then replacing the peeled off layer with white glue. This will hide the joints of the patch.

Minor damage to base frames seems inevitable, occurring mostly from contact with door frames. If chips and gouges on the flat surface are too shallow to hold spackle, drill small holes at these points to provide a binding condition. Fill, let dry, sand, and paint. Don't try open-sided fills of spackle at corners. It will chip out. Rather than this, cut out square sections and fill with pieces of the same wood. When the joints are dry, sand off the extra wood to a flush surface, fill any joint cracks with spackle, and repaint. This method is also good along top and bottom edges where an unsupported filler would tend to crumble out.

If the chips from damaged urethane foam are not available or cannot be glued back neatly, cut out square cavities around the damaged areas and fill with pieces of scrap urethane to fit snugly. If it is a display model with the open contours filled, ground cover may be in order to hide the joints that repainting will at least camouflage.

Separation of materials such as wood and cardboard glued with white glue (Ch. 34) is, for all practical purposes, impossible without severe damage to both surfaces. White glue is ineffective with nonabsorbing surfaces, so we have two good reasons to use contact glue as a general adhesive. If you have to separate the contact-glued joint between the layer of grading material and the base liner in model A (Ch. 9) for example, because the layer was not properly oriented on first contact, carefully pull the material as you cut the glue with a knife. Taking your time, you should be able to separate the surfaces without too serious an effect thereon. Then remove small lumps of glue with tweezers and a knife, aided if necessary by a sponged on application of glue solvent (Ch. 34). Bubbles which appear in Strathmore paper lining, for example, because of damp weather conditions and lack of glue coverage can be flattened out by slitting with a razor blade, inserting glue in the opening, and then rolling the surface. A hypodermic needle injecting glue at each bubble will cause less surface disturbance than the razor blade. The best remedy for this situation is to be sure to obtain complete adhesive coverage in the first place, and, where texture-permissible, to use a nonabsorbent material such as vinyl instead of paper.

Acrylic cover repair is limited to scratch removal and possibly resealing of joints that did not weld sufficiently. A broken cover must be done over unless your client can stand a welded piece broken out of a side edge. There is no way to hide the joint. Depending upon their severity, minor surface scratches can be rubbed out with finger pressure behind a wet rag dipped in a mild abrasive such as Dr. Lyon's tooth powder. Remember that you are removing material when you remove a scratch. If the scratch is deep, there will be a resulting depression in the surface, usually not as objectionable as the scratch. As scratches become deeper, use wet-and-dry sandpaper first, starting with the coarser grades and winding up with a very fine grade prior to polishing. See Ch. 24 for further details.

Cracked acrylic bodies of water should be replaced as there is no satisfactory way to camouflage joints. Cracked resin calls for removal and re-pouring of the lake or ocean. If the resin is opaque, you might get away with a carefully poured and disturbed patch over the surface side of the crack, but usually the depth of the crack will give you away.

REFURBISHING

After all repairs have been made to a damaged model, the next step is refurbishing which involves vacuuming, cleaning, painting, and restoration of landscaping.

Vacuuming: Vacuuming should be done first to remove all loose matter and reveal the fixed dirt to be washed off or covered with paint. Vacuum cleaning is rather a simple, basic operation, but there is a certain knack required peculiar to scale model cleaning. Generally you won't have much use for the fixed end of the hose because of its diameter. Start with the crevice tool (Ch. 36) keeping it *close to but away from* all the street surfaces, parking lots and other open areas including ground cover "planting". Carefully move the tool into spaces between houses and up over roofs, etc., to the extent that the size of the nozzle allows without scraping delicate structure or sucking up trees. Use the special nozzle (Ch. 36) for getting into all the minute pockets and around tree trunks, etc., being careful not to remove shrubbery and tree foliage. No matter how conscientiously dispersed and glued down, there will always be a small amount of shedding of ground cover material. When you remove the excess after the initial application, you could probably save it in some sort of netting over the nozzle, but here the small amount picked up wouldn't be worth the effort of saving, particularly since it is probably dirty.

Cleaning: Cleaning requires more judgment than soap. The latex and vinyl paints (Ch. 32) are washable with mild detergents, but think before you apply the "scrub brush". It may be easy to clean a complete section of street to even out appearance after creating a clean spot by removing a greasy smudge, but no one may ever notice that all those roofs, for example, are covered with smog. They may be a slightly different shade than the one you delivered, but they are all the same. A clean roof slope could stand out like a sore thumb in a housing development, requiring a time consuming task of cleaning *every* roof with its hard to reach valleys. This is not to say that you can ignore dirt to the detriment of a display, but that you should view the model with your clients and let them know that unless you remove every car, a "cleaned" parking lot may show every one sitting on an obvious dirty spot. Reach a meeting of minds before you embark on a "federal project" for which

you might have a hard time obtaining compensation. Use clean, damp rags with the mild detergent, and mop up with clean, damp rags only. Clean acrylic with the cleaner supplied by your plastics source (Ch. 35). Beware of anything stronger than alcohol when removing spots of unknown origin. Carefully applied contact glue solvent will remove minor visible glue missed before original delivery (Ch. 34). Wash the windows of your high-rise building with Q-Tips immersed in acrylic cleaner.

Painting: Painting should be done sparingly, with the same approach you took to cleaning. Don't repaint any more than necessary, since one stroke of the brush can snowball into an otherwise unnecessary complete new paint job. Carefully wet-and-dry sand the edges of chipped "holes" before filling with paint. On streets, parking lots, and sidewalks, you can most of the time blend a patch into the entourage by feather dry-brushing (Ch. 32). Touch up minute areas such as window mullions with a small, pointed brush, using as little paint as possible, or you will wind up with lumps which look worse than the chip. Let any paint on the windows dry before removing with a pointed or chiselled piece of wood. A Q-Tip applied to wet paint may smear it into the window frames making pristine appearance impossible.

When repainting of the model has been accomplished, repaint the base frame at least enough to cover the patches discussed previously under structural damage. Unless you are sure you can mask sufficiently with a handheld shield of cardboard, apply matte black latex instead of trying to spray Krylon (Ch. 32). The prospect of inadvertently spraying the model with black paint can give you nightmares!

Landscaping: Landscaping restoration can probably be limited to recovering "worn" areas of ground cover with new material and restoring or replacing damaged trees. If you made the mistake of using organic lichen which has dried out, replace it. I have had moderate success with shielded atomizer sprays of glycerine (Ch. 35) to "moisturize" lichen bushes, but it is hardly worth the effort. The metal armatures of trees squashed by cover replacement can usually be reformed with tweezers and recovered, but broken organic tree trunks (garden twigs) should be tossed in the round file and the complete tree replaced. About the only relatively short way to restore a landscape dulled by dust and smog is an overspray of the paint used originally. Areas of unobstructed ground cover can be brightened up with a fine spray of neutral green, being sure to shield the rest of the model. The better way, of course, is to scrape off the old ground cover, vacuum and replace with new. Pull each tree out individually, spray the foliage with its original color, and replace the tree immediately in its indicated spot. *Again, spray sparingly.* Just a mist will offset the "smoggy" appearance. See Ch. 25 for a more complete discussion of landscaping treatments.

In closing this section an important admonition from my experience is to insist that a damaged model be returned to your shop for repairs. I lucked out on my repair trip to Honolulu, for example (Ch. 19), because I had the use of another model builder's facilities, but nine times out of ten, no matter the anticipation, your traveling tool kit will lack at least one important item. Also, handling paints and glue at an upholstered display location is a bit precarious to say the least not to speak of the disconcerting effect on your nervous system. If your client insists, and you cannot get a reliable description of the damage, make a local inspection trip without tools and take it from there. After all, it would be a bit awkward to take your belt sander to the site.

43

Reference Library

Establish one or more loose-leaf folders to contain accumulated pamphlets, folders, and catalogues covering instructions and source lists with respect to materials, supplies, and equipment pertinent to shop operations. These would include instructions for resin casting, mold making, athletic field and court dimensions, accessory sources, electrical supply items with their component ratings and capabilities, etc. Each time you receive a pertinent catalog or buy a material that comes with instructions, place these in the proper binder for future reference. A year later it is often hard to remember proportions, drying times, and other critical information necessary to the proper use of a particular product. This is a good way to file machine instructions also. I have often had to refer back to instructions as to proper maintenance, adjustments, etc., with respect to power tools and equipment.

Construction manuals, trigonometric tables, and books on geometry, chemistry and physics have been useful. Also useful is a small loose-leaf binder with alphabetical index in which to glue business cards of suppliers. Enter these alphabetically by *subject* or *product* rather than by company name. If you have forgotten the name or location of your last supplier of commercial dyes, for example, find it under "D".

Purchase at least one good, complete book on trees and one covering shrubs. These will be invaluable in showing characteristic configuration, color and size in your struggle for authenticity. They also will enable you to trace trees and shrubs listed by Latin names in landscape architects' drawings. There are good books on landscaping model railroad layouts. Though you wouldn't want to follow all the hobbyist's directions, you may find good ideas to incorporate into your procedure.

Include decimal equivalent tables, metric conversion tables, and screw and bolt size schedules.

Refer to the Appendix, Ch. 50, for a few established names and sources.

44

Time Estimates

Assuming integrity of product, including consistent high quality, a reasonable price structure, and good working relations with your clients, the most important key to financial success lies in your estimates of time necessary for completion of model projects. This may sound elementary, but, from experience, it is easy to underestimate time in your desire to get the job. This is particularly true during your first years in the profession. On a going concern basis, all you should want is to be paid for your time and material — no more, no less.

After 25 years' experience, time estimates are still more difficult for me than model building. Unless you have to build duplicate models, as I have done on occasion because they had to be in different places at the same time, every model will be different from the last one. Every model has its own particular problems, simple or complicated; so all you can do is to base your estimate of time on experience with that *type* of model. There is no magic formula. You can't be guided, for example, by a current cost per square foot figure resulting from the economics of building construction. The time elements have no relation to model building. All you can do is to study the drawings in the light of the client's requirements, come up with a reasonable *monetary* time estimate for budget purposes,

and then ask for more *working* time, if possible, to cover the unknown. If it is your first model, and you have no friendly guidance from your guru, make a guess and hope! I will never forget the case of my first model, a church with interior, which of course took many more hours to complete than novicely estimated. When this was noted by my client, he advised me that I should learn to work faster. This was a stupid remark, particularly under the circumstances, and it is mentioned only to point out that no matter what your expertise and experience, there is no fast way to put out a high quality architectural scale model. You cannot pour an olio of materials into an automatic screw machine and expect a finished model to come out the other end. Most architectural clients will understand this, but expect to find clients who don't. True, there are faster methods which you will learn as you gain experience with materials, tool use, etc., but remember that with all the sophisticated help of modern power tools, scale model building is still hand work and takes time accordingly. No one yet has programmed a scale model into a computer to produce the three-dimensional object sitting on the conference room table, and no one is likely to in your life time.

From the drawings, break the job into separate

processes some of which may be very similar to those in a job for which you have detailed time cards on file (Ch. 46). You should know from experience fairly accurately how long it will take you to make the base. Look for components and facilities you have built in the past, considering the difference in form, texture, etc. Ask yourself, for example, if you should construct the railings or use acid-etched material, use one half a beach ball for that dome roof or have it spun, pour the ocean or use acrylic, use organic twigs for those trees or metal armatures, contour cut urethane foam or use one of the structural methods for grading (Ch. 9). Answers to such questions will help you arrive at a total estimated time, guided by past experience and possibly supported by time cards. Where removable roofs and interiors are required, initially accept the premise that such will at least *double* the time necessary for an exterior only model. Consider the extra time and costs of lighting. This requirement alone can double the time because of the engineering for installing ventilation, wire routing, etc.

When studying the drawings, keep yourself forewarned that there is likely "a snake in every barrel". Look for time consuming knotty problems such as complicated textures, structural situations with hard-to-hide model support, compound curves, etc. Some relatively insignificant but necessary component may take as long as all the others put together. There will be solutions, but it will take *time* to effect them. Beware of verbal oversimplification on the part of your clients. They are familiar with the job, and it is human nature to play down any apparent complications of structure. You are the expert in your field and know what you have to do to place a concept in three-dimensional form, so *study the drawings* and avoid the traps hidden therein! Be sure there are no additional required details to be supplied later.

If an announced deadline obviously will not permit enough time to complete a model properly, back off and save yourself a wrecked nervous system, not to speak of a possibly below par model because of the rush. A bit of overtime once in a while is in order in your effort to perfect a result, but pressure at 4 AM is for the birds and injurious to the results. Try to pin the clients down as to the seriousness of their "deadline". I have strained every fiber to complete a model for shipment across country, only to discover later that the model sat in its crate for two weeks before being shown. The model is apparently important to a display or your client wouldn't be spending money on it, so consideration should be given to the possibility that the deadline meeting could be postponed.

When you have established yourself as an honest operator who doesn't drag his or her feet and always endeavors to produce a model as expeditiously as possible, you may be fortunate enough to get a job on a time and material basis. This is ideal from the model builder's point of view, but hard to come by because, even though the clients are convinced of your integrity, they are probably controlled by a budget that demands a fixed price. This of course demands a fixed time estimate on your part. Some times you can work on a time and material basis with time and material accumulated to a maximum.

Always be prepared to give a little time. It is one of the hazards of the profession. It is far better in the long run to spend a few days more than your original estimate to produce your best effort than it is to slap a model together at the last minute. The results of such "rush" procedure are obvious. You can't of course make a practice of being late in the interests of your reputation, but of the two evils, the "unfinished" model is the less desirable. Your model is a monument to your professional skills, and a meeting delayed because of its late delivery will generally be forgotten sooner than evidence of poor workmanship sitting on the conference table long after the meeting is over. You can seldom hope to hit the nail on the head in time estimates, but keeping your wits about you and making experienced, educated guesses will hold uncompensated working time to a minimum.

Ideally you will build up a clientele which will return to the same stand, but even faithful clients may at times be required to obtain several bids for a model project. Your response to a request for a quotation should be the same as though you were the only supplier. The time it takes to pick up drawings and write unsuccessful proposals is a burden on shops with a small staff, particularly when that staff is busy on other projects, but such wheelspinning is one of the facts of life in any market place. If you should let your desire to do the job drive you into a ridiculously short time estimate, beware that you may later regret your action in obtaining an unprofitable job. Not only is your profit reduced, but because of being occupied, you cannot take on other profitable jobs. On the brighter side, the client who knows and likes your work may convince his client that the cheapest is not necessarily the best, thus possibly giving you the job. Sometimes sensing this will give you moral support for submitting consistently realistic estimates.

45

Contracts

It is an established fact that no contract can be written to cover every known possible contingency, much less the unknowns. However, in professional business relations, even if not traditional, it makes common sense to record at least a meeting of minds with respect to a given transaction. Such recording can save misunderstanding and possible "fisticuffs" later on, either in court or at dawn on the village green.

I have found that the proposal-contract letter has been very satisfactory. The combination eliminates extra paper work. The closing page 327 of this chapter is devoted to a sample letter and a sample change order. The first page would be on your letterhead, addressed to the clients, setting forth what you propose to do for them following preliminary discussions about the subject model. Be specific about identifiable items such as the project and the drawings upon which you are basing your price. Based upon your reputation which brought your client to accepting you, it is safe to assume that the amount of architectural detail will satisfy their requirements and that the "approximate" dimensions of the base will be within $1''$ of the stated figures, so you can hold verbage to a minimum. Allow their knowledge of your integrity to give you as much model builder's license as possible. The ex-

act number of cars and human figures can be decided during a visit by your clients while the model is in process. Obviously you will put the trees where the landscape drawings specify, etc. Any unused portion of your Page 1 is crosslined to conform to established practice of confining a contract to a specified number of pages. This is for clarity and protection for both of you.

Your Page 2, starting with "we will work from" can be a printed standard information form to be filled in. A space is left at the bottom for a closing friendly statement. The underlined portions of this sample form represent the information filled in.

Prices: FOB your shop clears you from having to pay delivery charges unless specified otherwise. Applicable taxes are basically sales taxes, but the phrase could cover any duties that might be imposed, etc. I have found that some clients not familiar with the tax laws have questioned the charging of sales taxes because of the "service" nature of a model business, but a product will normally carry a tax.

Terms: Though the amount may vary, it is customary to request an advance payment. I have always tried to have each model stand on its own cash feet, and the advance will usually cover required initial purchases of materials peculiar to a given job. Unless you are financed to allow 30 day accounts receivable, payment on delivery is necessary to keep yourself liquid. This does not mean that the client is supposed to hand you a check when they pick up a model. You probably haven't had time to make out a statement; as a practical matter, I expect payment within 10 days. In a few cases where the client was a large corporation, I have extended a small cash discount for payment within 10 days to speed up processing through an accounting department maze.

Delivery: Sometimes you cannot avoid a deadline date because of an important scheduled meeting at which the model is required, but it is only common sense to provide for a reasonable "cushion" whenever possible. See Ch. 44 for further discussion in this respect.

Changes, Outside Production, and Extras: In the interests of being specific to avoid later misunderstanding, it is wise to include a standard paragraph of this nature to define your obligation within the price of the model and the mutually accepted time limit. Because inconsistent "extras" would mean changing your rate of charge every time they occurred it is better to establish a fixed rate and provide for a surcharge when necessary. When the necessity for "extras" arises during a job, have at least a verbal understanding with your client before you perform them. Following the Proposal-Contract letter is a sample CHANGE ORDER for your use when the size of the change warrants it. Minor changes during the course of construction can usually be included in the quoted price, but where you are asked to change the shape of a building already assembled or make any other change of equal extra time demand, then some sort of written recognition is advisable.

A standard number of copies of a contract is 4 — original and one for your clients so that they can return a signed one to you, one for your client's architects, and one for your file.

Should a client, such as a large corporation, have to use their purchase order instead of signing your contract letter, be sure that such purchase order contains, or refers to, the basic provisions of your proposal. You have to be flexible. It would be hard, and not worth the effort, to get a General Motors to change their established purchasing procedure to conform to your system. You may even

have to forego the advance payment, *but always get something in writing.* As you establish long-time clients, you can operate on a more informal basis. You know what they expect, and they know what and how you produce. You don't have to establish a "meeting of the minds" every time. But don't let your administration deteriorate to the detriment of your relationship. Next time you may be dealing with a new job captain who knows nothing of you personally. Only once have I had to resort to court to be paid, not helped by the fact that there was nothing in writing as evidence of the agreement. Fortunately, it was a small claims court, so part settlement did not mean financial disaster. Just be awake and beware! On the other side of the coin, a written contract is only as good as the ability of the parties to perform. If you take on a model of a project for which financing is "in progress", do so at your own risk. The reputation of your prospective client, and the atmosphere at initial negotiation plus a bit of checking on the side should help you make the decision in a possibly "shaky" situation. Final collection might take years, if at all, and include litigation.

TIME CHARGES

You will note that the hourly rate in the sample contract letter has been deleted. This was done since it has no bearing on the subject as a specified amount. Rates will differ throughout the world, depending upon the location, the economic situation, and on the experience and track record of the model builder. However, it is well to say that you should be *consistent* with your time charges. If you want to do work for a nonprofit organization at a reduced rate, that is up to you, but charging "what the traffic will bear" is destructive of reputation and therefore not good for business. With nothing to prove your worth, you obviously cannot charge top price for your first model, but your first rise in rate can probably come soon after if your first model is a smashing success. Be reasonable in the light of your experience. Note that in the sample contract letter, "standard materials" are included in the price. Establish a rate to include such materials as wood, cardboard, plastics, paints, and glue expected to be used in any model. This will obviate the necessity for the time consuming recording of the cost of every nut and bolt.

Within the framework indicated in this chapter, you have to be competitive, remembering that being "competitive" is a moot subject. If you are putting out Cadillacs, you won't be able to compete pricewise with your competitor who is putting out Chevrolets. Unfortunately, the client who buys the cheaper model will never see the more expensive edition — another hazard of the market place.

SAMPLE PROPOSAL-CONTRACT LETTER

(Letterhead)

(Date)

XYZ Corp.
(Address)

Dear Sirs: (or Gentlemen)

Based upon discussions with Mr. J of (XYZ's architects) and upon a site plan and architectural drawings dated (date), we propose to construct for XYZ Corp. a (scale) scale exterior display model of their (project). We will show the administration building, three manufacturing buildings, and paint shop. Civil work at finished grade will include all traffic ways, steps, walls, and railings. We will include landscaping and a representative number of automobiles and human figures.

Including 1/2 the width of the two perimeter streets bordering the west and south sides of the property, the model will measure approximately (dimension X dimension).

We will supply an acrylic cover and shipping crate.

We will work from plans, elevations, and specifications to be supplied by your offices. (or architect's offices)

PRICES: FOB our shop, plus applicable taxes: $

                Acid etching

                Acrylic cover

                Crate   _____

                    Total $

TERMS: 1/3 ($) in advance;

        balance to be paid on delivery.

DELIVERY: We would like   weeks' working time from date of receipt of this contract and advance payment.

CHANGES, OUTSIDE PRODUCTION and EXTRAS: Except as specifically noted under "PRICES" above, such prices are for model-making services only (based upon a 40 hour work week), including standard materials, and based upon our timely receipt of complete working information. Any CHANGES from, or additions to original specifications, causing additional working time, will be charged for at the rate of $ .00 per non-overtime hour. OUTSIDE PRODUCTION for such as lighting equipment, acid etching, plexiglass covers, etc. will be charged for at cost plus 10%. Time for EXTRAS such as drafting, drawing research, survey, photography, traveling, etc. will be charged for at the rate of $ .00 per non-overtime hour, plus out of pocket expenses.

Your signature in the space provided below will signify your acceptance of our proposal, thereby establishing this letter as the controlling contract. Please return a signed copy for our files.

Thank you for this opportunity to be of service.

Accepted: Yours very truly,
                         (YOUR COMPANY NAME)

By: _____   (Representative signature)

CHANGE ORDER

TO: Date _____
PATTINSON MODELS   PM Job No. _____
219 South Glendale Ave.   Change Order No. _____
Glendale, California 91205   Client's No. _____
                    Price of Changes Below: _____

With respect to the _____ scale model of _____ _____ , and in consideration for the price shown above, please make the following changes:

46

Administration

This chapter is for the purpose of covering miscellaneous items, which, though important to a business, do not have direct relationship to model construction and do not warrant separate section headings.

SHOP

When you set up your own shop, try to obtain as much space as possible considering the local market and your budget. It is better to have a little extra room into which you can expand than have to move to get it. You of course do not have to have a fancy address since most of your clients will come through the telephone and not off the street. Consider proximity of supply houses such as hardware stores, plastics houses, lumber yards, stationers, etc. Be sure of good lighting. A skylight is great. A high ceiling is beneficial. Establish an enclosed area for an office to keep the sawdust off your paper work and allow at least semiprivacy for telephone conversations. A ventilating fan in one end and a vent in the other are great assets considering chemical odors and the moving of

hot air in the summertime. Depending upon the climate, consider the heating system. In Southern California I have found a small ceiling-hung circulating gas heater adequate, but of course in the snow country you will need a bit more Btu muscle. A sink with running water is a must, not to speak of a toilet. A profusion of electrical outlets will help efficiency. Lighting equipment is discussed in Ch. 38. Check the roof.

CIVIC AND STATE REQUIREMENTS

Before moving in, check with city offices with respect to licensing requirements, use and occupancy certificates, rubbish pickup, and fire regulations. If there is no private parking area, determine street parking restrictions. Obtain a state resale certificate for sales tax purposes.

RECORDS

Whether you are going to take care of financial record keeping yourself or have an outside accounting firm, too much stress cannot be placed on the importance of a complete set of records consistently maintained. Establish a working system and stay with it, keeping it up to date. You will have taxing authorities to deal with and probably payrolls to maintain so do not slight this part of the enterprise. Set up manila folder for each job, numbered so that you can refer to a particular one from a master chronologically accumulated list. I have found a loose-leaf system very useful, kept alphabetically by client, in which all pertinent telephone conversations, visits, etc. are listed. It is sometimes surprising how the record of a past telephone conversation with a client can help a current situation. Also I have found useful a loose-leaf alphabetical record of jobs by subject (that is, "hospitals", "hotels", "office buildings", etc.).

Have everyone keep time cards not only to support payroll but also to record time required on a model. This latter can be of help in the future in estimating time for a similar model.

I set up a manila folder for each job to hold applicable documents including the contract (Ch. 45), time cards, delivery receipt, data sheet, shipping memos, miscellaneous specifications not on the drawings and received separately during the job, etc. The data sheet is a 5-1/2" X 8-1/2" memorandum printed to provide for the information shown is Fig. 46-1. Always obtain a delivery receipt for a model when it is picked up by the clients or their representatives. The date of this document times the transfer of title and responsibility. Any standard receipt form can be used. I use a ready-made form in carboned triplicate with the company name stamped on the top.

INVENTORIES

I have never attempted to maintain inventory records of supplies. There is such a vast variety of items used in such relatively small quantities, that I have followed the practice of charging all model supply purchases to expense. See Ch. 38 for discussion of physical inventories.

INSURANCE

Check with your insurance broker as to what minimum coverage you should carry for your business. A blanket amount can include the models in progress, with extra amounts added in the case of unusually expensive models. Be sure to let your broker know of unusual circumstances in the interests of adequate coverage. Let your client know when their model leaves your shop so that they can obtain insurance coverage if they wish.

BILL PAYING

Set aside a specific weekly pay day and adhere to it for the economic well-being of and peace of mind for your employees. Cooperation in a temporary financial pinch may be willingly given, but an unpaid employee is neither a happy nor a productive one.

Also set aside a specific day of the month for paying your creditors. Promptness in paying your bills will maintain your good credit standing and save time consuming argument. If you anticipate requiring extended time on a purchase, make arrangements at time of purchase to forestall collection agencies and a lowered rating later on.

EXTENDING CREDIT

The advance payment discussed in Ch. 45 not only permits you to make model supply purchases for the job, but it also serves as good faith money on the part of the clients. It indicates that they are serious in wanting a model, and instills confidence in you that they will follow through with their part of the bargain. In the case of models which obviously are going to take more than say a month to complete, I usually ask for one or more interim payments, not only for the purpose of keeping jingle in the cash box but to add credence to the client's promise. The accumulated total of advance and interim payments should of course be supported by work done up to the most recent payment. Aside from the need for working capital on a sort of "pay-as-you-go" basis in a handmade, job order enterprise, you won't have to worry much about establishing clients insofar as their fulfilling their parts of contracts goes. In dealing with homo sapiens, however, you sometimes have to flavor faith with a bit of wariness. If in doubt about new clients, ask them for credit references before letting your zeal drive you into wasted effort. Some developers' dreams, for example, may be bigger than their cash supplies even though they are honest!

PDQ MODEL BUILDERS
(ADDRESS)

No.

Description:

Client:

Started:

Finished:

No. of Sections:

Sizes: (OD)

Section No.	Base	Frame 1	Frame 2	Box Cover	Plex. Cover

Drawings in File:

Remarks:

FIGURE 46-1 *Data sheet.*

BUSINESS STRUCTURE

From my own experience, the best business form at least in the beginning is the *sole proprietorship.* It is the least obligatory, and will give you a chance to get your feet on the ground and establish a clientele without having to account to somebody else for methods and results. You may be president, janitor, bookkeeper, public relations director, purchasing agent, and errand runner on top of being chief model builder, but all this has its rewards in self-accomplishment. Occasional necessary help can be engaged through contract, eliminating payroll keeping, and most suppliers will deliver, sometimes for a small fee.

If you have a friend with whom you are compatible, and you both wish to enter *partnership,* have a competent attorney draw up the partnership agreement for the protection of you both. Remember that a partnership is somewhat like getting married. The partners share expenses and profits, and many times the money sign suspended between them can ultimately make enemies out of friends. Your partner may be more interested in administration and public relations than in model building, resulting in a successful team, each one "staying out of the other's hair"!

When your enterprise grows to the point where you have a geographically widespread clientele, calling for an organization of numerous people of different talents, consider *incorporating.* This can reduce your personal liability with respect to the business and establish an impersonal entity in perpetuity. Your controlling interest can be sold or passed on to others, but remember that the practical "perpetuity" is only as good as the head and hands of the model builders following you.

47

Advertising and Publicity

If no one knows about your services, you might as well plan on confining expression of your urge to build scale models to an avocational effort in your basement. You must advertise to get customers, at least initially. This raises the question as to the best method for spreading the word and to whom it should be spread.

PRODUCT

Before answering this question, consider the type of service and product you plan to offer and the expected market. Professional architectural and industrial scale model building requires a specialized skill for producing a hand made product on a job-order basis. Except in very rare cases where you will build duplicates, no two models will be the same. You will not be producing a production line product to build up a finished goods inventory. You might accumulate an inventory of finished standard components to speed up future assembly, but you will never have a row of finished models for sale off a customer display shelf. The nearest thing to this might be a few tract house models made during slack times for sale or rent to real estate brokers for window display.

CLIENTELE

Considering the market, your clientele will never be greater than a minute portion of the total population. Mr. and Mrs. Citizen will not ring your door bell on their daily shopping expeditions, but with a reputation for consistent high quality at a reasonable price, you should be able to develop all the customers you can handle from those listed in the preface to this book. They will come mostly on an individually occasional basis not because you do not put out the best models available, but because the *requirement* is occasional. You may be fortunate enough to be the supplier of study models, for example, on a continuing basis for an architectural firm, but also there will be many clients who obtain a one and only display model from you simply because they have but a one-time demand. Most construction projects are long term capital investments and not daily expenses. Once the building is finished that piece of land will be occupied probably at least during your lifetime, cancelling any prospects for future development on that site.

APPROACH

Now that the type of product and the prospective clientele have been identified, attention must be given to the methods for getting business. Even though you may have advertising capital available for extended coverage, I advise feeling your way locally first. Paddle in the village pond before you tackle the ocean! Your first professional scale model will be an education, believe me. Concentrate on obtaining your first model contract by offering your services to local architects by telephone, by visits on appointment, and by mail. Tell all your friends, and when you answer the question "What do you do?" at a cocktail party, you may be talking to your first client.

ANNOUNCEMENT

Have a supply of business cards printed getting the advice if necessary from someone skilled in the advertising and display field. Also have a simple announcement printed with advice from the same person whose fee will be well worth the expenditure. This cannot list references or show pictures of work not yet done, but it can have a clever composition mentioning your qualifications such as "*x* years building models in (some one's shop)", "graduate of (scholastic institution)", etc. Mail these out to the architects listed in the Yellow Pages. In the case of the larger firms, take the time to find out beforehand the identity of the person responsible for obtaining models.

SALES AIDS

Make up a few sample scale model sections to show use of materials, sharp corners, civil work, landscaping, etc. You can probably get an architect friend to supply a set of old drawings from which to build a complete private residence, office building, or church model to mount in a carrying case. In the early days, I made such a sales aid in the form of a residential backyard with swimming pool, brickwork, glassed-in sun room with shingle roof, barbeque patio, and landscaping. Even though

your subject will not appeal to every architect, the effort shows seriousness of intent as well as evidence of your skills.

MAILERS

As you build up a track record of top quality at a reasonable price with a few local clients, start expanding your coverage. One way to do this is through the use of direct mail which has the advantage of allowing you to choose the recipients such as the architects, and landscape architects practicing in a given city. Obtain the advice of someone experienced in preparing mailers. They should be eye-catching, with the use of color if your budget allows, concise, to the point, and on a stock of high quality. If the mailer is a single sheet, make it 8 1/2" × 11" in size so that it will fit in the recipient's source file. You might consider sending the mailer in a file folder marked "Scale Models" ready to insert in such a file. Remember that the architects receiving your notice may not have model requirements for months following receipt, so you have to present them with information they *want to keep*. Every architect, for example, is a possible future client, so keep in mind periodic recircularization depending upon the size of your organization and work load.

I do not include any sample mailers because I do not want to confuse your ingenuity. What might be fitting in my area might not be acceptable in yours. Education in the use of scale models is a never-ending project for which the busy model builder does not have time. I have sent out "educational" folders listing the reasons models are useful such as those listed in the preface. Probably no worthwhile project will ever be cancelled simply because a model was not built, but it is constructive to remind architects, in effect, that though they obviously can visualize a project in three dimensions, their clients very likely cannot without a medium more realistic than a set of drawings or a rendering. This I know from experience. Other mailers have included sheets of small plates of models done with a covering letter, a miniature file folder filled with small plates, business card, and "model use" slip, and a single, letter size sheet showing a ghost photograph of a model overprinted with a list of types of models built and a list of references across the bottom. Anticipating the existence of a recipient's card file, attach your business card to the mailer.

YELLOW PAGES

A small advertisement in the local telephone Yellow Pages is a relatively inexpensive way to advertise. Your usual clients within the professional fields will have other sources of your identification, but I have had corporate clients find me through this source. One good model will more than pay for years of use of this medium!

REFERRALS

The best advertising for the model builder lies in an established good reputation which results in word-of-mouth referrals. This can resolve itself into a "which came first, the chicken or the egg?" situation at the beginning of your career. You can't get any work because you haven't done any work. Don't dismay! Pound on prospective clients' doors until you get your first job, and then, hopefully, you are off to the cumulative races. Word-of-mouth referral is confined pretty much to the local scene except in the cases of architects with foreign correspondents or branches. A corporation may sometime call a local architect for a reference, but corporate purchasing agents buying for their real estate development departments are generally hard nuts to crack unless you hit them at the model requirement minute. Let yourself be known rather to the resident architect or other real estate executive. He or she will understand better what models are and what their purpose is.

PERSONAL COMMUNICATION

Hold unannounced visits to a minimum. In the larger firms you probably won't get beyond the receptionist's desk unless of course you can charm him or her out of his or her wits, and the architect onto whom you open the front door in a small firm will likely be too busy to listen to you, thus making your presence an irritant (see Ch. 48).

Particularly if there has been a long spell of silence from an old client, call them up to remind them you are still in business to serve. Their employees responsible for models may have joined the firm since your last job with them. It is a fact of life that sometimes the right hand knoweth not what the left hand doeth. I once called a client who it could be assumed was in touch with neigh-

bors in the same profession, and for whom I had not done work for some time. This client was not aware that I had contour cutting facilities and asked for information because their eastern head office was in the middle of numerous projects for which contour models would be useful tools. So trod the old paths once in a while to keep past relationships alive.

LABELS

A subtle advertising medium is the identifying label you place on each finished model. Establish a simple, professional design, and have a supply made by a specialist. I use a thin aluminum label $1'' \times 3''$ in size which I attach with contact glue to a rear corner of the base frame or against the plywood on the vertical surface of the model structure at the rear. The latter is the better location because it prevents being rubbed off on contact with door frames, etc. Be prepared for newspaper photographers who will tear off your visible label lest they give someone unreimbursed exposure.

The last phrase of the preceding paragraph reminds me that a campaign is in order to get credit for model builders below published photographs of their work. Chances are that the architect will be credited with the subject of the photograph, and the photographer will have "Photo by so-and-so" at the bottom; why shouldn't the model builder get credit for his or her efforts? This is something for you to put in your "To Do" file.

WORK EXPOSURE

I have heard new clients say: "I've seen some of your work" implying that they were at least satisfied with what they saw or they would not be signing a contract with me, but don't count on immediate further business based upon the "publicity" of work exposure. It is logical to assume that the more widespread the distribution of a successful product, the longer the list of customers for that product, but since a scale model is an occasional, custom made rather than a continuing production line product, this maxim applies here with nebulous consistency and constancy. The "man in the street" does not normally buy the scale models concerning us here, and prospective clients don't buy a model until they have reached a preindeterminate point of time and circumstance.

They need their automobiles every day to get to their office, but they need a model only as their projects demand. A year later they likely have forgotten the identity of the builder of that beautiful model they saw on display. So don't fall under the spell of "Think of all the publicity this model is going to give you". This is of course a ploy to get you to reduce your price which not only insults your intelligence but advocates cheapening the value of your services.

A model builder needs advertising media other than work exposure because the viewers of a model are probably 99 times out of 100 more interested in the subject of the model than they are in the model presenting that subject. Creating interest in the subject is of course the reason why your client had the model built in the first place. A professionally built scale model is a means to an end, not the end itself. It is a relatively esoteric tool; esoteric because of the specialized field in which it is used and because of the specialized nature of its subject. The latter results sometimes in the ridiculous situation where you are not engaged to build a model of a church because all your work to date has involved other types of structures. So the display of an office building model to that prospective client won't get you their church business. Fortunately this tunnel vision is not prevalent, but I mention it as part of my experience. On the positive side, perhaps it is a recognition of the artistic as well as the structural ability required.

ADVERTISING CAMPAIGN

When your experience has given you the confidence to "take on the world" and you have established your quality standards, only then, in my opinion, should you consider engaging an advertising firm to put into effect a campaign to reach prospective customers outside your own bailiwick. This will be relatively costly, and serious consideration should be given to the expected return from your investment. This return involves not only money, but also your ability to maintain your established high quality in the larger volume, and your organizational ability in supervising multi-hand-built construction. Even a modest campaign could produce more customers than you could handle, requiring hard decisions and causing loss of at least some of your local clients because of your inability to continue giving the personal attention to which they have become accustomed. As your employees increase you will have to be alert to economic depression and falling off of business as architects' commissions drop and industrial expansion slows. This will require plans for "shrinking to size" or establishing satellite services to keep you afloat. The latter could sap the quality of your model work and harm your reputation.

I am not trying to present a case against progress which means, in the business world, expansion in varying degrees. I merely wish to present some of the pitfalls of trying to make too big a splash with a product which simply is not adaptable to mass production. In my opinion, your advertising funds are better spent as required through an agency which will accept you on a continuing "budget" basis with a flexible media coverage expanding outside the local scene only as your empty work tables demand. I have seen model building companies come and go for many reasons, including overexpansion.

48

Client Relations

In all human endeavor a pleasant atmosphere is important to the efficiency and longevity of any relationship. Cooperation is the key word, and your success as a professional model builder will depend upon it. You may negotiate with a client who signs the contract and pays for the model, but most of your communication will probably be with your client's architects from whom you take directions and obtain all working information. For the purposes of this chapter these are also considered as clients.

FIRST MEETING

Without any experience in the business world, you wouldn't be human if you entered your first client's offices for the first time without a certain amount of trepidation accentuated by a few large butterflies. The size of these butterflies isn't reduced by the lack of any model building track record behind you pitted against the fact that if your clients have been around a while they probably know more about model building than you do. A basic premeeting admonition comes, I believe,

from Plato who said: "Know thyself." If you tend to be a quiet person with not much visible response, command those gremlins inside to prod you into "Speak up!"; if you tend to be garrulous, prod yourself into "Shut up!" As you review the drawings with your client, listening can be very fruitful, not only in an education about the job you hope to undertake in miniature, but also in sifted out model building tips from someone who has possibly at least rubbed shoulders with more scale models than you will ever build. A display of self-confidence — a "can do" attitude — will help your client have confidence in you, but avoid any bluffing which will be read as such by your clients who know they are dealing with a novice. When the drawings have been explained and you have gotten answers to obvious questions which will arise, do not hesitate to ask to be allowed to take the drawings back to your shop for further analysis before you submit a price. Many times you will find that the flurry of a meeting will hide complicated structural problems to be covered in your quotation. When you are satisfied that you have a grasp of the whole picture, including the requirement for an acrylic cover and crate, submit your quotation over the phone first to see whether or not you are in the ball park. This procedure can possibly save unnecessary writing. If your price is accepted, write your proposal-contract letter (Ch. 45) and sharpen your mat knife!

Appearance: As time marches on, formality seems to march with it toward more casual attire, but keep in mind that you are meeting professional people who, particularly in the older, established firms, maintain an established decorum of dress which could make your work clothes reveal you in an unfavorable light. Until you hopefully become "one of the family", you will not go wrong wearing, if a man, a coat and tie, and if a woman, a dress. Above all, be neat and clean. Remember, if it is to be your first meeting with your first client, all he or she has to look at is you, except possibly for your business card and sales aid model (Ch. 47). Your client has not had the chance to be distracted by any professionally accomplished model inventory yet! Even after you have built up a record of many successful models, follow the same procedure in appearance for any first meeting with a new client. This admonition has a very practical purpose. Why jeopardize your image through an unfavorable impression created through personal appearance? An expensive suit or the latest from Paris will never make up for unacceptable model work, but attention to dressing for the occasion can at least forestall embarrassment from putting a crimp in the business at hand. With an established working relationship, you may be able to enter through a friendly back door to pick up a drawing during a job, but at any front office appearance beware and be dressed!

CONTINUING RELATIONS

As mentioned previously, cooperation is the key word. Without being obtrusive, try to work *with* your clients rather than *for*. To repeat some of the tips mentioned elsewhere in this book remember first and foremost that clients are busy people and do not have the time to hold your hand. Stay with your job and bother them only with intelligent questions the answers to which can't be found in the drawings. Inform them of apparent errors in the drawings. Correction could save their clients money. Let them know that you can incorporate changes if notified in time. At the beginning of a job be ready to help your client decide upon the best scale considering handling, size of display space, amount of detail required, etc. After learning the purpose of a model, consider with them the best type for that purpose. Don't try to lead them into a display model when you know that a study model will be adequate. Your honest proposal for a less expensive model will stand you in good stead in the future. When you anticipate late delivery, let your clients know far enough in advance so that they can change meeting dates, etc. Don't make it a practice to be late on delivery, but be late rather than inadequate. Occasional tardiness will be forgotten long before a sloppy job.

During your efforts to obtain new clients or just stay in touch with old ones (Ch. 47), beware of being a pest. You can lose business by becoming one. I will never forget the lesson I learned from a remark of a client's representative who said, in effect, that every time he looked up there was a representative of so-and-so standing there. I do not know that this was the reason but so-and-so was out of business not long thereafter. It would be nice if we could always happen to be present each time the requirement for a model arose, but without mental telepathy, all we can do is to find ways to keep our identities in the user's line of sight as through the use of periodic circularization and telephone calls (Ch. 47). You are selling a professional service; you have to be a salesperson—you have to be persistent without a perpetual foot-in-the-door approach.

49

Representative Models

The photographs of Pattinson models included in this section are for the purpose of exemplifying the results from application of construction tips covered in the text. They are numbered consecutively for text reference with no attempt at segregation by model subject.

Though certain parts of these models have been used as construction subjects, none have been completely rebuilt in discussion. The reason, as stated in the introduction, is that concentration on subjects never to be duplicated is not as useful as presenting proven methods to spark your imagination toward better solutions to any construction problems that may arise.

1. *Liquid fertilizer plant; scale 1/4" = 1'. Photo by Robert Blyth (Courtesy, Agriform Farm Supply, Inc.).*

2. *Transducer star element; scale: 20 times blowup. Designer, CEC Instruments. Photo by Robert Blyth (Courtesy, Philip S. Fogg).*

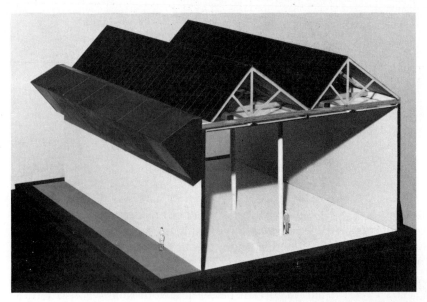

3. *Solar energy roof collector structure; scale: 1/2" = 1". Designer, Facilities Systems Engineering Corp. Photo by Herbert Bruce Cross (Courtesy, Spectrolab).*

4. *Church interior; scale: 1/4" = 1'. Architect, William Wollett. Photo by Robert Blyth (Courtesy, First Christian Church, Glendale, CA).*

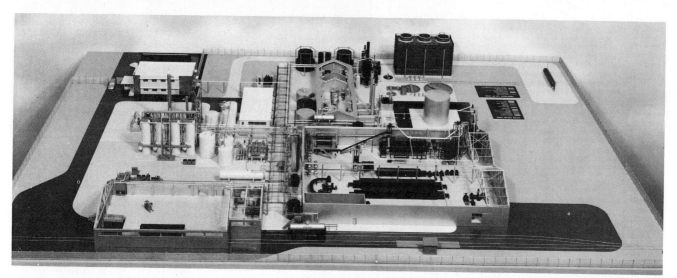

5. *Copper reclamation plant; scale: 1/10″ = 1′. Designer, Fluor Corporation. Photo by Dick Whittington (Courtesy, Fluor Corporation).*

6. *Manufacturing plant; scale: 1/32″ = 1′. Architect, George Vernon Russell FAIA & Associates. Photo by Solar Turbines International, an International Harvester Group (Courtesy, Solar Turbines International, an International Harvester Group).*

7. *Sanitation land fill; scale: 1/100″ = 1′. Designer, Los Angeles County Sanitation District (Courtesy, Los Angeles County Sanitation District).*

8. *Tract house interior; scale: 1/2"*
= 1'. Photo by Robert Blyth.

9. *Great America Park, Santa Clara,*
California; scale: 1/32" = 1'. De-
signer, R. Duell and Associates.
Photo by Adams Studio (Courtesy,
Marriott Corporation).

10. *Open contour model for resi-*
dential development study; scale
1/40" = 1'. Designer, Fargo Finan-
cial Corp. (Courtesy, Fargo Finan-
cial Corporation).

340

11. *Security Pacific National Bank Headquarters, L.A.; scale: 1/16″ = 1′. Architect, Albert C. Martin and Associates. Photo by Herbert Bruce Cross (Courtesy, Security Pacific National Bank).*

12. *Steel building sales model; scale: 1/4″ = 1′. Designer, Empire Steel Building Co. Photo by Robert Blyth (Courtesy, Arthur M. Andersen).*

14. *Building entrance study; scale: 1″ = 1′. Architect, Albert C. Martin and Associates (Courtesy, Albert C. Martin and Associates).*

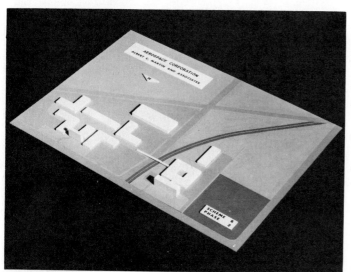

13. *Plant layout scheme; scale: 1/100″ = 1′. Architect, Albert C. Martin and Associates. Photo by Aerospace Corporation (Courtesy, Aerospace Corporation).*

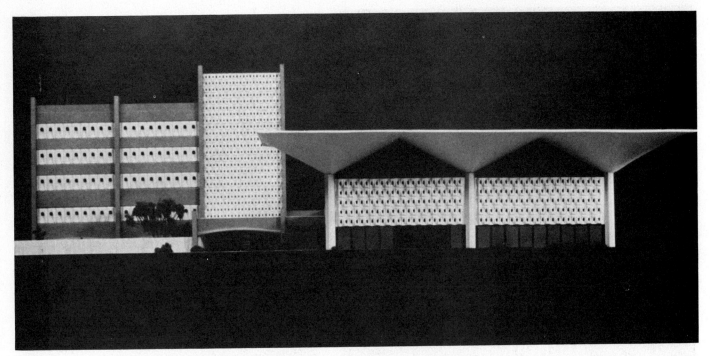

15. *Facade screen and colonnade study; scale: 1/4" = 1'. Architect, Robert E. Alexander FAIA. Photo by Julius Shulman, Inc. (Courtesy, University of California).*

16. *California Woods Condominium, Glendale, California; scale: 1/4" = 1'. Architect, Jones & Walton (Courtesy, Gregg-Gangi Development).*

17. *East Mall, Los Angeles, California (assembled); scale: 1/16" = 1'. Architect, Stanton & Stockwell. Photo by Herbert Bruce Cross (Courtesy, City of Los Angeles).*

18. *East Mall, Los Angeles, California (middle level); scale: 1/16″ = 1′. Architect, Stanton & Stockwell. Photo by Herbert Bruce Cross (Courtesy, City of Los Angeles).*

19. *East Mall, Los Angeles, California (bottom level); scale: 1/16″ = 1′. Architect, Stanton & Stockwell. Photo by Herbert Bruce Cross (Courtesy, City of Los Angeles).*

20. *Office interior study; scale: 1/2″ = 1′. Architect and Designer, Henry Eggers, Henry Dreyfus. Photo by Herbert Bruce Cross (Courtesy, United California Bank).*

343

21. *California Woods Condominium, Glendale, California; scale: 1/4" = 1'. Architect, Jones & Walton (Courtesy, Gregg-Gangi Development).*

22. *Commercial development study on aerial photo base; scale: 1/100" = 1'. Architect, Albert C. Martin and Associates. Photo by Herbert Bruce Cross (Courtesy, Albert C. Martin and Associates).*

23. *Channel Islands Apartments and Marina, Oxnard, California; scale: 1/20" = 1'. Architect, John Bartlett & Associates. Photo by Herbert Bruce Cross (Courtesy, Martin V. Smith & Associates).*

24. *Facade screen study; scale: 1/16″ = 1′. Architect, Albert C. Martin and Associates. Photo by Herbert Bruce Cross (Courtesy, Orthopaedic Hospital, Los Angeles, CA).*

25. *Research facility for American Cement Co.; scale: 1/16″ = 1′. Architect, Albert C. Martin and Associates. Photo by Herbert Bruce Cross (Courtesy, Amcord, Inc.).*

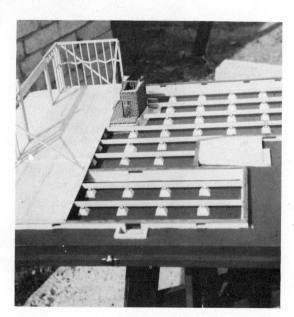

26. *Residential structures; scale: 3/4″ = 1′.*

27. *Transportable aircraft service equipment; scale: 1/2" = 1'. Designer, North American Aviation. Photo by Robert Blyth (Courtesy, Rockwell International).*

28. *Kitchen cabinet work; scale: 3/4" = 1'.*

29. *Master plan study model; scale: 1/100" = 1'. Architect, Albert C. Martin and Associates. Photo by Herbert Bruce Cross (Courtesy, Metro-Goldwyn-Mayer Film Co.).*

30. *Great America Park, Santa Clara, California; scale: 1/32" = 1'. Designer, R. Duell and Associates. Photo by Adams Studio (Courtesy, Marriott Corporation).*

31. *Waterfall, Busch Gardens, Van Nuys, California; scale: 1/32" = 1'. Designer, R. Duell and Associates (Courtesy, Anheuser Busch, Inc.).*

32. *World Trade Center, Los Angeles, California; scale: 1/16" = 1'. Architect, Conrad Associates. Photo by Herbert Bruce Cross (Courtesy, Equitec Properties Co.).*

347

33. *Airport village, Culver City, California; scale: 1/16″ = 1′. Photo by Robert Blyth (Courtesy, Robert Leonard).*

34. *Union Bank Headquarters, Los Angeles, California; scale: 1/16″ = 1′. Architect, Albert C. Martin and Associates. Photo by Herbert Bruce Cross (Courtesy, Galbreath-Ruffin Corporation).*

35. *Beverly Hillcrest Hotel, Los Angeles, California; scale: 1/8″ = 1′. Architect, Kite & Overpeck. Photo by Herbert Bruce Cross (Courtesy, Associated Hosts, Inc.).*

36. *Highrise apartment house, Los Angeles, California; scale: 1/16" = 1'. Architect, Kite & Overpeck. Photo by Herbert Bruce Cross (Courtesy, W. Frazier Overpeck, AIA).*

37. *University of California library San Diego, California; scale: 1/16" = 1'. Architect, William L. Pereira Associates. Photo by Marvin Rand (Courtesy, University of California).*

38. *Los Angeles Department of Water & Power Headquarters; scale: 1/16" = 1'. Architect, Albert C. Martin and Associates. Photo by Herbert Bruce Cross (Courtesy, Los Angeles Department of Water & Power).*

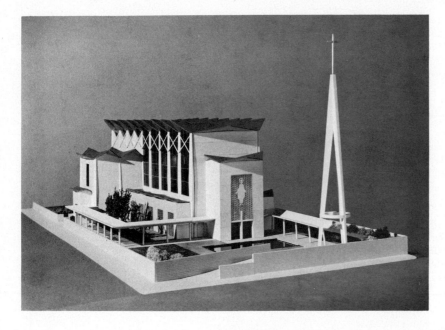

39. *First United Methodist Church, Glendale, California; scale: 1/8" = 1'. Architect, Flewelling & Moody. Photo by Herbert Bruce Cross (Courtesy, First United Methodist Church).*

40. *Private residence with copper roof; scale: 1/4" = 1'. Architect, Henry Eggers. Photo By S.C. Johnson & Son, Inc.*

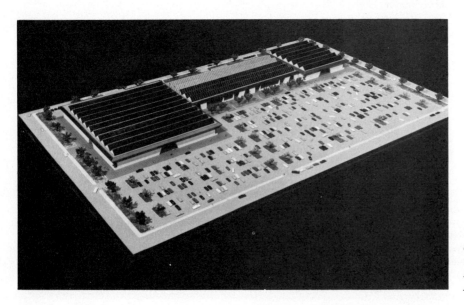

41. *Shopping center with solar energy roof arrays; scale: 1/20" = 1'. Designer, Facilities Systems Engineering Corp. Photo by Herbert Bruce Cross (Courtesy, Spectrolab).*

42. *Race track, Caracas, Venezuela; scale: 1/8" = 1'. Architect, Arthur Froehlich, FAIA. Photo by Jack Laxer (Courtesy, Hipodromo Nacional, Caracas, Venezuela).*

43. *Belmont Park race track, New York; scale: 1/32" = 1'. Architect, Arthur Froelich, FAIA. Photo by Herbert Bruce Cross (Courtesy, New York Racing Association).*

44. *Worldway Postal Center, L.A. International Airport, California; scale: 1/16" = 1'. Architect, Daniel, Mann, Johnson & Mendenhall. Photo by Herbert Bruce Cross (Courtesy, U.S. Postal Service).*

45. *Worldway Postal Center, L.A. International Airport, California; scale: 1/16″ = 1′. Architect, Daniel, Mann, Johnson & Mendenhall. Photo by Herbert Bruce Cross (Courtesy, U.S. Postal Service).*

46. *Ambassador College dining hall, Pasadena, California; scale: 1/8″ = 1′. Architect, Daniel, Mann, Johnson & Mendenhall. Photo by Ambassador College (Courtesy, Ambassador College).*

47. *Great America Park, Santa Clara, California; scale: 1/32″ = 1′. Designer, R. Duell and Associates. Photo by Adams Studio (Courtesy, Marriott Corporation).*

48. *Municipal Airport Master Plan, Santa Monica, California; scale: 1/40″ = 1′. Architect, Kite & Overpeck. Photo by Herbert Bruce Cross (Courtesy, City of Santa Monica).*

49. *Great America Park, Santa Clara, California; scale: 1/32″ = 1′. Designer, R. Duell and Associates. Photo by Adams Studio (Courtesy, Marriott Corporation).*

50. *Belmont Park race track, New York; scale: 1/32″ = 1′. Architect, Arthur Froelich FAIA. Photo by Herbert Bruce Cross (Courtesy, New York Racing Association).*

51. *Research facility for American Cement Co.; scale: 1/16" = 1'. Architect, Albert C. Martin and Associates. Photo by Herbert Bruce Cross (Courtesy, Amcord).*

52. *Mobile home and trailer park; scale: 1/16" = 1'. Designer, Trailer Coach Association. Photo by Herbert Bruce Cross (Courtesy, Mrs. John O'Conor).*

53. *Security Pacific National Bank Headquarters, L.A., California; scale: 1/16" = 1'. Architect, Albert C. Martin and Associates. Photo by Herbert Bruce Cross (Courtesy, Security Pacific National Bank).*

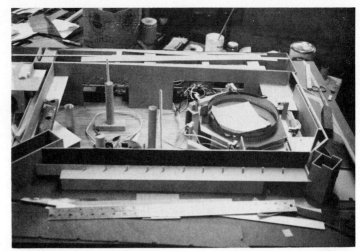

54. *Basement construction for lighted highrise building; scale: 1/16" = 1'. Architect, Albert C. Martin and Associates (Courtesy, Security Pacific National Bank).*

55. *Ambassador College dining hall, Pasadena, California; scale: 1/8" = 1'. Architect, Daniel, Mann, Johnson & Mendenhall. Photo by Ambassador College (Courtesy, Ambassador College).*

56. *Torch Junior Highschool; scale: 1/8" = 1'. Architect, Flewelling & Moody. Photo by Glenn Ward (Courtesy, Bassett School District, La Puente, California).*

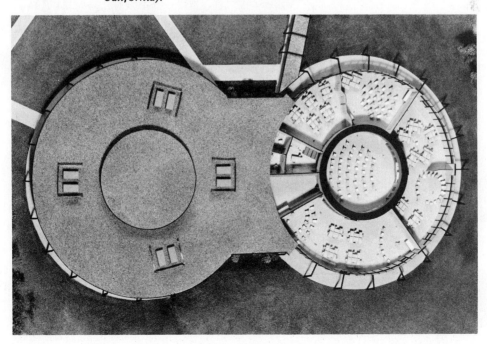

57. *Busch Gardens, Van Nuys, California; scale: 1/32″ = 1′. Designer, R. Duell and Associates. Photo by Herbert Bruce Cross (Courtesy, Anheuser Busch, Inc.).*

58. *Millikan Library, California Institute of Technology; scale: 1/8″ = 1′. Architect, Flewelling & Moody. Photo by California Institute of Technology (Courtesy, California Institute of Technology).*

59. *St. John's Seminary, Camarillo, California; scale: 1/16″ = 1′. Architect, Albert C. Martin and Associates. Photo by Herbert Bruce Cross (Courtesy, Archdiocese of Los Angeles, California).*

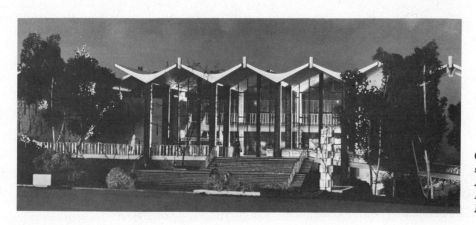

60. *University of Nevada Library; scale: 1/8″ = 1′. Architect, Robert Alexander, FAIA. Photo by Larry Frost (Courtesy, University of Nevada).*

50

Appendix

The specific sources listed in this section have, in my experience, a responsible attitude toward their customers and prospective longevity to assure availability to answer your requests for information or products. In some cases you will of course find comparable products nearer to your location, but those listed have been my mainstays for a long time, and their listing will at least start you on the right track.

ACCESSORIES

Accessories (Ch. 27) including vehicles and human figures at numerous scales, tree armatures, and office and industrial furnishings are cast in metal by Micro-form Models Inc., Webb Drive, Merrimack, NH 03054; telephone 603/883-6673. To my knowledge there are no distributors. Ask for their catalog to help you select items and order by number for prompt delivery. They will also cast to your specifications.

ACID-ETCHING

Acid-etching or photochemical machining (Ch. 17) is available from Merel Company Inc., 16809 South Gramercy Place, Gardena, CA 90247; telephone 213/321-9850. They work from your drawings of the desired screens or railings, etc.

ADHESIVES

Contact and white (water-base) glues (Ch. 34) are manufactured by Wilhold Glues, Santa Fe Springs, CA 90670. These are generic types, and you may find other brand names for the same purpose at your hardware store. Plastics cements will be obtainable at your plastic distributor's outlet. Mine is Gem-O'-Lite Plastics Corp., 5529 Cahuenga Boulevard, North Hollywood, CA 91601; telephone 213/877-1647. Bond Adhesives Company, Jersey City, NJ 07303 puts out its #527 multi-purpose glue in a tube which is excellent for water surface disturbance (Ch. 12). Good acrylic and vinyl cements are Weld-on #16 in a tube and #3 bottled liquid for brush wicking. These are manufactured by Industrial Polychemical Service, P.O. Box 471, Gardena, CA 90247. The cyanoacrylate or "Magic" glues, such as Eastman's 910, seem to be well distributed to hardware and large drug stores.

CASTING AND MOLDING MATERIALS

My trustworthy mold material, Blak-Stretchy (Syrup A) (Ch. 24) with catalyst is manufactured by Perma-Flex Mold Company, 1919 East Livingston Avenue, Columbus, OH 43209. My local source is Westwood Ceramic Supply Co., 14400 East Lomita Avenue, City of Industry, CA 91744; telephone 213/330-0631. Plasters suitable for molds as well as casting are put out by United States Gypsum, 101 South Wacker Drive, Chicago, IL 60606. Ask a local building supply company for their literature describing uses for U.S. Gypsum's various products. I happen to like Hydrostone because of its quick drying, density, and strength, but there are other types better for template forming, for example. Casting resin and catalyst can be obtained from your plastics supplier.

DYES

Dyes for acrylics (Ch. 33) can be found at your plastics supplier along with those for casting resin. The commercial powdered dyes I use for treating landscaping materials (Ch. 25) are made by Krieger Color & Chemical Co. Inc., 6531 Santa Monica Boulevard, Hollywood, CA 90038.

ENGINEERING MODELS

Excellent scale components for this specialized field (Ch. 2) are put out in plastic by Engineering Model Associates, 1020 S. Wallace Place, City of Industry CA 91748; telephone 213/261-8171; telex 67-3398. They also have assembly aids and training kits for those interested in models for the chemical processing, nuclear energy, and related fields. Their extensive catalog is a worthwhile addition to your reference library (Ch. 43) for the times when you have industrial requirements in-

cluding those for piping, tanks, stairs, ladders, handrails, motors, valves, pumps, structural beams, columns, etc. Most scale components are limited to 1/4″ scale or larger, but don't forget that a 1/16″ diameter pipe or column, for example, is a 6″ pipe or column at 1/8″ scale, and 12″ at 1/16″ scale. You may find a 1/4″ scale motor just right to symbolize a generator in your 1/8″ scale plant layout model, etc.

GEODESIC DOMES

See "Books" at the end of this section.

LIGHTING EQUIPMENT

Lighting equipment (Ch. 29) can be supplied by such companies as General Electric, Westinghouse, and Sylvania. I use components manufactured by General Electric whose catalogues have been useful in choosing bulbs, ballasts, starters, and transformers. Their fluorescent catalog will show wiring diagrams for various requirements. Check with an electrical supply house or advertising display company for sources of black light components in your area. Touch-Plate Electro-Systems, Inc. 16530 Garfield Avenue, Paramount CA 90723; telephone 213/636-8171 will identify their local representative for their low voltage control systems as noted in Ch. 30.

MASONITE

Masonite (Ch. 35) has apparently by usage incorrectly become a generic term for any similar pressed wood particle board available at your lumber yard. I always ask for Masonite, but there are suitable substitutes if it is not available.

MODEL COVERS

These (Ch. 39) are impractical to ship and will best be supplied by local plastics fabricators, but for a lead I have used Ray Products, 11565 Federal Dr., Elmonte, CA 91731; telephone 213/579-4250 who have supplied my acrylic covers for many years.

PAINT

There are many excellent paints (Ch. 32) on the market and I have become "hooked" on Pittsburgh's (P.P.G.) latex. They have a complete color range by custom mix formulas, including one called "grass" which is my basic countryside green, and they happen to be supplied by local hardware store. Krylon spray enamels manufactured by Borden Co., Columbus, OH 43215, are in my experience, the best of the pressure can colored enamels and worth the price for fast coverage. I use their matte black continually for model bases, and their matte spray will kill the sheen when necessary. They also have a matte (dull) "silver" (aluminum) which has been very useful. Illinois Bronze Powder and Paint Company of Lake Zurich, IL 60047 has an excellent line of metallic spray finishes including brass, copper, bronze, and gold for that anodized aluminum or copper roof requirement. Blair Art Products, Inc. of Memphis, TN has a useful Spray-matte for dulling purposes. You can find this product at your art supply store.

PAINT SPRAYER

The intermatic spray system (Ch. 32) is manufactured by W.R. Brown Co., Chicago Ill 60635. I have obtained mine from Standard Brands Paint Co., Inc., 401 N. Fair Oaks Ave., Pasadena, CA 91103; telephone 213/793-2994.

PATTINSON MILL

A shop drawing to guide you in construction of a Pattinson Mill is available from Pattinson Models, 219 S. Glendale Ave., Glendale, CA 91205. Send check or money order for $50.00 for postpaid delivery. California residents add $3.00 sales tax.

PLASTICS

Two of the most important plastics in the architectural field are acrylic and high impact sheet vinyl. Sheet acrylic plastic is manufactured by Rohm and Haas, Box 219, Bristol, PA 19007 as "Plexiglas" and by E.I. duPont de Nemours & Co., Wilmington, DE 19898 as "Lucite". Both are excellent for model fabrication. You will find acrylic products in the form of spheres, rod, and tubing. I have never seen a brand label on vinyl, but I believe Union Carbide is one manufacturer. I obtain high impact sheet vinyl in various thicknesses from Transparent Products Corp., 3410 S. La Cienega Boulevard, Los Angeles, CA 90016.

ROOFING

Real wood shingles and shakes (Ch. 33) at 1/4" scale are obtainable from Model Masterpieces Ltd., PO Box 1634, Englewood, CO 80150; telephone 303/988-6275. Ask for information about other items at the model railroad scales.

SOLAR CELLS

As the search for alternate energy systems expand, so will the availability of solar power equipment (Ch. 30). If your electronics store doesn't have solar cells, try Edmund Scientific, 101 East Gloucester Pike, Barrington, NJ 08007; telephone 609/547-8900.

TOOLS

Brookstone Company, 127 Vose Farm Road, (502) Peterborough, NH 03458; telephone 603/924-9511 has a great multitude of specialty tools, (Ch. 36) such as hemostats, tweezers, and small pliers that are just the answer for model building. Ask to be placed on their periodical catalog list.

URETHANE FOAM

Polyurethane foam (Ch. 10 and 35) obtainable in various densities is made as "Trymer Bun/board" by the CPR Division of The Upjohn Company, 555 Alaska Avenue, Torrance, CA 90503. I use the most dense or 4-lb product which I obtain from Vertex, Inc., 4200 Charter Street, Los Angeles, CA 90058, and from Foam Sales and Marketing, 1311 Airway, Glendale, CA 91201.

BOOKS

Geodesic Domes: *Paper Houses* by Sheppard, Threadgill, and Holmes; Shocken Books, New York, N.Y. *The Dome Builder's Handbook* edited by John Prenis; Running Press, Philadelphia, Pennsylvania.

Metric System: *VNR Metric Handbook* by Fairweather and Sliwa; Van Nostrand Reinhold Company, New York, N.Y.

Trees: International Book of Trees by Hugh Johnson; Simon and Schuster, Inc., New York.

Index